Between Eternities

Between Eternities

On the Tradition of Political Philosophy, Past, Present, and Future

Gregory Bruce Smith

LEXINGTON BOOKS

A division of
ROWMAN & LITTLEFIELD PUBLISHERS, INC.
Lanham • Boulder • New York • Toronto • Plymouth, UK

LEXINGTON BOOKS

A division of Rowman & Littlefield Publishers, Inc.
A wholly owned subsidiary of The Rowman & Littlefield Publishing Group, Inc.
4501 Forbes Boulevard, Suite 200
Lanham, MD 20706

Estover Road
Plymouth PL6 7PY
United Kingdom

British Library Cataloguing in Publication Information Available

Library of Congress Cataloging-in-Publication Data

Smith, Gregory B., 1949-
  Between eternities : on the tradition of political philosophy, past, present, and future /
Gregory Bruce Smith.
    p. cm.
  Includes bibliographical references and index.
  ISBN-13: 978-0-7391-2076-7 (cloth : alk. paper)
  ISBN-13: 978-0-7391-2077-4 (pbk. : alk. paper)
  ISBN-10: 0-7391-2076-X (cloth : alk. paper)
  ISBN-10: 0-7391-2077-8 (pbk. : alk. paper)
  1. Political science—Philosophy. I. Title.
JA71.S496 2007
320.01—dc22   2008001469

Printed in the United States of America

∞™ The paper used in this publication meets the minimum requirements of American
National Standard for Information Sciences—Permanence of Paper for Printed Library
Materials, ANSI/NISO Z39.48-1992.

For Joseph Cropsey:
My guide to the Tradition, with great respect and thanks

Contents

Acknowledgments

Several of the chapters below have been previously published. All have been changed more or less significantly for this volume so that they fit together as a complete whole. That said, the author gratefully acknowledges these prior venues.

Chapter 2, "The End of History or a Portal to the Future" appeared in *Francis Fukuyama and His Critics*, ed. Timothy Burns (Lanham: Rowman & Littlefield, 1994) as "The End of History or a Portal to the Future: Does anything Lie Beyond Late Modernity."

Chapter 3, "What Is Political Philosophy: A Phenomenological Approach," appeared in *Perspectives on Political Science*, Spring 2007 under the same title.

Chapter 4, "Machiavelli's *The Prince* and the Essence of Modernity" appeared in *Machiavelli Studies*, Vol. 2, 1988 as "Machiavelli's *The Prince* and the Abolition of the Political: A Preliminary Reflection."

Chapter 5, "Phenomenology or Constructivism: Robert Pippin's Modernity," was delivered as a convention paper at the Midwest Political Science Association meeting April 2005 as "Modernity and Constructivism: A Phenomenological Response to Pippin."

Chapter 6, "Cacophony or Silence: Derrida's Deconstructionism and the Possibility of Political Philosophy," appeared in *Political Science Reviewer*, Fall 1988 under the same title.

Chapter 7, "Who Was Leo Strauss?" appeared in *The American Scholar*, Winter 1997 under the same title.

Chapter 8, "Leo Strauss and the Straussians: An Anti-Democratic Cult?" appeared in *PS: Political Science and Politics*, June 1997 under the same title.

Chapter 9, "Athens and Washington: *Leo Strauss, the Straussians, and the American Regime*," appeared in Murley and Deutsch eds., *Leo Strauss, the*

Straussians, and the American Regime (Lanham: Rowman & Littlefield, 1999) under the same title.

Chapter 10, "On a Possible Epicurean Garden for Philosophy," appeared in *Political Science Reviewer*, Spring 2007 as "Philosophy and the City in the Thought of Leo Strauss: On a Possible Epicurean Garden for Philosophy."

Chapter 11, "On Cropsey's World," appeared in *Review of Politics*, Spring 1998 under the same title.

Chapter 12, "Leo Strauss and Martin Heidegger," was delivered as a convention paper at the American Political Science Association meeting September 2000 as "Leo Strauss and the Germans: Strauss's Post-Heideggerian Synthesis."

Chapter 13, "Dialogue and Dialectic in Plato's *Phaedo*," appeared in *Polis*, Winter 1992 as "Dialogue and Dialectic in the *Phaedo*: Plato as Metaphysician, Epistemologist, Ontologist and Political Philosopher."

Chapter 14, "Political Philosophy and Eros: Plato's Socrates in the *Symposium*," appeared in *Polis* Vol. 11, no. 2, 1993 as "Paths to and From Plato: A Reflection on the Origins of Political Philosophy: The Case of the *Symposium*."

Chapter 15, "*Plato's Parmenides*: Socratism and the Origins of Platonic Political Philosophy," was delivered as a convention paper at the Midwest Political Science Association Convention April 2001 under the title "The Origins of Socratism: The *Parmenides*."

Chapter 16, "Between Platonism and Postmodernism: Plato's Emendation of Socratism in the Trilogy," was delivered as a convention paper at the American Political Science Association Convention September 2000 under the title "Plato's Trilogy: Between Platonism and Postmodernism."

Chapter 17, "Aristotle on Reason and its Limits," appeared in *Polis*, Summer 1997 under the same title.

Chapter 18, "Legitimacy, International Morality and the Postmodern Global Future," was delivered as a convention paper at the Midwest Political Science Association Convention April 2004 under the title "Legitimacy, International Morality and the Postmodern Future."

Chapter 22, "Political Philosophy and Environmentalism: Recovering the Phenomenon 'Nature'," appeared in *Perspectives on Political Science* Winter 1998 under the title "Political Philosophy, Postmodernity and Environmentalism."

The Introduction, Conclusion, Chapters 19, 20, 21, and the Prefaces to the four sections of *Between Eternities* were all written specifically for this volume.

I also want to thank the Trinity College Faculty Research Fund for providing the funding, which helped to prepare this volume for publication, including production of the Index.

Chapter One

Introduction: Political Philosophy; Is There a Future Tradition?

Between Eternities takes up where my *Martin Heidegger: Paths Taken, Paths Opened*[1] leaves off. In the Conclusion to that volume I proposed that the Tradition of political philosophy is potentially still open. A vital, ongoing future for the Tradition of political philosophy is the prerequisite for the continuation of the West as something unique. But the continued possibility of the Tradition of political philosophy rests on openly rejoining questioning regarding its essential nature. My conclusion is that only if understood as itself proto-philosophy—that aims at a unitary account of the whole—can there be a future for the Tradition of political philosophy beyond what I argue is the closure of the modern variant of political philosophy. I see no basis upon which it makes any serious sense to go back to classical antiquity—albeit below I will propose a form of "second beginning." Our present situation is that we stand at the end of one age of the Tradition of political philosophy and at the possible commencement of another. We stand "Between Eternities."

A few prefatory words are required to explain how I arrive at some of these conclusions. In this volume, as with its predecessor, I begin from the premise that thought is always, in its point of departure, thrown and situated. This is not to say that we cannot dialectically transcend that thrown beginning to a greater or lesser extent. The thrown home of the Tradition of political philosophy is the West, and at the point at which we have now arrived it is also the home of commitments to freedom, equality, democracy, Scriptural norms and understandings, modern science, modern commerce and much more. That too is part of the situation into which we are thrown and it conditions our necessary point of departure. But at this point our situation is one of a Tradition that has culminated in not just a philosophical closure but, in significant ways,

1

everyday, practical, concrete closure. **If we try to will away these central facts of our contemporary thrownness we will stand nowhere and have nowhere to begin**. But that nowhere is precisely where modern philosophy has presumed to stand from the beginning, the nowhere of the self-legislating ego that constructs and projects it own basis. I will argue that that null projecting was the origin of our present closure. More to the point, it will be impotent in trying to transcend our present thrownness and open an ongoing future. We have been delivered over to the mindless and groundless competition of competing wills, Nietzsche's "fabling" of the world. That is precisely what we must escape.

Given the situated nature of all thought, even in trying to overcome what I will designate as the "Constructivism" of modern thought we need not give up the political and moral yield of modernity. We are equally situated within that. But lest we become caught in some variant of the End of History or of the inevitability of endless, changeless late modernity, with closure of novel possibilities as its most pregnant feature, we need to understand political philosophy in a way that [again?] allows it to be open to and capable of opening up the future as something unique. We must have a future toward which we are consciously moving. There is no other way to inform vital, energetic, unique practice in the present. And that is the prerequisite for the cross-generational perseverance we now so desperately need.

Without the possibility of unique forms of practice in the future, needed to meet the utterly unique situation that is coming, our existence as historical beings is at an end. That would alienate us from our essence as history making beings. We would be post-historical beings thrust into a post-human situation. It is as essentially historical beings that we must at this moment begin our efforts at self-understanding. I have, and will, argue that our essence as historical beings is determined by the "ecstatic temporality" that I have presented as central to Heidegger's phenomenological project, wherein we are most essentially ourselves as human when we bind together past, present and future in a creative fusion. We must stand in the present, lovingly appropriate our past and "open out" a future that can inform the conscious practice of fundamentally history making beings. It is that essential relation to temporality that has been lost in our age of closure.

Contrary to modern Constructivism—and that Constructivism is the only place where modernity has and can take its stand—I will designate the possibility I am trying to articulate as phenomenology, in a distinctive sense. In what follows, I will offer an understanding of political philosophy as simultaneously ecstatic, phenomenological and dialectical, and as a manifestation of a holistic proto-philosophy. The first section of essays deals with this distinction between modern Constructivism and phenomenology as I understand it.

Phenomenology as I use the term accepts that there are "phenomena" that in some fashion **present themselves** and that those phenomena are always our dialectical point of departure. Ultimately, modern Constructivism must reject that there are any phenomena of this kind until they are set forth in a self-grounded frame constructed by an autonomous theoretical ego. Even what has passed so far for Postmodernism is nothing but a furtive form of Constructivism—which is simultaneously contradictory and self-invalidating. I have argued, and will here continue to argue, that Constructivism leads inevitably to a slippery slide where the constructs that are presumed necessary to make reality present for us eventually leave us with nothing but pure idiosyncratic imagination projecting personal fantasies in an environment where multiple allegedly equal voices talk all at once—so clearly manifested in the work of Derrida which I consider below. From this cacophony of present voices no unique collective future can come forth and emerge, and the past will inevitably be forgotten in an a-historical descent into an unchanging present. We may still accomplish Nietzsche's longed for "innocence and forgetting." A present that has lost its past can have no future—that is the underlying lesson of the notion of "ecstatic" temporality.

Our present, increasingly lost in an a-historical cacophony of voices, is precisely the inevitable outcome Nietzsche predicted, an endless, monotonous, agitated closure, a present open to neither past nor future. Even a thinker of the greatness of Hegel, who tried to avoid this idiosyncratic cacophony by subsuming Will under Law, left us with the same closure of both practice and philosophy. It is the Constructivist move that leads to this closure. It implies the cessation of our fundamental humanity as history making beings.

In *Martin Heidegger*, I arrived at a series of premises, the *arche* for my present understanding. Therein I tried to draw a positive yield from Heidegger's work rather than the far more prevalent negative or deconstructionist yield. That yield is summarized here in the essay "What Is Political Philosophy: A Phenomenological Approach." I have tried to separate these positive premises from what I see as Heidegger's theoretically derivative, abstract, and frequently vaporous, late, "post-metaphysical" musings that lead us into nothing but silence and irresolute waiting.

I reject Heidegger's argument, which has become doctrinal in some circles, that Plato is the first metaphysician. From that understanding descends all manner of criticisms in contemporary thought of Plato as the origin of everything from nihilism to "logocentrism," and undoubtedly other inane theoretically derivative centrisms yet to be invented. I also reject that these understandings clarify the Tradition of political philosophy. I trace to modernity, or Aristotle, most of the problems Heidegger traces to Plato. In the essays that follow, I will argue that Plato was never metaphysical in the sense Heidegger adumbrates, but he was a phenomenologist in my sense.

I attempt to confront these charges, born in the thought of Heidegger, by a close reading of selected Platonic dialogues. My effort in those essays culminates in an attempt to show that Plato's thought represents a break from Socrates and an attempt to amend several of Socrates's **potentially** metaphysical tendencies. Another break in the tradition occurred directly after Plato, as Aristotle picked up and extended potentially metaphysical tendencies in the direction Socrates was already moving in a proto-fashion. Yet another break is between Plato's teaching and what came to be called neo-Platonism. My argument is that these breaks within antiquity were at least as great as the ancient-modern break which has traditionally received far greater notice.

The greatest break is to be found in Aristotle's **theoretical, and especially his logical,** works which represent the metaphysical flowering of incipient Socratism. A future phenomenological political philosophy must transcend those tendencies and return to the roots of the Tradition in the thought of Plato. An indication of how to do that can be found in the non-metaphysical Plato who is a quintessential phenomenologist.

I argue that the real Platonic intention was quickly covered over by Aristotle and was thereby substantially lost. Western thought was directed back onto the incipient Socratic path. This move had its full flowering in modernity. That said, I do argue that Aristotle's practical works represent classic efforts that deserve to be called phenomenological in my sense. Those phenomenological reflections culminate in an understanding of the proper place of *logos* or reason in practical life as well as indicate its limits. It is from Aristotle's theoretical works that much of what Heidegger attributes to Plato originates. His practical works are the more sanguine model upon which to build. They retain a phenomenological/dialectical point of departure.

My understanding of the ecstatic fashion in which the tradition must be enjoined is discussed in the essays in the third section on Leo Strauss and his successor Joseph Cropsey. I use these reflections as a model for how one must stand between past and future, linking the two. Leo Strauss started down a path similar to the one I am suggesting, but then diverted in directions that are not altogether consistent with his opening phenomenological moves and starting premises. My own understanding has evolved out a longstanding engagement with Strauss's thought. I try to show that Cropsey's thinking represents a similar engagement. It will become clear that I have picked up on some of the premises Cropsey developed as part of that engagement. I suspect I extend those premises in directions he would not go.

Strauss opens with what I call the phenomenological move. But in the end, I argue, Strauss adopted the Nietzschean understanding of the radical disjunction between theory and practice that is stated most clearly in Nietzsche's *On the Advantages and Disadvantages of History for Life*. This led Strauss to choose one or the other, theory or practice. I argue that he chose a primarily contemplative understanding of theory as the activity most worthy of pursuit. And I argue that he understood theory in an Aristotelian rather than phenomenological fashion—as a pure and autonomous activity. Faced with a similar, and I would argue false, dichotomy Hannah Arendt chose practice.

Strauss ultimately chose as his primary commitment theory understood as a detached theoretical activity that stares at and contemplates a fixed and unmovable ontological reality. It was this understanding of philosophy as a form of autonomous theory that his presentation of political philosophy is then depicted as defending. In that fashion political philosophy for Strauss became subsidiary to theoretical philosophy rather than architectonic proto-philosophy as I argue it must be.

Strauss's choice between theory and practice comes close to standing on the ground of the modern constructivist ego. From what other point can that choice be made? More to the point, because of his understanding of philosophy as ultimately theoretical, Strauss could not break through to an understanding of political philosophy as phenomenological, dialectical, architectonic, or as proto-philosophy. It seems to me that his successor Joseph Cropsey was closer to that breakthrough in his discussion of Plato's Trilogy and his understanding of the centrality of "caring." Again, it will become clear from my essay on Cropsey that I have built on and adapted a number of themes originated by Cropsey. My thought has been animated not only by Cropsey's dialectical relation to Strauss's corpus, but by my dialectical relation to both Strauss's and Cropsey's reflections. I simply must acknowledge my profound debt. From both thinkers I have taken themes, albeit frequently gone in directions that I am sure they would not. This is part of my understanding of how one ecstatically engages the Tradition.

I argue that phenomenology as I understand it presupposes a mutual and reciprocal "circular," dialectical relationship between what has customarily been designated theory and practice, in ways similar to an argument made by the allegedly "early" Heidegger about a necessary and fecund form of circularity that lurks within attempts at understanding Being itself. The clearest and most paradigmatic exemplar of what I am proposing was Plato. Plato's work fashioned together a unitary whole out of different fundamental theoretical positions, natural types of human beings, *logos* and *muthos*, as well as of ethics, politics, psychology, ontology and epistemology more generally.

By comparison, for Strauss, there is no basis for the poetic—it cannot be a manifestation of Truth and is defective as a form of speech in relation to theoretical *logos*—and hence no basis for creatively crafting a whole out of parts in the fashion one sees in Plato. Consequently, there is no place in Strauss for political philosophy in my holistic sense as proto-philosophy and poetic speech. And neither is Strauss a Platonist in the sense I will present. Strauss is a Socratic in the sense I believe Plato tried to amend.

I argue for what I see as the Platonic understanding of the mutual and reciprocal interpenetration of dialectical reason and poetic speech that fashions an account of the whole. This understanding is contrary to the approaches of both Heidegger and Strauss for both of whom a choice must be made between theoretical or poetic speech—in the end they simply made opposite choices. Finally, I try to show that Strauss, unlike Heidegger, cannot account for man's essence as a historical being understood not in the fashion of historicism but as a **history making** being. Political philosophy as the holistic enterprise I present has been a large part of the basis of that history making possibility, as the past Tradition in its relation to everyday life shows so clearly. It is the Tradition of political philosophy that has "opened the future" for Western human beings.

If political philosophy is to be architectonic, it must not only reflect on its relation to other possibilities that either aspire to that status or at least see themselves as autonomous undertakings, but it must actively take priority by fashioning the most comprehensive account of the whole, a whole that includes those other claimants. At the very least that involves a confrontation with other claimants like modern science—primarily contemporary theoretical physics and biology—and Theology. Throughout the modern era there has been an ongoing contest for priority between modern science and Theology. Indeed modernity was born of a unique confrontation with a manifestation of Christian Theology. That confrontation for supremacy, I will argue, is misguided. **Neither can be autonomous. Neither can be architectonic.** When I argue for the architectonic status of political philosophy, that means that everything from physics and biology to Theology becomes subsumed under political philosophy. Obviously, what that means needs to be clarified and fleshed out.

In the fourth section of this work, I try to show some of the ramifications of political philosophy being the architectonic science. Simultaneously, and in a variety of ways, I offer some provisional suggestions about how we might begin to think toward a future that is genuinely **post**modern. Given that the central "phenomenon" of modernity has undoubtedly become modern science—and in its rise it cut its teeth in opposition to revealed religion—and both clearly retain their power as phenomena in our world, these central **phenomena** must be confronted. From the modern beginnings through to contemporary "creationism" the tension between modern science and religion continues to express itself with each asserting not just autonomy but priority.

I will argue that many conundrums are avoided when political philosophy itself becomes the prior, architectonic undertaking.

It is clear that from the beginnings of modern science **in proto-modern philosophy**—for example in documents like Bacon's *New Atlantis*—modern science was never intended to gain autonomy from the oversight of philosophy, i.e., the philosophy that created it. Yet as constructivist, modern science always ran the risk of moving farther and farther away from the ultimate phenomena, it was unleashed to master rather than simply understand and explain ontologically. I will argue that we are beginning to see the ultimate ramifications of the detachment of modern science from phenomena, which will not only bring about the potential decay of modern science but have all manner of profoundly questionable everyday ramifications as well.

Eventually it will become clear, out in the open in the public arena of everyday speech, that modern science will not be able to maintain its pretensions to being primarily an **ontological** explanation regarding the nature of reality. It will then have to admit that it is primarily technological, able to predict, reproduce and manipulate phenomenal occurrences. As technological, manipulations and changes can only be judged from the perspective of moving from what is given to a state or situation that is better. Technology is always dependent upon a notion of the Good, and hence cannot be autonomous. This observation points our way toward the solution to Heidegger's conundrum regarding runaway autonomous technology and its enslaving and enervating consequences. Technology can never be autonomous.

I will try to suggest the ways in which only a phenomenological political philosophy can reign in the destructive movement of the sciences away from the phenomena as well as reign in any autonomy of technology. And only an architectonic political philosophy can take the Good as its primary subject matter. I will suggest that only political philosophy as I present it can save modern science and modern technology from themselves and their own ultimate self-dissolution, or our enslavement by them. In a similar vein, I will argue that revealed religion can have no more autonomy than modern science and modern technology. As ultimately dependent upon political philosophy, in the ways I will suggest, both science and religion are equals.

Further, there is no reason that we should, when it comes to religion and Theology, focus our attention upon never before seen possibilities like those presented by Nietzsche and Heidegger. We are already thrown into a Christian given. There is nowhere to stand to will that away. I will suggest that of the three revealed religions that accept the Hebrew Old Testament, Christianity in fact offers far more philosophical possibilities. It is not just that Christianity is our past, but it offers more, and less problematic, resources for being a future. Christianity remains our best alternative for the future.

I will argue that this superiority of Christianity has to do with the doctrine of the Trinity which simultaneously 1) gives us a relation to the core mystery of Being without being able to resolve it, 2) provides an opening to the fundamental problem of linking the One and the Many, 3) gives us a basis for having a respect for the natural whole beyond the injunction—so easy to co-opt technologically—to be fruitful, multiply and conquer the earth. It is also the case that 4) only Christianity has a need for political philosophy because of its doctrine of rendering unto Caesar what is Caesar's and unto Christ what is Christ's. And 5) only Christianity is open to man as temporally ecstatic, as a history making being projected between past and future—in the Christian context, between creation and *parousia*. 6) Neither Islam nor Judaism can grasp the essence of man as a history-making being or give us the possibility of openness to a novel concrete future. Finally, 7) I will suggest that our Western future need not require some choice between modern science and Christianity, but a loving refashioning of the relation between both.

I will conclude by suggesting that lurking "behind" all of the necessary thought projects that I will suggest in *Between Eternities* stands, as it always has, the necessary issue of the status of "nature." At that moment when modern science stands before nature, including human nature, armed with tools to transform or obliterate the natural, we have lost touch with the **phenomenon** nature. Modernity has increasingly alienated humanity from nature and we must begin by finding our way "back" to a new relationship. That ultimately leads me to argue, in different ways throughout all of the essays below, that we must recover nature as a "phenomenon" and not as a "concept" or "idea." Many readers will see that that conclusion brings me into a confrontation with Strauss's argument in *Natural Right and History* in the chapter "On the Origins of Natural Right." Therein Strauss repeatedly focuses on the "idea" of nature, and of the discovery of nature as an idea or concept. I am suggesting we now need to approach nature as a "phenomenon."

Having suggested that distinction, I will point out that my entering wedge for recovering "nature" is reflections on the "environment," man's relation to it, and consideration of some of the literature customarily dubbed environmentalist. Environmentalist thought usually begins with the modern, all too modern, conceptual split between man and the rest of the natural whole. It usually argues for as much autonomy for the natural whole as possible—allowing it to recover its own, allegedly static, self-presenting rhythms—while accepting radical constructivist intrusions into the human arena which has been conceptually abstracted from the natural whole. I will argue that we need to craft a way to view nature as a whole that includes man as a part of it and which sees nature itself as dynamic rather than static. That view of nature will then be in much closer touch with a view of man as a history making being rather than as a static, finished, materialistic or animal being.

The natural whole, which includes man, must be allowed to **present itself** in its ongoing dynamic tensions. This is in fact how both history making man and ever-changing nature **present themselves**. This is another way of saying that nature must be approached as a phenomenon that must never be obliterated in some constructivist fashion **nor assumed to be simply unchanging**.

Only after we recover the phenomena can we begin to reflect upon how to poetically articulate them. We must put ourselves back in a position similar to the one the Greeks faced when they confronted the phenomena directly, including the phenomenon nature. The poetic articulation of the phenomena, and especially of the concept nature that they offered is, I would suggest, **neither necessary nor inevitable**. The phenomena probably do not change at a core level except glacially; the poetic articulations of them have to change and far more frequently. Modern theoretical physics itself has become poetic, but it is increasingly a poetry divorced from the phenomena and available only to a few in an artificial language. Why should that artificial language assume either public or ontological priority?

I will offer another suggestion. If part of the natural whole includes man as a history making being, and we come to stand beyond the age of Constructivism, we will not only look forward to the reinvigoration of the political—**as a part of the natural whole**—but we will have to reflect on the ramifications of the political when freed from the artificial pursuit of the universal. In the end there can be no political philosophy that does not see **the centrality of the political, and the political as tied up with our nature as history making beings.** I enjoin this issue most openly through reflections on international relations theory in part 4 below.

Throughout, I try to show the importance of the continuation of the Tradition of political philosophy as "our" most unique possibility. Its existence is what has made Western civilization distinctive. Its continued existence is the only basis upon which the West can remain distinctive and thereby true to itself. Without being true to itself, the West will not survive and we are at present most assuredly in the midst of a moment of decision.

NOTE

1. Smith, Gregory Bruce, *Martin Heidegger: Paths Taken, Paths Opened* (Lanham: Rowman & Littlefield, 2007).

Part One

MODERN CONSTRUCTIVISM OR
PHENOMENOLOGY

Preface to Part 1:
Modernity and Its Closure

The essays that follow in this section explore the essence of modernity. That essence is to be found in "Constructivism," to which I oppose "phenomenology"—understood as a form of architectonic political philosophy—as the only viable alternative. It goes without saying that there has been an extensive literature on the nature of modernity and it simply cannot be enjoined here.[1] I will at present leave matters at saying that my understanding will leave me occupying different ground than a significant number of other reflections.

I accept the more or less conventional wisdom that modernity begins with the new political science of Machiavelli and the new natural science of Descartes. Of authors I will deal with below, I disagree with Pippin that modernity begins with the origins of what became German Idealism. I agree with Pippin, however, that the essence of modernity involves reliance on a notion of an autonomous, self-legislating ego and its posited freedom.[2] This notion is at the heart of what I am designating Constructivism. I want to argue, contrary to what I take to be Pippin's primary understanding, that constructivism can be traced back to Descartes, and somewhat more surprisingly, to Machiavelli as well.

I also disagree with Strauss who sees the essence of modernity in a transformed understanding of the good. Put another way, for Strauss the heart of modernity is to be found in ethics rather than a changed understanding of the nature of philosophy itself. I agree that at the origins of modernity there is a transformed understanding of what constitutes the human good, at least for the majority of human beings. But I see the essence of modernity as lurking primarily in a transformed understanding of Reason that increasingly attempts to emancipate itself not only from natural determination but from the encumbrance of "phenomena" as well.

13

In the essays that follow in this section I deal with the reasons why I think the attempted modern emancipation from "nature" and especially from "phenomena" is a mistake. Indeed, I will argue, despite the technical leverage it allows, that it is a mistake in every area from ethics and politics to epistemology and modern scientific speculation. As to the latter, in section four I will discuss what I see as the impending *reduction ad absurdum* we see within contemporary theoretical physics in string theory, but also the increasingly paradoxical ramifications within theoretical biology that have increasingly left the phenomena behind and have moved without trepidation into an arena where empirical validation becomes in principle impossible.

Modernity, in its very essence, leads to an increasing detachment from phenomena that can ultimately yield only silence or a cacophony of equal voices talking simultaneously creating a din that makes meaningful discourse impossible. And while it may not have been inevitable, at this point modernity has at the very least led irreversibly to a closure that we are now witnessing. I deal with this closure in the chapter on the End of History debate and the chapter on Derrida.

Despite the impending closure of the possibility of meaningful discourse to which I have alluded, any closure would also bring with it the end of the possibility of genuine, human historicality. In my *Martin Heidegger: Paths Taken, Paths Opened*[3] I have argued that genuine historicality is of the essence of our humanity. The continuation of the possibility of an ongoing historicality now rests on an architectonic, phenomenological political philosophy. In the chapter "What Is Political Philosophy: A Phenomenological Approach," I sketch the outlines of what I mean by this possibility. By architectonic I mean that political philosophy must fashion a whole of ethics, politics, psychology, ontology and epistemology. My argument is that these parts cannot ultimately, in any consistent fashion, be autonomous. They can in fact only "be" as part of a whole, either surreptitiously presupposed or fashioned self-consciously out in the light of day where the effort should take place—and that implies the use of everyday, public speech.

The closure of modernity presents us with the possibility of this architectonic political philosophy as I understand it. But it is not inevitable. As a possibility that exists beyond the closure of modernity, this possibility would deserve to be called postmodern. It is of the essence of any possible **post**-modernity, as opposed to the fragmentation of knowledge and discourse pointed to and frequently valorized as postmodern**ism,** to be unitary and "holistic."

The question remains, as a possible postmodern phenomenon could political philosophy as a public form of discourse offer possibilities distinct from what contemporary modernity can offer? Are there still possible goals and aspirations that lie beyond the increasingly actualized goals and aspirations of modernity or is modernity an end state, as many have argued since Hegel? Are there political forms, for example, as yet unseen, that will be more in line with the world that is coming than all past forms? Or are we confronted with endless modernity and the cessation of our fundamental historicality? Endless modernity and the cessation of historicality are very real if not inevitable possibilities. The possibility of something beyond endless modernity rests on the possibility of an architectonic, holistic, phenomenological political philosophy.

Contrary to a cacophonous closure of modernity that to my mind is the most likely outcome of endless modernity, Pippin believes that modernity can remain "rational" if the self-legislating ego has its freedom limited by law, as in the classic longing of German Idealism. I confess that I find this possibility unconvincing. But even if possible, it would mean the closure of modernity and the End of History. It would also mean a universal possibility that would imply the abolition of the political and simultaneously provide a rationalization for a quite possible global tyranny. At the very least, Pippin's possibility posits the end of novel future outcomes, and with it the end of man's historicality.[4] In that sense, we would arrive at an outcome that was both a post-historical and a post-human situation. I am not inclined to go quietly into what could only be an endless night of the human spirit.

There are a variety of philosophical notions central to modernity. My understanding is that after Heidegger, many of those central notions simply lack philosophical credibility. Hence, modernity can jettison those notions and still try to go on, or most likely, modernity can continue now only on the basis of maintaining many of those notions on the level of myth alone. But that is as much as to say that modernity can maintain itself only on the basis of irrationality, despite its constructivist rationalist longings.

I can offer two examples of what I have in mind. First, after Heidegger, I do not believe that modern philosophy can give any compelling articulation to the notion of a fully transparent, self-standing ego—which does not mean one cannot give credence to notions like intentionality conceptualized more along the lines of *phronesis* or practical wisdom. And second, I do not think that modernity will be able to give any philosophical credence to any further notions of History as linear in any respect—as opposed to radically, and somewhat mysteriously discontinuous.

As I suggest in section four, a crack in our belief in linear History will have significant ramifications for our understanding of International Relations. A crack in our belief in the self-legislating ego will have immense ramifications for our understanding of how self-consciously and ultimately prudently we will be able to deploy our exponentially expanding scientific/technological expertise. But what I see as the philosophically irreversible phenomena of the closure of modernity need not have any ramifications for the possibility of Reason understood phenomenologically in my sense. This latter issue will be slowly developed in all of the essays below in this section and beyond.

NOTES

1. I have enjoined the issue at greater length in my *Nietzsche, Heidegger and the Transition to Postmodernity,* (Chicago: University of Chicago Press, 1996).

2. As we will see in the chapter "On Cropsey's World," Joseph Cropsey finds the positing, self-legislating ego even in antiquity. He, like Pippin, albeit based on a different argument, sees a much greater break between early and later modernity than between early modernity and classical antiquity. I do not accept this position. As I have suggested in the Introduction, I see greater breaks within antiquity than within modernity which I see as fairly seamless—wherein I follow the implications of Strauss's "three waves" of modernity argument. See part 1 in my *Nietzsche, Heidegger and the Transition to Postmodernity.*

3. Smith, Gregory Bruce, *Martin Heidegger: Paths Taken, Paths Opened* (Lanham: Rowman & Littlefield, 2007).

4. Pippin, like Strauss, has no place for poetry.

Chapter Two

The "End of History" or a Portal to the Future: Does Anything Lie Beyond Late Modernity?

Rarely does one see so many take so much trouble responding to the arrival of a new book—and what for many was a new idea—as with the release of Francis Fukuyama's *The End of History and The Last Man*, especially in light of the almost universally critical, occasionally hyperbolic, nature of the responses. This was perhaps predictable in light of the controversy generated earlier by the article that launched the book. But prediction and explanation are two different things, and an explanation is harder to come by. However, I think they clearly protest too much.

If Fukuyama's argument impacted only one side of the contemporary political spectrum to the exclusion of the other, an easy explanation might present itself. Needless to say, liberal progressives were not intrigued by having the idea of History co-opted only to be told that individualism and free markets represent its terminus. And conservatives were less than thrilled to be told that the victory of the liberal West in the cold war might eventuate in the moral decay and spiritual hollowness of the Nietzschean last man. Since the negative responses cut across the political spectrum, it is reasonable to suppose that there may be more here than meets the eye; Fukuyama has apparently struck a nerve. I believe that there are several explanations for this phenomenon and that they tell us something of importance about our contemporary moral, intellectual and political environment.

On one level the End of History debate points to the frequent parochialism of the American academy. Similar debates, with far less fanfare, had already been conducted in France, Canada and elsewhere. For American academics, one part of the scandal was that this debate traced its roots to a German philosopher and one of his left bank Parisian commentators.[1] The continental roots of an argument are indictment enough in some circles. But the heat generated by the present debate, even in theaters where it had already played, indicates there is far more to the matter than American parochialism, especially as intelligent non-academics have also enjoined the debate. Needless to say, playing out the End of History debate at the end of the cold war was significant. The liberal West could no longer define itself simply as the demonstrably superior of two available options. The liberal West now has to look at itself in the mirror and define itself in relation to intrinsic, substantive goals and ideals—that is, articulate what we are *for* rather than take our bearings by what we are *against*. Therein lies one of the significant problems; neither the right nor the left seem well equipped at present to join that discussion.[2]

The End of History debate also came at the time of declining faith that History could be understood as linear and one-directional.[3] For a long time it has simply been assumed that the present is in principle superior to the past merely by having come later. That premise had worked its way out until it seemed like sound common sense for a series of generations.[4] But the "common sense" belief in linear History is by no means obvious when one looks at the actual grist of human affairs. Empirically, the past presents a spectacle of random occurrences. The faith that History has a meaning and direction requires a theoretical critique; it does not rest on empirical evidence. A theoretical frame must be brought to the empirical data from outside. It is precisely the status and origin of such frames—especially in the late modern world—that is at issue.

As I will argue throughout this essay, the fundamental issue with which we are confronted in the End of History debate is theoretical, not empirical. But after Hegel and Marx it has become increasingly difficult to accept the theoretical premises that underpin the notion of linear History. Nonetheless, political and moral life in the modern world has increasingly been driven by ideas. Many of those ideas lost theoretical credibility in previous generations; yet political and moral life continues to be driven by them. The premises that underlie our actions can remain suppressed for some time, but not indefinitely. When they are eventually brought to the light and seen as questionable a complicated situation arises. We live in one of those complicated times.

On the basis of a past theoretical faith in the linear, unidirectional movement of History, it was possible simply to begin from the prejudice that the past is a chronicle of ignorance and vice. To that could be added the gratifying notion that the present generation starts on a moral and political promontory simply by coming later. By extension, it was possible to adopt the conclusion that the future should in principle be superior to the present with or without re-actualizing necessary antecedent virtues and circumstances that made the present what it is. If we lose our faith in linear History, our easygoing faith in all manner of "common sense" opinions will be unhinged as well.[5]

This is where we had arrived prior to the End of History debate, without having publicly admitted it. "We" expected further progress, perhaps indefinitely; and Fukuyama suggested that we had more or less arrived at a terminus. Without History to support our aspirations we would have to defend our idea of the good far more explicitly. But at present, no one is in a particularly strong position to do so.[6]

An adequate rejoinder to the End of History thesis would require that one furnish a substantive discussion of the good that the future **should**, rather than **inevitably will**—or at present does—offer, along with the ways in which it is plausible to believe that it can be actualized. If History does not somehow underpin the movement toward the good, substantive argument or capitulation to the status quo are all that are left. No self-respecting progressive can ever publicly accept the status quo and most are loathe to turn to nature to underpin their arguments because the left generally does not like to admit that intransigent matter—human or otherwise—might limit its utopian agendas. The left prefers instead to believe in the relative indeterminacy and malleability of human beings, as well as material reality, at the hands of clever social manipulation, education and technological mastery.

But without a fixed nature that presupposes its own end or perfection, or an inevitable History that moves only in the desired direction, one is in a very awkward position in trying to justify one's idea of the good. The left is not alone in this predicament. Most conservatives sneak in a linear conception of History along with their various "invisible hands." Invisible hands have the effect of making it equally unnecessary to discuss substantive ends and explicitly justify them. Likewise, one need not consciously foster the political prudence and moral virtue that are the only alternatives to faith in mythical inevitability.[7] Fukuyama's thesis put many in the position of the emperor with no clothes. Being forced by Fukuyama to confront their substantive nakedness was not met with gratitude by either the left or the right.

That said, it was liberal progressives who were most discomfited. Theoretically, many had backed themselves into a corner by arguing for several generations that liberalism does not rest on a substantive teaching or point to distinctive liberal virtues.[8] According to this argument, liberalism is neutral as regards ways of life and substantive ends. It is fundamentally a set of procedural norms open to a diversity of ends. This fashionable variant of "antifoundationalism" is frequently secured by elements drawn from even more fashionable postmodernism in a way that yields an entirely jury rigged contraption.[9] However secured, this view represents the cul-de-sac that most on the present day left have decided to colonize. Hence being forced either to accept the End of History or be nudged into a substantive debate was particularly annoying in these circles.

Granted, arguing that History ends precisely where many neo-conservatives would wish it to end—in modern, commercial individualism—had the look of a "reactionary" maneuver. For many it was difficult to respond other than with outrage to the notion that History would not continue to progress even further in what had been assumed to be not only the desired but also the inevitable direction. The central point is this—and it is precisely the point Hegel made—one cannot know that History is linear and progressive except in light of the end toward which it moves. One cannot know of or about the end unless is has been, or soon will be, actualized. Without an End of History thesis the idea of a progressive linear History cannot stand.[10] It is impossible to conceptualize History progressing indefinitely. More to the point, if one rejects the End of History thesis, the only alternative is to show that we can somehow stand outside the flux of temporality at some fixed point. Only by standing at that a-temporal point could we then presume to measure temporal movement. That a-temporal standpoint is what is traditionally meant by the **concept** "nature."[11] Without being willing to openly accept the End of History, and refusing to accept Nature, the left is in a difficult position. The only consistent move that remains is to valorize "our own" as the good—and since at least Aristophanes, that has been the most traditional and conservative of maneuvers.[12]

While most on the left proceed from the assumption of the malleability and indeterminacy of man, Fukuyama has also been attacked by many, from both the right and the left, for not realizing that human nature does **not** change. History, they argue, cannot end because human nature will never allow itself to be satisfied by any substantive outcome, even prosperous liberal democracy. But that argument substantially begs the question. First, even such seeming absolutists on this question as Aristotle make clear that our nature requires completion by education and habit—that is, cultural variables—and those are obviously not static. It begs the question further by failing to mention that modern philosophical fellow travelers from John Locke and Jean Jacques Rousseau to Robert Nozick and John Rawls have told us we must quit the natural condition because the good for man exists only within an artificially constructed human arena. Debate in the modern era has focused explicitly on the relation between nature and the good and by and large has concluded that the human good requires quitting the natural condition. To simply assert nature as if it operated qua efficient causality in human affairs as it does for beavers, bees, ants and other social species does not hit the mark. The fact that there is a natural fabric to human existence does not immediately prove that it conduces to the good. The substantive question of the human good still has to be addressed even if we mechanically invoke nature.

Another variety of responses to the End of History thesis which invokes something empirically pre-given as an indication that History cannot end focuses on the renaissance of tribalism throughout the post Cold War world as clear evidence that secular, Western, liberal, technological, commercialism has not been, and will not be, globally victorious. In a similar vein, rising Islamic fundamentalism is put forward as empirical counter-evidence to the possibility of the End of History. This approach also begs the question.

The modern moral, political and technological juggernaut has confronted revealed religion before and an accommodation has been reached—and without the total secularization of religion. Someone would have to explain why Islam, which shares sacred texts and multiple principles with Judaism and Christianity, so differs from the other religions that accommodation will be impossible. Is not political marginality far more accountable for the frustration that presently finds vent in Islamic fundamentalism, for example, than simple moral outrage at the Western understanding of justice and the good? If that is the primary ground of frustration, there is no reason why accommodation is not possible. Otherwise, it would be necessary to explain why, even if a radical choice for or against Islam develops, the realities of the modern world would not force a decision for modern technological civilization.

As regards the hegemony of parochialism, ethnic tribalism and nationalism, what leads us to believe that present manifestations of tribalism will have greater staying power in their Balkan, African and Asian manifestations than they did in Western Europe? Has not the former Soviet experience demonstrated that one cannot ultimately retain any national autonomy in the modern world without at least free markets, and eventually liberal freedoms as well? And even if we anticipate a relative withering away of the modern nation-state, and the movement toward a more homogeneous, cosmopolitan, global civilization, there would predictably still be states competing to maintain their place in the cosmopolitan market. Kant's vision of a cosmopolitan federation of states is probably more plausible than any simple world state. Further, the tribal traditions to which our contemporaries turn in desperation represent a response to **present** difficult circumstances and resultant apprehensions. But such traditions emerged under entirely different concrete circumstances than those of increasingly global, modern technological civilization. As modernity consolidates, the future world will become increasingly foreign to the traditional world of the past. What leads us to believe that ancient traditions have any chance of maintaining themselves in a radically transformed environment?

Any tradition is born of an attempt to explain reality and support a shared conception of the good. It must be consistent with its concrete present, at least to some significant degree. The real question is, is not the modern world intrinsically at odds with the generation of stable customs and habits and hence with living additions to traditions generated in the past? If so, old traditions will become increasingly stale and out of touch. Why will the attempt to hold on to old traditions not become more and more of a parody with each passing generation? The mere fact that something is old does not make it good. It must also be reasonable and help explain life in the present. But will reason be able to substitute something in the place of decaying traditions? This latter question is another way of asking, will universal Enlightenment ever be able to take the place of a shared *ethos* in giving solidity to our lives?[13]

There is no doubt that we have habits in the modern, Western world. But our habits are ones that accommodate us to constant change.[14] There has never been a greater mechanism for constant change than free markets, conjoined with modern technology. This is especially true when they are likewise conjoined with an increasingly global mass media supported by ever-expanding information technologies. What could plausibly bring this mechanism to a grinding halt short of some form of holocaust? Is this not a steamroller that will crush everything that tries to congeal in its path, along with any remnants of past traditions? Put another way, is it possible for new traditions to form in this whirlwind?

Needless to say, near-term political and economic collapse remains a very real possibility, but how would it do anything but postpone the eventual march of modernity? Will Russia or its former satellites in Eastern Europe continue to turn to old traditions when they have become more successful at being modern, as seems a likely outcome sooner or later? To presume to prove empirically that History cannot end because of present manifestations of tribalism, fundamentalist religion or any other "facts," one would have to give persuasive answers to these questions and many more, not simply make empirical assertions.

The real issue is, what sovereign **theoretical** understanding leads us to believe in the imperviousness of present empirical givens in the undeveloped world, in an age of cascading global technological homogenization? Have we not created a world that will inevitably destroy old traditions without providing the circumstances for the generation of new ones? Are there any rational principles that can plausibly be thought to replace the shared *ethoi* that bind classes and generations together? If there were such rational principles, has our experience in the modern world heightened or destroyed our faith in universal Enlightenment?

If we have created a world of constant, monotonous change, History could end with ongoing, monotonous agitation. We would not have proved that History was some inevitable process. But we might be forced to conclude that our unique present obliterates past possibilities and simultaneously makes unique future possibilities unlikely.[15]

After a certain point humanity could very well arrive at a moment of **irreversibility**. The End of History need not require Hegelian **inevitability.** If we arrive at a moment of irreversibility, and movement forward seems implausible, we may have arrived at—at the very least—an extended hiatus of History. The question is: Is there some nexus of variables that makes liberal, commercial, technological civilization both plausible as a global outcome and difficult if not unlikely to transcend—at least for a very considerable period of time? And if transcended, would our movement be in the direction of "down" or "back"? That too would prove the End of History thesis; all novel possibilities have already been seen, while repetitions of past moments are still possible.[16]

If one is opposed to the possibility of historical novelty—opposed to the possibility of the generation of novel social and political forms and ends not yet longed for—then one should accept the End of History.[17] Either there is the possibility of historical novelty or we have seen all possibilities in morality, religion, poetry, art and politics, played out at least once already.

It could be argued that even if human nature, understood primarily qua efficient causality, is not simply operative, human imagination and creativity are indomitable. Here we arrive at an argument that is in its own way Hegelian; it rests on the premise that genuine, concrete historical change is preceded by the generation of novel ideas. When we generate new aspirations, goals and ideals we act differently and that eventually has concrete consequences in the world we share. But this approach also begs the question. The Hegelian point is that ideas and ideals sequence themselves in a way that leads from less comprehensive and more contradictory ideas to the most comprehensive and least contradictory ones, at which point the process of fundamental change stops because idea novelty stops. When idea novelty stops, and the latest ideas have been actualized in concrete institutions, History ends. Again, the only compelling empirical proof that this position is wrong would require the production of a novel ideal.[18] There simply is no evidence that has occurred since Hegel.

There have been post-Hegelian thinkers who have operated on a very high philosophical level—I have in mind especially Nietzsche and Heidegger— but they are fundamentally negative or merely hopeful. The central question is, what ideal is possible beyond a world devoted to universal equality (hence the pursuit of equal dignity and recognition), prosperity for all individuals, a secure, long, fear-free life, etc.? That ideal may not be fully manifested in present concrete reality, but what **ideal** could conceivably replace it that would win substantial acceptance? If no such ideal is imaginable, History could be at an end. If no novel ideals are possible our only alternative—other than to continue to globally actualize the reigning ideal—is to engage in sorties through past ideas and forms in acts of remembrance. Or we could try to patch old ideals and forms together into novel pastiches (i.e., practice the ironic, eclecticism of postmodernism).

The possibility of idea and ideal completion or exhaustion points in the direction of another fairly recent "end of" thesis—the end of political philosophy, a subject to which I will return in the next chapter. There has surely been revived interest in the history of political philosophy in recent years, and political theory abounds—that is, working out the ramifications of already manifest ideals—but where is the evidence of a novel speculative political philosophy? Much of fashionable postmodernism seems devoted to proving both the impossibility and undesirability of efforts to generate such political philosophies. What is at stake is the possibility of the generation of novel speculative political philosophies, especially ones that bind together the whole and are integrative and "holistic" in the fashion I will suggest below.

The proof that speculative political philosophy remains a possibility is an empirical one. But anyone trying to produce a truly novel speculative political philosophy will immediately see the difficulty. Again, precisely what is it one would wish for that we do not already have at least in theory? And, is there an interesting, non-atavistic faction in the world that wishes something other than a long, comfortable life, self-interested and self-sufficient, devoted primarily to an industrious acquisitiveness, freedom from pain and fear of violent death, with secularized institutions, great latitude of moral belief, and so on? Where is the comprehensive longing that lies beyond that modern dream that can offer a plausible object of aspiration? And even if there are a few who have such longings beyond the modern dream—and they would need someone to articulate that longing in a theoretically serious fashion—what is the likelihood of it gaining public manifestation rather than remaining a shared private fantasy of at most a few?[19] Is not the modern, bourgeois longing precisely what the majority of human beings desire everywhere and always? Other ideals are those of the few. What chance do the ideals of the few have of gaining ascendancy in an increasingly homogeneous, egalitarian age?

The two greatest philosophers of the post-Hegelian era, Nietzsche and Heidegger, give us no specific political philosophies, and Heidegger's thought, like much of contemporary philosophy, moves further and further away from concrete discussions.[20] Nietzsche, conceding Hegel's point, brings his thought to a culmination in willing the eternal recurrence of the same; in other words, Nietzsche simply wills a rerunning of History, not a novel moment. Heidegger, again conceding a Hegelian point, argues that at least an extended historical hiatus has arrived. He waits for a new god or a new dispensation of Being, neither of which, he admits, may come for a long time if at all. The record to date should not occasion great optimism for the early arrival of a genuinely **post**modern idea of justice, or a **post**modern articulation of the whole. Hence the end of History thesis is not as simple to dismiss as many on both the right and the left would lead us to believe. Simply to confront it would require that a different set of questions be addressed than those that have occupied most of Fukuyama's respondents.

It is certainly true that we have been witnessing the theoretical disintegration of faith in the principles that provide the foundation for the modern civilization that seems to be consolidating its gains globally.[21] But that fact only proves the ironic nature of our situation, not that counter-ideals exist. And when we are repeatedly told that modern liberal principles do not ground moral meaning, while allowing that meaning to intrude from a variety of traditional sources, we again see the irony of our situation. Will past traditions and norms become extinct and new ones become impossible, leaving global modern liberalism spiritually hollow—albeit materially comfortable and perhaps thereby acceptable to the majority?

Needless to say, the irony of our situation has caused more than a little shared inarticulate anxiety. The energetic responses Fukuyama has aroused are related to this pool of anxiety. But anxiety does not prove the possibility of a counter-ideal either. We should recall that the End of History thesis is just one of a series of parallel theses that we have witnessed as the twentieth century has unfolded. We could begin by pointing to the earlier twentieth century preoccupations with the end or decline of the West, add to that the far more academic discussions of the end of ideology or the end of political philosophy and make ourselves fashionably current by pointing to the various discussions of postmodern**ism** that will undoubtedly preoccupy us further into the twenty-first century. Add to these terms like postindustrial society, poststructuralism, the end of man, the decline of logo-centrism and like phrases that are all too familiar and one would have an odd mélange that seemingly shares only one idea: There is a more or less inarticulate sense that something out of the ordinary is occurring around us.

Beyond that vague sense, it remains unclear whether that which is occurring points toward a long period of stasis, a relatively quick transition to something novel, or the early stages of a novel future already deploying itself. Ambiguity always leads to uneasiness. Only a few, rare intellectuals could revel in irony and ambiguity as a way of life. Hence, anyone who revivifies an inarticulate uneasiness will run the risk of the kinds of responses Fukuyama received. But none of this proves the possibility of a novel postmodern ideal.

Many of Fukuyama's critics have been generous enough to recognize that his book-length treatment adds depth and subtlety to the initial articulation of his thesis. The price one pays for subtlety is frequently the introduction of new ambiguities. In the latest account, Fukuyama offers several different engines that move the dialectic of History. First, there is the dialectic of modern science and technology, which overlaps with and informs a dialectic of capitalist market economies. Something similar to the Heideggerian analysis of the inevitable and unidirectional march of modern technology seems to take hegemony in this part of the account—albeit in modern fashion technology is seen by Fukuyama as primarily emancipatory rather than alienating.

Second, there is also the spiritual or psychological dialectic of recognition, which is given two by no means identical articulations, one in **consciousness**—and here we come in contact with its modern Hegelian manifestation—and one in the **instinctive** love of honor—here we are confronted with Plato's discussion of *thumos*.[22] The spiritual dialectic leads Fukuyama to a reflection on the banality of bourgeois culture—shared substantially by authors from Tocqueville to Nietzsche, and many others. This part of the argument is in tension with the fundamentally optimistic faith in the emancipatory goodness of technology and markets. Many of the ambiguities of Fukuyama's account come from a failure to differentiate these different engines of History, or to explain how they might converge. Hegel does a better job in this regard.

Fukuyama's technological engine of History moves unavoidably in the direction of a global economy in which nation-states play a diminished role in the face of large-scale global, multinational institutions. This effect is magnified by the existence of the mass media, which increasingly gives everyone access to the same culturally homogenizing influences. In this fashion Western influences consolidate their hold globally. No nation can afford not to modernize or join the global economy or it will lose any chance for even minimal national autonomy, whether conceived in tribal terms or in some other fashion. Despite the growing global tribalism many of his critics glory in reciting, Fukuyama concludes that the parochial—whether conceived ethnically or religiously—is on a more or less gentle and extended slippery slide toward the universal. (Fukuyama clouds the issue somewhat by observing that this outcome may be mitigated in various Asian nations by Confucian traditions. Why that would be true requires further articulation.) Brute nature itself seems to pose the only potential barrier to this outcome, since limited resources might lead to the inevitability of a zero-sum economic game. While it would be imprudent to predict with certainty the near term outcome of the simultaneous globalization and tribalization which at present confront each other, the globalizing tendencies seem to have the upper hand.

As regards the dialectical movement of consciousness (recognition), Fukuyama openly follows Hegel—passed through the mediating lens of

Alexandre Kojève.[23] The fundamentally modern turn to **consciousness** that Kojève resolutely developed,[24] shared by many of Fukuyama's critics, is that man is not primarily a fixed, determinate being but a consciousness that changes and evolves and at each stage "outers" itself, achieving thereby various concrete manifestations in different religions, art forms, cultures, constitutions, and eventually the technological transformation of the natural world. Having passed through a multitude of stages and seen the various forms of narrowness of each successive stage, humanity would return to a previous stage only on the basis of error or forgetfulness rather than conscious rational choice.

Through an extended period of trial and error, which must be recorded in detail—and our historically conscious age is amazing in its ability to record and preserve—consciousness reaches ever more comprehensive and allegedly less contradictory states. Eventually it arrives at a point with which there is at least relatively high satisfaction on the part of the majority—taking into account the effects of the unavoidable pettiness, envy and jealousy that would remain—having transformed the external world to correspond with its internal consciousness. In the process of its journey, consciousness not only produces ideas, but acts upon them and concretely actualizes them. In this way consciousness transforms the external world—and any adequate theory of human reality must account for our ability to do this. Eventually the world we occupy bears primarily the stamp of a human creation. Consequently, the dialectic of consciousness should ultimately dovetail with the technological dialectic. Living in a humanized world, human beings allegedly achieve a satisfaction they could not achieve in the natural world. Again, this is the modern premise par excellence, whether we take Hobbes, Locke, Rousseau, Hegel or whomever as our favorite exemplar.

It is certainly true that Fukuyama adds a potential confusion by trying to synthesize the Hegelian discussion of recognition—a phenomenon primarily of consciousness—and Platonic *thumos*—primarily a phenomenon of fixed, instinctive being. As a result, Plato and Hegel cease to present us with fundamental alternatives. Further, Fukuyama's psychological dialectic eventually comes up against the empirical fact of significant if not universal alienation from modern, urban, global, technological civilization. That alienation can be accounted for in one of two more or less exclusive ways. Either the ideal that awaits at the end of the evolution of consciousness has not yet been perfectly manifested empirically on a sufficiently global basis, or man is not so much an evolving consciousness as a fixed being with a nature, suppression or sublimation of which within a technological civilization is necessarily alienating or dissatisfying. If the latter, nature could always rebel given the chance (barring the transformation of that nature by modern biological science). History might be irreversible, but it is never simply at an end as long as something deep in our being can repeatedly reassert itself.[25] History could be both irreversible and a terminus only if man was primarily a consciousness or if that part of his being that is fixed was irreversibly transformed.[26]

The central issue raised by the End of History debate has simply not been addressed by Fukuyama's critics: Is Fukuyama's point primarily theoretical or empirical? If both, how are the two related and/or which takes priority? By way of an answer, I would make the following fairly simple observation: To know that History, or anything else, had ended on a purely theoretical level would require us to know how the entirety of the human things—which is the subject matter of History—is integrated into the non-human. In other words, we would have to have complete knowledge of the Whole to make definitive statements about how any of the parts, particularly the human, fit into the Whole. We should admit that we will never have perfect knowledge about the Whole; hence we will never have finished knowledge about how the parts are articulated into the Whole. Likewise, we will never have final knowledge about the sense in which any of the parts could reach a terminus beyond which there is no novelty. Consequently, we cannot know with theoretical certainty whether History has or has not reached a terminus. But we can know that empirical evidence is never adequate to dispose of the issue. Where does that leave us?

This points to the fact that we should expect all articulations of the Whole to be partial. One would therefore expect a spectacle of repeated attempts to articulate the Whole, none of them perfectly adequate, with different ones publicly persuasive at different times and with the reasons that account for persuasiveness being somewhat unpredictable. If each attempt gives rise to various interpretations or "disseminations," with their own distinctive deferred ramifications and unpredictable practical consequences—as is reasonable to predict—one would expect novel ways of living to emerge. If we do not see evidence of that and see instead what looks like snowballing global homogenization, some at least temporary impasse or hiatus can legitimately be thought to have settled in and require explanation.[27] That explanation will be theoretical even though it can never be apodictic. Since it is unlikely that we will ever grasp the Whole, or if we did adequately grasp it—through some direct noetic act of apprehension—that we could articulate it comprehensively in some final form of public speech, it is unlikely we will ever arrive at the comparatively prosaic knowledge of the exact relationship between human consciousness or thought and our determinate natural being.[28] Hence perfect knowledge of precisely what we are as human is likely to remain a mystery—which is not to say that since we do not know everything, we do not know anything.

Further, as a theoretical matter it is necessary to state precisely what kind of terminus it is at which we are asserting History arrives when we say it ends. Is it the kind of end beyond which there is one or another form of nothingness or indeterminacy, or is it the kind of end that is understood as a perfection? In a significant way, Fukuyama thinks that something literally ceases in the sense that something that was part of the human scene hitherto will not be seen in the future. In another sense, Fukuyama wants to say that a form of perfection is reached, although the message is mixed, since a certain impoverishment is also possible, and the end of the possibility of novel ideas and ideals is posited as well. It would be helpful if Fukuyama could clarify the relationship between end understood teleologically and as terminus beyond which there is one kind of nothingness or another.[29] While it is plausible to project a terminus of History qua extended hiatus, it is not theoretically possible to project an end qua perfection given that we are not simply determinate beings moved only by efficient causality. If we were, there would be no History in any interesting sense. There can be History only because in some fashion we are historical beings.

These clarifications to the contrary notwithstanding, it should be admitted that one can "clarify" even a compelling idea out of existence and not thereby attend to what is truly compelling in it. What is it that is truly compelling in the end of History thesis? Let us begin by setting all "facts" aside and recognize that a theoretical frame cannot help but always be part of our approach to reality. That said, it should be recognized that it will be difficult to develop— or to mysteriously find ourselves equipped with—a post-Hegelian theoretical frame—here understood as a genuinely postmodern frame. Hence present empirical circumstances may be settling in for a long period. On this level, the End of History thesis can be **compelling** without being **conclusive.**

The End of History thesis presents a picture of an increasingly global, egalitarian, commercial, technological civilization emerging, one that at the very least may have great staying power. Yet two issues remain open: (1) Is it good? (2) If not, what is implied in the possibility of transcending it? Having arrived at those two questions, I would argue that the End of History debate would be better posed as an End of Modernity debate in which one seriously reconsiders the modern dream, the arguments in its favor and those against it. Such a reconsideration would occasion an explicit discussion of fundamental questions concerning the nature of justice and the human good. It would also require an explicit reflection on the place of the human within the larger Whole, knowing in advance that we cannot arrive at a definitive conclusion for all times as a result of those reflections. Reflections of this kind are necessary and ones which an increasingly technological and utilitarian civilization has tried to bury in the dustbin of History—while implicitly presupposing distinct answers.

I would argue that we should engage in a fundamental questioning of modernity not with an eye to pre-modernity as an alternative to the possibility of a late modern hiatus of History, but with an eye to the possibility of the genuinely **post**modern.[30] As long as a fundamental, essential kind of thinking of this sort remains possible and can find some public manifestation in the concrete world—in other words, as long as thinking does not choose, nor is forced, to retreat to some epicurean garden—History cannot end in any strong sense.[31] But if such essential reflection ceases to have a public echo we would have no right to glibly dismiss the End of History thesis. The End of History thesis points toward the need for—and reflections on the possibility of—speculative political philosophy. If it remains possible, all horizons are still open.

NOTES

1. The operative texts are G. W. F. Hegel, *Phenomenology of Spirit*, trans. A. V. Miller (New York: Oxford University Press, 1977); and Alexander Kojève, *Introduction to the Reading of Hegel*, trans. James Nichols (New York: Basic Books, 1969).

2. The End of History debate also comes at a time when there is increasing suspicion about the meaningfulness of traditional left-right or progressive-conservative dichotomies. Progressives frequently label everything that differs from their view as "reactionary," usually on the basis of a hidden End of History premise. They know they represent the cutting edge of History, hence only movement in the same direction they desire is legitimate. Anything that differs from the direction in which they wish to move must be a form of going back because there is nothing beyond their position that could come in the future. In this way the progressives become the defenders of the status quo. It is the conservatives who want change—either back or in some unclearly specified direction. The role reversals of progressives and conservatives may indicate the approaching end of the line for such distinctions. Terms that emerged as part of the fight for and against throne and altar, even when revamped for use in the confrontation between Marxist collectivism and Liberal capitalism, will not retain their force indefinitely.

3. See especially, Jacques Derrida, *Writing and Difference* (Chicago: University of Chicago Press, 1978); Michel Foucault, *The Order of Things* (New York; Vintage Books, 1973); and Jean Francois Lyotard, *The Post-Modern Condition* (Manchester: Manchester University Press, 1984) This can be seen clearly in the work of Nietzsche. However, History still retained a somewhat predictable circularity or repeatability for Nietzsche. It was Martin Heidegger who, in radically attacking the premises that support the Enlightenment faith in Progress, opened the door to the historically random and mysterious. Heidegger presents an account of the Whole (Being) dominated by various fated historical dispensations that are altogether unpredictable. In its comings and goings, presencings and absencings, Being is simply beyond human comprehension; consequently so is History. French epigones such as Michel Foucault and Jacques Derrida build on these Heideggerian premises to the same end. Man can no longer predict and

control existence as the modern thinkers had hoped. Fellow Frenchman Jean Francois Lyotard codifies these efforts and announces the end of the age of "metanarratives" (see *The Post-Modern Condition* [Minneapolis: University of Minnesota Press, 1984]).

4. What we call "common sense" is never something autonomous that we can use as a yardstick to measure theoretical frameworks. Today's common sense is the diluted, deferred ramification of a theory from the past. That is not to say that common sense is not more or less related to actual phenomena that show themselves in the present. Common sense, the shared understandings of a people that share a way of life, is not simply decayed theoretical overlay.

5. Obviously, progress in limited individual areas would remain possible, together with simultaneous retrogression in others. But the larger notion of simultaneous, linear Progress scientifically, morally, politically, socially, technologically, psychologically, etc., would be lost.

6. For example, if we think greater egalitarianism is necessary it must be defended substantively on the basis of an explicit discussion of such things as the nature of justice and the human good. To do so all manner of suppressed premises would have to be made explicit. Then we would immediately see the difficulties involved in enjoining the substantive debate.

7. One can accept the wisdom of unleashing human spontaneity from bureaucratic manipulation without falling prey to a mythic faith in an "invisible hand"—one permutation of which is not that far from Hegel's notion of the "cunning of reason."

8. One exception is William Galston's *Liberal Purposes: Goods, Virtues and Diversity in the Liberal State* (New York: Cambridge University Press, 1992). Fukuyama may still be correct that the kinds of virtues Galston catalogues are an uninspiring ensemble ill-equipped to hold the spiritual attention of the brightest and best, or even the majority.

9. Elsewhere I have differentiated what I believe could legitimately be called **post**modern from postmodernism. The latter is a straightforwardly late-modern phenomenon. See my *Nietzsche, Heidegger and the Transition to Postmodernity* (Chicago: University of Chicago Press, 1996).

10. The not so subtle irony is that many of those who attacked Fukuyama had been operating upon their own furtive, usually suppressed, End of History theses.

11. I will argue below for the need to recover "nature." But I will argue that what is needed in the recovery of the phenomenon nature, not the concept or idea nature. I will discuss the difference below.

12. This is precisely what a self-styled "postmodern, bourgeois ironist" like Richard Rorty does. See especially *Contingency, irony, solidarity* (New York: Cambridge University Press, 1991).

13. The central issue we confront at this point is one that cannot be adequately dealt with at present: What is the relation between reason, habit and tradition? The End of History thesis is the ultimate outcome of the Enlightenment faith that reason could replace habit and tradition completely. That was a fantastic hope from the beginning. But through acting upon that faith we have gone a long way toward destroying the habit background that is needed by any functioning society. Reason always requires law and habit as allies.

Even if reason is sufficient to grasp eternal questions and problems that does not prove that reason can be immediately manifested in the conventional arrangements needed for everyday life. Indeed, reason can be adequately manifested in more than one set of conventional arrangements—the doctrinaire, modern, absolutist faith to the contrary notwithstanding. That is substantially what Aristotle meant when he asserted that justice is natural even though it changes.

The relation between philosophic insight and the traditions and *ethoi* that support daily existence is complicated. Unless one retains an unbounded faith in Enlightenment, shared *ethoi* are needed and must be allowed to evolve slowly over many generations. We cannot simply will viable traditions even if we could grasp the Whole exhaustively. We always need to find the way to articulate the truth for our time and place. How that could be accomplished in our time of unprecedented simultaneous changeableness and creeping homogeneity remains the open question.

Even if we concluded that Plato, Aristotle, Aquinas or whomever had grasped the truth, it still has to be articulated publicly and manifested in laws, customs and habits. And the truth must be presented in ever-renewed poetic articulations. Where are the poetic articulations, habits and traditions for our time—the time at the end of the persuasiveness and plausibility of many *modern* beliefs and premises?

14. Consider in this regard, Alexis de Tocqueville, "How the Aspect of Society in the United States Is at Once Agitated and Monotonous," *Democracy in America*, trans. George Lawrence (New York: Doubleday and Co., 1969), pp. 614–16.

15. Of course, we can always believe in—or will—some version of the eternal recurrence. Even then we would be forced to explain what circumstance might return us to the beginnings. For us, the possibility of such a "return" probably would imply an apocalypse no sane person would wish for. But this would still not disprove the End of History thesis which claims only the impossibility of future novelty, not the impossibility of retrogression.

16. The collapse of Western (a.k.a. American) liberalism would in and of itself prove nothing. Likewise, natural catastrophes that reduce us to a more barbaric situation would prove nothing. The question would be, would we move to a novel set of historical possibilities, or "back" to ones that had already been lived? Having been pushed back to such a prior state, would we long for something novel in the future or would we then strive to get back to where we had already been? Everything comes back to the question, is there something novel—beyond late modernity—to long for? If not, the End of History thesis is plausible. The only point at which empirical evidence would be interesting is the empirical production of a novel ideal. We have seen none since Hegel.

17. If one accepts the argument that human nature is fixed and that there are a finite number of fundamental questions and human longings capable of playing themselves out, at some point History should have played out its finite possibilities. At that point only repetition or stagnation are possible.

18. It is no good saying that changes in material circumstances precede all changes in ideas, for one must still conceptualize, using ideas, what that change is/was. Worrying about the relation between ideas and material circumstances one quickly gets drawn into an unsolvable chicken-egg conundrum. Rather than be drawn into this use-

less discussion we should bring ourselves back to more manageable observations such as that ideas have concrete consequences and no ideas are formed in a vacuum. We should add to this the understanding that truly novel ideas are rare.

19. The same response can be made to those who say that "philosophy" represents a satisfactory response to present dissatisfaction with the moral and political contours of the late modern world. "Philosophy" is hardly an alternative for any but a few—to believe otherwise is Enlightenment at its silliest. Further, if philosophy exists only in some Epicurean garden, of what public interest is it? We may grant that philosophy should not be turned into a public weapon as it has in the modern world, but as an entirely private affair of the few it would be publicly irrelevant and hence irrelevant to the present discussion. Were the privatization of philosophy to occur we would have the Nietzschean picture of free-spirited overmen tripping quietly across the anthills that pass for civilization—what Nietzsche also termed the timeless "tombs of death." A deeper response would go to the nature of philosophy itself. Must not philosophy, in Socratic fashion, remain in the cave, and begin from speeches in the political community? If so, the epicurean alternative is destructive for philosophy itself. Once we recognize the need to speak, we recognize simultaneously the need to be persuasive. Then we are led back to the issues we have been discussing—what novel ideal can be persuasively argued for at present—surely not the universalization of philosophy?

20. This is not to say that in unhinging old presuppositions Heidegger's thought may not eventually have concrete, deferred ramifications. See in this regard my *Martin Heidegger: Paths Taken, Paths Opened* (Lanham: Rowman & Littlefield, 2007).

21. It is not at all easy to explain what accounts for the disintegration of faith in a moral or political dispensation—unless, of course, one turns to Hegelian premises. It is far too easy to say that it is because the old dispensation came to be seen as false. Does that mean that the reason for its initial persuasiveness was precisely its falsity? It seems to me that a dead end lurks in that direction. It is unlikely that reason is ever **fully** adequate to "prove" or "disprove" the persuasiveness of a political and moral dispensation. To claim that it is gets us in the awkward position of arguing that the "irrationalists" had, at one time, the stronger "reasons." And once again, even if we are capable of a noetic apprehension of the truth, it must still be put into speech, and unless you are Hegel, there is more than one way to do that. There is no reason to believe that what some of us might see as a compelling articulation of the truth will be publicly more persuasive than what some of us perceive to be false.

22. The idea that our fundamental humanity is to be found in our ego or consciousness rather than in our instinctive materiality is one of the central modern premises from Descartes to Hegel. By the time this modern idea had worked its way out to Kant and Hegel, our fundamental humanity was to be found not only in consciousness, but in conscious opposition to or negation of our instinctive materiality. This consciousness/instinct dichotomy is a distinctively modern invention.

23. Many critics of the End of History thesis have dismissed Kojève as a quaint and curious volume of increasingly forgotten lore. But the customary basis for those rejections is far from weighty—usually boiling down to the observation, correct if banal, that Anglo-American academics have paid him almost no attention. But Kojève is one of those rare individuals who truly deserves to be called a thinker. He knew how to take

a theoretical premise, isolate its key concepts and follow them resolutely to wherever might lead regardless of personal rooting interests. That kind of philosophical honesty is rare. It does not prove that Kojève is correct, but it does prove he deserves respect. By the same token, that most Hegel scholars dismiss Kojève's reading of Hegel does not prove that he is wrong. It is rare to find scholars who are honest brokers. One cannot fail to see the extent to which Hegel scholarship gives us a liberal, socialist, conservative or simply boring Hegel.

24. This could also, to use a term coined by Rousseau, be designated our "metaphysical freedom." This is *the* premise of late modernity—shared by Rousseau, Kant, Hegel, Marx, Existentialism, Critical Theory, etc. This is the idea upon which late modernity must make its stand. See in this regard my *Nietzsche, Heidegger and the Transition to Postmodernity*, Part 1, "The Essence of Modernity." According to this understanding, our metaphysical freedom is based on the fact that we are unlike all other species in that we are instinctively underdetermined. This allows us to determine ourselves, to a greater or lesser extent and more or less consciously, depending on the author. Unfortunately, the competition to determine man becomes increasingly hypothetical, abstract and artificial, at which point one senses that this line of argument has more or less reached its terminus. For an Anglo-American example of this artificiality consider John Rawls, *A Theory of Justice* (Cambridge: Harvard University Press, 1971), and his "Original Positions."

25. For reasons I will indicate shortly, I do not believe we should become overly delighted with the premise that human nature can always reassert itself. We live in a time when the mentality of limitlessness has taken hegemony. We are simultaneously equipped with techniques that allow us to assault natural limits—e.g., genetic engineering—and the desire to transcend all natural limits. Even if we could articulate what is fixed in our humanity, we are in a position to eradicate it. Hence the central question is one of ideas: should we or should we not continue further on the path to overcoming natural limits? We are then led right back into the kinds of issues we have been considering.

26. In my opinion, we are not confronted here by an either/or situation: The relationship between evolving consciousness and determinate materiality is complex. Fukuyama needs to work out more explicitly how the two are related. Perhaps he will return to this issue in a forthcoming sequel. The End of History debate confronts us with a version of the traditional nature/convention distinction. Is man primarily shaped by education, environment, culture, etc., or a genetically fixed and determinate being? This is in turn a version of what I would argue is an unsolvable chicken-egg problem of whether ideas cause changes in material reality or material changes prefigure changes in ideas. I believe it is best to conclude that the relationship is complex and that an either/or answer is not available. We have a fixed being that must be completed by habit, in a variety of different ways, albeit not an infinite variety. Our changing ideas have a significant influence on how that is accomplished.

Even here we are not confronted with a fundamentally empirical issue. Every modern "science" that presumes to speak about reality presupposes theories prior to the act of approaching empirical data; it would be naïve to think that those theories were morally and politically neutral. To try to deduce anything from scientific "facts" is simply to dig up what was presupposed from the very beginning. No science is morally, politically or metaphysically neutral. We should dismiss the contrary modern faith as a myth. I return thematically to this issue in part 4. Given that modern science cannot mediate the nature/convention issue, it is probably the case that we will never get beyond the conclusion that the relationship between evolving consciousness and determinate materiality is complex. Put another way, we will never get around the need to do speculative political philosophy.

27. As mentioned above, even if we find dissatisfaction by a few with the present world and the prevalent articulation of the Whole, it need not be interesting if global satisfaction by the majority remains. Living in a mass democratic age it would be unclear what ideas could come along to delegitimize the hegemony of the tastes, perceptions and desires of the majority. Who thinks there is a plausible basis for a newly legitimate Aristocracy; and from what direction might we expect its approach? Therein one may see one of the more compelling reasons why an extended hiatus of History is plausible.

28. This means we will never put to rest the fundamental nature/convention question and should be cautioned not to accept any simple invocation of either side of the equation.

29. For an important reflection on this subject see Joseph Cropsey, "The End of History in an Open-Ended Age?" in *If History Is Not Over, Then Where Is It Going? Reflections on Progress and Democracy*, eds. Arthur Melzer, Jerry Weinberger, and Richard Zinnman (Ithaca: Cornell University Press, 1994).

30. I have undertaken such a discussion in *Nietzsche, Heidegger and the Transition to Postmodernity*.

31. In other words, philosophy must always remain primarily dialectical political philosophy understood as proto-philosophy in the sense that I will propose in the next chapter. This necessity is for the sake of philosophy itself as well as the well-being of the rest of the world. The retreat to some garden of shared, private noetic apprehension—which always raises the question of whether or not one is engaged in some subjective fantasy—points toward an ultimate *alogon*, "blindness." Here we should recall the Socratic metaphor of trying to grasp Being directly as an inevitably blinding staring at the sun. Religion always runs the same risk of blindness as any simply noetic philosophy. Our noetic visions, whether based on grace or otherwise, must be brought to speech. Even faith in the words of the prophets raises the question of how to tell true from false prophets. All of our endeavors require dialectical speech. There is no way to transcend the dialogue that is intrinsic to being human. As dialectical and phenomenological in a sense I will propose, philosophy grows out of and is part of its shared world; and that ultimately means it must engage in shared public speech.

Chapter Three

What Is Political Philosophy: A Phenomenological Approach

What philosophy essentially can and must be is this; a thinking that breaks the paths and opens the perspectives of the knowledge . . . that kindles and necessitates all inquiries and thereby threatens all values . . . [T]he authentic function of philosophy [is] to challenge historical being-there and hence, in the last analysis, being pure and simple. It restores to things, to beings, their weight (Being).[1]

The now and the past on earth—alas, my friends, that is what I find most unendurable; and I should not know how to live if I were not also a seer of that which must come . . . I walk among men as among the fragments of the future—that future which I envisage . . . "It was"—that is the name of the will's gnashing of teeth and most secret melancholy. Powerless against what has been done, he is an angry spectator of all that is past . . . The spirit of revenge, my friends, has so far been the subject of man's best reflection; . . . [T]he will should at last redeem himself; and will should become not willing . . . All "it was" is a fragment, a riddle a dreadful accident—until the creative will says to it, "But thus I will it; thus shall I will it."[2]

PHILOSOPHY: PAST, PRESENT AND FUTURE

Fifty years ago there was considerable talk about the "End of Political Philosophy." At about the same time, it was also asserted that we had arrived at the parallel "End of Ideology." This was to lead to a spirited, if short-lived, debate about the "End of History."[3] All of these assertions exist within the orbit of the more comprehensive assertions about the "End of Philosophy." They belong to the same intellectual situation from which contemporary

37

thought must begin: Have we arrived at some significant end, beyond which certain features of past life, especially in the West, drop out? If so, why should we care?

Is it still possible for philosophy to open the future as something other than a stagnant, changeless repetition of the present or as the product of blind fate? Can Western humanity still open unique futures for itself by design? I will argue that intrinsic to our nature is our ability to generate unique manifestations of "historical existence." An endless, unchanging, stagnant repetition of the present would be tantamount to the extinction of our humanity. Further, I will argue that proto-philosophy, understood as political philosophy, is the prerequisite for our being historical beings. And, given that the engine of constant transformation born of the coming together of modern technology and global commerce will continue to radically change at least the material circumstances of life, I assume that an ossification of present social and political forms is not conducive to the just, the noble and the good in an environment of constant transformation. Are we not caught in that superficial present which Tocqueville described as "agitated and monotonous," alienated from both past and future? I have always been struck by Strauss's powerful formulation which so ably and economically depicts this possibility: "It means unity of the human race on the lowest level, complete emptiness of life, self-perpetuating doctrine without rhyme or reason; no leisure, no concentration, no elevation, no withdrawal; nothing but work and recreation; no individuals and no peoples, but instead "lonely crowds."[4]

But the continued existence of political philosophy is an issue that seems to excite the imagination of almost no one in our time. At the deepest level the reason why the question regarding the possibility of political philosophy is no longer even asked is the present hegemony of the "critique of metaphysics," and associated assertions about the "End of Philosophy." At its most profound level that critique comes from Martin Heidegger. It is that critique that must be confronted. The future possibility of political philosophy—of philosophy being of some public use in opening the future—can, I argue, only be clarified in our time by passing through a confrontation with Heidegger and, thus, not simply by rejecting him.

Only if man is understood as a historical being who must constantly adapt to his situation is political philosophy an ongoing necessity. Hence for political philosophy the future takes a certain priority to the past and present. The primary task is to secure the future, not to preserve the past. As even Aristotle observed, the old and the good are not identical. If the future moment always takes priority, political philosophy is not primarily a conservative undertaking—albeit it remains a task to conserve the essential elements of our humanity. If the future takes priority, philosophy will always be what Nietzsche designated as "untimely." But, I will argue, it is an undertaking that is impossible if in look-ing to the future we sever ourselves from affirming the past as being just as we would have wanted it, agreeing with Nietzsche that this is the only way to quit the "spirit of revenge."

If political philosophy requires that we be temporally projected both for-ward toward the future and back toward the past tradition, it requires the stance the "early" Heidegger designated as "authentic,"[5] an "ecstatic" tempo-ral stance that emerges again, in different form, in the allegedly "later" Hei-degger.[6] But after Heidegger no simple return to the past tradition of political philosophy is possible. Nonetheless, the past was **necessary** and we **are** our past.[7] Neither an attempted return to some allegedly perfect moment in past action or thought, nor a simple rejection of the past *in toto*—that stands nowhere and constructs future "frames" or "utopias" *ex nihilo*—represents an adequate temporal stance in **our** present. Finally, the thought that links past and future must grow out of "phenomena" as they **presently** present them-selves in the everyday perceptions and aspirations of the vast majority of hu-man beings. This suggested "phenomenological" beginning is intended to be an alternative to modern "constructivism" and implies that there are funda-mental issues that grow out of life itself.

POLITICAL PHILOSOPHY AND
THE PHENOMENA OF EVERYDAY LIFE

If there are phenomena that grow out of life itself, what are they? We can be-gin to see them in the **questions** that grow out of life itself. The unavoidable existential question is "How shall I live"? **Human** beings are the only beings confronted by this question because apparently we are not completely deter-mined by necessity. Further, the answer to this question is never obvious be-cause our possible ends transcend simple survival and self-preservation. This is especially true in civilizations that can produce plenty. Philosophy takes off from the question that no human being can avoid; hence it includes ethics as part of itself.

The first question is both the necessary and historical origin of questioning. Contrary to Heidegger, ethics takes priority to ontology. Avoiding this ques-tion is only possible on the basis of already having presupposed an answer— the best life is the unexamined life, the life I am already living, the conven-tional life lived by all or most, the life made necessary or unavoidable by present circumstances, the ancestral/traditional life, etc. If those answers were acceptable there would be no need for human beings to engage in question-ing. Repeatedly, those answers have proven to be unacceptable, certainly since Socrates. Hence I assume we are led unavoidably to the question "How shall I live?" or in more traditional terms "What is the good life"? Is there only one good life equally applicable to me and all others, is the good life dependent upon my historical circumstances or on unchanging underlying phenomena, and so on? Along that path an ensemble of other questions arises that needs not detain us at present. I am asserting that this unavoidable openness to questioning forms the basis of life for truly **human** beings, which means, historical beings who can live in qualitatively different ways. To live in different ways, and in different historical worlds, is of the essence of humanity. To cease to do so is to be at best post-human.

But this first ensemble of questions will inevitably involve us in a second set of questions. Given that we come forth into the world in groups, how does the existence of others affect the good life for me or you or the anonymous person indeterminately somewhere.[8] There is no reason to believe we were given a prior choice of our co-travelers any more than it is plausible to think that future human beings living in an increasingly crowded world will have such a choice. Hence we cannot avoid the question "How shall we live together?" In more traditional terms, "What is the best regime?" Does the best regime depend on the situation and the circumstances? Is the best regime large or small, "closed" or "open," etc.? These are the second set of questions that grow out of the phenomena themselves **without our theoretically constructing them**.

These two ensembles of questions about how we should live **are unavoidable**. And all answers simply are not equal. The life of a drug addict living in a commune of thieves has little to be said in its favor. No one could get through a day of his or her life without knowing this and many other things that imply knowledge of the good. It may or may not be true that ultimately we cannot have complete theoretical clarity about the good, but the fact that we do not have such complete knowledge does not mean that we do not know anything. Philosophy has no choice but to **begin** where life itself begins, with life's questions. This is especially true today given the rupture of the philosophic tradition. "We" are now forced to start from the beginning. But that beginning is where we are always already situated, in the phenomena.

It does not take long to realize that we cannot begin to answer either of these two questions until we know what kind of beings we are. Do we have a fixed "nature," are we changeable over time as a species, is each individual malleable within his or her own lifetime? What is the nature or essence of the beings who ask questions about how they should live? The existential questions force us toward questions about the nature of the being that raises those questions, about that which animates us toward that questioning, the soul, *psyche, anima*, which is to say, psychology. We move from ethics to political science to psychology. One can always despotically try to arbitrarily change the subject and wave away these questions as "metaphysical." But whether we are talking about Rorty, Derrida, a postmodernist feminist theorist or the garden-variety relativist at the local pub, all, in fact, presuppose answers to the questions posed above. One of the premises upon which I am operating is that the unexamined life is not the good life. But even if one asserts the opposite, he/she will still be drawn into the same questions. It is a regeneration of the discussion, **from the beginning(s), and that means from the phenomena**, that is necessary in our situation. And until we attempt it, we have no right to assume that we will simply repeat some past moment in thought, verifying thereby the eternal return of the same.

In due course it becomes clear that we cannot know our own essence without reflection upon how beings like ourselves are integrated into the more comprehensive whole of which we are a part. Hence we unavoidably must ask after the nature of the whole. One can assert that we cannot know the nature of the whole, but again, that person will either have to remain silent thereafter or in giving answers to any of the necessary existential and psychological questions presuppose ontological answers. In short, as Heidegger has argued, one always presupposes an ontology, and that in turn presupposes a doctrine of the Being of the beings who raise questions about Being as a whole. There is nothing to be gained by engaging these questions obliquely.

The final set of questions, both logically and historically, into which we are inevitably thrust are related to the question "How do we know?" We are unavoidably forced into questions about the nature of perception, apprehension and knowing. That said, I would argue that "epistemological" questions, while ultimately unavoidable, are the most derivative and last to arise and arise only at a high level of theoretical detachment from everyday life. That epistemology has become central for modern philosophy is a sign of its alienation from the phenomenological basis of everyday human understanding.

There are always "phenomena" from which we start and that are embedded in every activity we engage in as human beings whether we grasp this thematically or not. In our time, this understanding is most deeply and clearly presented by Heidegger who argued that all theoretical knowing takes off from a prior "everyday," **practical,** lived knowing and understanding. Whether we can or cannot get "beneath," "above," "outside," or "beyond" (*meta*) the phenomena as displayed in everyday life is an open question that in principle needs exploration. The very fact that we can stand back from our world, compare the thought of various thinkers and various civilizations, and even look at ourselves as if from outside seems to indicate that some detachment is possible. There is no reason to dismiss these phenomena in some self-invalidating reductionism; they need explanation.

The greatness of Heidegger's thought, even if this is not the entirety of what he was doing in his own mind,[9] was to show us the inevitability of fundamental questioning **and that it is an unavoidable unity**. The latter is certainly my conclusion. Heidegger opened the door to the recovery of political philosophy as the architectonic undertaking that affirms its past and cares for its future while necessarily addressing all the unavoidable questions **as a whole that includes all its parts**—ethics, politics, psychology, ontology, epistemology. My larger argument is that only a *logos* that can weave all of the parts of questioning together into a whole, and do so in the speech of the marketplace, will ever acquire any public persuasiveness. **Heidegger's thought most consistently points toward architectonic unity, not postmodernist fragmentation.**[10] All those who think we have outgrown this questioning, or think it is some situated prejudice of a particular race or gender are simply wrong and their own deeds and speeches will prove it when they become entangled in hopeless self-contradiction and litter their pages with self-invalidating premises.

What Heidegger has done is open the door to showing us the necessary unity of thought. For me, that highest unitary or holistic manifestation of philosophy is political philosophy. That various philosophers, for their various reasons, abdicated parts of the whole and set them off on allegedly autonomous paths—and Aristotle was one of the first and most mischievous in this regard—does not prove the necessity of those diremptions and abdications.[11] Political philosophy is the thematic reflection on the questions that every human being answers either consciously or unconsciously, and is the activity that fashions a persuasive, **public** articulation and integration of the whole.

This undertaking should lead to novelty if for no other reason than that it is unlikely that the answer to the question how shall we live together will be the same at all times. How could it be when at one time we lived in relatively closed communities of roughly 50,000, and we now live in an increasingly global world of ever multiplying billions linked by computer technology? Change one part of the whole and the whole must itself change and be rearticulated.[12] Furthermore, how could there be no significant change in the **public** articulation of philosophical reflection over time when the situation of thought itself, which is part of the whole, is in principle different with each addition to the whole—e.g., a tradition of thought is an open-ended undertaking which never simply overcomes its past? Admitting these facts does not lead us into relativism. It leads us only to the conclusion that the activity that is proto-philosophy—i.e., political philosophy—must be ever renewed and repeatedly brought to reflect on its unique situation as its necessary point of departure.

There is no doubt that the enterprise of thinking was a risky business at the time of the origins of the philosophic tradition. Socrates' fate testifies to that fact, as does the fate of countless victims of later inquisitions. Is political philosophy as risky a business in the present world? Of course not; in fact it is largely ignored. Might it become a risky undertaking again in the future? Possibly. Does the situation from which what I have presented as unavoidable questioning necessarily **begins** determine the way it is publicly disseminated in speech? Of course. But the ensembles of questions themselves remain the same and they are the substance of political philosophy, not the public *poiesis* through which political philosophy presents itself any more than the situation to which that rhetoric responds—both of which change. For example, I believe Strauss is absolutely correct that the situation in which political philosophy arose required a defensive posture. But that does not mean that that situation will always hold as primary. It may be the task of political philosophy at the present time not to defend itself against the city, but to defend the possibility of ongoing historical *praxis*, to defend the city against some of the philosophers.[13]

Strauss also observed that "there is no room for political philosophy in Heidegger's work."[14] Strauss was asserting that Heidegger had made traditional political philosophy impossible and was, furthermore, the most substantial critic of the philosophic tradition who ever lived. These assertions are correct as applied to the **past** tradition or to political philosophy understood as a branch of philosophy as Strauss asserts.[15] But I want to argue that Heidegger also opens a door toward the re-establishment of political philosophy in the future as an **architectonic** *poiesis* rather than deductive enterprise. Heidegger opens the door to seeing political philosophy as proto-philosophy. The speculative ideas of great thinkers like Heidegger change the entire landscape of thought.[16] They can be ignored only by adopting the stance of the ostrich. But that will not limit their influence, quite the contrary. Even in openly opposing the **substance** of the thought of Heidegger one is forced into playing the game on his home turf.

After Heidegger's path-breaking thought, no one will be able to present philosophy intellectually in any of its past métiers or rhetorical permutations. We have clearly seen ample evidence of this already. This does not in my view mean philosophy ends as Heidegger somewhat hyperbolically asserts, it merely must adapt to a changed situation. After all, one of the central features of philosophy is to reflect on the nature of philosophy itself. At the very least, that ongoing discussion always has to be conducted in the métier of its own time. But it can never avoid the fundamental questions in their unity that I posed above.

ON THE NATURE AND ORIGINS OF CONSTRUCTIVISM

Heidegger called our age the "Age of the World Picture," which for him is the same as saying it is the age dominated by "constructivism." Heidegger designates the constructivist essence of the modern age as "Enframing"

(*Gestell*). For Heidegger, late modern philosophy had finally consummated the transformation of Being into something that is entirely our construction and our projection. By "our" is meant the projection of a non-situated, self-grounding self or ego: whether that was the ego of an individual, a group or some species-being was left open. Ours is the constructivist age with the self-grounding, autonomous self as the ultimate ground and foundation of all that is. For Heidegger, this transformation to the constructivist age was allegedly prefigured in the Greek origins of the tradition of philosophy, but he is clear that strictly speaking there was never such a thing as an ancient or medieval "world view" or "frame," for neither the ancients nor the medievals viewed Being as **our** projection or construction any more than they viewed man as the self-grounding, un-situated "subject" that made these projections. Both saw Being as **self**-presenting (*physis*) and man as the being who apprehends (*noein*) that which **shows itself**.

At the heart of Heidegger's philosophical undertaking is the attempt to show that the original philosophical enterprise grew out of a pre-philosophic, "everyday" experience of Being. In bringing that experience to "scientific" speech in the way they did the earliest philosophers opened a door to a transformation of the everyday understanding of Being as *physis*—**emerging** into appearing that simultaneously holds itself back in concealment—to Being as *ousia*—fully accomplished, self-standing **presence**. For Heidegger, that transformation was the prerequisite for the eventual transformation of Being into a mere projection made by a fully present and self-transparent human "subject"—most notably originating in the philosophy of Descartes.

This understanding of the tradition led to Heidegger's unique understanding of what is meant by "metaphysics." For Heidegger, the entire tradition is metaphysical, even that modern part that saw itself as transcending metaphysics as traditionally understood. The traditional understanding presented metaphysics as the study of that which was beyond (*meta*) or transcendent of the physical world grasped by the senses. But for Heidegger any understanding is metaphysical that has a "doctrine of Being as presence," indeed as full, finished, perfectly accessible presence. The Platonic ideas were allegedly fully present to the mind, Descartes's ego was fully, self-transparently present to the thinker; Hegel's Absolute Spirit eventually was fully present in the world. The original pre-philosophic conception of Being as *physis*, as emergence, saw Being as both present and absent at the same time, unconcealed and concealed simultaneously. There was the permanent threat, if not necessity, of things repeatedly falling back into concealment since they could not achieve full permanence and presence. The metaphysical tradition allegedly changed all this and took away the threat of Nothingness, where the Not had originally belonged to emergent Being itself.

While I do not accept Heidegger's reading of, for example, Plato, in calling our attention to the questionable status of modern "metaphysical" beliefs, especially things like the fully present subject or ego, Heidegger has made it almost impossible for future thought to put its faith in the modern constructivist approach except as a pure article of faith. This approach will not be cast aside overnight, but it is predictable that there will be a law of diminishing returns. One of the few benign effects of the work of Heidegger's French epigones has been to speed this process. Put another way, the life span of constructivist thought is now limited. And almost everything that passes for political philosophy in our time—albeit it best deserves to be called political "theory"—is constructivist. And by that I mean that even those attempts that presume to go back to some previous author and adopt his stance are engaged in constructivism. It is a self-conscious ego standing at some fully present Archimedean point that is making these choices, whether they be for Aristotle, Locke, Kant, Hegel, whomever. The possibility of political philosophy as I understand it—not constructivist political "theory"—now and in the future exists only in a post-constructivist environment and Heidegger has opened the door to that possibility.

Heidegger's understanding that original philosophy had its foundation in a pre-philosophic understanding of everyday life is a significant discovery. If this is correct, it means that in its beginnings philosophy was situated, and since philosophy can never will away its past, it is always going to carry its beginnings with it. Hence, no pure, self-grounding subjectivity is ever possible. That said, just as I have serious reservations about whether the seeds of modern constructivism were sown in Plato, I have profound reservations about Heidegger's various experiments with non- or post-metaphysical thinking. To my mind they lead us into various vaporous musings that I predict will never have any flowering or issue precisely because they have no phenomenological basis. If, as I strongly suspect, non-metaphysical thought can have no manifestation, then the attempt to go about trying to gut every substantive effort at thinking of allegedly metaphysical elements can have no **positive** issue whatsoever. Working down that path seems to me to lead to an utter blind alley in which we are forced into silence or sneaking in the back door concrete conclusions to which a genuine non-metaphysician would never be entitled.[17]

To my mind the most profound core of Heidegger's project is to be found in several core elements of his thought: 1) the phenomenology of everydayness, although I will argue that Strauss, Arendt and others have developed this insight in a far more concrete moral and political direction; 2) Heidegger's showing of the priority of the practical to the theoretical; how the theoretical always grows out of some specific, situated articulation of the everyday. Consequently, for Heidegger, the practical is a "prior" arena of "truth" and knowledge, and theory, which is derivative, has no autonomous right to dictate to or to negate that knowledge and truth; 3) which leads to Heidegger's deconstruction/ overcoming of the tradition which as *Uberwindung* (an unwinding or de-sedimentation which is similar to Hegelian *Aufhebung,* in reverse) which should be understood as an unpacking and re-appropriation qua *Andenken*— understood as a remembrance or thinking back rather than a total rejection; 4) All of which points to Heidegger's discussion of primordial spatiality and es-pecially primordial temporality qua ecstatic temporality which fits in with everything from his explorations of primal Christianity to the "resoluteness" of *Being and Time* to the possibility of "building" and *Gelassenheit.* **I will argue that this ecstatic temporality is the necessary temporality of political phi-losophy**; 5) Finally, central to the future of political philosophy is Heidegger's seminal critique of constructivism. I will begin with some remarks about con-structivism and then move to a consideration of the other four elements. These remarks will have to be brief because my present interest is in returning to my discussion of the future of political philosophy.

In Heidegger's presentation of the tradition, the same essential thought and the same essential understanding of Being exists throughout modernity from Descartes to Nietzsche. Nietzsche's doctrine of the Will-to-Power is the apotheosis of Descartes's projection of Being as spatio-temporal magnitudes, a projection self-grounded by a fully transparent subject. Starting from the projection of Being as quantitatively spatio-temporal made it possible to so set upon Being that it could be unlocked and transformed into "standing re-serve," by which Heidegger means that all of Being is transformed into non-appearing abstractions like capital and energy. Being as *physis*/emerging had appearing as part of its essence. But at the end of the constructivist age the realm of appearance no longer has any self-standing solidity or Truth. Hence Being no longer appears or stands at all.

Being qua "standing reserve" is utterly abstract and absent. Yet it totally determines our existence. Even man can only be revealed technologically, as a calculable cog in a global technological system that has neither rhyme nor reason other than to continue to expand. Like external nature, man merely "stands by" ready to be bureaucratically sallied forth in the various projects of a runaway technological world. Increasingly those projects no longer pro-ceed from any comprehensive or even comprehensible end other than the in-tensification of ongoing manipulation of Being. There is no remaining self-standing "objectivity' and we cannot be, therefore, any longer self-defining, autonomous, transparent "subjects"; we are merely pawns. A subject cannot exist without objects (*gegenstand*), and objects must "appear."

According to Heidegger, no Nietzschean overman could will the overcom-ing of this present situation because everyone is already, before the fact, surrounded by a world that is technologically determined and which in turn determines our being and our own self-understanding. We cannot reveal ourselves or the world in any way other than technologically. We can no longer dwell peacefully on the Earth and beneath the Heavens as mortals who know we are not gods. The technological world is the deferred ramification of previous constructivist projections. But that world has gained such inertial force that no further self-conscious projections can instrumentally control it. We are no longer surrounded by phenomena that truly show "themselves." The constructivist age creates for itself a room with no windows or doors. When man tried to be the ground of Being, Being (qua *physis*) began to withdraw. The withdrawal of Being is nihilism.

There were of course important stages between Descartes and the allegedly completed metaphysics of Nietzsche and modern technology. Kant made the transcendental ego the ground not only of objective Being as it presents itself in "empirical intuition" but also of the Ought which was likewise the projection of the human Will. While both objectivity and subjectivity had their ground in the Will, Being and the Ought nonetheless became severed. Once that was accomplished, it eventually allowed the Will to be emancipated from Kant's merely idiosyncratic invocation of the universal; this led to the Ought being seen as based on mere "values" that were no longer intrinsically valuable because they had no ontological ground in objective Being. Remove the Kantian projection of universality and the related cosmopolitan prejudice, for that is all it could still be, and we have the unbridled confrontation of Nietzschean wills that will the particular rather than the universal. Hegel tried to ward off this outcome by making History itself the necessary ontological ground of the evolving Ought. But when History was stripped of the idea of Necessity, we were left with mere historicism, the belief that values change over time with no predictability—leaving us the victims of blind fate. The constructivist age began with Descartes's faith in the power of the self-transparent will of the human ego and ended with the hegemony of a blind fate no will can master.

The most straightforward, and seemingly benign, manifestation of the constructivist projection of frames upon reality in contemporary political theory is to be found in the thought of John Rawls. Rawls projects his "original position" with its "veil of ignorance" and its definition of rationality and then proceeds to deduce what justice is. When it is pointed out that the end is already implied in the utterly artificial beginnings we are told that the premises of the projection are in fact the premises that individuals already hold—there is an attempted phenomenological move. All that is being done, allegedly, is to more articulately point out what follows from the already shared principles. But the circularity of the undertaking remains all too obvious, and if in fact everyone did accept the Rawlsian premises—which is false—we really would not need the theory in the first place. The point of constructivist political theories is to help us change reality not explain it. But even if we did accept the premises Rawls builds on, we are still left with the conclusion that we have a universal, rational, cosmopolitan theory applicable everywhere and always. Hence the tradition of political philosophy is at an end because we already have our final premises. Under those circumstances, the good is the endless repetition of the present in perpetuity—the End of History.

Such universalist premises destroy the possibility of political philosophy by making it impossible to see man as a historical being who must repeatedly re-confront the changing phenomena of the time and reconnect past and future. To repeat, I assume that being historical beings, beings able to generate different historical worlds, is of the essence of man. To remove that possibility is to transform man into an unchanging, highly administered pet. I assume that the comfort that might be possible thereby is bought at far too high a price. The price of trading in our humanity and becoming both post-historical and post-human is simply too steep. Only if man is seen as a historical being who must continually reenact fundamental questioning within a changing situation is political philosophy possible or an ongoing necessity.

Obviously not all forms of contemporary constructivism are universalist as is the case of Rawls. Almost all those who argue that race, class and gender are "social constructs" do so as a deconstructive prelude to reconstructing the categories of contemporary discourse in the way they see fit. Again, the point of their theories is to change reality, not describe it. They wish to project a frame (*Gestell*) upon reality. This is constructivism.[18] It only makes sense on the presupposition of an autonomous projecting subject, whether the author sees this or not. It is a metaphysical undertaking in Heidegger's sense. Many contemporary theorists—from multiculturalists to deconstructionists—want to construct a form of particularism, seeing the hegemony of the universal as destructive of the good—how they know the nature of the good is almost always inexplicable on their premises. But they are no less constructivist merely because they eschew the universal. For example, we see a version of particularist constructivism from the so-called communitarians who invariably want to construct a good liberal form of "community" with all the hard edges of nationalism and closed societies leveled off, even though universalistic, cosmopolitan, radically individualistic liberalism is what they see as the problem they are trying to confront.   ·

Even the quintessential deconstructionist Jacques Derrida, despite all of his protestations, is a constructivist and thereby on his own terms a metaphysician. Ultimately deconstructionism implies an autonomous ego, the ego that decides whether or not to deconstruct. Deconstruction is presumed to bring about an effect that is good. All of Derrida's efforts are in the service therefore of projecting a vision of the good. This became increasingly clear in Derrida's later works such as *Spectres of Marx* and *Politics of Friendship*. As Derrida sees matters, the good is to be found in an environment like that of Marx's predicted communist future, where friendship can replace coercive justice, and where as many determinative structures as possible are dissolved as much and as for long as possible—state, ethnicity, gender, religion, etc., all the things Marx predicted would dissolve inevitably. The good, even if not completely actualizable once and for all, toward which ongoing deconstruction must struggle is the breakdown of "metaphysical" structures, which is to say, it is in the service of anarchism as the good (especially in the precise sense of without *arche*). Marx's explanation/prediction of how we would necessarily arrive at the anarchist good at the End of History is replaced by an allegedly post-metaphysical explanation aimed at getting us to the same place using ongoing deconstruction. But the underlying question is, **why should I self-consciously deconstruct**? The answer: because it leads to the good, which is still projected as a classless, nationless, cosmopolitan anarchism. That good is being projected upon the future as a frame. How one knows this is the good, especially for beings that are allegedly without a fixed nature or metaphysical presence, as Derrida asserts, is never explained. Everything Derrida does is in the service of projecting a vision of the good. It is as a self-standing ego that he does this. This is constructivism. Hence, this deconstructive attempt to invert metaphysics is still metaphysical, all too metaphysical in Heidegger's sense.

We have arrived precisely where Nietzsche predicted we would, at the groundless competition of wills, the "fabling of the world." "Postmodernism" has not gotten one millimeter beyond the situation Nietzsche predicted. At best it is the latest basis of interest group politics operating within a Madisonian extended republic. At worst its operation will become enervating, bring down scorn on philosophy itself, and more than likely political and moral chaos. I believe that after Heidegger's critique, constructivist willing in all of its forms will look thinner and thinner to anyone with even a short-term historical perspective. But is there an alternative? Is not all concern for the future constructivist in one way or the other? This question leads us in the direction of "phenomenology."

PHENOMENOLOGY AND MAN'S HISTORICALITY

In general terms, the alternative to the constructivist approach is the "phenomenological" approach. Heidegger argues that "phenomena" are the things that will "show themselves" if man properly opens himself to them. But phenomena also simultaneously conceal themselves requiring an active effort to bring them out into the open and to keep them there. The phenomenologist is the **theorist** who brings these things that show themselves, but not always or completely, out into the open, which means into the open in speech. For Heidegger, the phenomena of phenomenology are theoretical categories like those he brings to a showing in *Being and Time*. They include all of the structures of facticity he develops from thrownness and falling to primordial ecstatic temporality and primordial spatiality. For Heidegger, these structures are determinative of all human existence throughout all its historical transformations.

But Heidegger also observes that there are what he calls pre-phenomenological "phenomena." It is these kinds of phenomena that he links with notions like the Fourfold, the "releasement toward things" of *Gelassenheit* or the discussions of "building and dwelling" that interest me most and condition my understanding of phenomenology. At the core of Heidegger's philosophical understanding is the premise that all theoretical discourse is grounded in these pre-theoretical phenomena. Without a prior "showing" of Being which occurs in shared everyday life, there would literally be nothing for the theorist to stare at, talk about, or try to conceptually articulate. One of the truly great insights of Heidegger is to show how the philosophical tradition grew out of **a specific** pre-philosophic revelation of reality and that the entire philosophic tradition has carried with it large remnants of that initial phenomenal showing, and it can never simply cast these remnants aside. For even in trying to consciously oppose them, one is precisely determined by them and in forgetting them one is determined even more completely.

Heidegger also argues that reality always presents itself in a shared, **group** revelation of Being. This could be a global revelation of reality only if there could be a universal, cosmopolitan group. Given the full nature of Heidegger's understanding that should be an impossibility. If, contrary to the metaphysical tradition, especially in its constructivist variant, appearance is an arena of Truth and part of Being, the mere fact of different geographical locations and climates should condition different revelations of reality on a purely phenomenological level. But that is only the tip of the phenomenological iceberg.

If Heidegger is correct, all theoretical constructivism comes along too late in attempting to consciously construct reality. In refusing to let pre-theoretical reality constitute and present **itself**, the theorist is engaged in a self-defeating circular undertaking. The constructivist theorist thereby merely destroys the possibility of any genuine future openness and uniqueness, ensuring the End of History, denying man the chance to be a historical being. Ongoing constructivism, especially in its universalist form, promises a future that would predictably offer an increasingly flattened and uniform, groundless and colorless everyday reality to live in, without vivacity or novelty. If the good for human beings is to live in a world that is in fact genuinely open-ended, theoretical constructivism wards off the human good. If one believes that a good exists in the closure of that openness—the End of History—at this point in time that has to be argued explicitly rather than accepted as obvious.

My argument is that the task of political philosophy **now** is to "step back" from the constructivism which—and here Heidegger is correct—wards off every unique possibility, leaving us with nothing but an endless repetition of increasingly narrow willing. Does not this "step back" rest on the assumption that human life constitutes itself if left alone? Yes. For example, the ancient Egyptians, Persians, Japanese and Chinese needed no constructivist theorists to have a high culture. But is not evil part of what comes forth out of a *praxis* which is left to its own devices without restraints? Yes. Should not evil be opposed? Yes. But the recognition of and reaction to evil grows out of life itself. Put another way, the reaction to injustice and evil does not require a theory. Knowledge of the noble, the just, the good and the holy are parts of life itself. They must be allowed to show themselves. If they were not part of the phenomena already, no one could theoretically construct them out of thin air. In fact, the theorist would not know what the subject matter of something like evil was if it was not already present in a pre-theoretical revelation of things.

The phenomenological part of Heidegger's corpus—as opposed to his "post-metaphysical" musings—argued that the metaphysical tradition had diverted thought from the factical richness of primordial spatiality and primordial ecstatic temporality into a primary concern for an a-spatial, a-temporal abstract eternity. In the process, the metaphysical tradition lowered the truth status of poetry, religion, statesmanship, art and "thinking" vis-à-vis metaphysical thinking and logic, and ultimately vis-à-vis modern mathematical, technological science.[19] But Heidegger the phenomenologist is always diverted by his concern not to allow his thought to fall into metaphysics when his main effort should be to emancipate everyday life from its constructivist stranglehold so that phenomena can show themselves. Heidegger's competing concerns make it difficult for him to articulate everyday life in its phenomenological richness in any but formal terms. One cannot be phenomenological and "post-metaphysical" simultaneously. This is where it has always seemed to me that someone like Strauss, not subject to the same anti-metaphysical predilections—not that I think he was a metaphysician[20]—has pushed Heidegger's phenomenological insights in a far more concrete and therefore useful and profound direction. Strauss uses concrete moral and political categories as a point of departure.

Strauss's mature studies of "everydayness," found in his works on Xenophon, Thucydides, Aristophanes, Plato and Aristotle, were attempts, in a precisely Heideggerian vein, to articulate the pre-theoretical awareness that conditioned the origins of philosophy. In the process Strauss concretely pointed out all manner of things that were/are central to the pre-theoretical revelation of reality that Heidegger only circled in vague or formal terms. But for both, the pre-philosophic revelation of Being was moral, political and religious, showing an unavoidable understanding of rank ordering, the unavoidability of a commitment to "one's own," and much more. The everyday in our time still shows all of these elements, as is clear from some of the determined constructivist, **theoretical** attempts to overturn their hegemony. But I would argue the present phenomena are not identical to those initial phenomena that conditioned the origins of the tradition. Hence we should not **initially** label the Greek phenomena or our own as either natural or conventional; they just are, they just show themselves. That should be our point of **departure**. I do not doubt that we will along this path rediscover "nature," but in our time it needs to be rediscovered from the beginnings. We will need **first** to rediscover "nature" as a phenomenon, not as a concept or idea.

Being and Time, as the title signaled, was Heidegger's attempt to show that man was a historical being because he was linked inextricably with Being which was itself historical, coming to presence in various distinctive happenings or events. During the philosophical tradition, Being qua *ousia* had come to be linked with eternity and seen as unchanging and a-temporal. Heidegger wanted to think Being in a way more consistent with the original revelation of Being as *physis*, as repeatedly emerging through various distinctive revelatory events or "foundings." He claimed that implicit in that original determination of Being was a temporal component. Being was simultaneously an **emerging** forth into **presence,** which held itself back in a mysterious **absence**. Presence and absence were inextricably temporal concepts even if no one grasped this at the time, or for that matter, until Heidegger.

According to Heidegger, the interweaving of presence and absence determines the sense in which Being is temporal and not the "inauthentic" understanding of temporality that developed in the tradition. As the understanding of Being was transformed from *physis* to *ousia*, from repeated emergings to a total presence—thereby obliterating absence from Being—the door was opened to seeing time as a qualitatively uniform passing of nows. The past was the no longer present. The future was the not yet present. Neither the past nor the future, qua absent, had any Being—they both were Not. Only the fleeting present moment had Being but it constantly passed and would not stand still. Only by removing Being from the evanescence of the relentless fleeting present moments could Being be secured. Only an eternal present could truly have

Being. Being was removed from any relation to temporality and Time was reduced to an endless, relentless, uniform passing of nows. Heidegger wanted to reposition Being in a qualitatively discontinuous temporality of happenings/events. And he wanted to set loose the *praxis* and *poiesis* that would be not so much the cause but the "site" for those events if those acts were ecstatically temporal. In ecstatic temporality, both past and future can be present.

Originally, Being qua *physis* was seen to include within itself both appearing and becoming as well as absence and the Not. But when Being came to be associated with eternity, appearing and becoming became associated with the Not-Being that had been expelled from Being. In the process, Being was cut off from the temporal. Once all attention was focused on the eternal, the temporal was so lowered in status that it could no longer be taken seriously; it was not the venue of Being or Truth. Action was lowered in status vis-à-vis detached contemplation of the fully present eternal. Human *praxis* was no longer a site through which Being emerged from absence into presence. Heidegger argued that at that point it became impossible to understand man as a historical being, the being who makes history, or put differently, as the site for historical existence to happen. Heidegger looked for an "authentic" understanding of human temporality that could relate human temporality and the temporality of Being as both present and absent as presencing through qualitatively unique events. This led to the discussion of ecstatic temporality in the second part of *Being and Time*.

At one time, in his early years, before receiving his Full Professorship at Marburg, Heidegger promised a work on the phenomenology of religion. It appears that that work would have focused on an analysis of "primal Christianity." Following Luther, Heidegger believed that the intrusion of Greek philosophy into Christian theology completely overwhelmed the original existential understanding of Christianity which included a heightened experience of passion, hope, despair, longing, tension and anguish. The primal Christian lived preoccupied with the past life, death and resurrection of Christ. But the primal Christian was also projected forward toward the future second coming. This concerned occupation of the present moment (*Augenblick*) made the past and future passionately co-present. While in their own way absent, the past and future moments of temporality were also actively present in the vivid, high tension of the co-presence of the three "ecstasies" of temporality. Life was lived "ecstatically," outside itself—understood as a biological phenomenon—outside the mere inauthentic temporality that only granted Being to the present moment. The fusion of the three moments of temporality is precisely what Heidegger meant by the authentic temporality of "resoluteness" in *Being and Time*.

Once invaded by Greek philosophy, Christian theology became focused on contemplating the tranquil presence of eternity and utterly lost the primal

relation to the ultimate mystery of the Godhead. It was replaced by the tranquil contemplation of eternal presence. Instead of a life that was rooted, anxious, involved and intense, one stood back detachedly and contemplated a
fully present Godhead. This path led to Hegel and the Godhead made fully
actual and present in the world. For Heidegger such a tranquilized existence
never makes history. Christianity, which was itself historical in its beginnings, eventually helped destroy man's essential historicality. The Christian,
like the Greek philosopher, came to sit back and merely "awaited" the future
in an extreme, detached tranquility. In all theoretical/contemplative detachment, nothing gets accomplished, nothing is affirmed, and humanity is delivered over to endless historical drift.

In Heidegger's treatment of ontology as an analysis of Dasein's facticity,
we get the famous critique of the "falling" into the "they-self" which is Heidegger's version of Nietzsche's critique of the "last man." One falls away
from the high tension of authentic life into a tranquilized drifting along that
accepts the dulled down, shared conventional understandings of a mass society. In Heidegger's account, this leveled off averageness manifested itself in
endless "idle talk" about the frivolous and trivial, "ambiguity" as to one's
roots and a flitting "curiosity" that darts from one thing to the next, with a dilettantish refusal to ever stand its ground and take anything seriously. This
stance leads to an endless, a-historical drifting along toward the future. It
merely "awaits" the future in a way that does not anxiously anticipate it with
active concern and care. The future is not present. In forgetfulness neither is
the past. In the process, life is lived in an endless succession of qualitatively
unchanging present nows—the End of History.

Against this drifting along, Heidegger juxtaposed the resolutely authentic
individual who in the high tension of the true "moment of vision" (*Augenblick*) held together and made present the past and future. In this fashion one
was forced to take seriously one's true "situation" and past "tradition" and the
possibilities both allowed as well as the limitations they imposed. The ecstatically authentic person understood that he was "thrown" into a co-determination with certain distinct others and delivered over to a fated tradition. But
this person would also adopt the stance of being responsible for the continuation of that tradition by taking over the responsibility of opening future possibilities that were latent in that "thrownness." Such a person neither sits back
and unconcernedly awaits the future nor believes that it can be constructed *ex
nihilo* or *de novo*. This is the ecstatically temporal being who can be historical. For Heidegger, it is through such a being that Being itself comes to presence. History is the arena of the coming to presence of Being from out of
some mysterious abode. That coming to presence takes place in a linking together of past and future and the "opening" out of the present that it allows.

But in an environment dominated by detached theoretical staring (the pre-supposition for Constructivism) we get an endless succession of identical nows. As a result Being "withdraws" and stays away not coming to presence in any fashion.

Heidegger's accounts of throwness and falling, of ecstatic temporality and authenticity, and all his categories of facticity, are ontological in that they determine the ways in which Being reveals itself to and **through** man. Looked at from the side of humanity alone, those categories imply that in our very being we are determined by the specific group of individuals, distinct tradition and contemporary situation in which we find ourselves "always already." We do not choose, or construct this co-determination—for example, in some "communitarian" fashion; we always already **are** this situated co-determination. We are not autonomous subjectivities to which is then merely added the accident of various external historical determinations. We **are** our group, tradition, situation and future set of possibilities.[21]

We can simply get lost in our present situation, or we can relate to it in a way in which we ecstatically also stand out from it toward the past and future. Our throwness is never simply a fossilized given. Every tradition is open-ended both forwards and backwards. It is open-ended forward as long as we do not drift along in the endless repetition of the present. It is open-ended backwards as long as we can re-appropriate our past and not merely genuflect to something frozen for all time or merely dismiss it entirely in some constructivist fashion. Heidegger's discussion of ecstatic temporality implies a dynamic, caring, loving, affirmative relation to both the past and the future. We **lovingly** affirm the past as part of what we **are** and actively **care** for the future by keeping it open-ended and capable of multiple possibilities for those who are to come. But we are always prone to a tranquilized indifference and unconcern about the past or future—or Nietzsche's angry spirit of revenge toward the past. In our specific time, we are especially prone to a revengeful rejection of the past from some presupposed Archimedean point outside the present.

Heidegger tries to link his discussion of ecstatic temporality with his phenomenological analysis of our pre-theoretical relations to Being/beings. The pre-theoretical relation to life comes forth in a primordial spatiality as well as a primordial, ecstatic temporality. Primordial space can only be explicated by *poiesis*, not by mathematical constructions, since it is qualitatively discontinuous.[22] If Heidegger is correct regarding the discontinuous fashion through which space first opens up for human beings, the quantitatively uniform understanding of space is derivative and is only possible after a theoretical standing back from an already revealed spatiality. This qualitatively uniform space is in principle the spatiality of unconcern. It is a dulled down and leveled off revelation of spatiality. Likewise, temporality reveals itself primordially in a qualitatively discontinuous "ecstatic" fashion. Only the person passionately concerned to open out the future occupies primordial temporality—the original Christian being Heidegger's most concrete example. As ecstatically temporal one could also quite easily add Lincoln who had an authentic relation to the past founding and attempted to extend its **essential** features into a novel future freed from slavery.

The issue of ecstatic temporality leads us thematically to Heidegger's relation to the past tradition. This relation has been greatly misunderstood. Far too much emphasis has been put on the hyperbolic connotation of Heidegger's word *Destruktion*. It is easy to read this term as implying an angry antipathy to the past. Heidegger's later terminology is far more precise. It becomes clear that Heidegger's form of "deconstruction" is an *Uberwindung* ("overcoming" qua "unwinding" or unpacking) as well as an *Andenken* (a thinking back qua ongoing remembering where thinking remains a thanking, *denken als danken*). Leo Strauss has captured what Heidegger had in mind in his observation that Heidegger disinterred the roots of the tradition and brought them into the light for inspection in a way that had never occurred before.[23] Again, I think Strauss perfectly articulated this undertaking: We must engage in a "loyal and loving reshaping or reinterpretation of the inherited."[24]

Heidegger's aim was to unwind the tradition and work back through its sedimented layers to get to the simple, primordial defining experiences that initially determined it. After the unwinding, we can explore latent past possibilities—"second beginnings"—or explore instead concrete possibilities within the **present situation**. Either way we have to work **from within**. We have no way whatsoever to even prophesy non-metaphysical thought for it has never existed and, I would argue, in principle never could. The attempt to pursue the non- or anti-metaphysical will always lead to constructivism. It is precisely constructivism into which all of those quasi-Heideggerians fall when they make antagonism to metaphysics and the projecting of utterly novel un-metaphysical, non-concrete **new beginnings** their only endeavor.

HISTORICALITY, NATURE AND POLITICAL PHILOSOPHY

Where do these reflections really leave us? Does stressing that man is in his essence a historical being, a history making being, completely destroy a relationship to or orientation toward "nature" and hence deliver us over to relativism and historicism? No. First, given that human beings play out their humanity in such different ways in different places and at different times, it is necessary to explain the historical feature of our humanity, i.e., our ability to make history in qualitatively different fashions. We cannot ignore man's historicality and presume to have explained the whole. This historicality is, I would argue, the primary feature that differentiates us from all other social species—e.g., for good reasons no one would ever write a book about the history of beaver society, even though they are social creatures who build.

We cannot dismiss the possibility that a variety of features intrinsic to human existence may recur or stay unchanged in the midst of our historicality. But we cannot begin there either. We begin with the phenomena and see where we arrive. There is undoubtedly something called "nature." The questions are: how do the operative phenomena show up for us, how do we articulate them, why must "nature" show itself as at odds with our human historicality and why must "nature" be aligned with what is static? If one takes the nature of our planet as an example, tectonic plates shift, continents form and break up, volcanoes create new islands, ice ages come and go, mountain ranges and river valleys are created and destroyed, "old growth" forests come into existence—and relatively recently—replacing, indeed destroying what was there before. This is the dynamic "nature" of our planet. **There is such a thing as nature; but as a phenomena—not as a concept—it clearly is not static.** As a part of the larger natural whole, the same is undoubtedly true of nature as it shows itself and plays itself out in humanity as well. Further, if nature is a "phenomenon," then it is something we approach not theoretically, but in a phenomenological fashion. Phenomenological nature cannot, therefore, be reduced to a concept, even though it must be articulated in speech, a speech that will be more like *poiesis* than logical or representational speech.

As a phenomenon—and at this point in the philosophical tradition that is the only level upon which nature can be recovered—"nature" must continually be re-appropriated and rearticulated in speech. There is a phenomenon "nature," but to believe that it can be brought to presence fully in representational speech is an error. Hence the "idea" of nature can never be fully captured once and for all and stored away in a cupboard. This is not devastating news if Heidegger is correct that *poiesis* can be an arena of Truth. I am asserting that it is not possible to get it totally "right" on the subject of "nature" once and for all. Hence we must continually re-enjoin the phenomena and re-articulate those phenomena in speech. That undertaking itself will be historical without being historicist. We need only admit that there are phenomena, not that they need to be static and unchanging, to avoid relativism. And hence, man's historicality—which must unavoidably be dealt with anyway—is not at odds with "nature."

What is implied in stepping back from Constructivism in the direction of the phenomena is a particular form of moderation. I would accept that there was a form of moderation in antiquity born of a prudential understanding of the exposed position of the philosophers such that it was prudent to avoid elaborate idealistic prescriptions about how to transform already existing political life. Likewise, as philosophy attempted its rapprochement with the theological authorities in the Middle Ages, a significant moderation was required. But modernity has been so radically transformative that no return to earlier forms of moderation is either plausible or capable of being useful. We need a new form of philosophical moderation if we are to avoid the endless repetition of the present or a simple blind, fate-driven wandering into the future. We need to be naïve again and thrust back into a substantive, open encounter with the ensemble of phenomenological questions that is political philosophy freed from all of the constructivist objections—to say nothing of deconstructivist. That is the issue before us at present. Despite protestations that I can predict, that simply is not being done in our time because of the omnipresence of a determination to be anti-metaphysical as a point of departure for thought.

To conclude, let me summarize some of my central premises regarding what political philosophy needs to be after Heidegger if it is to be a unique, ongoing, open-ended, architectonic, which is to say holistic, enterprise:

1. It would explain how man is a historical being. Further, it would assume that the preservation of the human requires the preservation of the possibility of actual ongoing historicality.[25]
2. Political philosophy itself **includes** ethics, politics, psychology, ontology/cosmology and epistemology as part of itself, as part of a whole. These undertakings that have been cast off by the past tradition to a presumed autonomy must be brought back into a whole. Otherwise, we will merely presuppose answers to parts that we ignore.
3. Political philosophy would cease to be Constructivist and unleash the phenomena from further theoretical subjugation. That requires an initial act of postmodern moderation.
4. Political philosophy would be neither autonomous nor **theoretical** (qua representational speech)—it would exist as a reflection upon and dialectical movement out of pre-theoretical understanding which is its only point of departure.
5. As phenomenological, political philosophy would be more than merely the **defense** of the possibility of solitary autonomous **theoretical** activity. It would be *poiesis* caring and concerned for the future.
6. Future political philosophy would not be a mere going back and picking and choosing from past authors. That is Constructivist and presupposes standing at some Archimedean point to make the choice, a choice made by a self-grounding ego. That kind of movement back also closes down the

future as a co-present moment and more or less destroys the possibility of human historicality.

7. In our time, the fascination with or determination to be non- or post-metaphysical can only be constructivist and will lead to silence or the furtive ideological incorporation of presuppositions that should in fact be matters for discussion. That discussion itself is part of what opens the future.

8. Modern science is derivative from a prior decision of political philosophy. It cannot be architectonic nor a foundation for deducing outcomes applicable in other areas, especially concerning human *praxis*, ethics, politics, or psychology. Modern science is not and never has been morally, metaphysically or ethically neutral. There can be no such thing as an autonomous ontology or cosmology. That follows from political philosophy being holistic.

9. The only feasible "ground" or point of departure for political philosophy is the pre-theoretical phenomenology of everyday life. This fact can be waved away only on the basis of a constructivism that is in fact a permutation of modern subjectivism which can no longer be maintained.

10. The hegemony of the pre-theoretical phenomena does not require that we go back and assume that the initial pre-theoretical roots from which the philosophical tradition emerged were the only "natural" ones. We can always begin from the phenomena in our time, and in fact that is what we always do one way or the other.

11. Political philosophy is dialectical to the extent it inevitably moves away from the initial phenomenal showing of everydayness. That moving away toward an architectonic articulation of the whole incorporates an element of poetic speech. There is no autonomous **theoretical** stance from which to debunk the poetic, which is an at least co-equal arena of Truth, albeit probably primary.

12. The previous implies that political philosophy would be both Socratic/dialectical and poetic. The Socratic either/or choice between *logos* and *poiesis*—still accepted by Nietzsche just inverted—would be rejected. This is a move already made by Plato as I will develop below.

13. The appropriate temporal stance of political philosophy is to bind together past and future. It avoids both a static conservative affirmation of the past and the contemporary spirit of revenge against the entire past as an arena only of error.

NOTES

1. Martin Heidegger, *An Introduction to Metaphysics*, trans. Ralph Manheim (New Haven: Yale University Press, 1959), 10–11.

2. Friedrich Nietzsche, *Thus Spoke Zarathustra*, in *The Portable Nietzsche*, trans. Walter Kaufman (New York: Penguin Books, 1959), 250–53.

3. See my "The End of History or a Portal to the Future: Does Anything Lie Beyond Late Modernity?" in *After History: Francis Fukuyama and his Critics*, ed. Timothy Burns (Lanham: Rowman & Littlefield, 1994).

4. "An Introduction to Heideggerian Existentialism," in *The Rebirth of Classical Political Rationalism: An Introduction to the Thought of Leo Strauss*, selected and edited by Thomas L. Pangle (Chicago: University of Chicago Press, 1989), 42.

5. I consider Heidegger's argument regarding "ecstatic" temporality to be paradigmatic for political philosophy. I will return to this issue thematically below.

6. I have questioned the validity of the alleged "reversal" in Heidegger's thought in both my *Nietzsche, Heidegger and the Transition to Postmodernity* (Chicago: University of Chicago Press, 1996), and *Martin Heidegger: Paths Taken, Paths Opened* (Lanham: Rowman & Littlefield, 2007).

7. Again, I stress Nietzsche's argument in "On Redemption," in *Thus Spoke Zarathustra*. Only by emancipating ourselves from the spirit of revenge against the past and our temporality more generally—with its constant movement—can we hope to open a future that is not the projection of our anger and spirit for revenge. For Nietzsche that required that we accept the past as being precisely as we would have willed it. Only then can we be emancipated in the present and future from taking our revenge against it. Much of what passes for political theory in our time is a straightforward manifestation of the spirit of revenge against the past.

8. In fact, it does not make any sense to even talk about human beings who are anonymous and without particular traits and not situated someplace distinct, contrary to authors like Rawls and many others.

9. Nietzsche makes the apropos comment that great thinkers never have a right to truly understand themselves. See *Beyond Good and Evil,* trans. Walter Kaufmann (New York: Vintage Books, 1966) *#256.*

10. For the best statement regarding postmodern fragmentation see Jean Francois Lyotard, *The Postmodern Condition* (Minneapolis: University of Minneapolis Press, 1984).

11. Spelling this point out in detail would require a work far larger than the present undertaking. Hence I am going to have to assume at present that this point has certain self-evidence. My general point is that it is the existential questions about how shall I live and how shall we live together that take a certain **temporal and logical** priority and lead on to psychological, ontological and epistemological issues. All of the parts mutually imply a whole, either thematically or surreptitiously through necessary presuppositions. It is this wholeness of thinking that I am arguing that Heidegger makes manifest. But to give the barest of indications of what I have in mind here, Aristotle separated theory and practice, opening a door to a faith in the autonomy of theory, Descartes cast off from political philosophy reflection on the nature of the whole just as Adam Smith cast off economics to an alleged autonomy and Rousseau supplied the premises for an independent anthropology. Specific moments in the tradition can be seen where various parts of the whole of fundamental thinking

were cast off to a supposed autonomy. Heidegger opens the door to a return to what, for want of a better term, can be called a holistic approach.

12. If thought is unavoidably a whole, and we must repeatedly reassess the question how shall we live together, then the other parts of the whole of thought—ethics, epistemology, psychology, ontology—must be repeatedly reintegrated anew into a novel whole. I am arguing that it is the unavoidable existential questions that assure philosophical open-endedness.

13. According to Strauss, Heidegger had revealed the roots of the tradition and made it possible "thus perhaps to know, what so many merely believe, that those roots are the only natural and healthy roots." "An Unspoken Prologue," *Interpretation*, Vol. 7, no. 3, p. 2. As with regards to Strauss, I have never been able to completely satisfy myself whether Strauss was asserting that the tension between philosophy and the city is a necessary and eternal tension or indicative only of the situation at the origins. And I have never been able to completely satisfy myself whether Strauss was calling for a return to everyday experience as the basis of philosophy or a return to the "natural" experience exemplified in the world that existed before philosophy emerged. I am inclined to the opinion that Strauss thought that there is an **eternal** tension between philosophy and the city and that only the initial, pre-theoretical understanding at the origins is "natural." If that is correct, I am parting ways as regards both of those conclusions. I am arguing that we begin from our own situation. Further, I would argue that on a larger plane, there have been at least **four pivotal situations** that have determined thought: 1) That at the origins of the tradition in ancient Greece; 2) that which occurred during the confrontation with Revelation especially within Christianity; 3) that at the origins of the modern epoch during its break with the stranglehold of theology; and 4) our present, post-Heideggerian situation.

14. In Strauss, "Philosophy as Rigorous Science and Political Philosophy," *Leo Strauss: Studies in Platonic Political Philosophy* (Chicago: University of Chicago Press, 1983), p. 30.

15. These assertions only apply to political philosophy if it is seen as an undertaking that deduces the political and ethical from the theoretical—i.e. the ontological. Elsewhere I have argued that for Plato psychology was foundational, not metaphysics or ontology. See chapter 16 on Plato's Trilogy. It was Aristotle who opened the door for the later tradition to take ontology as foundational. Strauss seems to me to confuse matters by on the one hand seeming to say that the deductive model for doing political philosophy applies universally to the essence of political philosophy while simultaneously adopting the Heideggerian "phenomenological" approach which I believe leads elsewhere—toward what I call a holistic rather than deductive model. See the chapters on Strauss in part 2 especially chapter 12 on Heidegger and Strauss.

My argument is that after Heidegger we must realize that metaphysics and ontology cannot be taken as foundational but can only be seen as parts that must be integrated into a presentation of a whole. That is entirely different than seeing them as prior in status as grounds or foundations from which other things are deduced. If anything is prior, I am arguing, and here I am **not** following Heidegger, it is the existential questions how shall I live, how shall we live. Heidegger's mistake was to start from ontology and only then to move toward ethics and politics, a destination at which he never arrived. My position is that we must start from the existential issues and work **toward** a position that integrates the ontological, psychological and episte-mological into a whole. That integration implies an element of *poiesis*.

16. Strauss's statement is particularly striking: "[T]he only great thinker in our time is Heidegger." (p. 29) And, "Heidegger is the only man who has an inkling of the dimensions of the problem of a world society" (p. 43), in "An Introduction to Hei-deggerian Existentialism," pp. 27–46, in *The Rebirth of Classical Political Rational-ism*.

17. Again, I have dealt with these issues at much greater length in my *Martin Hei-degger: Paths Taken, Paths Opened*.

18. To make another long story short, my argument is that there is a difference be-tween "ecstatically" **opening** the future—which links past, present and future—and imposing a frame or construction upon it.

19. It is not possible at present to explore Heidegger's understanding of *alētheia* or truth in depth. But a brief word is necessary. For Heidegger, *alētheia* originally meant "to be unconcealed." It went along with the concept of Being as *physis*, that which emerges from concealment. That which had emerged into the open was unconcealed or had truth, *alētheia*. Hence truth had an element of appearing and becoming. It was not associated with a transcendent eternally present reality. Toward the end, in one of his post-metaphysical suggestions, Heidegger said that perhaps thought should try to move beyond this initial understanding of truth that he seemed to have co-opted him-self. He suggested that perhaps we could think "clearing and presence" rather than be-ing and truth, unconcealing and concealing. But without his concept of *alētheia*, truth as unconcealed, almost none of Heidegger's later work makes any sense. The think-ing of "clearing and presence" is one of those vaporous suggestions I do not believe can have any issue. Further, the original sense of *alētheia*, emerged **from** everyday experience. It is hard to see how "clearing and presence" could come to have any everyday resonance.

20. See my "On a Possible Epicurean Garden for Philosophy: Philosophy and the City in the Thought of Leo Strauss," below in chapter 10.

21. While we are certainly embedded in such determinations as our point of de-parture, because of his concerns about falling into metaphysics, as I have suggested, I think Heidegger radically understates the actual phenomenon of detachment of which we are capable. It goes far beyond what Heidegger attests in the category "be-ing-toward-death." Detachment is an actual phenomenon that needs to be explained and articulated. It does not need to be **theoretically** proved.

22. In this regard, let us think for one moment of the example of a parent contem-plating a beloved infant who crawls about across the room from the sofa that the par-ent occupies. If, as Heidegger claims, spatiality in its primordial revelation opens out in the mode of concernful nearness and farness, the infant is by far nearer than the glasses the parent views it through or the sofa upon which he or she is sitting. This is the nearness of "deseverance." Spatiality opens up out of our concernful dealings. The things we are in no way concerned with at any particular moment are not present at all—the eyeglasses—and fall off into absence and have no space. Space opens up in

qualitatively discontinuous ways and in qualitatively different "regions." This is why the infant is closer than the glasses, just as the *agora* and the sacred places could be two qualitatively different kinds of spaces into which different things come forward into presence.

23. "By uprooting and not simply rejecting the tradition of philosophy, [Heidegger] made it possible for the first time after many centuries . . . to see the roots of the tradition as they are." Strauss, "An Unspoken Prologue," *Interpretation*, Vol. 7, no. 3.

24. Leo Strauss, *Spinoza's Critique of Religion* (New York: Schocken Books, 1965), p. 25.

25. It may be the case that this understanding is easiest to maintain in a Christian environment. For example, a historical element cannot as easily be incorporated into Islam or Judaism where there is a fixed law. That has massive implications for the relation between Christianity and the future. See chapter 19.

Chapter Four

Machiavelli's *The Prince* and the Essence of Modernity[1]

While pretending to give lessons to kings, he gave great ones to the people. Machiavelli's *The Prince* is the book of Republicans.[2]

But what means a prince, whose sole motive is lust of mastery, should use to establish and maintain his dominion, the most ingenious Machiavelli has set forth at large, but with what design one can hardly be sure. If, however, he had some good design, as one should believe of a learned man, it seems to have been to show, with how little foresight many attempt to remove a tyrant, though thereby the causes which make the prince a tyrant can in no wise be removed but, on the contrary, are so much the more established, as the prince is given more cause to fear. . . Moreover, he perhaps wished to show how cautious a free multitude should be of entrusting its welfare absolutely to one man, who unless in his vanity he thinks he can please everybody, must be in daily fear of plots . . . I am the more led to this opinion concerning that most far-seeing man, because it is known that he was favorable to liberty, for the maintenance of which he has besides given the most wholesome advice.[3]

Throughout *Between Eternities* I will subscribe to a version of the understanding that sees Machiavelli as the father of modern political philosophy[4] while Descartes is the father of modern natural philosophy.[5] But what is this essential modernity that these two seemingly different authors share? On the one hand, Descartes is the father of the self-grounding, self-legislating theoretical ego that projects the Being of the world out of itself. On the other, Machiavelli is the realist who gives hard-headed, at times devious and duplicitous, advice about how to pursue personal ambition and glory as a means to national acquisition and expansion. Seemingly, far from being a theoretical philosopher with an epistemology and cosmology/ontology, Machiavelli

65

openly eschews "imagined republics" in the name of focusing on the "effectual truth" of the sinew and ligature of everyday political competition. Hence where is the common inspiration operating in Machiavelli and Descartes? The shared modernity of Machiavelli and Descartes can be found in their shared, negative determination to make a break with the pre-modern past, but what underlying positive understanding, sentiment or attitude do they share that makes them equally moderns?

One thing the modern age has done is to bring about an enlargement of the unavoidable interpenetration of thought and everyday life, such that philosophy always has major reverberations within our public world even as thinking unavoidably sets off from a shared everyday given. Hence as a part of our modern public life we must continually reflect upon the underlying shared premises that determine us all. Because of this increased interpenetration of thought and life—and Machiavelli lies at the heart of that modern phenomenon—we live in an epoch that oscillates between resolute self-forgetting and intense critical self-examination. Our self-forgetting attempts complete indifference to the principles that silently determine our existence. But that self-forgetting is necessarily punctuated by an ongoing critical disinterring of our roots that is unprecedented. There is no sign that either of these tendencies will yield to the other in the foreseeable future. We seem committed to alternate indifferent floating and drift and an almost pathological, microscopic auto-analysis. In one respect, therefore, critics of our age, like Nietzsche and Heidegger, who fear the complete hegemony of the self-forgetting of the "last man" or "they-self" seem to have underestimated the role of the thinker and critic in determining our public life. Whether healthy civilizations require the good conscience that the self-forgetting of a closed society entails is at present irrelevant, for there is no sign that our ongoing, modern, critical self-examination is about to abate and be replaced by the parameters of a closed, traditional city.

Undoubtedly there is a variety of intellectual crosscurrents within modern life, but one cannot dismiss that the modern age was set in motion by the desire for a conscious break with the past and the traditions of the past in both action and thought. On some level the opposite of the modern is the traditional. Put another way, modernity was set in motion by thought, and remains primarily moved by it. Once unleashed, thought is unlikely to rest with a comfortable acceptance of its present. Modernity looks to supply by conscious thought what was previously supplied by the slow accretions of accident that make up a tradition. But this gets us only so far. I want to argue that a significant part of the modern longing was set in motion by an attempt to limit the sphere of Chance and accident as much as to overcome the hegemony of Necessity. But I also want to argue that the ultimate limitation if not abolition of the political was seen as intrinsic to that task.

In this regard, Descartes is instructive. Descartes hoped that his new science would allow mankind to deal with the two features of human life that he saw as leading to political competition: lack of security and material scarcity. If one could lengthen life, secure it in peace, and emancipate it from competition over scarce necessities, one could achieve the good. If those things could be accomplished by a new science one could look forward to an abolition of the political with its competition and war. For Descartes this was true because a peaceful and secure life was the good life. What was primarily needed was a new science, properly deployed, that could so conquer nature that it could reveal regularities which when gathered up and reproduced as needed could overcome scarcity, and perhaps death. The good could be achieved without political competition.

If we turn in a pre-modern direction, to Plato's *Republic,* we see the extent to which the political *per se*, as well as its perfection, deals with more than scarcity and security. For example, one must accept the spirited and the erotic within the city because these represent needs of the human soul. One could be secure and awash in plenty and still not be fully satisfied or human. In fact, of Socrates's three parts of the soul, the spirited (*thumos*) is presented as the primary wellspring of the distinctively political. Desire (*epithumia*) points primarily to the private realm of the *oikos* or household for its gratification, and thought (*dianoia*), belongs to the city only when it is tamed and diluted, existing in its pure form only when substantially privatized.

Contrary to Descartes, Machiavelli of all authors would seem to be a spokesman for those elements of the soul that link up with ambition, the longing for glory and greatness, and competition for recognition in all its forms. But I am going to argue that contrary to appearances, while Machiavelli is willing to use and manipulate these human traits, his view of the good ultimately longs to undermine their hegemony. It is a shared notion of the good that Machiavelli and Descartes have in common that constitutes their fundamental modernity. Likewise, they both see a proper understanding of Necessity as central to the conquering of Chance. They differ in that Descartes pursues their shared conception of the good using a new natural science, while Machiavelli pursues it using a new political science.[6] It is in Hobbes that we see the first attempt to synthesize the new political science and the method of the new natural science. The pure sources however remain those displayed in Descartes (and to a lesser degree Bacon) and Machiavelli.

I will argue that Machiavelli's emancipation of the pursuit of ambition and glory from traditional moral and religious restraints, while central to his teaching, has to be understood in light of the end it intends to advance. Machiavelli's "lowering of the sights" is not the essential core of his modernity. Machiavelli, as many have argued, gives an empirical account of the "is" that is emancipated from concern for the "ought." Thereby he is frequently presented as the father of modern value-free political science, which limits itself to description and eschews prescription. By this understanding, Machiavelli limits his analysis to an elaboration of *raison d'état* and power politics.[7] He is said to accept the "low" bases of human action without casting moral aspersions rather than attempting to habituate man to the "high."[8] Machiavelli tries to build the high—rule of law, self-sovereignty, and national prosperity—upon the low, a self-serving love of preeminence by the few and a calculating fear in the many. This allegedly links him with other modern authors who try to build on the well-known "low but firm base," e.g., Hobbes on fear, Smith on greed, Rousseau on inarticulate sentiment or sexuality, and so on.

But I want to argue that this seeming value-free teaching is value laden and in the service of pursuing a distinct, modern vision of the good. Everything that is distinctively Machiavellian is the means to that good. Machiavelli's teaching is in the service of pursuing a transition to a novel future that captures and incorporates a novel view of the good. While consciously projected transitions are altogether modern phenomenon, it is the end—a new understanding of the good—that most conditions the essence of modernity.[9] When one looks carefully it is clear that Machiavelli in no way limits himself to mere description. Far from being a hard-nosed realist, Machiavelli is one of the first of the great modern idealists who longed to transform the traditional, pre-modern world.

Machiavelli's attempted break with the past can be seen quite clearly in the opening chapter of *The Prince*. His attack on pre-modernity represents Machiavelli's negative modernity. Machiavelli could count on the fact that every educated person in his time would have been raised on the teachings of Aristotle. The schools, and that meant the Church, taught not just Aristotle's political and moral teachings, or his metaphysics, but even Aristotle's physics, logic and rhetoric. That was the core of every curriculum. When Machiavelli said that all regimes that are or ever have existed have been either Republics or Principalities he knew this would be compared with Aristotle's division of regimes into three good regimes and three corrupted regimes.

In Aristotle's scheme, one asked, "who rules" with the answers being one, a few or the many. And one asked whether they ruled for the benefit of themselves or the benefit of the entire community. But for Machiavelli, all regimes are divided into either Principalities, the rule of one, or Republics, the rule of the few. This simple statement speaks volumes. It makes clear that according to Machiavelli the many never rule. Even in what might look like democracies, a few will always remain in effective control. Machiavellian Republics are not Democracies. At most one will have competing groups of the few jockeying for power. And Machiavelli makes clear as well that no one ever rules in the public interest. Rulers always rule in their own interest. That is the effective truth of political life.

Machiavelli claims that in *The Prince* he will not deal with Republics. That proves to be a false statement, as Rousseau and Spinoza so clearly saw. But the man who openly teaches duplicity can hardly be blamed if he engages in it himself. What sensible person would expect any less? Regarding Principalities Machiavelli asserts that there are two kinds, old or hereditary and new. The hereditary principalities are called "natural." They can be maintained with ease if one sticks to the observance of traditional laws and customs. Unlike new princes, old princes can be "loved," held in place by natural affection.

It quickly becomes clear that old princes can prudently expand their holdings only so far if they wish to maintain their "natural" advantages. They are limited to minor annexations of territories that are "naturally" alike in language, custom, religion and ethnic stock. Machiavelli makes it clear that "natural" regimes can only be relatively small. Aristotle argued that the best regime was small. And the best of small regimes, the Polity, mixed the competing elements of Oligarchy and Democracy, the rule of the few and the many respectively. Machiavelli wishes to transcend all of this. He wants a large Republic, initiated by "new" princes who of necessity negate all of the old, traditional laws and introduce, from scratch, "new modes and orders." The best regime will be a large, homogeneous Republic ruled by a few. It will be an artificially constructed regime consciously projected. But even there another novelty will be introduced. The few Machiavelli has in mind are not the traditional few found among the wealthy and socially notable.

The underlying positive proto-modernity of Machiavelli can be seen in the penultimate chapter of *The Prince* where Machiavelli discusses "How Much Fortune Can Do in Human Affairs, and in What Mode It May Be Opposed."[10] Machiavelli states that he opposes the common view that worldly affairs are determined by Chance or by God. He opposes that notion "in order that our free will not be eliminated" (p. 98). If there is to be a realm in which our human free will can be efficacious, a "realm of Freedom," calculating human prudence must understand and manipulate Necessity so that it can align human affairs so that Chance, and presumably God as well, cannot overwhelm the human will. If this is done artfully, Machiavelli asserts, the human realm can come to encompass about fifty percent of the whole. Machiavelli hopes to reach a stand-off with Chance. This seems like a more modest goal than that pursued by Descartes or Bacon who clearly desire an almost complete conquest of Nature. But even here it is Machiavelli's will operating as the primary given. This is a will that is much like Descartes' autonomous ego.

It would appear that for Machiavelli the creation of a human realm of Freedom requires primarily a political reordering. He seems to approach his novel, modern end, a human realm of Freedom, in a traditional fashion, i.e., through the questions of who rules, how one should rule, and how the city should be organized. Machiavelli would seem to reject those approaches to the conquest of Chance, which rely on nonpolitical means, e.g., on modern technological science (Descartes, Bacon, et al.) or on man's transforming labor (Hegel, Marx). Nonetheless, we can say that it is his longing for the certainty that is made possible by the creation of a human realm of Freedom that binds Machiavelli to the rest of modernity, that shared by Descartes, Bacon, Hobbes, Locke, Rousseau, Kant, Hegel, and Marx, to name a few.

Machiavelli offers the analogy of a flooding river. When it is in full flood there is nothing to be done. Human beings are the pawns of Necessity. But in quiet times dams and dikes can be constructed to channel the flood according to one's will. In political terms the flood is unchecked human passions and emotions, especially runaway ambition and fear more than elements of greed and sensuality that rarely sneak into Machiavelli's account. The dams and dikes are consciously constructed "new modes and orders" that order the new, artificial, large Republics Machiavelli attempts to construct. Unleashed from the old modes and orders that cast moral opprobrium on human passions, they can be allowed to flood. Chance is conquered by consciously channeling those unleashed passions and emotions in a predictable direction. Unleashing Necessity controls Chance. But we need to return to the details of how Machiavelli hopes to bring this about.

It is his longing for a human realm, an arena for the play of free will, rather than his alleged scientific realism, or "lowering of the sights," that makes Machiavelli a modern. It is attention to this longing that helps unlock Machiavelli's teaching in *The Prince*. For example, it explains the inadequacy of the rule of traditional princes—or traditional regimes more generally—who oversee ancestral systems of customary law. As mentioned, Machiavelli admits that the rule of such princes is "natural"; he calls the old prince the "natural" prince (p. 7). Hereditary princes administer ancestral laws and as a reward are "loved." Furthermore, natural princes have the benefit of "legitimacy" and the tranquil domestic politics it helps ensure. But this hegemony of Nature makes impossible the realm of Freedom and the operation of the free will, which pops up more than once as a theme in *The Prince*. The politics of old principalities is ruled by natural catastrophes, economic trends beyond control and the unpredictable machinations of external enemies. Machiavelli's prescription is that old princes must be replaced by new princes, albeit not, as we will see, *ad infinitum*. New princes are a transitional tool.

The great advantage of old principalities, their "legitimacy," will be maintained if the hereditary prince refrains from innovations and merely applies ancient laws in his inherited principality. Slow change and continuity erase the memory of innovation and foster the maintenance of legitimacy. When that legitimacy is removed, it has to be replaced with fear. The new prince, and the means by which he comes to power and remains in power, are the basis of that fear. Again, if we follow the logic of Machiavelli's advice and examples, it becomes clear that it is not prudent for old princes to try to enlarge their kingdoms or embark on the creation of large empires ("composite" or "mixed" principalities).[11] For example, if a desired conquest has similar customs, the same language and racial origins (Natural bases of society), it can be easily annexed. Expansion beyond that scope, which provides a natural limit to size, brings with it great difficulties.

If the language, customs and race of a proposed annexation differ, the prince must go in person and live in the annexed province. In this way he can see disorders as they arise and respond in a prompt and efficient manner. But this is an inconvenience at best, or more likely, a potential danger to one's rule at home. For now the advantage of on the site administration is vitiated in one's hereditary province. The alternatives to going to the annexed province in person are: (1) maintain expensive armies in the annexed lands—which drains the homeland's treasury; (2) completely destroy the annexed country—which hardly makes it a desirable possession, except perhaps occasionally for some needed resources; or (3) send out an oligarchy to rule in one's place—which in effect creates potential rivals. The logic of the argument seems to be that if an old prince wishes to maintain himself he should refrain from both innovation and anything but limited expansion. Hence an old prince is limited as to how large his state can become, i.e., limited by Nature.

It is clear from *The Prince* that the conquest of Chance requires large nation-states that can be more immune to natural and external threats than the small, ancestral *ancien regime*. New princes, following their desire for glory, and Machiavelli's advice, will pick out an old principality as the object for their conquests. This is the logic of Machiavelli's argument. The old princes, who have limited incentives for change or for enlarging their territory, at best can fight a holding action, waiting to become obsolete at the hands of a world of large, new principalities. The logic of Machiavelli's *Prince* moves toward the replacement of old princes by new ones.[12]

Once new princes come to power, they are advised to destroy the old, legitimate ruling class, along with the traditional laws that support their states (pp. 20–21). New Princes must introduce "new orders and modes" (p. 22). Theirs is then to improvise, with great latitude; they are limited, if they are prudent, in only two areas—the inviolability of women and inheritance—with inheritance being the most inviolable (p. 67). This ability to transcend tradition and start from scratch is what allows new princes the possibility of expansion that is not available to old princes. They can use force in a way old princes never could if they wished to remain legitimate. Fear and human force replace the softer natural ties of loyalty and love. The new prince, who comes to power by his own *virtú* and arms, can level the past and pave the way for a unique future that better conquers Chance. The man moved by love of glory, by the desire for the immortality that comes with being a founder, a natural motive, is the efficient cause of the Machiavellian realm of Freedom. Machiavelli has in mind someone precisely like Napoleon who in one stroke levels off the *ancien regime* making it necessary consciously to write new laws—e.g., the Code Napoleon. Such new princes have littered the modern landscape: Lenin and Mao being prominent examples that could be added to Napoleon.

The new prince must risk all, his life, whatever property he may have, and even his moral reputation, in the name of his one overriding passion.[13] He must judiciously lie, cheat, murder, and commit all manner of prudent cruelties and crimes, some directly, others through accomplices that he must turn on if it becomes useful. The new prince must show traditional virtue when it is useful, and traditional vice when necessary. He must even prefer to be feared rather than loved; all he must do is avoid hatred (accruing to those who are rapacious) (p. 68) and contempt (the latter accruing to those who are effeminate and irresolute). In short, a new prince is to behave in a Machiavellian fashion.

As far as Machiavelli is concerned, foundings are always brutal, yet premoral (awaiting as they do new modes and orders), especially those in the service of the conquest of Chance. One cannot rely on the accidents that lie at the foundation of traditional, ancestral cities; modern foundings must be conscious acts upon which new laws and a new morality can be constructed. In this fashion, Machiavelli prepares the way for the modern transformation of the status of Reason whereby the typically modern alliance of Reason and Will is established. Reason is to become active and creative.

The surface, "Machiavellian," side of Machiavelli's teaching is well-known and has been amply explored, and need be reviewed no further. Let us look, however, in a different direction. Let us look closely at the dialectic that occurs after the founding if all the actors behave as Machiavelli predicts and advises. The greater part of the advice in *The Prince* is not advice on acquisitions, but on consolidation and building a base for future expansion. We must see what happens to our new prince after the founding if he follows precisely Machiavelli's advice on consolidation: Will he, like the old prince, become a "sitting duck"? My suggestion is that he will undermine not only himself, but the ongoing possibility of new princes as well. The constant flux of founding and refounding is not what Machiavelli aimed at. In the resulting chaos the conquest of Chance would be impossible.

One of the more significant pieces of advice on consolidation is gleaned from the comparison of the government of the Turks and that of France in chapter 4, "Why the Kingdom of Darius Which Alexander Seized Did Not Rebel from His Successors after Alexander's Death."[14] Machiavelli compares the kingdom of the Turks, where all power is centralized, with that of France, where it is decentralized and shared with the landed barons. Machiavelli argues that it is difficult to defeat the Turks because with one ruler there is always unified planning plus a lack of disgruntled nobles to help give a foothold to an invader. But once the Turkish King is defeated, the nation belongs safely to the conqueror, for there remain no alternate sources of authority to launch a counter-coup. On the other hand, Machiavelli claims it is easier initially to defeat the French, for there will be bickering on policy and disgruntled nobles to help give the potential conqueror an opening. But once the French are defeated, it is hard to consolidate and hold the winnings, for there is a variety of legitimate sources of authority to rally around, and it would be impossible to kill all of them.

A prudent new prince will draw certain lessons from this story in picking a target for his new principality. But a new prince bent on consolidating his power would have to draw a different lesson. The moral of this comparison for an aspiring prince is: Attack a centralized, traditional power if you wish to be able to maximize the chance to consolidate your conquest; however, the staying power of your founding depends on the ultimate decentralization of authority. The new prince, the one moved primarily by the love of glory, will be more likely to grasp the first teaching rather than the latter. In fact, the latter teaching is something about which an aspiring new prince should probably not be overly clear before he risks all; were he more clearsighted he might choose a less paradoxical occupation. Few men will risk all if they realize that the best way to keep their winnings is to parcel out their authority. This point is reinforced when Machiavelli makes it clear that it is not fruitful to attack Republics where there is "greater life, greater hatred, more desire for revenge" (p. 21). Someone with political wisdom would not only not attack Republics, he would look to them as his model for consolidation if he desired to maximize the staying power of his founding. Of course the longevity of the society as a whole and that of the prince are two different things. Indeed, the founder may even eventually be rebuked for his cruelty, as were such new princes as Lenin and Stalin.

Very early in Machiavelli's *The Prince,* therefore, we are alerted to the possibility that Machiavelli's deviousness may cut deeper than that which he advises quite openly. New princes are needed to level the past and begin the march toward the conquest of Chance, but it is not clear that they will ever get what they long for, which is to consolidate their power, rule in their own behalf, and choose their own successor, if not found a hereditary state—we should keep in mind that there are no discussions of succession in *The Prince*.[15] Nonetheless, Machiavelli, manipulating new princes, gets what he longs for. We should realize that if the new prince merely becomes the founder of yet another "old" principality, Machiavelli will have failed at his attempt at a radical new beginning. Again, new princes are just tools to level the old and open the possibility of the radically new.

Another intimation of the problems new princes face, in principle, can be gleaned from the advice Machiavelli gives regarding the constitution of armies. Initially the new prince is advised to rely on his own arms and fighting prowess. Since, as Machiavelli's examples show, most new princes will be drawn from the military, what is meant by having one's own arms probably means one's prior comrades in arms. Given Machiavelli's view of human nature, their motivation will no doubt be a desire for personal gain. However, to maintain the principality after having achieved power, the new prince is told he must have a militia and arm his people, i.e., those he has robbed of their ancestral laws, forced to endure examples of butchery and cruelty and probably the loss of property. The new prince must jettison his comrades in arms, for they will be hard to satisfy, be a drain on his resources, and provide a breeding ground for future rivals. Nonetheless, militias or armed citizens clearly represent a form of decentralization of power. But since it is asserted that neither mercenaries nor foreign troops are to be relied upon there is no alternative. You must arm those you have assaulted in their quiet appreciation of ancient modes and orders.

We should also consider Machiavelli's general advice regarding not relying on fortresses, but relying rather on the armed populace going out to meet the enemy at the border.

> Therefore the best fortress there is, is not to be hated by the people, because although you may have fortresses, if the people hold you in hatred fortresses do not save you; for to peoples who have taken up arms foreigners will never be lacking to come to their aid. (p. 87)

We are also told that fortresses are only useful for princes who fear their people more than foreign enemies. But if one fears one's own people, being locked up inside a fortress with them is not the best alternative, and being surrounded by them is no alternative at all (pp. 86–87). Hence the main point seems to be that it is necessary for a prince "to have the people friendly; otherwise he has no remedy in adversity" (p. 41). To accomplish this, the prince must always align himself with the people rather than the great (whether of birth, wealth or special natural endowment).

> One cannot satisfy the great with decency and without injury to others, but one can satisfy the people; for the end of the people is more decent than that of the great, since the great want to oppress and the people want not to be oppressed. Furthermore, a prince can never secure himself against a hostile people, as they are too many; against the great, he can secure himself, as they are few. (p. 39)

Finally, one gains favor with the people not only by arming them and opposing the great, but by refraining from excessive taxation. The latter is accomplished by not being overly generous—i.e., by making the people self-sufficient rather than dependent on the prince's largesse (p. 64). Clearly there is a certain decentralizing, democratizing tendency inherent in the consolidation of large, non-natural, new states.

These observations may represent excellent means to the strengthening of the new nation itself, but are disadvantageous to a new prince who has turned over ancient customs and created animosity through the crime and cruelty we are told he cannot avoid. If the new prince follows Machiavelli's advice on consolidation, he will do things that will surely preserve what he has founded, but parcel out his glory, undermine his rule, and make him or his heirs eventually superfluous.

An armed and independent people might quickly wonder why they still needed a prince who had given them ample examples of how ruthlessly he was prepared to act. Of course, one might respond that love for and loyalty to the new prince might mitigate this line of argument. But Machiavelli gives no advice whatsoever on how new princes come to be loved. It is old princes that he explicitly says are loved. They are the ones that can rely on such traditional, "natural" supports as loyalty, honor and patriotism. As we have seen, Machiavelli asserts that it is only necessary for a new prince to be feared, as long as he is not hated or held in contempt.

Machiavelli gives considerable advice to his new prince on how to become feared. In building his teaching on the "effectual truth," Machiavelli consciously eschews reliance on the supports of those who begin from "imagined Republics," i.e., the traditional political philosophy he is attempting to transcend and make obsolete (p. 61). Machiavelli does not rely on patriotism and loyalty, at least not on the part of the people toward the new prince.

We can see that the teaching of *The Prince* on consolidating new modern foundings, undertaken in the service of the conquest of Chance, leads not only in the direction of decentralization, but also toward the need for a self-sufficient citizenry, armed and capable of defending itself. Another argument reinforces the point about self-sufficiency. The new prince is advised to give public recognition to the "virtuous" and "excellent" among the common men.

> [The prince] should inspire his citizens to follow their pursuits quietly, in trade
> and in agriculture and in every other pursuit of men, so that one person does not
> fear to adorn his possessions lest they be taken away front him, and another to
> open up a trade for fear of taxes. But he should prepare rewards for whoever
> wants to do these things, and for anyone who thinks up any way of expanding
> his city or his state. (p. 91)

The new prince should foster the arts (and presumably philosophy), commerce, and trade. Thereby he can be the prince of a wealthy and magnificent state, which will increase his glory. But simultaneously he will come to have as subjects those with independent wealth and public reputations, which are neither dependent upon nor emanate from him. Is there not an inexorable dialectic in this movement that Machiavelli sets in motion? In effect, the new prince is advised to set in motion the movement from the small, traditional city-state to the large, heterogeneous wealthy commercial nation-state with consciously written laws based on a new spirit of the laws, Machiavelli's new modes and orders. We still have not dealt with who is going to supply those laws once the *ancien regime* is overturned.

That the new prince is intended to become obsolete can be approached from yet another direction. He is advised to go forth as captain and lead his army himself (p. 49). Also, "a prince should have *no* other object, nor *any other* thought, nor take anything else as his art but the art of war and its orders and discipline; for that is the *only* art which is of concern to one who commands" (p. 58; italics mine). Machiavelli also asserts, without qualification, that the education of the new prince should be entirely in war, its history, and strategy. Furthermore, the new prince should spend most of his time in the countryside doing the things that conduce to heartiness:

> Besides keeping his armies well ordered and exercised, he should always be out
> hunting, and through this accustom the body to hardships; and meanwhile he
> should learn the nature of sites, and recognize how mountains rise, how valleys
> open up, how plains lie, and understand the nature of rivers and marshes—and
> in this invest the greatest care. (p. 59)

In short, the new prince must assume the role of a relatively rustic commander-in-chief, and remain in the provinces more than in the capital.

We should recall that the new prince has founded a principality that can enlarge itself in a way the "Natural" city it succeeds could not. Having leveled the past, this new state will need new, consciously constructed codes and administrative appurtenances that were previously unnecessary. There is no suggestion that the new prince should study treatises on day-to-day legislation or public administration; his only non-rustic study is history, but even then only the history of war and strategy. And he only studies that history because Machiavelli says the new prince needs to find someone to imitate; he gives as examples Alexander, Achilles, Caesar, Scipio, and Cyrus (p. 60). It is not clear that there is much of value regarding legislation or administration that can be learned from those five warrior/leaders.

As part of his study of history, the prince is explicitly advised to read Xenophon, and presumably not Xenophon's Socratic discourses. Given the reference to Cyrus we might fruitfully turn to Xenophon's *Education of Cyrus,* where we find that after considerable military success, Cyrus's consolidation consists of barricading himself in his castle, parceling out his authority to Satraps, constantly looking over his shoulder, fearful of coups and generally fearful for his life. The longevity of the rule of Alexander and his lack of success at consolidation (consider again the odd title of chapter 4) and the end met by Caesar are likewise hardly reassuring for a new prince.

In another argument that leads in the same direction, Machiavelli cites four new princes "who have become princes by their own virtue and not by fortune"; he repeats the example of Cyrus and adds Romulus, Theseus and Moses (p. 22). The example of Moses is perhaps most striking. Moses takes his people out of bondage and on a tortuous journey at the end of which he is not allowed to enter the promised land (consolidate). The examples of Romulus and Theseus are equally instructive, and in different ways reinforce the same point. There is a cloud hanging over the prospects of even the most successful new prince. In fact, each of Machiavelli's ancient examples reinforces our thesis that while the new prince will act as founder, he will hardly be the one who consolidates that founding. Given that it is unlikely that he will gain a reputation for honor and virtue, he may even be renounced during the consolidation, again in the fashion of Lenin and Stalin.

These observations shed even more light given Machiavelli's famous metaphor of the "lion and the fox." "You must know that there are two kinds of combat: one with *laws*, the other with *force*. The first is proper to *man* the second to *beasts*" (p. 69; italics mine). The metaphor is complicated by the fact that both fox and lion are put on the side of the beasts, leaving one wondering who represents the human. Presumably it is the one who deals with laws, and even further in the background, the new modes and orders that inform the new laws. Machiavelli says that both lion and fox are necessary, as are combat with force and laws. He makes it seem as if it might be the same person who exercises all of these possibilities. But is it likely that the intrepid, rustic new prince will be the one who can be both? He surely knows how to play the part of the beast qua lion and perhaps some will even play the fox and use duplicity along with overt force. But one must also know how to do combat "with laws." These are undoubtedly the ones that Machiavelli refers to as the ones who "know." The knowers who stand in the background eventually come into our view if we take the time to look for them.

We have already wondered who will attend to the necessary administrative details the new prince will not handle directly. It is not until the end of *The Prince* that we find a potential answer about where we shall find such a person. Chapter 22, "Of Those Whom Princes Have as Secretaries," and chapter 23, "In What Mode Flatterers Are to Be Avoided" provide some clues and, seen in the proper light, are quite amusing.

The new prince is told that the choice of ministers is of immense importance to him. It is categorically asserted that the wisdom and intelligence of the prince will be judged entirely in relation to the advisors he has around him—in other words, not on the basis of any intrinsic wisdom or intelligence of the prince himself. Machiavelli gives the example of a particular prince whom everyone judged as "a most worthy man," because of the minister he had chosen (p. 92). Without that minister the judgment of the new prince would have been different. Let us put this observation in a distinctive light. The relatively rustic commander-in-chief who has been advised to spend most of his time, especially in peace, on maneuvers and bivouac away from the capital, is advised to keep a houseful of wise advisors—those who know—back in the capital. He is told that his own wisdom will be judged entirely in relation to the wisdom of those he has as ministers.

Those advisors who dominate the life of the capital are the ones who will deal with administrative matters like education, roads, bridges, taxes, budgets, and so on—in other words, all the things left un-discussed in *The Prince* that touch the lives of ordinary citizens in the most massive ways and on a day-to-day basis. If a new prince were perspicacious enough to follow through the ramifications of the advice on advisors, he might come to question the prudence of having them as potential rivals. But he is in no position to do without them, for he has leveled the past where they were not necessary and launched a world of large modern regimes stripped of tradition where they will be unavoidable. The new prince creates a new, non-natural city, arms it, fosters its prosperity, and then leaves it to the administration of what without distortion we can call "intellectuals." The larger and more sophisticated the regime, the more it will require those who know.

What the new prince does is create the circumstances which will eventually make him less relevant if not simply obsolete. If he is successful, the new world, the growth of which he has set in motion, will have conquered Chance in a way no previous regime could, become more orderly and pacific, and will not need warrior/leaders like the new prince except on increasingly rare occasions. For unlike old principalities, the new "modes and orders" make possible a size and prosperity that makes the new nation-state substantially more immune to external forces as well as natural ones. Perhaps new princes will still be out front on the stage, but it will not ultimately be they who rule.

Following this line of argument we might note the rule of thumb Machiavelli offers the rustic warrior/prince for judging which wise ministers he can trust. He must find ministers who think more of him than of themselves. Machiavelli asserts that the way to assure that this is accomplished is to profusely honor one's ministers, make them rich, and share glory with them so they see that they cannot possibly have more riches or honors by leaving or opposing the prince (pp. 92–93). This is tantamount to the maxim that to assure loyalty one should "give them the gold before they take it." This is a maxim that works well from the perspective of the advisors, but if we invoke the wisdom of Hobbes, if the desires are insatiable and proceed from one to another endlessly, ceasing only in death, we see it does not necessarily work to the advantage of the prince.[16] One will never truly satisfy the advisors.

In the same vein, the prince is given advice on how to avoid flatterers. He must make sure that advisors can see no advantage in dissembling. The only way to accomplish this is said to be to make sure that the advisors have an incentive to always say what they truly think. This is accomplished by granting them unlimited freedom of speech, albeit on only those subjects about which the prince inquires.

> But [the prince] should ask them about everything and listen to their opinions; then he should decide by himself, in his own mode; and with these councils and with each member of them he should behave in such a mode that everyone knows that the more freely he speaks, the more he will be accepted. (p. 94)

Herein lies the basis of intellectual freedom, freed from the limitations of religious doctrine and ministering only to the well being of the secular state. If the new prince follows Machiavelli's advice, he will make his advisors wealthy, honored, and unlimited in their speech and more or less alone in the capital dealing with day-to-day affairs. The advisors reap a harvest greater than that of the general citizenry. And the new prince gains even more rivals, rivals he cannot do without. Hence the new regime truly will be a Republic ruled by the few. Yet it is the few who are knowers. Whether a prince is out front on the stage is largely superfluous. The new regime can be called a princely Republic or a republican Principality. It will in reality be the rule of the few who know.

Again the example of Cesare Borgia is instructive. He plays a central role in *The Prince*. Cesare came to power through the aid of his father rather than entirely through his own arms and virtue, so he is not a true new prince who rises from private station by his own devices. Nonetheless, in his attempt to

consolidate he follows all of Machiavelli's advice. Only Agathocles and Oliv-
erotto rival his clever ruthlessness. "And if his orders did not bring profit to
him, it was not his fault, because this arose from an extraordinary and extreme malignity of fortune" (p. 27). "If at the death of Alexander [Cesare] had
been healthy, everything would have been easy for him. . . . He had thought
about what might happen when his father was dying, and had found a remedy
for everything, except that he never thought that at his death he himself would
also be on the point of dying" (p. 32). What ultimately thwarts Cesare's efforts is a simple natural phenomenon—death. Death is something that no individual can outstrip, not even one who comes to power by virtue and his own
arms.

   To depend on individuals beyond the founding, no matter how Machiavellian
that founding may be, is always to remain in the grasp of Chance. Only laws
can gain a duration that allows Chance to be conquered. Despite Machiavelli's
praise of the individual desire for personal glory that moves the founder prince,
laws must eventually replace the will and discretion of such founders. And as
we have seen, the realm of law will be the arena of those who know, the realm
of the advisors. A large, wealthy, self-sufficient citizenry under consciously created laws that are administered by "intellectuals" is the way to conquer Chance.
The eventual overcoming of the warrior/princes is inevitable.[17]

   In one way, I have suggested that Machiavelli's teaching in *The Prince* is
compatible with Rousseau's more republican arguments of *The Discourses,*
albeit not in any conventional sense. For it is not a conventional Republic toward which Machiavelli is pointing. Machiavelli uses the new prince like a
puppet to level the past and create a new world that is better suited to the rule
of men like Machiavelli—who decries his own malignity of fortune—than to
the rule of truly political men moved by simply political motives. This is not
to say that Machiavelli is not moved by ambition. But it is an ambition of such
a magnitude that it represents a quantum leap from the ambition of simple political actors and an ambition greater than that of the ancient philosophers. Ultimately, Machiavelli's longing to create a human realm of Freedom is not a
political motive. The end Machiavelli longs for actually paves the way for the
abolition of the political as traditionally understood. What looks like a praise
of the autonomy of politics and political action from morality and religion in
fact prepares the way for the dialectical overcoming of the political. What is
left in its place is the politics of competing philosophical programs that gains
its eventual codification in Nietzsche. Machiavelli provides the opening
movement in the modern, all too modern, symphony. Far from being the realist, he is the ultimate idealist who craves the actualization of the rule of the
philosopher-king in a way Plato would have never thought possible.

   In this light let us consider one final example. Machiavelli observes:

There are three kinds of brains: one that understands by itself, another that discerns what others understand, the third that understands neither by itself nor through others; the first is the most excellent, the second excellent, and the third useless. (p. 92)

The highest praise is not reserved for the intellect of even the best new prince. Such a prince can only aspire to see the highest intelligence in others. Further, there is no indication anywhere in Machiavelli's thought that there is more than one kind of wisdom—as Aristotle distinguishes between the theoretical and the practical—one that the political man like the prince participates in and one that the thinker like Machiavelli has. There is one kind of wisdom and Machiavelli and his kind possess it. Therefore, no subtle articulation of the theoretical and the practical is required in Machiavelli's modern solution.

Machiavelli does not need the on-the-spot action of the genuinely political man to apply a watered down version of the highest wisdom as is true in ancient political philosophy. Since there is only one kind of wisdom, those who have it, Machiavelli and his kind, have, thereby, the most legitimate claim to rule—not the spirited, glory-seeking political man. While he will undoubtedly rule from behind the scenes, the philosopher is in command qua philosopher.

Again, far from being the great realist, Machiavelli is, therefore, the first thinker who attempted to recreate the world in such a way that it would make possible the *actualization* of the rule of the philosopher-king, although in the guise of the intellectual-administrator. My suggestion is that this is, in Machiavelli's understanding, the only appropriate means to the conquest of Chance. At most, the political man reigns, but does not rule. The philosophic man rules, albeit perhaps not out in the open. In this way Machiavelli transforms the status of the philosopher from contemplative knower to active participant. It remains necessary to conquer only part of Chance if the philosopher is to retain his hegemony. Without that ongoing task he would be brought out far too clearly into the open. Hence Machiavelli does not try for the complete victory of other modern thinkers. That limitation comes from self-interest not, moderation.

Nonetheless, within modern political philosophy we can also see clear parallels of this Machiavellian approach. In Bacon's *New Atlantis* we see pictured a society administered to and ruled by intellectuals, in that case scientists and inventors. In Rousseau's *First Discourse,* an argument, it should be recalled, against the public dissemination of wisdom, we have the following argument for the appropriate integration of wisdom into the city.

May kings not disdain to allow into their councils the men most capable of advising them well; may they renounce the old prejudice, invented by the pride of the great, that the art of leading people is more difficult than that of enlightening them, as if it were easier to engage men to do good willingly than to constrain them to do it by force. May learned men of the first rank find honorable asylum in their courts. . . . *So long as power is alone on the one side, intellect and wisdom alone on the other,* learned men will rarely think of great things, Princes will more rarely do noble ones, and the people will continue to be vile, corrupt, and unhappy.[18]

And in Hegel's *Philosophy of Right* we have the veritable codification of the legitimacy of the rule of intellectual administrators in a large Republic that conquers chance.

My suggestion is that Machiavelli tries to transcend the rule of the purely political man in favor of rule by "knowers." Hence fellow philosophers need not in the future be put in the galling position he depicts in the dedicatory letter to *The Prince* where one who has no right rules, and one who, through knowledge has the right, does not. This overcoming of a natural injustice is at the heart of Machiavelli's understanding of how to conquer Chance. The main debate within modernity has been whether the ranks of the new philosopher-kings will be filled primarily by a scientific/technological intelligentsia or by what we might call a "humanistic" elite. In other words, under what mask should the new philosophers hide themselves since in the new modes and orders it will no longer be as gentlemen or priests, as was true with classic and medieval political philosophy? Needless to say, there have been reactions against this anti-political tendency, most notably in Nietzsche. But those reactions have only intensified the dialectic of modernity, not reversed it. And in Nietzsche we see the full, self-conscious flowering of Machiavelli's audacious pride and desire to rule from just off stage.

Contrary to Machiavelli, I would suggest that if there is a political and moral crisis in our time, it is linked with the abolition of the political, and that in turn is tied up with the sublimation of the spirited and honor loving. If the overcoming of the political and spirited are a necessary means to the actualization of the realm of Freedom, and that realm comes to be seen as unlivable, then perhaps we must rethink the relationship between the spirited and political, on the one hand, and the existence of the realm of Freedom, on the other. We must wonder if the abolition of the political really leads to the conquest of Chance, or merely to the hegemony of Chance in a new more powerful and frightening form. The world of the twenty-first century seems increasingly ruled by events beyond human control, which were nonetheless unleashed by previous human choices. Have we really conquered Chance, or opened Pandora's box in such a way that we are increasingly ruled by a Fate and Destiny beyond the conscious control Machiavelli and other moderns so extolled?

If what I have suggested has substance, it would be unwise to seek in Machiavelli for the spirited and political possibilities modernity may now require. In fact it would be unwise to look for the political in Machiavelli either. If Machiavelli in some way speaks for the spirit of modernity, it is a spirit ultimately antagonistic to the enspiriting and the political. Unless another modern source can be found we may be forced to turn elsewhere in our search for the ground of the spirited and the political. In the process we may be forced to question the realm of Freedom and gain a new appreciation for Nature. But I doubt that antiquity offers all the resources necessary for a postmodern world already unfolding.

Any search for spiritedness, which may be required for a healthy public existence, may lead us in the direction of a profound paradox. In other words, we must decide what price we are willing to pay to be, on the one hand, enspirited, or on the other, residents of the realm of Freedom which may constitute our new slavery. Perhaps we may wish to strike a balance that differs from the way it has been done especially within modernity. Be this as it may, we remain better off in our *public* existence for having knowledge of our paradoxical situation, for we become aware thereby of the delicate balance that must be maintained to pursue a public well-being that is consistent with *our* late-modern world.

NOTES

1. This chapter is a substantial reworking of an article that originally appeared as Machiavelli's *The Prince and the Abolition of the Political: A Preliminary Reflection*, in *Machiavelli Studies*, Volume 2, 1988.

2. Rousseau, *On the Social Contract*, trans. by Judith R. Masters, ed. Roger Masters (New York: St. Martin's Press, 1978), p. 88.

3. Spinoza, *Political Treatise*, in *Works of Spinoza*, Vol. 1, trans. Elwes (New York: Dover Publications, 1951), p. 315.

4. Exceptions to this include Pocock, Skinner and Coby among others. See J. Patrick Coby, *Machiavelli's Romans* (Lanham: Lexington Books, 1999), Quentin Skinner, *Machiavelli* (New York: Hill and Wang, 1981), and J. G. A. Pocock, *The Machiavellian Moment* (Princeton: Princeton University Press, 1975).

5. A serious dissent from this view can be found in Robert Pippin, *Idealism as Modernism* (New York: Cambridge University Press, 1997).

6. *Within modernity,* there are three authors who appear to be the most straightforward spokespersons for eros, spiritedness, ambition and the pursuit of glory: Machiavelli, Rousseau and Nietzsche. But despite his praise of a Spartan-like political whole, Rousseau may ultimately be a spokesman alternately for the domestic and the solitary contemplative rather than the political. At least such has been his primary public influence. Nietzsche presents a variety of problems in this regard, which at present I think it best to ignore, but in the end he may be the only modern—albeit a modern determined to make a transition to post-modernity—who actually speaks for the political. I have dealt with this in my *Nietzsche, Heidegger and the Transition to Postmodernity.*

7. In this light consider Sheldon Wolin, *The Politics of Vision* (Boston: Little, Brown, 1960), pp. 220–35.

8. See for example Leo Strauss, *What Is Political Philosophy?* (Glencoe, IL: Free Press, 1959), pp. 41; 46.

9. For a contrary view see Harvey Mansfield, *Machiavelli's Virtue* (Chicago: University of Chicago Press, 1996).

10. Niccoló Machiavelli, *The Prince,* trans., with intro., by Harvey C. Mansfield, Jr. (Chicago: University of Chicago Press, 1985). All page citations in the text refer to this edition.

11. For the discussion of old principalities, See *The Prince*, chapters 2 and 3, "Of Mixed Principalities."

12. For a similar, albeit not identical, observation, see Pocock, *The Machiavellian Moment*, p. 158; more generally, pp. 156–82.

13. It is not obvious that the new prince achieves happiness as a result of pursuing his one passion. In this regard consider G. W. F. Hegel, *Lectures on the Philosophy of World History: Introduction* (New York: Cambridge University Press, 1980), pp. 85–86.

14. The paradoxical nature of the chapter title should not be neglected.

15. The example of Cesare Borgia is instructive here. He is said to have done everything correctly. But he ultimately failed because first his father, the Pope who gave him his start, and then he himself died. But death is a natural fact that cannot be outstripped. In the life of states the only thing that is relatively deathless is modes and orders. Laws may succeed themselves where individuals do not. Those laws point toward not only Republics but the individuals who can promulgate and write them. As we will see, that is unlikely to be the tough and relatively rustic new prince. And behind the specific laws themselves lies the "new modes and orders," or what Montesquieu called the "spirit of the laws." That clearly proceeds from the likes of a Machiavelli.

16. Machiavelli holds a particularly Hobbesian view of the commonality. The vast majorities are uninteresting to Machiavelli precisely because they are always "obedient to present necessities" (p. 70). They want to be left alone to pursue their domestic existence. Only occasionally must one manipulate them, and then through the use of fear; otherwise they are not a major political problem. The only "higher" sentiment in the Machiavellian universe is that displayed by the spirited and ambitious new prince.

17. It could be argued that, contrary to my presentation, what is anticipated by Machiavelli is something like the ongoing competition that allows "ambition to check ambition," i.e., something like the system of checks and balances. But none of the participants in the system of checks and balances is a "new prince," nor do any of those constitutional competitors aspire to destroy the system so a new founding becomes repeatedly necessary. Their competition is closer to that of law-abiding citizens jostling for a bigger piece of the pie. Such is not the stuff of which new princes are made. And such is nowhere near the stuff of which Machiavellian ambition is made. This kind of competition does not fit the example of warrior/princes bent on the immortal glory that comes from being a founder. And it does not fit the model of those who long to introduce new modes and orders.

18. Jean-Jacques Rousseau, *First Discourse,* in The *First and Second Discourses, ed., with intro. and notes by Roger D. Masters, trans.* Roger D. and Judith R. Masters (New York: St. Martin's Press, 19(4), p. 63–64. [my emphasis]

Chapter Five

Phenomenology or Constructivism: Robert Pippin's Modernity

Philosophy, like every other activity, has to begin somewhere. That somewhere is the topic of my reflections. Of course, for those of us who arrive in the midst of what is already an almost 2,500-year-old tradition, we begin almost unavoidably in mid-stream. Any pure autonomy from the past tradition is in practical terms impossible. Perhaps, in their own way, even the initial Greek thinkers began in mid-stream. If we take the suggestion of Heidegger seriously, even the Greek philosophers co-opted and built upon a series of understandings that had evolved inarticulately in Greek, "everyday," or "ordinary," living itself. But at some point in its history philosophy turned its efforts into a reflexive activity and thematically considered the nature of its own undertaking as at least as important as reflection upon its surroundings. Whenever that moment occurred—and in my understanding it was long before the beginning of modernity and the turn toward the self-legislating ego—thereafter, the self-analysis of philosophy came to be at the very heart of its own reflections. I would suggest that we are living in a moment when that self-reflection is unavoidably even more primary than might otherwise be customary. It is obvious that in getting underway with a reflection upon how philosophy itself gets underway I have begun in mid-stream. And in my reflections below I will not get much beyond the issue of how to make a beginning. Obviously there is more to the story, but the rest will have to be told another time. As the old saying goes, the beginning may be more than half the whole, but in this instance I would ask that judgment about my beginning be reserved until my argument can be seen as a whole.

At present, I want to approach my issue by a reflection upon an argument made by Robert Pippin in his recent essay, "The Unavailability of the

Ordinary," which extends an argument he has made elsewhere, especially in his *Idealism as Modernism*.[1] I have selected Pippin because I think he is one of the best contemporary spokespersons for a fundamental philosophical alternative; one I reject that is nonetheless compelling.

Pippin is a spokesperson for the modern philosophical position that grounds itself on the self-legislating ego. He also is a proponent of the modern moral and political understanding that takes freedom as the central concept in modern moral and political life. He attempts both to save and to conjoin these two modern positions with a version of Idealism which seems to be most consistent with Hegelianism, albeit as far as I can see, a Hegelianism that is shorn of the End of History thesis and indeed of inevitability more generally, not to mention the Absolute Ego. In the essay in question Pippin takes on Leo Strauss. Pippin construes Strauss to be arguing that philosophy begins not from a self-legislating ego but from a "natural consciousness." Strauss' studies of the Greeks were undertaken to get back to this natural understanding that had become occluded in the modern age precisely by the projections of the modern self-legislating ego. It is this "natural consciousness" of Strauss'—albeit I believe the term takes on the connotations it has for Strauss for the first time in Hegel's *Phenomenology*—that Pippin equates with his term "the ordinary."

I want to argue that at the deepest level what is at issue here is really a confrontation with Heidegger and not Strauss. What is at stake is Heidegger's assertion of the priority of pre-theoretical, "everyday" understandings to any thematic theoretical discourse. If Heidegger is correct, any belief that there can be such a thing as an autonomous, self-legislating ego is a chimera. I would argue that Pippin's critique of Strauss's derivative permutation of this argument for the priority of the pre-theoretical is substantially correct. But Pippin's critique of Strauss does not get to the more fundamental point that Heidegger is making, especially when amended in a way I will suggest.

In short, for Heidegger there are always already "phenomena" that "show themselves" and into which we are always already "thrown." These phenomena create the horizon of the "ordinary," or as Heidegger puts it our "everyday" immersion in doing and making (in the *pragmata*). It is this immersion that informs our initial openness to reality which can never be completely cast aside. These "phenomena" need not be "natural" in the sense of unchanging or historically primordial, but they are nonetheless primary. Pippin's argument does not displace the primacy of the "ordinary" in Heidegger's sense. Further, Heidegger's presentation of Being as *physis,* as that which repeatedly emerges and shows **itself,** transcends the traditional, **theoretical** nature/convention distinction that I will argue both Strauss and Pippin share and that is, I will further argue, not a phenomenological point of departure. The derivative nature of the nature/convention distinction is already clear in Strauss discussion of its origin in *Natural Right and History*.

In a straightforward sense, Pippin is a conservative trying to defend already extant modern moral and political life—coalescing around his understanding of the primacy of "spontaneous" freedom—using modern philosophical tools. In his own way, Pippin also begins with the given—the modern moral, political and philosophical stance—and is not interested in transcending it in the direction of something novel that might evolve in the future. Hence in his own way, there is an end of history thesis lurking in Pippin's thought.

Heidegger's critique of the modern is that it leads not to freedom but to the most complete slavery humanity has ever seen. That slavery is the result of the "constructivism" or "Enframing" of the modern self-legislating ego, which so transforms its world that nothing any longer "stands" forth and shows **itself** in our time. According to Heidegger, man and everything else have come to be set forth universally, and only, as raw material to be transformed and held in waiting to be sallied forth in the projects of a runaway technological juggernaut that no longer has any other end than its own intensification. Once this occurs, no human will can reign in this technological juggernaut because it is the willfulness of the self-legislating, constructivist ego that set this universal revelation of reality in place in the first place. To deploy the will as a cure against the effects of the will is like struggling in quicksand. Heidegger would like a world that again "shows **itself**," and allows man a place for his political and moral life to be played out free from the total hegemony of the universal technological revelation of reality.

I would suggest that ultimately Pippin's response to Heidegger would have to show that there is never anything that "shows itself" in Heidegger's sense. The alternative argument to Heidegger's is that until the self-legislating ego, in its spontaneous autonomy and freedom, projects what things "are," they have no Being of their own—hence they cannot show themselves at all. Only, I will suggest, in this way could one dismiss the primacy of the "ordinary." Further, I would suggest that Pippin would have to show that the will can in fact have some substantive bearings for its willing in our time other than the technological transformation of man and nature—i.e., that an autonomous moral and political realm can still exist. In other words, he would need to show how in the modern world acts of the will can avoid getting immediately reified. Can one still will an Ideal that remains unactualized as an ongoing object of aspiration?

To put the matter in Hegelian terms, Pippin would have to show how a dialectic between the Real and the Ideal could continue to exist so that the Hegelian dialectic could continue to ground our spontaneous freedom in a way

that avoids the Heideggerian technological juggernaut or the Nietzschean idio-
syncrasy of the Will-to-Power but without the inevitability and endedness of
the Hegelian account.[2] I would suggest that this is the same problem Marcuse
struggled with in his attempts to avoid "one-dimensionality." But, without historical endedness and inevitability the Hegelian dialectic cannot be saved as
the basis for substantive guidance for the will. I would argue that the Hegelian
is the most consistent manifestation of Idealism. Without something like the
Hegelian dialectic, the spontaneous, self-legislating will could offer nothing
other than Nietzsche's ongoing, unguided idiosyncratic Will-to-Power or Heidegger's determinacy of the hegemony of blind technological fate.

STRAUSS, PIPPIN AND
THE NATURE/CONVENTION DISTINCTION

I am prepared to stipulate that Pippin gives a clear and altogether fair depiction of Strauss' position. For Strauss, the classical understanding is a primary,
originary or "natural" understanding in a way that no post-classical (which
means post-Greek) understanding could be. The classical authors were still in
touch with the "natural," "lived experience" of engaged participants in political life. This Straussian "natural" understanding is what Pippin associates
with his phrase "the ordinary." By contrast, Strauss sees especially late modern understandings—his "third wave"—as artificial. Those late modern understandings have occluded the natural in a way that allows us living in the
present no immediate access to our allegedly primary relationship to the
world. We have been "screened" from that understanding.

The modern world is thereby for Strauss so artificial that we cannot get our
bearings. In the modern world we are in danger of "forgetting" once and for
all what human scale and measure are like. Hence the only way to begin is to
recover a sense of the natural as it is displayed in the original, pre-artificial
understanding of those Greeks still capable of a direct confrontation with primary reality. For Strauss, that can at this point only be accomplished by a
careful reading of the texts of Greek political philosophy. This hermeneutic
propaedeutic provides us with the means of access to a "remembering" that
in our time is prior to any possible access to the natural. And all of this is
needed because of a moral and political crisis that has descended upon us because of the artificiality of our modern situation.

Pippin makes the perfectly straightforward observation that there is a circularity operating here that undermines Strauss' position. If we do not have
access to what is meant by the natural in the present, we have no hopes of dis-

covering or remembering it when we see it in the Greek texts. And if we already have at least an intimation of the natural in the present then we should simply turn immediately to an interrogation of the present and the "phenomena" that already present themselves. I also agree with Pippin that what Strauss does is make the original showing of things as manifested in Greek thought the primary, natural or ordinary understanding that has to be repeatedly recovered by an act of remembering and going back. Therefore, in this understanding there is only one manifestation of the ordinary for all times.

For Strauss, the modern approach to reality represents a view that is artificial, conventional and occluded, while the Greek understanding represents the natural understanding. This nature/convention distinction—which in *Natural Right and History* Strauss openly admits is theoretically derivative of various prior everyday perceptions,[3] **despite in his own terms being theoretically derivative rather than natural or ordinary**—is the basis of Strauss's position. Here is, I would argue, the real focal point of the problem, and Pippin misses it because he shares a version of the same distinction—albeit in his case it is a permutation of the modern Freedom/Nature distinction.

This is where Heidegger's notion of Being as *physis* is far more useful as a point of departure than the nature/convention distinction in that there can by Heidegger's understanding always, at least potentially, be an ongoing showing of the ordinary or everyday that emerges and shows itself.[4] While I would suggest that there are difficulties implied in the notion that there are multiple showings of the ordinary, the most useful point to be derived from Heidegger's doctrine of Being as *physis* is that the ordinary always exists no matter what the time period.

Without the nature/convention distinction, all one can say of that which emerges and shows itself is that it "is." I want to argue, contrary to both Strauss and Pippin, that the most important distinction is not nature/convention but between those things that show **themselves** and those that "stand" only after a constructivist "Enframing" (*Gestell*). This distinction a) "shows itself," versus b) Enframed—or put differently, between phenomenological and constructivist—is a different distinction than what is contained in the nature/convention dichotomy. There is no phenomenological need for the ordinary/everyday to be something that is historically first, primary or primordial.

As part of his critique, Pippin goes on to chide Strauss that the ordinary revelation of reality is "full of gods, angels, ghosts, wretched probability expectations, primitive fears, and banality." (336) Clearly Pippin, like Strauss, associates the "ordinary" with the original and primordial. Shortly, it becomes clear as well that Pippin associates the term original with the pre-reflexive. This is all perfectly Hegelian and indeed informs the basis of Hegel's *Phenomenology* where the natural consciousness is the early, pre-theoretical consciousness, prior in fact to "self-consciousness." Pippin's diminishment of the ordinary as rudimentary and pre-reflexive, no matter how conceived, is also consistent with his conclusion that the ordinary or natural is not the source of the good. Pippin rejects Strauss's version of "phenomenology" in favor of his own version of self-legislating constructivism as the only viable, "anti-natural" ground of the good.

In line with the "Idealism" with which he sides, Pippin argues that we as moderns must side with the realm of Freedom and not the realm of Nature—and the origin of modernity is precisely to be found, according to Pippin, in the Idealism especially of Kant and Hegel, and not in what is usually seen as the proto-modernity of Machiavelli, Descartes or Hobbes. But in adopting his version of the Freedom/Nature distinction, Pippin has simply proceeded on his own version of the nature/convention distinction he shares with Strauss. In effect Pippin chooses convention—the products of the human will. Strauss at least seems to choose Nature. **Each would have to explain where he presumes to stand in making this choice, and I would argue that ultimately neither can.**

I would argue that the author who best explains this is Heidegger, the author who thematically explains the place of thrown, resolute choosing. In the end, I believe both Pippin and Strauss are forced into a stance of groundless choosing. Pippin stands on the self-legislating ego that accepts no natural limitations or guidelines except perhaps negatively. One simply chooses Freedom. Strauss, especially in his discussions of Reason and Revelation, makes it perfectly clear that the choice for one or the other is a groundless choice, an act of faith as he calls it. I am arguing, and I derive this from Heidegger, that there are always "phenomena" that present themselves (*physis*) in the present. One is always "thrown" into them. One can neither choose for or against that thrownness. Thrownness is, before the fact, the thrown basis. And one cannot begin by categorizing that thrownness and its associated phenomena as either natural or conventional, they just "are." Those phenomena may very well prove to be unclear and contradictory, but that is precisely why they will always point beyond themselves toward more thematic philosophical reflection. And it is why a dialectical approach to philosophy is always unavoidable.

To return to Pippin, he shows his nature/convention commitment in a variety of straightforward ways. As yet another example, he argues that Strauss' understanding of the status of the ordinary commits him to the conclusion that the ordinary has only one manifestation for all times. Pippin, siding with Hegel and his moderns who, he asserts, see "History" as a primary modern phenomena, argues instead for "historically multiply" manifestations of reality. Pippin asserts that the central issue is to distinguish between a picture in which the everyday has been forgotten but is recoverable, layered over or screened behind artificial constructs and fantasies, and a picture in which there can be no such contrast, in which there are historically multiple (if sometimes continuous) everydays, not primordial and derivative experiences. The deepest and most comprehensive version of the latter picture is Hegel's and so involves the right way to understand what it means to tie philosophy, when understood as reflection on the meaning of human experience, to history, all as opposed to what I regard as this persistent dream of a lost (but findable) everyday, human experience of the human. (p. 337)

First, to say that there are historically multiple experiences is only possible on the basis of an assumption of some permutation of a primary, originary or "natural" position, or from the standpoint of some other unmoving and unchanging point outside historical movement. Only by comparison to some fixed point can one assure oneself that what look on the surface like "multiple" and hence categorically different experiences, are not just endless repetitions of the same.

Without the assumption of some unmoving point, Pippin could not show that there is not ultimately something underlying what appears to be surface change that remains changeless in the ongoing panoply of the surface phenomena. Ultimately, I would argue that for Pippin that fixed point is some originary position that is recoverable by thought albeit benighted and to be rejected and transcended in the name of the products of an autonomous self-legislating will. The will needs an ongoing "other" from which it is constantly emancipating itself to ground itself. And that same point is needed to prove historical movement rather than stasis. Without some fixed point—either primordial "nature" at the beginning or some perfected state at the end—the appearance of historical change may be a thoroughgoing illusion.

A simple metaphor is useful here. If someone were on the ocean adrift on one of its main currents, out of sight of the shore, incapable of seeing the bottom, and under a cloudy sky, that person would have no idea if he or she were moving or not. The shore, the ocean bottom, a fixed star, some unmoving point is required to even fathom motion. The same is true of History if one is to prove there is uniqueness or multiplicity. This is why the consistent authors of History, like Hegel, posit that fixed point outside of historical movement. For Hegel it is the Absolute Spirit. But as far as I can see, Pippin wants nothing to do with anything as metaphysical as an Absolute Spirit. And hence he is forced to posit some "originary other" that is to be negated by the self-legislating of a spontaneously free self—Freedom versus Nature. There may be an element of Hegelian negation operating here, but how it avoids the slippery slide into the Nietzschean Will-to-Power or of Heideggerian technological Enframing, and its resultant slavery, is not clear.

I would suggest that one can never make the hard case for historical uniqueness or multiplicity without a Hegelian-like assumption of standing at some privileged moment when the movement has, or soon will, stop or by positing an altogether unchanging primary nature. It seems to me that Pippin rejects the End of History and assumes the latter stance, merely taking Nature as benighted. If, on the other hand, one concludes that there are always phenomena into which we are thrown that we can dialectically engage, the problem disappears. We simply have to stop calling those phenomena natural or conventional, ordinary or occlusive, the product of a self-legislating will rather than benighted Nature, and on and on. They just "are" and we just begin by articulating and interrogating those phenomena. I would call this approach a dialectical, phenomenological philosophy. One might also designate this point of departure as "naïve." This is where we must make our beginning. Where we go after the beginning is another story.

HISTORY AND PHENOMENA

Pippin argues that what is distinctive about us moderns is that we view our ordinary experience as historical. On one level I would agree. But I doubt that this is true on any interesting level for the majority of, for example, ordinary, everyday, middle-class, American citizens. It is a well-known fact that Americans know far less about history generally, or even their own history, than citizens of various countries in Europe or Asia. Tocqueville long ago remarked on this fact of the fundamental a-historicality of Americans. He argued that it is aristocratic cultures that venerate the past and hence have a reason to study history. But in a democratic society, with considerable class mobility, and by historical standards limited class consciousness—especially in an increasingly universal middle-class society—life seems to begin anew with each generation. Change is rapid and interest in the past is of no particular utility in "getting ahead" in life. Pippin is correct that historical consciousness is at the core of intellectual and more generally theoretical culture in the modern age. But beyond the upper tiers of various intellectual and cultural elites, the experience of History simply does not determine the ordinary consciousness of the vast majority of middle-class Americans. To say, therefore, that all moderns view everyday experience as historical is an observation that is not faithful to the ordinary and everyday phenomena as they present themselves.

Pippin's observation about the moderns viewing ordinary experience as historical is part of what paradoxically amounts to a phenomenological reproach of Strauss. If Pippin's assertion is true, he believes it refutes Strauss's view that there is in ordinary experience only one primary, primordial, natural, ordinary (the terms are interchangeable) understanding of reality. But what Pippin has really done with this phenomenological assertion is point out the perfectly straightforward **phenomenon** in the late modern world of the increasing disconnect between high intellectual perceptions and majority everyday perceptions.

I would argue that this disconnect is precisely one of the phenomena to interrogate. But I see no need, nor any basis, upon which to designate for example, the high intellectual perception as "natural" or the majority view as "artificial," or vice versa. I see no basis upon which to "preference" one or the other. One simply begins by honestly articulating the phenomena.

Clearly Pippin wants to preference the high intellectual perception of reality and the equally high intellectual distinction between Nature and Freedom. I see no basis, initially at least, to do anything more than simply say that the two "are." As far as I am concerned that is what follows from the phenomenological/dialectical move I am suggesting. That said, I would say that as part of the priority of the phenomenological move, I believe Pippin is being a good phenomenologist when he asserts that our contemporaries see freedom as one of the core values of "our" civilization. But I would assert quite strongly that it is phenomenologically incorrect to assert that the majority conceptualizes Freedom as self-legislating or as involving the Freedom/Nature dichotomy.

Freedom is conceptualized by the majority of everyday citizens in far more commonsensical Lockean or Madisonian ways, where freedom means no more than what it did for Hobbes, freedom from external impediments. That could easily be a Freedom consistent with following our natural instincts free from external impediment. But that is a view of Freedom an Idealist like Pippin cannot accept as true Freedom. As with Kant, the true Idealist will always have to measure Freedom precisely in terms of its being anti-natural. We prove that a choice is free by proving it has transcended, indeed negated, all natural determination. Be that as it may, what is at stake here is the phenomena and how **they show themselves.** For the vast majority, freedom does not show itself as self-legislating. Pippin cannot ground his notion of freedom in the phenomena even though he makes what amount to phenomenological moves. The larger issue is can one be an Idealist without being a Constructivist in my sense; **and at what point will every Constructivist make an unavoidable phenomenological move without admitting it.**

None of these criticisms of Pippin, however, in any way help re-enthrone Strauss's view that there is only one manifestation of truly pre-theoretical or "natural" phenomena. I am arguing that we simply cannot know. We can always begin by interrogating how things present themselves **publicly** to the vast majority in the present. That may or may not, when thematically articulated, present us with something like the way the Greeks viewed the world. We cannot know; certainly not before the fact. We simply begin with the "ordinary" phenomena in our time. And in his own way, so does Pippin without being willing to accept the ultimate consequences of doing so.

We cannot **begin** phenomenologically from either the nature/convention distinction; nor can we begin from the Freedom/Nature distinction, nor the "inside/outside" distinction with which Pippin ends his article. These kinds of distinctions are all theoretically derivative and in no way immediately supported by the phenomena. And we have absolutely no theoretical way of knowing if the present phenomena are historically determined distinctions without being able to prove that we stand somehow outside of History. The phenomena simply "are." To assert anything more is to assume more than we are entitled to assume.

Phenomenologically, I agree completely with Pippin that modern life is an outgrowth of the experience of the inadequacies of the pre-modern. I agree as well that part of the phenomena of modernity include the subordination of art and religion to science together with the primacy of an un-heroic everyday reality of nuclear families, market economies, increasing classlessness and on and on—albeit, everyday reality does not categorize the phenomena in these theoretical terms. I only question Pippin's right to co-opt Hegel's term "rational"—which is to say that everyday life is now infused with high self-consciousness and a limitation of contradictions—to depict these phenomena rather than starting by asserting no more than that they "are." We will know if they are experienced as "rational" by the vast majority only after we interrogate how everyday individuals experience their lives in the present. For example, do they experience those lives as satisfying or alienating? And what we mean by satisfying and alienating will have to be generated internally from out of the phenomena themselves.

Phenomenologically, I also agree with Pippin that modernity has experienced itself since its beginnings, and continues to experience itself into the present, as a striving to get beyond the given. But if I understand correctly, what Pippin is arguing is a version of the Hegelian position that modernity as presently constituted in fact already presents us with both a rational understanding of reality and a rational hierarchy of objects of aspiration. For Pippin, modernity in its presently constituted aspirations, even if not in its extant actuality, represents the final good.

As far as I can see, Pippin is arguing for the rationality of endless modernity, but that paradoxically means an endlessly striving to get beyond the present given. **But that latter perception and striving could only make sense if the given were not rational.** The alleged "rationality" of the present is precisely a death knell for the phenomenological longing of modernity to continually transcend the given. Beyond this contradiction, what Pippin sees as the rationality of modernity would mean the impossibility of ever again striving in the present for the actualization in the future of genuinely **novel,** which is to say non-modern, outcomes. Modernity must endlessly strive to get beyond the given while simultaneously striving only for modern, "rational" outcomes.

Pippin's understanding actually inevitably implies the end of human historicality. I would argue that phenomenologically what moderns long for, if interrogated carefully, is ongoing historicality in a genuine sense and that Pippin is offering precisely the cessation of unique historicality. Further, Pippin argues that for his position to truly operate in the world, the will must be subsumed under law; otherwise we get the idiosyncratic Nietzschean Will-to-Power and with it the hegemony of the irrational. But that means that if there is to be rationality there can ultimately be only **one** law universally. And that one law will have to define itself as anti-natural if it is to make possible Freedom. I would suggest that to maintain this position, Kant and his notion of regulative ideas and the necessity of a world state will keep popping up for Pippin far more than he would like. Be that as it may, at best all Pippin, like Hegel, can offer is the greater geographical and demographic spread, or greater intensification, of principles and aspirations already extant. But that means that the underlying aspiration is precisely the End of History.

PHILOSOPHY AND THE CITY
(A.K.A. ORDINARY EXISTENCE)

Pippin observes that even if Strauss is correct that there is one ordinary or natural perception of reality we are still left with the question "why should we care." Why should we not obliterate the ordinary understanding in the name of the good, seeing the ordinary or natural as atavistic, as the arena of witches, goblins, suffocating ignorance and, in short, generally benighted. In a similar vein, Pippin makes the observation that even if we could isolate an originary understanding, "so what," given that for all we know the Tradition of modern political philosophy might have been irrelevant to the alleged occlusion of that reality and equally irrelevant and uninteresting to any moral or political crisis that might exist in the present. Indeed, the everyday world might go on uninterested and unaffected no matter what occurs in the realm of thought. Herein Pippin is raising a version of Strauss's question about the relation between Philosophy and the City. Do they really have any cross-fertilizing relationship whether healthy or not? Should they be related? Or might they simply go on about their business in some kind of parallel isolation, and so be it?

As to the latter, it is perfectly clear that Pippin believes nothing of the kind. He obviously thinks it is of moral and political interest and even importance that we adopt not only the modern stance but his Idealistic version of it. He makes it perfectly clear that he sees a nexus between philosophy and everyday life and that philosophy should take the lead in informing everyday existence. Philosophy is not only important but effectual. Philosophers should assist the everyday world in "constructing" its understanding of itself and its understanding of the appropriate objects of its aspiration.

But where does Strauss really stand on this issue? I would suggest that Strauss's view of this nexus between philosophy and the city is more complicated than is ordinarily seen. Characteristically, on this subject as elsewhere, Pippin gets quickly to the heart of the matter. Pippin presents a very clear picture of Strauss's ambivalence regarding the ordinary and everyday understanding of things. For Strauss, the ordinary and everyday is a cave. The best life, the **truly natural** life, transcends the ordinary. It is clear that Strauss's recovery of the ordinary view of life is a propaedeutic maneuver. Strauss wishes to pass through it in order to get to a praise of philosophy as the best life. Regardless of whatever moral and political crisis may exist in the present, it is clear that for Strauss the greatest danger at present is the possible abolition of philosophy.

Like Nietzsche and Heidegger, and Hegel for that matter, Strauss sees philosophy imperiled in our time by having reached an end. Between these various authors, what is at stake is how that end is conceptualized. For Strauss, when we go back to the origins we find that in the natural articulation of things there is, within ordinary experience, a sense that philosophy is dangerous. Strauss is presenting this as one of the natural phenomena, the ordinary perception versus the philosophic perception of reality such that philosophy is always endangered and therefore in need of circumspection. I would argue that while philosophy and everyday perception always present themselves as different, the phenomena in our time no longer present this element of dangerousness and endangerment. The problem is that philosophy is ignored and dismissed as trivial and ineffectual in our increasingly scientific, technological, utilitarian civilization.

I have argued repeatedly elsewhere that Strauss ultimately adopted the Nietzschean stance regarding the appropriate relation between philosophy and the city, at least the stance of Strauss's Nietzsche.[5] Strauss's Nietzsche, and I admit I accept this view of Nietzsche's teaching, did not long to be a philosopher-king as so many conclude. He longed for a future epicureanization of philosophy, by which I mean a withdrawal into a solitary, contemplative, theoretical activity conducted out of the public view and with almost no public duties, in some postmodern epicurean garden.

Like his Nietzsche, Strauss saw the solution to the modern political and moral predicament requiring the philosophers to withdraw from the modern stance of theoretically dictating to practice and of constructing everyday perception. Like his Nietzsche, Strauss saw theory as bad for practice, especially modern theory. Ultimately, like his Nietzsche, Strauss saw practice as capable of constituting itself "internally" or "naturally" if left alone—and with nowhere near the mercilessness and brutality of Nietzsche's account. In this, there is to be found an optimistic element of Burkean conservatism in Strauss. Philosophy could be saved in the late modern world by becoming a private activity conducted among friends. Philosophy so understood is a form of contemplative theoretical activity.

I would argue that the tension in Strauss's thought is to be found in the competing elements he drew from Nietzsche and Heidegger—and even from Hegel—not to mention from Plato, Aristotle and others. Pippin quite justly points to the influences of the post-Hegelian authors from whom Strauss drew, but I would argue, misses the ultimate synthesis that is so distinctively Straussian.

To summarize an argument I have made elsewhere,[6] Strauss took the idea of a "natural consciousness" from Hegel. He then grafted it onto Heidegger's phenomenological move that posits the priority of the practical revelation of reality to the theoretical in everyday doing and making. He then, entirely opposing the Heideggerian inclination, adopted the Nietzschean view of philosophy as a pure theory that had to isolate itself from practice for the sake of both theory and practice. In the end these competing elements could not hold together especially when conjoined with positing the Aristotelian understanding of *praxis* and practical wisdom.

What Strauss got right was the phenomenological fact of the repeated tension between theory and practice. It need not be the tension of dangerousness and endangerment. The tension need only be the tension of different perceptions with the philosophical being based on a dialectical move away from the everyday. I would argue that this difference can never be resolved. But this difference is not only practically useful, it is the very basis of human historicality.

It is the dialectical relation between everyday perceptions and theoretical articulations that drives history. Pippin, following Hegel, comes much closer to presuming a possible resolution of the tension between theory and practice. Presumably with it would come a synthesis of theoretical and everyday experiences. This is Hegel's point—practice increasingly becomes more theoretical, and theory increasingly becomes more practical, until they merge. I would argue that Strauss is on phenomenologically sounder ground in seeing an ongoing difference and tension. But it is not the tension of necessary dangerousness and implacable foes that ultimately need to be separated for their mutual and reciprocal wellbeing.

Pippin rightly points out that when Strauss articulates the "ordinary" understanding of the Greeks, a central element becomes an articulation of the perceptions of "gentlemen." Like Nietzsche, Strauss felt that if stripped of theoretical intrusion, experience presents itself in a fashion that is hierarchically ordered. There is, as Nietzsche put it, always—especially with gentlemen—a "pathos of distance," and its associated "looking down." I would argue, contrary to Strauss and Nietzsche, that this element of hierarchy will show itself as part of the everyday perceptions of the vast majority in the middle class in modern democratic societies as well. Hence one need not go back to aristocratic societies, or will the "noble" as Nietzsche would have it, to find this phenomenological element of hierarchy. It is only an autonomous, self-legislating Constructivism that could presume to eradicate this element of everyday perception.

Be that as it may, it is perfectly straightforward that the views of Athenian gentlemen would have been shaped by habits that would be supported by traditional customs. Aristotle admits as much about all moral virtue when he says that its basis is habit rather than the Socratic injunction that virtue is knowledge. Pippin stresses that this formative importance of habit means that the perceptions of everyday Athenian gentlemen had a social and historical basis. Here again I would stress that Pippin is assuming too much in reaching this conclusion. Once again, he is presupposing the same nature/convention distinction Strauss posits. In this case Pippin wants to use it as evidence that the "natural" perceptions that Strauss elicits are not "ordinary" or "natural," but in fact conventional—i.e., they are historically determined. Hence, he concludes, as with all social conditions, they occur in time and can hardly be the basis of trans-historical "nature." But one cannot presume to know, as Pippin does, that something is "merely" conventional without knowing the natural understood as that which **produces itself, everywhere and always** and does not change— the fixed point that does not move that we discussed above.

But what if what we had with the perceptions of the Greeks was Heideggerian *physis* manifesting itself, i.e., phenomena presenting themselves. Those phenomena just were, just as our present phenomena simply are? We cannot even know if they are ultimately different at a deeper level. They both just are. Given that the present, and the things that are present now already "are," their process of "becoming" is rather irrelevant to those of us thrown into the present. The allegedly natural and the allegedly conventional things have equal impact on our existence. They are equally givens.[7]

This is the paradigm for our relation to all phenomena: even those from the past only present themselves in the present. There is a "situation" in the present. For example, the everyday now presents itself through the perceptions of a majority middle class society, which is educated and possesses various shared perceptions and aspirations. As educated and cultivated those aspirations are capable of more or less self-conscious articulation. In Athens the only educated individuals were gentlemen; hence they were the only audience for thematic discussions to address. The "ordinary" always must be interrogated and having done so philosophy must publicly disseminate its thematic efforts to articulate those perceptions. In the process philosophy establishes its **difference** from the ordinary presentation of reality. When the philosophic articulation of things is disseminated, a dialectical interaction is set loose between the two different perceptions. Hence one need not recur to some prior, originary or primordial manifestation of the ordinary as is true for Strauss, and neither is one forced to make an either/or choice for theory or practice as do Strauss and Nietzsche, and in his own way Pippin. Theory need not stake out a position of opposition and negation toward the everyday; one of difference will always produce itself.

I am suggesting that we simply start from the everyday perceptions of the present and articulate them. We do not in advance characterize them as natural or conventional, primary or occluded. And we do not praise them as morally superior perceptions nor stigmatize them as benighted. We simply begin. The thematic articulations we arrive at will be different than the everyday perceptions, in principle. As different, there will in principle always be a built-in dialectical tension between the everyday and the detached, thematic articulation of what is contained in the everyday. Hence there will always be a dialectical tension between philosophy and the everyday that is unavoidable. But this difference does not and cannot prove the possibility of autonomy. And it cannot be theoretically proved that this relation is either unchanging or changeable. And it is not necessary that the relation be one of danger and endangerment. Hence, one should just begin and get on with it. In the process we avoid both metaphysics and any lurking is/ought problems. We do not try to go back to some perfect moment nor presume some perfect autonomy.

Pippin, pointing to Hegel, quite correctly observes that the "ordinary ordinarily tears itself apart." But the same is true for all theoretical positions of which I am aware. There will never be a contradiction–free theoretical articulation of the whole. For Pippin the observation about the ordinary perception of things tearing itself apart is intended to show the inferiority and unreliability of the ordinary perception of things. I would agree that the ordinary perceptions are always contradictory. But leaving aside the fact that I am unaware of any theory that has so far presented itself in a contradiction-free fashion, **this contradictoriness contained in "the ordinary" is precisely the repeatable basis upon which philosophy itself always comes to be, and necessarily comes to be dialectically.** Without the example of a philosophical theory that has so far succeeded in freeing itself from contradiction theory has no right to look down on the everyday for its contradictoriness especially since that contradictoriness is the very basis of the possibility of philosophy.

In his own way, Pippin, like Strauss, denigrates the ordinary as a cave. I am making no such assumption. Phenomenologically all one should say is that it "is," at least initially as part of making a start. And of any thematic philosophical articulation all one can say is that it is different than the ordinary. Thematic articulations should be judged not in light of their "objectivity" nor their relation to some "ought," but in relation to their phenomenological richness and "disclosiveness"—a term I cannot now pause to articulate.

As a phenomenological fact, I would assert that most people will never assume the stance of thematic detachment from the ordinary articulation of reality. And they will get through their lives quite adequately and in most cases quite happily. I cannot even say that those of us who by a kind of necessity are led toward thematic, philosophical detachment are better off. We too just are and we are different. The phenomenological nature of reality includes this split. It simply is. And the dialectic that is set off because of it should be ongoing if we do not theoretically short-circuit it on the basis of a theory that, I would argue, has no autonomous place to stand in doing so. The possibility of ongoing historicality, phenomenologically a part of modernity's self-understanding as Pippin rightly points out, is built into the constitution of the human situation if we do not short-circuit it.

PIPPIN'S MODERNITY AND
DIALECTICAL PHENOMENOLOGY

My conclusion is that Pippin gains his theoretical leverage for asserting his view only on the basis of opposition to an "other." In this instance that other is Strauss but also primary "nature" which he depicts as benighted. And Pippin gets further purchase to assert his position by showing the difficulties and circularities of Strauss's position. Now in fairness to Pippin, in the article in question, he is perfectly explicit that he is merely **asserting** his position. But in light of his other work, it seems to me that he cannot ground his position except as a negation of other positions that are "inadequate" because contradictory, or on a "nature" or an "ordinary" that are likewise posited as inadequate. Pippin's argument for the primacy of a self-legislating ego rests on the negation of "nature," or the "ordinary" as inadequate. Then an either/or choice between Nature and Freedom is set in motion. No such either/or choices are necessary.

In response to Pippin I am arguing that Strauss' presentation of the philosophical "primacy of the ordinary" is not the best presentation of that position and hence dismissing Strauss does not dismiss the primacy of the ordinary. I have even suggested that in the end Strauss' invocation of the ordinary is actually only a rhetorical propaedeutic maneuver anyway. He too needs the ordinary as a foil or other. Strauss ultimately accepts the autonomy of the theoretical, but contrary to Pippin understood it as contemplative rather than legislative and constructivist. It would be interesting to have both Strauss and Pippin explain their respective choices without recourse to the primacy of the phenomenological in my sense. My ultimate conclusion is that what I am offering under the rubric dialectical phenomenology is a better alternative **for contemporary moderns, as moderns,** than either Strauss's teaching or Pippin's self-legislating constructivism. Those two do not represent an either/or choice.

Furthermore, Pippin relies heavily on conclusions drawn from Hegel to which he ultimately is not entitled. As I have suggested above, Pippin seems to me to be unwilling to incorporate those elements of Hegel's teaching that involve endedness, inevitability and an Absolute Spirit. That said, central to Pippin's Hegelian claims is the assertion that modern life is more "reflexive" than pre-modern life. (351) I would suggest that precisely what is being asserted here is not clear. Is it being asserted that modern philosophy is more reflexive than pre-modern? As I will argue, contrary to Hegel's reading of Plato, philosophy had already been raised to a level of full self-conscious reflexivity in the Platonic dialogues as I will argue in section three below. Furthermore, philosophical reflexivity does not require autonomy in the modern sense nor a self-legislating ego; all it requires is honest reflection by philosophy on its own nature and doings.

Or is the assertion being made that the vast majority of middle class citizens in the modern world are more self-conscious and reflexive than any citizens in the past? If that is the claim, I would question it empirically, just as I question the existence of a historical consciousness on the part of the vast majority of present day middle class citizens. There is a great danger of projecting the consciousness of an elite few onto the everyday many, even if there are diluted public reverberations of that elite consciousness. When one asserts the sameness of the few and the many in this regard that comes very close to arguing what "ought" to be the case rather than what phenomenologically "is" the case. Without getting into the "is/ought" conundrum, I can merely ask why the consciousness of the few ought to be made that of the many.

Pippin elaborates upon his claim that we moderns are more self-conscious and reflexive than anyone in the past by asserting that we moderns assume our roles more self-consciously as "ours" than pre-moderns who presumably acted more on blind habit and instinct. Again, I question the phenomenological solidity of this assertion. I agree with Tocqueville that in modern, democratic, increasingly classless societies it is amorphous public opinion that determines the tastes, aspirations and perceptions of the vast majority and that this public opinion is ruled by a massive, idiosyncratic faddishness that tyrannizes individual perceptions and aspirations. But beyond that, like human beings of all times, most moderns are not prone intrinsically toward philosophical detachment. Most contemporary perceptions are formed by habits and reigning public opinion just like those of their predecessors. Given that those habits work more silently and in a softly despotic fashion in the modern world, they may work more seamlessly than at any time in the past. Actual ongoing confrontation with pain and tyranny foster a detachment that probably leads to more reflexivity than the soft despotism of our time.

Modern morality may **presume** to rest on self-legislation, but its precepts descend into the consciousnesses of the vast majority in a perfectly habitual and unself-conscious fashion. Pippin's assertion about the uniqueness of modernity, where our roles are allegedly "assumed" rather than "inhabited," is phenomenologically questionable. Nietzschean, Tocquevillean and Heideggerian analyses of the "last man," "soft despotism" and the "they-self" seem much more phenomenologically compelling. So the issue really boils down to whether what Pippin is saying is really something about the "is" or in reality primarily about the "ought." Is he really saying moderns ought to proceed "as-if" they were more self-conscious than pre-moderns? Is a Kantian "as-if" what is really lurking here?

I do not see the evidence that the vast majority of moderns self-consciously adopt their understandings as their own, as "roles" that they give themselves. Maybe they should. As both Hegel and Heidegger argue in their different ways, we moderns—like, I would argue, our predecessors—are an "I" only as a "we."[8] *Moralitat* really does, for the most part, get overpowered by *Sittlichkeit*. Hence I do not see that there is a dichotomy, requiring a choice, between a natural consciousness that is unself-conscious and a fully autonomous self-consciousness. This is a phenomenologically false distinction. Likewise, I do not see Pippin's distinction that juxtaposes morality based on a self-legislating ego on the one hand and "dogmatism" on the other. All of the proponents of the self-legislating ego from Descartes to Kant and beyond seem to me to have ended up with teachings that are altogether dogmatic. Heidegger appears more correct in arguing that the self-legislating ego is intrinsically linked not only to metaphysics but to what always has to be metaphysical in his terms, systematic philosophy and dogmatism.

I also question the argument that the experience of living a thoughtful, reflexive and more or less self-conscious life could not have been available in antiquity. In fact, it seems to me that the undemocratic social conditions, and freedom from want and labor provided for a few, may have granted an independence to some few pre-moderns that is greater than most moderns, no matter how wealthy, can now accomplish in an age when there are so many new forms of dependence. **That the past was inegalitarian does not mean it was unreflexive.** At any rate, in the modern world a liberal education in the classic sense, which helps foster the possibility of a detachment from the dominant forms of public opinion, is every bit as necessary now as in any other age of man. Whether it is more available now is an open question. On Pippin's premises, that detachment is somehow the birthright of moderns and presumably in far less need of cultivation.

We must confront the issue of autonomy versus detachment. Can we have the total autonomy Pippin seems to assume as his starting point, or only the relative detachment from the reigning opinions, a detachment won at significant and ongoing dialectical expense and effort? I would suggest that if the spontaneous, unsullied autonomy Pippin posits cannot be phenomenologically defended, the normative necessity of the moral self-legislation that Pippin asserts as of the essence of modernity runs the risk of simply being a modern myth that informs distinctively modern habits. But as dominated by habit, or natural instinct, moderns are no more self-conscious or autonomous than anyone in the past, the myth that may have occasioned those habits to the contrary notwithstanding.

Pippin twice quotes the following statement of Strauss, once calling it his favorite: "[E]ven by proving that a certain view is indispensable in living well, one merely proves that the view in question is a salutary myth; one does not prove it to be true. Utility and truth are two entirely different things." It seems to me the same thought may ultimately apply to Pippin's substantive alternative to Strauss as well. Is the "spontaneous," self-conscious, self-legislating self he espouses clearly discernable in the phenomena or a useful modern myth?

Pippin is a remarkably clear and honest author. He sees and points to the ultimate danger in his position and in all Idealism. The spontaneity and autonomy he espouses, if incapable of being linked with law, as was attempted in different ways by all the Idealists, opens the door to a slippery slide that goes from spontaneity to pure imagination to Will-to-Power and blind fate-driven technological mastery. (353) I would argue that without something like Kantian universalism and the "as-if" or Hegelian inevitability and endedness, that slippery slide is inevitable. **And both alternatives undermine the possibility of ongoing human historicality.** Both the Kantian and Hegelian solutions seem to me to be at odds with the actual phenomenological aspiration for future openness for which moderns indeed do long. Both point toward universalist closure. Moderns need the possibility of ongoing historicality far more than the myth of the self-legislating ego.

I would suggest that modernity can best be saved phenomenologically with the dialectical version of phenomenology I have suggested here and throughout this volume. It vouches for the possibility of ongoing historicality without the danger of groundless willfulness. Modernity's concern for freedom, equality, fairness, open-endedness and many other things are all already built into the perceptions of the everyday and the ordinary. They do not have to be willed; there is no need to reinvent the wheel. The "ordinary" as Pippin understands it is, therefore, a perfect point of departure **precisely for a good modern**. But that is true only after the ordinary has been freed from various theoretically constructed artificialities. We simply start. The dialectic that we need for both ongoing everyday historicality and ongoing philosophy is phenomenologically built into the fact that while most are locked habitually into the ordinary and everyday—and that has more than one manifestation—some strive to thematically articulate that everydayness and gain thereby detachment from it. That dialectical tension between not so much the Real and the Ideal, but the ordinary and the thematic, will remain as long as the philosophers eschew epicurean detachment and continue to publicly disseminate their ideas. But that public dissemination requires more than a little fidelity to everyday perceptions if it is to be publicly persuasive. Hence there is something to be said for the formula, "to the phenomena themselves," to which may be added, "as they show themselves."

NOTES

1. Robert Pippin, "The Unavailability of the Ordinary," in *Political Theory*, Vol. 31, No. 3, June 2003, pp. 335–58; and Pippin, *Idealism as Modernism: Hegelian Variations* (Cambridge: Cambridge University Press, 1997). One could also consult his *Hegel's Idealism: The Satisfactions of Self-Consciousness* (New York: Cambridge University Press, 1989) and *Modernism as a Philosophical Problem* (Cambridge: Basil Blackwell, 1991).

2. My understanding is that Pippin is unwilling to simply recur to the Kantian application of the universal to solve these problems and hence needs some element of Hegelian dialectic. This emerges in his essays on Kant and Hegel in *Idealism as Modernism* and his argument in *Hegel's Idealism*.

3. I explore this in depth in the chapters on Strauss in part 2 of this volume. For Strauss, the everyday perceptions that eventually yield the nature/convention distinction grow out of awareness of the things that emerge on their own rather than through human intervention, the priority of seeing with one's own eyes rather than accepting hearsay, that fire burns the same in Persia and Athens and so on. Properly combined these everyday perceptions yield the "idea of nature."

4. I agree with Pippin that Strauss's notion of "occluding" or "forgetting" is derivative from Heidegger. I would go on to argue that Heidegger betrays his own core

premises when he argues that we could live in a time when there is a total forgetting of Being or "phenomena" that show themselves. I would argue that there is always something that shows itself and it is precisely from those ordinary "phenomena" that one must always begin. Heidegger too comes close to falling back on a hidden nature/convention distinction. I make this argument in my *Martin Heidegger: Paths Taken, Paths Opened* (Lanham: Rowman & Littlefield, 2007). See also my earlier *Nietzsche, Heidegger and the Transition to Postmodernity* (Chicago: University of Chicago Press, 1986).

5. See particularly "On a Possible Epicurean Garden for Philosophy," chapter 10, as well as "Athens and Washington: Leo Strauss and the American Regime," chapter 9, and "On the Tradition of Political Philosophy in the Future," chapter 12, all in part 2.

6. See previous footnote plus chapter 12 of my *Martin Heidegger.*

7. I am aware that if time and space permitted, far more would have to be said here to defend myself from the charge of circularity. At present I will leave it at saying that by adopting the stance of Heideggerian thrownness, I am in advance adopting the stance of unavoidable circularity in precisely the same way that Heidegger thematically enjoins that issue in *Being and Time*. I would simply assert that that circularity and some level of detachment (not autonomy) are possible simultaneously.

8. It is never clear "who" the self-legislating ego is supposed to be. Is it an individual "I," a political or cultural "we," the modern "we," a great philosophical legislator, the Absolute Self?

Chapter Six

Cacophony or Silence:
Derrida's Deconstructionism and the
Possibility of Political Philosophy

Discussing Jacques Derrida in a volume on the tradition of political philosophy and its future requires a few prefatory remarks. Until several of his last works, like *Specters of Marx* and *The Politics of Friendship*, Derrida seemed to stay away from political and moral discussions. Whether these late efforts are consistent with the principles that gained Derrida renown is a question to which we will return. A prior question is whether or not Derrida's core principles make the continuance of the tradition of political philosophy impossible. His work certainly seems to call into question the systematic manifestation of political philosophy that has had prominence in the Tradition. He seems sworn to taking apart and "deconstructing" all past systematic efforts as metaphysical and thereby as the handmaiden of the devil.

There are straightforward tactical reasons why Derrida wrote no explicit political texts. He had concluded that the good for man was to be found in as anarchistic a situation as possible, where as few structures as possible had as little hegemony as possible. How he could know this was the good on his principles remains an open question. Contemporary students of political philosophy are confronted with two significant phenomena. First, we see the increasingly abstract nature of philosophy. Contemporary philosophy occupies itself with very rarified, and at times seemingly artificial puzzles; on the other hand—witness the later work of Heidegger—philosophy has not only lost concrete content but has even attempted to stand outside the exigencies of concrete language. Philosophy has increasingly detached itself from any relation to everyday phenomena as they show up in everyday existence.

The opposite side of this coin is that political discussion has become increasingly divorced from philosophical grounding. This is true not only of empirical research, but of contemporary political theory as well, which frequently takes off from shared conventional premises, ignoring the philosophical status of those premises. On occasion the shared, fundamental premises are those of a segment of the political community, at other times those shared by a plurality of professors. Either way this approach leaves contemporary political theory to build its house in midair. When roots are sought, it is invariably in a scandalously undefended notion of "History" that still lurks in the background of the thought of so many. Even many who accept most of what is taught by Nietzsche and Heidegger still remain "progressives," a dicey undertaking for those who don't believe in History and a meaningful movement of humanity through time.

These phenomena, the increasingly abstract nature of philosophy, especially at its peaks, and the increasingly ungrounded nature of political action are connected. This is not to say that contemporary political discussion is without philosophic presuppositions any more than it is to say that contemporary philosophy is without political intentions. The work of Derrida is a case in point. While seldom even tangentially approaching the sinew and ligature of actual political and moral existence, he is explicit, as we will see, that his work has a political intention. In short, Derrida attempts to deconstruct the foundations of all contemporary moral and political institutions. And while this does not simply mean destroy, it clearly intends to expose the ultimate error of believing that those institutions have any objective ground. Presumably one does not deconstruct what one loves, respects and wishes to sustain. Derrida's intentions are thoroughly revolutionary. His work is a sign of what happens when philosophy becomes simultaneously politicized and abstracted from concrete political and moral categories. The obverse is the anticipated lack of a thoughtful, philosophical foundation for political and moral life, an end Derrida desires and actively pursues. He is an anarchist in the sense of wanting to consciously live without *arche*.

It is in light of this cessation of fundamental (phenomenological) philosophical reflection on concrete existence and the related increasingly thoughtless nature of political discussion that we will approach the work of Derrida. It is from Derrida that so many in recent generations have learned the politics of deconstructionism with its edicts from avoiding metaphysics to avoiding all manner of –centrisims to the origins of the politics of diversity. In the process we get a disconnect between actual everyday existence and the allegedly high politics of the academy. I will argue that what we are really witnessing is the dissolution of modernity. As I have argued above, the essence of modernity is to be found in constructivism, and deconstructivism is just a novel permutation of that undertaking that tries to get by without ever openly discussing the good it intends to pursue or ever coming close to the categories of everyday discourse. It leads either to total silence or the babble of the cacophony of competing equal voices that all talk simultaneously. This may not have been the inevitable outcome of modernity, but I would argue that it is now the more or less irreversible outcome of modernity.

Derrida's alleged postmodernism is ultimately modern, all too modern. It will destroy the possibility of the tradition of political philosophy not because it destroys the possibility of "foundationalism," but because it is built on a total disconnect from everyday phenomena and everyday speech. In the space at hand, what follows can at best be a propaedeutic to the reading and interpretation of Derrida's individual texts, each of which requires a lengthy effort as well as a close familiarity with the original texts Derrida is analyzing. Derrida never discusses actual phenomena, he only discusses speeches about them. Because I believe this approach is ultimately part of Derrida's sleight of hand, we will move, with more dispatch than might otherwise be justified, to the substantive issues that concern us. Likewise, while some attention to Derrida's distinctive terminology will be necessary, we will avoid, as much as possible, a descent into the jargon peddling to which his thought gives rise, which at its best can never be mistaken for genuine interpretation and analysis, and, as will be seen, would be an approach which runs in the face of the primary phenomenological intentions of this volume.[1]

THE CLOSURE OF THE WEST

The idea of the "closure" or completion of the West gains its codification in the work of Hegel and then receives transformed manifestations in the work of Nietzsche and Heidegger. Derrida's thought operates within this constellation of ideas. He accepts without much further ado that this closure has already occurred.

Hegel attempted to demonstrate that history was driven by the desire of Spirit to attain full, universal, rational self-consciousness. This was to be accomplished through a dialectical process in which contradictory *logoi* become "sublated" (*Aufhebung*) and raised to a higher synthesis, thereby overcoming contradictions without simply obliterating them. History is the linear progression which moves teleologically toward the overcoming of negation, opposition, and contradiction. Through a long tutelary process Spirit rises to absolute self-consciousness, conscious of itself as rational (devoid of contradiction) and as expressed in all things, i.e., it achieves Identity with all that is and conquers the Difference into which it was first dispersed at the origins of History. History culminates in a finished *logos* that is present to Spirit primarily in law, religion, philosophy and art, but to a lesser extent in the modern technological world that overcomes its natural predecessor.

More concretely, philosophy, the love of wisdom that had led to a variety of contradictory *logoi* and philosophies, is replaced by finished wisdom: i.e., Hegelian philosophy beyond which there will be no novel philosophies. The various forms of religion manifest in the past are replaced by the one religion that views Spirit as one, self-conscious and present in the world: i.e., Protestant Christianity. Politics culminates in a society governed by universal, rational laws that the individual would freely choose and will for him or herself: for the first time law and will coincide. This universal rational code of law would be manifest in a society dominated by the most universal and least natural classes—i.e., the commercial classes, especially the middle class, the bourgeoisie—and administered by the most rational class, the bureaucracy—i.e., the class where self-interest and public interest most coincide.

The rational state, the one that fully self-conscious individuals would choose and will, is a bureaucratic, Protestant, bourgeois society that is supported by the modern scientific/technological victory of Reason/Spirit over Nature—Spirit so transforms the objective world that it comes to see the objective world as a manifestation of itself. This state would become ever more universal in scope, eventually claiming every hinterland as its own, even if there remained individual, sovereign states. The oppositions between spirit/nature, human/divine, will/law, nation/nation, race/race, male/female, East/West, etc., would be overcome in a universal, bourgeois, Christian, bureaucratic, technological civilization. For Hegel, this represented the spiritual *telos* of the West, hence its completion or closure qua perfection. This end could not be negated or transcended except through spiritual retrogression. We need not rehearse here the Marxist transformation of this notion other than to say that Marx's vision of History likewise culminates in a universalism in which difference and contradiction are overcome (e.g., class difference, national difference, religious difference) and is likewise a universalism predicated upon the victory of modern technology and thereby the emancipation of man from Nature.

Nietzsche's response to both versions of universalism was to categorize them as manifestations of the "last man." The last man aspires to nothing beyond material comfort and the mere preservation of life. Nietzsche saw the hegemony of the last man as the victory of a uniform mediocrity and the destruction of the possibility of greatness. In place of the self-conscious rational Spirit of Hegel, Nietzsche posited the spontaneous, unself-conscious, "Will-to-Power." The Will-to-Power manifests itself through "instinct" rather than self-consciousness. For Nietzsche the self-conscious "subject" is the preserve of the plebian last man, and the ground upon which envious mediocrity could overcome the instinctive, "noble" few.

For Nietzsche, self-consciousness is the arena for the exercise of *ressentiment* and the "spirit of revenge" of the ignoble many who try to topple the more instinctive noble few. The ground of the eventual hegemony of the ignoble was laid by Socrates and hence is imbedded deep within the interstices of Western thought. Socrates is the self-conscious plebian who founds a form of contest (*agon*)—dialectic—at which he could surpass the noble, instinctive few. He forces them to explain and give reasons for their instinctive behavior. When they cannot produce those reasons and are silenced by Socrates, they stand vanquished in the eyes of the young. According to Nietzsche, the Socratic will-to-truth and the imperative to develop a rational discourse to justify action is a manifestation of the spirit of revenge against those better endowed, those more in touch with the primal force, the Will-to-Power.

But Nietzsche announces that this victory of Socrates has reached its end, for "God is dead." By this phrase Nietzsche intends to say that there is no Being, no God, no transcendent realm, no soul, no truth, no Nature, no History in any meaningful sense; in short, there is nothing that transcends the realm of appearance and grounds the world. While this has always been true, a variety of life-giving illusions have shielded man from realizing it. But now man is forced to confront this fact and it is paralyzing. All is Becoming, flux, change, based on the ongoing permutations of the Will-to-Power. There is no reality behind appearance, and all that appears is determined by the horizon or perspective that reigns, which is something the individual cannot master, but can be "willed" by the "Overman."

Reason, the great shibboleth of the Socratic West—the highest manifestation of self-consciousness—is shown to be but a manifestation of the instinctive Will-to-Power, and is an attempt by the philosopher to impose his own forms on a formless reality. Even in the most self-conscious of men, Socrates, instinct held sway, albeit a decadent and resentful instinct. Socrates' decadent instincts, which announce the will to truth and to the hegemony of discursivity, eventually stifle the fecundity of spontaneous creativity and cause it to atrophy. Consequently, no new forms are imposed on the river of Becoming and a dangerous time of formless decadence and stagnation arrives. This is the closure of the West caused by resentful Socratic dialectic and the commitment to truth and Reason.

Nietzsche attempts to demonstrate—perhaps cajole and intoxicate is more correct—that not only is the unconscious the only ground of form and meaning, but that there is no such thing as a subject, a self, self-consciousness, or anything like a voluntary, intentional actor. Even Socrates, the great proponent of the self, fell prey to his own peculiar, plebeian, decadent instincts. This is true of all thought which is always dominated by unconscious forces and by a pre-existing horizon of meaning. All thought, and all that is, is a form of interpretation rather than discovery or explanation. Reason is a form of interpretation, explanation is a form of will. But will and interpretation are

unconscious forces; hence Nietzsche attacks not only the concept of intentionality, but of causality, substance, volition and freedom.

When Nietzsche calls for the unleashing of "instinct," of the Dionysian, of the
unself-conscious Will-to-Power of a new caste of masters, he is calling on what
he sees as the only ground for imposing new forms on the river of Becoming.
The Socratic, Western forms—especially in their Hegelian manifestation—are
moribund. What once was life-giving must now be replaced for it has become
life-destroying. Nietzsche points beyond the inevitability of the universality of
bourgeois, bureaucratic, technological Christian Europe to a new aristocratic society where noble actors would without guilt impose their values on the many
and thereby reinstitute "monumental history." With this would come the emergence of post-historical difference and diversity, a new diversity of classes, values, nations, religions and on and on.

Heidegger continues the assault on self-consciousness and the rationality
of the closure Hegel enthrones. The early Heidegger presents the human situation as one dominated by the existential category "being-in-the-world."
The World as Heidegger conceives of it is the *a priori* structure of meaning
that makes it possible for us to encounter or be familiar with things that surround us, whether they be tools, natural objects or other human beings. This
existential category World is never present for our inspection, but without it
nothing else would be present. The ground for the possibility of presence is
itself absent. For Heidegger the multiplicity of Worlds is not the product of
conscious human subjectivity but rather the mysterious dispensation of Being
itself. Being presences through World. Being is not only not present itself but
cannot be confused with self-conscious Hegelian Spirit, nor is it possessed of
will even in the unconscious form posited in Nietzsche's Will-to-Power. It is
not a being and nothing can be predicated of it. Being so conceived is the
ground of Worlds. We are always already "thrown" into such a fated dispensation and can never do anything to master it, either in its coming into being
or its passing away.

The fated dispensation that rules in our time is that of objectivizing science,
technological constructivism (Enframing) and the rational organization of human beings. This organization of all life, both human and non-human, for the
purpose of domination and manipulation is what uproots modern man and
alienates him from his primordial openness to both Being and beings. Man
should be the being who is open to and in the nearness of Being and in the
nearness of beings infused with Being. According to Heidegger, this contemporary uprootedness is the ultimate outcome of Western metaphysics, begun
by Plato and finding its highest manifestation in the technological West. For
Heidegger, as for Hegel, this was the end toward which Western philosophy
pointed from the beginning. But where Hegel presents it as the overcoming

of all alienation, Heidegger sees it as our greatest alienation from an increasingly concealed and absent Being.

The withdrawal of Being and man's uprooted alienation were prepared by the Western conception of self-conscious Reason which was based on a doctrine of "Being as presence." Armed with this notion, Western thinking turned its back on the ground of presence, the real "object" to be thought. The early Heidegger tries to prepare a conception of Being not qua presence, but as the *a priori* precondition of presence. But Heidegger came to believe that to use the traditional term Being for this new notion was misleading. He also came to see that his early work could be accused of a kind of Nietzschean voluntarism and of transcendental subjectivism.

Being, if it can still be called that, is that absence that stands before presence; "It" gives (*es gibt*) or grants presence but withdraws and remains concealed. It is the ground of unconcealment or appearance which remains self-concealed, unlike Hegel's self-revealing, self-manifesting Spirit. Being must be linked with the primordial meaning of *alētheia*, Heidegger argues. Being is the "uncovering, which is simultaneously a "veiling." Heidegger experimented with a variety of locutions that could express this Nothing in non-metaphysical terms free from the language of subjectivity. He finally arrived at the locution: Being "under erasure," (~~Being~~) signifying the absence which mysteriously remains the reason for presence.

For Heidegger, our age of technological and organizational frenzy was working itself out in identical fashion in both Moscow and Washington. The great ideological divide of the twentieth century was a metaphysical canard as the two contestants were equivalent at the deepest level. He looked for a third way. To transcend this inevitable end of metaphysics the later Heidegger increasingly preached a quiet, reticent, silent openness to Being, *Gelassenheit.* With the concept *Gelassenheit* Heidegger aimed at overcoming voluntarism and transcendental subjectivity which he saw as still controlling the thought of Nietzsche as well as infecting his own early work — at least that is how many interpret him.[2]

Furthermore, Heidegger, at least on the surface, construed Nietzsche's doctrine of the Will-to-Power as a traditional metaphysical doctrine of the Being of beings, and concluded that by merely inverting the metaphysical priority of Being over Becoming, Nietzsche remained within the grips of metaphysics. Heidegger accused Nietzsche of being the last metaphysician. He tried to accomplish the transcendence of metaphysics at which Nietzsche had allegedly failed. Unlike the early Heidegger who talked about the centrality of authenticity and resoluteness, the later Heidegger's new form of thought, *Gelassenheit,* argued that we had to await a new allegedly post-metaphysical dispensation of Being. Heidegger claimed that he was only "on the way" to this new mode of thought and that he merely prepared the way and then waited, along with the rest of us, for the new beginning that would free the West from the end of metaphysics and its practical ramifications. Heidegger waits for the mysterious healing power of what is absent and remains veiled and concealed. Being as the absent and fecund Nothingness—it presents itself as Nothing in that it must come to presence through beings as what it is not, it is not a present being. Present beings like concepts, objects, laws, words, whatever cannot be our primary focus. Trying self-consciously to change them misses the point that Being itself must bring a mysterious change first before any human action can be fruitful. For Heidegger, the path toward transcending the will to dominate all things, which represents the closure of the West, is to begin to contemplate Being as the mysterious absent source.

MEANING AND SIGN, WRITING AND SPEECH

It is at this point that Derrida enters the discussion. It is within this complex of ideas and concepts about the closure of the West that Derrida's work takes its stand. Nonetheless, Derrida approaches these ideas through discussions that are far less concrete than even the work of the later Heidegger. The movement from Hegel to Nietzsche to Heidegger to Derrida is a movement in the direction of abstraction in which we move farther and farther from a phenomenological point of departure. While there are substantive moral and political issues lurking in the background—issues that give meaning to Derrida's entire undertaking—he almost never confronts them directly, certainly not using the speech of everyday discussion. His discussions focus on such topics as signs and semiology, language and linguistics, writing and speech.

In reconsidering the traditional treatments of these topics Derrida is led to his characteristic, close textual analyses of authors from Plato, Rousseau, Hegel, Nietzsche, Husserl and Heidegger to Freud, Mellarme, and Levinas. His central problematic, which he attempts to apply in all his specific textual readings, can be seen in fairly complete outline in one of his early works, *Speech and Phenomena: and Other Essays on Husserl's Theory of Signs.*[3]

Contrary to Husserl's own **self**-understanding, Derrida tries to show that Husserl's work is dominated by metaphysical presuppositions. Husserl understood the term metaphysics to involve a pointing beyond the immanent world (as the traditional translation of the "meta" would lead one to believe). Husserl saw his own work as, in this sense, anti-metaphysical, as an attack on the transcendent or any world or structures that are "beyond." Husserl saw himself as aiming at an "immanent" analysis.

But Derrida tries to show that Husserl's work is dominated by metaphysics in Heidegger's redefined sense. A metaphysical understanding is one that conceives of Being as presence. In Heidegger's presentation, Being has more about it of absence than of presence. The new meaning of metaphysics almost reverses the traditional meaning of the term that pointed toward transcendence. Using Heidegger's redefinition of metaphysics allows Derrida to classify Husserl's thought as dominated by metaphysical concepts from which he cannot extricate himself even though he consciously tries. This, indeed, is one of the core notions of Derrida's deconstructionism, that thinkers are ruled unconsciously by structural necessities they are unaware of, cannot articulate, and can never self-consciously transcend. Furthermore, authors say more than they intend, have effects they cannot calculate ("deferral") and engender interpretations they cannot predict. Of course in a consistent philosophical world, if true, all of these strictures would apply to Derrida as well.

Derrida focuses on Husserl's theory of signs. For Husserl, signs re-present (as in make present a second time), stand in the place of, or "signify" ideas. There are two forms of signifying, "indication" and "expression." For Husserl, indication signifies or represents another signifier or sign. As a result, indication carries no meaning (*Bedeutung*), in the sense in which Husserl uses the term. Only expression carries or conveys meaning in the strict sense for it signifies or represents originary ideas. Only ideas give a ground for meaning. Husserl's ideas are ideal entities standing outside time and place. Furthermore, the ideas stand in necessary relationships to each other, as do the signs that represent them. The ideas are the real, albeit transcendental, entities, the signs (expressions) are mere copies. The relation of the ideal realm of transcendental ideas to the world of sense experience is complicated and it is here that Derrida tries to show that Husserl becomes trapped in a blind alley and ends in a necessary complication from which he cannot extricate himself.

Words are signs for ideas which lodge in the transcendental as opposed to empirical self. But, Husserl admits, words are also used within the spatio-temporal empirical world of appearance. Within the spatio-temporal matrix the meaning of words is determined by the historical context which shifts over time. Husserlean man seems divided so as to exist in two realms, the convergence of which is unclear. Husserl presents a philosophy of ideality (transcendental philosophy) and an empirical philosophy of life (phenomenology). Empirical life and transcendental life seem to reproduce, in a novel fashion, either the metaphysical dualism of Kant or a new form of the body/soul duality. For Derrida, as for Heidegger, both are equally metaphysical. But this is not the main thrust of Derrida's analysis.

Derrida argues that the reason that Husserl is forced toward what seems like a problem is due to his unwitting reliance on the key metaphysical concept of

Being as presence. For Husserl what is fully present are the ideas grasped by the transcendental self. Derrida argues that Husserl tried to preserve the originally silent, pre-expressive stratum of experience. For Husserl, there is a direct relation to, grasping of and non-empirical perception of the ideas, unmediated by anything spatial or temporal. This immediate intuition is also true for one's relation to self-presence. All language, signs and acts merely re-present (make present a second time) what is initially grasped immediately. Hence meaning, for Husserl, is based on the possibility of abstracting from the phenomenal world, which is always grasped immediately, and getting in touch with some self-standing, fully present given, immediately. It is reliance on the metaphysical concept of presence—here a pure, unmediated ideal presence—that, according to Derrida, dominates Husserl's thinking and determines its direction. The underlying doctrine of Being as presence is something Husserl allegedly shared with the entire Western tradition. The subtle twist Derrida eventually gives this analysis is that even Heidegger fell victim to this doctrine of Being. Only Derrida transcends this tragic, shared doctrine.

Husserl admits that in ordinary speech, expression always takes on a component of indication, and hence is sullied by the historical, spatio-temporal dimension. Everyday speech is never ruled completely by transcendental ideality. Yet he holds fast to the ideal realm knowing it is the only arena in which he can ground pure presence, or what he eventually calls "rigorous science." But according to Derrida, Husserl can never bridge the gap between ideal objects and empirical objects. It is the need to preserve a relation to the metaphysics of presence that makes him attempt, unsuccessfully, to link the two.

Throughout his work, Derrida tries to show that there is nothing that is totally or purely present. Any doctrine of meaning, such as Husserl's, which is grounded upon a doctrine of pure presence must fail. For Derrida, meaning emerges from the relation of one sign to another, and from the relations of an entire nexus of signs held together in a totality. And all such totalities are evanescent and fleeting, constantly transforming into something new. Hence there can never be identity between a sign and some absolute, objective presence. At best one has likeness, but even then the sign participates in both same and other, in contradiction, in Not-Being, in Nothingness. And since two things that are only like each other are *not* the same, in all meaning there is an element not only of Not-Being but of non-identity. All meaning is infected with both Identity and Difference, Being and Not-Being. On this level, all things are the Same. That Parmenides beat Derrida to these gymnastics is straightforward. See the discussion of Plato's *Parmenides* in part 3.

If in all "meaning" there is never complete Identity, then nothing is ever completely present. As a result, no act of meaning can ever be simply repeated. One cannot over time repeat the same meaning by using the same sign. Hence meaning, like signs, and language in general, changes over time; the evanescent historical context is central to the meaning process. Because of his attempt to ground meaning in a doctrine of pure presence, Husserl can never adequately treat the temporal and phenomenal features of signs and speech without falling into contradiction. At least this is what Derrida asserts. Derrida feels he can better account for the actual, phenomenal meaning process. This can allegedly be done while jettisoning every form of transcendental ideality.

For Derrida's Husserl, there are pure, immediate, non-contradictory, simple ideal things that are instantly graspable and fully present to the transcendental self. While that self is not a traditional soul it has no phenomenal character. Without such an objective ground there is no simple, unchanging referent that can ground meaning. That is precisely Derrida's point. He never "proves" this;[4] his method is instead to show that those who maintain the opposite are always led to ruin, to say nothing of a doctrine of Being as presence—that is always Derrida's trump card. In this fashion Derrida tries to rid himself of such notions as "natural experience," "transcendental experience," "pre-philosophic experience," and so on. There is nothing underlying—or as Pippin puts it, nothing "ordinary." Having cast off the transcendental, with this maneuver one casts off the solidity of anything originary in my phenomenological sense as well. Strictly speaking, there are no "phenomena," hence there can be no phenomenology.

Signs always signify only other signs, signifiers never have an ultimate signified. Meaning emerges only from the relation between signs, which is fleeting and changes over time. As with Heidegger, we are always already beings thrown into an evolving world of meaning which grounds the possibility of our experience. There is no prior, "natural" experience of things which we share as human beings.

Derrida tries to point out that all metaphysical thought has the same structure, speech is an **ex**-pression or **re**-presentation of something immediately present. Writing is always presented as a **re**-presentation of speech. Hence throughout metaphysics, from Plato to Saussure's linguistics, writing stands at the furthest remove from what is ultimately signified and hence its dignity is diminished accordingly. But for Derrida, as for Heidegger and Nietzsche, at the most primordial level, experience and language are always already historically shaped. Speech merely points toward or signifies that already shaped evolving meaning structure—what Heidegger designated by thrownness.[5]

There is no simple correspondence or identity between speech and what it signifies, or between speech and writing. Hence there cannot be a "correspondence theory" of truth. The initial, primordial shaping of what passes for a meaning structure, evanescent and changing,[6] is what Derrida calls "Writing." (Henceforth, to differentiate it from writing in the traditional, everyday, phenomenal sense, Derrida's use of the term will always be capitalized.)

Writing so understood stands prior to both speech and writing in their more traditional usages. There is no immediate grasping or experience prior to Writing; all experience, signifying and meaning are made possible by it. Writing takes the place of Heidegger's concept World. It is that absent "thing" that is the cause of all that is phenomenally present. By using the term Writing, Derrida thinks he can accomplish what Heidegger attempts with the concept World, but without any ontological encumbrances.[7]

DIFFÉRANCE, THE TRACE AND *SOUS RATURE*

If it is true, as Heidegger asserts, that every great thinker thinks but one central thought, Derrida's central thought is Writing, a concept which emerges from his reflections on the relationship between speech and writing in the tradition of metaphysics with its doctrine of Being qua presence. In thematically developing the concept Writing in *Of Grammatology* Derrida says the following:

> Perhaps patient meditation and painstaking investigation on and around what is still provisionally called writing, far from falling short of a science of writing or of hastily dismissing it by some obscurantist reaction, letting it rather develop its positivity as far as possible, are the wanderings of a way of thinking that is faithful and attentive to the ineluctable world of the future which proclaims itself at present, beyond the closure of knowledge. The future can only be anticipated in the form of an absolute danger. It is that which breaks absolutely with constituted normality and can only be proclaimed, presented, as a sort of monstrosity.[8] (OG 4–5)

Derrida is clear that in trying to point out the underlying uniformity of past metaphysical thought, he is clearing the way for a new understanding of thinking, which necessarily must do violence to the old conception, and will, no doubt, occasion violence of a different sort. Derrida is in no way furtive about his desire to bring down the concrete world that surrounds, built as he believes, on metaphysical principles. He is far more restrained in announcing what he wishes to replace it with. But underlying the entire project is clearly a conception of the good. The present world is a monstrosity; a post-metaphysical world will conduce to the human good as this does not. But where does Derrida get the right to a notion of an underlying human good?

Derrida claims that the same pattern he attempts to demonstrate in the thought of Husserl applies in Western thought since its beginnings in Plato and Aristotle. Spoken words are seen as the symbols of mental experiences that have an immediacy to them and written words are the symbols of the spoken. Derrida asserts that this is as true to Aristotle's *De interpretatione* as it is of Husserl's theory of language or Saussure's linguistics (OG 11).

Allegedly throughout the metaphysical tradition, initial mental experience "mirrors" things through natural resemblance. There is an order or *logos* in natural things that is available immediately to experience. The experience of the *logos* is immediately present. This is true whether we are speaking of the *logos* that orders the cosmos, the Word of God, or the "book of Nature" whose pages the scientists read.

There is always the *logos* prior to speech. Hence all Western thought is "logocentric." And since speech is the first signifier of the *logos* grasped by the mind, the voice has immediate proximity to the mind. Writing merely represents the sounds produced by the voice. Hence given the priority of speech and voice, all Western thought is also fundamentally "phonocentric": there is a necessary relationship between the *logos* and the *phone*. The *gramme*, or written mark, is at a second remove from the *logos*. Logocentric metaphysics and phonetic writing go together.

Furthermore, "phonetic writing, the medium of the great metaphysical, scientific, technical, and economic adventure of the West, is limited in space and time and limits itself even as it is in the process of imposing its laws upon the cultural areas that had escaped it. But this non-fortuitous conjunction of cybernetics and the 'human sciences' of writing leads to a more profound reversal" (OG 10). Technological Enframing, metaphysics, logocentrism and phonocentrism are all inexorably linked together. Agreeing with Heidegger, Derrida concludes that the West culminates in technological mastery, economic rationality and bureaucratic organization which upon reaching its necessary closure points to the possibility of a reversal. That reversal points beyond our technological age to a non-logocentric and non-phonetic future, whatever that might mean. These locutions are Derrida's substitutes for Heidegger's experiments with non-metaphysical thinking, a thinking the outlines of which one cannot even sketch except negatively.

One intimation of what this future portends is what Derrida calls the "death of the civilization of the book" (OG 8), i.e., the death of what he will call "linear writing." Linear writing is the writing that presumes that all meaning is carried by the specific words found on the line of a text. Derrida asserts, however, that at least, if not more, meaning lodges in the "spaces" between the lines and in the "margins." Hence there is more meaning in what is not said than in what is. To emphasize this Derrida even experiments with novel, non-traditional ways of presenting page formatting; e.g., in *Spurs* as well as in the opening essay "Tympan" in *Margins Of Philosophy.*

Derrida also tries to show that temporal or human writing is always presented as fallen, debased, or misleading (OG 17). This allegedly becomes necessary when one sees the primary kind of "writing" as non-temporal and non-human, i.e., divine writing or natural writing ("book of Nature"). Derrida wishes to enhance the status of human, temporal writing; indeed, he wishes to make it primary. To do so he thinks it is necessary to free everyday writing from its dependence on such notions as *logos,* truth and the belief in a primary signified. Derrida points toward a Writing that is constitutive rather than derivative, at the heart of the meaning process rather than a fallen debased form of representation that takes place at some distance from a primary signified.

Derrida sees even Heidegger as still within the grips of metaphysical logocentrism. For Heidegger, the process of unconcealment (*alētheia*) operates in such a way that unconcealment is caused by Being. And Being happens or takes place as History through the *logoi* of the great thinkers. Even as absent, Being retains a quasi-substantive quality, and the *logos* still retains a certain priority, at least according to Derrida. For Derrida, it is Nietzsche who is closer to the passage to the new epoch with his notion that the reading of any text is an ongoing originary operation, that Writing in its primordial form is not based on the existence of an absolute signified, but is rather always an unconscious form of "interpretation." For Nietzsche, as for Derrida, this is even true of the Writing of modern physics (cf. *Beyond Good and Evil* no. 14).

Since for Derrida Writing is not "an instrument enslaved to a full and originarily spoken language" (OG 29), one can do away with the notion of writing as an "outside" or "exterior" enslaved by a pre-given *logos* which is the "interior" or "inside." As Derrida says, "the Outside is (under erasure) the Inside" (OG 44). When writing is conceived in that way, the science of language sees its task as recovering the natural, original, "inside" source, much as is true of Rousseau, from whom, Derrida tries to show, emanates the inspiration that leads to the founding of the science of linguistics.

Likewise, the notion that writing is conventional and exterior to the real source of meaning allegedly links it to a specific notion of politics, which puts politics in an exterior, secondary and derivative light. In its own way politics always Writes, it must write laws and promulgate edicts. But those concrete laws and public statements are seen as derivative from a prior source, and exterior to that source. Politics is, allegedly, always seen as causing violence to the true *logos* (OG 36). Politics is a "cave," and is seen as destructive of the truth. Politics causes "forgetting" while the source is seen as in need of "recovery." Philosophy is seen as the means to recovery or "remembering."

For Derrida, "deconstructing this tradition will . . . not consist of reversing it, of making writing innocent. Rather of showing why the violence of writing does not befall an innocent language. There is an originary violence of writing because language is first, in a sense I shall gradually reveal, [W]riting" (OG 37). Derrida wants a conception of both Writing and of politics that is primary and constitutive. Armed with such a notion of politics, the traditional distinction between politics and philosophy will dissolve. Indeed, as we will see, Derrida's philosophic activity is itself politics understood as part of a process of constitutive Writing. By placing Writing more generally at the very heart of the meaning process rather than exterior to it, both philosophy and politics become forms of Writing. As such, philosophy and politics in no way differ.

Derrida argues, against what he terms the logo- and phono-centric tradition, that when we see that signs are never identical to that which they signify, all signs signify only other signs, the lock of the traditional notion of truth will be broken. On the contrary, since all signs always announce something other than themselves, there can be no Identity. Hence the sign always announces what it is *not,* what is absent. Nonetheless, this announcing always bears a "Trace" of what it signifies, a Trace of what is absent. But there can never be complete correspondence or Identity between the Trace and that toward which it points. This is true of all signs in relation to the absence toward which they point. It is true of all speech and writing as well. Indeed it would be doubly true of Writing, where both the author and the referent are absent (OG 10–11).

Derrida argues that both writing and speech are necessarily constituted by absence. In this crucial respect, there is no difference between them. Furthermore, contrary to the metaphysical tradition, no simply phonetic writing ever exists. Speech can never pronounce absence, the Nothing, the Trace of the absent signified or author. Both speech and writing are constituted by the not. Furthermore, writing can never be a simple phonetic representation of speech, for the possibility of meaning rests on the non-phonetic, e.g., line spacing and punctuation. These are not mere accessories but co-equal and necessary to the meaning process with the letters. The not, spacing, the absent, the margin, the Trace, the evanescent author, etc., all make Writing possible.

We are led to ask, therefore, how the Trace operates, whether it is random in its "movement" or bound by structural necessities.

> The instituted trace is "unmotivated" but not capricious. Like the word "arbitrary" according to Saussure, it "should not imply that the choice of the signifier is left entirely to the speaker." Simply, it has no "natural attachment" to the signified within reality. For us, the rupture of that "natural attachment" puts in question the idea of naturalness rather than that of attachment.
>
> . . . The "unmotivatedness" of the sign requires a synthesis in which the completely other is announced as such—without any simplicity, any identity, any resemblance or continuity—within what is not it. *Is announced as such:* there we have all *history,* from what metaphysics has defined as "non-living" up to "consciousness," passing through all levels of animal organization. The trace, where the relationship with the other is marked, articulates its possibility in the entire

field of the entity, which metaphysics has defined as the being-present starting from the occulted movement of the trace. The trace must be thought before the entity. But the movement of the trace is necessarily occulted, it produces itself as self-occultation. When the other announces itself as such, it presents itself in the dissimulation of itself. (OG 46–47)

Following Heidegger's discussion of "It" that "gives" more than he would wish to admit, Derrida asserts that his notion of the Trace points to something mysterious and absent that stands behind all signs and inhabits them, and everything is a sign for Derrida. This primordial absence that is nonetheless responsible for whatever vapor trail is present to us produces itself through "self-occultation," or in Heidegger's terms, veiling and concealment. The self-concealing Trace accounts for the movement of historicizing as well as language understood as the total nexus of Writing. Writing, in Derrida's sense is the dynamic of producing itself as Other. But where Heidegger talks about Being, Derrida also talks about *différance*. Writing is another word for the operation by which the *différance* produces the Trace, the closest thing to presence we have. Contrary to metaphysics, the origin is absent, and what is semi-present, the Trace, is always riddled through and through with absence, with the not. But if signs refer only to other signs, then this is as much as to say that absence refers primarily to absence, Trace to Trace. This endless process is Writing, the process by which *différance* creates difference and differentiation. What takes the place of the ultimate signified, *différance*, can never be said or written for it is self-concealing. Hence like Heidegger's Being, the ultimate source can only be referred to "under erasure" (*sous rature*). All writing and speech are equally dominated by erasure, the mark of the absent author or source.

History cannot end, the meaning process is endless, but that also means the absence process is endless. History is endless, but random and without predictable order; it is neither teleological nor does it repeat. The existence of difference is endless, but without fixed determination. It is only now that we realize this **truth**, now that Derrida announces it. Of course, the announcing itself is caught in the dynamic of *différance* and is but a Trace. How it will be interpreted and transformed by future Writing cannot he predicted, because for Derrida, every time one reads a text, one writes another; that is one of the mechanisms by which Writing "moves." Every human activity is a form of Writing. All reading and speaking changes what it operates on, its "text." Each new text is endlessly operated on in this fashion. Every book, natural object, political constitution, and one's own "self" are all texts in this sense, and are all a mere Trace, determined by the operation of *différance*.

The movement of the Trace, which is simultaneously the absence of any transcendental or transcendent signified, is termed by Derrida, "play" (*jou*). The play of the Trace causes all difference; hence all difference is fluid (OG 65). This play is the absolute origin of all sense and meaning. Hence Writing is not an undertaking that any author can completely or consciously master. As Derrida puts it in his attack on Hegelian self-consciousness, Writing is the becoming absent and becoming unconscious of the subject (OG 69). There is no "subject" to engage in "Enframing" and no "object" to be Enframed. The message seems to be "lighten up," quit worrying about it. Gender, nation, race, religion, honor, morality, you name it, they are all Traces, vapor trails hardly above the threshold of Nothingness. Quit taking it all so seriously, it's all just play. Of course, the next truly playful, rather than primarily angry, deconstructionist one finds should be reported to the popular press simply due to their novelty.

Writing, as an ultimately unconscious process, must be opposed to the conscious subjectivity of the metaphysics of presence. The preeminence of the self-consciousness from Descartes to Hegel is to be overcome. When one deconstructs the metaphysics of presence, one is left with an unpredictable hegemony of unconscious forces intersecting and interpenetrating each other in unpredictable ways. The whole unpredictable process yields only evanescent Traces. Ultimately, as with Gertrude Stein's Oakland, there is no real There there.

As mentioned above, it is not only in traditional textual interpretation that one finds this dynamic, or as regards oneself, but in politics as well. For if everything is a text ruled by the Trace and the operation of *différance,* this is equally true of law, whether it is written or customary. If no law can mean the same thing to two people or over time, the rule of law dissolves. The dissolution of law can only leave in its place the unconscious interaction of individuals. While Derrida clearly looks forward to a form of self-regulating anarchism, it is impossible to see how this would differ from power politics, the rule of the strongest—or at least the loudest. Why would this not create an environment of violence, and the unconscious imposition of order by some on others, and in precisely the fashion Nietzsche predicts is coming. Derrida refrains from giving any concrete discussion of these things, unlike Nietzsche who is more forthright and courageous in spelling out what follows from the fact that "God is dead." In "Ends of Man" (MP 111), Derrida flirts with such topics as the overman and monumental history but they play no part in his teaching. The absence of the overman from Derrida's account may be no more than an egalitarian prejudice, or a rhetorical necessity for an author who wishes to have an effect. But on his own terms, what that effect might be will surely remain a mystery for there can be no prediction in a world ruled by *différance* and Traces. Derrida believes he is opening the transition to a new conception of writing, which is non-phonetic, non-representational, independent of the *logos* and thereby transcends the metaphysics of presence. It is this new understanding that will help foster the *transition* to a new, post-metaphysical epoch. In principle Derrida cannot predict what that new epoch will look like, only *différance* itself will determine it.

The victory of deconstructionism, which undoes the hegemony of logocentrism and phonocentrism, simultaneously destroys the basis of modern science. There is no science that transcends the dynamic of Writing any more than politics does. There is no meaning that can be repeated between scientists and across time, and that is absolutely required if science is to exist. As he initially called it, "Grammatology" is the new discipline that replaces all the old disciplines. Grammatology is to become the new queen of the sciences, and presumably would take the central place in the universities of the Derridean post-West. Grammatology is the new discipline that demonstrates that there is absolutely no graspable or repeatable meaning, no origin or author. Needless to say, in transcending metaphysics Grammatology simultaneously overcomes theology. As we will see, Derrida reserves some of his harshest words for theology. And yet in some of his last works he comes around to an odd pointing toward the place of some generic kind of religiosity.

As I have said, with Grammatology (one wonders how Derrida is entitled to use the suffix deriving from *logos*) comes the end of linear writing, the end of the epoch of the book (OG 86). We come to realize there is meaning in the margins and between the lines that is at least as, if not more, significant than that on the line. We begin to read and write outside the lines. We know, in other words, that meaning is not simply present anywhere. It somehow lurks in some nebulous environs. As a result, we begin to reread all old texts differently, and will continue to reread them endlessly. This becomes our relation to both past and present. The future mysteriously takes care of itself. This hermeneutic rewriting will be the main occupation of grammatologists, supported in the universities in comfort, paradoxically, by those they are sworn to vanquish. For without texts to cannibalize, the deconstructionist would have no grist for his mill.

The grammatologist realizes that what is thought today can only be thought under erasure and therefore cannot be written according to linear writing, but only within a pluri-dimensional text (OG 87). But this new writing does not point toward esotericism. The possibility of esotericism implies a conscious intention on the part of the author and the ability to reproduce that understanding on the part of the reader. Derrida rejects both possibilities because reading and writing are always forms of Writing, i.e., the creation of a new text. Since nothing is ever simply present, neither the self of the author nor a textual product, the intention of the author is never present, to either the author or the reader. How Derrida presumes therefore, seemingly in a conscious fashion, to stand outside this dynamic and consciously foster a new epoch using a new science is not clear. Hence how he knows a new epoch is possible is not clear. And how he knows that closure has arrived is least clear of all. Derrida seems to presume more than his own principles allow. To paraphrase the poet, expel "nature" as vociferously as you like, it will always sneak back in through the back door.

Once again, we should keep in mind that what takes the place of proof in this kind of theoretical undertaking is not discursive argumentation, to which Derrida cannot appeal, but rather Derrida's distinctive deconstructive readings of the texts of the metaphysical tradition. Without them Derrida would have no matter upon which to operate. His "proofs" are his attempts to show that despite themselves, metaphysical authors point in precisely the direction Derrida points, even though they proceed from contrary premises. The proofs of the existence of *différance* and the Trace are their operation in all past thought no matter how narrow and convoluted the showing may be.

DERRIDA AND THE LATE MODERN INTELLECTUAL COSMOS

Clearly Derrida rejects all doctrines of Nature, and hence the doctrine of Natural Law or of Natural Right whether Thomistic, Aristotelian or Lockean liberal. In this Derrida is far from original, he is but a drop in the late modern flood. His opposition to metaphysics also takes the form of the opposition to what Heidegger called onto-theology. His antipathy to theology and religion is manifest: "the theological motif par excellence is decidedly the one to be destroyed."[8] Further, the attempt by capitalism to generate wealth can only be built on a misguided reliance on presence and the desire to foster a particular constellation of presence, founded as well upon a fairly straightforward doctrine of human nature.

But "God is dead," and Derrida does not see the refutation of Nature as a major problem. Derrida simply takes that as a given. Yet the focus of Derrida's work is clearly anti-Hegelian. He wishes to overturn the philosophy of self-consciousness. He also attempts to show that not only can there be no Hegelian overcoming of binary opposition, but the traditional binary pairs that are allegedly central to Western thought are an illusion: e.g., speech/writing, good/evil, body/soul, being/becoming, subject/object, *logos/muthos,* theory/practice, matter/form, matter/spirit, nature/convention, freedom/nature, signifier/signified. There can be no simple opposition, hence there is no *Aufhebung* or *relever* (POS 43).

Derrida is also at pains to oppose, and tries to deconstruct, all permutations of the sovereign notion of the age, the idea of History. He rejects any linear conception of History whether the liberal notion of progress, the teleological notions of Hegel and Marx, or the cyclical History of Nietzsche with its eternal return of the same. They are all the result of the metaphysics of presence. "I am very wary of the concept of history. . . . As for linearism, you know very well that it is not my strong point. I have always, and very precisely, associated it with logocentrism, phonocentrism, semanticism, and idealism" (POS 50).

Accordingly, Derrida rejects the possibility of predicting the future, just as he must accept the necessity of continually rewriting the past. The past is like any text; all of life is a text, written and rewritten. Consequently, Derrida says there is no "absolute autonomy of the history of philosophy" in the mode of either Hegel or Heidegger (POS 50). Derrida's relation to the idea of History raises the question of his relation to Marxism.[9] For example, if the history of philosophy is not autonomous, might other variables like economics or class struggle have that autonomy? Derrida is explicitly pushed on this point by Jean-Louis Houdebine in an interview reported in *Positions*. Derrida's response is somewhat indirect. He argues that since logocentrism is always an idealism, to dismantle the hegemony of the *logos* is to dismantle idealism. Since he and dialectical materialism have this in common, they are not at odds. But when pushed on whether he is a materialist or not, he is forced to follow the logic of his argument. For Derrida, there can never be any fixed or finished presence. This precludes the possibility of any simple materialism. Derrida says he would accept any materialism that understands that "matter" is determined by the dynamic of Writing (POS 64). Whether Marx's materialism—for example, consider the discussion in *Theses on Feuerbach*—fits this definition, Derrida does not say. Derrida is consistent and does say that no text of Marx, Engels, or Lenin avoids the dynamic of Writing, and hence there can be no fixed or finished meaning to their texts (POS 63). And he is explicit that Marx does not escape from metaphysics, for example, in his historical teleology and eschatology, or for that matter, in his discussion of classes (POS 75).

Perhaps the key to Derrida's relation to Marx is his relationship to the concept of "base and superstructure." For Marx the base phenomenon is economic and the basic dynamic is that of class struggle, determined by man's relation to the reigning mode of production. For Marx everything else is secondary, the superstructure is determined by the base. Politics, art, religion, and philosophy are all epiphenomenal superstructures. Changes in the superstructure are not autonomous but rather dependent upon the base. But for Derrida the base is Writing. The superstructure can never be more than the Trace of *différance*. And since Writing includes all human activity it includes all of the things Marx would assign to the superstructure. (For a tangential discussion of this issue, see POS 90.) And the notion of base is startlingly like an ultimate signified. Derrida will never come out and say what he should say;

Marx is a logocentrist and metaphysician. In his late work, *Specters of Marx*, he does say that those of us in the present owe much to the Marx that is, as it were, a brooding omnipresence in the sky. But who the "us" is beyond French, left-bank, left intellectuals is not clear. And why that us is itself more than a Trace is not clear either. In the end, Derrida simply comes off as too delicate to hurt the feelings of his left intellectual fellow travelers.

Finally, Marxism presumes the victory of modern technology over Nature and over the "idiocy" of Natural forms of existence. That is the prerequisite for the proletarian revolution as well as the prerequisite for establishing a classless society. But that technological victory is based on the success of modern science, a success built upon the metaphysics of presence. When "truth," *logos* and presence are dismantled, so are science and technology. This is a sword that cuts against Marxism as much as it cuts against liberal capitalism or any other modern dispensation. To dismantle the *logos* is to dismantle universal reason, but also to dismantle universalism and cosmopolitanism in all forms, Marxist and liberal. The pursuit of difference and the hegemony of *différance* cannot lead to the cosmopolitan politics of either Moscow or Washington. And yet categories like race, class, nation or people are not available to Derrida. So where he should end up in his longings is hard to say. Yet it is clear he longs for some form of cosmopolitan anarchism.[10]

Derrida's relation to Nietzsche's philosophy is simultaneously close and partial. He borrows heavily from Nietzsche's discussion that what passes for reason is always interpretation, even in physics. He also borrows from Nietzsche's argument that the will to truth always grows out of irrational sources, and hence that those opposites always go together. The concept of *différance* bears some resemblance to Nietzsche's concept of the brooding, unconscious force of the Dionysian qua Will-to-Power. Derrida builds on Nietzsche's attacks on the idea of the self as a voluntary actor and hence upon Nietzsche's discussions about the hegemony of the unconscious. As previously mentioned, in "Ends of Man" Derrida flirts ambiguously with concepts like "active forgetfulness," the "overman" and "monumental history," but seemingly does not adopt them. Without going any further we can say that Derrida borrows heavily from Nietzsche's psychological and epistemological discussions, but he appears to borrow very little from Nietzsche's discussion of politics and morals. Nietzsche's stern, hierarchical, aristocratic politics is nowhere in evidence. The discussions of good/bad, good/evil, the Will-to-Power, Eternal Recurrence, *ressentiment* and the spirit of revenge are not prominent. Perhaps this goes hand in hand with what Derrida calls his "feminist" reading of Nietzsche in the bilingual volume *Spurs: Nietzsche's Styles/ Eperons: Les Styles de Nietzsche*. The stern and masculine part of the teaching is dropped. How someone with Derrida's principles presumes to make a self-conscious choice for one part of Nietzsche against another is not clear. The self, like Nature, keeps sneaking in the back door with Derrida.

Derrida does confront Heidegger's reading of Nietzsche, wherein Heidegger accuses Nietzsche of being the last metaphysician, the last proponent of onto-theology. He also confronts the Heideggerian accusation that Nietzsche remains a proponent of subjectivism and the autonomy of the Will. Derrida tries to defend Nietzsche against these charges and in fact tries to turn the argument against Heidegger. He co-opts central Heideggerian categories, but seemingly to accomplish a return to Nietzsche, if only his primarily feminist Nietzsche. And indeed, Derrida seems more faithful to Nietzsche than Heidegger, especially in his focus on the place of the unconscious. For Derrida, Heidegger, with his quasi-substantive discussions of Being, and his invocation of terms like "spirit," is more metaphysical than Nietzsche.[11]

Derrida's relation to Nietzsche goes a long way toward explaining his relation to Freud. Like Nietzsche, Freud develops the problematic of the unconscious. Clearly the unconscious cannot be dominated by an Id or any instinctive, Natural base for that would imply the metaphysics of presence. The Freudian doctrine of the Superego can be construed as compatible with Derrida's concept of Writing. Obviously Derrida cannot accept, on any level, the existence of a self-conscious Ego. Hence Derrida's attempted appropriation of and accommodation to Freud is, to say the least, in need of a subtle presentation (cf. "Freud and the Scene of Writing," in WD 196). The reasons for trying to appropriate Freud are clearer than Derrida's precise relation to him. Derrida must in some way accommodate himself to Nietzsche, Freud and Marx, the *ménage à trois* without which there would be no contemporary intellectual Left in France, for that is the very air a left-bank French intellectual breathes. Nonetheless, it should be clear, his relationship has to be unorthodox; although that probably means self-consciously rhetorical.

Despite the fact that Derrida pushes the right buttons in his opposition to the Vietnam War, opposing Western "ethnocentrism," support for the Civil Rights movement, feminism and Third World revolutions, his relation to the contemporary Left is far from clear. A pure conjecture, based entirely on a reading of his books, is that his delicately balanced stance, given Derrida's academic venue, may be almost obligatory. Nonetheless, whenever the Left stands on a doctrine of presence, Derrida's teaching will undermine it. That leaves one to wonder if Derrida's teaching can ultimately be used by others for anything but negative purposes, i.e., trying to deconstruct and de-legitimize the teachings of others.

Derrida's relation to Heidegger is equally complicated. He simply takes off from, without feeling the need to prove, Heidegger's conclusion that Western thought is dominated by the conception of Being as presence and by onto-theology. But again, as with Nietzsche, he seems to stay away from the political and moral themes that dominate Heidegger's thought. He relies on neither the early Heideggerian discussion of authenticity and resoluteness nor the later discussion of autochthony and *Gelassenheit*. Derrida does dismiss as insignificant Heidegger's Nazi flirtation. But beyond that he is silent about the political and moral themes so evident in Heidegger's thought. Heidegger certainly had no cosmopolitan or anarchistic longings, either modern or postmodern. Yet in the end, it appears that Derrida longs for some form of postmodern cosmopolitan anarchism.

Derrida tries to show that Heidegger is still dominated by the doctrine of Being as presence, and hence still determined by onto-theology. He substitutes his notions of Trace and *différance* for Heidegger's Being, but with the hope of conveying the idea in a fashion that avoids the problems he asserts Heidegger still has. In every case where Derrida tries to go beyond Heidegger, and avoid the reappearance of *logos* and presence, he does so at the cost of becoming even less concrete than Heidegger. Derrida is just about the only author that can outdo Heidegger in abstract jargon-peddling.

The real difference between Derrida and Heidegger emerges when we juxtapose the concepts Writing and *Gelassenheit*. *Gelassenheit* is usually translated as "openness" and "releasement." It is a stance of quiet anticipation and hopeful waiting for the "silent call" of the self-concealing, withdrawn and absent source. This stance literally leaves the Heideggerian thinker speechless. Indeed what the thinker waits to hear will have no sound. There is no indication of how one bridges the gap between what will be heard in silence and speech in the spatio-temporal world. The Heideggerian, post-Western thinker has nothing to say, must wait and cannot avoid silence, perhaps even after the anticipated call. Given the dynamic of Writing, the Derridean post-Western thinker absolutely must keep speaking, must keep Writing or fall into the abyss of meaninglessness and nothingness. Where the late, hopeful Heidegger cannot speak, Derrida cannot keep silent. Derrida must Write, even though, precisely because, there is no objective ground or foundation for meaning. And others must continue to Write as well, a cacophony of Writing without hope of an arbiter. Between Heidegger and Derrida we are left with the antimony cacophony or silence.

In the late Heideggerian notion of *Gelassenheit* there is also a notion of an openness to beings. This picks up the early Heideggerian notion of openness to "phenomena" that "show themselves." In Derrida there are no phenomena, and nothing shows itself. The "phenomenological" part of Heidegger's teaching still allows one to be open to a world of things and meanings that stand still far more than under the auspices of Derridean Writing and Traces.

DERRIDA'S PLATO

Despite the amazing number and variety of authors analyzed by Derrida in an attempt to "prove" his theory, the centerpiece of his deconstructive analyses is Plato. Plato is for Derrida, as for Heidegger, the acknowledged father of the tradition of Western thought. He is proclaimed everywhere as the spokesman for absolute, objective, unchanging ideas. Those ideas, like Husserl's, are reputedly available to the mind through an unmediated, noetic presence. Such is the traditional understanding as well as, to a large extent, Derrida's. Derrida, like Heidegger, adds that Plato is the father of the metaphysics of presence. Given this account it is curious that one of Derrida's operative texts is not the *Republic, Sophist* or *Phaedo* but rather the *Phaedrus* (cf. "Plato's Pharmacy," in *Dissemination*).

Central to Derrida's analysis of the *Phaedrus* is the attempt to show Plato's preference for speech over writing. As we have already seen this preference goes hand in hand with logocentrism, phonocentrism and the metaphysics of presence. This alleged preference for speech is, no doubt, what occasions Derrida's decision to deconstruct the *Phaedrus*. As he always does, Derrida tries to show that even in Plato *différance* operates and determines the course of Plato's writing without him knowing it. Hence, in Derrida's sense, even Plato is a manifestation of Writing.

Derrida is particularly fascinated by the frequency of the use of the Greek word *pharmakon*. He points out that in the *Phaedrus* the word takes on a variety of meanings, the two most prominent of which are antithetical: on the one hand the term signifies an "aid" or "remedy," while on the other hand it means "poison." Derrida sees this as an indication of his thesis that there is never simple identity or univocity of meaning in anything. All of life is a text and texts are always dominated by evanescent traces the author cannot dominate. The interpenetration of opposites is the very nature of Writing. In spite of himself Plato cannot suppress its operation. The prominence of the term *pharmakon* is neither an accident nor is it the manifestation of a conscious choice on Plato's part; it points to the operation of a structural necessity. As is true of any text, what operates on the subconscious level, driven by *différance,* leaves its Trace. The intention of the author is always subordinate to the operation of these necessities. In this respect, the privileged stance of the deconstructionist allows understanding the author better than that author understands him or herself. But how is this possible if the same necessities are operating in the author who "discovers" these necessities? Are these necessities that will always operate or only in the present moment of *différance*? Does any of this imply that we are living in a distinctive or privileged moment?

Derrida asserts that the operation of the same structural necessities can be seen in the speeches of Socrates. For example, Socrates argues that speech is preferable to writing because writing can never defend itself as speech can. Writing can never make on the spot adjustments taking into account the audience or the unique circumstances because the "father" of the *logos* is absent (DIS 77). Needless to say the father of the dialogues is absent. The father of Socrates's speeches is never present in any of his works. Others carry Plato's speeches and we are left to understand the meaning of the spectacle that is put before us. In this respect Derrida's point is well taken.

But has not Plato written in such a way, dialogues, that he does speak differently to different readers? Has not Plato solved the problem Socrates speaks of in the *Phaedrus*? And does not the fact that Plato writes dialogues represent a criticism of Socrates' position rather than an acceptance of it? In other words, contrary to Derrida, is there not a *conscious* criticism of Socrates operating in the *Phaedrus* as I will argue in part 3 below? Indeed without Plato, the speeches of Socrates would not have to defend themselves and his total absence might be assured, i.e., there might have been no Western philosophy. Derrida does not seem to see any dramatic reflection upon Socrates and what he stands for on the part of Plato. His gaze is cast elsewhere.

Derrida tries to show that the contradiction between writing and speech and the Socratic condemnation of writing is a manifestation of *différance*. He rightly observes that the "father of speech" that Socrates has in mind is not the mortal author but the Good (*agathon*), especially as it is presented by Socrates in the *Republic* (DIS 81). The Good is the Source or father of all *logoi*. In the *Republic* Socrates makes it clear that the Good cannot be grasped directly; it blinds the eye of the soul as the sun blinds the eye of sense. In the *Phaedo* we learn that to avoid intellectual blindness Socrates turned away from the attempt to apprehend the Good directly. He turned from the attempt to look directly at Being to interrogating beings by interrogating speeches about beings.

These *logoi* take the place of what is absent or unavailable, the Good. Thus is established a chain moving as follows: The Good — Ideas — Visible Things — Speeches about Things. Derrida asserts that the chain is set up in such a way that each is a copy of the former. The true author, the Good, is present within but different from the speeches that presume to be copies of it. On the one hand the speeches are not the same as the author; on the other hand they are what they are only on the basis of what they are not. Once again, Derrida claims that this outcome is a Trace of the operation of *différance* within the Platonic text, i.e., the necessary penetration of the is and the is not, presence and absence.

Derrida goes on to argue that for Plato speech suffers from the same problem as writing, the absence of the author. The distinction between speech and writing thereby collapses, they both bear the Trace of what is absent, they are both forms of Writing. Again, Plato and his dramatic Socrates are determined by structural laws of which they are unaware but which Derrida is privileged to be able to articulate.

Yet another place in the text where Derrida sees the unmistakable Trace of *différance* is in the Platonic distinction between *muthos* and *logos*. Derrida claims it is impossible to maintain this distinction. According to Plato's account, both myth and philosophic speech are imitations or copies of the absent source. Derrida claims that if the difference between myth and philosophy dissolves, as he thinks, the distinction between philosophy and sophistry likewise dissolves and so does that between philosophy and poetry. Plato unconsciously undermines the central aim of his work.

Let us take one final example of Derrida's analysis. In the myth of Theus and Thamus, Socrates relates the argument that writing is primarily beneficial as an aid to memory (*pharmakon* qua remedy). But Thamus is then made to argue that rather than aid memory writing replaces it and allows it to atrophy (*pharmakon* qua poison). With the atrophy of memory comes our alienation from the true father. Hence writing cuts one off from the source it presumes to copy. Derrida argues that this myth is not a conscious construction of Plato's but rather something that was absolutely imposed upon him and in precisely the place where it appears. Once again the structural logic of Writing imposed itself upon Plato to the detriment of the surface argument.

Derrida multiplies analyses like these but we need not present them further for we can now report what Derrida sees as the yield from this deconstruction. Binary opposites that are central to the surface of Plato's argument—true/false, sophistry/philosophy, speech/writing, "father"/copy, myth/*logos*, true opinion/false opinion, Being/Not Being—intermingle and interpenetrate each other in Plato's text, despite the surface teaching. Plato, like everyone else, is caught in the web of Writing and *différance.*

This is not the place for a substantive confrontation with Derrida's analysis but several points can be made.[12] First, Derrida seems to miss the dynamic which the *Phaedrus* more than any other dialogue presents, the confrontation between Plato and Socrates. Hence he misses the idea that Plato is trying to show that he has invented a form of writing that solves the problem his dramatic Socrates presents. If this is true, Derrida's reading proves that the dialogue does speak differently to different readers, and in such a way as to protect the author from the potential moral and political outrage of the city.

Second, while the *Phaedrus* is about speech and writing, it is at least coequally about Eros. Derrida seems to miss completely the place of wonder or awe (*thaumazein*) and Eros in Platonic thought. Eros (all longing caused by a perceived lack or deficiency) is presented by Plato as the engine that lifts the soul beyond preoccupation with mundane existence, or presence, i.e., to an amazed and awe-struck pursuit of that which is lacking. This is a straightforward "phenomena" of human existence, as understandable to us today as it was to Plato's readers in his own time. Hence there must be some enduring presence or "nature."

Derrida, in trying to turn Plato into a proto-Hegel, misses the fact that the **pursuit** of wisdom implies that one does not already have it but nonetheless is driven by the desire to acquire it. In this respect the feeling of ignorance is similar to sexual longing. The existence in the soul of the erotic desire for wisdom does not prove that it is attainable any more than lust assures one of a mate. The erotic longing may be altogether tragic. Failing to see the place of the phenomenon Eros, Derrida fails to see philosophy as a way of life rather than as a discursive body of knowledge that re-presents unchanging truths. As a result Derrida fails to see the altogether non-political basis of philosophy in Plato's thought. Likewise he does not see that it is the experience of lacking in an erotic soul that differentiates the philosopher from the sophist in Plato's teaching, not the existence or non-existence of an apodictic *logos*. It is the sophist who is locked within presence and a desire to be a political actor and dominate the mundane world, not Plato's philosopher.

Third, Derrida rightly presents the ambiguous relation between Being and Not-being, Same and Other, and Identity and Difference in Platonic thought. But this ambiguity points not to the necessary operation of *différance* but to the fact that Platonic dialogues present fundamental alternatives, and forces them to confront each other. Plato consciously presents oppositions, but there is no *Aufhebung* in Plato, no attempt to synthesize or overcome them. The erotic soul is left to reflect on what may be fundamentally irreducible oppositions, or no oppositions at all. Contrary to Derrida, this points to the fact that Plato refrains from presenting a metaphysical or ontological teaching; he refrains from taking sides on the confrontation between fundamental alternatives. This points toward Plato's primary teaching, the central element of which is moderation. As I will argue in the chapters of part 3, not only is there no metaphysics of presence in Plato, there is no metaphysics or ontology whatsoever, and that for a conscious reason. Hence there is no absolute political or moral teaching that can he deduced from apodictic first premises.

Plato's dialogues are not metaphysical, ontological or epistemological; those are constructions imposed upon Plato after the fact. The Platonic dialogues are fundamentally manifestations of political philosophy in the holistic sense I presented above. How Plato relates to the tradition of Western thought is therefore far more complicated than the picture Derrida—or Nietzsche or Heidegger—presents. That tradition has had far more breaks and discontinuities than any of those three authors will admit.

Not only does Plato juxtapose fundamental metaphysical alternatives without taking sides, but he presents a world populated by fundamentally different souls. Plato is an impresario, he brings various souls on stage for our inspection. And he is much more concrete than late modern thought, especially that of Derrida. He tries to show dramatically that different types of souls are moved by different principles. Furthermore, individual souls are torn by competing internal principles. Plato makes it clear that taking these irreducible differences into account is central to any sane understanding of human existence. Put another way, Plato takes account of genuine difference.

Finally, the two types of souls Plato presents as in most fundamental opposition are the ones of most political interest. They are represented by Socrates on the one hand and partisans of one's own like Meletus and Anytus on the other, with those like Glaucon and Alcibiades hanging in the balance somewhere in the middle. Derrida recognizes that Plato's thought has a political intention, but he misses completely that that intention is to make the world safe for both Socrates and Meletus. We might say, therefore, that it is in Plato that we see the real defender of difference, and not the kind that has to be invented by the "post-modern" thinker after he deconstructs all the forms that already show themselves.

There is difference all around the post-modern thinker Derrida, but he will not accept it. Instead we are told to pursue a form of difference that has never been seen and cannot be outlined in any way. Herein we see that the "post-modern" Derrida is really just another modern, following modernity's animus against Nature, and against any phenomena that show themselves. The attack on the metaphysics of presence merely carries that modern hatred of Nature to a higher power. It is a form of what Nietzsche called the spirit of revenge.

To conclude, for Plato there can be no final, apodictic *logos*; to believe so is to be Hegel. Hence it cannot be said that Plato is simply logocentric, for he presents quite clearly that poetry and myth are needed to fill in the gaps where *logos* has nothing to say. Derrida is correct that upon closer inspection the line between philosophy and poetry blurs, and that the two interpenetrate each other, but he is wrong in thinking that Plato is unaware of the fact, or that presenting this ambiguity is not part of Plato's conscious intention.

Derrida is prevented from seeing these things in Plato by his prior commitment to eschew all attachment to presence. Hence he cannot grasp the presence of Eros, see the variety of souls, or see the fundamental, if irreducible, multiplicity of *logoi*. The deconstructionist sees *less,* not more, than the author he deconstructs.

CONCLUSION: DERRIDA AND THE POSSIBILITY OF POLITICAL PHILOSOPHY

Derrida's philosophy clearly intends to have a political effect. In that respect it could be called a form of political philosophy.

Why engage in a work of deconstruction, rather than leave things the way they are, etc.? Nothing here, without a "show of force" somewhere. Deconstruction, I have insisted, is not neutral. It *intervenes*. (POS 93)

All of this is not without, it is not to all of you I will have to teach this, political consequences. They are still difficult to calculate.[13]

[The] historical and political horizon would call for a long analysis. I have simply found it necessary to mark, date, and make known to you the historical circumstances in which I prepared this communication. These circumstances appear to me to belong, by all rights, to the field and problematic of our colloquium. (MP 114)

There is no need to multiply these examples; the point is perfectly evident. Derrida's conception of philosophy forces him to pursue a political intention, for there is no object that philosophy can grasp that leads to knowledge or wisdom that can be contemplated. Therefore, philosophy cannot be an end in itself, a way of life, a private undertaking. It is part of, indeed if we are honest it is intended to be the leading part, of the Writing that constitutes the Traces that pass for presence in our world. Philosophy is a form of activism. And that activism operates on an understanding of the good. Derrida somehow "knows" that the good is not to be found in the modern, technological, secular, liberal capitalist societies that allow deconstructionists to speak. It is to be found in some vague postmodern cosmopolitan anarchism. How Derrida knows this is the good, or how he can predict that his activities can foster it are absolutely impossible to explain on his premises. But he clearly presumes to act far more self-consciously than his principles will allow. And there is an underlying imperative that cannot be explained either: "Thou shall deconstruct." And thou shall do so endlessly. Why? Because that is the means to the good.

When philosophy becomes a straightforward form of activism and merges with everyday politics it loses its soul. Philosophy for Derrida is a form of action, a form of making, indeed it is a making and constituting of "reality." It is a form of constructivism and therefore it is a form of metaphysics in the sense of Heidegger that Derrida shares. The deconstructivist is just a furtive constructivist. At the deepest level, therefore, the distinction between philosophy and politics dissolves, both philosophers and non-philosophers Write, and neither can be said to do so with any greater sovereignty. In the process philosophy becomes politicized, it can no longer be an awe-inspired, erotic love of the pursuit of wisdom among equal friends. Derrida does not so much engage in political philosophy as produce politicized philosophy. He certainly cannot produce the weaving together of the whole that must be real political philosophy. He does not even see the necessity of the task. I will return to this issue in my discussion of Plato's Trilogy.

This is absolutely necessary and consistent for Derrida. It is the necessary correlate to his rejection of all versions of unmediated, "original" or "natural" experience that stand outside the shifting river of meaning produced by Writing and *différance*. Philosophy qua deconstructionism Writes, even if its effect is, as Derrida argues, deferred. Derrida makes much of the similarity in speech of the words differ and defer (cf. *différance* in MP). For Derrida, *différance* operates simultaneously to create "difference" and "deferral." Applied to philosophy this is as much as to say that philosophy is propagandistic, having its full effect after its dissemination has had time to percolate. And this is precisely how Derrida presents his relation to the future epoch for which he longs. But given his understanding of the process of deferral, Derrida should not be able to predict what a future epoch will look like; he cannot predict the deferred effect of his propaganda. He should not even be able to say that the future will be different; different compared to what? Everything is a Trace, everything is the deferred ramification of previous Writing. Everything is the same.

Still, Derrida is operating on a perfectly modern understanding of philosophy; philosophy makes, it does not discover. This is the unmistakable ramification of Derrida's teaching about Writing. But this is most assuredly not a novel idea, it is the insight of "modern" philosophy, more to the point of modern political philosophy. Hence, Derrida is just the deferred ramification of the Writing of modern political philosophy. Derrida's depiction of all of life as a text, the product of the ever-changing river *différance*, is likewise not novel. Derrida's novelty is to wed the modern notion that philosophy is a form of making to ancient Protagoreanism and Heracliteanism. It is a wedding of the newest and the oldest. Its novelty lies in a novel permutation of fundamentally finite possibilities; in short it lies in a form of repetition, a phenomenon that for Derrida should not exist.

While Derrida cannot predict specifically what the deferred results of his thought will be, in general terms we can construct an accurate picture of what he does *not* want politically as well as some of the broad brush strokes of what he does want. Derrida wishes to overcome the uniformity and destruction of difference in the modern world. And he wishes to overcome the technological domination and bureaucratic manipulation that supports the modern world. In putting a premium on the play of *différance,* and of the value of difference, Derridean politics hopes to foster individuality in the sense of the spontaneous individuality of an unconscious actor, not that of conscious, responsible, intentional subjects. Hence Derrida's politics would unhinge the notions of responsibility and accountability.

In a fashion that is simultaneously less substantive and poetic than the Nietzschean account, Derrida looks hopefully to the great creative wellsprings of the dark, the mysterious, the unconscious, the Dionysian. Standing in opposition to whatever stifles spontaneity, creativity and difference, Derrida stands opposed to the suffocating uniformity he sees in the liberal West, opposed to the fundamentally classless—dominated by a majority middle class—society, regimented in the service of economic rationality, supported by the organizational sophistication of modern bureaucratic institutions and the domination of nature performed by modern technological science. But his work should only be a propaedeutic, for he should not be able to predict what *différance* will disgorge. For reasons that are unclear, Derrida seems to predict that metaphysical structures will continue to repeatedly reproduce themselves. Hence ongoing deconstruction will be necessary in perpetuity. Yet occasionally he seems to offer the possibility that we may pass through a window of forgetting. If so, perhaps we need not be deconstructionists forever. Deconstructionism might be forgotten in the new epoch. (Consider Derrida's remarks on "active forgetfulness." [MP 136]) But it is always unclear how on his principles Derrida is entitled to any predictions one way or the other. Either there will be suffocating closure, or there can be renewed spontaneity, or endless repetition of the present, or a spontaneous novelty.

Derrida is far from being the first thinker to reflect on the uniformity of modern life. Tocqueville, for example, provides a more concrete depiction of the problems inherent in modern uniformity: e.g., majority tyranny, not the occlusion of *différance,* or the suffocation of unpredictable spontaneity. Tocqueville talks about greed, fear, patriotism, the family, the army, relations between the sexes, and so on. In short, he talks about what I have called phenomena that show themselves, the concrete sinew and ligature of political life, topics cast aside by Derrida as an unhygienic immersion in presence. Unlike Derrida, Tocqueville can talk about concrete alternatives and remedies— religion, voluntary associations, freedom of the press, federalism, lawyers, etc. Derrida's philosophy is politicized but it is not really political, and hence it is in danger of remaining destructive without the assurance that it can be constructive, it merely hopes that future spontaneous creativity will be constructive in some mysterious fashion. That is a very big gamble for very high stakes.

Beyond the great watershed that deconstructionism prepares, how can Derrida, given his understanding, know the future will be better than the present? What could a "better" future mean to a deconstructionist? What could it mean to any antagonist of the metaphysics of presence for whom there is no fixed human presence, no human nature that allows one to judge? It is striking that those who praise the spontaneity of life and the unconscious immersion therein are too fastidious to actually discuss concrete human existence and its variety of possibilities. Is that a manifestation of self-conscious prudence or personal hygiene?

How would a concrete political philosophy proceed? It would ask the questions: Is the hierarchical, bureaucratically rational organization of human beings good for them? Is the technological domination, manipulation and transformation of Nature, including human nature, advantageous? Are the increasingly uniform mass societies, dominated by bureaucracy and technology, advantageous? There is no doubt that when thus posed, it becomes incumbent upon the thinker to articulate a view of what is advantageous and disadvantageous, to look to the priority of the good. Such a discussion is impossible if there is no such thing as the essentially "human" that can in some fashion be grasped and articulated. A concrete discussion of the issues with which Derrida is clearly concerned would inevitably lead one into a variety of questions, but first and foremost, questions about the nature of man, of the soul, in short psychology. And it would lead on to a reflection on how man is integrated into the larger whole. It would lead to a holistic account of the five fundamental questions I posed above in chapter 2. As I will argue in the fourth section, in some fashion the issue of "nature" will have to be addressed and the "phenomenon of nature" recovered. I will return to this issue below.

Derrida's thought is far from trivial. He is clearly concerned with important issues. But he finesses enjoining those issues openly by proclaiming the need to avoid the metaphysics of presence. But that does not save him. Presence, or Nature, sneaks in through the back door repeatedly, which explains how Derrida knows what is better and worse for human beings and why it is justifiable to unleash the deconstructionist flood. His refusal to openly discuss these issues is because he is still ruled by the modern anti-Nature animus but is unwilling to confront it directly.

Derrida's work is a manifestation of the most intense form of modernity's stance toward Nature in all its permutations; e.g., the desire to conquer fortune, quit the state of nature, proclaim the realm of freedom and all the variations on a theme prior to him. Derrida does not so much stand in opposition to the ancient formulation of thought in Plato, which he sees reigning in all later thinkers, as he perfects the *telos* of modern political philosophy. Modern political philosophy could only end in the praise of unrestrained human creativity, call it spontaneity moved by *différance.* With no remaining phenomena to tie one's aspirations to, the necessary outcome of the modern hatred of Nature eventuates in either cacophony or silence. We have nothing to say, or we all talk at once because our voices are in principle equal. The outcome of Derrida's version of egalitarianism is to all talk at once. And yet he knows his Writing is superior to most.

The deconstructionist presumes to unpack the hidden premises that have reigned from Plato to Heidegger in a uniform progression unmarked by discontinuities. Consequently Derrida rejects the distinction between ancients and moderns and fails thereby to see the extent to which he remains a prisoner of modernity, the very modernity the ultimate political ramifications of which he wishes to transcend.

Derrida is the father of the high intellectual variants of multiculturalism and the politics of diversity. The first move is to dissolve the solidity of the mantra-like categories "race, class and gender," and with them nation, religion, and on and on. The second move is to remove from existence any ultimate signified that can allow discernment of the hierarchial quality of speaking and writing. The outcome is to put forth un-situated individuals, incapable of self-conscious action, whose speeches are in principle equal. The underlying moral imperative in those circumstances is that everyone should spontaneously express themselves simultaneously, with each voice equal. And again, everyone talks at once to help foster the Writing that puts in place the Traces that constitute existence for us. Of course, what is meant by "us" becomes very vague.

Deconstructionism is the attempt to play the part not of the courageous and forthright debater and fellow citizen, but of the surreptitious intellectual change agent qua aspiring leader who actually tyrannizes the process from off stage. For in the last analysis the dynamic of Derridean philosophy is not persuasion but power, to dominate the outcome. Like the politician the philosopher desires power. Derrida will not allow outcomes that he considers metaphysical, and that is what actual discourse among non-Derridean citizens would produce. Derrida can propose no difference between the philosopher and the tyrant, for he can see no difference between philosophy and politics. What we see in Derrida is the latest manifestation of the modern politicization of philosophy.

In Derrida we still see modern philosophy trying to recreate the world. But what the late modern philosopher now flees in horror is the world that is the deferred ramification of early modern thought. What we are seeing is not the end of the metaphysics of presence born of Plato, but the death throes of modern philosophy alienated from the concrete world it was responsible for creating. Yet the late modern remains caught in the modern web, with a deep anti-Nature animus and convinced that all of life is making and power. To transcend the world that was created on those premises, Derrida is forced to spin more and more vaporous webs of speech to take the place of that from which man has become alienated. He remains caught in this web because of the firm belief that to admit anything else is to unleash the most hideous forms of inequality, domination, racism, sexism and the general reign of brutality and ignorance because that is all that the metaphysics of presence can offer.

We, should mention here that pre-modern thought does not point toward mastery or domination, whether political, moral, technological or bureaucratic.

It points instead to a non-politicized philosophy and a moderate politics that would eschew domination precisely because of its understanding of the limits of the political. This cannot be construed to mean that anyone could believe that pre-modern thought is in any way immediately applicable to, or a panacea for our present ills. Nothing follows beyond the fact that modern thought, even in its most intense contemporary forms, has utterly failed to prove its superiority.

Derrida is left in a difficult position; reacting against modern universalism, and the modern version of rationalism, especially in its Hegelian form, he longs for *différance*, and that can only mean he longs for particularism. But all forms of particularism are metaphysical and there is an imperative to deconstruct them. He wants "difference" but it has to be a constantly reconstituting difference because Derrida claims that racism, sexism, nationalism and cultural chauvinism are the result of Western ethno-, logo- and phono-centrism. He assumes that following his deconstruction of the old forms of parochialism nothing comparable will be reproduced. But how can he know that?[13]

Derrida's response to late modernity is to posit the hegemony of unpredictable flux, and counsel us not to defend our own. A perfectly predictable concrete yield of such a dynamic is the political collapse of the West, global chaos, and eventual tyranny, not the universalization of creative spontaneity. No one could so believe in the formless fluidity of existence not to see that the yield of this teaching will be power politics, the politics of violence, the politics of the hatred of the West, with no competitor in the free-for-all more right than the next.

Nevertheless, having stated these reservations we must admit that Derrida confronts a number of issues central to the nature of our time, and his reflections point us to a variety of important and unavoidable questions. The study of philosophy and political philosophy has assumed an increasingly heavy reliance on the interpretation of texts. Philosophy has in a substantial manner become hermeneutical. It is as if the text has become the primary given, replacing the concrete lived experience of individuals in the world as the fundamental given. In one sense Derrida seems right; life has become a text for us. He seems correct in another sense; the hegemony of hermeneutics seems to point in the direction of something that is absent or lacking, at least something presently occluded for contemporary human beings. This fact cannot simply be dismissed and must be analyzed and questioned.

Derrida forces us as well to look anew at the relation between philosophic texts and concrete practice. Derrida forces us to wonder why some texts have staying power (in his terms why they take on meaning) while others do not. Is it not clear that the deepest and most penetrating texts always have the greatest influence? Even if we conclude that an author has grasped an essential truth that accounts for the influence of a text, Derrida forces us to raise a central question in the sociology of knowledge. Is it not true that pivotal philosophic texts have their primary influence through epigonal dilutions, i.e., through a process of "dissemination" that waters down the original teaching (i.e., writes a new text) and makes it possible for it to have a "deferred" impact?[14] Derrida would undoubtedly counter that we cannot make this distinction between primary text and "watered down" distillation, or secondary text. For all writing is a re-writing of a previous text. But Derrida is not really entitled to this rejoinder. How can one know that all writing is always re-writing if one does not know the original text and what it means in and of itself?[15]

These and other interesting questions aside, I have ended this section with an extended discussion of Derrida because despite being designated a postmodern author I believe he represents the latest extension of modern thought. And I believe he represents the dissolution of modern thought. Modernity set out to transform the world. I have tried to show in Machiavelli, and it is even easier to show in Descartes, that this understanding rests on an anti-Nature animus and a constructivist understanding of philosophy. That undertaking has been highly successful. But what has occurred is that the constructions that have been projected unto the world have been so successful that the world around us increasingly bears only the imprint of those constructions. Hence wherever we look, in effect, we see only ourselves.

Our world no longer seems self-standing. We have increasingly lost faith in the value of those constructions and even in our ability to continue to project them in self-conscious and predictable ways. This comes when the world takes on an increasingly abstract and vaporous quality. There seems to be little left that presents itself, no world, no phenomena. My suggestion is that while this may not have been the necessary and **inevitable** *telos* of modernity, it is at this point probably the **irreversible** outcome of modernity; and it is an untenable outcome. Derrida is representative of the dead end and closure of modernity in a vaporous world that cannot take its bearings. There may be no further uniquely modern moves. I have argued that constructivism is of the essence of modernity and that deconstructivism is nothing but constructivism by another name. This leads me to conclude that at this point there is no possibility of going back to any previous moments of modernity and trying to strike off in different directions. There is no point within modernity that is not constructivist. I offer as an alternative what I have been putting forth as phenomenology and political philosophy. I will explore the ramifications of this distinction in the following sections.

NOTES

1. The reader is directed to two recent complementary works on Derrida that came out after the original essay upon which this chapter is based was completed. The first is Stanley Rosen's *Hermeneutics as Politics* (New York: Oxford University Press,

1987). Chapter 2, "Platonic Reconstruction," deals specifically with Derrida, in a fashion that supplements the present essay, going beyond it in the pursuit of numerous important philosophical issues. It is of particular value. Also valuable is Catherine Zuckert's *Postmodern Platos* (Chicago: University of Chicago Press, 1996), which has a chapter on Derrida.

2. Ultimately, I see this "turn" from early to late as primarily rhetorical, conditioned by Heidegger's need to get reinstated after the War. I develop this thesis at length in *Martin Heidegger: Paths Taken, Paths Opened* (Lanham: Rowman & Littlefield, 2007).

3. Jacques Derrida, *Speech and Phenomena: And Other Essays on Husserl's Theory of Signs.* trans. by David B. Allison (Evanston: Northwestern University Press, 1973). While Derrida was extraordinarily prolific in the number of books he penned, his "philosophy" came forth in four key texts. Very little in the way of principle changed thereafter. In English translation, see *Of Grammatology*, trans. by Gayatri Chakravorty Spivak (Baltimore: The Johns Hopkins University Press, 1976), cited in this text as OG with a page number; *Margins of Philosophy*, trans. by Alan Bass (Chicago: The University of Chicago Press, 1978), cited as MP; *Writing and Difference*, trans. by Alan Bass (Chicago: The University of Chicago Press, 1978), cited as WD; *Dissemination*, trans. by Barbara Johnson (Chicago: The University of Chicago Press, 1981), cited as DIS.

4. Strictly speaking, how could anyone with Derrida's doctrine prove anything in any hard sense? Since "proof" in any apodictic fashion is out of the question, one must understand that Derrida's undertaking is based entirely on rhetoric. As rhetorical, how can it not be self-conscious? But Derrida is publicly as great an opponent of self-consciousness as Nietzsche and Heidegger. The last great proponent of self-consciousness was Hegel.

5. The only question is, how does one see it and designate it as thrownness without some form of transcendence? Heidegger tries to deal with this question in his discussion of Being-Toward-Death. I do not think Derrida can deal with it, at least not in a consistent fashion.

6. Again, how does one know it is changing except from the vantage point of something that doesn't change? Derrida keeps sneaking in these sleights of hand throughout his corpus. Perhaps it is rhetorically clever, but it is certainly inconsistent to rely on premises to which one is not entitled on the basis of one's teaching.

7. At this point, despite the veritable library that Derrida produced, we have more or less encapsulated the relatively simple thought that underlies all of Derrida's abstract and jargon prone efforts.

8. See Jacques Derrida, *Positions*, trans. by Alan Bass (Chicago: The University of Chicago Press, 1981), cited as POS. With notions like "absolute danger" and "monstrosity," Derrida appeals to a fundamental phenomenal given that has a status almost identical to Heideggerian "moods." As such, Derrida bases himself on what is, after all, a shared, pre-theoretical experience that has presence. This is precisely a reliance on Heideggerian "phenomena" or what Strauss will call everything from "natural consciousness" to "pre-theoretical experience" to "pre-scientific awareness." Once again

Derrida sneaks something in the back door to which he is not entitled on the basis of his teaching.

9. See one of Derrida's last works where he paradoxically associates himself with Marxist longings: *Specters of Marx: The State of Debt, the Work of Mourning, and the New International*, trans. by Peggy Kamuf (New York: Routledge, 1994). How Derrida is entitled to be an heir to these longings is not clear.

10. Derrida looks to replacing justice with a-political friendship. See *Politics of Friendship* (London: Verso, 1997).

11. See Jacques Derrida, *Of Spirit: Heidegger and the Question*, trans. by Geoffrey Bennington and Rachel Bowlby (Chicago: The University of Chicago Press, 1989).

12. For a more complete response see Rosen and Zuckert cited above in note 1.

13. Jacques Derrida, *The Postcard: From Socrates to Freud and Beyond*, trans. by Alan Bass (Chicago: The University of Chicago Press, 1987), p. 21. An older form of Western thought guarded against the worst forms of parochialism with the belief that there is an essence as either rational or as the children of God shared by all human beings. There is a brotherhood and sisterhood of essential selves. In jettisoning those pre-modern notions, condemned as "onto-theology," how can Derrida assure himself that the new form of difference will not be despicable and cruel, i.e., precisely what he claims he wishes to transcend?

14. Let us give an example. Granting, as Derrida would not, that an author, say Plato, had a conscious intention and a serious student could recover that intention, is it not true that those who have misunderstood or transformed Plato are the ones who have had the greatest effect? To be provocative, is it not Plato the ontologist who allegedly actually believes in the doctrine of the ideas, who has had the public effect throughout History? Does this mean that Plato's effect has been the result of a mistake? Is it true that the public meaning of a text is more important than the intention of the author, which is available perhaps only to a private few? Is it not true therefore that the politicization or at least vulgarization of texts is inevitable? Is it true that the effect of the most serious authors is in fact always deferred, happening long after the author is in a position to defend it? The Nietzsche who could publish almost nothing in his lifetime, and "disseminate" even less, is a case in point. Is it true that what we would call the secondary literature inserts itself into the primary text and in effect becomes the text? Is the effect of the secondary literature the one that has the primary public effect?

15. Of course these questions raise more issues for someone like me who thinks the original text can be fathomed than it does for Derrida. Even if one does admit the distinction between primary text and secondary literature, is it true that how one is read is more important than what was consciously intended? This would be the same as saying that the history of Philosophy is the history of mistakes. Would we be forced to conclude that History has been an accident? Even granting the existence of a Natural substratum to existence, thought clearly overlays that substratum and has its effects. Nature provides no total immunization against the practical ramifications of thought. We can raise one final question that necessarily follows. Is it possible that these issues only arise in, and are only pertinent to, the age of mass societies? We live

in the fairly recent and unique age of the universal, public dissemination of all speech and knowledge. Texts are more immune to being rewritten when they are not publicly disseminated. The necessary foundation for the universal public dissemination of all knowledge is the modern bureaucratic and technological sophistication that makes mass equality possible.

Part Two

LEO STRAUSS AND THE TRADITION; AN ENGAGEMENT

Preface to Part 2:
Remembrance and Tradition

We always stand between past and future. We can do so consciously or inarticulately. And while we always must open ourselves to the concrete moral and political phenomena of our time, we also always stand within a tradition that we did not will and cannot will away. It is precisely these features of "thrownness" that modernity tried to transcend through positing an ego that stands nowhere and wills its world from out of nothing. That neither the proto-moderns, nor anyone who followed, in fact achieved anything resembling this desired immaculate foundation is beside the point. They put in motion a series of moves that culminated in a late modernity that poses the greatest threat to the Tradition since its inception. We are threatened with a thoroughgoing forgetting and rootlessness.

My argument is that unavoidably political philosophy must adopt the stance of "ecstatic temporality" holding together past, present and future. Put another way, the political philosopher must always stand in the present, lovingly remembering the past, and from out of that past open possible futures by way of crafting the holistic account I detailed in the last section. Given my own personal thrownness, access to the tradition of political philosophy was initially through the work of Leo Strauss and in many ways has continued to progress through an ongoing confrontation with his thought. As quoted previously, Strauss once observed that what was needed was a loving reinterpretation of the tradition. Hence his corpus includes the *Andenken* or Remembrance that I see as necessary and as a model for where we must always begin. But I do not see that Strauss opened anything in the way of publicly shared future possibilities.

Over time I have come to question the one thing that Strauss seems to be projecting for the future—a renewed privacy and solitude for a form of autonomous theoretical philosophy. I have come to question Strauss's understanding of proto-philosophy as a **theoretical** contemplation of the "first things." Likewise I have come to question his conceptualization of political philosophy as either a politic defense of private, theoretical philosophy or as but a subsidiary branch of proto-philosophy more generally. I argue that political philosophy as I present it is proto-philosophy and it cannot be reduced to just a contemplation of first things, a subsidiary activity, or mere politic esotericism. None of those understandings will get us to the future. Further, the poetic element that I see as a necessary part of political philosophy, and so clearly a part of Platonic political philosophy, as I will try to present it in the next section, is missing in the work of Strauss.

Finally, I have come to reject Strauss's association of pre-theoretical phenomena with the "natural experience" that Strauss presents as displayed only at the beginnings. I argue that the "phenomena" in the present are in fact always pre-theoretical and that it is only in the present that we will be able to find the phenomenon "nature." It is to present phenomena that we must always turn as our point of departure. Our task is to strip away the theoretical impediments to the phenomena showing themselves, not go back to some allegedly primordial showing of the phenomena.

My own teacher, Joseph Cropsey, also painstakingly reflected on the Tradition, as did his mentor, Strauss. In the process he also reflected on Strauss's teaching. That reflection was so dignified, and quiet, that most have missed the radical nature of the questioning Cropsey produced. In a number of ways I am closer to Cropsey than Strauss. In other ways I have diverged. As I have already tried to develop, I believe the origin of the tradition of political philosophy, and its essential exemplar, is to be found in the Platonic correction of Socratism, a correction quickly reversed by Aristotle. That understanding had room for what Cropsey called "caring." And that caring requires an element of the poetic, a poetry wed to the phenomena, with which Strauss cannot deal.

As I mentioned above, and will try to demonstrate in the next section, I see the breaks between Socrates and Plato, and between Plato and Aristotle, as in many ways greater than later breaks like that of proto-modernity breaking with medieval thought. Unlike Pippin and Cropsey I do not see the break between proto-modernity and what Strauss called the "second wave" of modernity as crucial. I am much closer to Strauss's "three wave" argument. Cropsey had already seen that there were breaks in the tradition that were greater than the ancients-moderns break. I see a bigger theoretical break between Plato and Aristotle, and between the ancients and moderns, than Cropsey who, for example, sees a closeness between Aristotle and Hobbes that does not, in Cropsey's understanding exist between Hobbes and medieval thought where there is a more radical break.

In my terminology, the break that occurred at the beginning of modernity can be seen as the rise of a unique Constructivism, a break from phenomenology, as I posed that distinction in part 1. I see that Constructivism as essential to modernity and working itself out in increasingly destructive fashion. This understanding leads me to be less sympathetic to proto-modernity than Cropsey, even though I am willing to accept that there is a certain wisdom of the moderns. I also see more available resources in the philosophical post-modernity of Nietzsche and Heidegger than Cropsey. Cropsey sees a radical break between proto-modernity and late modernity with Nietzsche and Heidegger as primarily late moderns. I have an openness to authors like Nietzsche and Heidegger that is closer to Strauss who, I will argue in the chapters below, drew important themes and major bearings from those two authors.

These dialectical distinctions about the nature of the past tradition emerge in the essays that follow in this section. Distinctions like the ones that emerge in the forthcoming essays condition my understanding that theoretically essential modernity is at an end but that we are not without resources to transcend it. But it must be transcended with an eye to the future, not with an eye to going back to the past, except to get a running start.

But the fashion in which Strauss painstakingly engaged the tradition, and Cropsey engaged the tradition and the thought of Strauss, is for me the model of that necessary component of *Andenken* or Remembrance that is part of architectonic, holistic political philosophy as I understand it. I present this questioning of the past tradition as a model of the relation to the past that is necessary as the only healthy basis for opening out the future in a non-constructivist fashion. My own thinking emerges from a dialectical confrontation with those who went immediately before me and who opened the door to the tradition for me. One can but hope to become one link in that ongoing chain no matter how small or weak the link may be. In that way one may hope to be a path to the Tradition for someone better who will come in the future. In at least that small way one can stand in the present and link past and future.

Chapter Seven

Who Was Leo Strauss?

Leo Strauss remains an enigmatic and controversial figure. Commentators, both friendly and hostile, have variously found the pivot point of Strauss's thought in a desired return to Greek thought—in some permutations complete with the elitism of the rule of philosopher-kings; or in a conservative defense of modern, liberal democracy, especially against Marxist communism; or in a furtive, esoteric, historicist, Nietzschean nihilism hidden behind a clever, rhetorical public teaching on the one hand; or in a dogmatic, hierarchical, inegalitarian understanding of unchanging Nature on the other; in the reflections of a fundamentally Jewish thinker; or in a Socratic skepticism; and on and on.

Since his death Strauss has even been attacked in the popular press, an odd phenomenon for a man who seldom declaimed in public and, despite a sense of professional obligation to his university and his students, clearly preferred the withdrawn, quiet, private, contemplative life. It would be difficult to find a man less likely to want to be a philosopher-king, or to want to have any public persona whatsoever. That Strauss has become so controversial has to be traced ultimately to the untimely nature of his thinking, and his willingness to question openly the philosophical orthodoxies of his time. But to an equal extent, the controversies surrounding Strauss must be traced to the idiosyncrasies of unpredictable changes in moral, cultural, and political fashions. Because of the unpredictable nature of such fashions, how Strauss' influence will evolve in the future is difficult to predict.

Leo Strauss was born in Kirchhain, Hessen, Germany, in 1899. He received a traditional gymnasium education. He reports that as a young man he read and re-read the works of Nietzsche. He was also much attracted to Zionism. After serving in the German army during World War I, he returned to study philosophy, mathematics, and natural science at the universities of Marburg,

Frankfurt, Berlin, and Hamburg. Upon completing his formal education, he was a researcher in the reform institute for Jewish studies in Berlin, where he examined seventeenth century biblical criticism, especially that of Spinoza. From these studies came Strauss' first major work, *Spinoza's Critique of Religion.* After completing his doctorate, Strauss sat in on the courses offered by the phenomenologist Edmund Husserl (1859–1938), who was teaching at Freiburg. Husserl was famous for the philosophical injunction to get "to the things themselves," a premise that, in altered form, Strauss himself adopted. It was at Freiburg that Strauss also sat in on the courses of Husserl's assistant, Martin Heidegger (1889–1976), whose influence on Strauss was far greater than is usually seen. Heidegger, like Nietzsche, had launched a theoretical critique of the origins of late-modern nihilism. In a parallel fashion, Strauss was much preoccupied with the "Crisis of the West."

In 1932 Strauss left Germany to avoid Nazi oppression, returning thereafter for only a brief period. After two years in France on a Rockefeller Foundation fellowship, and four lean years in England, he came to the United States in 1938, where he remained until his death in 1973. Between 1949 and 1968 Strauss taught political philosophy at the University of Chicago; there he wrote an impressive number of terse and intensely erudite books and articles about such authors as Aristophanes, Xenophon, Plato, Aristotle, Farabi, Maimonides, Machiavelli, Hobbes, Spinoza, Locke, Nietzsche, and Husserl. Even a cursory attempt to confront these works presents one with themes that lie far from contemporary public debates: the relation between Reason and Revelation, the battle between the ancients and the moderns, the nature of esoteric philosophic writing, the origins of late-modern historicism. It is an odd legacy for such a man to have somehow become taken as the arch-enemy of democracy and be made responsible for controversial positions on everything from multiculturalism to Supreme Court nominations to debates about social justice and American foreign policy.

It is always dangerous to try to deduce too much from the origins and personal history of a thinker. In the classic model of philosophy, especially as Strauss understood it, the thinker seeks to stand outside his place and time, not in order to negate the world he lives in but to gain the widest possible perspective on it. Strauss strove for that detachment. But he hardly could have avoided being influenced by his experience as a German Jew, born to an orthodox family. From the very beginning, Leo Strauss was a profound, fervent supporter of liberal democracy as the best political dispensation available in the modern world. He had seen the inadequacies of other modern regimes, such as fascism, at first hand, and he viewed communism as straightforward tyranny.

Strauss was especially impressed with the American variant of liberal democracy and studied its history, its Constitution, and the writings of its founders and statesmen. While he never wrote on these subjects, he saw a rare genius in the **practice** of American political life. But his scholarly work on modern political philosophy forced him to conclude that the modern **philosophical** premises that supported liberal democracy were inadequate; and if not transcended, they would weaken attachment to a fundamentally just and decent way of life. Beginning with his work on Hobbes—*The Political Philosophy of Hobbes,* completed while he was still in England—and proceeding through his studies of Locke and Machiavelli, as well as in his pivotal *Natural Right and History,* Strauss tried to understand the essence of modern political philosophy and how it could lead to such radically different offspring as liberal democracy, Fascism, and Marxist communism. Eventually Strauss was led back to Greek thought in hopes of finding an alternative to the nihilism he saw as implicit in modern thought. This led to the attempt to give life back to the confrontation between the ancients and the moderns. It is by addressing the major philosophical themes that occupied Strauss's scholarly efforts that his influence can be confronted at the deepest and least accidental level.

Strauss's scholarly work initially tried to confront the nihilism of what he would eventually call the "third wave of modernity" by addressing itself to that component of Nietzsche's claim that "God is dead" which implied that belief in a transcendent God and His revelations had become impossible for future humanity. In *Spinoza's Critique of Religion,* Strauss tried to show that none of the modern critiques of the possibility of revealed religion was definitive. Thus the possibility of taking revealed religion and its wisdom seriously remained open. From Spinoza, Strauss was led to the great medieval Jewish thinker Moses Maimonides (1135–1204), whom Spinoza had taken as one of his major opponents. It was from Maimonides that Strauss learned about the esoteric or secret writing that became one of his major scholarly themes. Thereafter, he never left behind the question of the relation between Reason and Revelation, or "Athens and Jerusalem."

In the face of late-modern irrationalism, which he saw as the inevitable outcome of **modern** rationalism, Strauss also tried to reconsider the other central component of Western civilization, Greek rationalism. He repeatedly made clear that the heart and soul of Western civilization was to be found in the irresolvable tension between Revelation and Rationalism. Strauss's argument was that the modern philosophical attacks on classical Reason and Revelation were not conclusive; he never claimed much more certainty than that. Strauss hoped to reopen questions that had been presumed conclusively closed. He did not presume to substitute a new closure for that openness. Despite his discussions of Natural Right and Natural Law, Strauss never asserted the existence of rigid moral absolutes. It is especially paradoxical, therefore, that Strauss should be seen as a dogmatic partisan.

Strauss did make clear, however, that in his mind the viability of Western civilization—with Western liberal democracy being one of its central components—rested on the ever-renewed reinvigoration of the West's distinctive tension between Reason and Revelation. Both were under assault in his time. Strauss was equally clear that the tension could never be resolved in favor of either Reason or Revelation. In general terms, Strauss encouraged an openness to this tension, not dogmatism or irrationalism—or what comes close to the same thing as irrationalism, secret writing and esoteric misdirection.

Modern philosophy and modern political philosophy had attempted to transcend both Greek rationalism and biblical Revelation. Strauss invested a major part of his scholarly life in trying to understand the nature of the break modernity attempted. He eventually concluded that the primary change that took place at the dawn of modernity was a moral change—one that rested on a transformed conception of the good for mankind. From the beginning, and this could be seen clearly in Machiavelli, the moderns tried to "lower the sights." Rather than aim at the grand and inspiring virtues that pre-modern thought—in both its Greek and biblical variants—took as the appropriate end of political action, the moderns were prepared to emancipate and channel the spontaneously occurring passions and emotions, among them fear, ambition, narrow self-interest and greed. The hope was that a more accessible and egalitarian goal could be substituted for the grand aims of the pre-moderns, which ultimately were accessible only to a few.

The moderns came to see comfort, affluence, and the avoidance of death as fundamental to the good life, secured by a new science that saw its end not as perfecting the rational faculty by striving for understanding but as gaining power over nature. The good life, they claimed, could be actualized for all in a prosperous society supported by modern science. The pre-moderns rejected, before the fact, this idea of the good because they saw human desires as unlimited. Hence prosperity alone would not make human beings happy; it would merely lead to the invention of new desires, an endless round whereby human beings would become moral slaves. Further, the mere possession of scientific power, without knowledge of ends other than vulgar hedonism, could never be a simple good. In fact, such power could transform itself into a threat to our very humanity. The reduction of humanity to desirous slaves armed with a powerful new science pointed toward a never before seen tyranny rather than emancipation—a conclusion reached by many in the twentieth century on both the right and the left.

Less visibly, Strauss also confronted the philosophical component of modernity posited by Descartes. To lay the foundation for the new science that could master nature, Cartesian Idealism tried to abstract from the data of the senses and ground itself in the thinking self, or the abstract ego. From the beginning, the moderns doubted the reliability of the data of the senses as well as the veracity of common sense or "the way things appear for all"—what Strauss came to call the natural, pre-theoretical, or pre-scientific articulation of things. It was necessary for the moderns, therefore, to substitute conscious theoretical constructions for the natural awareness present to all in everyday life. Much of Strauss's scholarly labors went into an attempt to transcend this modern "constructivism" and find a way back to what he believed was the natural articulation of reality.

For Strauss, modern political philosophy had by stages moved from a more or less benign beginning to a final intensification and radicalization in late modernity. An initial peak was reached in Lockean liberal democracy, which represented the culmination of the "first wave" of modernity. But with the thought of Rousseau, modern political philosophy took a more radical turn and Strauss's "second wave" was initiated. The first wave of modernity still believed in the existence of a fixed human nature that had to be accommodated because it could not be transcended. It saw quitting the natural condition as good, but nature still remained as a guide or limit for human affairs. Strauss's second wave posited the malleability, changeability, and historicality of human existence. In doing so, Rousseau initiated an understanding that, after passing through Kant, culminated in Hegel's depiction of an inevitable movement of history that brought with it an inevitable transformation of man and of the natural environment. This "progressive" understanding—shared by Marx—saw human history as linear, inevitable, and moving from lower to higher stages.

With the commencement of Strauss's "third wave" of modernity, faith in the changeability and historicality of human existence remained but was now stripped of any linearity, necessity, or progressivity. This was the wave initiated by Friedrich Nietzsche. With Nietzsche, the problem Strauss designated "historicism" raised its head. Nietzsche asserted that all knowledge—especially of good and evil—was dependent upon the altogether arbitrary historical perspective into which one was thrown. And all perspectives were transitory. With Nietzsche, history came to be accidental in its unfolding, if not regressive and nihilistic.

All past understandings of reality came to be seen as merely human constructions, albeit unconscious ones. But with the insight that all past conceptions of reality were merely human constructions came the possibility that in the future those constructions could be consciously willed. The third wave brought with it the age of what Nietzsche called the politics of the Will-to-Power—actually competing wills to power with no possible arbiter other than force more or less overtly deployed. Everyone would compete to posit his personal construction of reality—a fundamental premise that underlies many contemporary intellectual phenomena.

Malleable man himself could now be consciously transformed. But there was no guidance for this transformation other than an entirely arbitrary contest of wills, eventually won by the momentarily strongest. With this premise, Strauss believed that Nietzsche opened the door to Heidegger's even more thoroughgoing historicism, where faith in the self-conscious will waned, to be replaced by the hegemony of the blind, overpowering fate and destiny of the nihilism of universal, global, technological civilization. And after Heidegger, Strauss predicted that we would see the spectacle of even more radical relativisms—which would have been Strauss's understanding of everything from deconstructionism to various forms of feminism.[1]

According to Strauss, the inevitable outcome of modern thought was a humanity that no longer believed in Divine Revelation, eternal Nature, or inevitable History as providing any standards for judgment. In such an intellectual environment, Strauss believed that liberal democracy, despite all its practical decency, would come to be seen as just one moral and political dispensation among many, and theoretically no better than its alternatives. Strauss believed that this would inevitably sap the commitment to liberal democracy that was needed in the face of the immoderate political dispensations that were the result of the second and third waves of modernity—Communism and Fascism respectively.

Strauss dedicated his mature scholarly efforts to trying to find a non-historicist alternative that could help provide the basis for a defense for liberal democracy that he believed could not be found within modern thought. In this search he turned to a painstaking attempt to understand what he saw as the non-historicist Greek authors at the origins of the Western philosophic tradition in hopes that they would provide insights into how to transcend our late-modern impasse. This led to Strauss's most mature works on Thucydides, Aristophanes, Xenophon, Plato, Socrates, and Aristotle.

Strauss had discovered the idea of esoteric writing in his studies of Maimonides, so that when he went back to the Greeks to find an alternative to late-modern irrationalism, he arrived at a very novel reading of Plato—in his mind a more authentic understanding of Plato than that contained in conventional, Anglo-American scholarship. When reflecting on the esoteric writing style of Plato, Strauss reached a slightly different conclusion than in his studies of Maimonides. Instead of concentrating on the confrontation between philosophy and revealed religion, Plato dealt with the tension between open philosophical inquiry and the needs of a closed political community. Political communities, according to Strauss's Plato, were always closed and particular and could not withstand the glare of the universal truth, which was the object of philosophy. Political communities were caves; philosophers longed to transcend the cave. This unavoidable tension between political life and philosophy—after all, the Athenians had condemned Socrates to death—led Plato to use the dialogue form, embellished by beautiful myths, as his distinctive mode of speech.

Similarly, Strauss applied his understanding of esoteric writing to the texts of Farabi (873–950), the Islamic medieval philosopher par excellence. Strauss's Farabi also saw the need to adopt an esoteric mode of speech and engage in secret writing. He used yet another set of devices to confront his special environment. Strauss's conclusion seems to have been that different environments required the use of different literary devices, which were needed to accomplish the same end of simultaneously speaking to different audiences while conveying more than one message—but not for the sake of conveying the identical message.

Yet it was the Greek authors who remained central for Strauss. When the Greek philosophers were read carefully, Strauss thought that they offered a non-historicist alternative to the nihilism encountered by late-modern thought. The moderns had constructed an abstract relation to life; Strauss believed that the ancient Greeks were still in contact with a rich, concrete, and "natural" understanding of life.[2] Strauss saw in the Socratic dialectical method—which begins from concrete questions and answers—the only way of approaching that concrete richness of life without destroying it. Hence much of Strauss's later scholarly work centered on an attempt to understand Socrates and what his new philosophic method represented, approached not only from the perspective of Plato, but through the eyes of such contemporaries as Aristophanes and Xenophon.

For Strauss, the Platonic dialogues were not primarily ontological or metaphysical documents but rich articulations about the things that interest human beings most, including the nature of the best life and the best regime, the meaning of virtue, the possibility of happiness. In the Platonic dialogues, one finds the presentation of various distinctive kinds of lives, all of which present themselves as the best—the private life of virtue, the public life of the statesman or sophist, the life of philosophy, the life devoted to physical pleasure, and so on. Since there were different political communities, political life also came to light as a debate between different regimes, each pursuing a different conception of the good. In Strauss's understanding, nature articulates itself through different human beings with different aspirations, and through different regimes that preference different ends. Within these natural limits, life presents **itself**—without the imposition of willed human constructions. The modern attempt to transcend these limits using constructivist interventions ultimately led to an alienated and nihilistic life within a very abstract world. Strauss concluded that the ancient Greeks demonstrated that there was an unchanging, natural articulation of reality that could be recovered. When this task of recovery was accomplished, it would become apparent that there were always a number of unchanging givens that could nonetheless be ordered in a variety of ways. **It was the diverse, natural, human possibilities, not a specific ordering of those possibilities, that Strauss wanted to recover.**

According to Strauss, the nature of the best regime depends on the circumstances. Strauss believed that the Greeks had adequately articulated the essence of our various natural perceptions and aspirations. They did not necessarily offer the best articulation of all possibilities, an issue that cannot be addressed except in light of present circumstances. What is always needed is flexibility; there is no one best regime everywhere and always, but there are natural possibilities that should always be allowed to manifest themselves. Hence, in *Natural Right and History,* Strauss tried to differentiate his understanding of a flexible "Natural Right" teaching from the more dogmatic and rigid "Natural Law" teachings of such philosophers as Aquinas and Hobbes.

Strauss argued for the need to recover a Socratic, dialectical understanding of philosophy, which when turned loose on a transformed modern world—transformed, as Strauss argued repeatedly, by the successes of modern political philosophy—might yield different articulations than those reached by previous thinkers.

> We cannot reasonably expect that a fresh understanding of classical political philosophy will supply us with recipes for today's use. For the relative success of modern political philosophy has brought into being a kind of society wholly unknown to the classics, a kind of society to which the classical principles as stated and elaborated by the classics are not immediately applicable. Only we living today can possibly find a solution to the problems of today. But an adequate understanding of the principles as elaborated by the classics may be the indispensable *starting point* for an adequate analysis, to be achieved by us, of present-day society in its peculiar character, and for the wise application, to be achieved by us, of these principles to our tasks.[3]

Strauss believed that there was a natural fabric to human existence, even though late-modern human beings had become alienated from it. But that natural articulation of reality was not always operative or immediately available at all times. This understanding represented Strauss's more concrete manifestation of the Heideggerian thought contained in the idea of "the withdrawal of Being." Strauss was explicit that late-modern life, was *contra naturum*. His was a scholarly attempt to open a path to a recovery of what had become substantially absent for his contemporaries. This experience of absence was one that Strauss ironically shared with a diverse group of thinkers that included not only Heidegger but many of Heidegger's descendants down to Jacques Derrida, the father of deconstructionism. But Strauss's response was far more concrete.

Strauss first became controversial among academics in the 1950s as part of his critique of the then dominant behavioralism in the social sciences, especially as it manifested itself in academic political science, which, technically, was Strauss's departmental home. Behavioralist political science began from the modern Cartesian premise that in order to understand political life it was necessary to project consciously constructed, "scientific" categories in place of the categories that arise in the marketplace of everyday, commonsense discussion. Strauss tried to show—especially in his essay "Epilogue"—that the behavioralist attempt to substitute an "objective," scientific account of reality for the one embedded in common sense was a mistake. Far from arriving at an understanding that was deeper and more profound, this undertaking was trivial, reductionist and distorting. It could never arrive at the scientific detachment and objectivity it desired, because it always began by taking for granted commonsense, pre-theoretical presuppositions from which it could never emancipate itself.

This was the basis of Strauss's critique of the dominant fact-value dichotomy. There are no such things as value-free facts. Facts first present themselves to us as part of our acting, doing, and making, which are always evaluative. Without this evaluative, commonsense criteria of relevance embedded in our shared experience, no science could ever judge the difference between the relevant and the trivial.

According to Strauss, our primary, natural relation to life is always determined by the regime in which we live and by our shared understandings of the just, the noble, and the good—especially as those principles are articulated in constitutions, public documents, and the speeches of great statesmen. This natural world is better understood by citizens and statesmen than it is by detached scientific observers. Strauss concluded that, far from being superior to the older political science that emanated from Aristotle and included the traditional political philosophers, the new political science was in fact not only trivial, but deluded about its own foundations and ultimately incapable of clarity. All it could do was undermine the pre-scientific perspective shared by citizens and that was totally destructive of democracy.

With these arguments, Strauss first came to be seen as a conservative. Behavioralist political science was almost exclusively the preserve of a liberal academic establishment. It was a method by which all substantive moral debates could be put aside in favor of discussing the means to ends that were already built into the political system. It represented a surreptitious way of defending a moral position without having to do so substantively. Having presupposed one's understanding of the best life and the best regime—the modern progressivist understanding—one tried to limit debate to allegedly factual observations. It is no small irony that, after Strauss had made his critique of behavioralism, a similar critique was made by the New Left, which was that behavioralist political science operated under a hidden "conservative" agenda. This is only one among many areas where Strauss made common cause with thinkers customarily seen to be of the left.

According to Strauss, the real danger of behavioralist political science was that it shielded itself from the truly fundamental questions of the day. For those who lived in the West, especially after World War II, everyday political reality was determined by the confrontation between liberal democracy and Marxist despotism. Only by an abstraction that led in the direction of less rather than more clarity could one conclude, as behavioralist political science did, that the difference between democracy and totalitarianism was a difference between quantums of coercion, or a difference in the nature of the group interactions that determined policy.

Despite his profound respect for Heidegger's philosophical mind, Strauss ultimately offered a criticism of his thought similar to that which he made of behavioralism. Heidegger had reached the conclusion that the liberal democratic West and the Marxist communist East—"Washington and Moscow"—were "metaphysically equal." For Strauss, this abstract conclusion was an affront to what was obvious—the clear superiority of living in a liberal democracy rather than a Marxist despotism. According to Strauss, our natural, pre-theoretical, commonsense relation to reality had to be defended and its primacy had to be justified and taken seriously. If there is one key that unlocks Strauss's difficult corpus, it is to be found in his attempt to show the priority of a very diverse, natural, pre-theoretical articulation of reality. And for Strauss that always meant the fundamentally political and moral way in which reality is revealed to all.

By contrast, in Strauss's view of Heidegger, our pre-theoretical relation to reality is determined by a series of fated worldviews that come and go mysteriously and unpredictably. For Strauss, this was pure relativism. Despite his respect for Heidegger's philosophical depth, Heidegger remained for Strauss the ultimate historicist. Just as he had tried to confront the relativism of the fact-value dichotomy of social science behavioralism, Strauss tried to confront the historicism that he saw as the ultimate and inevitable outcome of modern thought. But in many ways, his confrontation with historicism was far more provisional.

First, Strauss tried to show how historicism evolved necessarily from previous moments in modern thought. While the first and second waves of modernity were less virulent, they led, unavoidably, to the third historicist moment, and so consequently it was not feasible to simply go back to one of the prior moments of modern thought. Strauss further tried to show that on its own terms historicism had not made a case for its superiority to non-historicist thought. It need not, therefore, be taken as the dogmatic given that it had become for so many of Strauss's contemporaries—a veritable legion since his death.

But Strauss never presumed to have simply transcended historicism; there remain historicist components in Strauss's thought. For example, he never gives any simple invocation of a nature that is **always** operative. For Strauss, nature does not operate as simple mechanical causality, and it is never immediately available—in the manner of the color green—without study. In fact, there are ages like our own during which nature is occluded and, thereby, to a significant extent inoperative. This is why it was so important for Strauss to try to recover an understanding of the Greek writers who remained in closer touch with nature than the late moderns. This was the basis of Strauss's veneration of the "Great Books." They provide access to experiences that have been lost as well as to a serious debate about the alternate conclusions regarding the nature of the best life, alternatives that had ceased to be part of present debates.

While not being a simple ahistoricist, Strauss nevertheless saw radical historicism as the greatest problem confronting contemporary humanity. It constituted what he meant by the "Crisis of the West." According to Strauss, that crisis consisted of the West no longer being able to take itself and its aspirations seriously. Transcending radical historicism was for Strauss the highest task, but that could not be done by rhetoric, mythmaking, or esoteric misdirection—as many of Strauss's detractors claim was his intention. Historicism could only be transcended by engaging in the painstaking scholarly reconstructions that could help us give concrete articulation to the vague intimations with which we are left. Strauss may have been wrong in his perception of our time and of what was required to transcend it, but he never fell back on the abject banality of believing that late modernity could be overcome by what amounted to clever lies.

Like so many twentieth century thinkers, Leo Strauss's critique of modernity remains far clearer and more telling than the alternative he offers. In the last analysis, I believe Strauss has no concrete recipes to offer. His detractors, and some of his sympathizers, have constructed far more concrete positions for him than he himself would have been willing to accept. But it is around issues concerning the place of religion in Strauss's teaching and his rediscovery of esoteric or secret writing that most of the wilder and more polemical claims brought against him can be found—down to the accusations that

Strauss ultimately is an atheist who nonetheless thought it was necessary for the non-philosophic to be told various religious fictions by an elite to keep them in line. Even some of Strauss's students seem to have arrived at a similar point that stresses the central importance of **civil** religion, which says more about his students than about Strauss.

Further, many have concluded—detractors and admirers alike—that a man who spent so much time pointing out the esoteric techniques of others must have written esoterically himself. They have similarly concluded that Strauss must have done so for the same reasons as those who operated in entirely different environments: in other words, primarily because of the inexorable tension between political life and philosophy that Strauss attributed to Plato; or the inexorable tension between philosophy and revealed religion that he found operating in Maimonides; or the need to keep unpalatable moral truths silent, as did Machiavelli. And, they conclude, he must have used the same devices they used. If this is true, Strauss must have had all the subtlety of a magician who explains his trick before performing it. If Strauss was actually engaged in esoteric speech, his real message absolutely must have been something other than what he asserted quite openly. His revelation of previous reasons for esotericism, and previous devices used, must have been the smoke screen under which he hid his deeper truths.

In the present world, where everything is said openly, only an extreme paranoid could think he might be persecuted for observing with Plato that there was a tension between philosophy and politics, or with Maimonides that there was a tension between philosophy and religion. In the contemporary West, we live at a time when we do not have closed political communities, God has been openly proclaimed dead, simple hedonism is advanced as the good life, and many assert we have arrived at the end of philosophy. Precisely what devastating truth is still to be revealed that is not already part of the public domain? That certain realities in Athens, medieval Europe, or Islam, early modernity, or whenever, led to esoteric writing for previous writers seems irrelevant in our changed circumstance.

I do not know if Strauss had an esoteric teaching. But I am confident that if he did, his detractors—and more than a few of his admirers—have been taken in by his surface teaching. With more partisanship than insight or honesty, many have laboriously dug up Strauss's perfectly obvious surface teaching and proclaimed it his great secret, or reveled in saying that the sphinx had no secret.

There is no doubt that Strauss was a fervent defender of liberal commercialism. This alone made him anathema to many on the left. That they would search for reasons to attack him—no matter how implausible—is understandable. Strauss certainly ran against the tide of the dominant progressive intellectual currents of his time, all of which accepted uncritically the doctrine that history moves in a linear fashion, with later stages being necessarily more complete and higher than those that had gone before. This notion allowed many to be sympathetic to the claims of not only democratic socialism but also Marxist communism as being higher stages of social and political evolution since they came after the emergence of liberal capitalism. It was even common to see some intellectuals overlook the realities of Stalinist oppression and be mesmerized by the claims of their abstract theory of history. Strauss simply had no patience with the kind of thinking that could so theoretically anesthetize itself that it emerged intellectually numb to obvious oppression and brutality. For many, Strauss was seen, therefore, to make common cause with the devil. If the progressivist view of democracy was the only plausible one, anyone who questioned it must be anti-democratic. That the more fashionable post-modernist Left eventually came along to question those same progressivist presuppositions as did Strauss is another interesting irony.

In this regard, it is pertinent to recall Strauss's famous exchange with Alexandre Kojève, a Russian émigré who settled in Paris at about the time Strauss passed through on the way to the United States. He and Strauss met there before World War II and kept up an active correspondence thereafter. Strauss considered him a significant thinker and sent several of his students to seek out Kojève. Kojève gave a series of influential lectures on Hegel that were attended by seemingly everyone who became anyone in French academic circles from the 1930s to the 1980s. He developed a unique reading of Hegel that accepted that the end of history had arrived: the final wisdom had been revealed, if not totally actualized; all coherent aspirations could now be satisfied. According to Kojève, the only conclusion that could be reached was that all societies would now strive to actualize the modern, liberal, commercial, bureaucratic state. The outcome would be a cosmopolitan world society along the lines of secular, Western, bureaucratic, technological, liberal, commercial societies.

Strauss concluded that such a universal, cosmopolitan society, far from opening the possibility of a truly human, satisfying existence, created the specter of a universal tyranny in which all man's higher, natural possibilities and aspirations would be strangled. Such a state would have far more resources at its command than Nazi Germany or Stalinist Russia and would leave no oases for émigrés. For Strauss a world state would at best be prone to the creeping conformism and gentle slide into "soft despotism" that Tocqueville envisioned, or, at worst, Nietzsche's nightmare of a future dominated by the "last man" who aspires to nothing other than comfortable self-preservation. Strauss did not believe that such a state was possible. But even if it were, it did not represent a coherent object of aspiration.

Strauss's critique of the end of history thesis—long before Francis Fukuyama brought the subject to public attention—was simultaneously a critique of the modern, cosmopolitan aspirations of the dominant progressivism that accepted a cosmopolitan outcome as the only rational object of political and moral striving. Strauss's objections were taken as prima facia evidence of his anti-progressive and therewith reactionary and anti-democratic tendencies. It was assumed by proponents of progressivist cosmopolitanism that the only alternative to their view was a narrow, parochial, ethnic nationalism, which was defined as, in principle, fascistic. But Strauss did not accept that a cosmopolitan/fascist dichotomy exhausted the available options. He was a proponent of neither. Strauss becomes a reactionary, anti-Enlightenment conservative only for those incapable of escaping the cosmopolitan/fascist dichotomy—a dichotomy that unfortunately remains all too prevalent.

The extent to which a teacher should be held responsible for the deeds of his students or disciples is an open question. Serious thinkers frequently die the death of a thousand students. Since it is impossible for even the greatest of teachers to predict who their disciples will be or in what direction they will strike off, it would seem unreasonable to hold a teacher responsible for everyone who claimed to have been influenced by him. Yet Strauss has been blamed for all manner of things said by his students. Those students have struck off in a variety of directions to explore a variety of themes that Strauss opened up. Even a cursory glance at the work of the so-called Straussians shows such diversity, to say nothing of disagreement, that, at the very least, the Straussians represent a very factious "cult" possessed of an extremely lax policing mechanism.

So diverse are Strauss's students that some have taken his argument for the superiority of Aristotelian political science to its contemporary, behavioralist successor as a simple endorsement of Aristotle as having arrived at the final wisdom. Others, taking off from his observation that the first wave of modernity was more commonsensical than what followed, have tried to reappropriate first-wave authors like Locke and Montesquieu as exemplary of a final wisdom. To put the matter succinctly, Strauss's students include proponents respectively of both the ancients and the moderns. Other Straussians try to generate grand syntheses whereby Locke, for example, is transformed into an Aristotelian. Still others argue that a pastiche of ancient rationalism and modern republicanism can somehow be constructed. Still others see Strauss as a primarily Jewish, religious thinker and plumb those aspects of his work. Some Straussians are ardent supporters of liberal bourgeois civilization; others are critics in the mode of Tocqueville or Nietzsche. In the last analysis, an honest observer would have to conclude that it is impossible to find a unified doctrine lurking in the work of Strauss's students. What one sees is a very diverse body of philosophical literature. Again, what is shared are questions, not answers. Those who thought a great number of those questions had been answered or transcended have not been pleased to see them reopened. That explains a significant part of the hostility to Strauss and his students.

When one looks at Strauss's own large and complicated corpus, one primarily sees a great number of novel thought experiments. One sees a questioning of accepted orthodoxies and a desire to try to approach the phenomena of human existence afresh. That is the philosophic longing that must be ever re-enacted as long as we remain merely mortal beings. That questioning is a sign of the ability to exist in the tension of openness that exhilarates us all, but which, unfortunately, few of us are capable of sustaining for any extended period of time. Philosophic questioning manifests itself in a refusal either to be dogmatic or to give in to a skepticism that is dogmatically relativist.

Leo Strauss reopened many questions that had been presumed closed once and for all. One pays deference to the legacy of Strauss by keeping the questions open, not by trying dogmatically to close them anew. Strauss's thinking points toward a high-level, serious skepticism, albeit absolutely not the kind of skepticism that moves from the openness and tension appropriate to a serious questioning to the banal, flaccid somnambulism of everyday, garden-variety relativism. In the modern world, such philosophical skepticism will not destroy moral and political commitment; the fact that we do not know everything does not mean that we do not know anything.

No serious thinker ever has or ever will be suffered gladly by those who have already arrived at their final truths. From beginning to end, Leo Strauss was an iconoclast and an enigma. He will no doubt remain both as he will no doubt remain controversial. His ultimate influence is impossible to predict. But continuing, open-minded discussion seems to me to constitute the appropriate legacy for such a thinker.

NOTES

1. I do not agree with Strauss that relativism is all that is lurking in Heidegger. I have argued that the phenomenological Heidegger in fact begins in precisely the same place as Strauss, with what Heidegger calls "everyday" experience and Strauss calls "pre-scientific" experience. Below I will argue that Strauss took this premise from Heidegger.

2. Unlike what appears to be Strauss's position, I believe that understanding is always potentially available in the present.

3. See Leo Strauss, *The City and Man* (Chicago: Rand McNally & Co., 1964), p. 11.

Chapter Eight

Leo Strauss and the Straussians: An Anti-Democratic Cult?[1]

In both scholarly and popular venues, the political philosopher Leo Strauss has emerged as the alleged father of an anti-democratic cult at odds with the principles of American democracy. The relative suddenness and uniformity of this recently evolving sentiment is intriguing. Certainly, Strauss's name and those of his self-avowed "followers" have surfaced in public before recent years.[2] That Strauss was a controversial and iconoclastic *scholar* during his lifetime is certainly true, but primarily on issues such as how to read Machiavelli or the appropriate way to approach the study of the social sciences. His recent *public* impact, especially since his death, was therefore hardly predictable. Strauss simply was not a public man. He seldom declaimed in public, and despite a sense of professional obligation to his university and his students, clearly preferred the withdrawn, quiet, contemplative life. He showed no desire to have a public persona.[3]

It is difficult to explain, therefore, how Strauss could occasion such intemperate remarks as those printed in the *New York Times,* under the heading "Undemocratic Vistas: The Sinister Vogue of Leo Strauss." Author Brent Staples stated that "Leo Strauss contended that the Philosopher-kings (himself included) were born to rule, servants were born to serve and that only disaster came of letting the rabble get above its station. Strauss, then, was unapologetically elitist and anti-democratic. His ideas have survived him and crept into vogue in American politics."[4] The author was repeating charges that were already in the air, charges of anti-democratic cultism that have become common in both the popular press and in academia.[5] As recently as thirty years ago, the general view of Strauss and Straussians was that they agreed on the appropriate method for studying philosophic texts, or more generally how to confront the study and practice of political life. Now, Strauss's

167

influence is increasingly seen as politically and morally sinister. What accounts for the changed perception? Who was Leo Strauss? What did he stand for? Is there *a philosophic* basis for recent criticism?

STRAUSS AND HIS WORK IN CONTEXT

It is always dangerous to try to deduce too much from the personal history of a thinker. In the classical model of philosophy, especially as Strauss understood it, the thinker seeks to stand outside his place and time in order to grasp it in the widest possible perspective. But Strauss could hardly have avoided being influenced by his experience as a German Jew, born to an orthodox family. He lived through the period between the World Wars and witnessed the rise of Nazism. Hence it is not surprising that he was a fervent supporter of Liberal Democracy as the best political dispensation available in the modern world. He had seen the inadequacies of modern regimes like Fascism first hand and Communism offered nothing but tyranny in his understanding.

Strauss was especially impressed with the American variant of Liberal Democracy, studying its history, its Constitution, and the writings of its founders and statesmen. But in his scholarly work on modern political philosophy he concluded that the modern philosophical premises of Liberal Democracy were inadequate and, if not transcended, would weaken attachment to a fundamentally just and decent way of life. Though an ardent supporter of modern liberal democratic practice, he criticized the modern philosophic premises that gave rise to that practice, a dilemma in which a great number of recent thinkers have found themselves. Beginning with *The Political Philosophy of Hobbes* and proceeding through his studies of Locke and Machiavelli, as well as in his pivotal *Natural Right and History.*[6] Strauss examined how modern political philosophy could lead to such radically different offspring as Liberal Democracy, Fascism, and Marxist Communism. Eventually, Strauss went to Greek thought in hopes of finding an alternative to the nihilism he saw as implicit in modern thought.

To confront this nihilism, Strauss initially sought to address that aspect of Nietzsche's claim that "God is dead," which implied that belief in a transcendent God and His revelations had become impossible for future humanity. Strauss found these origins in the early-modern critiques of the Biblical dispensation, taking Spinoza as the classic exemplar of this critique. In his *Spinoza's Critique of Religion,* Strauss argued that modern critiques were not definitive; the possibility of taking seriously Revelation and its wisdom remained open. From Spinoza, Strauss moved to the medieval Jewish thinker Moses Maimonides (1135–1204 CE), a major opponent of Spinoza. According to Strauss, Maimonides was as much committed to the Enlightenment as Spinoza was, yet Maimonides achieved a rapprochement with the Biblical dispensation. Further, it is arguable that it was from Maimonides that Strauss learned about the esoteric or secret writing which became one of his major scholarly themes. Thereafter, Strauss continually addressed the irresolvable tension between Reason and Revelation, or "Athens and Jerusalem."

According to Strauss, modern thought led Western philosophy into a crisis by questioning the validity of the twin wellsprings of Western Civilization— the Biblical dispensation and the pre-modern versions of Enlightenment and Rationalism, especially in their Greek manifestations. The full ramifications of this questioning became evident in late-modern irrationalism, which Strauss saw as the inevitable outcome of modern rationalism. Strauss argued that modern philosophical attacks on Reason and Revelation were not conclusive. By doing so, he hoped to reopen questions that were presumed closed by modern thought. He did not presume, as many recent detractors claim, to substitute a new closure for that openness. Strauss argued that the viability of Western Civilization—with Western Liberal Democracy being one of its central components—rested on a continual reinvigoration of the West's distinctive tension between Reason and Revelation, both of which were under assault in his time. He posited that that tension could never be resolved in favor of either Reason or Revelation. Moreover, Strauss encouraged an openness to this tension, discouraging dogmatism, irrationalism or what amounts to the same thing as irrationalism, secret writing and esoteric misdirection administered by cultist priests.

That Strauss has became so controversial can be traced ultimately to the untimely nature of his thinking and his willingness to question the philosophical orthodoxies of his time which dismissed Revelation, and increasingly in our time, Reason—in both pre-modern and modern permutations. Furthermore, Strauss's work was undertaken in the midst of a profound tidal shift in thought that has been underway for at least a century and is unlike anything that has occurred since the beginning of the modern age five centuries ago.[7] It will be a long time before we gain clarity about the full import of that tidal shift. It goes without saying that such shifts cause anxiety and apprehension in proponents of both old and new pieties.

CONFRONTING MODERNITY

A major part of Strauss's scholarship seeks to address the nature of the break modernity attempted. He ultimately concluded that the change that took place at the dawn of modernity was primarily a moral change that rested on a transformed conception of the good. From the beginning—and for Strauss this could be seen clearly in Machiavelli—the moderns tried to "lower the sights." Rather than aim at the grand and inspiring high virtues that pre-modern thought took as the appropriate end of political action, the moderns were prepared to emancipate and channel the spontaneously occurring passions and emotions like fear, ambition, and greed. A more accessible and egalitarian goal was substituted for the grand aims of the pre-moderns, which were ultimately accessible to only a few.

The moderns came to see comfort, affluence, and the avoidance of death as intrinsic to the good life, secured by a new science that saw its end not as perfecting the rational faculty by striving for understanding, but as gaining power over nature. The good life, they claimed, could be actualized for all in a prosperous society supported by modern science. Pre-moderns rejected this idea of the good before the fact because they saw human desires as unlimited. Hence prosperity alone would not make human beings happy; it would merely lead to the invention of new desires, an endless process whereby human beings would become moral slaves. Further, the mere possession of scientific power, without knowledge of ends other than vulgar hedonism, could never be a simple good. In fact, such power could transform itself into a threat to our very humanity. Reduced to desirous slaves and armed with a powerful new science, modernity pointed toward unprecedented tyranny rather than emancipation—a conclusion reached by many on both the "right" and the "left."

Less visibly, Strauss also confronted the philosophical component of modernity posited by Descartes. To lay the foundation for the new science that could master nature, Cartesian Idealism tried to abstract from the "data of the senses" and became grounded in the thinking self—the abstract ego. From the beginning, the moderns doubted the reliability of the data of the senses as well as the veracity of common sense or "the way things appear for all," what Strauss came to call the natural, pre-theoretical, or pre-scientific articulation of things. It was necessary for the moderns, therefore, to substitute conscious mental constructions for the natural awareness allegedly present to all in everyday life. Much of Strauss's scholarship attempts to transcend this modern "constructivism"—what Heidegger called "The Age of the World View"—and find a way back to what he believed was the natural articulation of reality.[8] Strauss argued that, if given a chance, reality presents *itself* prior to the artificial ways reality is presented by modern theoretical constructivism.

For Strauss, the conjunction of the changed modern moral understanding and the new scientific, constructivist relation to the world led in an inevitable direction, toward twentieth century relativism and nihilism and, as a result, political tyranny. That late modernity represented an inevitable yet untenable moment was an idea shared by thinkers from Nietzsche and Heidegger to Adorno and Marcuse. But where authors on the "left" like Adorno pursued this idea under rubrics like "The Dialectic of Enlightenment," Strauss articulated it under the rubric "The Three Waves of Modernity."

For Strauss, modern political philosophy had by stages moved from a more or less benign beginning to a final intensification and radicalization in late modernity. An initial peak was reached in Lockean liberal democracy which represented the culmination of the first wave of modernity. With Rousseau, modern political philosophy took a more radical turn and the second wave was initiated. The first wave of modernity still believed in the existence of a fixed human nature that had to be accommodated because it could not be transcended. It saw quitting the natural condition as good, but nature still remained as a guide or limit for human affairs, albeit only as a foil. The second wave stressed the malleability, changeability, and historicality of human existence. In so doing, Rousseau initiated an understanding that, after passing through Kant, culminated in Hegel's depiction of an inevitable movement of History that brought with it an inevitable transformation of man and of the natural environment. This "progressive" understanding—shared by Marx— saw human History as linear, inevitable, and as proceeding from lower to higher stages.

With the commencement of Strauss's third wave of modernity, faith in the changeability and historicality of human existence remained, but was stripped of any linearity, necessity, or progressivity. This wave began with Nietzsche. With Nietzsche, the problem Strauss designated "historicism" raised its head. Nietzsche asserted that all knowledge—especially that of good and evil—was dependent upon the altogether arbitrary historical perspective into which one was thrown. And all perspectives were transitory. With Nietzsche, history came to be accidental in its unfolding, if not regressive and nihilistic. With the suggestion that all past conceptions of reality were merely human constructions came the possibility that in the future those constructions could, for the first time, be consciously willed. The third wave brought with it the age of what Nietzsche called the politics of the Will-to-Power—competing wills to power with no possible arbiter other than force more or less overtly deployed. Everyone would compete to advance his or her construction of reality—a fundamental premise that underlies many contemporary phenomena from multiculturalism to various forms of feminism.

Malleable humanity could now be consciously transformed. But there was no guidance for this transformation other than an entirely arbitrary contest of wills won by the momentarily strongest. Strauss believed that Nietzsche's philosophy opened the door to Heidegger's even more thoroughgoing historicism where faith in the efficacy of self-conscious action waned, replaced by the hegemony of blind, overpowering fate, and the nihilism of an inevitable, universal, global, nihilistic, technological civilization.

According to Strauss, the inevitable outcome of modern thought was a humanity that no longer believed in Divine Revelation, eternal Nature, or inevitable History as providing any standards for judgment. In such an intellectual environment, Liberal Democracy would come to be seen as just one moral and political dispensation among many, and theoretically no better than its alternatives. Strauss argued that this would inevitably sap the energy needed to defend Liberal Democracy that was needed in the face of the immoderate political dispensations that resulted from the second and third waves of modernity: Communism and Fascism, respectively.

In much of his work, Strauss sought to find a non-historicist alternative to help defend Liberal Democracy, an alternative not to be found within modern thought. Strauss did not believe Liberal Democracy was the only just and decent political possibility for all times. But it was the only decent alternative on the immediate horizon. To provide a ground for Liberal Democracy that avoided the pitfalls of modern thought, Strauss made a painstaking attempt to understand those allegedly non-historicist Greek authors at the origins of the Western philosophic tradition in hopes that they would provide insights into how to begin to transcend the late-modern impasse. This led to Strauss's works on Thucydides, Aristophanes, Xenophon, Plato, Socrates, and Aristotle—works which, to a significant degree, have been ignored by both the scholarly community and his polemical detractors.

Having discovered the idea of esoteric writing in his study of Maimonides, Strauss arrived at a very novel reading of Plato—in his mind a more authentic understanding of Plato than that contained in conventional, Anglo-American scholarship. When reflecting on the esoteric writing style of Plato, instead of focusing on the confrontation between philosophy and revealed religion, Strauss found a tension between open philosophical inquiry and the needs of a closed political community. Political communities, according to Strauss's reading of Plato, were always closed and particular and could not withstand the glare of the universal truth, which was the object of philosophy. This tension between political life and philosophy led Plato to use the dialogue form, embellished by myths, as his distinctive mode of speech. Likewise, Strauss applied his understanding of esoteric writing to the texts of Farabi (873–950 CE), the Islamic medieval philosopher. Farabi also adopted an esoteric mode of speech and engaged in secret writing. Strauss's conclusion seems to have been that different environments required the use of different literary devices; these devices were needed to accomplish the end of simultaneously speaking to different audiences while conveying more than one message—but not for the sake of conveying the identical message in all circumstances no matter how different.

When the Greek philosophers were read carefully, Strauss believed they offered a non-historicist alternative to the nihilism of late-modern thought. The moderns had constructed an abstract, constructivist understanding of the world; Strauss believed that the ancient Greeks had a rich, concrete, and "natural" understanding of life free from modern abstractions. In the Socratic dialectical method—which begins from concrete question and answer—was to be found the most fruitful way of approaching that concrete richness without destroying it. Hence much of Strauss's later scholarly work centered on an attempt to understand Socrates and what his new philosophic method represented, approached from the perspective not only of Plato, but also through contemporaries like Aristophanes and Xenophon.

For Strauss, the Platonic dialogues were not primarily ontological or metaphysical documents as much of postmodernism would have it, but rich articulations about the things that interest human beings most, including the nature of the best life and the best regime, the nature of moral virtue, and the possibility of happiness. In the Platonic dialogues, one finds the presentation of various distinctive kinds of lives all of which present themselves as the best—the private life of virtue, the public life of the statesman or sophist, the life of philosophy, and so on. Since there are always different political communities, political life is also a debate between competing regimes, each pursuing a different conception of the good. In Strauss's understanding, Nature articulates itself through different human beings with different aspirations, and through different regimes that favor different ends. Within these natural limits, life presents itself—without the imposition of willed, human constructions. Though modern thought led to an alienated and nihilistic life within a very abstract world, the ancient Greeks demonstrated that there was an unchanging, natural articulation of reality that could be recovered. It was the diverse, natural, human possibilities—not a specific ordering of those possibilities—that Strauss wanted to recover. There is no dogmatism here; in fact, there is considerable fluidity.

According to Strauss, the nature of the best regime depends on changing circumstances. Strauss believed that the Greeks had adequately articulated the essence of our diverse natural perceptions and aspirations. They did not, however, necessarily offer the best articulation of all possibilities for all times. Strauss understood that political philosophy must repeatedly weave together the diverse natural elements in creative ways that are consistent with present possibilities. Flexibility is always necessary; there is no one best regime everywhere and always, but there are natural possibilities that should always be allowed to manifest themselves. Hence, in *Natural Right and History*, Strauss tried to differentiate his understanding of a flexible "Natural Right" teaching from the more dogmatic and rigid "Natural Law" teachings of authors like Aquinas and Hobbes.

Strauss argued for the need to recover a Socratic, dialectical understanding of philosophy, which, when turned loose on the modern world—transformed, as he argued repeatedly, by the successes of modern political philosophy—would yield entirely different philosophical articulations than those reached by previous thinkers.[9] It was never Strauss's understanding that one went back to the ancients or medievals to recover all the conclusions that they had reached or the poetic articulations of reality they offered. Strauss no more intended to assert the desirability of the rule of philosopher-kings than he meant to assert the modern viability of the *polis*, or the need to pray again to Zeus. Strauss argued for the need to recover a lost way of *relating to reality*. The precise, late-modern application of the wisdom of the classics would have to await the efforts of those freed from the artificialities of late modern discourse. Strauss was in no position to say what those articulations would be in the future; that was the jurisdiction of political philosophy, and he saw his work as a scholarly propaedeutic to the possibility of its restoration.

Strauss's main problem was that the natural articulation of reality was not always operative or immediately available. This understanding represented Strauss's more concrete manifestation of the Heideggerian thought contained in the idea of "the withdrawal of Being." Strauss was explicit that late modern life was *contra naturum*. His was a scholarly attempt to help recover what had become substantially absent for his contemporaries. This experience of absence was one that Strauss ironically shared with a diverse group of thinkers that included Heidegger and even Derrida, the father of deconstructionism. But Strauss's response was far more concrete.

Armed with his new understanding of the pre-moderns, Strauss wanted to reinvigorate the quarrel between the ancients and the moderns on the issues that naturally most concern all individuals: How shall we live? What is happiness? How is happiness best achieved? Strauss believed that a conscious break had taken place at the origins of modernity and wanted to oppose that view to the prevalent, contemporary, philosophic view that the history of Western thought was seamless from beginning to end. The latter idea reached a peak with the thought of Hegel, where the seamless movement of prior thought was seen as progress toward higher stages of understanding and freedom. This idea would be inverted by authors like Nietzsche, Heidegger, and their descendants who claimed a seamless decline. In our time, almost all of the fashionable dismissals of Western civilization draw whatever philosophical credibility they possess from Nietzschean and Heideggerian philosophies of history. Strauss rejected the notion that history is seamless, and he thought not only that there had been a radical break at the beginning of modernity, but that, far from being more comprehensive, much of late modern thought had forgotten many things previously understood. The fact of past, substantive breaks indicated future ones might be possible as well.

CULTIST LEADER?

Strauss first became controversial in the academic community in the 1950s as part of his critique of the then-dominant behavioralism in the social sciences. Behavioralist political science began from the Cartesian premise that in order to understand political life, it was necessary to project consciously constructed, "scientific" categories, in place of the categories that arise in the marketplace of everyday discussion. Strauss tried to show—especially in his essay "Epilogue"—that the behavioralist attempt to substitute an "objective," scientific account of reality, especially political reality, for the one embedded in everyday experience and discourse was a mistake. Furthermore, it could never arrive at the scientific detachment and objectivity it desired because it always took for granted a variety of pretheoretical presuppositions from which it could never be free. This was the basis of Strauss's critique of the dominant fact-value dichotomy. There are no such things as value-free facts. Facts first present themselves to us as part of our acting, doing, and making— which are always evaluative.[10] Without these evaluative, common sense criteria of relevance embedded in our shared experience, no science could ever judge the difference between the relevant and the trivial.

For Strauss, behavioralist political science represented a method by which all substantive moral and political debates could be placed aside in favor of discussing the means to ends that were already built into the political system. Having presupposed an understanding of the best life and the best regime— the modern progressivist understanding—behavioralism tried to limit debate to factual observations. By opposing behavioralism, Strauss could be made to look like a conservative if one assumed that there were only two alternatives available. It is no small irony that after Strauss had made his critique of behavioralism, a similar critique was made by the "New Left," which argued that behavioralist political science operated with a hidden "conservative" agenda.

According to Strauss, the real danger of behavioralist political science was that it shielded itself from the truly fundamental questions of the day. For those who lived in the West, especially after World War II, "everyday" political reality was determined by the confrontation between Liberal Democracy and

Marxist despotism. Only by an abstraction that led in the direction of less rather than more clarity could one conclude, as behavioralist political science did, that the difference between democracy and totalitarianism was a difference between quantums of power—a perfectly modern, Newtonian category—or a difference in the nature of the group interactions that determined policy, or other similar "scientific" explanations.

Despite his profound respect for Heidegger, Strauss offered a criticism of Heidegger similar to his critique of behavioralism.[11] Heidegger had reached the conclusion that the Liberal Democratic West and the Marxist Communist East—"Washington and Moscow"—were "metaphysically equal." For Strauss, this abstract conclusion was an affront to what was obviously the clear superiority of living in a Liberal Democracy rather than a Marxist despotism. Furthermore, despite his respect for Heidegger's philosophical depth, Strauss considered Heidegger the ultimate historicist. Just as he had tried to confront what he saw as the relativism of the fact-value dichotomy of social science behavioralism, Strauss tried to confront the historicism he saw as the ultimate and inevitable outcome of modern thought. But in many ways, his confrontation with historicism was far more provisional. First, he tried to show how historicism evolved necessarily from previous moments in modern thought. Yet while the first and second waves of modernity were less virulent, they led unavoidably to the third, and hence it was not feasible to return to one of the prior waves. Strauss further argued that, on its own terms, historicism had made no compelling philosophical case for its superiority to non-historicist thought. Therefore, it need not be taken as the dogmatic given it has become for so many third wave moderns.

There remain historicist components in Strauss's thought. For example, he never gives any simple invocation of a Nature that is *always* operative. For Strauss, Nature does not operate as simple mechanical causality and it is never immediately available—in the manner of the color green—without study. In fact, there are ages like our own during which Nature is occluded, and thereby, to a significant extent inoperative. This is why it was so important for Strauss to recover an understanding of the Greek authors who remained in closer touch with Nature than the late moderns. This was also the basis of Strauss's veneration of the "Great Books." They provide access to experiences that have been lost as well as to serious debate about the alternate conclusions regarding the nature of the best life, many of which had dropped out of present debates and contemporary life.

While not a pure ahistoricist, Strauss nevertheless considered radical historicism the greatest problem confronting contemporary humanity. It constituted what he called the "Crisis of the West." According to Strauss, that crisis consisted of the West's inability to take itself and its aspirations seriously. Transcending radical historicism was for Strauss the highest task, but that could not be done by rhetoric, myth-making, or esoteric misdirection as many of Strauss's detractors claim was his intention. Historicism could be transcended only by painstaking scholarly reconstructions that help us give concrete articulation to the vague intimations of Nature with which we are left. Strauss may have been wrong in his perception of our time and of what was required to transcend it, but he never fell back on the abject banality of believing that late-modernity could be overcome by what amounted to clever lies by cultist Straussian priests.

Strauss was primarily a thinker and scholar. He had no concrete recipes or plans to offer. His detractors, even some of his sympathizers, have constructed concrete positions for him that he would not have accepted. But it is around the place of religion or myths in Strauss's teaching and his "rediscovery" of esoteric or secret writing that the more polemical claims brought against him center. The accusation that Strauss ultimately was an atheist who nonetheless thought it necessary for the non-philosophic to be told various religious fictions to keep them in line is a case in point. Some of his students now stress the central importance of "civil religion," but this says more about his students than about Strauss.[12] Equally incorrect is the argument increasingly posited by admirers that he is primarily a Jewish, religious thinker. Understanding Strauss as a fundamentally religious thinker, while perhaps saving him from the charge of being an esoteric nihilist, suggests that he simply gave up on Rationalism—which he never did.

Further, detractors and admirers alike have concluded that because he spent so much time pointing out the esoteric techniques of others, he must have written esoterically himself. They have likewise concluded that Strauss did so primarily due to the inexorable tension between political life and philosophy Strauss attributed to Plato; or the inexorable tension between philosophy and revealed religion he found operating in Maimonides; or the need to keep unpalatable moral truths silent like Machiavelli. And, they conclude, he must have used the same devices these thinkers used. Yet if this is true, Strauss had all the subtlety of a magician who explains his trick before performing it, unless the actual trick lies hidden somewhere else entirely.

STRAUSS AND THE STRAUSSIANS

There is no doubt that Strauss was a fervent defender of a classical or Federalist version of liberal commercialism. In this, Strauss certainly ran against the tide of the dominant progressive intellectual currents of his time, all of which accepted uncritically the doctrine that History moves in a linear fashion, with later stages being necessarily more complete and higher than those that had gone before. This notion allowed some to be sympathetic to the claims of everything from Democratic Socialism to Marxist Communism as being higher stages of social and political evolution since they came after the emergence of Liberal Capitalism. It should be remembered that some intellectuals even overlooked the realities of Stalinist oppression and were mesmerized by the promises of an abstract, progressivist theory of History. Strauss had no patience with thinkers who could be anesthetized to obvious oppression and brutality. For many, Strauss was seen, therefore, to make common cause with the devil. If the progressivist and increasingly egalitarian view of democracy was by definition the only legitimate one, anyone who questioned it must be anti-democratic. That the postmodern left, like Strauss, has come to question those same progressivist presuppositions—or metanarratives—is yet another grand irony.

In this regard, it is pertinent to call attention to Strauss's famous exchange with Alexandre Kojève. The two met in Paris before World War II and kept up an active correspondence thereafter. Kojève gave a series of influential lectures on Hegel attended by seemingly everyone who became anyone in The French academy from the 1930s to the 1980s. He developed a unique reading of Hegel that accepted that the end of History had arrived. The final wisdom had been revealed, if not totally actualized; all coherent aspirations could now be satisfied by modern science and the modern bureaucratic state. But Strauss concluded that, far from opening the possibility of a truly human, satisfying existence, such a universal, cosmopolitan society offered the specter of a universal tyranny in which all man's higher possibilities and aspirations would be strangled. Such a state would have far more resources at its command than Nazi Germany or Stalinist Russia, and leave no oases for émigrés.

For Strauss, a world state would, at best, be prone to the creeping conformism and gentle slide into the "soft despotism" that Tocqueville envisioned, at worst, to Nietzsche's nightmare of a future dominated by the "last man" who aspires to nothing other than comfortable self-preservation. Strauss did not believe that such a state was possible. But even if it were it did not represent a coherent object of aspiration. Strauss's critique of the End of History thesis—long before Francis Fukuyama brought the subject to public attention—was simultaneously a critique of the modern, cosmopolitan aspirations of the dominant progressivism which accepted a cosmopolitan outcome as the only rational object of political and moral striving. Strauss's objections were taken as *prima facie* evidence of his anti-progressive and therefore reactionary and anti-democratic tendencies. It was assumed by proponents of progressivist cosmopolitanism that the only alternative to their view was a narrow, parochial, ethnic nationalism, fascistic in principle. But Strauss did not accept that a cosmopolitan/fascist dichotomy exhausted the available options. He was a proponent of neither. Strauss is a reactionary, anti-Enlightenment conservative only for those all too many who do not look beyond the cosmopolitanism/fascism dichotomy.

Of course, many of Strauss's students championed what are often termed conservative causes.[13] But the extent to which a teacher should be held responsible for the deeds of his students or disciples is still an open question. Yet Strauss has been blamed for all manner of things said by his students.[14] Aside from those who have entered the public arena, Strauss had an unusually large number of students who became teachers and authors that struck off in a variety of directions to explore themes opened by Strauss. The work of the so-called Straussians shows such diversity—to say nothing of disagreement—that, at most, the Straussians represent a very factious "cult" possessed of an extremely lax policing mechanism.

So diverse are Strauss's students that some have taken his argument for the superiority of Aristotelian political science over behavioralism as a claim that Aristotle possessed the final wisdom. Others, taking off from his observation that the first wave of modernity was more benign than what followed, reappropriate first wave authors like Locke and Montesquieu as keepers of the final wisdom. Other Straussians try to generate grand syntheses whereby Locke, for example, is transformed into an Aristotelian. Still others, like Thomas Pangle, argue that a pastiche of ancient rationalism and modern republicanism can somehow be constructed. Still others see Strauss as a primarily Jewish, religious thinker and plumb those aspects of his work. Some Straussians are ardent supporters of liberal bourgeois civilization; others are critics in the mode of both Tocqueville and Nietzsche.

An honest observer would have to conclude that it is impossible to find a unified doctrine lurking in the work of Strauss's students. What one sees is a very diverse body of literature. What is shared are questions, not answers. Intellectuals who thought those questions were answered or transcended have not been pleased to see them re-opened. That explains a significant part of the hostility to Strauss's students; they will not stick to orthodox paradigms.

Strauss and his students have also been responsible for a large body of scholarly work on specific authors. The interpretations inspired by Strauss's work have been controversial because unlike some contemporary approaches which proceed from the assumption that one knows that past understandings are false or at least inferior to present ones, Straussian approaches proceed on the assumption that the author might be correct, and that it is important to try to understand authors as those authors understood themselves rather than from some presumed superior stance. Straussians assume that authors have intentions and that careful and honest readers can penetrate those intentions, which flies in the face of the self-invalidating assertions of fashionable deconstructionism. Perhaps the largest number of such interpretations have been painstaking explorations of individual Platonic dialogues—Bloom's translation and interpretative essay on Plato's *Republic* being the best known—but modern authors have also been subjected to close Straussian readings. This growing body of textual scholarship has forced reconsideration of a number of academic orthodoxies, most notably the Anglo-American trusteeship of Plato complete with its "development" theory. But whether it has been a reconsideration of Plato, Machiavelli or whomever, even dissenting scholars have been forced to confront the new, detailed readings. The result has been an invigoration of contemporary scholarly debates.

It has been asserted—by Straussians and non-Straussians alike—that there is one major divide that has opened up among those influenced by Strauss. That divide is between so-called political and philosophical Straussians (a.k.a., western and eastern Straussians). This was indicated in a debate that spilled over into the *National Review* between Walter Berns and Harry Jaffa. Strauss's method opens up the possibility of this debate. Since Strauss's point of departure is the way reality is initially revealed for everyone collectively, and that articulation is presented as being intrinsically political, one must take seriously the common sense, political articulation of things. Followers like Jaffa and his students are sometimes accused of never getting beyond political discussions and political categories to philosophical analysis. Jaffa and his students have, in turn, accused others like Bloom and Pangle of moving too quickly beyond common sense categories, thereby undermining the moral and political perspective of the citizen.

But it could be argued that the citizen perspective was merely Strauss's point of departure. One's point of departure and destination are two different things. Strauss clearly intended to move dialectically from the common sense perception of reality to a more philosophical articulation. Strauss intended to do philosophy, albeit for him the highest and most comprehensive manifestation of philosophy was political philosophy. Nor was political philosophy just an exercise in esoterics. To him, it *was* philosophy. This may not be the last word on the nature of philosophy, but however the issue between the so-called political and philosophical Straussians is resolved, since the debate follows fairly logically from Strauss's explicitly stated method it is a debate that is perfectly logical, far more logical than taking sides on the ancients/moderns dispute. Strauss tried to reinvigorate the latter dichotomy primarily as a point of departure in an attempt to show that radical breaks have been possible in the past and could be equally possible in the future. Ancients and moderns did not represent for Strauss the only two possibilities in a closed set any more than the unmediated citizen perspective was never to be transcended.

CONCLUSION

Strauss was not a political partisan. When one looks at his large and complicated corpus, one primarily sees a great number of novel thought experiments undertaken in the service of resurrecting the *possibility* of political philosophy. As a citizen, Strauss defended Liberal Democracy, but that was not his highest concern. This becomes clear when one looks at the radical questioning of accepted orthodoxies that lies at the heart of Strauss's enterprise, a questioning which in principle cannot come to an end.

Strauss attempted to break out of contemporary categories and approach the phenomena of human existence in a fresh fashion. That is the philosophic longing which must be ever reenacted among finite, mortal beings. Genuine philosophic questioning manifests itself in a refusal to be either dogmatic or to succumb to a skepticism which is dogmatically relativist. One pays deference to Strauss by keeping the questions open, not by trying to close them dogmatically. The existence of a sectarian cult would have dismayed Strauss immensely for its existence represents the cessation of questioning. Indeed, while there are many Straussians, there can be no such thing as Straussianism.

Beyond a shared hermeneutic commitment to taking texts seriously as they present themselves, or in putting forward the ongoing need for political philosophy, there is no such thing as Straussianism. As I stated before, there is no consensus or agreement among Strauss's students and followers. That there is debate and discussion, and at times even heated disagreement, is a sign of healthy openness, not of cultist closure.

Leo Strauss and the Straussians will no doubt remain controversial because from beginning to end Strauss was an iconoclast. In the long run, Strauss's influence is impossible to predict, but, to be sure, presently fashionable opinions about him are far from the last word.

NOTES

1. This is an expanded version of an article that initially appeared in *The American Scholar*, Winter 1997. Bibliographic information for Strauss's works can be found at the end of chapter 10.

2. Clearly, there is growing public interest in Strauss and those he influenced. Allan Bloom, Strauss's publicly best known student, author of the best seller *The Closing of the American Mind,* became a lightning rod for criticism, especially for his spirited critique of America's liberal culture. Bloom traced the decline of American culture to a turn away from traditional education, especially as it finds a peak in the serious study of the "Great Books." Others like Francis Fukuyama, in *The End of History and the Last Man,* also brought Strauss's influence into public view.

Fukuyama argued that the end of the Cold War signaled the global victory of liberal capitalism over the "progressive" teachings of communism, democratic socialism, and other leftist aspirations. Fukuyama attracted spirited rejoinders as well. Strauss's press clippings have even gone international. The influential Strauss-Cropsey textbook on the history of political philosophy has been translated into French and reviewed in *Le Monde;* during the 1992 presidential election *Die Zeit* even ran a piece on Bill Kristol, Dan Quayle, Murphy Brown, and Leo Strauss.

Students of Strauss, or those influenced by his work, have also been in the public arena for some time—from Harry Jaffa, who worked for Goldwater, to Robert Goldwin in the Ford administration, Paul Wolfowitz in both Bush administrations, Bill Galston in the Clinton administration, to Republican strategist Bill Kristol and presidential candidate Alan Keyes, who have been the objects of attack pieces in the *New Republic* for their Straussianism. And Strauss's students teach in numerous colleges and universities and are published widely in scholarly journals.

3. Strauss's student Allan Bloom described him as a man who "knew many interesting men and women and spent much time talking to students, but the core of his being was the solitary, continuous, meticulous study of the questions he believed most important. . . . He was active in no organization, served in no position of authority, and had no ambitions other than to understand and help others who might also be able to do so." Allan Bloom, "Leo Strauss: September 20, 1973," *Giants and Dwarfs: Essays 1960–1990* (New York: Simon and Schuster, 1990), p. 235.

4. Staples concluded that Strauss believed the ruling philosopher-kings should keep the "rabble" in their place, a conclusion that does not fit with Strauss's reading of Plato's *Republic.* Strauss presented the controversial argument that Plato intended to show precisely why the rule of the philosopher-king was impossible. As best I can ascertain, Strauss only spoke of the "rabble" while describing Nietzsche's usage of that term to apply to those who live without a sense of honor. He never used it in his own philosophical work.

5. Stephen Holmes, in *The Anatomy of Antiliberalism,* has given a more scholarly patina to this argument. Charging that Strauss is anti-democratic, he also asserts that Strauss felt that only philosophers like himself and his students could understand the whole truth. Since average citizens could not fully understand truth, they had to be told myths, primarily through religion. In Holmes's eyes, Strauss's students represent a cult purveying these myths. Yet Holmes arrives at his conclusions only by engaging in a rhetorical juxtaposition of Strauss with the likes of Joseph de Maistre and the Nazi theorist Carl Schmitt. That method raises some serious questions as to objectivity through its use of guilt by dubious association.

Another version of this line of argument is presented by Shadia Drury in *The Political Ideas of Leo Strauss.* She goes even further, asserting that Strauss was a furtive atheist and Nietzschean nihilist who thought that the truth of nihilism had to be kept from the unphilosophic. Like Holmes, she focuses on Strauss's studies of esoteric or secret writing, presented in such works as *Persecution and the Art of Writing.* Holmes, Drury, and others paint a picture of a Strauss who is primarily a conservative, anti-liberal, anti-Enlightenment thinker who believed in the existence of natural hierarchies and who took the distinction between philosophers and non-philosophers as the only interesting human dichotomy.

Not all of the critical responses to Strauss's work have been of a primarily political nature, although even scholarly debates about his work have often become polemical. In a debate played out in the popular press—this time the *New York Review of Books*—Plato scholar Myles Burnyeat took exception with Strauss's iconoclastic reading of the Platonic dialogues. A flurry of responses and counter-responses ensued. Scholars like J. G. A. Pocock have taken Strauss to task for his unique reading of Machiavelli—as presented in *Thoughts Concerning Machiavelli*—as an esoteric author with a secret teaching. Strauss's students have also begun to debate his influence, debates which at times have likewise spilled over into the popular press, such as the *National Review's* debate between Harry Jaffa and Walter Berns.

6. In *Natural Right and History*, Strauss presented modernity as a reaction against the dogmatic Natural *Law* teachings of medieval authors like Aquinas. That reaction brought forth the equally dogmatic teachings of authors like Hobbes. Later modernity in turn was in many ways a reaction to this modern dogmatism. Strauss saw the far more flexible Greek Natural *Right* teachings as an alternative to medieval and modern dogmatism.

7. I deal with this issue at greater length in my *Nietzsche, Heidegger and the Transition to Postmodernity* (Chicago: University of Chicago Press, 1996).

8. Strauss took off from the reflections of Husserl and Heidegger. Husserl's attempt to get to "the things themselves" remained caught in Cartesian Idealism and even Kantian Transcendental Idealism. For Husserl, the things themselves had remained transcendental ideas, grasped by a pure, abstract ego. In Heidegger's critique of Husserl, Strauss saw an attempt to find the basis for approaching the things themselves through "empirical intuition"—i.e., how reality is revealed collectively to the eyes of all in everyday life. Strauss saw this as opening a door to a richer, more concrete relation to "everydayness."

As part of his complicated deconstruction of the Western philosophic tradition, Heidegger tried to argue that truth has its locus and advent in appearance, not primarily in abstract ideas or logical statements. Strauss too wanted to find truth in appearance, in empirical intuition, his natural, pre-theoretical revelation of reality. Unlike Heidegger, Strauss came to see that possibility already deployed in Socratic dialectic. Strauss thought it was necessary to take seriously the "data of the senses," especially as articulated in ordinary public speech and the common sense articulation of reality toward which everyday speech pointed. For Strauss, the modern philosophy that emanated from Descartes had become too abstract and ceased to interrogate everyday understandings of reality as had Socrates. Heidegger's thought remained too abstract as well by failing to grasp the fundamentally moral and political articulation of natural experience which was so important for Strauss. Strauss hoped to reverse the modern tendency to abstractions.

9. "We cannot reasonably expect that a fresh understanding of classical political philosophy will supply us with recipes for today's use. For the relative success of modern political philosophy has brought into being a kind of society wholly unknown to

the classics, a kind of society to which the classical principles as stated and elaborated by the classics are not immediately applicable. Only we living today can possibly find a solution to the problems of today. But an adequate understanding of the principles as elaborated by the classics may be the indispensable starting point for an adequate analysis, to be achieved by us, of the present-day society in its peculiar character, and for the wise application, to be achieved by us, of these principle to our tasks" (Leo Strauss, *City and Man* [Chicago: Rand McNally, 1964]), p. 11.

10. According to Strauss, our natural relation to life is always determined by the regime in which we live and by our shared understandings of the just, the noble, and the good—especially as those principles are articulated in constitutions, public documents, and the speeches of great leaders. This allegedly natural articulation of reality is better understood by citizens and leaders than it is by detached scientific observers. Hence Strauss concluded that, far from being superior to the older political science that emanated from Aristotle and included the traditional political philosophers, the new political science was deluded about its own foundations and ultimately incapable of clarity.

11. In Strauss's understanding, no thinker in the twentieth century rivaled Heidegger's philosophical acumen and rigorous honesty. Heidegger's thought remained central for Strauss in a way that is seldom appreciated by either his supporters or detractors. As Strauss sat in on Heidegger's lectures in the 1930s, he became especially impressed with the meticulous care Heidegger showed in dissecting every detail of the texts about which he lectured—a method of teaching for which Strauss became famous. Many years thereafter, Strauss observed that nothing so affected his thinking at its most formative period as the thought of Heidegger. Strauss would tell a story of how his lifelong friend Jacob Klein observed that Heidegger had, without attempting to, opened a door back to the ancients that had perhaps never previously been open. Strauss appears to have passed through that door. Throughout his written works, Strauss is clearly responding to Heidegger, even when his name is never mentioned, as it rarely is. An example would be the initial chapters of *Natural Right and History*.

12. Arguments for "civil religion" almost necessarily presuppose that Revelation is non-existent or false—which Strauss was unwilling to assert. Further, it is hard to see why anyone would need to hide an understanding that law-abidingness and the inculcation of moral habits might benefit from the support of religion. The defense of religion for its usefulness, as opposed to its truth, is a cat that has long been out of the bag. It is hard to fathom why any sensible person would think it necessary to dissemble on this subject and deploy esoteric speech to keep it quiet. Strauss limited himself to the conclusion that no one had succeeded in proving the impossibility of Revelation.

13. While a significant number of prominent students of Strauss have been conservatives, or at least aligned with some causes customarily seen as conservative, I see no necessity for this in Strauss's work. In Strauss's understanding, a great deal always depends on evanescent circumstances. With the end of the Cold War, circumstances have already changed radically since Strauss's death. What Strauss's understanding would be in these changed circumstances is a fascinating subject for conjecture, but I see no reason why he could not easily make cause **against** those who have

now positioned themselves on the right. Further, there is certainly no philosophical basis for historically transient modern dichotomies like left/right or liberal/conservative. While Strauss defended a traditional, Federalist view of liberal democracy as the best available alternative in his time, there is no reason to believe the future will not present other alternatives. Strauss would never have accepted any version of an End of History thesis. He tried philosophically to confront the political and moral possibilities that existed in his time, a task that must be repeated by each generation.

14. One example concerns the charge that Strauss had secret teachings that were atheistic and hedonistic, regarding pleasure as the highest good while believing philosophers, the greatest of the hedonists, should not share this conclusion with non-philosophers. The origin of this assertion may be Bloom's influential essay appended to his translation of Plato's *Republic*. Bloom stresses that the *Republic* can be read as a juxtaposition of the tyrannical life and the philosophic life. Socrates allegedly tries to convince Glaucon that the philosophic life is more choiceworthy because its pleasures are more intense, long-lasting, and self-sufficient. Hence the choice turns on which is more hedonistic. One will look long and hard to find a defense of hedonism anywhere in Strauss's writings—certainly not in those writings that repeatedly argue for the natural basis of nobility, shame, inhibition, and the natural sociality of humans. And nothing in the way Strauss led his personal life would be termed hedonistic by the average observer.

Chapter Nine

Athens and Washington:
Leo Strauss and the
American Regime

The one-hundredth anniversary of Leo Strauss's birth arrived one year before the impending millennium. That year also marked the twenty-sixth anniversary of his death. In the intellectual life span of significant thinkers, both are short periods of time. But already we can look back at a very diverse group of interpretative confrontations with Strauss's thought. There is every reason to believe there will be more diversity to come. To date, various interpreters have asserted that Strauss's thought is a manifestation of everything from a naïve attempt to return to the Greek *polis*, to an elitist teaching regarding the existence of a rigid natural hierarchy that must be given direct political manifestation, to a conservative defense of modern, liberal capitalism, to a Nietzschean nihilism hiding behind an esoteric natural right teaching, to a Machiavellian atheism, to the efforts of a medieval rabbi in disguise. In light of this interpretative diversity—and there is some textual support for all these positions, and others besides—it is difficult to assess with any precision Strauss's exact relation to the present and future American regime. This is especially true if we are hoping for guidance on everyday policy decisions.

While it is altogether fair to call Strauss a supporter of American political life, if his thought is of any lasting significance it will be because it transcends the confines of any particular regime or time. Surely Strauss knew that everything that comes into being passes away, especially political dispensations. And Strauss would never have accepted the End of History thesis, as his exchange with Alexander Kojève makes clear.[1] Hence the ongoing need for both continuity and change remains a given. Strauss was a proponent of *both* continuity and change.

Strauss once pointed toward the need for the "loyal and loving reshaping or reinterpretation of the inherited."[2] In short, what is needed is to plot a course into the future, which remains loyal to the spirit, if not always the letter, of the past. Hence Strauss, like all the serious thinkers he deals with, was "untimely" in that his thinking was projected beyond the present and into the future, the only moment of temporality a thinker can in any way affect. Whether philosophy is ultimately a contemplative activity remains an open question, but Strauss of all people knew that when serious individuals write books they intend to accomplish more than to simply foster private reflection. Books are unavoidably public documents aimed at present and future generations. But everything depends on what the aim of the loving interpretation is intended to be.

It is clear from his many works that Strauss reflected upon the issue of *transitions* from past to future and how the thinker is implicated in them. He understood the unprecedented and untenable nature of our time. But again, if Strauss is a significant thinker, ultimately he was primarily a proponent of political philosophy itself rather than any particular moral, political or religious dispensation past, present or future, although, as any reader of Strauss knows, these concerns are far from being mutually exclusive.[3] My assertion will be that it is precisely because of his understanding of philosophy and its future prospects that Strauss could be a genuine, sympathetic supporter of the present-day American regime as well as someone capable of wishing it well into the future. Yet to my mind the most interesting issue that reflection on Strauss's thought opens for us as lovers of our own is: What is required to keep the American regime worthy of a serious philosophic defense into the future?

The title of this essay, "Athens and Washington," is intended to evoke two dichotomies simultaneously. The first is the dichotomy Athens and Jerusalem, which has gained a certain prominence in recent interpretations of Strauss's work. The other is the dichotomy Moscow and Washington which points toward the Heideggerian, and more generally postmodernist, conclusion regarding the metaphysical equality and thereby questionableness of all modern political dispensations. Again, while I will stipulate that most of the prominent interpretative efforts to untangle Strauss's enigmatic corpus to date have rested on at least an element of the truth, I will argue that it is only through grasping the iconoclastic fashion in which Strauss was a proponent of "Athens" that one can understand his ultimate support for the American regime and thereby his most profound practical influence. It may be a very long time before we can begin to judge his ultimate philosophical influence.

Given the nature of Strauss's difficult corpus, it is almost impossible to arrive at any easy conclusions. At some point a more or less well-founded speculative leap is required. But that leap must take off from substantial textual facts. On the assumption that it is true that the beginning is more than half the whole, let us on this occasion begin with the straightforward clues that

Strauss gives us about the beginnings of his own thought. Strauss once observed that at the formative period of his thought he was totally absorbed in the reading of Nietzsche.[4] Strauss even makes the striking observation that he not only read the work of Nietzsche voraciously, but that he simply believed *everything* he thought he understood: "Nietzsche so dominated and charmed me between my 22nd and 30th years, that I literally believed everything I understood of him."[5]

At the very end of his life Strauss returned to Nietzsche in an essay on *Beyond Good and Evil*. In that essay, Strauss prominently observed that Nietzsche's writings went out of their way to call attention to "Mr. Nietzsche." Strauss never did anything of the kind. He never wrote anything resembling *Ecce Homo* telling us about Mr. Strauss or how to interpret his various books. The rare occasions when Strauss calls attention to himself autobiographically are therefore doubly significant. They amount to an attempt to call attention to something Strauss thought had been overlooked. This, taken together with the series of indications Strauss gave of how to read other significant thinkers, gives us our present point of departure.

Was Strauss a Nietzschean? Yes and No. He was a Nietzschean in line with everything he thought he understood of Nietzsche. But Strauss's Nietzsche would not be recognizable as the Nietzsche presented in most contemporary scholarship. To take but one example, Strauss could have cared less about who was more "metaphysical," Nietzsche or Heidegger. That would have been an utterly superficial, derivative and obscurantist issue for him. Nor would Strauss have accepted that at the heart of Nietzsche's thought was to be found only the will of an esoteric nihilist.[6] Strauss's Nietzsche intended a paradoxical "return" to Nature, not the customarily announced emancipation from it. And perhaps even more iconoclastic, Strauss's Nietzsche was a Platonist.[7] Indeed, it is in understanding what Strauss meant by Platonism that we simultaneously grasp what he owes to Nietzsche.

Strauss discovered Nietzsche's Platonism before he turned to the systematic study of Jewish thought that occupied a good deal of his early scholarly efforts.[8] Strauss discovered Nietzsche's Platonism before he systematically confronted the work of Farabi who allegedly so massively influenced his reading of Maimonides. My assertion is that before Strauss turned to Farabi, Maimonides, and ultimately Plato, he already had his understanding of Platonism in hand. Why he presented that Platonism through the lens of, for example, his Maimonides rather than Nietzsche is an open question. An equally important question is why Strauss presented the *tension* between Jerusalem and Athens in such a way that serious commentators think it reasonable to conclude that he ultimately chose Jerusalem. Before we can assess what to make of Strauss's work on various Jewish thinkers, and long before we can proclaim Strauss a "Jewish thinker" himself, we must attend to the Platonism Strauss found in Nietzsche.

We have only one text of Strauss's specifically addressed to a Nietzschean work. It is his later essay, "A Note on the Plan of Nietzsche's *Beyond Good and Evil*."[9] It would be misleading to immediately assume that whatever is ultimately presented in that text represents what Strauss thought he understood fifty years earlier. But if there are central clues in that essay that point back to themes that were crucial in Strauss's works in the 1930s, 1940s and beyond, highlighting those convergences will prove to be valuable.

Strauss's late interpretation of Nietzsche comes into boldest relief when seen in the light of customary interpretations. Most noteworthy is the central position of God and religion as co-topics in Strauss's reading. Equally noteworthy is the importance given to the issue of a "transition" to a future where man is translated "back" into nature albeit paradoxically becoming "natural" for the first time. Strauss's interpretation runs in the face of those attempts to use Nietzsche to pursue a perfectly straightforward modern desire for the autonomy afforded by the freedom from nature. Finally, Strauss brings into high relief Nietzsche's longing for a total transformation of philosophy—and not just a transformation of its *public* persona. The future philosophers become the peak of existence in whose being all of existence is justified. Those new philosophers are said to rule in subtle and indirect ways as priests of a new religiosity. Behind these more priestly public philosophers, however, lurks another breed of philosophers in the freedom of a high solitude. God, religion, the high solitude of future philosophy, "nature" and the need for a transition to a unique future become the central themes. Strauss's Nietzsche is not the conventional Nietzsche.

For Strauss's Nietzsche, at least as matters come to light in *Beyond Good and Evil*,[10] the central issue is whether future philosophy will rule over religion or religion over philosophy. By comparison, Strauss asserts that for Plato and Aristotle the central issue was the rule of the city over philosophy or philosophy over the city. For Plato and Aristotle, religion is subsumed under the city. Strauss would have us believe that religion is taken to a higher plane by Nietzsche and in the process politics is transported to a lower plane. Yet the assertion is far from obvious. Indeed, Strauss goes to some pains to point out that the first chapters of *Beyond Good and Evil* are about philosophy and religion, while the later chapters are about politics and morals. Hence by Strauss's own reckoning, the organization of the book seems to point toward the confrontation between philosophy/religion on the one hand and politics/ morals that have been emancipated from philosophy on the other.

Complicating matters further, religion is discussed in chapters whose titles make them appear to be about political matters and political matters are discussed in the chapter "Das Religiose Wesen." The same can be said for the way the topic of philosophy is interspersed in all of the chapters. Further, just as *Beyond Good and Evil* criticizes all past philosophy while projecting a categorically different future philosophy, modern politics is criticized and a new, aristocratic, postmodern politics is held out as a redemptive possibility beyond the age-old spirit of revenge. I want to argue that the chasm between philosophy and the city, central to Strauss's conception of Platonism, was learned from Nietzsche. One of the first indications of this is seen in his interpretation of the order of the chapters in *Beyond Good and Evil*. Therein, Strauss stresses the chasm between philosophy and city. Yet Strauss seems determined to focus our attention on the future relation between philosophy and religion.

The mature Strauss's lifework on Aristophanes, Socrates, Xenophon, Thucydides, Plato, etc., seems to be built around the attempt to recover the experiences out of which philosophy initially grew. Those experiences are alternately designated pre-scientific, pre-theoretical or "natural."

When Strauss is finished trying to articulate those natural experiences it turns out that philosophy initially emerged in the midst of the experience of an unavoidable antagonism between philosophy and the laws, customs and gods of particular cities. The city was seen as intrinsically closed and particular; philosophy as open, skeptical and longing for knowledge of the universal. There are places in his corpus where Strauss makes it appear that this is the central and untranscendable tension for all time—a "natural" tension.

But if the abolition of the political is at all thinkable, then this tension is not natural in the sense of always emerging on its own in all circumstances. One can speculate that what Strauss is signaling in his late piece on Nietzsche is the possibility or even expectation that religion will in the future rise in importance as the political wanes. Any consciously plotted transition to the future would have to take that into account, accentuating its positive possibilities, limiting its negative ones.

In the aftermath of the collapse of modern rationalism—and Strauss shares with Nietzsche, Heidegger and many others the understanding that this has already happened—perhaps there is a logic that takes over that gains powerful momentum. Perhaps part of what is implied in that momentum is that politics will wane and an ambiguous religiosity will become ascendant. It is ambiguous because the object of that religiosity remains an open question. For example, with Nietzsche there is an attempt to attach it to the god Dionysus who will be a manifestation of the eternal, this-worldly circularity of the Will-to-Power. With Heidegger it is attached to a vague longing for yet unseen gods. From Strauss we get a particular manifestation of Jerusalem, as brought forth by the Hebrew prophets, as lovingly reinterpreted by Strauss.

The possible rise of a new religiosity seems linked with Strauss's understanding that the modern longing to abolish the political could be successful even though the modern rationalism that fostered it has collapsed. Strauss repeatedly argued that the resulting World State would lend itself to the degradation and dehumanization of man and a possible tyranny of immense proportions because the abolition of the political would require that mankind cease to strive to understand the good, the just and the noble and pursue them in action. That pursuit would cease because the state would insist that it already incorporates the final wisdom.

At one point Strauss says in praise of Heidegger that he is the only man who has an inkling of what is implied in the technological world civilization that is coming.[11] Strauss tells us that Heidegger believed that every great civilization in the past has had a religious foundation. But according to Strauss, in his search for a new god to save us, Heidegger had gone over to the side of the gods of the poets. Philosophy had thereby abdicated. It was in Nietzsche that the desire to have philosophy rule over religion is to be found. In this, Strauss apparently took the side of Nietzsche.

Like both his Nietzsche and his Heidegger, Strauss points to the impending significance of religion in the age after the collapse of modern rationalism when a worldwide technological civilization looms. But unlike either his Nietzsche or his Heidegger, Strauss still points to the importance of retaining, indeed retrieving, the political. He also points to the need to retain ties with the traditions of the past even as we move to a unique future that will need to be confronted in unique ways. A loving reinterpretation of past traditions is needed to make a successful transition to the future. Strauss apparently believed that the unique future that was coming should be both religious and political. As we will see, the two converge in a way that allows continuity with the past. In this regard we have something resembling the eternal return of the same.

In the English translation of his early work on Spinoza, Strauss bookends his confrontation with the "theological-political problem" first published in 1930 with an autobiographical piece added in 1962 that confronts the nature of the "Jewish problem" and a respectful piece on Carl Schmitt's *Der Begriff Des Politischen*. The theological-political problem was a life-long theme for Strauss. The "problem" concerns the irresolvable tension between the claims of philosophy and Revelation. Each claims to have the ultimate wisdom and the only genuine understanding of the good life. Strauss tried to show that despite his self-understanding, Spinoza had not refuted Revelation, and by extension, neither had anyone else.

The autobiographical discussion that prefaces the Spinoza critique discusses the problem confronted by Jews in Nazi Germany. Because of their precarious situation, they were forced to question the essential nature of their fundamental identity and how to maintain it. For example, did its maintenance require the creation of a secular Jewish state, moving to a tolerant liberal state, assimilationism of one kind or another, a return to "cultural" principles, or a return to the traditional, orthodox faith in miracles, creation *ex nihilo*, and the existence of a mysterious, willful, voluntaristic God? In this autobiographical piece philosophy, politics, and religion are brought together in a distinctive way.

In Strauss's account of "Jerusalem," and this is true throughout his corpus, it is not the orthodox faith in miracles, creation *ex nihilo* and the existence of a willful mysterious God qua lawgiver that is central to Revelation as he presents it, but the phenomenon of the prophet. Strauss's prophet is a human lawgiver who through his poetic speech orders a community. The prophets are depicted as philosophers in the city.[12] The primacy of the political is preserved in Strauss's rendition of Hebrew Revelation—law and lawgivers, obedience and law followers become central.[13]

Strauss eventually argued that the "Jewish problem" is identical to a universal human problem; in other words, there can be no contradiction-free society as the moderns hoped—least of all a global, technological state. Whenever Strauss turned to an explicit discussion of what was at the essential core of Jewishness, he never argued that it was to be found in membership in a particular tribe. And he never argued that it had anything to do with a return to traditional orthodoxy or Jewish "culture." In fact, in spite of his youthful fascination with Zionism, he came to argue that the existence of a specific Jewish state would in no way solve the "Jewish problem" as he articulated it. What Strauss defended is precisely the *rational* elements in the Jewish law, especially as interpreted by commentators like Maimonides. Strauss repeatedly argued that Judaism was always legalistic, hence rationalistic.[14] Further, Strauss argued that the Jewish God was always seen as the true God for all mankind, not merely the God of that particular tribe with which He initially covenanted. This is, to say the least, an argument not shared by all.[15]

Strauss repeatedly observed that in the Bible the beginning of wisdom is fear of the Lord, where for the Greeks the route to wisdom begins in wonder. The foundational necessity of fear was never in evidence in Strauss's work. And he knew perfectly well that all manner of dangerous nonsense could be advanced under the umbrella of divine inspiration or Revelation. The difference between true and false prophets had to be maintained and could only be discerned by the "intrinsic quality of revelation," i.e., its rationality.[16] Revelation needs philosophy. But philosophy cannot give an apodictic proof of the impossibility of Revelation and hence of philosophy's superiority. But that incapacity to dismiss Revelation is hardly a crippling blow for any philosophy that knows its own limitations and like Revelation realizes there is a mystery at the core of Being.

Strauss's longtime philosophic friend Jacob Klein once asserted that Strauss belonged to two worlds. The implication was that he was both a philosopher and a Jew. But in Strauss's terms that ultimately reduces to the fact that Strauss, like everyone else, had roots, belonged to a specific tradition and had a fated particularity: the love of one's own has its own beauty and fascination. Put another way, that meant no more than that Strauss was both a philosopher and a political man.

Having rationalized Revelation and Judaism, Strauss nonetheless turned around and argued paradoxically that the Bible is "the East within us."[17] This is part of his argument that at the heart of Western Civilization lies the energizing tension between Athens and Jerusalem, at least his lovingly reinterpreted variants of them. But it is also a response to Heidegger's attempt to import an Eastern element to help save the West by turning toward either a "second beginning" that takes off from the pre-Socratics or by importing something like non-subjectivist Buddhism. Strauss responded that we already have, and always have had, an Eastern, which is to say non-rationalist, element in the very heart of the West.

Without presently trying to resolve the seeming contradiction between depicting Judaism, and hence Biblical Revelation, as both rational and non-rational, Strauss seems to be trying to argue that after the collapse of modern rationalism, the West would be well served by the energizing tension of his own variants of Athens and Jerusalem. This is all part of Strauss's transition to a future that remains in touch with its past rather than having effected a radical break. Past and future are linked.[18] We do not need a "*destruktion*" or "deconstruction" of the West in either a Nietzschean or Heideggerian variant. We need only instead a "loving reinterpretation" of our tradition.[19]

We will return to Strauss's understanding of Athens in a moment, but we should note that Strauss makes it clear that he did not expect to ever see a perfect philosophic system that could explain the Whole. Hence we will never have perfect knowledge of man's place in the Whole. Barring such a perfect philosophic system, Strauss asserted that it may be true that the world could never be perfectly intelligible without the premise of a mysterious God.[20] Thereby, Strauss publicly defended at least one of the tenets of orthodoxy and by extension, the life of the orthodox believer. He defended that life, just as he defended a **substantive** vision of the political against Schmitt's formalism, but he did not choose either for himself as the central venue of his life. His is the benevolent act of a man on behalf of some of his destiny-mates. But it is also an act of honesty on the part of a man who was committed to the philosophic life while understanding in a deep and penetrating fashion the limits of rationalism. Perhaps he understood those limits even more profoundly than Socrates. For Socrates there was still an early, not altogether explored, faith in Reason. Strauss, however, had been a witness to the shipwreck of modern rationalism.

Despite his attempts to rationalize Judaism and Revelation, Strauss seems frequently to circle back in the direction of the mysterious, willful God of orthodoxy. At the heart of all that is, as with Heidegger, a mysterious absence that human *logos* cannot penetrate.[21] Yet Strauss could still remain committed to rationalism. Strauss left matters at saying that "it is unwise to say farewell to Reason."[22] Since modern reason had self-destructed, Strauss made it appear that we had to go back to a previous rationalism. But he was really looking forward to a future rationalism born of the novel tensions he proposed. The point at which Strauss stood in proposing those tensions—especially that between Athens and Jerusalem—was *outside* of both.[23]

To return from the Spinoza book to Strauss's essay on *Beyond Good and Evil*, following Nietzsche's lead, Strauss calls attention to the differences between all past "prejudiced" philosophers, present "free spirits" and the so-called philosophers of the future. All past philosophers were prejudiced and went astray in a variety of ways that need not detain us at this time.[24] Present philosophers are free from past prejudices but as their precursors, they are not yet the philosophers of the future. The "philosophers of the future" will have the overall obligation to rule and will for all intents and purposes be priests of a new life and nature affirming religion. Strauss stresses that for Nietzsche, while belief in the old God is dead, religiosity itself is growing and will only continue to grow into the future. This is put forward as a consistent outcome following the collapse of faith in modern rationalism. But despite the growing religiosity, for an extended period into the future, mankind will be left in a transitional period of atheism, left, that is, to worship the Nothing.

Strauss asserts that worshiping the Nothing is not where Nietzsche wants to leave the matter. He wants to make a transition from the No-saying of the present and immediate future to a Yes-saying, affirmative stance toward reality in the more distant future. The growing religiosity must be made compatible with this affirmative stance. There must be a religion of the Will-to-Power—understood as a vindication of a this-worldly circular god—that will be administered by the philosophers of the future who will be religious in a way no past philosophers have been.

The curious fact about the philosophers of the future is that in many ways they will not be as free and clear-sighted—and certainly not as capable of freely chosen solitude—as the prejudice-free "free spirits" of the present. Those free spirits seem to occupy a privileged moment.[25] Their response to that moment is to be the precursors to a different kind of philosopher. But their kind of philosophy will survive into the future, hidden deep within the interstices of the world where the philosophers of the future will be far more visible.

The freest philosophers must not only be shielded from what elsewhere in *Beyond Good and Evil* is called the "necessary dirt of all politics," but from any public persona or public function whatsoever. They must freely choose solitude, unlike involuntary solitaries of the past such as Spinoza or Giordano Bruno. That is best accomplished by the existence of a long ladder of different types of individuals. To the extent that free-spirited philosophy becomes in the process a skeptical, questioning "way of life" without public responsibilities or fixed metaphysical doctrines, it will tend to withdraw into solitude ruling over the religious philosophers of the future in a subtle and indirect fashion, publicly allowing religion to rule over what remains of politics.[26] What is Strauss trying to signal by this unique interpretation of Nietzsche?

One can only speculate about precisely what Strauss most appreciated in Nietzsche when he was young and reading him both voraciously and surreptitiously. But I would point to two texts to which Strauss only rarely thematically alludes. They are two of Nietzsche's earliest works—*The Birth of Tragedy* and *Untimely Meditations*. In the latter, Nietzsche discusses at length the ways in which the will to truth—i.e., philosophy—is inimical to life. Nietzsche's assertion is that we should choose life over truth. The philosophic longing for truth must not be allowed to destroy life, which requires all manner of tensions, contradictions and sheltering half-truths or outright myths and lies. One might note that for Nietzsche, the historical sense that contemporary man is so proud of, and Nietzsche is more than willing to use it to his advantage, is one of the truths from which we should be shielded. Strauss was likewise a public opponent of what he called historicism.

Yet despite making this argument, Nietzsche never tired of praising the clear-sightedness of free-spirited philosophy. What he ends up doing is positing a great chasm between what is good for life for most and what is an unavoidable "instinct" for some. Fortunately, according to Strauss's Nietzsche, that instinct of the few is what gives meaning to life for others if it is exercised with discretion. This chasm between philosophy and life, or alternately put, between philosophy and the city, is what became central to what Strauss meant by Platonism.[27] I suggest that Strauss learned it from Nietzsche. One ramification for both Strauss and Nietzsche was the need for esoteric speech and philosophic solitude.

In *The Birth of Tragedy*, Nietzsche points out the ways in which Greek civilization was energized if not constituted by the tension between Apollonian and Dionysian tendencies. This was part of Nietzsche's critique of modern rationalist civilization which had attempted to overcome all the tensions and contradictions which healthy civilizations require. The Greeks gave this particular tension to themselves—Nietzsche goes so far as to assert that they invented both of the tendencies symbolized by Apollo and Dionysus—in the height of their spiritual strength. In a parallel fashion, Strauss repeatedly argued that at the heart of Western Civilization was to be found the energizing tension between Reason and Revelation, Athens and Jerusalem. Strauss asserted that as long as that tension remained in place Western Civilization need not die. Asserting the life giving need for a central tension is not the same as asserting the simple truth of either of the participants in the tension.

We should recall the understanding Strauss attributes to Xenophon that even after the "Socratic Turn," the real Socrates continued to free-spiritedly think about all things, human, cosmic and presumably divine. That open and questioning philosopher need never show himself on the public stage if he is prudent like Nietzsche's future free spirits. As Nietzsche would have it, a public persona or mask can go forth into the world. Perhaps more to the point, the real philosopher may, for the first time, be able to withdraw and have no responsibility except to himself if things are arranged correctly. A present danger may point to a future possibility that has never yet existed, the actual possibility of solitary contemplation without public duties. This is a far cry from wanting to be a philosopher-king in any but the most remote and indirect fashion.

It is in this light that we should look at Strauss's argument in favor of the plausibility of Revelation. Its possibility had to be defended *philosophically* and the wisdom of Athens had to be depicted as a rationalism that knew its limits; it could not get to the ultimate mystery at the core of Being. Beyond the collapse of modern rationalism lies the tension between a specific, rationalist view of Jerusalem and a unique kind of rationalism. I suggest that Strauss got the underlying idea for this necessary tension from Nietzsche and long before he turned to Maimonides, Farabi, or Plato.

Apparently, what is required now is not to accentuate the original tension between philosophy and the city—although Strauss repeatedly returns to that theme—but primarily the tension between philosophy understood as a particular "way of life," and a somewhat un-traditional variant of Biblical religion that can be seen to have a rational leaning. Both leave an element of the mysterious at the core of Being. In different ways, this mysteriousness is at the heart of the public teachings of both Nietzsche and Heidegger; it is not at the heart of the public teachings of either Farabi or Maimonides.

Once one begins to look closely, it becomes more difficult to say precisely what the metaphor Athens meant for Strauss than what he intended by the term Jerusalem. We cannot leave matters at the easy-going statement that Athens stands for rationalism. For Strauss there are different variants of rationalism and a certain incommensurability between the modern and non-modern forms. For example, Strauss publicly rejected the premise, advanced by Heidegger among others, that modern rationalism descends in a direct line from Greek rationalism. "Athens" represents a specific variant of rationalism for Strauss. What I will assert is that there is a postmodern variant of rationalism toward which Strauss points. Athens is the metaphor for that postmodern rationalism as much as it is for the elements drawn from Greek thinkers.

In line with his depiction of the *Socratic* Socrates, Strauss initially presents the rationalism indicative of the metaphor Athens as a search for the "nature" or "natures" of the various categories or "tribes" of things "visible" publicly to all. This is what follows from interrogating what is alternately called the pre-theoretical, pre-philosophic, "natural" or common sense experience of reality.[28] Strauss asserted that using this approach we could gain considerable knowledge regarding the heterogeneity of the multiplicity of tribes even if we could have at best limited knowledge of homogeneity, the ultimate One of the whole cosmos.

But according to Strauss, Greek philosophy, and thereby "Athens," is also connected with the discovery of an even more generic philosophic concept "nature." According to this argument, the concept nature was discovered by reflecting upon such common sense experiences as the multiplicity of *nomoi* or conventions in the various cities, as well as through consideration of what follows from such distinctions as the difference between hearsay and what we see with our own eyes. In the former case, central to the idea of nature is the *nomos/physis* dichotomy. In the latter case, nature is associated with that which an individual can vouch for independent of commonly held and repeated opinions.[29] "Nature" so understood now has more in common with homogeneity (the One) than with heterogeneity (the multiplicity of the tribes or "whats"). The Socratic approach to "nature," which seeks the heterogeneity of the various tribes, seems to be a consciously adopted form of moderation in the face of the initial, more radical search for "nature" qua One.[30]

Be that as it may, the first complication we confront is that Strauss also links terms like pre-philosophic or pre-theoretical experience with "natural" experience. Much of Strauss's later work is devoted to trying to recover this pre-philosophic, "natural" awareness. I would argue that this undertaking is a decidedly postmodern maneuver that takes off from a specific modification of the German phenomenological tradition—especially as it is articulated by Heidegger.[31] The very task is decidedly un-Greek. This phenomenological task of unpacking leads to a "recovery" of *an* idea of "nature" that is different than the concept of nature Strauss asserts the Greek philosophers discovered precisely **in opposition** to pre-theoretical awareness.

If the concept "nature" has a historical element, as would seem to be indicated, why should the initial Greek manifestation, or its Socratic modification/moderation, be taken as the definitive manifestation? More to the point, I would maintain Strauss is ultimately grafting different notions of "nature" side by side. As I will argue in a moment, Strauss got the initial impetus for this idea from Nietzsche.

Using the Bible as his exemplar, Strauss asserts that in the pre-theoretical horizon man is not meant to be a knowing, wondering or contemplative being. It is "natural" to live a simple life in compliance with the law.[32] Straussian Platonists also understand that there is everywhere and always an arena of law, opinion and custom.[33] That too is "natural." The detachment from this pre-theoretical everydayness that is intrinsic to philosophy is thereby "unnatural" in that it rests on a detachment and alienation from primary, pre-philosophic attachments. These "natural" bonds formed the necessary background against which philosophy launched its initial pursuit of wisdom, i.e., the discovery of the philosophic concept or idea of "nature." But we can immediately turn the last point around yet again by observing that the wonder driven pursuit of wisdom, to the extent that it is driven by the powerful inclination of a distinctive or unique kind of being, is also "natural."

Obviously there is an extraordinary fluidity to the term "nature" in Strauss's thought that is similar to the fluidity in *Beyond Good and Evil*. My suggestion is that Strauss eventually follows his Nietzsche in seeing a variant of "nature" in pre-history, another historical variant initiated by the Greeks, modified in the "Socratic turn," and yet another that is possible in the future. All of these notions coexist in the metaphor Athens.[34] Athens, as it comes from the hand of Strauss, is a hybrid constructed of elements taken most notably from Plato, Xenophon, Aristotle, Nietzsche, and Heidegger.

Strauss's discussion of pre-theoretical awareness parallels Heidegger's discussion of "everydayness." For Heidegger, everyday perception is pre-theoretical and shaped by a distinctive "World." That pre-theoretical revelation of reality is always prior to any theoretical perception or philosophic detachment. Theoretical detachment is, therefore, always derivative and if not unnatural, at least "inauthentic." What Strauss does is give this abstract Heideggerian account of everydayness substantive manifestation by passing it through various Greek writers. For example, Strauss not only adds the flesh and blood of distinctive kinds of individuals with competing ends taken from the Platonic dialogues, but he also articulates Heidegger's "World" by importing a large element of what Aristotle meant by "regimes."

When Strauss is done, Heideggerian everydayness is determined by the substantive ends that distinctive tribes of individuals pursue which in turn are shaped by the shared view of the good of a particular group that shares a specific regime. To reduce the matter to a formula, Strauss makes Heidegger's abstract Phenomenological accounts of "everydayness" and "World" more concretely political. Strauss is also at pains to remind us that we are always confronted with competing regimes with different constellations of ends and different views of the ultimate good. This is what forms the very sinew of the political—contrary to Schmitt, for example, who sees political differences grounded in the generic "dangerousness" of man or the formal need for the we/they dichotomy.

Strauss not only gives sinew and ligature to Heidegger's account, he turns the issue of everydayness against Heidegger. Here, he borrows an element from the Socratic turn. Again, in interrogating everyday experience we always find that the world comes forth as a multiplicity of tribes or "whats." But eventually, even in the Socratic variant of the interrogation of everydayness, one is led to speculate on the origin or "cause" of the multiplicity of tribes. The Socratic response to this "natural" inclination is, according to Strauss, to make the tribe or class to which things belong the cause of the tribes. The answer to the question "what is" a certain thing points toward its essential nature which it shares with the other members of its tribe. The "what" of the various things defines their Being—they *are* this what. Pre-Socratic thought, already driven toward pursuing a concept of "nature" as cause, tried to think the cause directly and in abstraction from determinate beings— i.e., qua Fire, Water, Air, One, Number, etc. Like the pre-Socratics, Heidegger tried to think Being in abstraction from determinate beings.[35]

But Strauss does not stop here. He complicates matters by admitting that the thinking of the "real," non-Socratic Socrates went beyond working out the articulation of the multiplicity of things, the ensemble of "whats." The real Socrates did not stop with the easygoing conclusion that the tribes of the various things are their causes. Real philosophy always attempts to grasp the Whole and to think the origin of the Whole qua One. For Strauss this means that philosophy is always led in the direction of the question *quid sit deus*. But Strauss is almost completely silent regarding the noetic foundation of the seemingly necessary speculations toward which he alleges that "real" philosophy always moves. Strauss is just as silent in this regard as is Nietzsche about the life of the real thinkers who stand behind the "philosophers of the future." Hence it remains unclear whether for Strauss there is any continuity between philosophy in its Socratic manifestation and in its more comprehensive "speculative" or purely theoretical mode. What Strauss is doing is signaling that, like Nietzsche, he believes that all real philosophy is theoretical and solitary. The rest is public veneer. Still, philosophy, no matter how construed, does not and never can culminate in a public system of knowledge; it culminates in a "way of life" pursued by human beings of a very distinctive kind. This is precisely Nietzsche's conclusion.

It is also apparently Strauss's position that real, theoretical philosophy is eventually driven away from reflecting primarily on "external" reality and toward an interrogation of the nature of the inquirer. To again reduce the matter to a formula, mind or soul comes to take precedence over "nature" understood as concrete matter. According to Strauss, this happened at Athens. It goes without saying that a thinker like Hegel would concur that mature thought becomes reflexive; he would not accept that this occurred until long after Athens—the turn to reflexivity being prepared by Christianity through its deepening of self-consciousness that is then deepened further by Cartesian modernity. This may or may not give added credence to the idea that what Strauss meant by Athens was a hybrid of Greek and late modern (i.e. German) elements. However we deal with the historical question, high reflexivity is also an element of what Strauss means by his catch-all concept Athens. True philosophy is reflexive.

With the turn toward reflexivity, regardless of when it originated, the philosophic enterprise itself comes to take center stage. Henceforth the philosopher scrutinizes not only what he does in thinking, but also reflects on the very possibility of his enterprise and why it is of any value. Philosophy, born of a questioning and wondering instinct, to some extent rises above that instinct on the wings of its reflexivity, a reflexivity that is precisely what Revelation rules out of court before the fact. Reflexively interrogating itself, thinking points toward articulating the ground and very possibility of thinking. This almost inevitably leads away from everyday experience.

What we have said to this point has to be made consistent with Strauss's central argument that what happened in Athens at the dawn of philosophy was the simultaneous turn to *political* philosophy. Political philosophy as Strauss uses that designation is precisely what follows from reflexivity. Strauss argues that the turn to political philosophy was primarily undertaken for prudent or defensive reasons and thereby involved a newfound concern for political rhetoric—rather than because of any unavoidable epistemic dependence of thought on everyday experience, as the Socratic method seems to imply—not to mention the Heideggerian priority of the pre-theoretical.[36]

Its self-conscious concerns presuppose that philosophy as it turned to political philosophy had already become reflexive enough to see itself with self-conscious clarity as in principle in rebellion against the city and the various conceptions of justice of the various cities. Political philosophy is a fully self-conscious brand of philosophy. In a parallel fashion, Nietzsche depicted past, prejudiced philosophy as an initially instinctive activity which rises to reflexive clarity about itself, its presuppositions, and its needs only with the free-spirited philosophers of the present. For Nietzsche, there are many historical manifestations of philosophy. They occupy rungs on a ladder leading to a fully self-conscious philosophy. Both Strauss and Nietzsche point toward the need for a full, self-conscious brand of philosophy. Each sees it as culminating in a distinctive way of life outside and beyond everyday experience.

Strauss is never clear about just how dependent thought ultimately is on pre-theoretical awareness. From Heidegger we get a clearer answer regarding the relation between philosophy and everydayness. Everydayness is simply determinative. Every form of theoretical detachment takes off from the world revealed to us in our collective doing and making. For Strauss, it appears that philosophy can stand far enough outside its world to contemplate intelligibles of some sort.[37] In this, Strauss seems much closer to his Nietzsche than to Heidegger. Heidegger denied to philosophy this level of self-consciousness.

Whether philosophy can ever completely emancipate itself epistemically from everyday experience and primary associations, and hence how much purchase it can get on modifying the future, remains an open question. At present, all I want to suggest, for proving the matter is beyond the scope of the present undertaking, is that what Strauss means by Athens is a synthesis of elements drawn from the Greeks and the Germans. The Germans set the task; the Greeks supply substance and moderation.

Returning to Strauss's essay on *Beyond Good and Evil*, we have dealt with the prominence Strauss gives to religion, the need for a transition to a uniquely constituted future, and the various gradations of "philosophy." We have compared Strauss's Nietzsche with his own reflections on Athens and Jerusalem. We must now thematically attend to what Strauss designates the "problem of nature." I have already suggested the complicated, if not conflicting, ways Strauss uses the term "nature." Again, in the last analysis I believe Strauss follows his Nietzsche in significant ways.

Strauss asserts that for Nietzsche "nature" is something to be hoped for in the future when we can become natural for the first time. While it can be argued, as the moderns did, that we find the natural in the beginnings of human history, it is primarily at the end of history, or in the post-historical world, that Strauss's Nietzsche hoped to encounter the natural. Strauss twice repeats the observation that nature is a problem for Nietzsche but that he cannot do without it. The same appears to be true for Strauss. The Greek philosophers carved out and polished a concept of nature, linking it with the universal and unchanging. The moderns eventually made nature problematic by unleashing a new natural science and a new political science that had as their end, from the beginning, the eradication of unchanging nature and thereby of natural limits. We now see that those sciences themselves are without assignable limits at a time when nature dissolves as even a foil. Both Nietzsche and Strauss try to respond to this problem.

Nietzsche's response was to will the eternal recurrence which has as its end the "reintegration of man into nature." Despite the term "**re**-integration,"

Strauss makes much of Nietzsche's claim that man has never yet been natural. For Nietzsche, Strauss asserts, even in the pre-theoretical period prior to the origin of philosophy, man was not natural. Paradoxical as it might initially seem, the reason for this assertion is that at that time man had no end that differentiated him from the beasts. Furthermore, until the day after tomorrow, it will not be possible for mankind to affirm all that is and has been. We have feared, despised and revengefully attempted to transcend temporal reality from the beginning. Never yet has there been a self-conscious, affirmative, yes-saying to this world. That possibility still awaits us in the future as our end. Pursuing that end or *telos* is what will make us "natural" for the first time.

While Nietzsche asserts that mankind has never yet been natural, he does admit that at one time we were "instinctive," and for him that is at least a very close cousin of the natural. Nevertheless, following Aristotle, Nietzsche puts the primary locus of the natural in the end or *telos* and not in our beginnings or the simple, mechanical or efficient causality we share with the beasts. But the matter is more complicated. The Aristotelian ends are, in some compli-cated fashion, built into the constitution of the various things. The Niet-zschean end is not pregiven and has nothing about it of necessity, whether telic or efficient. Its coming to be depends on a unique prior history that leads up to the intervention of Nietzsche and a merely possible future.

Nietzsche seems to praise the instinctive. He says that late-modern hu-manity has ceased to be instinctive, becoming "de-natured" and timid. In re-sponse, he seems to praise the high, unself-conscious instinctiveness of a Caesar or an Alcibiades. This praise goes so far as to praise even their cruelty, the opposite of our present, de-natured timidity and compassion. By this ar-gument, the un-reflexive assertiveness of a few distinct individuals is closely akin to the "natural."

The benefit to life of their assertiveness and even cruelty, for the two are unavoidably linked, is that they can become the basis of a long-term compul-sion against the "natural," utilitarian impulse to immediate gratification and pleasure. We share that latter tendency with the beasts. This long-term com-pulsion impresses a form or "nature" upon mankind through habits. Conven-tional behavior eventually congeals as "nature"—*nomos* becomes *physis*. All form-giving, and this includes especially morality, is dependent upon this kind of tyranny against "nature" which simultaneously forms our "nature." But we moderns have fled this form-giving tyranny and are "de-natured." We must be "reintegrated into nature."

What Strauss stresses is that for Nietzsche, "nature" is ultimately some-thing to pursue that we can actualize in the future, not by going back to some manifestation of instinctiveness from the past. To get to that future, we must rise above the un-reflexive Caesars and Alcibiadeses of the past to the

philosophers of the future—Caesar with the soul of Christ. Those philosophers of the future are allegedly the most comprehensive beings in whose existence all of Being is affirmed. They have as their goal the overall development of mankind. Using the old *nomos/physis* distinction, Nietzsche plots a
path to a new conception of "nature," to be found in the future, where *nomos*
and *physis* in their traditional usages merge. If this merger is possible, the initial showing of "nature" as the other of convention should not be taken as the
last word.

Strauss makes a point of observing that the chapter title "Natural History
of Morals" is the only chapter title that explicitly refers to nature.[38] It is in this
chapter that Nietzsche makes much of morality being based on a tyranny
against "nature." In the discussion of philosophy and religion in the prior
chapters, both had been posited by Nietzsche as powerful "instincts." The
philosophers of the future will be less instinctive than their traditional predecessors, but also less reflexive than the free spirits. Strauss concludes that
"the subjugation of nature depends on men with a certain nature." They will
become the future basis of law, and long-term compulsion. Everything aims
at the justification of **these** "philosophers." They are the linchpins of the project to bring unbounded affirmation and with it the return of a sense of the noble and the related faith in rank and hierarchy. There is a striking resemblance
between this outcome and where Strauss arrives in his discussion of classical
Natural Right.

Strauss's "Natural Right" position must be differentiated from his discussion of the "Natural Law" tradition, which in many ways represents a betrayal
of its ancestor. Unlike the Natural Law tradition, Natural Right does not culminate in a specific universal morality or a best regime valid everywhere and
always. The Natural Right position is far more flexible because the focus is
primarily on the existence of a hierarchy of "natural" types of human beings
with the philosopher at the peak. Moral and political matters must be adjusted
to ever changing circumstances in light of the need to maintain that natural
hierarchy. On this, Nietzsche and Strauss are in almost perfect agreement.[39]
Beyond that, Natural Right also stands for the same things Strauss means by
Platonism. Politics, religion, and morality are "natural" dimensions of life, as
is genuine philosophy. Philosophy is the highest and most self-sufficient life,
but laws are still needed. Hence lawgivers are needed. Philosophy itself cannot give those laws; hence it must justify those who must. All of this is part
of Strauss's understanding of Platonism. Strauss's Nietzsche stands for all of
these things.

When Strauss is finished interpreting Nietzsche, Nietzsche stands for a future that is "natural," in that there will be a long ladder of rank and hierarchy,
at a peak of which stands the philosophers of the future. They are the justifi-

cation of all of existence because on a rung just above them, invisible from the base, are the true Nietzschean free spirited philosophers. One may say of Nietzsche's ladder that it is a conventional construction, in the traditional sense, except for the one rung at the top that is "natural." Without the peak, the rest of the ladder would have no meaning whatsoever; it would be a ladder to Nothing.

Moralities and regimes are "conventional," albeit the need for them is "natural." They must be judged in light of the extent to which the highest of human possibilities remains possible. To that end, an attempt may need to be made to argue that there is continuity between morality, law, religion and philosophy. But the continuity is questionable. The only way we can take our bearings regarding the Whole is to judge it in light of its highest manifestation—highest because it is **most comprehensive and reflexive**. Perhaps that highest possibility can only truly come to pass for the first time in the future.[40] That would make the future "natural" for the first time. All of past history would be a movement toward that possibility. The accidental past would be redeemed and have meaning only if this new naturalness came to pass. There was a close cousin of nature in the beginning—instinct—and there is nature in the future as an end to pursue. There is, therefore, something resembling eternal return.

What Strauss presents as the classical Natural Right position was quickly swamped by the rigidities of the Natural Law tradition. That Natural Law tradition reached its first peak in Aquinas. The rigidities of his teaching were reproduced in a reaction against it in the modern Natural Law teaching of Hobbes. The reaction to the modern Natural Law tradition led through a series of wave-like intensifications to the birth and expansion of the historical consciousness, which both Strauss and his Nietzsche oppose by attempting a move forward into a novel future. In Strauss's case, the move includes a loving reinterpretation of both Jerusalem and Athens. With that reinterpretation comes the return of the Natural Right tradition in a permutation never before seen. Nature "is" a diverse set of tribes with a hierarchal articulation.

Beyond the call to wonder, to questioning and searching, seen as a manifestation of the highest "way of life," what kind of concrete "project" has Strauss bequeathed?[41] Taken in panoramic perspective Strauss appears to have purposely left us with the untranscendability of various tensions: Philosophy and the City, Athens and Jerusalem, Ancients and Moderns, and more than a few others that are less prominently displayed. Strauss has concluded that life is best served by the ongoing, healthy interplay of irresolvable tensions. Much as life and truth come into opposition for Nietzsche, they do for Strauss as well. What is good for everyday life is not simply the final truth for philosophy, which concludes among other things that its own activity is the most comprehensive. Philosophy is a mysterious part of the natural whole. Like every other natural species or tribe, this one always runs the risk of becoming extinct. It is impossible to predict, as any environmentalist will testify, how the natural whole is affected by the elimination of one of its parts.

But if, as both Strauss and his Nietzsche thought, philosophy is nature's highest and most comprehensive part because through it mind comes reflexively into the Whole, its loss could be devastating. Strauss seems to have concluded that if the present momentum of the increasingly global West is not reversed, the future might not continue to be conducive to philosophy. Nietzsche's *willing* of the eternal recurrence and hope for a new breed of philosophers implies the same thing.

Strauss's late text on Nietzsche signals predictions regarding what is to come. In that vision, forthcoming is a diminution of the tension between philosophy and the city. Because of the success of modern philosophy, we can predict the possible abolition of the political, especially if modern science were to eradicate the natural diversity that stands as its ground. That still hangs in the balance. To preserve its own distinctive form of diversity, philosophy must speak up on behalf of diversity *per se*. To continue to defend itself **against** the city as it did in its first manifestation would leave philosophy aiming its cannons in the wrong direction. The political should be defended. Likewise, to continue to rail against philosophy being diminished if it even appeared to be the handmaiden to theology, as was reasonable at the end of the middle ages, would represent a misallocation of resources in the world that is coming. Philosophy must defend Jerusalem or give way to ambiguous new gods. It should be kept in mind that the defender is clearly higher than the defended.

Defending philosophy primarily against either theology or the city has become an antiquarian undertaking. Contrary to either of those antiquarian undertakings, Strauss posits unavoidable tensions between Philosophy and the Political and between Philosophy and Revelation at a time when all the parties are in danger of extinction. I have tried to suggest that both Strauss's Athens and his Jerusalem represent amalgams of ancient and modern elements. It is not surprising therefore that there have been such diverse interpretations of his work. **I maintain that most of those diverse interpretations are consistent with the tensions Strauss wants to put in place.**[42] I believe that Strauss thought he needed a variety of different positions to be adopted—i.e., taken seriously—if he was to modify the features of the future he saw coming.[43] It was imperative that there be believers, lawgivers, patriots, thinkers of all stripes and colors, and on and on. The existence of this diversity is the presupposition of both Strauss's Natural Right position, and the project of his Nietzsche.

While Strauss thought that it was necessary to hold on to rationalism in the age of the collapse of modern rationalism, it was also necessary that there be laws. To the extent that, contrary to modern philosophy, philosophy is transformed into a mysterious *way of life* rather than a public *system of knowledge*—and Nietzsche is at the forefront of this undertaking—future philosophers in principle will not be lawgivers in any but the most indirect and detached way. Strauss understood as well as Heidegger that a global, technological civilization was coming wherein we would be possessed of immense power with no assignable limits to its exercise. He does not appear to have believed that some form of autonomous theoretical philosophy can ultimately assign those limits any more than did Heidegger. That leaves in its wake a concrete political and moral problem. There is a need for laws and lawgivers. But there is no need to quit serviceable ones that already exist. They can be lovingly modified.

The solution to the problem of limits seems to presuppose the need for the existence of different individuals able to pursue different ends—i.e., different visions of the good life.[44] That in turn would bring with it serious debate about the most important things. Therein the political would remain a feature of the future world, no matter how local or global the venue of the debate. **For Strauss, the political implies a serious conflict over the nature of the good which given the mystery at the core of Being can never yield apodictic answers**. The debate can be eternal, albeit all publicly adopted answers are doomed to being replaced eventually. There need not be armed camps and war. But there will be some degree of conflict and confrontation. That is intrinsic to both our nature and the nature of the Whole.

While the necessary interplay of genuine diversity could easily be quite unpredictable, Strauss was unwilling to let matters eventuate in the amorphous possibilities he attributed to both Nietzsche and Heidegger. He wanted to link future possibilities to past traditions. Far more than the late modern authors from whom he draws, Strauss wanted a more or less predictable future. In the end, the belief in the possibility of predictability seems to rest on the presupposition of an unchanging nature. But Strauss was always reticent to simply assert that theoretical possibility. Therein lies the problem of nature in Strauss's thought, which, I believe, remains unresolved.

Be that as it may, there is no mystery why, in the aftermath of Nazi inhumanity, and throughout the Cold War threat of universal tyranny, Strauss could be a perfectly unproblematic defender of Washington. Openness to debate about the good was precluded by both modern, totalitarian options. Acceptance of natural human diversity, no matter how defined, was openly opposed. Washington still allowed openness to a more "natural" form of politics. To the extent that openness remains, Strauss would continue to defend Washington as should any sensible human being. But there is a problem here for Strauss. Moscow, Berlin and Washington all rested on the efforts of modern philosophy which for Strauss moved with wave-like necessity from its more modest beginnings to its destructive end. To reject modern rationalism would seem to carry with it the conclusion that all of the political and moral dispensations descending from it must be rejected as well.

But Strauss asserted that it was an affront to common sense not to see the clear superiority of Washington to either Moscow or Berlin, to which we might now add Tehran and Beijing. The superiority of Washington to any available alternative was and is true whether we look at the matter from the rarefied perspective of a philosopher, or from the more straightforward common sense articulation of reality shared by millions of individuals in everyday life.

The problem for Strauss is that this common sense conclusion seems to give greater priority to everyday experience and the **practical reason** that emanates from it over the theoretical or speculative reason whose solitude Strauss seems to want to defend in the future. I know of nowhere in his corpus where Strauss defends anything like the priority of practical reason to theoretical reason that this understanding requires. We are back to the troubling question of where the philosopher stands who puts in place all the tensions he presumes are beneficial to life. Is it not practical wisdom rather than theoretical or speculative reasoning that tells him what is necessary?

By the same token, I see no statement of Strauss's anywhere that points out the noetic foundation of a truly autonomous speculative philosophy even though in the last analysis I think he follows Nietzsche in positing a certain detached solitude for future philosophy. Perhaps there is some middle ground here, but Strauss remains silent regarding what it is. Maybe in line with what Klein indicated, Strauss did try to live in two worlds, if not precisely the two Klein had in mind. But the relation of those two worlds—the everyday and the speculative—remains obscure in Strauss. As a result, the ultimate philosophical ground of Strauss's defense of Washington remains unclear.[45]

That said, let us assert the following: For Strauss, Washington stood for a form of practice that was far more "natural" than the available alternatives. And this is true despite the fact that its Constitution is descended from the modern theoretical principles that aimed at routing nature. Beyond that, Strauss's Washington is open to and indeed already linked with Jerusalem; we are already formed by the scriptural tradition. Strauss repeatedly quoted Nietzsche's observation that it was impossible to have Biblical morality without the Biblical God. But for Strauss there is no need to construct some synthesis of Caesar with the soul of Christ to retain that link.

The link to the Biblical tradition is already imbedded in the practice of Washington.[46] What was needed was to defend the dignity of the life of the believer. One does not have to create a new belief or wait for new gods with no assurance that either would be forthcoming or sanguine. Finally, Washington, at its best, offers an environment where modern constructivism does not so virulently unleash itself that the natural articulation of reality with its everyday understanding and primary attachments gets routed, despite Washington being a child of the Enlightenment. Washington is potentially more immune to the excesses of modernity than any of the other modern alternatives yet seen, to say nothing of the virulently anti-modern alternatives. **But without some new future, postmodern end to pursue, it may not remain immune forever.**

That said, in the aftermath of the Cold War, with no sign of a revitalized Fascism on the horizon, Strauss's relation to Washington would have changed. In this new environment, Strauss would be free to criticize elements in the moral and political life of Washington that would have been irresponsible in a different environment. American political life is becoming less and less natural—and moral discourse is becoming increasingly abstract, and the vitality of concern for things like honor, morality and the holy is precarious.

Beyond that, Strauss would surely criticize the creeping uniformity of late-modern civilization. Indeed, it would be the moral and cultural underpinnings of late modern civilization that Strauss would have criticized more than its parchment regime or concrete laws which are perfectly serviceable. He would, however, probably oppose the transfer of more and more issues that were strictly political into administrative and bureaucratic venues. And he would no doubt wish a reversal of contemporary trends in theology, wishing to see Jerusalem interpreted more in the direction of resoluteness and fortitude than what he would see as an easygoing, democratizing latitudinarianism.

But I think it is inappropriate to drive Strauss very hard in the direction of specific policy issues because he would have shied away from allowing political philosophy to become confused with political ideology, no matter how dignified the ideology or the regime it supported. For Strauss there could never be a perfect regime or contradiction free society. And political philosophy had to remain an open-ended undertaking. In the last analysis, Strauss was a partisan of philosophy rather than of any specific regime.

To the extent that the American regime remains open to diverse natural possibilities, our past Western tradition, *and* the need for change, it would in Strauss's eyes remain worthy of a serious philosophical defense. But to do so, Washington would have to remain open to *both* continuity and change. Depending on that openness, Washington would remain either a threat or a shelter for future humanity, a prison or a haven.

NOTES

1. See Leo Strauss *On Tyranny: Including the Strauss-Kojève Correspondence*, ed. Victor Gourevitch and Michael S. Roth (New York: Free Press, 1991). See also chapter 2.

2. Leo Strauss, *Spinoza's Critique of Religion* (New York: Schocken Books, 1965), p. 2.

3. I will return to the question of what Strauss thought the future of philosophy should be in the next essay.

4. Leo Strauss, "Correspondence of Karl Löwith and Leo Strauss," trans. George Elliot Tucker, *Independent Journal of Philosophy* 5/6, 1988, pp. 177–92. We should also note that Strauss says something similar regarding Heidegger. He claimed that nothing so massively affected him "in the years in which [my] mind took [its] lasting direction as the thought of Heidegger." He also says of Heidegger that he is the only "great thinker" of the twentieth century. Leo Strauss, "An Unspoken Prologue," *Interpretation*, Vol. 7/3 (September 1978), pg. 2. See Leo Strauss's *The Rebirth of Classical Political Rationalism* (Chicago: University of Chicago Press, 1989), pg. 29. See also Leo Strauss *What Is Political Philosophy?* (Chicago: University of Chicago Press, 1988), p. 246. We will return to the issue of Heidegger below, although on this occasion, reflection on Nietzsche's influence will take the lead.

5. *Independent Journal*, p. 183.

6. Shadia Drury has attributed such a position to Strauss. See her *The Political Ideas of Leo Strauss* (New York: St. Martin's Press, 1988). While this argument has become a staple for the *New York Times* whenever it mentions Strauss's name, as well as in the essays of individuals like the liberal polemicist Stephen Holmes, I agree with Robert Pippin regarding the abject superficiality of this position. "The idea of Strauss's 'philosopher' as Nietzschean 'superman,' 'creating values,' is an absurd overstatement and misses a very central issue in Strauss's account, the problem of nature, nowhere explored with any sensitivity in Drury's book." I will argue below that Pippin is quite correct in seeing the "Problem of Nature" as a, if not the, central issue linking Nietzsche and Strauss. See Robert Pippin, *Idealism as Modernism* (New York: Cambridge University Press, 1997), p. 212.

7. Laurence Lampert is one of the first to see this in his subtle account in *Leo Strauss and Nietzsche* (Chicago: University of Chicago Press, 1996). While Lampert sees some of the elements Strauss and Nietzsche share, he ultimately takes Strauss to task for not following what he (Lampert) sees as the logic of where Nietzscheanism leads. In effect, he accuses Strauss of a certain cowardice that eventuates in a conservatism that refuses to speak the truth in public. Lampert's Nietzsche, on the other hand, intended a general "enlightenment" and emancipation from myth. Humanity was to resolutely stare into the abyss en masse. It seems to me that Lampert may have missed the real thrust of **Nietzsche's** project. To a certain extent, he seems to understand Strauss better than Nietzsche.

8. Indeed, as Lampert notes, Nietzsche's presence is massive in Strauss's early work *Philosophy and Law*. It can be seen prominently as well in his early work on

Spinoza and in later works such as *Natural Right and History* (Chicago: University of Chicago Press, 1950), especially pp. 9–80.

9. The essay is included as one of the central chapters in Strauss's last book, *Studies in Platonic Political Philosophy* (Chicago: University of Chicago Press, 1983), pp. 174–91. That Strauss designated the essays in this volume "Platonic" is another key to what Platonism meant for him.

10. In comparing *Beyond Good and Evil* and *Zarathustra* Strauss says that *Beyond Good and Evil* had always seemed to him to be Nietzsche's most "beautiful" work. He notes that Nietzsche thought that *Zarathustra* was his most "profound" work. Strauss observes that profound and beautiful are two different things. He seems to have purposely avoided using Nietzsche's most profound work as his vehicle. In short, Strauss purposely chose not to deal with Nietzsche's most philosophic text.

11. See "Heideggerian Existentialism," in *Rebirth of Classical Political Rationalism* (Chicago: University of Chicago Press, 1989), p. 43.

12. See especially in this regard *Philosophy and Law* and the "Introduction" in *Persecution and the Art of Writing* (Glencoe, IL:Free Press, 1952).

13. Indeed, Strauss points out that one of the most significant differences between the Jewish and Christian traditions is that the one is legalistic and the other arrives at a more or less apolitical set of tenets of faith. For what it is worth, authors like Machiavelli and Nietzsche who took on scholarly significance for Strauss had argued that Christianity undermined the political. Be that as it may, Strauss is clear that the ultimate outcome of modernity, whether as secularized Christianity or not, is a threat to abolish the political. Hebrew Revelation in Strauss's rendition does not.

14. Strauss even cites Deuteronomy 4:6 in support (*Spinoza's Critique of Religion*, p. 30).

15. Yet Strauss could still make a more visceral argument that it is "honorable" to love one's own—i.e., to affirm the lot in life into which one is unavoidably thrown. One must keep in mind the status of honor in Strauss's thought. See Leo Strauss, "Why We Remain Jews," in *Leo Strauss: Political Philosopher and Jewish Thinker*, ed. Walter Nigorski and Kenneth L. Deutsch, (Lanham, MD: Rowman & Littlefield, 1994).

16. See "Progress or Return," in *Rebirth of Classical Political Rationalism*, p. 264.

17. *Rebirth of Classical Political Rationalism*, p. 44.

18. This comes close to the element of "ecstatic temporality" that I have argued is the appropriate stance for political philosophy. See chapter 3 "What is Political Philosophy" above.

19. We should keep in mind the assertion that Strauss explicitly made that the concern with past and future intrinsic to modern thought, and especially late modern thought, comes at the expense of the primacy of the eternal. See "Progress or Return," in *Rebirth of Classical Political Rationalism*, p. 239. My version of ecstatic temporality requires a recognition of the place of the temporal together with an openness to the eternal, which is part of how the phenomena present themselves. As I will try to show in the next chapter, I believe this is exactly what Strauss does. Strauss, like his Nietzsche, was concerned with the past and future and the possibility of a transition

that could link them with some degree of continuity. That is an openness to the place of the temporal.

20. *Spinoza's Critique of Religion*, p. 29.

21. The moderns tried to eliminate the mysterious core by replacing the visible world with a hypothetical one constructed by the mind. In that effort, Strauss argued, it remained precisely as hypothetical as orthodoxy and every bit as much based on faith. That world theoretically constructed by man could never be totally successful in explaining the whole, which would be the only philosophical, as opposed to technological, argument in its favor. As we will see shortly, from Heidegger Strauss learned a powerful critique of that constructivism and a way back to the visible world that shows itself, and thereby back to "nature." That opening informed his vision of Athens.

22. *Spinoza's Critique of Religion*, p. 31.

23. I will argue that Strauss's loving reinterpretation was a synthesis born of a Platonism learned from Nietzsche, informed by theoretical insights taken from Heidegger, projected back on selected ancient and medieval authors as part of fostering a transition to a novel future. Therein lay Strauss's novelty.

24. I deal with this at greater length in my *Nietzsche, Heidegger and the Transition to Postmodernity* (Chicago: University of Chicago Press, 1996), pp. 135–171.

25. Strauss also seems to point to the present as a privileged moment. See *The City and Man* (Chicago: Rand McNally, 1964), p. 9: "[T]he crisis of our time may have the accidental advantage of enabling us to understand in an untraditional or fresh manner what was hitherto understood only in a traditional or derivative manner. This may apply especially to classical political philosophy."

26. For Nietzsche that meant, at least initially, the "great politics" hegemonized by a united Europe that would usher in global rule for the first time.

27. Strauss clearly never accepted that the doctrine of the ideas was central to Platonism, or even that Plato had any specific metaphysical doctrine.

28. Prior to the discovery of the philosophic concept or idea of nature—already approached by the Sophists—"pre-philosophic" awareness focused on the "custom" or "way" of the various individual things. In this fashion, the custom or way of a dog was equated with that of trees, Persians, athletes and so on. All things belong to a "tribe" and have a custom or unique way. As is true of his depiction of the pre-Socratics, Strauss asserts that there is no philosophic concept or idea like "nature" in the Bible. The Bible also discusses "custom" or "way," not "nature." In this regard, the Bible is "pre-philosophic" or "pre-theoretical." This is a conclusion that even some who consider themselves Straussians are want to reject. See Hadley Arkes, "Athens and Jerusalem: The Legacy of Leo Strauss," in *Leo Strauss and Judaism*, ed. David Novak (Lanham, MD: Rowman & Littlefield, 1996), pp. 1–23.

29. *National Right and History*, pp. 81–120.

30. I deal with this subject at greater length in the next chapter.

31. Husserl had argued that there was pre-theoretical awareness. All scientific knowledge was derivative from this "primary" knowledge of the world. But Husserl ultimately linked that awareness to an openness to pure essences grasped by a decidedly modern, abstract, theoretical ego. Heidegger deflected Husserl's insight in the di-

rection of the "everydayness" of sensibly perceived, publicly shared reality. See "Philosophy as Rigorous Science and Political Philosophy" in *Studies in Platonic Political Philosophy*, pp. 29–37, and "An Introduction to Heideggerian Existentialism" in *Rebirth of Classical Political Rationalism*, pp. 27–46. Strauss follows Heidegger in that he wants to lodge the pre-theoretical in a publicly shared reality. I also develop this theme further in the next chapter.

32. Drawing from Heidegger, Strauss also argued that pre-theoretical experience is not only political and moral, but always contains an element of the holy. This is what Strauss borrowed most significantly and then modified most creatively, Heidegger's understanding that the everyday articulation of things unavoidably contains an element of the holy—e.g., the "Fourfold." Strauss deflects this notion in the direction of his discussion of Revelation. Strauss and Heidegger both see the pre-philosophic lifeworld as a world of nations (hence politics), morality and faith. But Strauss is always far more substantive in articulating what this means.

33. Straussian Platonists further know that while the philosophic pursuit of wisdom may be instrumental in changing the everyday content of opinion, it will never lead to the overcoming of opinion and its replacement by universal wisdom.

34. In between the Greek beginning and the future we have Christianity and Modernity, both of which attempted a journey *away* from "nature."

35. Heidegger argued for the need to get directly to the issue of Being without passing through the determinate particularity of any distinct things. He felt that any doctrine that focused on beings led inevitably to the mastery and domination of beings intrinsic to modern technology. Strauss's unstated response to Heidegger is that one must always ask the question, "What is *this* thing?" For Strauss, one cannot, or at least should not, try to get to the Being of a thing except by proceeding through discrete beings. Or to cast the matter in a Heideggerian light, one cannot get to Being in abstraction from beings.

36. For Strauss, alternately, political philosophy is either the reflexive defense of pure philosophy—understood as pure theory—or one of the branches of pure philosophy. This is where I part ways with Strauss. I argue that political philosophy is proto-philosophy.

37. I reflect on the nature of these intelligibles in the next chapter.

38. Strauss then, seemingly nonsequitously, wonders out loud if nature could be the theme of the entire second half of *Beyond Good and Evil*.

39. An unavoidable question remains: Upon what foundation does the person making the practical adjustments called for by this understanding of Natural Right stand?

40. Strauss did assert that no one had *ever* spoken more magnificently about what a philosopher was than Nietzsche. And Nietzsche's discussion of philosophy, in Strauss's eyes, leads up to the philosophers of the future.

41. We might note that to say that philosophy is primarily a "way of life" presents a metaphor that hardly basks in the light of full substantive clarity.

42. Needless to say, a few of the prominent interpretations are based on the inability to understand either Strauss or the sources he attempts to hold in tension.

43. It is not necessary that Strauss saw how all the parts would fit into a whole all at once. That clarity may have come over time.

44. The diversity toward which Strauss points was not the now fashionable group diversity associated with the mantra of race, class, gender and ethnicity. Strauss pointed toward the diversity of genuinely different types of individuals who pursue different ends.

45. I try to transcend these problems that come from accepting the theoretical/practical split that descends from the teaching of Aristotle. I believe my notion of political philosophy as proto-philosophy accomplishes that task.

46. I will argue below that there is much to be gained by stressing the Christian element of that tradition far more than Strauss did.

Chapter Ten

On a Possible Epicurean Garden for Philosophy: Philosophy and the City in the Thought of Leo Strauss

An evolving interpretative context has pitted interpretations of Strauss as a furtive Nietzschean nihilist on the one hand against an understanding that he was primarily a Jewish thinker on the other. I will argue that he was neither. Strauss was attempting to recover what he categorized as the original **idea** of philosophy as theoretical and contemplative. But given the novel late modern situation of philosophy, that required that theory be reconceptualized. Further, following his own understanding of Nietzsche, he wished to separate future philosophy from the city, sending it off to a new found detachment in a postmodern epicurean garden. Far from aiming at unleashing a new band of philosopher kings, Strauss aimed at epicureanizing philosophy by separating future philosophy from the constructivist interventionist stance it adopted during the modern epoch. That separation required, however, that the political be given a new found autonomy, beyond the possibility of the End of History.

Nature, we have heard the accusation that has arisen recently that Leo Strauss was really a furtive Nietzschean nihilist and atheist operating under the esoteric cover of discussions of Natural Right and Revelation.[1] Surprisingly, we also have an expanding literature on Strauss as a "Jewish thinker."[2] My position is that Strauss was neither a Nietzschean nihilist nor a Jewish thinker. He was primarily trying to rethink the nature of philosophy and what it could be in the future. This rethinking took on a "political" element because Strauss saw philosophy in its **origins** as born out of a confrontation between philosophy and the city. And in its **present** situation, Strauss saw philosophy as endangered by the modern longing for the End of History and the abolition of the political it implied. Reflections on day-to-day political matters were not Strauss's primary focus; those reflections were derivative from his primary concerns regarding the nature and future of philosophy.

But to say that for Strauss philosophy was the central concern does not immediately solve all problems. We would still have to determine if Strauss saw philosophy primarily as a form of activism (perhaps along the lines of a Nietzschean voluntarism) or as a form of contemplation? Assuming as I do that the answer is ultimately the latter, did Strauss understand contemplation as the detached theoretical reflection upon unchanging metaphysical and ontological realities—"Nature" or "Being"—or was contemplation understood differently? Once again, my conclusion is that the second possibility is where Strauss comes to take his stand.

Strauss complicates matters by arguing that the point of **departure** for philosophy is always "phenomenological," in the sense of grounded in the "everyday" articulation of things. Almost always this understanding is deflected by Strauss in the direction of an allegedly Socratic, dialectical position. This leads in a direction wherein philosophy would appear to be incapable of being a simply theoretical activity unless it can leave its point of departure behind completely. But Strauss also presents philosophy as a theoretical contemplation of unchanging "fundamental questions." And he presents philosophy as an activity that always has to defend itself against the city. So understood, that which is defended would appear to have to be a **detached** theoretical activity. When all is said and done, these various indications are not mutually consistent or capable of being synthesized.

It is curious that debates about Strauss in recent years have been transformed into a confrontation between Strauss as Nietzschean atheist versus Strauss as religious thinker given that a prior generation of commentators posed the issue in such a significantly different fashion. For them, the issue was whether Strauss was a defender of liberal, Lockean modernity, especially in its American liberal capitalist permutation, or an antidemocratic, anti-liberal, absolutist "ancient."

We should recall that in the American academy, Strauss was one of the leading generals in the battle against social science positivism and the ascendancy of the fact-value dichotomy (see Storing, Rothman and Cropsey). By arguing that modern, social science positivism was relativist in a way that would inevitably lead to historicism, Strauss emerged, by a hasty dualistic process of elimination, as an antiquarian and absolutist (see Gunnell 1978). In response, Strauss argued that most of his allegedly objectivist, positivist opponents were in reality just closet liberals who furtively brought their liberal "values" in the back door (see "Epilogue," in Storing). No doubt this confrontation helps explain why in his opponents' eyes Strauss was a conservative, and in the minds of some, thereby necessarily anti-democratic—i.e., primarily a political thinker.

Strauss's scholarly explorations of classical political thought and the Natural Right tradition, along with his criticism of the philosophic foundations of historicism—which he saw as implicit in proto-liberalism—also brought forth the accusation of absolutism and anti-democratic sympathies. It was argued that at the heart of liberalism lay voluntarism, toleration and diversity. Any attempt to suggest that there was a natural fabric to human existence or a natural hierarchy of human types of life would jeopardize the toleration needed to foster competing and diverse voluntarily chosen lifestyles.

In one defense of liberalism it was argued that relativism, academically referred to as "anti-foundationalism," was the prerequisite for legitimizing the necessary, democratic, voluntarist acts of pure choice. Strauss threatened this commitment and thereby became an anti-democratic, backward looking conservative in the eyes of his detractors. On the other hand, many self-proclaimed supporters saw in the possibility of a **recovery** of a classical Natural Right position the means to overcoming what they saw as a deepening moral and political crisis—either of modernity or of Western civilization more generally. They looked on favorably at the possibility of recovering absolute standards (see Jaffa 1982).

Hence it is all the odder that the contemporary orthodoxy among detractors makes Strauss a Nietzschean nihilist and atheist (Drury, Ferry, Holmes, Rosen). All of Strauss's discussions of Natural Right, Athens and Jerusalem, the limitations of positivism and historicism—in short, all of the things that previously got him labeled an absolutist—are now seen as no more than an exoteric surface constructed for the sake of misdirection. The point of this misdirection, however, is still held to be the pursuit of a conservative, anti-democratic political agenda. Again, Strauss is reduced to being primarily a political thinker.

The newer Strauss allegedly believes that philosophy is the only intrinsically valuable life. But since philosophy rests on no natural or trans-historical foundation—and hence has nothing unchanging to theoretically contemplate—all it can do is engage in Nietzschean acts of will that stand in mid air and impose a world of "values" on the non-philosophic many. Philosophy is reduced to a form of voluntarist activism on the part of a new breed of philosopher-kings who must dictate to non-philosophers how they should live.

Along the previous battle lines, it was Strauss's liberal opponents who were the Nietzschean voluntarists; now it is Strauss. A curious reversal. But the outcome is the same. In each case Strauss becomes an anti-democratic conservative, political thinker. Either he is an absolutist who undermines self-defining democratic individualism or he is an elitist voluntarist who sees no alternative to the imposition of a groundless order on the unwashed many by the wise few—a few, it is feared, made up entirely of a secret order of "Straussians."

This position has evoked an emerging counter-orthodoxy among a number of Strauss's supporters that by comparison with earlier supporters, inflates the importance of Strauss's discussion of "Athens and Jerusalem."[3] Many now conclude that in the "tension" between Athens and Jerusalem, Strauss chose Jerusalem and hence some now see Strauss as primarily a "Jewish thinker." In short, the new debate between Strauss's supporters and detractors seems to be focusing on the issue of Strauss's belief in God and Revelation rather than his commitment to unchanging Nature as a standard for absolutist political norms.

It is fascinating that Strauss has elicited so many widely divergent interpretations. I want to argue that they are all made possible by the central core of Strauss's thought which, following Strauss, I will designate "Platonist."[4] But Strauss's Platonism is of a kind that could only be possible after the tradition shattering thought of the last one hundred and fifty years. The only vague recognition of this influence is by those who attribute Nietzscheanism to Strauss. But they have failed to pay proper attention to Strauss's own interpretation of Nietzsche. Strauss's Nietzsche is not a voluntarist but rather a Platonist. Central to Strauss's Nietzsche is an attempt to recover "Nature." His Nietzsche focuses on the possibility of a future breed of philosophers who—unlike the modern philosophers—would again adopt a detached theoretical stance rather than public activism/constructivism—i.e., a new form of Epicureanism with the philosophers withdrawing from the political arena. Finally, while Strauss's Nietzsche focuses on the future status of religion in the aftermath of the collapse of modern rationalism, that Nietzsche clearly sides with philosophy.[5]

Strauss was not a Nietzschean in the conventional sense his detractors propose, nor a historicist in his own sense of the word. And as I have argued elsewhere, the alleged tension between Athens and Jerusalem rather quickly dissolves on a theoretical level—Strauss's depictions of Reason and Revelation make both Platonic.[6] Strauss, like his Nietzsche—and his Heidegger—understood that the present situation of philosophy was unique and precarious. It is this understanding that conditions all of Strauss's efforts.

In his one, late, extended interpretation of a Nietzschean text, Strauss asserts that for Nietzsche Nature was a problem but it was nonetheless a concept he could not do without. (Strauss 1983, pp. 174–91) I believe the same is true for Strauss. Paradoxically, the issue of Nature is framed theoretically by Strauss using a philosophical problematic he took from the author he asserted was the quintessential historicist, Heidegger. While on some rhetorical occasions Nietzsche was presented by Strauss as a historicist, his "late" presentation of Nietzsche stresses the importance of "reintegrating man and Nature." Heidegger, on the other hand, was for Strauss, in several public pronouncements, the author who had completely expelled Nature, and thereby eternity, making philosophy as a theoretical activity impossible. It is most assuredly in opposition to radical historicism that Strauss undertook all his mature explorations of Socrates, Aristophanes, Thucydides, Xenophon and Plato in an attempt to recover the "natural experience" of reality. **"Nature" had to be recovered if "contemplation" was to be the end of philosophy.**

Yet Strauss makes it clear as well that even though philosophy grew out of what he presents as a "natural consciousness" or "natural understanding," it was initially conditioned by a specific historical situation that included a distinctive tradition of authority in opposition to which philosophy emerged. Hence even if we conceptualize "natural consciousness" as in some fashion "universal," there appear to be both universal and particular factors conditioning at least the **origins** of philosophy.

Strauss uses terms such as "natural consciousness," "natural awareness," "natural world," "pre-scientific understanding," "pre-theoretical understanding," interchangeably. While these terms are used to explain the situation or understanding from which philosophy allegedly emerged, they are all decidedly non-Greek. They would never have been used by Plato or Aristotle let alone the pre-Socratics. Indeed, these terms have a pedigree, and it is straightforwardly late modern. To put the matter succinctly, these terms emerge in a discourse conditioned by the late modern situation we occupy, not that at the origins of the tradition of philosophy.

For example, the idea of a "natural consciousness" plays an important role in Hegel's *Phenomenology*.[7] Hegel uses the term to designate the early consciousness of man where experience is allegedly unmediated by conceptuality. It exists on the level of "immediacy."[8] Immediate consciousness is dominated by the senses and results in a naïve realism that takes external objects as totally self-subsistent and independent of man's thinking. Hegel's *Phenomenology* is an attempt to show why this immediate consciousness points beyond itself toward higher more comprehensive forms of consciousness because immediate consciousness can never arrive at a consistent understanding. Once we rise to a realization that the constituting principles of our experience of reality are in us, in thought, we transcend once and for all the *naïveté* of this natural consciousness—not that significant numbers of individuals might not always remain mired in its narrowness.

Strauss uses terms like pre-scientific and pre-theoretical interchangeably with terms like natural consciousness and natural experience. But these terms have a later origin in the varied and ambiguous intellectual tradition known as phenomenology.[9] For present purposes the two most important exemplars of phenomenology for Strauss were Husserl and Heidegger. Strauss took courses from both and refers to both in his published writings. Both Husserl and Heidegger argued that modern science arose out of and always carried along with it presuppositions taken from "pre-scientific" awareness, an awareness which, in Hegelian terms would nonetheless exist at a temporal point well beyond the "natural consciousness." Husserl was led to the precipice of concluding that modern science grew out of a particular practical situation, and by carrying with it the presuppositions of that origin, could never be "objective." If so, no "methodology" could ever remove the hegemony of these presuppositions. But Husserl drew back from the precipice in a desperate last minute attempt to generate a "rigorous science." Nietzsche took a similar thought and carried it to the more logical conclusion that modern science was just one interpretation among many and of no greater dignity than others. Nietzsche in fact went so far as to assert that the understanding of modern science rested on a slavish and plebeian "spirit of revenge."

Still hoping to ground science or philosophy as a "rigorous" theoretical science, Husserl's ultimate, objective foundation remained, in Cartesian and Kantian fashion, a transcendental ego. Despite all his talk about "lived experience" and the "life world" the pre-scientific awareness for Husserl was a **theoretical** awareness. It was Heidegger who argued for the absolute epistemic priority of the practical revelation of reality. Hence for Heidegger, pre-scientific awareness was simultaneously "pre-theoretical." Strauss repeatedly pointed to Heidegger's greater depth in realizing that the initial, practical revelation of things is not as mere objects theoretically grasped (which is what they are after being set up by socratic "what is" questions), but as *pragmata,* the things we deal with actively in our doing and making. (Strauss 1983, p. 29–37 and 1989, p. 29)[10]

For Heidegger, there is always an *a priori*, foundational, practical, lived, "everyday" experience of reality. All detached theoretical staring contemplates objects already revealed within a practical world that is a whole and is constituted prior to theoretical detachment. For Heidegger, this practical revelation of reality is conditioned by the distinctive shared Worlds of unique historical groups of individuals. Hence, pre-theoretical reality is not fixed once and for all times. The various peoples and their Worlds come and go unpredictably even if they leave residues, which are passed on to others.

For Heidegger, everything that comes out into the open and becomes "visible" and has a shared appearance is dependent upon that which does not appear, the "World." The difficulty arises when a World has become moribund and a new one has not mysteriously come to pass and enclosed a charmed group of individuals within it. In fact, the more sobering danger in Heidegger's eyes was the possible loss of worldliness *per se* in the impending hegemony of the monolithic revelation of reality lurking in the increasing autonomy of a global technological civilization.[11]

For Heidegger, the very possibility of things coming forward into presence for us is always determined by something, which is absent. As absent "It" can never be self-consciously mastered or projected. No autonomous willing by "legislators," philosopher-kings or overmen could ever be efficacious for their acts of willing always come along too late and are determined by a prior revelation of reality even if it is decaying or moribund. Even though Heidegger recognized the likelihood of an impending global, technological civilization, he hoped worldliness itself might still be regenerated as a determinative category of our humanity, or our humanity would be lost. But on the basis of his philosophy that could never be more than a hope despite all his efforts as midwife. Hence for Heidegger, "Only a god can save us now."

By making terms such as natural consciousness and pre-theoretical awareness co-terminus in the way he does, Strauss has affected one of many of his syntheses. Specifically, he has synthesized Hegel and Heidegger. Strauss's entire mature undertaking to explore the pre-philosophic origins out of which philosophy grew makes sense only if it is possible to recover a pre-theoretical relation to the world that is not determined mysteriously and idiosyncratically by Heideggerian Worlds. For Strauss, natural experience must be pre-theoretical in Heidegger's sense, but "natural" in something like Hegel's sense qua primary. There must be a primary relation to the world, which is recoverable at least by thought, if not simply repeatable in practice. That relation to the world also has to have a foundational status. In some fashion it must be a "natural" given.[12] "We are natural beings who live and think under unnatural conditions—we must recall our natural being in order to remove the unnatural conditions of thought." (Strauss 1988, p. 184)[13]

The unavoidable issue that emerges is one specifically raised by Hegel. Would not the natural, pre-philosophic consciousness so partake of contradiction and confusion that it would inevitably point beyond itself? For Strauss the answer is yes. Inherent in natural consciousness as he presents it is precisely an intrinsic contradictoriness. As Strauss poses the matter, reflecting on the things visible to all **citizens** in pre-theoretical awareness—especially as articulated in **publicly shared opinions and speeches**—points toward philosophical reflection precisely because of the contradictoriness. Unlike Hegel, for Strauss it is necessary to recover the only "natural" origin repeatedly. Perhaps this is because, among other things, philosophy needs the dialectical experience of confronting and culling the contradictoriness of the pre-theoretical presentation of things. It is that "natural" **self**-showing that conditions the possibility of philosophy. Otherwise we are thrust into a groundless modern constructivism where World and mind become one yet groundless and arbitrary. Another way of putting this is that philosophy needs the experience of contradictoriness, tension and perhaps even strife as much for Strauss as for Nietzsche and Heidegger.

My point so far is that Strauss's undertaking makes sense only on the basis of a philosophic problematic that rests on premises drawn from late modern philosophy and not primarily from ancient, medieval or proto-modern philosophy. It should also be clear that such a problematic makes no sense whatsoever on the basis of a Scriptural dispensation, although if the holy is intrinsically part of natural experience—as I would argue both Strauss and Heidegger believe—philosophy can never eradicate or replace the experience of the holy.

Armed with this philosophic problematic for the recovery of the natural, we can move to Strauss's reflections on the origins of the philosophic tradition out of natural experience.[14] Despite having posited a pre-theoretical "natural" articulation of reality, Strauss begins by stating unequivocally that the discovery of the **idea** of Nature is the work of philosophy. There is, in short, no experience of the **idea** of Nature in "natural experience," just as there is no acceptance of the naturalness of natural experience among those who discovered the "**idea** of Nature."[15] For the philosophers natural experience was "conventional" (*nomos* vs. *physis*). Nonetheless, natural consciousness and natural experience—or "common sense," another equivalent term Strauss introduces, which specifically points toward a shared worldliness—point **toward** the concept or "**idea** of Nature."[16] It is only in this fashion that they are linked.

In explaining how the **idea** of Nature was discovered, Strauss points to such common sense experiences as the priority that will "naturally" be given to evidence one has seen with one's own eyes as opposed to that which originates from second hand accounts or hearsay. To this Strauss adds that since the arts have been known from the beginning of human existence, the distinction between the man-made and that which is not man-made is "natural" for the natural consciousness. Indeed, the things not made by man are designated "natural" by natural experience. Nature, so understood, refers to the things that emerge into presence for us on their own, without human intervention, thereby pointing to the existence of an origin or cause other than man. Hence for natural experience, "to be" is "to be self-caused," or at least to proceed from a mysterious cause that is not man.[17] Finally, Strauss points out that natural experience was eventually confronted with the existence of different laws in different places together with the realization that fire burns in the same way everywhere.

Properly combined, these "natural" perceptions yield the **idea** of Nature. In its essence philosophy comes into view as a contemplative theoretical grasping by the mind directed toward a/the first cause. Since it appears to the mind and not the senses this cause has the status of an "intelligible."[18] To the extent the first cause is not man-made or conventional it can seem to point in the direction of an unchanging first cause. Consequently, in the initial manifestation of philosophy, "to be is to be eternal," and simultaneously "to be is to be intelligible." While eternality and intelligibility are conditioned by the situation of philosophy's Greek origin, they remain, in various permutations, re-appropriated throughout the tradition of philosophy in different ways. Strauss attempts to re-appropriate them anew.

Common sense or natural experience never put two and two together in the way initial philosophy did, hence it never discovered the **idea** of Nature. It is only a detached theoretical attitude that could do this. Why it took so long for this stance to emerge is anybody's guess—i.e., why the theoretical attitude took so long to emerge and then emerged precisely where it did. But it is only the theoretical attitude that raises the question of whether or not there exists something that is true everywhere, that is its own cause and can be grasped by an individual with the "mind's eye," such that the **idea** of Nature came forth initially as the self-caused eternal *arche* that is graspable directly by thought. With the discovery of the **idea** of Nature came the **idea** of philosophy as the **theoretical** search for Nature or Being understood as cause. Strauss frequently acts as if this represents the eternal paradigm for philosophy. But by his own deeds he shows that this conclusion is incorrect.

For the Greeks, and perhaps for pre-philosophic experience everywhere, the good came forth as determined by a combination of what is old and what is one's own, i.e., as ancestral or traditional. But deferring to our predecessors in this fashion only makes sense if those who came before were higher or better than we are. That is possible only if our predecessors were in direct contact with the gods or were gods themselves. Hence natural experience traces the good back to a cause that is not human in origin, indeed is supra-human. Initial philosophy, further conditioned by this "natural" origin, does something similar by moving back **in time** in search of its first cause and seeing it as the basis of the good. Hence, the good and the true are associated with what is simply first, from which everything else derives.[19]

But if we follow the logic of Strauss's argument, everything changes with the "Socratic turn." The Socratic/Platonic conception of philosophy departs from the **idea** of philosophy. Pre-Socratic philosophy wished to theoretically grasp the first things directly, in pure thought in abstraction from the senses. Socratic/Platonic philosophy, as Strauss presents it, concludes that this approach leads to "blindness" or "madness." It may be a divine madness, but it is madness just the same. Consequently, Socratic/Platonic philosophy develops not only a new conception of philosophy but a new conception of Nature, cause and truth as well.[20]

In the Socratic/Platonic approach, as presented by Strauss, one begins by interrogating the data of the senses especially as the visible world is informed by the publicly shared opinions about things. Public speech takes foundational priority. Hence Strauss presents the Socratic/Platonic approach as "phenomenological." Using this point of departure, the Socratic/Platonic approach implies that there is no such thing as an unmediated natural consciousness as Hegel presents the matter. There is an admission that there is always an element of thought that co-mingles with the senses through the element of shared opinions. Those shared opinions are intimately linked with the becoming visible of things. Platonic/Socratic philosophy **begins** with the way things are publicly present for all, or what is "first for us" and not by pursuing "what is first *per se*."

When interrogated theoretically, pre-theoretical awareness presents itself as a world composed of a multiplicity of discrete tribes of things. "To be is to be a thing." The world presents **itself** as a heterogeneity of things that sort themselves out into discrete groups or tribes of things. These tribes of things, or visible *eidē*, are elicited by the Socratic "what is" questions. According to this new approach, the whole is a whole made of parts. In the process, the ultimate cause of the whole becomes inaccessible or at least is no longer the primary object of reflection. But the question regarding the ultimate ordering or articulation of the parts points toward what lies beyond them as their cause. Hence, over time there will be various speculations about the articulation of the whole or its cause, but Socratic/Platonic philosophy can get no further than asserting that it knows what it cannot know—i.e., the first cause *per se* cannot be known even though we cannot help poetically speculating about it.

By starting from what is **first for us** we appear to preclude definitively getting to what is first simply. To the extent that what is first simply is unavailable, theoretical contemplation is called into question since according to the **idea** of philosophy it requires an object qua first cause. Either theory must be abandoned or re-conceptualized. Aristotle tried to return to a conception of pure theory, contemplating the first cause. So did much of the philosophic tradition. When that notion of theory collapsed authors like Kierkegaard, Nietzsche and especially Heidegger, according to Strauss, dropped theory in favor of *praxis*.[21] My argument is that Strauss tries to rethink the possibilities of an autonomous theory using phenomenological premises. And it is precisely his post-Heideggerian conceptualization of the Socratic turn that allows him to do this.

In Strauss's version of the Platonic/Socratic approach, we get a philosophy that understands the extent to which theory is dependent on a prior practical articulation of reality that comes forth in shared, everyday experience. This leads to the following conclusion: If we associate the term Being with that which is first simply, and it is unavailable, "to be is to be always mysterious." Socratic/Platonic philosophy, as presented by Strauss, concurs with both Scriptural Revelation and Heidegger, the first things are mysterious. So conceived, Platonic/Socratic philosophy is an eternal affront to the **idea** of philosophy which presumes to grasp Being as the first cause, a cause graspable in thought. It is precisely this understanding of theory that Aristotle re-enthrones with his radical separation of theory from practice and theoretical wisdom from practical wisdom.[22] This latter view of autonomous theory, shaped by the pre-Socratics and re-opened by Aristotle, conditions the philosophic tradition, apparently having short-circuited Strauss's version of the Platonic-Socratic move almost immediately.

Strauss's version of Socratic/Platonic philosophy concludes that the cause or the Being of things is associated with the "what" or "essence" of the individual tribes of things. Hence by concluding that "to be is to be a thing" we are shielded from the theoretical blindness or madness threatened by the formula "to be is to be eternal and intelligible." But this shielding is simultaneously the destruction of the **idea** of philosophy. To the extent that the **idea** of Nature or Being is transferred from the first cause to the multiplicity of the essences of the various tribes, the first cause *per se* in principle has the status of Not-Being or Nothing. Everything that "is" is caused or surrounded by Nothing. The resonance of Heidegger is again unmistakable. But the resonance of the Plato of the *Republic* where the Idea of the Good is beyond Being is also clear. Again, in principle at the core of reality is a mystery, which brings Platonic/Socratic philosophy into the vicinity of religion, if not completely "going over" to the side of religion, and certainly not the religion of the poets, an accusation Strauss hurled at Heidegger. We are saved from contemplating the Nothing only by theoretically moving the locus of Being to the multiplicity of whats or essences. This may be no more than a theoretical sleight of hand.

Following Heidegger, Strauss's depiction of Socratic/Platonic philosophy posits the epistemic priority of the practical revelation of reality and hence the dependence of philosophy upon something that is not "intelligible." Strauss's Socratic/Platonic understanding of philosophy, while directing us away from the **idea** of philosophy, nonetheless tries to salvage the **idea** of Nature by transforming it into an ensemble or heterogeneity of natures. But the matter becomes more complicated when we reflect on the ramifications of Strauss's equation of the doctrine of the *eidē* (i.e. Being qua the ensemble and heterogeneity of "whats") with his famous, if seemingly paradoxical, assertion that the doctrine of ideas reduces to the eternal ensemble of "fundamental questions."

Strauss argues that in the history of philosophy what inevitably emerges is a set of "fundamental" theoretical positions each of which elicits sects devoted to them as the last word. (Strauss 1963/1991, pp. 194–96)[23] This sectarianism undermines the Socratic/Platonic approach to philosophy, which, it turns out, not only phenomenologically articulates the heterogeneity of *eidē* that are publicly displayed but also contemplates various fundamental metaphysical positions and practical alternatives.[24] It is precisely these fundamental issues that become the object of theory and not the potentially blinding attempt to directly grasp the first things, the whole, the first cause or the allegedly ultimate question *quid sit deus*.[25]

In short, Strauss's conception of theory does not have Being or Nature qua cause as its object. It has the spectacle of recurrent human doings as its object. Such contemplation is ontological only to the extent that one transforms ontology in the way a Hegel does into the study of the history of thought and deed.[26] But the thoughts and deeds are, for Strauss in Nietzschean fashion, recurrent rather than sequential.

To this point we can reach two conclusions. First, much of what I have presented so far of Strauss's attempted recovery of the origins of philosophy not only is conditioned by Heidegger's problematic regarding the priority of the pre-theoretical but it represents an ongoing dialogue with Heidegger regarding the true origins of the philosophic tradition whereby Strauss attributes to the pre-Socratics much of what Heidegger attributes to Plato. In the process there is the positing of the pre-theoretical as "natural" even though in philosophic terms it is "conventional." Second, we should notice the variety of different usages of "nature" that we have already confronted. My argument is that Strauss attempts to craft a novel usage that can line up with a novel understanding of future philosophy, an idea, I will argue, that Strauss gets from his Nietzsche—e.g., Nietzsche's idea that only in the future can humanity become natural for the first time.[27]

It seems to be Strauss's position that Nature presents itself in different ways—e.g., pre-theoretically and in the **idea** of Nature. Further, Nature always presents **itself** in some fashion. One might expect therefore that the present situation would also present a conception of Nature. But according to Strauss it does not because it is obliterated by the **theoretical** perspective of historicism that has become conventional wisdom. As a theoretical perspective, historicism, like all theoretical perspectives, is derivative from a practical revelation of reality—and Strauss argues specifically that the origin of the historical consciousness *per se* comes from the conservative attempts to defend practice against the effects of the French Revolution which were of theoretical origin. In other words, historicism is contingent. Emancipated from historicism's hegemony we should, by this understanding, re-discover Nature in some fashion. This is precisely what Strauss attempts, **not the recovery of some previous permutation of Nature**. Strauss's Nietzsche helps us see this. He presents us with an attempt to find our "naturalness" in the future.

Strauss's Nietzsche is, from the perspective of conventional scholarship, as iconoclastic as his Plato. But it is precisely by comparing Strauss's late interpretation (in Strauss 1983) with the conventional view of Nietzsche as a voluntarist nihilist,[28] that we see what is distinctive. (See chapter 9.) When we do so we are struck by the extent to which Strauss's Nietzsche is not a voluntarist nihilist who thinks philosophers should will "values" *ex nihilo*, but is rather engaged in an attempt to recover Nature. By contrast, the voluntarist tradition wishes precisely to emancipate man from Nature. Central to Strauss's treatment of Nietzsche is also the uncharacteristic centrality of religion. Strauss's Nietzsche looks forward to an unavoidable increase of religiosity in the future. Yet perhaps precisely because of this Strauss's Nietzsche also looks forward to the need for a new form of future philosophy to rule that religiosity that is categorically different than past manifestations of philosophy. What is really distinctive is that for Strauss, as for his Nietzsche, that future form of philosophy will in fact be a detached theoretical activity. Finally, Strauss's Nietzsche is a Platonist.[29]

Strauss argues that for Nietzsche the central philosophic issue was a concern that in the future philosophy needed to rule over religion rather than vice versa. Strauss says that this contrasts with the situation at the **origins** of the philosophic tradition where the central issue was to assure the rule of philosophy over the city. Initially, religion was subsumed under the city and its laws. Only later, due to the Scriptural tradition, did religion gain autonomy and pose an independent problem for philosophy, a problem confronted by medieval thought and presumed to have been transcended by modern thought. By comparison with his Nietzsche, Strauss says that Heidegger simply went over to the side of what amounts to the religion of the poets, leaving no place for philosophy qua theory. Strauss sided with his Nietzsche.

For Strauss, as for his Nietzsche, the prediction that the future would include a newly robust and assertive religiosity seems to follow from the collapse of modern rationalism. With the decline in faith in reason, nothing would stand in the way of a newly assertive, if nonetheless post-scriptural, religiosity. This is especially true if one has concluded that the natural consciousness always includes an element of the holy—a premise Strauss shared with Heidegger.

The danger was that future religiosity would build upon the autonomy religion gained through the separation of religion from politics that emerged in the modern era, to assert not just its autonomy but hegemony once its other—reason—declined. This hegemony might well be aided by a decline, if not abolition, of the political toward which global modern technological civilization points. Strauss's Nietzsche argues that if future philosophy is in fact to rule over a uniquely assertive religiosity it would need to be radically transformed. None of the past permutations of philosophy could have performed the task—albeit Strauss's Maimonides, as the spokesman for the "natural" understanding of rationalism, might in Strauss's mind give some clues to how

this might be accomplished. (Strauss 1935/1987, p. 3) But in the end, most of
the needed clues are more clearly deployed in Nietzsche.

Strauss and his Nietzsche see a recurring, perhaps eternal, tension between
religion and philosophy. This tension is designated by Strauss as the theological-political problem, or the tension between Reason and Revelation, Athens
and Jerusalem. It may be more eternal than the tension between philosophy
and the city that seems so central to Strauss's teaching. Only if one took one's
bearings by the **origins** of the philosophical tradition could one see the tension between philosophy and the city as forever primary. Contrary to Alexander Kojève, who saw the abolition of the political not only as the end toward
which History aimed, but as good, Strauss saw its possibility as a threat to our
very humanity. But that such an abolition was bad did not prove it was entirely impossible. By predicting the possible hegemony of a newly robust, autonomous religiosity in the future, Strauss and Nietzsche point to the possibility of the decline in importance of the political, or put another way, the End
of History.

If the political declines, only philosophy could limit a potentially autonomous religion. But philosophy could only do so once it was emancipated
from the "prejudices" of all past philosophy. According to Strauss's Nietzsche, the entirety of the past tradition of philosophy was narrow and prejudiced, incapable of seeing its errors and limitations. But contemporary "Free
Spirits," among whom Nietzsche clearly places himself, have gained the
strength, self-consciousness and clarity to put off past prejudices and see the
world as it is.

Strauss makes much of Nietzsche's use of the term "philosophers of the future." According to Strauss's Nietzsche, these future philosophers will be religious in a way no past philosophers have been—not just adopting the public stance of religious exegetes like medieval philosophers—but actually
being religious. But as post-scriptural "philosophers," they will believe in a
this-worldly circular god conceived of as the Will-to-Power which eternally
recurs as appearance. It is clear that these "philosophers" will be incapable of
the high self-consciousness and free-spiritedness of present philosophers like
Nietzsche.

But behind, outside, or "above" the "philosophers of the future" will remain the Free Spirits of the future in a high theoretical solitude emancipated
from any but rare public functions or tasks. **They will be anything but activist philosopher-kings**. Perhaps for the first time, philosophy could be
emancipated from the city to pursue a pure contemplative vocation, to pursue
the **idea** of Nature and the **idea** of Philosophy. But this would be possible
only if the Free Spirits subtly and indirectly ruled through the philosophers of
the future and their future religiosity. Strauss himself is moving in the same

direction as his Nietzsche, towards the recovery of a conception of Nature and the emancipation of philosophy to a future contemplative solitude—although as I have suggested, theory must be re-conceptualized in a non-cosmological and non-metaphysical fashion.

We should consider two other examples from Nietzsche, which are not explicitly Strauss's but nonetheless line up with Strauss's own teaching. In his *Advantages and Disadvantages of History for Life*, Nietzsche argues that there is an untranscendable tension between the requirements of everyday life and the needs and desires of free-spirited philosophy. In Strauss's terms an untranscendable tension between philosophy and the city exists. Again, this is a tenet central to what Strauss meant by Platonism. Strauss's Nietzsche proposes as a solution to insulate everyday life and self-conscious thought through the intermediacy of the priestly philosophers of the future. Strauss is moving in the same direction.

Through his argument about the unavoidable tension between Reason and Revelation or Philosophy and the City, Strauss makes a move reminiscent of one Nietzsche made in *The Birth of Tragedy*. For Nietzsche, the central tension in Greek civilization was presented as that between Dionysian and Apollonian tendencies. Tellingly, Nietzsche observed that the Greeks gave both tendencies to themselves, in other words invented them, in the height of their strength. We must note that far from making a choice for either Reason or Revelation, Strauss publicly asserts the life-giving energy that Western Civilization has drawn from the irresolvable **tension** between Reason and Revelation. Strauss argues that Western Civilization need not come to an end as long as that tension exists. It is all too obvious, however, that in proposing this tension Strauss theoretically stands outside either of its components at some third point.

If we put together the idea of necessary tensions—Philosophy and the City, Reason and Revelation, with the idea of a hierarchy of human ends and types of human beings,[30] and the resultant need for esoteric speech—we arrive, figuratively speaking, at half of what Strauss meant by Platonism, which overlaps with what Strauss means by Natural Right.[31] The other "half" is to be found in Strauss's distinctive presentation of the epistemic nature of the Socratic turn, which I have argued is a synthesis of elements drawn from both the classical Greeks and the modern Germans. **To the extent that "Platonism" so understood rests on a synthesis of elements drawn from across the philosophic tradition, it is a novel synthesis and in no fashion a "return."** As such, Strauss's Platonism, like the understanding of his Nietzsche, points forward to a novel, fully "awake," permutation of philosophy to become manifest in the future.[32] There is ample evidence that Strauss looks forward to a novel future manifestation of philosophy. But in his case it is a postmodern "rationalism" born of a post-Heideggerian synthesis. This rationalism would **not** be a return to classical, medieval or modern rationalism. It would be a rationalism that is contemplative in a new sense such that the future philosopher will in no way be, or long to be, a king.[33]

Finally, Strauss's Nietzsche—far from being the voluntarist nihilist who qua philosopher-king wills moral and political dispensations *ex nihilo*—longs for a "re-integration of man into nature." But the "re-" is misleading. Strauss emphasizes that his Nietzsche thinks that only in the future can man be natural **for the first time**. For Nietzsche, only at the end, freed from the accident of our animal past, can we have a truly human end, thereby becoming natural for the first time. Yet Nietzsche argues that in the past there was a close cousin of "nature" to be found in instinct. But instinct does not propel us toward **human** ends, which are ends that we must in a fully awake self-consciousness give ourselves. This really means ends given by someone like Nietzsche.

In the present, Nietzsche sees us as totally "de-natured" because Christianity and modern philosophy were both moved by an anti-nature animus, which robbed us of our instincts. At present we have neither instinct nor a truly human end. We are totally de-natured. For Strauss's Nietzsche there is a past showing of Nature and a future showing of Nature. Nature has more than one possible historical showing of itself. I have already argued that we find the same thing in Strauss. There is a pre-philosophic showing of Nature; a pre-Socratic showing; a Socratic showing; a possible post-Heideggerian showing; etc.

For Strauss, contemporary humanity is totally alienated from the **idea** of Nature and hence in need of historical studies to recover it. But this is a propaedeutic to a new deployment or showing of Nature. Since Strauss asserts that Natural Right requires the **idea** of philosophy, which in turn requires the **idea** of Nature, the future recovery of Nature opens the possibility of the future return of Natural Right, which in its initial permutations was eventually betrayed.

To this point I have largely abstracted from the issue that Strauss is probably most associated with, his argument regarding the origin and nature of political philosophy. Strauss links the Socratic turn with the origins of political philosophy. Socratic/Platonic philosophy, and Strauss never really disentangles the two, came to **self-conscious** clarity about the ways in which philosophy intrinsically threatened the city and was in turn threatened. With the origins of Socratic/Platonic philosophy came a higher reflexivity and "awakeness" than anything prior. Thought turned to thinking itself and its conditions. Strauss clearly attributes to Socratic/Platonic philosophy a higher degree of self-consciousness than would Hegel. The level of reflexivity Strauss attributes to Socrates/Plato occurred much later in Hegel's understanding, in fact with the advent of modern philosophy. Some might argue that Strauss consciously projected backwards unto Socrates/Plato a degree of reflexivity that is questionable. But I would argue that there was a great deal more self-conscious clarity in the thought of Plato than is usually seen, although in a different way than Strauss presents.[34]

Be that as it may, Strauss argues that the higher reflexivity of Socratic/Platonic philosophy, compared to pre-Socratic thought, is what made it concern itself far more with rhetoric than had pre-Socratic thought. Hence it explicitly addressed the need to speak in the language of the city. Hence we arrive at Strauss's characteristic argument that the newly emergent political philosophy represents the **politic defense of the philosophers before the political community.** This seems to leave matters at the fact that the moral and political prescriptions made by political philosophy are largely self-interested. To that extent its principles are in the service of a good outside the moral and political arena. That would make it look as if in reality exists no rational basis for any actual moral and political prescriptions. They are based on misdirection and myth in the service of the good of the philosophers.

This appearance is what gives ammunition to those who argue that Strauss's Natural Right teaching reduces to nothing more than philosophers manipulating life for their own benefit with total disregard for the moral and political good. It also opens a path to the charge that Strauss's teaching has no real foundation and is no more than prudent esoteric rhetoric.[35] Pushing this line of attack further, it is asserted that according to Strauss the good life is the pleasant life and only the life of philosophy is a pleasant life. Hence justice is not only a lie projected in the service of the philosopher's pleasure but there is a complete disconnect between the naturally good, which is allegedly pleasure, and justice—with justice and morality being seen as intrinsically unpleasant. So the story goes; the political has no other point than to be manipulated for the pleasure of the few. And that is the position ascribed to the conventional understanding of Nietzsche as well.

But if Strauss is a Nietzschean nihilist **in the conventional sense**, then he believes that there is nothing unchanging, no "Nature," no real object of thought, hence no such thing as the **idea** of philosophy. Consequently, fully awake philosophy can only consist of awareness of the abyss conjoined with the personal desire for pleasure. But the awareness of the abyss seems far more consistent with the anguish and anxiety associated with the alleged teachings of Nietzsche and Heidegger than the pleasure of philosophy pointed to by Strauss's detractors. It would be a rare human being indeed who could make abysmal anguish the basis of pleasure. But unlike Heidegger, who specifically argues that the origin of contemporary thinking is anxiety, not the wonder of classical thought,[36] Strauss never wavers from placing the origin of philosophy in wonder (the Greek *thaumazein*). Finally, what is the point of putting all of one's efforts in the service of defending philosophy if in fact it has no object? Under those circumstances all a fully awake person could do is choose another life.

Beyond these and other inconsistencies into which the position, which has Strauss as merely an esoteric nihilist, is driven, I believe it is called into question by several substantive facts. The first is Strauss's grounding of the philosophic enterprise in the epistemically prior, practical revelation of reality—which for Strauss means the moral, political and religious revelation of reality. The second is the extent to which Strauss's detractors miss the subtlety of his presentation of the issue of Nature and the Natural Right tradition. Strauss's depiction of Natural Right shows that it has multiple permutations conditioned by multiple starting points. Finally, Strauss differentiates between Natural Right and Natural Law and he positively does not long for the return of the Natural Law tradition. It is that tradition, and not how Strauss understands Natural Right, that is absolutist.[37]

Strauss asserts that the commonly observable given from which all Natural Right positions begin is the heterogeneity of the human kind. Modern philosophy attempts to transcend this pre-theoretical given through a constructivism that posits an equally shared abstract individuality that stands in the place of the observable heterogeneity. Natural Right, like philosophy itself, must be grounded in a pre-given autonomous reality in all its heterogeneity, in this case human nature as it is displayed in everyday understanding.[38]

But some past Natural Right teachings also began by **abstracting** from natural difference, beginning instead from what is **common** to the heterogeneity of humanity. Hence there were actually two strains of Natural Right, one that while acknowledging heterogeneity looked for the commonality beneath it and one that accentuated what is distinctive to different types of human beings rather than what is shared. Strauss attempted to show that different Natural Right teachings descended from each point of departure. If one starts from human commonality, this points toward taking human sociality and man's political nature as central. Proceeding from the distinctiveness and heterogeneity of human beings led to ranking the individual types of lives hierarchically with the most complete or perfect at the top. It is this latter approach that Strauss's detractors take as paradigmatic of his own position. While Strauss at times seems to lean in this latter direction—a position he attributes to his Nietzsche—*Natural Right and History* is in fact surprisingly neutral toward the various starting points and the various permutations of Natural Right.

After the Natural Right tradition developed, the two pure starting points were transformed. Starting from the ideal of man's perfection pointed toward philosophy as man's highest excellence. Starting from the notion of what is shared commonly pointed toward man's political and social nature as central. This latter approach eventually pointed toward the perfection of justice as the highest good. **This move eventually spun off the Natural Law tradition which Strauss argues inevitably tried to generate a law universally applicable to all in a world *polis* that could only be ruled by God.** This led toward the possibility of bringing together Natural Law and Divine Law. But in this direction also lay the secular world state of modernity and the End of History. It is at this point that Strauss's neutrality ceases. According to Strauss, one way or the other the Natural Law tradition inevitably led toward moral and political rigidity and some version of cosmopolitanism.[39] Both the rigidity and the cosmopolitanism were betrayals of the Natural Right tradition.

While the Natural Law tradition descended from that branch of Natural Right that begins from the commonality of man as a social and political being, it seems to point toward the abolition of the political. Perhaps this is why Strauss vastly prefers the Natural Right tradition in any of its permutations to the Natural Law tradition. But what he really hopes will ensue from his historical efforts is that in the future we will plumb possibilities that were never developed because they were closed off and abandoned by the Natural Law tradition. This has about it an element of a "second beginning."

Strauss discusses one further maneuver of the past Natural Right tradition. This permutation of the classical Natural Right tradition blended or mixed the two original paths. The perfection of individuals and the commonality of humanity when taken together pointed toward mixing elements of both. The "mixed regime" grew out of this move wherein both philosophy and justice could prosper but only by toning down the demand for perfect justice. Strauss seems best disposed to this move among the **prior** Natural Right positions. The mixed regime as the best regime can never be perfectly just and does not take its bearings by perfect justice as does the Natural Law tradition. But neither does it put moral and political life in the service of a trans-political end—philosophy—as many of Strauss's detractors claim he does. For the mixed regime to exist one must balance the competing claims of justice and pure theory. This balancing effort seems to point, therefore, toward the hegemony of practical wisdom as the faculty that does this balancing. That in turn would undermine the higher dignity of contemplation by in effect making practical wisdom prior and higher, as some of Strauss's commentators have also claimed is his understanding.

The possible hegemony of practical wisdom only follows from taking the "mixed regime" approach as Strauss's last word. But rather than siding with any past permutation of Natural Right Strauss is primarily interested in recovering the **idea** of Nature as the basis for a future Natural Right position.

That position need not be a replay from the past. As a historian, Strauss's neutrality only seems to flag when it comes to the Natural Law tradition to which he is not friendly. My argument is that Strauss points toward a post-modern deployment of Natural Right that is consistent with a postmodern deployment of Nature, an idea he got from his reading of Nietzsche. As regards the possibility of Natural Right in any deployment Strauss asserts unequivocally that "Natural Right presupposes philosophy in its full and original meaning." (Strauss 1950, p. 31) As I have already shown, the **idea** of philosophy makes it a contemplative pursuit. Its object is Nature understood as in some fashion eternal and intelligible if not primarily as first cause.[40] Hence the direction Strauss is heading requires a new manifestation of the **idea** of philosophy.

We should keep in mind that for Strauss, the **idea** of philosophy rests on a theoretical directedness toward the **idea** of Nature. My argument is that this is Strauss's highest end, a new, postmodern basis for theory and contemplation. How does this relate to Natural Right? Just as Heidegger set himself the task of thinking Being in the hopes that its recovery from oblivion would have unpredictable yet sanguine practical ramifications, Strauss wished to recover Nature. He sees that as the propaedeutic to recovering Natural Right. I do not believe he thought this out in anything resembling concrete terms. What might follow was for others to work out. His primary concern was the future of philosophy.

If we limit ourselves to general outlines and paint with a broad brush, we can sketch a picture of what may well have been Strauss's understanding of the history of philosophy. Pre-Socratic philosophy grew out of a specific historical situation. It co-opted, extended, synthesized and extrapolated from elements drawn out of the everyday, common sense experience of the world in which it existed—albeit it did not do this with full self-conscious clarity. Why this philosophical culling of common experience originated when and where it did is simply a mystery. It was a unique undertaking that was done with almost no self-consciousness or reflexivity. There was an element of madness in this initial manifestation of philosophy in its attempt to grasp the first things directly.

The Socratic/Platonic transformation of philosophy attempted to defend philosophy against this madness and the public opprobrium it occasioned. But the Platonic/Socratic transformation of philosophy was almost immediately betrayed by Aristotle who, contrary to Strauss's Plato, enthroned an autonomous theory that directly tried to think Being, and was thereby forced to posit an autonomous practical wisdom and political science. Given Strauss's phenomenological understanding, such a separation should not be possible.

Nonetheless, Strauss attempts a similar separation in a fashion which I believe is contradictory and betrays his phenomenological point of departure.

Throughout the classical period various attempts were made to generate a Natural Right position, permutations of which we have discussed, none of which were entirely successful. This undertaking was conditioned by the fact that law and justice were problematic issues in the classical period. This Natural Right tradition, by the time of Rome, generated the first manifestations of the Natural Law tradition. At about the same time began the epochal confrontation of philosophy with the Scriptural tradition. In this tradition, especially in Judaism and Islam, the law was no longer problematic. Hence the philosophers could draw the distinction between prophet and philosopher, leaving the prophet to deal with law and justice and leaving philosophers to pursue theoretical contemplation. What this amounts to is philosophy returning to the **idea** of philosophy as pure theory together with a novel permutation of Aristotle's division between theory and practice and theoretical and practical wisdom.

The confrontation between philosophy and Christianity yielded a different outcome. Within Christianity the day-to-day law remained problematic, since Christians are called to accept articles of faith but not specific legal institutions. Finding its roots in the Roman Empire, Christianity had ready to hand an embryonic Natural Law tradition that it embraced and expanded. A millennium later this led to a rigid absolutism that strangled both practice and theory. In other words, neither could come forth in anything resembling its "natural" manifestations. The resultant reaction launched modernity.

Modernity launched two initially separate reactions against the tradition it inherited which rather quickly merged. The first reaction attempted to emancipate political practice from its theoretical/theological stranglehold and launched modern political philosophy via Machiavelli. Modern theory in turn tried to emancipate itself from theological determination as well and hence tried to return autonomy to theory but in the process launched modern technological science instead, which was just a new form of practice masquerading as theory.

Various other novelties emerged that would require a diversion into Strauss's reading of modernity which is not consistent with our primary purpose at the moment. But, for example, despite his attempts to return autonomy to practice, Machiavelli did not simply recover **natural** *praxis* which presupposes human heterogeneity. By building on the common element shared by human beings—understood now as consisting of fear, greed and ambition rather than natural sociality—Machiavelli and later moderns "lowered the sights." At the origins of modernity, therefore, is not so much a theoretical change of perspective as a moral one.

In its own attempt at autonomy, modern theory quickly put itself in the service of modern practice—modern science always had as its end the emancipation of humanity from physical need and want, seeing that as the primary means to the human good. In the process, modern theory projected what would count as reality, casting off into indifference the pursuit of the actual whole, which is to say, the **idea** of Nature or Being. By another paradoxical twist, however, this new permutation of theory eventually came to take away the autonomy of practice, practice being put in the service of actualizing the modern theoretical end of the conquest of nature.

For Strauss, Hegel is the last modern author because he is the spokesman par excellence for the modern end of the conquest of nature by spirit. He is the last Christian thinker because he is the last to posit God as the object of thought—*quid sit deus*—albeit what this really means is he posited contemplation of the path and completion of the mind of God already made actual as the end of philosophy. Philosophy was reduced to contemplating what had happened in history—a premise still shared, after a fashion, by Heidegger's notion of *seinsgeschichte*. For Hegel, at the end of history, the spiritual or ideal had become actual. In practical terms that meant the final understanding of justice had arrived and could be bureaucratically administered—hence the abolition of the political. Not only was practice in the stranglehold of theory, it eventually disappears.

Then to break the modern stranglehold of theory over practice that leads toward a universal, cosmopolitan practice and World State, Strauss's Kierkegaard and Heidegger attempted to save a practice that could be novel by not just transforming but by **destroying** theory as Strauss understood it. Kierkegaard, Nietzsche and Heidegger were eventually so successful in their assault on Hegel that they consummated the utter collapse of modern rationalism which had from the beginning turned its back on articulating the actual world in favor on constructing it in thought and transforming it.

But when modern man's theoretical constructions ceased to have any veneer of objectivity, being just the interpretations of their individual constructors, humanity was confronted with an utterly unprecedented situation. For the first time since the pre-Socratics the very possibility of theory—the **idea** of philosophy—was problematic, perhaps lying in ruins. Simultaneously we were faced with the possible obliteration of practice in the face of an impeding global technological civilization and World State. This is the unique situation that conditions Strauss's post-Heideggerian synthesis wherein he paradoxically attempted to recover theory by phenomenologically asserting the epistemic priority of practice.

Strauss both accepts and rejects elements of each of the stages in this history, Platonic, medieval and modern. Yet he draws elements where he can to construct his novel synthesis. But his most massive borrowings are from German philosophy, not from classical philosophy or medieval Jewish thought. How could it be otherwise? The present situation has little in common with the classical or medieval situations.

As far as I can see, the epistemic component of what Strauss depicts as the Socratic turn, which is simultaneously the turn away from the **idea** of philosophy, has its only basis in the Heideggerian phenomenological positing of the priority of the practical revelation of reality. Heidegger opened a door for Strauss back to recovering and then amending the Socratic turn as an amalgam of Socrates, Plato and German philosophy. Strauss's attempted "return" to the beginnings is in order to get to a novel future that has elements of a "second beginning." Strauss re-appropriates the origins in a fashion that need not be deflected in the same direction as in the prior tradition, which seems to have reached a dead end. Where Heidegger attempted his "second beginning" from the opening provided by his version of the pre-Socratics, Strauss strikes off from his version of Socrates/Plato. But this "return" is precisely to help get to a novel "natural" future in significant ways like that depicted by his Nietzsche.

Strauss once wrote an essay entitled "Progress or Return." (Strauss 1989, pp. 227–270) Ultimately, Strauss intended neither. Progress in the strict sense was not a possibility for any post-Hegelian who accepted the truth of the collapse of modern rationalism and the likelihood of an impeding global nihilism as did Strauss. Strauss never believed in the possibility of "return" in the sense of going back and taking up a ready-made position for immediate adoption. He was in search of a novel future possibility that reappropriated the **idea** of philosophy as contemplative, the **idea** of Nature as in some way linked with eternity and intelligibility, and a permutation of the **idea** of Natural Right. In this sense, Strauss was a postmodern thinker, not a classical, medieval, Jewish or late-modern one.

Strauss gives us other hints of where he is headed. For example, we should attend to Strauss's straightforward assertion in *Natural Right and History* that no competent thinker of the present would take as simply true anything said by any thinker in the past (Strauss 1950, p. 20). This alone is ample evidence that Strauss was intending no simple return in an attempt to recapture a past position. Second, and here only an informed speculation is possible, we need to attend to the ramifications of the following, seemingly modest, observation:

> We scholars live in a charmed circle, . . . protected against problems by the great thinkers. The scholar becomes possible through the fact that the great thinkers disagree. Their disagreement creates a possibility for us to reason about their differences. . . . We may think that the possible alternatives are exhausted by the great thinkers of the past. We may try to classify their doctrines," and so on less to our present purpose. (Strauss 1989, p. 30)

We must recognize that it is in the "philosophies" of the great thinkers so conceived that one finds the basis for what Strauss puts forward as the "fundamental issues." Those "great thinkers" become a significant part of the object of contemplation for the new theory of the future. But who represents the higher phenomenon, the great thinkers or the ones who reflect on their doings? For example, those great thinkers, not knowing they are giving permutations of fundamental positions—thinking in each case that they are original—are not as "awake" as those who contemplate the comings and goings of those positions.

For Strauss the highest manifestation of philosophy is the most fully awake and self-conscious. The "great thinkers" as Strauss presents them seem to have the status of phenomena of Nature. To the extent that thought can now so completely transform physical Nature, to attempt to contemplate Nature directly becomes a derivative enterprise. The great thinkers henceforth become the primary data for it is their thinking that is the only real given.

Since it is around the ideas of the great thinkers that sects form for true believers, and since each great thinker must in principle think he is correct, as a partisan of his own ideas, he too must be a true believer. It is precisely such true belief that Strauss says destroys the new **idea** of philosophy understood as a fully awake awareness of the fundamental issues. Must we not conclude that the actual proponents of the fundamental positions, the "great thinkers," are in fact less clear, less awake, less philosophic than those who give manifestation to the new **idea** of philosophy by contemplating the fundamental issues understood as eternal positions that recur? There is only one conclusion: Such a contemplator sees himself as higher than anyone from Plato to Heidegger.

"Awakeness," like Nietzschean "Free Spiritedness," becomes the standard for the philosophers of the future. And human thoughts and political and moral doings and the associated *poiesis,* not cosmology, ontology or metaphysics, become the object of theoretical contemplation. In this newly fashioned manifestation of the **idea** of philosophy, future philosophy will contemplate the theoretical, and to a lesser extent practical, doings of which must give manifestation to its own fundamental possibilities. Hence future theory requires as its object—and hence presupposes for its existence—the doings of the various great thinkers and the moral and political deeds of the non-philosophic. Implied is the Nietzschean understanding that we have eternally recurrent outcomes, not teleological sequencing. Strauss sides with Nietzsche against Hegel. But Strauss agrees with Hegel that the object of philosophy becomes theoretical and practical deeds. The theorist who contemplates these things is more self-consciously awake than the actual doers or thinkers yet remains dependent upon them. Hence the new theory will not be epistemically autonomous as it was for Aristotle and the theoretical tradition that descends from him. And the new theory will have a hard time informing practice as did the prior tradition of political philosophy, especially modern political philosophy. Again, the new theory will not be cosmological or metaphysical, simply political or moral.

I am suggesting that what Strauss has done is turn theory away from the contemplation of first things qua reflection on *archai* or cosmological or metaphysical issues, which was the basis of the original permutation of the **idea** of philosophy, toward contemplating the recurring patterns found in the deeds and thoughts of human beings. What becomes eternal is the eternality of human doings as they sort themselves out into at least semi-predictable patterns that repeat. Hence we have a version of what Strauss attributes to Nietzsche as the meaning of eternal return.[41] We have our new object for detached contemplation. And we have no real basis for the continuation of modern philosophical activism and constructivism.

What we also have is a position that shares more than a surface similarity with a position Strauss attributes to Hegel: "There came into being a new type of theory . . . having as its highest theme human action and its product rather than the whole." Delete the controversial Hegelian idea of ultimate completion and we close in on Strauss's post-Heideggerian position. As I have already noted, having deleted the idea of completion we are not that far from what is implied in Heidegger's doctrine of *seinsgeschichte*, that the history of Being is the history of the way in which Being comes to presence in human doings. For Heidegger the primary object of thought is Being. But it is not an abstract detached Being but rather one which primarily comes to presence or manifests itself through the thought of the great thinkers and poets who are both rooted in the historical revelation of reality of specific peoples and contributors to the shaping of those peoples. "Language is the house of Being," and language for Heidegger is always the language shaped by great thinkers.

But for Strauss there is less mystery in Being than there is for Heidegger because there is significant repeatability as is true for Nietzsche. Nonetheless, Strauss once observed that Nietzsche's thought culminated in myth where Heidegger's culminated in a submission to fate. Strauss is much closer to submitting to fate, his detractors who think he wants to be a philosopher-king to the contrary notwithstanding. As he presents the matter, there is contingency in the origins of individual moments of the philosophic tradition, but there is inevitability in the movement between those moments and their predictable outcomes—as in the modern "three wave" march to nihilism or the movement of the Natural Law tradition toward rigidity and absolutism. Between the novel moments of thought there is an inevitability for Strauss, because precisely as in Hegel, when thought becomes manifest in the World it has determinate ramifications. But since for Strauss there is recurrence there is also an element of eternity, i.e., of the **idea** of Nature.[42]

In turning theory toward the contemplation of the thought of past great thinkers and the recurrent patterns they manifest—with **occasional** intrusions of novelty—like much of contemporary thought Strauss turns theory toward hermeneutics. But for Strauss hermeneutics is **not** a practical activity as it is, for example, for Gadamer. It is a **theoretical** activity. The recovery of theory in novel circumstances is precisely Strauss's aim. But it is not a recovery of classical or medieval conceptions of theory—and certainly not the modern constructivist conception. Strauss aims at finding a postmodern, **theoretical** stance for philosophy.[43]

Far from being a Jewish or classical thinker, or a modern thinker, or even a late modern thinker, Strauss is a decidedly post-Heideggerian thinker. It was not primarily his predicament as a young Jew in Germany that set his thought in motion, it was the situation of the collapse of modern rationalism that conditioned his thought, a collapse that, like Nietzsche and Heidegger, Strauss believed had already irreversibly happened. Strauss was neither the moral absolutist that he would have attributed to the Natural Law tradition—and that some of his supporters and detractors attribute to him—nor a voluntarist. He was determined to recover and give manifestation anew to the **idea** of philosophy. While transcending radical historicism and its self-invalidating assertions that nothing stands still in the swirl of temporality, he understood that thought was historically conditioned, not only in its beginnings but now and always. What was not conditioned was the need to repeatedly give manifestation to the **idea** of philosophy and the **idea** of Nature.

NOTES

1. See for example, Burneyat, Drury, Holmes 1989, 1993, Lampert 1996, and Rosen 1987. For citations, see the list of references at the end of this chapter.

2. See in this regard Danhauser, Deutsche and Nicgorski, Green, Novak, Orr, and S. Smith.

3. The earliest notes of this new approach seem to be sounded in Pangle and Tarcov 1988. The philosophically deepest exploration of this thesis can be found in Green. See also Dannhauser, Novak, Orr and the essays in the Deutsche and Nicgorski volume.

4. That Strauss's view of Platonism is iconoclastic is evidenced by the hostility of those who are the defenders of the traditional Anglo-American understanding of Platonic Scholarship. See Burneyat and Hall with the response to Hall by Bloom 1977. See my 1999 article "Athens and Washington."

5. The primary text for Strauss's view of Nietzsche is "Note on the Plan of Nietzsche's *Beyond Good and Evil*," in Strauss 1983.

6. See chapter 9, "Athens and Washington."

7. While Strauss rarely offers extended thematic treatments of Hegel, there are a variety of places where Hegel is clearly in the background. The discussion of Burke in *Natural Right and History* is one instance. Strauss probably used Burke instead of Hegel to end his discussion of the historical consciousness to press his point that the historical consciousness has a practical origin rather than emerging out of theoretical necessities. Strauss's understanding of Hegel is displayed throughout his corpus in ways that have not been adequately explored. A useful point of departure for seeing Hegel's influence is to be found in Strauss's letters, especially in his correspondence with Kojève and Löwith.

As regards courses taught, Strauss only publicly taught courses on the *Philosophy of Right*, defending the exclusion of other more purely theoretical texts by pointing to his venue in a political science department. But we know that he read Hegel's theoretical works. Indeed, in the mid-1950s he hosted a discussion group on the *Logic* at his home, which included, among others, Joseph Cropsey and Alan Bloom. This information comes to me from Joseph Cropsey.

8. Hegel deals with natural consciousness in the section of the *Phenomenology of Spirit* designated "Consciousness," which is eventually surpassed by "Self-consciousness" and so on, ultimately culminating in "Absolute Consciousness."

9. Consider in this regard Strauss's favorable disposition to what he terms phenomenology. "For Hegel is only the end of modern and probably also Christian philosophy—but not of the philosophical tradition as such. . . . I don't think as unfavorably as you do of the academic philosophy of the nineteenth century: from this arose phenomenology!" (Strauss, 1988, p. 190)

10. Strauss clearly signals us that he was significantly influenced by Heidegger. "Nothing so affected our minds as profoundly in the years in which they took their lasting directions as the thought of Heidegger. . . . Heidegger who surpasses in speculative intelligence all his contemporaries . . . attempts to go a way not yet trodden by anyone or rather to think in a way in which philosophers at any rate have never thought before. Certain it is that no one has questioned the premise of philosophy as radically as Heidegger. . . . Klein alone saw why Heidegger is truly important: by uprooting and not simply rejecting the tradition of philosophy, he made it possible for the first time after many centuries . . . to see the roots of the tradition as they are and thus perhaps to know, what so many merely believe, that those roots are the only natural and healthy roots." (Strauss 1978, p. 2)

11. Strauss's view of modern science is that it is technological to the core, and his reservations about it are very similar to Heidegger's. Consider the following controversial observation regarding Aristotle: "One may say, however, that [Aristotle] could not have conceived of a world state. But why? The world state presupposes such a development of technology as Aristotle could never have dreamed of. That technological development, in its turn, required that science be regarded as essentially in the service of the 'conquest of nature' and that technology be emancipated from any moral and political supervision. Aristotle did not conceive of a world state because he was absolutely certain that science is essentially theoretical and that the liberation of technology from moral and political control would lead to disastrous consequences." (Strauss 1950, p. 23) This must be put together with Strauss's other famous observation: "The

fundamental dilemma, in whose grip we are, is caused by the victory of modern natural science. An adequate solution to the problem of natural right cannot be found before this basic problem has been solved." (Strauss 1950, p. 8) But the problem is not, as usually thought, the existence of a non-teleological science. Strauss's phenomenological move solves that problem given that the "natural" everyday articulation of reality **is** teleological. Non-teleological science is derivative of a particular everyday prescientific experience. The problem is the intertwining of science and technology. Herein Strauss follows Heidegger.

12. Why Nature cannot be seen in the present world, and instead requires historical studies, is never entirely clear. There is a theoretical difficulty lurking here. If Nature is not visible in the present world, how will we know it when we see it in the past? Perhaps Strauss's historical studies are primarily a propaedeutic for those who do not see the natural in the present.

13. Interestingly, shortly thereafter Strauss asserts, "By the way: I am **not** an orthodox Jew."

14. This is developed in *Natural Right and History*, especially the chapter "The Origin of the **Idea** of Natural Right." [my emphasis]

15. On the frequent and obtrusive use of such locutions as the "**idea** of nature," the **idea** of Natural Right and the "**idea** of philosophy" see Kennington. I believe this frequent and obtrusive use of "idea" is of key importance. To my mind it offers Strauss a way to argue that there can be different deployments of "Nature," "Natural Right" and "philosophy" that nonetheless share a core "idea" and thereby point beyond situational particularity in the direction of a shared universal.

16. Put another way, the term "common sense," a phrase of Latin origins, clearly points in the direction of a shared, practical, group perception of reality. The old saw that today's common sense is a decayed permutation of the writings of some dead scribbler points toward the ultimate lack of autonomy of "natural experience," once philosophy is past its origins, or even once there is poetry.

17. This is an understanding Heidegger seems intent on recovering.

18. Heidegger would call such an understanding "metaphysical." It should be noted that in these terms it is natural experience that is metaphysical; the origin of metaphysics is not the philosophical tradition as Heidegger asserts; it is "natural experience" in Strauss's terms.

19. In this light, we can see "Idea of the Good" as it is depicted in Plato's *Republic* as an extrapolation from natural experience.

20. Those familiar with Heidegger's critique of the tradition might note the extent to which Strauss attributes to the pre-Socratics most of the elements that Heidegger criticizes as originating in Plato. Strauss's analysis frees Socrates/Plato from Heidegger's charges.

21. "The revolts against Hegelianism on the part of Kierkegaard and Nietzsche . . . appear as attempts to recover the possibility of practice. . . . But these attempts increased the confusion, since they destroyed, as far as in them lay, the very possibility of theory." (Strauss 1950, pp. 320–21)

22. Consider the following: "Plato *does not permit* the philosophers 'what is now permitted them,' namely, the life in philosophizing or lingering in the contemplation

of truth." (Strauss 1935/1987, p. 110) Given his phenomenological argument, Strauss likewise will not allow theory to be epistemically autonomous in the way Aristotle does. But he is determined to turn it again toward contemplation. As I will argue, it seems that Strauss must follow Aristotle in positing the relative autonomy of practice if not the simple autonomy of theory. This Aristotelian move is at odds with Strauss's Platonic/Socratic phenomenological move.

23. Strauss also calls the "fundamental questions" the "eternal and unsolved problems." (1963/1991, p. 211) "Philosophy is . . . nothing but genuine awareness of the problems, i.e., of the fundamental and comprehensive problems." (1963/1991, p. 196) Further: "If the fundamental problems persist in all historical change, human thought is capable of transcending its historical limitations or of grasping something trans-historical." (Strauss 1950, p. 24)

24. Strauss eventually admits that the fundamental positions are not eternally finite: "We cannot exclude the possibility that other great thinkers might arise in the future—in 2200 in Burma—the possibility of whose thought has in no way been provided for in our schemata." (Strauss 1989, p. 30)

25. One might note that while the Platonic/Socratic approach to philosophy as presented by Strauss may be metaphysical in the sense that it goes "beyond" the data of the senses and articulates what is embedded in it, or presupposed in the everyday articulation of reality, it is not metaphysico-theological in Heidegger's sense. That change makes more sense when applied to pre-Socratic thought or Aristotle's thought.

26. Consider the following: "There came into being a new type of theory . . . having as its highest theme human action and its **product** rather than the whole . . . Philosophy of history was primarily theory, i.e., contemplation of human action." [my emphasis] (Strauss 1950, pp 320–21) Heidegger accomplishes a similar transformation of ontology into the analysis of facticity and of the various events of Being throughout man's history—i.e., his theory of *Ereignis*.

27. So far we have confronted a pre-philosophic equation of the natural with that which presents itself, as opposed to the products of art that presuppose man. We have seen the pre-Socratic articulation of the **idea** of Nature as eternal, self-grounding first cause. We have seen the Socratic/Platonic equation of "nature" with the ensemble or heterogeneity of *eidē*. And we have approached the post-Heideggerian articulation of the pre-theoretical as "natural consciousness" qua pre-theoretical.

28. I agree with Lampert (1996) that earlier treatments of Nietzsche by Strauss are largely rhetorical. Interestingly, even a thinker as radical as Heidegger ultimately adopts the conventional view of Nietzsche as a voluntarist, subjectivist metaphysician. By comparison, it will become clear that Strauss's view is more radical. That said, Strauss borrowed heavily from what he understood of Nietzsche. "Nietzsche so dominated and bewitched me between my 22nd and 30th years, that I literally believed everything that I understood of him." (Strauss 1988, p. 183) I believe that Strauss's Nietzsche is closer to the real Nietzsche than almost any other extant interpretation.

29. I have argued elsewhere in chapter 9 that Strauss learned his "Platonism" from Nietzsche long before he encountered Farabi, Maimonides or Plato. What Strauss means by Platonism centers largely around the tension between philosophy and the city at the origins of the philosophic tradition and what follows from that tension. I

also believe Gourevitch (1968) is correct that this tension forms one of the tenets of what Strauss means by Natural Right. This points to the close relationship for Strauss between what he means by the terms Platonism and Natural Right.

30. Compare the following: "Gentlemen have this in common with the wise man, that they 'look down' on many things which are highly esteemed by the vulgar or that they are experienced in things noble and beautiful." (Strauss 1950, p. 142) "Without that *pathos of distance* which grows out of the ingrained difference between strata—when the ruling caste constantly looks afar and looks down . . . the other, more mysterious pathos could not have grown up either—the craving for an ever new widening distances within the soul itself." Nietzsche, *Beyond Good and Evil* (New York: Vintage Books, 1960), p. 201. But this in turn should be compared with Strauss's observation that since the nineteenth century, the philosophical advantages of the gentlemen have simply dissolved. (Strauss 1950, p. 143) That does not mean that philosophy should not defend itself by constructing a hierarchy with itself out of sight at the top.

31. One should keep in mind how this differs from what Strauss presents as the past permutations of classical Natural Right, an issue I will return to shortly.

32. "Awakeness" seems to be the clue to Strauss's understanding of the nature of true philosophy at its highest. It is amazing how often the term arises in his corpus. As one example consider: "The good life simply, is the life in which the requirements of man's natural inclinations are fulfilled in the proper order to the highest possible degree, the life of a man who is awake to the highest possible degree, the life of a man in whose soul nothing lies waste." (Strauss 1950, p. 127) This is more than a little reminiscent of the place of high self-consciousness as the defining character of philosophy in the thought of Hegel and Nietzsche where Absolute Self-Consciousness and Free-Spiritedness respectively represent peaks of philosophy. **Herein Strauss clearly parts company with Heidegger** whose critique of the possibility of fully awake and transparent self-consciousness and subjectivity is legend.

33. Stanley Rosen argues that Strauss's understanding ultimately rests on a turn to the primacy of practical wisdom in its choosing between and balancing of different moral and political options. This is allegedly necessary because for Strauss, consistent with the more conventional view of Nietzsche, there remains nothing to contemplate theoretically. As I will argue more fully below, Strauss, like his Nietzsche, is trying to recast theory as an end in itself and looks toward a future where philosophy, perhaps for the first time, can precisely withdraw from political and moral responsibilities to a contemplative solitude. This is possible precisely because philosophy in the future need not adopt the same defensive posture vis-à-vis the city as a result of the relative abolition of the political that is coming. (Rosen 1987, passim)

34. I will present this understanding in the essays on Plato in Part 3. I argue that Plato attempted a self-conscious break from Socrates.

35. Even a supporter like Pangle seems to come very close to this position. (Pangle 1983, 1989)

36. See Martin Heidegger, *Contributions to Philosophy* (*From Ereignis*) (Bloomington: Indiana University Press, 1999), pp. 15–17, 32, and passim. This is a translation of *Beitrage zur Philosophie (Vom Ereignis)* (Frankfurt am Main: Vittorio Klostermann, 1989).

37. Strauss goes no further toward the Natural Law tradition than the following: "There is a universally valid hierarchy of ends, but there are no valid rules of action." (Strauss 1950, p. 162) The Natural Law tradition desired to, and did, deduce rules of action.

38. While it may be true that one cannot ultimately understand the human without understanding the whole of which it is a part, or for that matter without understanding it in relation to the divine, it nonetheless appears that Strauss's understanding of Natural Right descends largely from a conception of human nature in its self-presenting heterogeneity. It is not an understanding that is cosmologically or metaphysically grounded. The human soul—its desires, needs, and ultimate good—is the ground. Hence, phenomenology trumps cosmology and metaphysics.

39. This is not the only point in history where Strauss concluded that an initially contingent choice led in an inevitable direction. His "Three Waves of Modernity" thesis shows the same kind of necessity operating. (Strauss 1975 II, pp. 81–98)

40. As I will argue shortly, I do not think that this in any way leads Strauss in the direction of metaphysics, cosmology or ontology as it may appear to have done with prior philosophy.

41. One should also reflect on Strauss's stunning observation regarding the ramifications of the doctrine of the eternal return: "[I]f one considers what decisive importance the dogma of creation and providence has for all of post-ancient philosophy, then one comprehends that liberation from this dogma was only to be brought about through the 'superhuman' effort of the teaching of the eternal return. Once this liberation— liberation from an unbelievable *pampering* of the human race—is achieved, then the eternal return can be taught calmly . . . In any case, true philosophizing is possible only on the assumption that the eternal return is taken seriously as a possibility and is endured. . . . Concerning deliverance from 'It was' in Descartes (!) see my Spinoza book p. 168f." (Strauss 1988, p. 190)

42. What follows for Strauss is the same as what follows for Heidegger: the abolition of man would simultaneously bring with it the abolition of Being.

43. In turning future philosophy toward a withdrawn, epicureanized, theoretical contemplation, as does his Nietzsche, Strauss seems forced to accept the relative autonomy of practice once theory again becomes contemplative rather than activist as it became in its modern permutation. But unlike Aristotle, Strauss does not posit the **simple** autonomy of theory. He sees that when made public, theoretical positions have practical ramifications. Whether a move like this ultimately saves theory is an open question. But contrary to commentators like Drury, Holmes and Rosen, Strauss is clearly trying to get theory out of the business of dictating to practice as it has for so long, especially in the modern era.

REFERENCES

Anastoplo, George, 1974, "On Leo Strauss: A Yahrzeit Remembrance," *University of Chicago Magazine*, Vol. 67 (Winter 1974).

Berns, Laurence, 1991, "The Prescientific World and Historicism: Some Reflections on Strauss, Heidegger and Husserl," in Udoff below.

Berns, Walter, 1973, "The Achievement of Leo Strauss," *National Review*, Vol. 25 (7 December).

Bloom, Alan, 1974, "Leo Strauss." *Political Theory* (November), pp. 372-92.

———. 1977, "Aristophanes and Socrates: A Response to Hall," *Political Theory*, Vol. 5.

Burneyat, Myles, 1985, "Sphinx Without a Secret," *New York Review of Books*, Vol. 32, no. 9 (May 30, 1985).

Cropsey, Joseph, 1962, "Reply to Rothman," *American Political Science Review*, Vol. 56.

Dallmayr, Fred R., 1987, "Politics Against Philosophy: Strauss and Drury," *Political Theory*, Vol. 15, no. 3.

Dannhauser, Werner, 1974, "Leo Strauss: Becoming Naïve Again," *American Scholar*, Vol. 44.

———. 1991, "Leo Strauss as Citizen and Jew," *Interpretation*, Vol. 17, no. 3.

Deutsche, Kenneth L., and John A. Murley, editors, 1999, *Leo Strauss, the Straussians and the American Regime*. Lanham: Rowman & Littlefield.

Deutsche, Kenneth L., and Walter Nicgorski, editors, 1994, *Leo Strauss: Political Philosopher and Jewish Thinker*. Lanham: Rowman & Littlefield.

Drury, Shadia, 1988, *The Political Ideas of Leo Strauss*. New York: St. Martin's Press.

Ferry, Luc, 1990, in *Political Philosophy, Volume 1, Rights—The New Quarrel Between the Ancients and the Moderns*. Chicago: University of Chicago Press.

Gourevitch, Victor, 1968, "Philosophy and Politics I," and "Philosophy and Politics II," *Review of Metaphysics* Vol. 22, nos. 1 and 2.

Green, Kenneth Hart, 1993, *Jew and Philosopher: The Return to Maimonides in the Jewish Thought of Leo Strauss*. Albany: State University of New York Press.

Gunnell, John, 1978, "The Myth of the Tradition," *American Political Science Review*, Vol. 72.

———. 1985, "Political Theory and Politics: The Case of Leo Strauss," *Political Theory*, Vol. 13, no. 3 (August).

Hall, Dale, 1977, The Republic and the 'Limits of Politics,'" *Political Theory*, Vol. 5.

Heidegger, Martin, 1999, *Plato's Sophist*. Bloomington: Indiana University Press.

Holmes, Stephen, 1989, "Truths for Philosophers Alone," *Times Literary Supplement* (December).

———. 1993, *The Anatomy of Antiliberalism*. Cambridge: Harvard University Press.

Jaffa, Harry, 1982, "The Legacy of Leo Strauss," *Claremont Review of Books*, Vol. 3, no. 3 (Fall 1984).

———. 1987, "Crisis of the Strauss Divided: The Legacy Reconsidered," *Social Research*, Vol. 54.

———. 1987, "Dear Professor Drury." *Political Theory*, Vol. 15, no. 3.

Jung, Hwa Yol, 1964, "A Post-Polemic," *American Political Science Review*, Vol. 58 (June).

———. 1967, "Strauss's Conception of Political Philosophy: A Critique," *Review of Politics*, Vol. 29 (October).

———. 1978, "The Life-World, Historicity, and Truth: Reflections on Leo Strauss's Encounter with Heidegger and Husserl," *Journal of the British Society for Phenomenology*, Vol. 9, no. 1.

――. 1978, Two Critics of Scientism: Leo Strauss and Edmund Husserl," *Independent Journal of Philosophy*, Vol 3.

Kennington, Richard, 1981, "Strauss's *Natural Right and History,*" *Review of Metaphysics*, Vol. 35.

Lampert, Laurence, 1978, "The Argument of Leo Strauss in *What Is Political Philosophy?*" *Modern Age*, Vol. 22.

――. 1996, *Leo Strauss and Nietzsche*. Chicago: University of Chicago Press.

Levine, David L., 1991, "Without Malice but With Forethought: A Response to Burnyeat," *Review of Politics*, Vol. 53, no. 1.

Manent, Pierre, 1989, "Strauss et Nietzsche," *Revue de Metaphysique et de Morale*, Vol. 94, no. 3.

Marshall, Terrence, 1985, "Leo Strauss, la philosophie et la science politique," *Revue francaise de science politique*, Vol. 35.

Miller, Eugene F., 1976, "Leo Strauss: The Recovery of Political Philosophy," in *Contemporary Political Philosophers*, ed. Anthony de Crespigny and Kenneth Minogue. London: Methuen and Co.

Novak, David, 1996, *Leo Strauss and Judaism: Jerusalem and Athens Critically Revisited*. Lanham: Rowman & Littlefield.

Orr Susan, 1995, *Jerusalem and Athens: Reason and Revelation in the Works* of Leo Strauss. Lanham: Rowman & Littlefield.

Pangle, Thomas and Nathan Tarcov, 1988, "Epilogue: Leo Strauss and the History of Political Philosophy," in *History of Political Philosophy*, 3rd edition. Chicago: University of Chicago Press.

Pangle, Thomas, 1983, "Introduction," in *Studies in Platonic Political Philosophy*, Chicago: University of Chicago Press.

――. 1989, "Introduction," in *The Rebirth of Classical Political Rationalism,*" by Leo Strauss. Chicago: University of Chicago Press.

Pippin, Robert B., 1992, "The Modern World of Leo Strauss," *Political Theory*, Vol. 20, no. 3.

Pocock, J.G.A., 1975, "Prophet and Inquisitor, or, A Church Built Upon Bayonets Cannot Stand: A Comment on Mansfield's 'Strauss's Machiavelli,'" *Political Theory*, Vol. 3.

Rosen, Stanley, 1987, *Hermeneutics as Politics*. New York: Oxford University Press.

――. 1991, "Is Metaphysics Possible?" *Review of Metaphysics*, Vol. 45.

Rothman, Stanley, 1962, "The Revival of Classical Political Philosophy: A Critique," and "A Rejoinder to Cropsey," *American Political Science Review*, Vol. 56.

Smith, Gregory Bruce, 1997, "Leo Strauss and the Straussians: An Anti-Democratic Cult?" in *PS: Political Science and Politics*, and this volume.

――. 1999, "Athens and Washington: Leo Strauss and the American Regime," in *Deutsche and Murley* 1999, and this volume.

Smith, Steven B., 1991, "'Leo Strauss' Between Athens and Jerusalem," *Review of Politics*, Vol. 53, no. 1.

Storing, Herbert, 1962, *Essays in the Scientific Study of Politics*, edited by Herbert Storing. Chicago: Holt, Rinehart and Winston.

Strauss, Leo, 1930, *Die Religionskritik Spinozas als Grunlage seiner Bibelwis-senschaft Untersuchungen zu Spinozas Theologishe-Politischem Traktat.* Translated in 1965 as *Spinoza's Critique of Religion.* New York: Schocken Books.

——. 1935, *Philosophie und Gesetz.* Translated in 1987 as *Philosophy and Law.* Philadelphia: The Jewish Publication Society.

——. 1936, *The Political Philosophy of Hobbes.* Oxford: Clarendon Press. And also in 1952 by Chicago: University of Chicago Press.

——. 1950, *Natural Right and History.* Chicago: University of Chicago Press.

——. 1952, *Persecution and the Art of Writing.* Glencoe, IL: The Free Press.

——. 1958, *Thoughts on Machiavelli.* Glencoe, IL: The Free Press.

——. 1959, *What Is Political Philosophy?* Glencoe, IL: The Free Press.

——. 1963, *On Tyranny.* Glencoe, IL: The Free Press. And also in 1991 a revised and expanded edition edited by Victor Gourevitch and Michael Roth. New York: The Free Press. The latter edition will be cited.

——. 1964, *The City and Man.* Chicago: Rand McNally.

——. 1966, *Socrates and Aristophanes.* New York: Basic Books.

——. 1968, *Liberalism: Ancient and Modern.* New York: Basic Books.

——. 1970, *Xenophon's Socratic Discourse.* Ithaca: Cornell University Press.

——. 1972, *Xenophon's Socrates.* Ithaca: Cornell University Press.

——. 1975, *The Argument and the Action of Plato's Laws.* Chicago: University of Chicago Press.

——. 1975 II, *Political Philosophy: Six Essays by Leo Strauss*, edited by Hilail Gildin. Indianapolis: Pegasus Books.

——. 1978, "An Unspoken Prologue," *Interpretation,* Vol. 7, no. 3.

——. 1983, *Studies in Platonic Political Philosophy.* Chicago: University of Chicago Press.

——. 1988, "Correspondence with Karl Löwith," *Independent Journal of Philosophy,* Vol. 5/6.

——. 1989, *The Rebirth of Classical Political Rationalism.* Chicago: University of Chicago Press.

Udoff, Alan, 1991, *Leo Strauss's Thought: Toward a Critical Engagement,* edited by Alan Udoff. Boulder: Lynne Rienner Publishers.

Ward, James, 1980, "Experience and Political Philosophy: Notes on Reading Leo Strauss," *Polity,* Vol. 13.

——. 1987, "Political Philosophy and History: Links Between Strauss and Heidegger," *Polity,* Vol. 20, no. 2.

Chapter Eleven

On Cropsey's World: Joseph Cropsey and the Tradition of Political Philosophy

"Fortunate is the political society in which the healthiest instincts resonate to the deepest insights." (SASA 41)*

Throughout a distinguished academic career spanning five decades, Joseph Cropsey has reflected upon the meaning of political philosophy and its complex tradition. Those reflections can be fruitfully approached under four headings. First, he questions the nature and origins of political philosophy as well as its cosmological or metaphysical foundations. Second, Cropsey questions the customary periodizations of the tradition of political philosophy. He especially questions the usefulness of the ancients-moderns distinction. Third, Cropsey reflects upon the relation between the tradition of political philosophy and concrete political life past and present. In the process, he tries to show the ways in which comprehensive constellations of ideas work their way into and inform everyday life. Fourth, he reflects upon the nature of the American regime and its prospects for the future. Throughout, it becomes clear that Cropsey has engaged in an ongoing dialogue with his mentor Leo Strauss. Finally, it also becomes clear, contrary to recent assertions made in response to his *Plato's World,* that Cropsey engages in a series of subtle critiques of Nietzschean and Heideggerian historicism and thereby of contemporary postmodernism as well.

From his first book on Adam Smith which appeared in 1957 to his controversial book on Plato which appeared in 1995, Cropsey has left an impressive written record of those reflections. One consistently sees not only significant clarity, penetration and precision but the recurrence of several central themes.

References to Cropset's writings are cited by abbreviated titles, followed by the page number. For full citations see the bibliography at the end of the article.

First, from beginning to end, Cropsey has reflected upon the nature of political philosophy. He has repeatedly tried to show that, contrary to much post-Heideggerian thought, ontological, cosmological or metaphysical reflection is a necessary **part** of political philosophy and can be transcended only by a more or less self-conscious suppression of tacitly held premises, whereby an author runs the risk of inconsistency. Cropsey has tried to show that all of the great political philosophers have reflected on the nature of the whole and on the relation between humanity and that comprehensive cosmic or natural whole of which we are a part. I will suggest that the way Cropsey engages this issue makes political philosophy architectonic, making it thereby the very peak or essence of the philosophic enterprise.[1]

Second, throughout Cropsey's corpus there is an ongoing series of reflections on the adequacy of the customary periodizations of the tradition of political philosophy. For example, Cropsey seems to question repeatedly the usefulness of the ancients-moderns distinction. He sees divisions within both antiquity, and especially within modernity, that are at times far greater than those existing between some moderns and some ancients. There is also an ongoing series of reflections on the relation between ancient and modern proponents of natural reason on the one hand and the Hebrew and Christian scriptural traditions on the other. As we will see, questioning distinctions like these can have far-reaching ramifications.

Third, as part of his reflections on the relation between the tradition of political philosophy and political life, past and present, Cropsey repeatedly discusses the ways in which the thoughts of the most comprehensive thinkers work their way out into the world and have practical ramifications. He argues that through a somewhat unpredictable process ideas inevitably get filtered, distorted, simplified and vulgarized on their way to concrete manifestation. Only in this fashion do comprehensive constellations of ideas work their way into the interstices of everyday life which they unavoidably inform.[2] Cropsey repeatedly argues that concrete lived experience always has complex overlays of different and even competing simplifications of comprehensive systems of thought.[3] This is a phenomenon that has accelerated in the modern age. These reflections have obvious ramifications for the possibility of total enlightenment and lead to Cropsey's conclusions regarding the need for an enlightenment of modest expectations.

Finally, and the list is intended to be indicative, not exhaustive, Cropsey has repeatedly reflected upon the nature of the American regime and its prospects for the future. He conducts those reflections in light of his understanding of the nature and necessity of political philosophy, and of the unavoidable relation between high thought and everyday life. Seen from that panoramic perspective, Cropsey offers a sobering yet ennobling vision of what is possible and what is not to be expected in our third century. Cropsey's vision is neither optimistic nor pessimistic, neither progressive nor inevitably tragic. These four themes, seen in Cropsey's work from beginning to end, will form the axes around which the following remarks will revolve.

Ever mindful of the comic element in the picture of various counterpoised, spinning whirls that inhabit the inner workings of the cosmos in various Platonic dialogues, I nevertheless wish to propose three further axes around which Cropsey's life work can be seen to revolve. These three axes are formed by specific authors rather than general themes. Again, the list is indicative rather than exhaustive. First, it almost goes without saying that the name of Joseph Cropsey is inextricably linked with that of Leo Strauss. It was largely through the efforts of Leo Strauss that the tradition of political philosophy was disinterred and brought back, if not as a corpse from the grave, at least from the danger of imminent suffocation. That patrimony was passed to Cropsey among others. He shares with Strauss a concern regarding the necessity of political philosophy, that modern political philosophy has led to a series of intensifications, and that late modernity is theoretically problematic while in significant respects, informs decent practice.

Yet for all Cropsey shares with Strauss, it would be a mistake to see his work as a simple repetition. He recasts many of Strauss's themes as well as quietly diverges from him on important, substantive issues. But this should not be surprising. Serious thought requires more than simple repetition. I want to suggest specifically that Cropsey has a different view than Strauss of the nature of political philosophy and of its founder, Socrates. Further, Cropsey's understanding of the relation between the ancients and the moderns differs, as does his understanding of the relation between the secular and scriptural components of the tradition. Other differences will emerge as we progress.

The second and third authors who can be seen as significant foils for Cropsey's thought are Friedrich Nietzsche and Martin Heidegger. Despite engaging in the kind of comprehensive reflections about man's place in the whole that Cropsey presents as necessary, each attempted to be a grave digger for the tradition of political philosophy. Each in his own way thought that he had discovered something that had escaped all prior thinkers and thereby made the tradition of political philosophy obsolete. In one way or another, implicitly or overtly, Cropsey's corpus can be seen as a response to these presumptions of closure and overcoming (EOH).[4] Cropsey denies that such closure is possible. Further, he painstakingly demonstrates, contrary to the reigning historicism, that there was nothing in principle unavailable to prior thinkers—ancient or modern—that was first discovered by Nietzsche, Heidegger or anyone else. In that fashion, Cropsey attempts to confront the claims of Nietzsche and Heidegger at the deepest philosophical level.

Cropsey's initial published works reflected primarily on modern political philosophy and how it informed modern practice. In these works, as well as throughout his corpus, one is struck by the movement back and forth between reflections on high thought and on the concrete issues informed by it (cf. MB, RFA, USP, RR). Cropsey's initial academic training was in technical economics, but it is clear that he was almost immediately led beyond technical analysis to an inspection of the suppressed theoretical premises that animated it (cf. WE, PSE). He shows how, by ignoring questions regarding human nature and substantive human ends, technical economic analysis is always blind to what it can and cannot legitimately accomplish. Economics as an allegedly autonomous science came into existence only on the basis of a decision by modern political philosophy which concluded that political life could fruitfully be reduced to the competition of various interests—that is, politics was substantially reduced to economics. Simultaneously, the natural whole of which man was a part had to be recreated, which is to say theoretically reconceptualized. The conclusion that Cropsey draws from these reflections is characteristic of his thought from beginning to end. Neither economic activity nor concrete political life—nor their respective modern scientific treatments—are autonomous activities. Only political philosophy is autonomous.[5]

Despite genuine respect for the proto-modern project that lies at the basis of capitalism and liberal democracy, Cropsey nonetheless retains a significant skepticism regarding the sufficiency of self-interest as an autonomous principle when divorced from a concern for virtue or human excellence.[6] But this never led him to extravagant or utopian claims in the name of virtue, for he never saw any such claims offered even by the sober ancient authors who are frequently seen to be proponents of utopian schemes in the name of virtue. For Cropsey, political life has always been seen to be precariously balanced upon a natural base which threatens man's moral well-being.[7] We will return thematically to this issue in a moment.

Cropsey seems to have drawn some encouragement from the fact that even Adam Smith, the theoretical father of capitalism, did not ultimately abstract from considerations about virtue. In *Polity and Economy,* Cropsey argues that in the name of virtue even Smith offered some of the same reservations against commerce as the ancients.[8] Cropsey points out that Smith followed Hobbes in positing a morally indifferent natural whole ruled by simple cause and effect into which man was integrated in a straightforward or "simple" fashion not through reason but by the passions. For Hobbesean fear, Smith tried to substitute the desire to better one's condition and the existence of natural sympathy. Smith believed that economic competition could replace fear of others or a powerful sovereign, while still emancipating the passions from the constraints of ecclesiastical authority. His publicly articulated vision was that the good life consisted of a primarily active life of labor which could do without citizen participation or pursuit of the grand virtues of the ancients.

Cropsey argues that Smith hoped that humanity could purchase freedom from ecclesiastical rule which, he somewhat iconoclastically points out, was the primary end sought by his espousal of what came to be called capitalism. Capitalism was always seen as a means to an end other than itself. But that end was not primarily profit as Marx and many others have argued. According to Cropsey, Smith's primary end was freedom from Christian, ecclesiastical authority, not profit, or for that matter, emancipation from the moral teaching of the heathen ancients. Indeed, elsewhere Cropsey asserts that the early moderns simply misunderstood, and were wrong about, the ancients, in effect, wrongly conflating them with the Christians (cf. AM, pp. 47–51; PLNO passim). Herein Cropsey arrives at one of his central themes, a theme that seems to separate him from Strauss. Modernity was born not in opposition to pagan antiquity, but in opposition to Christian ecclesiastical authority and the disastrous politics to which it led.

Despite his project for liberation, Cropsey's Smith was profoundly worried about the moral implications of capitalism. Being a means rather than an end, capitalism always remains an utterly empty vessel until it is filled with moral content from without. In *Polity and Economy,* Cropsey argues that for Smith that external content proved to be a traditional understanding of virtue and the good. The open question is whether this was a moral content to which Smith was entitled on the basis of his teaching.[9] Smith could not jettison a commitment to traditional virtue because he feared many of the same things as Nietzsche.

Smith was concerned that capitalism would bring with it a decline of martial spirit, moral strength and moral independence leaving instead the reign of general, moral indolence. Whether Smith's conceptualization of nature adequately resolved these seemingly competing concerns remains an open question. Regardless of the answer, Cropsey believes that confusions and contradictions emanating from the potentially conflicting claims of self-interest and virtue remain embedded in liberal, democratic thought and practice to this day. Whether a recurrence to Smith's rendition of capitalism is what is primarily needed to confront these contradictions, or a move to some other foundation remains an open question as well.[10]

Cropsey's Hobbes, the first liberal, if not the first capitalist, frequently seems more theoretically resolute and thereby less prone to contradiction than Smith. Perhaps this is why Cropsey repeatedly returns to Hobbes.[11] Further, Hobbes was not as prone to the unprecedented "spasm of optimism," which Cropsey attributes to most of later modernity (AM, p. 49). Like his Smith, Cropsey's Hobbes saw ecclesiastical authority as the principal antagonist.

Hence he attempted to assert the primacy of nature over supernature, and thereby the primacy of natural reason over revelation. In this, Cropsey observes, he followed the ancients—albeit for the ancients the principal dichotomy was between nature and convention. Between natural reason and revelation, Cropsey asserts, there is no possible synthesis (HTM 295).

Cropsey's Hobbes sides with Aristotle not only on the primacy of natural reason but also on the necessity of secular supremacy. This is conjoined with an attempt to present God primarily in the limited role of first cause of the whole. Throughout, Cropsey tries to show that the gap between Hobbes and the ancients—Aristotle is in this instance the primary exemplar—is nowhere near as great as that between Hobbes and the Christian, scriptural dispensation. The modern-revelation split is accentuated, not the ancient-modern dichotomy, where the gap is substantially closed.[12] Cropsey argues that what Hobbes attempted was a "rectification within the tradition," at least as much as he could, by providing a "displacement of revelation" in the service of natural reason. In short, Hobbes rejected part of the tradition in the name of another part.

In an essay that appeared twenty-six years later than the initial Hobbes essay, Cropsey argues that a, if not the, task of political philosophy is to bring about repeated revisions, reorganizations, renewals, and "ingatherings" of one's traditional patrimony (AM 45).[13] He fits this idea under the rubric of a discussion of "enlightenment." Cropsey asserts that there have been *four* enlightenments in the West: Hebrew, Greek, Christian, and modern. On its face this might seem to be a paradoxical use of the term *enlightenment.* But this is only true if one associates the term enlightenment with an unmitigated commitment to rationalism, as is usually done in interpreting the modern enlightenment. The modern enlightenment used the scriptural tradition as its foil in the process making it appear "irrational," while elevating its own depiction of reason to hegemony.

Cropsey tries to show that the proto-modern enlightenment itself took over elements from pagan antiquity, and Scripture as well, and reorganized them, thereby giving them a novel bearing. This reorganizing of the patrimony is true not only of Hobbes and presumably Smith, but of thinkers like Descartes and Spinoza as well.[14] As we will see shortly, Cropsey uses the same rubric of enlightenment to present the doings of his Socrates who synthesizes and moderates elements of thought that came down to him from Parmenides, Heraclitus, Anaxagoras, Pythagoreanism, Protagoreanism, etc.[15] As "reorganizations" or "mixings," "enlightenments" are many and varied and do not require a total public commitment to "rationalism." These mixings must presumably be understood as forms of poetry. I would suggest that Cropsey's own work could be cast as a late-modern enlightenment in precisely his terms, a reorganization of the patrimony to date. Some elements from the past ascend, others decline in importance. It is not clear, however, if there is any possibility of novelty.

To return to Hobbes, Cropsey argues that a scriptural component taken from the tradition was reappropriated through an attempt to show that nothing in Scripture was at odds with natural reason. The name of Spinoza could be added to this effort as well. If, the proto-modern enlightenment argued, God is a good and rational God, then His creation and His deeds must be rational. Christianity opened a door. But the Christian argument also led to destructive politics. Hobbes reorganized his patrimony to transcend this destructiveness. On this level, Hobbes thought that a synthesis of natural reason and Scripture had some plausibility. What is again to be noted is that Cropsey's Hobbes is not primarily affecting a break with antiquity so much as attempting a return to continuity with it.

While Cropsey is at pains to show the ways in which Hobbes's thought represents a return to the ancients, he does argue that in one significant respect there is a difference. While Hobbes returns to the ancient understanding that the life in accord with reason—as opposed to revelation—is the best life, he seems to reject what the ancients thought followed from that fact. According to Hobbes's public teaching, an active and productive life is best, rather than the philosophical life devoted to reasoning. The life *according* to reason is best but the life *of* reason is not the highest excellence.

Cropsey observes that this contradiction reigns throughout proto-modernity. As a result, where Aristotle and Plato allowed a claim to privacy that existed above the law in philosophy, Hobbes only admitted a realm of privacy below the law in passion and ultimately only in the passion for self-preservation. And to ground secular sovereignty, Hobbes, like all the proto-moderns, fully integrated man into a morally indifferent natural whole of strict causality. The passions were our point of linkage to nature, not reason. For Hobbes, since that natural whole was so at odds with human well-being, it had to give way to a conventional sovereignty with total authority, admitting no private appeals to religion, philosophy, or anything else except self-preservation.

Cropsey argues that having accomplished this exhaustive, mechanical integration of man into nature, later modernity was left to struggle to find a place for freedom in an all-encompassing natural whole.[16] That struggle led almost inevitably to Kant and the convoluted politics that descends from his work, especially via students like Marx. Having passed through Kant, modernity was so transformed that Cropsey asserts that the gap between early and late modernity is far wider than that between proto-modernity and antiquity. He goes so far as to suggest that the two are simply incommensurable (cf. CDMS). Herein Cropsey departs from the logic of Strauss's "three waves of modernity" argument. Within modernity is to be found one of the most note-worthy gaps or fissures in the tradition, more significant than that between an-cients and proto-moderns. It is a fissure more significant as well than that be-tween the proto-moderns and the Christian scriptural elements of the tradition.[17]

Cropsey's Descartes adds further brush strokes to his proto-modern canvas. His Descartes emerges as more philosophically daring than Hobbes's. But like Cropsey's Hobbes and Smith, he too is shown to be in pursuit of a goal shared with antiquity.[18] His was the audacious soul that posited a method "based on the unflattering notion that between himself and the rest there is a colossal inequality" (PPIP 275). He understood as well as the ancients that thought thinking itself represented the best life, and that solitude and private resoluteness were its prerequisites. Like the ancients, he saw the highest free-dom coming from thought thinking itself. Also like the ancients, Descartes saw the rule of the philosopher as the best rule, albeit from a distance, and over subjects rather than equals (PPIP 278). Actually, in this he may have been far more audacious, and less democratic, than the ancients.

According to Cropsey, Descartes' teaching rested on the understanding that "the existence of the thing being wholly in the mind, the clear and distinct definition of it is the real being" (PPIP 286). Hence, as is true in the common, textbook picture of Plato, for Descartes the being of things is grounded in ideas, albeit not self-subsistent ideas existing in a separate realm rather than the human mind. Given the precise ideas that Descartes posited, Cropsey goes on to argue that his projection of clear and distinct ideas is only consistent with a corporealist monism, like that of Hobbes, Smith and Spinoza, and not the customary dualism that is attributed to him. Be this as it may, what we see again is Cropsey's attempt to soften the ancients-moderns distinction sub-stantially. Perhaps most interestingly, Cropsey's Descartes comes far closer to *openly* positing the life of thought as the best life than other proto-moderns, Smith and Hobbes included.[19]

For Cropsey, the most substantial ground for the distinction between the ancients and the moderns has to be found somewhere other than where it is usually placed—for example somewhere other than seeing the ancients as idealists who posited "imagined republics" while the moderns were hard-headed realists. That more substantial ground emerges thematically in Cropsey's 1961 article, "Political Life and a Natural Order," which is one of the quintessential examples of the dialectical mode of reasoning that Cropsey frequently deploys. Cropsey lays out various popular premises and resolutely traces out where they lead, how one is driven into confusion or obscurity and hence why the initial premises need to be recast and reconsidered. One is then driven to new premises which are considered in the same fashion in search of a premise that can stand its ground. We cannot reproduce that dialectic here; we can report the outcome.

Cropsey starts from the venerable distinction between natural and artificial things.[20] He depicts the natural things as coming into being through a process of necessity or causality, with the obscurity of the natural things resting in the ultimate obscurity of the first cause. The artificial things, including laws, are based on man's contrivance. The obscurity of the artificial things rests in their seeming to lack necessity, resting instead on the potentially arbitrary will of man. In some respects the artificial things seem more intelligible; in other aspects it is the natural things. Neither basks in total intelligibility. Necessity vouches for the regularity of the natural things but seems thereby to preclude choice and morality; natural necessity is seemingly amoral. The existence of the artificial things might be seen to vouch for the possibility of something that escapes simple necessity, but from a moral point of view seems to point toward the arbitrary rather than the necessary. Hence law and morality might seem arbitrary. Cropsey presents this as the fundamental conundrum present to all thought, rational or scriptural, ancient or modern. How are we to articulate the relation between the natural and the conventional, the necessary and the free, the arbitrary and its opposite?

Cropsey argues that man's distinctiveness arises from resisting the natural necessity which he shares with all other beings.[21] This need for resistance was understood by the ancients at least as clearly as by the moderns, but they confronted it differently. Proving that this is true becomes one of the animating principles of Cropsey's later works on Plato. Unlike the moderns, Cropsey's ancients were primarily led toward a prideful, moral assertion against nature in the name of the possibility of human excellence, understood as a "noble simulation of independence" (PPIP 226). His moderns were led toward a contradictory public project of moral capitulation to natural necessity and an attempted scientific mastery of it (PPIP 6).[22] For the ancients, it was precisely the dual or complex organization of the whole—which included both man and natural necessity—that was taken as the model for political life. Both intelligence and corporeal necessity had to be incorporated into the whole. Put another way, the passions, which could be resisted but not extinguished, had to submit to a prideful assertion on the part of mind or intelligence. Hence the cosmic whole was seen as having humanity as its culminating part, with mind or intelligence thereby operating in the whole primarily through man.

For the ancients, the complex cosmic whole was the model for man's political and moral resistance to necessity in the name of excellence. Cropsey argues that the moderns, on the other hand, posited a unitary, mechanical, exhaustive natural whole into which man was simply integrated by the passions. For the moderns there was allegedly nothing but necessity conceived as the power of efficient causality. Hence the model for the moral and political had to be found elsewhere than in a complex integration into nature. This view eventually led to far greater conundrums than the first. Modern political science—exemplified by the likes of Hobbes, Smith, and Spinoza—argued that mankind must capitulate to the unitary nature that flowed through it.

Yet modern science tried to triumph over unitary nature by creating its own order from out of the mind, implying thereby a duality. Unfortunately, the modern unitary view cannot account for the existence of modern science. The complexity raised by the existence of modern science was not taken as a model for political and moral existence. In some ways the ancient view provided a more consistent model for the complex understanding that emerged in modernity than the modern unitary view of the whole.

A few modern authors to the contrary notwithstanding, the moral and political world ceased to be a venue for the strenuous rebellion against nature. That became the task of a natural philosophy that posited order in the mind and eschewed the task of grasping the pre-given whole which remained utterly mysterious. As a result, natural philosophy ceased to be a wonder-driven striving for union with the natural whole. In the process, modernity gave up any public manifestation of a gallant, prideful struggle to keep alive the hope of excellence—it was left for those solitary, resolute individuals such as Descartes, Spinoza, or Rousseau alone, but only in their private lives.

Cropsey's understanding of the nature of modern political philosophy and of the inevitable relation between high thought and everyday life conditions his reflections on the American regime. He sees the central contradictions in contemporary American life as having descended from complications always inherent in proto-modern thought, especially in light of the contradictions incident to the efforts of later modern thought to resolve the earlier tensions. Given that Cropsey rejects the textbook view that the ancients understood the natural whole in a simple or unitary fashion that supports human existence in an equally simple fashion, he is not given to offering any easy solutions. By the same token, he is thereby moved to give modernity a far more sympathetic hearing despite its inherent contradictions (cf. AM 51). For example, Cropsey seems to experiment with various creative returns to authors like Hobbes and Smith.

Cropsey's critique of the American situation can be summed up in his conclusion that in the strict sense used by the ancients, the United States is not a regime (PPIP 211). A regime, strictly speaking, provides the organizing or constituting principles of the way of life or *ethos* of a people. While the principles of proto-modernity are embedded in our Constitution, that document does not presume to constitute every aspect of life. It sets the parameters that make considerable moral and political freedom possible. But freedom is a substanceless end until it is filled by concrete objects of aspiration.

Since there is no specific morality that is the necessary adjunct of our parchment regime, nothing specific exists which necessarily informs the everyday lives of American citizens. Large segments of life are left to the private conditioning performed by everything from art and religion to philosophy. Cropsey's argument rests on the distinction between our *parchment* regime or written constituting documents and our *effective* regime or the everyday way that concrete lives are lived. The two diverge. The proto-modern philosophy of authors like Hobbes, Spinoza, and Smith is clearly mixed with our parchment regime. Later modern thought informs much of everyday life. The two are inconsistent. This is the source of our self-dissatisfaction.

Once again, it is Hobbes to whom Cropsey turns as the exemplar of the central premises underlying our parchment regime. Those premises are reduced to moral relativism, concern for personal freedom, constitutionalism upon which a strong conventional sovereignty is built, and egalitarianism.[23] Were we to be totally informed by proto-modern principles, there would be some consistency in our regime. But as an "open society" we are open to more than proto-modernity. Within modernity there is both unity and diversity. Throughout modern thought there is a unitary view of a morally evacuated nature of which man is a simple part. But there is also a theoretical longing to find a basis for freedom which unfortunately gets deflected into the moral and political arena. Proto-modernity attempted an uneasy **accommodation** of its view of nature and freedom; later modernity tried to elevate freedom **above** nature and hence above the operation of the passions and the concern for self-preservation. Eventually, late modernity not only tried to elevate freedom above nature but to move it entirely **outside** nature (CDMS 17).

Cropsey argues that throughout late modernity there is a great confusion about the relation between nature and freedom, which produces the split within modernity that is greater than the split between proto-modernity and antiquity (CDMS 18).[24] This split leads not so much to the alienation that Marxism posits—which Cropsey argues is not a very useful theoretical category (AA) but to a loss of national unity and patriotism and to confused, demoralized, and dispirited citizens. The greatest danger is not alienation but the destruction of magnanimity and self-regard (cf. AA, PPIP 205–17).

One antidote Cropsey proposes for the problems that exist within modernity involves stressing the Hobbesean elements in our parchment regime, especially the emphasis on the need for strong conventional sovereignty.[25] Hobbes saw the need for strong conventions as a response to a morally neutral and fundamentally unorderly natural whole. Cropsey sees that as a consistent response. But later moderns reject strong sovereignty, for they saw convention as alienating and therefore as a greater threat to freedom than immersion in a unitary, morally indifferent, natural whole. Cropsey sees no easy way around this problem because late modernity can never overcome its confusion about the relation between nature and convention or nature and freedom. But when late moderns try to absolutize idiosyncratic will as a means to freedom while retaining proto-modernity's view of the moral indifference of nature, they threaten the endurance of a fundamentally decent regime.

With an atrophying commitment to strong conventions and sovereignty, Cropsey believes that our parchment regime cannot maintain itself against the ongoing onslaught of external opinions and influences that wash over us like waves over a defenseless shore. As examples, Cropsey points to such phenomena as existentialism and psychoanalysis, but he means all those movements of thought that descend from Rousseau, Kant, Hegel, Marx, Nietzsche, Freud, Heidegger, et al. He argues that what one sees is that even initially stern modern moral teachings eventually foster outcomes that serve the indolent rather than the inspiriting. This loosening of conventional moral restraints leads toward chaos and the abyss of unguided will or potential despotism.

In concluding his discussion of the American regime, Cropsey asserts, without further elaboration, that politics originates nothing (PPIP 15). The American regime is the playground for various incompatible elements drawn from a modernity which is still working itself out. The scene is further complicated by the existence of decayed elements drawn from Scripture and antiquity. This complicated environment of mutually exclusive crosscurrents is what shapes our effective regime. It cannot be made compatible with our parchment regime. As a result we are caught in the embrace of chance as our extended regime contains elements that are ungovernable and unpredictable. These ungovernable elements are the source of our ongoing self-dissatisfaction; it does not emanate from our laws or Constitution, nor can it be dealt with by them. We are a microcosm of self-dissatisfied modernity as it tries to resolve the tensions inherent in its original constituting principles. As a general formula, Cropsey offers that whatever hope we have must come from drawing from the inspiriting wellsprings of modernity, which seems to mean those that can emancipate us from the unmediated longing for survival, security, self-indulgence and general bourgeoisification. Unfortunately, in Cropsey's own analysis, those wellsprings seem few and far between within modernity and they may not be accessible to more than the likes of Hobbes, Descartes, Spinoza, Rousseau, etc. as a private solution.

To return to a theme we have already confronted, the real solution to our dissatisfaction—our loss of exaltation, vivacity and high-heartedness—may ultimately have to come from thought, and in Cropsey's mind any number of modern thinkers understood this perfectly well, despite the fact that they repeatedly posited the priority of action over thought as intrinsic to the good life.[26] Cropsey painstakingly points out how many modern authors still saw contemplation as the highest solace. Even if we are totally immersed within a morally evacuated nature, contemplation of that fact creates detachment and thereby freedom. According to Cropsey, thought is free to the extent that it makes itself its object, as many moderns from Descartes to Hegel make clear. Thought, by reflecting on thought, rather than through random, idiosyncratic spasms of will, discovers freedom.

But as modernity evolves, thought is eventually transformed into will. From Rousseau to Nietzsche we see the apotheosis of will asserting itself against nature in the form of the proud act of a single individual. Therein lies the central problem for late modern political philosophy. By the time that grand, if mad, idea works its way to the political arena, it comes forth as the idea that convention is a bigger restraint on will than nature, an idea that destroys liberalism's commitment to conventional sovereignty and subjects the regime to every ill considered wave of thought in the name of the openness of an open society which is not substantively open to anything in particular.

For Cropsey, as for pre-modern thought, true regimes require some degree of closure which we late moderns do not possess. Cropsey sees the openness that we sometimes praise in adding up the benefits of modern democracy as a potential danger. Yet he sees perfectly well the need for some form of openness. One totalitarian regime after another in this century has shown the danger in the modern world of attempting total closure. In his reflections on the nature of openness, Cropsey suggests that the idea of openness can be given no consistent meaning without linking it to the genuine openness of philosophy (cf. APOS). As far as he is concerned, that is in no way inconsistent with the existence of something closer to a genuine regime with its strong sovereignty and moral conventions. But to the extent that a society openly based on philosophy is a chimera, as Plato-Socrates show in the *Republic*, the openness of any society that has the possibility of endurance is at best precarious. Cropsey presents endurance and openness as competing goods. He offers no easy theoretical solution beyond awareness of the problem and the need to balance those goods.

The kind of "caring" statesmanship that might be able to deal with a tension like this is given concrete form in a number of Cropsey's philosophical reflections on concrete policy issues, as well as theoretical articulation in *Plato's World*. I will limit the discussion to two of Cropsey's concrete examples. As regards the potentially volatile issue of religion in American political life, Cropsey observes that while we are a nation founded by Christians, which still contains a majority that is Christian, we were never intended to be a constitutionally Christian land (cf. RCE). Christianity is not written into our parchment regime; Hobbesean liberalism is. Yet we do benefit from the moral virtue Christianity offers via the private realm. We have "the privilege of enjoying the blessings of two separate worlds" (RCE 35).

Cropsey has no intention of advising that a hoped for, reinvigorated sovereignty imposes traditional Christian morality—assuming one could figure out precisely what that implied. His point is not the Machiavellian one that Christianity enervates—a position transformed by Nietzsche into the belief that Christianity is a hate-filled resentment against the high-spirited—but closer to the proto-modern realization that while necessary, religion is potentially inflammatory. Power corrupts; absolute power corrupts absolutely whether wielded for secular or ecclesiastical purposes.[27]

The other side of the coin is that in an age of the hegemony of the idiosyncratic will one cannot have the authoritative meaning of Scripture publicly advanced by every David Koresh or Jim Jones who unpredictably wanders onto the scene. Natural reason must be the judge. Ours is a regime that needs moral principles to enter from without. But that "without" should be judged by political philosophy. What is required of a philosophically informed statesmanship is to defend sovereignty and convention, avoid despotism, invigorate and inspirit, remain open to philosophy. To say the least, that requires a delicate practical balancing act, not theoretical or moral dogmatism. On the success of that delicate balance rests the practicality of a durable, decent regime.

In a similar vein, in his reflections on contemporary liberal and conservative ideologies, Cropsey points out the theoretical contradictions inherent in each as they deploy themselves in everyday political life (cf. CL). Again, contemporary liberals have strong reservations against convention, while rarely being led toward nature. They praise freedom, self-expression and creativity shorn of both natural and conventional limits. But while they want to cultivate freedom, they also retain a faith that this can somehow simultaneously, indeed spontaneously, coalesce into fraternity, community, and sociality rather than simple mass, assertive, idiosyncratic egoism. In short, they are for liberty, but also for fraternity, and its adjunct, equality. Such contradictions cannot stand theoretically.

Contemporary conservatives on the other hand customarily see nature as morally indifferent, hence pointing toward a competitive, even aggressive, free-for-all if not controlled by strong moral and political conventions. Yet they also desire unlimited economic competition. They are further committed to the idea that conventions need to grow imperceptibly over a long period of time and should therefore not be overthrown by autonomous reason. Hence traditional conventions become quasi-natural. Conservatives simultaneously espouse capitalist competition and precapitalist tradition. They are for liberty but also for constraints on liberty in the name of virtue. These contradictions cannot theoretically stand either.

On one level there is an equivalence between contemporary liberalism and conservatism. They are both residues of competing elements drawn from past political philosophies. They are both constructed of discordant principles. The solution Cropsey proposes is a fruitful balancing of the two, not in the name of noncontradiction or the public manifestation of the entire truth, but in the name of moderation. Prudence dictates that neither should be allowed to annihilate the other. With an appropriate balance in place, one could hope to avoid both dogmatism and anarchism. Again, a high level philosophic statesmanship is needed that points toward constructing a "temperate equilibrium of error" (PPIP 130). This statesmanship should not, of course, be confused with political philosophy itself, to which it is subordinate. Unfortunately, such high-level statesmanship, above simple partisanship, while greatly needed is rarely seen.

On the more philosophic level, Cropsey observes that the modern "flight from nature" was, in one respect, on the right course. Constructing an egress from nature is always what is philosophically required (APOS 26).[28] In different ways, such an egress was attempted not only by the moderns but by both Scripture and the ancients. But in neither of those latter cases did that egress culminate in the hegemony of will. Cropsey argues that we must find an egress from dehumanizing nature that culminates neither in the abyss of unguided will nor in despotism. His search for that egress led him to the Platonic dialogues. In a series of articles on specific dialogues, and in *Plato's World,* Cropsey has looked for an alternative to the contradictory theoretical situation left to us by modernity. Once again we will have to limit ourselves to reporting on outcomes rather than rehearsing the details.

In his treatment of the *Philebus,* Cropsey iconoclastically points out the ways in which Socrates takes the side of multiplicity rather than unity or the One (cf. PHG). He argues that throughout the dialogue it becomes clear there are no uncompounded unities, not even the Good. He goes on to show how Socrates also presents the soul as primarily moved by a desire to preserve its motion, which prompts Cropsey to observe that Socrates seems to have discovered Hobbes (PHG 181–82). He demonstrates how the dialogue differentiates the use of the term cosmos, as referring to the world of Becoming, and the term nature, as referring to the realm of Truth and the faculty related to it (PHG 189). He argues that there is a tension that emerges between what exists in the cosmos (Being) and what exists in thought. Needless to say, this treatment diverges from conventional understandings of Socratic dogma.

Cropsey tries to show how Socrates reaches the conclusion that neither pleasure nor mind alone are synonymous with or lead to the good life. The existence of the Good requires good mixing for its coming to be, for example, the mixing of pleasure and mind, among other things. Since mixing implies a mixer, it becomes clear that the existence of the good requires artifice. It is further shown that no matter what other elements are needed, the mixture that brings the Good to be always requires Measure and Proportion. Cropsey then argues that Truth, to the extent it is a necessary part of any mixture, rests on rational, fabricating mind for its coming to be. The echo of an idea usually attributed to Descartes becomes clear. Plato was capable of confronting the same fundamental idea as the proto-modern Descartes, albeit he gave it a different, perhaps more comprehensive, articulation.

Cropsey concludes that rational mind, in the *Philebus* at least, is the indispensable mixer. His interpretation of the *Statesman* will arrive at a similar point. Shorn of any cosmogonic elements, and remembering that Measure and Proportion—which implies Beauty—must be part of any rationally compounded whole, perhaps we can see the ways in which this picture would diverge from that presented by various modern authors. It is easy to see how it diverges from the picture presented by Nietzsche, who posits the opposites of Measure, Proportion, and Beauty. Further, the Good requires a mixture; it is a multiplicity considered as a One by having a single Idea stamped upon it (PHG 190). Fabricating mind is the cause. While pleasure is needed to ground self-preservation, contrary to Hobbes, it is not self-sufficient as a principle. Mind is needed for the existence of the Good. But Mind is ultimately operative only in a few, from which Cropsey draws the practical conclusion that the difference between man and beast is revealed only in philosophy understood as the activity of fabricating mind that mixes necessary elements.[29]

Humanity itself is a compound of parts separated by profound incommensurability—a diversity which is paralleled in many individuals. In this regard, mankind is a microcosm of the whole which exercises Mind only through man. Mankind forms the last link or part of the whole through its exercise of Mind. In that fashion, far more than by the operation of simply repetitive blind necessity, there is rationality in the whole. But by the same token, in both the whole and within the part mankind, there is simultaneously incommensurability or irrationality. The truth of the cosmos becomes a mixture of reason and irreason.[30]

Whether this understanding Cropsey presents is entirely Socrates', whether it is Plato's, or whether it is Cropsey's remains an open question. Assuming it is entirely Socrates's, does Plato entirely agree? Assuming that this understanding is Plato's correction of Socratism, what is the precise nature of Socratism? The subject of the relation between Plato and Socrates, and hence of the nature and origin of the tradition of political philosophy, is engaged thematically in Cropsey's treatment of Plato's *Phaedrus* (PPIP 231–51). These reflections return elsewhere in Cropsey's treatment of Plato and represent some of his most original contributions to scholarship.[31]

At one point, Cropsey injects the phrase "The Problem of Socrates," which is both a chapter heading used by Nietzsche and a lecture given by Strauss (PPIP 233). What is that problem? Cropsey points to several possible responses. Socrates' invocation of Isocrates as his best pupil certainly raises questions regarding his judgment. The fact that he speaks against the value of writing in a written dialogue, points toward another possible Platonic critique. Cropsey also raises the issue of whether Socrates ever arrived at the trans-verbal insight that is achieved allegedly only in an act of positing the very thing itself, or if he remained merely a midwife to Plato—a role he seems to accept in the *Theaetetus*. If the highest truth comes only to a few in noetic insight, then from a purely philosophic point of view perhaps it need not be written down for recollection. If, on the other hand, the highest philosophic insight comes in an act of positing, it may be necessary to preserve it or at the very least one might run the risk of giving in to a certain evanescence of Being not unlike that pointed to by Protagoras. If this latter is the case, Socrates's refusal to write would be a sign he lacked *theoretical* clarity.

In trying to unlock the structure of the *Phaedrus*, Cropsey interprets Socrates' first speech as positing nature as being unitary, exhaustive, and implying a universal predatoriness. In this speech, nature is power, compulsion and necessity, totally devoid of beauty or nobility, to say nothing of Measure and Proportion. But in his second speech, or recantation, Socrates posits beauty, philosophy and nobility and in the process totally reconstructs nature. Cropsey argues that this amounts to rescuing mankind from morally repellent nature. But who is it who performs the necessary task of rescuing mankind from repellent, morally indifferent nature, Socrates or Plato?

What should be noted in this vein is that Cropsey is trying to suggest that Plato-Socrates—taking them for the moment as indistinguishable—on some level may be operating on the same view of nature as the moderns—for example, Hobbes, Descartes, and Spinoza. Nature is posited as necessity, causation and blind power, albeit none of the moderns claims that this is simply true of the whole since the thing-in-itself remains mysterious. Modernity posits nature in a certain way and closes itself off to reality in itself as ultimately unknowable.[32]

But Plato-Socrates also go beyond the modern position and posit a refashioned view of nature as a model for human striving. Is the real issue between the ancients and the moderns primarily a practical difference, given that both may see the whole in roughly the same light? Is it possible that it is the same practical difference that separates Socrates and Plato, or is there primarily a theoretical difference?[33] These, and many more, are the issues that Cropsey's reflections on Plato open for us.

Finally, before turning to a reflection on *Plato's World,* it should be noted that the specific origin of the idea for the book seems to have been percolating for more than a decade as indicated by Cropsey's 1987 article "The Dramatic End of Plato's Socrates" (DES). The insight into dramatically linking, and hence interpreting as a whole, seven Platonic dialogues that deal with everything from the nature of knowledge to statesmanship and the trial and death of Socrates, so obvious once someone has pointed it out, but hard to find anywhere in the literature prior to Cropsey, is already deployed. And with it comes Cropsey's interpretative understanding that grasping Plato's **intention** is far more important than discovering any alleged **development**, even if we had evidence based on something more than the speculative, pseudo-science to which appeal is customarily made.

In the first written incarnation of the idea, Cropsey goes so far as to state that the Platonic corpus is simply the appraisal of Socrates (DES 158). As in the essay "Ancients and Moderns," Socrates again becomes a moderate figure who translates prior "Greek philosophy onto the plane of sobriety" (DES 174). For example, Socrates domesticated Pythagoreanism with its cultist extremes and drastically restricted pre-Socratic political pretensions—the pre-Socratics were the ones who really longed for the philosopher-kings, not Socrates or Plato. Unlike modernity, which as time went by radicalized its sources, Socrates deradicalized his as part of his rearranging of his patrimony. While there is surely advice to late moderns contained in this observation, one wonders if Socrates has not become almost too moderate as a result.[34]

In the question concerning the nature of Socratism and of Socrates' doings lurks the issue of the nature of political philosophy and what it should do now. Is political philosophy born of positing a noetic cosmological insight about the nature of the whole and man's integration into it, or is it the less soaring, mixing, and rearrangement of the patrimony which in the last analysis originates nothing? Or is some synthesis of the two models possible?

What is the noetic status of political philosophy? Is it primarily a practical or theoretical activity? Does political philosophy primarily *descend* from theoretical insight or work *up* from experience and practical wisdom—or is the distinction a false one? Or must practical wisdom always operate within the horizon of theoretical insight? Again, we have a family of fascinating progeny which at present we must leave orphaned.

Lurking in all of these questions is the issue of whether political philosophy ever actually originates anything. For if political philosophy originates nothing, and as Cropsey asserts elsewhere, politics originates nothing, is there any originary source, or is the whole locked in an eternal return of elements that are all present from the beginning? Is it possible that a pure, speculative, daimonic philosophy, that is in no way moderate, and not to be confused with political philosophy, is an originary source? If so, would not too much moderation destroy it? Or is nature itself an originary source, especially if it is leavened with chance and irreason? Cropsey's extraordinarily penetrating analyses raise all these primary questions for us. Perhaps we should simply be thankful for a patrimony that consists of a handful of grand and inspiring questions, rather than an entire cosmos of final answers that cannot, precisely because of their finality, lend themselves to anything but banality. Putting aside this last issue for a moment, I believe some answers to the questions regarding the nature of political philosophy are to be found in *Plato's World*.

Plato's World consistently carries forward themes that have occupied Cropsey from the beginning. His presentation of Plato develops a complex view of the relation between man and the whole. We also see the ways in which Plato is better equipped than most in the tradition of political philosophy to deal with the unavoidable dilution of thought on its way to informing everyday life. And we see political philosophy presented as an actively caring enterprise that cannot come to an end, and whose "mixing" must be ever repeated. And unlike conventional scholarly readings more generally,[35] from Cropsey we receive a Plato who can still speak with us as an unrivaled teacher rather than as the brightest among the adolescents during philosophy's infancy or as the unwitting father of all manner of ideas that allegedly lead eventually to nihilism, "logocentrism," the end of philosophy, and even the End of History. Cropsey's Plato is an enduring spokesman for recurrent possibilities, which makes it clear that nothing of significance has come to an end in human affairs and there is nothing of significance which was only available in previous times and is absent for us or has temporarily withdrawn from presence. This understanding puts Cropsey at odds with such seemingly disparate thinkers as Heidegger and Strauss, to saying nothing of the most radical spokesman for eternal absence, Derrida.[36]

In Cropsey's work on Plato, we continue to see a manifestation of the idea that the moderns were aware of absolutely nothing that was not already known by Aristotle, Thucydides, Xenophon, and especially Plato.[37] In *Plato's World* we see this understanding explicitly deployed with regard to authors like Hobbes, Spinoza, and Descartes and less explicitly deployed in the final chapters that see Being-toward-death and its philosophic, moral, and political significance as central to the fundamental human condition. Indeed, Cropsey goes on to show Plato dealing with a number of issues more commonly associated with late modern authors. Being and Not-Being are shown to intermingle (PW 103). Philosophy is said to originate in the question "what is a thing" (PW 97). Being is said to be present in all things only as a mystery (PW 90–91). Plato shows that Being cannot be a being, and so on. This attempt to show that a mind can grasp fundamental positions at any point in history is central to Cropsey's critique of historicism. Far from siding with the late moderns, Cropsey's position can be shown to be a critique of Nietzschean and Heideggerian historicism. Not only is postmodernism confronted, with Heidegger as its principal exemplar, but the Nietzschean argument that philosophy must consist of a large component of *poiesis is* confronted as well. Plato is shown to see the ways in which *logos* must be supplemented by *muthos* and *poiesis* without dissolving into either. Cropsey thereby responds to Derrida's assertion as well that Plato presents a logocentrism wherein *logos* is shown to be in simple opposition to other terms such as *muthos* and *poiesis.*

Once again, in *Plato's World* the issue of the relation between Socrates and Plato is opened. Cropsey's argument is that the Platonic corpus represents a high-level inspection of all of the important alternatives available in his time, Socrates included. In *Plato's World,* Cropsey points out that Plato understands that Socrates is imprudent and impolitic, he has an unsupportable inclination to utopianism, and ultimately comes to stand on a questionable consequentialist hedonism. All of this represents an elaboration of investigations into this issue begun by Cropsey twenty years earlier in his essay on the *Phaedrus* and returned to frequently in the interim.

In *Plato's World* Cropsey is also at pains to show the reasons why the human predicament inevitably points toward a theological-political analysis.[38] For Cropsey this is built into the nature of the human condition. This comes out especially in his treatment of the *Euthyphro* (PW 177). Very little is made of the confrontation between reason and revelation, although the attempt to show the unavoidability of recurrent, necessary, theoretical conundrums might quite easily point toward revelation's plausibility. But Cropsey does not take this tack.[39] What is noteworthy about Cropsey's treatment of the gods is that like several variants of existentialism, he points to Plato's reflections on the importance of confronting the situation left by a *deus absconditus* who leaves behind no revelations. As to textual fidelity, this seems to be an unavoidable issue for anyone who attends to the myth of the reversal in the *Statesman.*

Throughout his career in his studies of modernity, Cropsey has pointed out that modernity has presented both an inspiriting alternative and an indulgent one. In his controversial essay on the United States as regime Cropsey concluded by observing that in its coming third century, America's prospects rested on a need to draw from the less frequented, spirited wellsprings **of modernity** (PPIP 1–15). The issue of inspiriting is again persistent throughout the latest text on Plato. Cropsey is now explicit that it is primarily the philosopher who must be spirited and courageous in the face of the mysteries of existence. One wonders what the more general political and moral ramifications of this insistence are.

While Cropsey points out that the Eleatic Stranger calls for a "weaving" together of the hard and the soft, of spiritedness and temperance, very few concrete indications of where those intimations might lead are insinuated into the analysis. How the courageous and spirited philosophic ethic relates to a possible, larger, non-philosophic, moral and political ethic remains open to further thought. Perhaps it points back to Cropsey's various experiments with Hobbes and Smith.

In this same vein, more than a few have had the suspicion that in the last analysis Strauss, like Nietzsche, expected a protracted dark age through which the philosophers would have to protect themselves by invoking both immense circumspection and physical withdrawal into some version of a modern epicurean garden. This could also explain Cropsey's stress on the need for an inspiriting philosophic ethic. But when all is said and done, I do not think this is Cropsey's primary point for the following reason: where Strauss opens a significant chasm between philosophy and the city, Cropsey points toward a possible reconciliation. He shows how all of the finite, possible, fundamental epistemological and ontological positions fail to be persuasive—for example, his "statics" and "kinetics." This points to the need for various synthetic positions—for example, the *eidē* both combine and are separate; Being and Not-Being interpenetrate. Cropsey seems to argue that the needed synthetic positions are precisely commensurate with what follows from the interrogation of common experience. Philosophy and the city arrive at the same place and occupy the same ground not through noble lies and philosophic misdirection but for straightforward theoretical reasons. Hence the philosopher is tied to the city for theoretical reasons, not merely due to whatever psychological or moral imperative it is that forces philosophers to care for others.

I would point to what I believe *may* represent another dialogue with Strauss that occurs in *Plato's World*—and on this issue, with Heidegger as well. This occurs in the central part of the book (PW 99–105). Therein, Cropsey discusses the relative merits of Being and Nature as philosophic categories and the ways in which these categories are reached by approaching philosophic questioning from different directions. One is immediately reminded of a statement Strauss made in concluding his dialogue on tyranny with Alexandre Kojève: "Both of us appear to turn our attention away from Being and toward tyranny because we saw that those who lacked the courage to face the consequences of tyranny, who, therefore, *et humiliter serviebant et superbe dominabantur* [Livy: themselves obsequiously subservient while arrogantly lording it over others], were at the same time forced to escape the consequences of Being precisely because they did nothing but speak about Being."[40] The person Strauss has in mind here who got confused about tyranny while talking incessantly about Being was clearly the Heidegger, who attempted to understand Being directly without approaching it through the interrogation of beings. Strauss's *announced* methodology is to proceed through an interrogation of things by asking the "what is" questions that elicit the essences or **natures** of the individual things. Cropsey seems to question whether either approach to philosophic questioning—through the concept Being or the concept nature—is ultimately satisfactory by itself. It is possible that at one point Cropsey may suggest a way in which the two approaches can be combined or even dissolve into each other.[41]

Finally, Cropsey is at some pains to explain why philosophy's highest manifestation as political philosophy is never sectarian. True political philosophy never takes its stand on any of the finite, repeatable, philosophic positions, of which none can be proven apodictically. Beyond its need to care, posit and mix, political philosophy also becomes a dignified inspection of all the possible, albeit finite, sects, all of the finite, possible regimes, all of the finite, disparate types of individuals and all the manifestations of the same from the past. Political philosophy thereby becomes a contemplative activity.[42] Two questions arise: How does this relate to the analysis of the *Philebus* and the mixing that the cosmos requires? And how does one get from the contemplative component of political philosophy to political philosophy in the conventional sense of discussing the best regime and the best life for the non-philosophic, or to Cropsey's understanding of a creative caring or mixing reappropriation of the patrimony?

In *Plato's World,* Cropsey continues to make it clear that he sees an extremely important practical task for political philosophy. The task of political philosophy is to "weave." To do so political philosophy must come forth as *poiesis* if it is to care for man and supplement other absent sources of order. But does Cropsey do more than point to that need? Is there political philosophy being presented here in more than a detached contemplative sense? That contemplative understanding, which can be the ground for moderating the dangers intrinsic to unrealistic utopian aspirations, can also, from a purely political and moral point of view, run the risk of causing enervation. Which is the greatest danger in our time, overly enthusiastic utopianism or the deep frustration of a dispirited and enervated mass society?

In pursuit of an answer to this final issue, I would point to the surface of Cropsey's Plato text. Despite being a commentary on Plato, one cannot help but notice the profound divergence between the surface of Plato's dialogues and the surface of Cropsey's text—after all, superficial as it was, the neo-Platonic deflection of Platonic thought was hardly dreamed up out of thin air. This question of the surface or outer veneer of a work is unavoidable for anyone influenced by Strauss and his hermeneutic principles. There is no attempt in *Plato's World* to dissemble about what might seem to some to be unpalatable truths. Of course all of those possibly unpalatable truths are already part of the public domain in our time. Let me advance a conjecture. After the thought of Nietzsche and Heidegger and the various trains of thought that have descended from them, it will never again be possible to adopt the traditional public stance of either political philosophy or its prior public persona. Those things will have to be reconsidered. I think it is likely that Cropsey has given more than a little consideration to this issue. Political philosophy must always adopt a public stance consistent with its own time, even if, perhaps precisely if, it wants to transcend it. That means that political philosophy must be more than a simple repetition of what has been said on the surface by previous authors. Precisely if it includes an element of *poiesis,* political philosophy must adapt to the experiences of its own time.

NOTES

1. In his discussion of the nature of political philosophy, Leo Strauss asserted that political philosophy was a subset of philosophy. See in this regard, Leo Strauss *What Is Political Philosophy* (Chicago: University of Chicago Press, 1988), pp 10–12. This conclusion puts Strauss within a tradition that sees metaphysics, cosmology, or whatever one wants to call the study of the whole, as first philosophy. That in turn reduces political philosophy to a subordinate position, at most architectonic vis-à-vis practical sciences.

Let me simply assert at this point that that distinction descends from Aristotelian assumptions far more than from Platonic assumptions. Without being at leisure to pursue the matter more fully here, I want to suggest in what follows that Cropsey may see political philosophy as architectonic in the highest sense such that it represents the peak of the philosophic enterprise. I do not think he conceptualizes the matter in the same way that I do in the chapter "What Is Political Philosophy." For Cropsey, it is political philosophy that must posit the whole and weave together not only the diverse human elements of the whole—the hard and soft elements of Plato's *Statesman*—but weave together as well the articulation of the human and the non-human components of the whole. If this assumption has merit, one of the things that follows is that political philosophy is far more than a merely politic esotericism presented publicly for primarily defensive purposes, as I have argued repeatedly.

2. Cropsey gives no indication that there is a primordial or "natural" situation wherein there could be a politics for which there is no intermingling of ideas that

descend from prior thought. Needless to say, ideas overlay a natural substratum informed by the passions. That said, it should be recalled that the attempt to disinter the "natural consciousness" is what seems to inform Strauss's later works on Plato, Aristophanes, Thucydides and Xenophon It is not clear that Cropsey would accept the validity of that project if by natural consciousness one implies a relation to a reality unmediated by ideas. If this is his position, I agree with Cropsey against Strauss.

3. The idea that politics might be largely — i.e., in its most interesting features — a distillation of thoughts at one point leads Cropsey to wonder if he has reinvented Hegel. He concludes that he has not. The reason he offers for this conclusion is that he rejects the Hegelian idea that an ascent or progress is implied on the side of either ideas or political reality.

4. I will suggest that herein we find another point of departure between Strauss and Cropsey. Strauss's longing to recover an understanding that he posits was once available but is now concealed implies that something has been forgotten. I would suggest there is more than a superficial parallel between this thought and Heidegger's more abstract conception of the "withdrawal of Being." Cropsey seems to believe that nothing of importance has ever been unavailable to thought.

5. Herein we again approach the question of the architectonic status of political philosophy. Assuming that the whole is not knowable in any apodictic fashion, the good for everyday life cannot be deduced in any simple way from a more or less mysterious source. But as Cropsey's modern authors show, the whole still needs to be posited in some fashion as an extension of one's reflections regarding the well-being of the human. Cropsey also stresses the way in which modern political philosophy has felt constrained to operate within the proto-modern scientific understanding of nature as dominated by causal necessity.

6. This concern leads Cropsey to show great respect for Smith's project to conceptualize nature as exhaustive and mechanical, yet nonetheless incorporating an element of moral teleology. Cropsey's Smith thereby reconciles selfish impulses with the good for all, morality with preservation (cf. PPIP). Significant is Cropsey's admission that "natural philosophy can resemble high mythologizing" (PPIP 84).

7. Is it true that without knowing the whole completely, one can still extrapolate from significant, if less than complete, evidence that the cosmic whole is not in any simple sense supportive of human well-being? Or is there another principle underlying the philosophical construction of nature? Cropsey makes it clear that "nature is always a construction" of the world of empirical data. Nature itself never appears directly. This leads him to ask the question regarding what the philosopher may legitimately add to empirical evidence in construing nature. The formula offered by Cropsey in response is, "whatever makes the world intelligible" (PPIP 84). This is clearly what Cropsey sees proto-modern authors like Smith doing.

8. In a significant later essay on Smith, "The Invisible Hand: Moral and Political Considerations" (PPIP 76–89), Cropsey either extends or modifies this early position to argue that Smith's construction of nature allows him to see it as the ground for both the engine of self-interest and the distinctions between right and wrong. In the latter essay, Cropsey concludes that Smith primarily agrees with the ancients in seeing na-

ture as exhaustive and mankind as integrated into it—admitting no power, human or divine, either above or outside its comprehensive wholeness. Like Cropsey's ancients, Smith thereby synthesizes teleology and a potentially ambiguous understanding of the moral supportiveness of the natural. According to Cropsey, this makes capitalism more amenable to the moral benefits usually attributed to "the tradition" than is usually realized (PPIP 87). This seems to present a more sanguine view of Smith's teaching, and thereby of the prospects for liberal capitalism, than the more ambiguous treatment of *Polity and Economy* which will inform the following remarks.

9. Compare *Polity and Economy* and "The Invisible Hand" (PPIP 76–89) for two differently nuanced answers to this question.

10. Be this as it may, Cropsey does seem to draw the conclusion that contemporary liberal democracy not only contains no substantive moral regimen of its own, but it eventually erodes commitment to traditional sources of morality, leaving itself to wash about in a series of complicated, frequently contradictory moral and intellectual eddies and crosscurrents (cf. PPIP 1–15).

11. At one point Cropsey seems to suggest that a solution to contemporary confusion is to "ascend to Hobbes" (LNC 27). He even suggests that the tradeoffs made by the proto-modern enlightenment offered by Hobbes may have been worthwhile (AM 51). Cropsey clearly sees greater moral and political value in the teachings of the pre-Rousseauian proto-moderns. Of the proto-moderns, Smith and Hobbes seem to take priority for Cropsey; which stands highest remains hard to say. Noticeable by their relative absence are the projects of proto-moderns like Locke and Machiavelli.

12. This argument is particularly interesting in that it is prosecuted primarily in an article included in a volume entitled *Ancients and Moderns,* which was presented to Leo Strauss as a *festschrift.* Two things should be remembered. Strauss made much of the ancients-moderns split and the fact that the proto-moderns saw *themselves* as breaking with the ancients. Strauss is relatively silent about Christianity. When he discusses reason and revelation it is almost always in conjunction with the Hebrew Old Testament. By focusing on the Hebrew component of Scripture, Strauss could make it appear that even if no synthesis between Reason and Revelation was possible, an uneasy rapprochement could possibly be constructed. By focusing on the Christian component of Scripture, Cropsey emerges with what appears to be a straightforward either/or choice.

13. This is Cropsey's version of Strauss's argument for a "loving reinterpretation" of the tradition.

14. As noted above, largely absent in Cropsey's account of the origins of modernity is the Machiavelli who Strauss ultimately came to see as the father of modernity.

15. The details of precisely how the idea of enlightenment could be concretely applied to the Hebrew and Christian enlightenments will have to be left for another occasion.

16. Throughout, Cropsey sees the politics that descend from the freedom/ nature split as simply destructive. It leads to the pursuit of an "imaginary human emancipation" that brings with it a "palpable political servitude" (PPIP 87). At one point he goes so far as to suggest that the issue of freedom conceived as emancipation from exhaustive, mechanical nature does not arise spontaneously but only in the aftermath

of various modern presuppositions. The argument is that the idea of bondage requires a domination wherein this one is "over-against" another. But if mankind is integrated into an all-inclusive whole, there is no over-against implied in the relation between mankind and the rest of the natural whole. Consequently, to be included is not to be dominated. At any rate, Cropsey makes it clear that if mankind is an integrated part of the whole as modernity posits, no political or moral project would be in any way useful in offering emancipation. Therefore, it is far better to stick to the more common sense, everyday view of the freedom-domination issue wherein it is political servitude that is the problem. That approach leads more efficaciously in the direction of decent politics (cf. PPIP 76–89). We will address the issue of how the question of freedom should present itself from a purely philosophical point of view below. But even philosophically, Cropsey is very skeptical of the freedom-nature conceptualization of modernity from Rousseau on.

17. Again, it is also a fissure more significant than Strauss's more or less seamless and inevitable moves from first to second to third "waves" of modernity.

18. Compare Cropsey's discussion of Descartes with PHG. Despite his audacity, it appears that Descartes came up with absolutely nothing that had not already been understood by Plato. Indeed, what is customarily seen as Descartes' invention was explored by Plato in a far more sophisticated form, as Cropsey tries to make clear in his treatment of the *Philebus,* to which we will return shortly.

19. This seems to overlook the fact that thought has become active and productive for Descartes, rather than contemplative.

20. One could profitably compare Cropsey's analysis with Strauss's discussion of the origin of the idea of nature in *Natural Right and History* (Chicago: University of Chicago Press, 1953), pp. 81–119.

21. This discussion needs to be compared with the implications of the discussion of freedom in "The Invisible Hand" (PPIP 76–89).

22. There remained, however, a quieter *theoretical* "noble simulation of independence" by the philosophic few. The problems emerged when the independence of the few became the political and moral beacon for the many.

23. It should now be noted that Cropsey's Hobbes is far more libertarian than in some treatments, as well as more open to a significant arena for private property and perhaps even a right to revolution. Compare HTM, LNC, SASA.

24. Herein lies Cropsey's response to Heidegger's assertion—followed by much of postmodernism—regarding the metaphysical equality of Moscow and Washington. For Cropsey, communism and liberal democracy descend from incompatible moments within modernity. Beyond that, Cropsey argues that one should primarily look at the types of human beings that different regimes create. Regimes like communism and liberal democracy create different kinds of citizens. Finally, grand observations like Nietzsche's that all of modernity creates hate driven and resentful human beings, or Heidegger's that all of modernity creates similar technological and bureaucratic outcomes, are rejected by Cropsey. See especially CDMS.

25. See in this regard "Joseph Cropsey: Modernity and the American Regime," by Christopher Colmo, in *Leo Strauss, the Straussians, and the American Regime,* ed. Kenneth L. Deutsch and John A. Murley (Lanham, MD: Rowman & Littlefield,

1999), 221–34. Another experiment involves trying to show that Smith's vision of liberal democracy is more open to traditional virtue than many think (PPIP 76–89).

26. Cropsey goes so far as to assert that all of high modernity has attempted man's emancipation through thought (LNC 24). Hence the real animus of modernity is to attempt man's emancipation through mind or spirit albeit only for a rare few. Again this is a possibility that may be vouched for better by antiquity than modernity itself, Hegel to the contrary notwithstanding.

27. It should be recalled that Cropsey sees the hegemony of secular sovereignty as a dictate of natural reason shared by Hobbes and the ancients.

28. This should be compared with what appears to be Cropsey's later argument on Smith, which seems to experiment with arguing for the plausibility of a public teaching based on immersion or integration into an exhaustive natural whole (PPIP 76–89).

29. There is no indication whatsoever that mind creates the elements *ex nihilo*.

30. Is this duality being asserted by Cropsey as fact or posited as a necessary part of a necessary mixing? For example, Nietzsche argued that a tension between the Dionysian and Apollonian animated Greek society. Nietzsche also asserted that the Greeks posited *both*.

31. I would suggest that it is not entirely clear what Cropsey's ultimate conclusion is regarding the relation between Plato and Socrates. Does Socrates represent the moderating of pre-Socratic elements that is advanced in "Ancients and Moderns," by way of transforming and mixing elements from his patrimony, or are there problematic elements in his thought, like the Protagoreanism Cropsey attributes to him, which had to be moderated by the fabricating mind of Plato? In "Plato's *Phaedrus* and Plato's Socrates," Cropsey seems to approach the latter conclusion. In *Plato's World* potential criticisms of Socrates seem to emerge again, but they are not precisely the same. Does *Plato's World* represent Cropsey's final resolution of the question?

32. On this level even our allegedly open society is closed in the most important respect.

33. Unfortunately, gaining any precise understanding of the matter is very difficult. Cropsey admits that plumbing the nature of Socratism leaves one trying to mine "rhetorical hints" (PPIP 250). But he does assert that Socrates seems to have had a problem in keeping heaven and earth from flying apart. Did Plato transcend that problem? Did the proto-moderns? Questions like these are the ones we must address to *Plato's World*.

34. It would be most useful if a future scholar compared Cropsey's understanding of Socrates with that of Strauss, wherein Socrates becomes a much more questionable figure. Strauss's treatment of Socrates is undertaken in conjunction with an analysis of his ancient critic Aristophanes who saw Socrates as an enemy of the city, its morality and its gods. Despite the fact that it is also undertaken in conjunction with an interpretation of the much more positively inclined Xenophon, the view that emerges from Strauss is that Socrates and the way he pursued philosophy was in fact at odds with the city. This is consistent with Strauss's prominent theme regarding the tension between philosophy and the city. Strauss saw that tension as central to the origins of political philosophy. The philosophers had to be more subtle in their dealings with the

city for the sake of the well-being of both. Strauss's Socrates, and this is accentuated by the stress Strauss puts on the lengths to which Xenophon went to try to transform him into a gentleman, had not yet learned how to engage in politic philosophy.

Strauss argued that political philosophy could be understood either as the philosophic treatment of politics, or as the politic presentation of philosophy before the city. The latter especially points toward the esotericism that was such a central part of Strauss's teaching. Strauss also tried to strip Socrates of a cosmological teaching, and on the surface at least, seemed to buy into the Socratic method that Socrates presents in the *Phaedo* as his "second sailing." One asks the "what is" questions, and by interrogating common experience in this fashion is led toward a multiplicity of essences. On the surface Strauss tried to make the Socratic method metaphysically and ontologically neutral, despite the fact that Strauss's Xenophon indicates that Socrates continued to study nature directly throughout his life—much, one presumes, as Heidegger tried to study Being directly. Strauss criticizes Heidegger for that undertaking. These are deep waters, and we can do little more at present than point to issues worthy of further thought.

While Cropsey is certainly aware of the issues Strauss raised, and in his own way deals with them, he puts emphasis neither on the tension between philosophy and the city nor on the issue of esotericism. And on the methodological idea implied in Socrates' "second sailing," Cropsey seems to heap considerable scorn (DES 170). Cropsey puts emphasis on the necessity of an ontological vision of the whole and of man's place in it. He repeatedly attempts to draw out what must have been Socrates' understanding in that regard. Cropsey re-ontologizes both Socrates and political philosophy. This is due to more than a change of emphasis. There is a different understanding of Socrates emerging in Cropsey's thought and a different understanding of the nature of political philosophy. Consequently, one would presume there is a different understanding of what political philosophy should do *now*.

35. In *Plato's World,* Cropsey presents a Plato who has seemed unconventional to some in light of the orthodox position of the still dominant Anglo-American Platonic establishment—for example, that exemplified by Vlastos and Burnyeat. But the conventional reading, which descends from the neo-Platonic deflection of Plato's thought—complete with its reassuringly orderly cosmos and access to the changeless, disembodied Ideas—has been under assault for more than a century, going back at least to Nietzsche, accelerating in our century with the readings of Heidegger, Derrida, Strauss and many others. In light of that assault, it is fair to wonder if these conventions and traditions, like so many others that have been devoured in this century, may soon be replaced.

36. I deal with this issue in my article, "Leo Strauss and the Straussians: An Anti-democratic Cult," in chapter 8.

37. One should also note that for Cropsey, while there may be shared understandings, the ancients do not represent any single, easily abstractable, unified position, anymore than they present us with a mere syrupy set of platitudes about how nature operating as efficient causality simply supports human existence as it does for the ants, bees or beavers. As we have seen, this lack of unity is true of the moderns as well.

38. A comparison with Strauss on this issue is unavoidable. Cropsey and Strauss could quite fruitfully be compared on the issue of the fundamental nature of the political-theological question as it presents itself to *natural* reason.

39. As an aside, one cannot help remark the curious fact that despite descending from the thought of the Heidegger, for whom the absence of the gods and hope for their return is central, for most of postmodernism the issue of the gods and their presence or absence completely drops out. Not so for Cropsey.

40. Leo Strauss, On *Tyranny,* ed. Victor Gourevitch and Michael S. Roth (New York: Free Press, 1991), p. 212.

41. Is there a third path being offered? I point to this as yet another subject for further investigation. It should be investigated along with the curious way in which Cropsey circles back to what could be seen as a soft resurrection of the Ideas—which for example, never happens in Strauss, who unsatisfyingly reduces the Platonic Ideas to the fundamental unchanging questions confronting humanity and makes them go away completely in his interpretation of Farabi's Plato.

42. For a competing vision that may put the emphasis elsewhere consider the last words from the last essay on Rousseau in *Political Philosophy and the Issues of Politics*: "To speak by reference to Plato, in Rousseau's scheme the principle of one man one job is replaced by versatility; gymnastic is replaced by labor; music is replaced by love, and communism is replaced by domesticity. Rule appears to remain in the hand of the philosopher" (PPIP 329).

INCLUSIVE BIBLIOGRAPHY FOR JOSEPH CROPSEY

Books

Ancients and Moderns: Essays on the Tradition of Political Philosophy in Honor of Leo Strauss, editor and contributor (Chicago: University of Chicago Press, 1964). (PPLS)

History of Political Philosophy, with Leo Strauss (Chicago: Rand McNally, 1962, 1972, University of Chicago Press, 1987). (HPP)

Hobbes's A Dialogue Between A Philosopher and A Student of the Common Laws of England, edited with an Introduction (Chicago: University of Chicago Press, 1977). (HD)

Plato's World, Man's Place in the Cosmos (Chicago: University of Chicago Press, 1995). (PW)

Political Philosophy and the Issues of Politics (Chicago: University of Chicago Press, 1977). (PPIP)

Polity and Economy: An Interpretation of the Principles of Adam Smith (The Hague: Martinus Nijhoff, 1957). (PE)

Articles

"Activity, Philosophy and the Open Society," in *Order, Freedom, and the Polity,* ed. George W. Carey (Boston: University Press of America, 1986). (APOS)

"Adam Smith," in *History* of *Political Philosophy.* (AS)

Commentary on "Revolutions and Copernican Revolutions," by Carl Cohen, in *Science and Society,* ed. N. H. Steneck (Ann Arbor: University of Michigan Press, 1975).

"Conservatism and Liberalism," in *Left, Right and Center,* ed. Robert A. Goldwin, (Chicago: Rand McNally, 1967). (CL)

"The Dramatic End of Plato's Socrates," *Interpretation* 14, no. 2 (1987). (DES)

"The End of History in the Open-Ended Age? The Life Expectancy of Self Evident Truth," in *History and the Idea of Progress,* ed. A. M. Melzer, J. Weinberger, M. R. Zulman (Ithaca and London: Cornell University Press, 1995). (EOH)

"Hobbes and the Transition to Modernity," in *Ancients and Moderns* (New York: Basic Books, 1964). (HTM)

"Karl Marx," in *History of Political Philosophy.* (KM)

"Liberalism, Nature and Convention," *Independent Journal of Philosophy, vol.* 4. (LNC)

"Liberalism, Self-Abnegation and Self-Assertion," in *The Prospects of Liberalism,* ed. Timothy Fuller (Colorado Springs: Colorado College Studies, No. 20, 1984). (SASA)

"The Moral Basis of International Action," in *America Armed,* ed. Robert A. Goldwin (Chicago: Rand McNally, 1963). (MB)

"On Ancients and Moderns," *Interpretation* 18, no. 1 (1990). (AM)

"On Descartes's Discourse on Method," *Interpretation 1,* no. 2 (1970). (DOM)

"On Pleasure and the Human Good: Plato's *Philebus,*" *Interpretation* 16, no. 2 (989). (PHG)

"On Situation Ethics," *Perspectives* 3, no. 1 (1967). (OSE)

"On the Mutual Compatibility of Democracy and Marxian Socialism," *Social Philosophy and Policy 3,* no. 2 (1986). (CDMS)

"On the Relation of Political Science and Economics," *American Political Science Review* 54, no. 1 (1960). (PSE)

"Political Life and a Natural Order," *Journal of Politics* 23, no. 1(1961). (PLNO)

"Radicalism and Its Roots," *Public Policy* 28, no. 3 (1970). (RR)

"Religion, the Constitution, and the Enlightenment," in *Understanding the United States Constitution, 1787–1987,* ed. Timothy Fuller (Colorado Springs: Colorado College Studies, No. 24, 1988). (RCE)

"Reply to Rothman," *American Political Science Review* 56, no. 2 (1962). (RTR)

"The Right of Foreign Aid," in *Why Foreign Aid,* ed. Robert A. Goldwin (Chicago: Rand McNally, 1963). (RFA)

"Smith, Adam," in *Encyclopedia American.*

"Ueber Die Alten und die Modernen," in *Zur Diagnose der Moderne,* ed. Heinrich Meier (Munich/Zurich: Piper, 1990).

"United States Policy and the Meaning of Modernity," in *American Foreign Policy and Revolutionary Change,* ed. Jack B. Gabbert (Pullman: Washington State University Press, 1968). (USP)

"Virtue and Knowledge: On the *Protagoras,*" *Interpretation* 19, no. 2 (1991–92). (VK)

"Wealth of Nations," *Encyclopedia American,* 30th ed., 1968. (WN)

"What Is Welfare Economics?" *Ethics,* no. 2 (1955). (WE)

"The Whole as Setting for Man: On Plato's *Timaeus,*" *Interpretation* 17, no. 2 (1990). (WSM)

Chapter Twelve

On the Tradition of Political Philosophy in the Future: Leo Strauss and Martin Heidegger

There is no room for political philosophy in Heidegger's work, and this may well be due to the fact that the room in question is occupied by gods or the gods. (SPPP 30)[1]

In our age, . . . politics has in fact become universal. . . . Simultaneously political philosophy has disappeared. (SPPP 29)

We hardly exaggerate when we say that today political philosophy does not exist anymore. (WPP 12)

Certain it is that a simple continuation of the tradition of classical political philosophy—of a tradition, which was hitherto never entirely interrupted—is no longer possible. (CM 2)

Classical political philosophy is non-traditional, because it belongs to the fertile **moment** [*Augenblick*?] when all political traditions were shaken, and there was not yet in existence a tradition of political philosophy. (WPP 24) [my emphasis]

Political philosophy is that **branch** of philosophy which is closest to political life, . . . [P]olitical philosophy is a **branch** of philosophy [understood as] quest for wisdom, is quest for universal knowledge, for knowledge of the whole. . . . The absence of knowledge of the whole does not mean, however, that men do not have thoughts about the whole: philosophy is necessarily preceded by opinions about the whole. . . .

Philosophy is essentially not possession of the truth, but quest for the truth. . . . Of philosophy so understood, political philosophy is a **branch**. Political philosophy will then be the attempt to replace opinion about the nature of political things by knowledge of the nature of political things. (PP 4-5) [my emphasis]

[Political philosophy] cannot be dealt with scientifically but only dialectically. And dialectical treatment necessarily begins from **prescientific** knowledge and takes it most seriously. (PP 21) [my emphasis]

The exoteric teaching was needed for protecting philosophy. It was the armor in which philosophy had to appear. It was needed for political reasons. It was the form in which philosophy became visible to the political community. It was the political aspect of philosophy. It was "political" philosophy. (PAW 18)

In the last century, no one has done more to revive **interest** in the tradition of political philosophy than Leo Strauss. But he concluded explicitly and categorically that the tradition of political philosophy has disappeared. And he publicly implicated Heidegger—his quintessential "radical historicist"—in that disappearance. Yet I want to argue that no one in the last century has given us more by way of philosophical resources to address this problem, no one has opened more doors to the possible recovery of political philosophy, than Martin Heidegger. This is the paradox I want to explore. Contrary to Strauss's public statements, I also want to argue that Heidegger opens several philosophical doors that are necessary to the resumption of the tradition of political philosophy that Strauss correctly sees as at a moment of decision in our time. Heidegger himself never went through the doors he opened but for my present purposes that is not relevant.

Strauss states categorically that Heidegger's work makes political philosophy impossible. This goes hand in hand with Strauss's repeated assertion that political philosophy requires philosophy **in its original sense** understood as the "quest" for ["ontological"] "knowledge of the whole"—i.e., knowledge of God, the world and man (PP 38). That knowledge would be, in traditional Aristotelian terms, "theoretical." What Heidegger has made problematic is philosophy understood as theoretical, contemplative and system building. But this is definitive for political philosophy only if, for example, it deduces its prescriptions from theoretical premises. Strauss comes close to asserting something of the kind in making political philosophy a "branch" of philosophy. Thereby, theoretical philosophy grasps the comprehensive whole; political philosophy is a mere peripheral or derivative activity. Philosophy as theoretical quest is the comprehensive activity.

It appears to be philosophy understood as a comprehensive theoretical activity that Strauss sees as having been publicly defended by the politic rhetoric of past "political" philosophers. This politic defense of theoretical philosophy is one of Strauss's definitions of what political philosophy is in its very being. Alternately, Strauss defines political philosophy as comprehensive knowledge of the political things. Whether that "comprehensive" knowledge is theoretical or practical, in, for example, Aristotelian terms, is not clear.

But if political philosophy begins not from theoretical premises but from "pre-scientific," "pre-theoretical" awareness as Strauss also asserts, the questionability of philosophy as an autonomous theoretical activity might be irrelevant to political philosophy. If political philosophy looks to articulate the awareness embedded in pre-scientific, non-theoretical awareness, everything changes. Strictly speaking, that activity would be "phenomenological," not ontological. This notion of the autonomy and priority of the pre-theoretical is taken by Strauss from the path-breaking work of Heidegger. For Heidegger, philosophy necessarily grows out of pre-theoretical awareness from which it can never emancipate itself. Philosophy, like human life in general, is "thrown." Hence the origin can never be theoretically mastered. All that can happen, according to Heidegger, is that we can forget this unavoidable foundation.

The theoretical is always derivative. If we proceed on this phenomenological premise, it is in no way clear why Heidegger destroys the possibility of political philosophy if political philosophy is primarily phenomenological. Heidegger attempted to recover that which is, in Strauss's terms, the "natural" ground of both philosophy and everyday life. Strauss's treatment of the origins of the tradition of political philosophy depicts it as "dialectical," as growing out of a pre-philosophic awareness. This is most assuredly a Heideggerian move. But Strauss also depicts political philosophy as the defensive public face of philosophy, a subsidiary undertaking that defends pure, autonomous theoretical activity. This taps into Strauss's analyses of the esoteric nature of philosophic texts.

Strauss never argues that political philosophy deduces its prescriptions from pure, theoretical premises, or from the theoretical/ontological understanding of the whole striven for in his picture of pure philosophy. Hence it is not clear why political philosophy presupposes philosophy in this "original sense." And Strauss never really explains the basis of the forward-looking ecstatic temporality that **is and must be** political philosophy in its **essential nature** if it is to have an **ongoing tradition**. Strauss talks about a "loving reinterpretation" of the tradition. But obviously that must be undertaken for the sake of the future. But it is Heidegger who argues for the necessity of this ecstatic relation to temporality, binding together past, present and future.

If political philosophy is primarily a defensive public face for philosophy, the **underlying** philosophy is the primary phenomenon and political philosophy does not really open any future possibilities in any essential fashion as its primary activity. Accidental outcomes may descend from its defensive activities; but that is something entirely different. If political philosophy is a dialectical enterprise plumbing pre-philosophic awareness, it takes on an autonomy from the theoretical it does not otherwise possess. **Two fundamental Straussian premises move in different directions.** The one takes philosophy qua quest for theoretical knowledge of the whole as primary, understood as the quest for unchanging ontological knowledge. If this is proto-philosophy, political philosophy becomes at best a derivative **branch** of philosophy. The other approach takes political philosophy as based on a foundation that is prior and it is the theoretical that becomes derivative from the pre-theoretical, as in Heidegger's account.

I have argued throughout that political philosophy is the architectonic undertaking qua foundational and is in fact proto-philosophy. Heidegger may destroy philosophy as a traditional, theoretical activity. I will argue he **opens the door** to political philosophy as proto-philosophy. I will grant that Heidegger did not go through that door himself. In the end, I believe Strauss sees philosophy qua theoretical as the primary activity, and hence for him political philosophy can ultimately only be derivative despite his occasional depictions of it that seem to lead to the conclusion that political philosophy, like philosophy itself, grows out of and dialectically culls a pre-theoretical awareness that is foundational. Heidegger opened the door to this later understanding of philosophy, an understanding that is "phenomenological" in the sense that it grows out of a pre-theoretical presentation of phenomena into which we are always already thrown.[2]

Strauss's hermeneutic corpus builds on the notion that there is a pre-scientific revelation of reality that is foundational. But ultimately he fell back toward a position that longed for the primacy of philosophy as theoretical, contemplative and ontological. Hence he fell back toward a position he attributed to Nietzsche, in his quite iconoclastic reading of Nietzsche.[3] Strauss's Nietzsche longed to cast off human practice to an a-theoretical autonomy so that he could withdraw to a future contemplative philosophy in some private, post-modern epicurean garden. I have argued that this interpretation of Nietzsche points in fact to Strauss's projection of the future status of philosophy as private, theoretical and contemplative. This vision certainly fits well with Strauss's depiction of classical philosophy. It is modern philosophy, in Strauss's depiction, that turned private, contemplative theory into a form of practice and brought with it all of the problems Heidegger associated with the technological relation to reality and the constructivism of "Enframing" (*Gestell*).

Strauss wanted future philosophy to cease to be a form of practice as it had become in modernity and again be contemplative. Like his Nietzsche, for

Strauss *praxis* appears to be cast off to a certain autonomy, based on growing out of a projected pre-theoretical or "natural" everydayness. Hence the philosopher need not push through to any form of *poiesis*. Like his Nietzsche, Strauss was led to choose between theory and *praxis*, philosophy and the city.[4] Like his Nietzsche, he chose philosophy as a private theoretical activity. Unlike Nietzsche, Strauss makes no bow to *poiesis*.

Hence for Strauss, political philosophy never becomes a poetic casting forward of future possibilities. Without that possibility, the tradition of political philosophy is at an end. As Strauss observes, by way of discussing Aristotle, separating theory and practice implies that human action must have principles independently graspable. Practical science must not depend on theoretical science. Theory can then be autonomous contemplation, as it was for Aristotle, thereby avoiding the dangers that come from transforming philosophy into an assault on nature—e.g., by both modern science and technology and by the modern political science that descends from Machiavelli. Strauss positions philosophy as theoretical, private and contemplative in both its premodern form and his projected post-modern form. In that environment political philosophy is at an end.

By this path, Strauss ultimately arrived at a critique of modernity in many ways similar to Heidegger's. Modernity destroys what "is" by projecting theoretical frames upon reality. As mentioned, Strauss also iconoclastically observes that Aristotle would have rejected the modern approach because he would never have accepted the moral and political autonomy of *technē*. Further, *praxis*, as independent, requires that it be determined by "natural ends." Strauss tries to link the "pre-scientific" and everyday awareness with "natural ends"—i.e., he tries to link phenomenology and teleology—a precarious maneuver I would argue. In that regard see the essay on contemporary biology, chapter 21 in Part 4 where I argue that phenomenology implies the priority of the formal to the final cause.

Theory, Strauss says, is in the service of an independent "natural" practice only to the extent that it should defend *praxis* and *phronesis* from damaging theories. The theory that defends is not the basis of *praxis* or its dictatorial sovereign. Theory intervenes not to open up possibilities for *praxis*, but for self-interested defensive purposes, or to maintain a presumed autonomy of *praxis*. I want to challenge this understanding. **I want to see what is implied if political philosophy is to both open future possibilities for mankind and be proto-philosophy without becoming constructivist and determined by Heideggerian "Enframing."**

My argument will be that philosophy does in fact grow out of pre-theoretical awareness, which shows itself. This has all manner of ramifications, not the least of which being that the model of philosophy as autonomous theory based on autonomous ontological knowledge of the whole, is a mistake. Here is where Heidegger's articulation of pre-theoretical awareness as being intrinsically prior and "ecstatic," is important. Only on such a basis can one argue that man is intrinsically a historical being. If he is not, there is no need for political philosophy as an opening of future possibilities. I do not believe that Strauss can adequately account for man's historicality, which I believe is part of his essential nature.

Paradoxically, Strauss gives manifestation to an understanding of ecstatic temporality in his discussions of **modern** political philosophy, especially in his discussion of Machiavelli as the first political philosopher who engaged in "propaganda," understood as the attempt to project forward a self-consciously calculated posthumous effect. Strauss argued that Machiavelli learned this propaganda approach from the Christians. The propagandist is engaged in ecstatic temporality by standing in the present, projected toward both the past that one wants to transcend and the future one wants to open, making them co-present in a temporal "fusion."[5] A truly ecstatic person simultaneously looks back to the past and forward to a novel future. Heidegger also saw that temporal relation originating within Christianity. Heidegger opens this philosophical door. I believe it is one of the necessary philosophical presuppositions for the future resumption of the tradition of political philosophy which must somehow be grounded as an ongoing, repeatable activity. So understood, it need not be a mere repetition of traditional political philosophy, especially classical political philosophy. Even Strauss says that no competent person in the present would accept as simply true any past philosophical teaching.

To be an ongoing, repeatable public activity, political philosophy must be more than a contemplative knowledge about the nature of political things, although it certainly should incorporate the knowledge of the phenomena that fit under that designation. Political philosophy incorporates such knowledge, but it must be more than this. Otherwise we run the risk of the End of History — qua endless repetition of the present — or the eternal return of the same — the attempt to simply reproduce a past moment — whether that be Aristotle, Aquinas, Locke, Marx, the *polis*, Rome the Middle Ages. Political philosophy must be able to open **novel futures** if it is to be an ongoing tradition.

Given his critique of modernity, Strauss runs away from the ecstatic stance of his Machiavelli toward a contemplative philosophy that eschews political philosophy as an "opening" of the future. Hence Strauss can do no more than leave the tradition of political philosophy at an end and hence non-existent. Strauss does nothing to re-start the tradition of political philosophy as anything but veneration for past moments in its history together with what can only be a groundless choice among past authors — a modified version of the eternal return of the same. **Strauss cannot open the future moment for political philoso-**

phy. Heidegger opens the future moment but cannot walk through that door toward political philosophy because of his theoretically derivative strictures against metaphysical thinking.[6] Hence he can do no more than wait for some mysterious future dispensation of fate, some "event" that will open novel futures. **That waiting is not political philosophy**. But neither is political philosophy a mere, presuppositionless standing in mid air and projecting of "utopias"—this is no more than the subjectivism and Enframing constructivism that Heidegger rightly criticizes. To reduce the matter to a formula: political philosophy needs to be ecstatic, without being constructivist. It needs to ground itself on the past while opening the future. On what basis is that possible?

My contention is that the possibility of a future tradition of political philosophy needs philosophical presuppositions that in our time only Heidegger can supply. Throughout I will continue to use Strauss as a foil because I believe he drew from many of those presuppositions—in one case, I will argue, improving upon Heidegger's treatment. But Strauss cannot adequately deal with two central issues that Heidegger deals with thematically, the essence and necessity of a poetic element in political philosophy and an explanation of how man is capable of being a historical being. The latter requires that we be able to explain man so as to explain how, unlike all other species, we have been able to live in uniquely different "worlds." Unlike what seems to be a necessary conclusion for Heidegger, I do not think we are reduced to having to say that all such worlds are equal.

The central, necessary, philosophical presupposition that Heidegger opens for us is what I have called above the "phenomenological move." This argument is made thematically in *Being and Time*. There are pre-theoretical (Heidegger confuses matters by also calling them pre-phenomenological) "phenomena" determined by our thrown, shared, being-with others. That shared being-in and being-with includes not only our local horizon of meaning but the comprehensive tradition that determines how the world and others are "opened out" or "brought near" for us. This pre-theoretical understanding is always primary and incapable of being transcended except in partial fashion. Unfortunately, the crucial issue of transcendence is one we will have to bypass at present. But it is an issue where Heidegger's own phenomenological account remains most vulnerable. The main point, however, is that even transcendence has to be explained phenomenologically, not from the presupposition of an autonomous theory that stands nowhere and posits self-standing objects of thought.

Whenever we adopt the theoretical attitude and stare at **already** present things, this is a derivative mode of relating to things that always presupposes their prior revelation in our pre-articulate doing and making **together**. This phenomenological understanding informs Heidegger's early lecture courses leading up to *Being and Time*, all of the discussions of art and poetry, and even the "late" work, *Gelassenheit*.[7] Heidegger betrays this phenomenological insight only in his theoretically derivative preoccupations with avoiding metaphysical thinking and projecting something utterly unphenomenological like post-metaphysical thinking. If our "primary" or "primordial" relation to reality is in our doing and making, theoretical issues like post-metaphysical thinking only arise in detached theoretical staring which is in principle derivative from a particular pre-theoretical world.

For Heidegger, the philosophic tradition itself is derivative of the pre-theoretical awareness of the Greeks. Unlike Heidegger, I would argue that one can always begin from the pre-theoretical, shared, lived experience that reigns at the time. One need not go back to Greek pre-theoretical awareness in hopes of launching a "second beginning." Strauss comes close to projecting what amounts to a similar second beginning in his argument that Greek pre-theoretical awareness is in fact "natural," which is to say the trans-historical, quintessential pre-theoretical revelation of reality. But in our time, with the collapse of the tradition that both Strauss and Heidegger believed had already happened, all we really need to do is clear away the theoretical constructions that keep us from accessing primary pre-theoretical awareness. Unfortunately, depicting Greek pre-theoretical experience as either "primordial" as Heidegger does or "natural" as Strauss does is a theoretical projection, which will occlude access to the pre-theoretical.

Even though our present reality has been conditioned in many ways by past theoretical constructions, there is still a nexus of everyday doing and making that forms the perceptions of those with whom we share an unavoidable destiny. And the vast majority of human beings, not being "theorists," relate to reality in this pre-articulate, pre-theoretical fashion. If we are to avoid the endless competition of subjectivist, theoretical constructions—which is what Nietzsche described as the groundless competition of competing wills to power—then the pre-theoretical is the only foundation for philosophy, the only place for philosophy to **start**. Failure to recognize this leads to all manner of self-invalidating, mid-air, theoretical tap dances. To the extent that pre-theoretical reality is inevitably shaped in a moral, religious and political fashion—all of which presuppose an understanding of the whole—its articulation is part of political philosophy understood as proto-philosophy. Political philosophy must ultimately, poetically, articulate the whole that is already revealed to it. If this is done in a persuasive, holistic, public fashion it will open the future as a deferred ramification.

Heidegger's own articulation of this phenomenological position leads to very formal and abstract categories, from those in *Being and Time* to such presentations as the "Fourfold" and the strife of "World and Earth," to "releasement to things and releasement to the mystery" in *Gelassenheit*. This is one place where Strauss takes the Heideggerian phenomenological move and develops it in a far more useful fashion. From Strauss's articulation in *Natural Right and History* of the "origin" of the idea of nature and natural right to all of his mature treatments of Aristophanes, Thucydides, Aristotle, Xenophon and Plato we have attempts to show the grounding of past thinkers in pre-theoretical awareness that is moral, religious and political in a concrete fashion. Strauss's treatment, unlike Heidegger's, is richer in the actual detail of everyday life, and the categories of everyday perception and speech. But as complicated and subtle, and even phenomenological, as Strauss's treatment of "nature" is, in the end his designation of Greek awareness alone as "natural" precludes him from being able to explain how man continues to be a historical being, changes his world, and with it his pre-theoretical perception of reality and his relation to "nature."

From the phenomenological move we are led to a second philosophical resource that Heidegger offers, the critique of what he calls "Enframing," that we can more straightforwardly designate as a critique of modern constructivism. Heidegger frequently talks about "letting beings be." We, in our time, relate to reality almost exclusively through the filtering lens of especially modern theoretical constructions. In the process we have become increasingly alienated from the real depth phenomena of our existence. More to the point, the whole process of modern constructivism leads eventually not so much to a situation where everything in the world "stands" only as an object for our subjectivity, but due to the success of modern technology, and its relation to reality as "standing reserve," eventually nothing stands at all on its own or presents itself. As "standing reserve" all of reality is transformed into raw material, standing by ready to be used in our technological projects. In the process everything is transformed into an abstract standing about shorn of any phenomenal presence whatsoever. We are surrounded by shadows and traces of reality (absence); all novel phenomenal coming to presence is blocked. Not only do novel future forms of presence become impossible, nothing really is for us except the **process** of technological transformation that has become totally divorced from any ends other than its own preservation and intensification as process. Things can no longer present themselves with any moral, religious or political significance. As a result, it is not so much that everything is permitted as Nietzsche said, but that nothing really "is" and hence nothing really matters—"The Unbearable Lightness of Being."

Heidegger attempts to chart a course beyond the hegemony of this theoretical Enframing, "back" to a world infused with more self-showing significance and phenomenal presence. He does this primarily by his critique of the entire epoch of constructivist Enframing, and attempts to show there is a more "phenomenological" relation to that which somehow "presents itself." I would be the first to admit that Heidegger gets caught in some problems here, and they go beyond the "circularity" that he himself admits. But his critique of Enframing puts the modern stance of constructivism in a novel light and brings it to presence for us in a way that will not allow us henceforth to take it as the quintessential philosophical stance ever again. The Cartesian move stands ready to be replaced. Hence Heidegger opens up the philosophical landscape and turns our thinking toward alternatives.

Interestingly, Strauss also picks up on this critique. He uses it in his attack on behavioralism in his essay "An Epilogue." (PP pp. 99–129) He argues that before the social science positivist projects his theoretical frames upon the phenomena, he already knows what the significant phenomena are because of a pre-theoretical awareness that is the basis of all meaning and significance. Hence Strauss points to the derivative status of the theoretical Enframing of social science positivism. With positivism's status as pure and autonomous knowledge debunked, Strauss can legitimately turn to articulating pre-theoretical awareness as the primary undertaking.

The point for both Strauss and Heidegger is that a theoretical critique of constructivism can free or open the space in which something previously occluded can "show itself." My point here, and obviously more is needed than to merely assert this, is that the possibility of an ongoing tradition of political philosophy lies beyond modern constructivism where phenomena can be allowed to "show themselves." Unlike Strauss, I do not think we should start by differentiating some of those phenomena as "natural" before the fact and then find them only in some prior pre-theoretical showing. **That strikes me as itself a form of Enframing or constructivism.** We just start and turn ourselves toward the phenomena of our time and how they show themselves.

The way the world reveals itself to most in a shared fashion just "is." Categorizing some phenomena as "natural" and others as "conventional" is theoretically derivative and should not be part of any **initial** phenomenological articulation. Even Strauss admits that the idea or concept of nature emerged from the phenomena at a specific historical moment in the past. "Nature" could again emerge from the phenomena. The "Idea of Nature" is not, however, a concept with which one should start. Granted, the phenomena do not truly "show" themselves when they are inarticulate background phenomena in our doing and making. They need to be explicitly articulated, or "made present" **in speech** to be what they "are"—this is what Heidegger means by his prophetic observation that "language is the house of Being." But one does not do that by initially thematically imposing frames like natural/conventional. Phenomena must be articulated **as they are, and as they show themselves**. The phenomenologist should just begin; thematic (i.e., poetic) articulations will follow, down the road. One must conceptually differentiate the two stages.

This brings us to the status of poetry, or *poiesis* more generally. One of the central things that Heidegger tries to accomplish is to make poetry a phenomenon that is at least as closely related to Truth as "thinking." In Plato's *Republic*, we have the paradox that poetry is both attacked as at a significant remove from the Truth, and then magnificently deployed in everything from the allegory of the cave to the myth of Er. With the latter undertaking, poetry is presented as a means of conveying the Truth. Plato clearly understands that there must be an interpenetration of philosophy and poetry, as I will try to show in the next section. Yet the *Republic* is taken by many to indicate the priority of philosophy to poetry as regards its closeness to the Truth. In the course of the philosophic tradition, from the perspective of Truth, poetry was downgraded to something that only deals with the pleasures of the senses, and eventually it was transformed into a mere expression of idiosyncratic personal experience. Nietzsche raised the status of the poets, but he still understood philosophy and poetry as opposites. At that point, Nietzsche made a groundless choice for poetry as the basis of necessary horizons of meaning. But Nietzsche did this in the name of life, not in the name of Truth. The resulting projected horizons are posed by Nietzsche as in principle being untrue. In a choice between Truth and life, Nietzsche chose life and untruth, with poetry as the basis of necessary myths/untruths.

Heidegger attempted to make poetry and philosophy (or as he sometimes calls philosophy, "thinking") co-equal as regards the Truth. **Some such argument is absolutely necessary if there is to be a tradition of political philosophy that is ongoing in the five-fold holistic sense I posed above**. I can schematically pose the matter in the following fashion. The "phenomenological move" presupposes that there is always a prior, shared, inarticulate horizon of meaning that informs all of our doing and making. It must be brought to speech and made manifest rather than left inarticulate. This is part of what political philosophy as phenomenological must do. But there is no one, pure, simple, representationally correct way to do this. The making explicit or present of what is inarticulate or absent is not done through some simple correspondence between public speech and some pure, pre-articulate "grasping," or to use Heidegger's term, "understanding." Every interpretation of a pre-articulate understanding is in principle poetic to the extent that it cannot be representational. Heidegger arms us to see this with his critique of representational thinking and of correspondence theories of Truth.

To the extent that one remains true to pre-theoretical experience, articulating rather than imposing a frame upon it, one will have given a poetic articulation. Let me here borrow two terms associated with the thought of Derrida. The terms are "dissemination" and "deferral." I intend to use them in a way that seems to me to be perfectly straightforward and that does not imply any further Derridean gymnastics. Whenever we disseminate something in public in speech we have brought something new to presence. We have established a new phenomenon. We have changed the world toward which we are publicly related. Hence, disseminating speech will always necessarily change the way we act and perceive. This will have deferred ramifications, not all of which will be predictable. One way or the other, we have "opened" a way forward toward future possibilities and future "showings." To the extent that we remain true to the phenomena we are articulating, this is not a form of constructivist, subjectivist Enframing. It is a form of opening out and bringing the world to presence.

A truly artful phenomenological poetry can open up future possibilities. In the most general terms, political philosophy must be phenomenological and poetic if it is to be an ongoing activity, **rather than one that culminates in a finished wisdom, locked in a representationally correct speech that can then inform nothing but an unchanging** *praxis.* The more phenomenologically rich the speech, the more it will be able to predict at least some of the contours of the future it is opening. If all one can do is randomly open indefinite future possibilities, there is no need to dignify the activity as being part of a tradition of political philosophy. That is the critique we can apply to Heidegger's hopeful waiting for Being or new gods.

For the possibility of political philosophy, one must be capable of some efficacy in linking past, present and future. That this observation rests on a series of presuppositions is something of which I am perfectly aware. At another time all of those presuppositions would have to be explicitly confronted. At present I point to two that I think are central. First, poetry must be a form of Truth. Second, man must be **both** a "who" and a "what" simultaneously.[8] Heidegger can account for man being a "who," but cannot explain the myriad ways in which "nature" shows itself in and through human existence. Perhaps Strauss can account for man being a "what," but cannot account for how man is capable of being a historical being—one of the presuppositions for political philosophy as an ongoing activity that opens future possibilities. Heidegger can explain poetry as a form of Truth but not how to judge between different forms of poetry. Strauss can better deal with the latter, but cannot explain the place of poetry in the whole. That inability is Strauss's central blind spot.[9]

If political philosophy grows out of a phenomenological showing, necessarily plumbing and culling a prior, shared, pre-theoretical experience (doing so dialectically, by culling the **implications** of public speeches), it points toward a public articulation of its researches that will not culminate in "logical" or representational speech, but in poetic speech. This strikes me as something Plato understood perfectly well which I will explore in the next section. Plato's Socrates deploys his own dialectical adjunct to phenomenology, but never gets beyond *aporia* because he **only** deploys dialectic and is incapable of moving on to poetic speech. Plato is far less one-sided than Socrates. Plato is something of a model for us. We, of course, could not deploy the same poetic articulations as Plato even if we concluded that the underlying pre-theoretical phenomena were identical. I do not assume that the underlying phenomena are entirely identical, nor entirely different. So one could not simply repeat Platonic political philosophy as it was made present in his works, even though—in fact, precisely because—we are the deferred ramifications of Plato, and others. Each successive generation is the deferred ramification of those that went before as well as the wider constellation of phenomena which present themselves in the present. No one can be totally emancipated from this determination. In each successive generation, the phenomena have changing showings and always will as long as we remain historical beings—i.e., history making beings.

It does us no initial good to try to sort out those things in "our" pre-articulate phenomena that trace themselves to "nature," and those that trace themselves to past speech. Precisely because there has been a tradition, the phenomena are different for us than those at the beginning. And I am not remotely presupposing that the prior tradition took a "necessary" path. There are far too many accidents that condition human existence to believe that. One always starts from the present. One tries to bring the shared revelation of reality in our time to speech in an articulate fashion. If one does so artfully, and not with some narrow, immediate political outcome in mind, one can poetically articulate the phenomena so as to open the future in a novel way. This is what the great artists in speech of the past did, whether they explicitly understood this or not. Those great artists were the political philosophers of the past tradition. Ours is not simply to genuflect to them, but to carry on that tradition.

I believe that Strauss is correct, and here he agrees with both Nietzsche and Heidegger, and a host of others, that the tradition has in our time been if not destroyed at least suspended. That is now one of the phenomena that we can neither ignore nor dance around. Strauss, therefore, is correct that our time is in one respect like that at the origin of the philosophic tradition. **We in the present** exist in a moment when the philosophic tradition is, at least momentarily, no longer a given. **Those at the beginning of the tradition** existed at a moment when all past political traditions were called into question and no tradition of thought yet existed. Ours has a prior tradition, but no tradition in the present.

From a phenomenological point of view, the technological transformation of the world cannot be ignored. It is not an epiphenomena superimposed over an essential and recoverable reality. It informs our pre-theoretical experience of reality. To make a phenomenological start, we cannot presume to go back to some pure moment.[10] We have to just start. If we cannot discover "path-marks" in the pre-theoretical way we experience reality—for example, feeling anxious about our alienation from the "natural" world, or from primary attachments to others—then we are simply lost. I do assume that we experience phenomena like nobility, the sacred, outrage, anxiety, wonder, and on and on. We should not try to make those phenomena go away theoretically nor begin by theoretically designating their status. They just "are" and they must be found phenomenologically and brought to speech poetically in the present.

I have argued above and elsewhere that Heidegger's central philosophical insight, as regards the possibility of political philosophy, is his understanding of the essence of man as linked to "ecstatic temporality." Heidegger tries to show that pre-theoretical awareness itself is related to time and space in a unique fashion. This understanding is manifested in Heidegger's "early" discussions of "primal Christianity," in the "anticipatory resoluteness" of *Being and Time*, in the activity of the poet who projects forward future "preservers" in "Origin of the Work of Art," and a number of other places.[11] It forms the basis of Heidegger's understanding that man is essentially a historical being. Ecstatic temporality is in fact only true of historical man, and does not apply to what one might call pre-historical man, nor would it to "post-historical" man.

Heidegger traces primordial spatiality to man's very capacity to be related to the world. This possibility is found in "deseverence," our capacity to bring things "near" in our concerned action.[12] The beloved infant is "near" even if at the far side of the room. The glasses through which the infant is viewed are likely entirely absent as they do not concern us at all. Heidegger wants to explain this capacity we have to bring things near, to be related to them in our concerned doing and making. In our very being, we make things present for ourselves while other things fall away and are absent. Despite the seeming spatial nature of this ability, for Heidegger this relation between presence and absence conditions our **primal temporality**.

Only in making things present do we open up space for them. Primordial spatiality presupposes primordial temporality. Only because we are beings who are concernfully absorbed in things in the world do we experience space and time. Space understood as uniform extension is a derivative form of spatiality. Primordial, pre-theoretical space is opened in different, discontinuous, qualitative regions of concern. Only when we lose this concern and stand back detachedly can we experience space as uniform, an experience that is theoretically derivative. Likewise, primordial temporality is discontinuous. Some moments of time stand out with a vivacity and duration that other moments lack. The birth of a first child is not comparable to the time spent mowing the lawn.

Only in theoretical detachment from primordial time and space, both of which imply the interpenetration of presence and absence, do we experience time as a uniform passing of equal moments or nows. Primordial temporality (the temporality of presence and absence) is experienced in the discontinuous openings of space for unique things to come near to us. This "happening" of space and time always presupposes the shared existence of a "world" that conditions our shared revelation of reality with distinct others.

For Heidegger, in the theoretically derivative experience of time, the present moment is the only moment invested with Being. The future and the past are dominated by the Not, Not-Being, the Nothing. The past "is" the **no** longer present. The future "is" the **not** yet present. In the derivative experience of time as uniform, the past and future have no Being. But this is not how man immediately experiences life. Just as the baby can be nearer than the eyeglasses, the past or future can be more present to our concern than the immediate present. Heidegger felt that this was how the early Christians experienced reality. Life was experienced in the daily tension of being projected back toward the death and resurrection of Christ and forward toward the promised second coming.

In this primordial Christian understanding, past and future were more present in concern than the mundane dealings one had in the immediate present qua now. The present was at best an alienated dream, a veil of tears that one could not invest with significance. It had to be endured for the sake of eternity. For Heidegger, when Christianity was invaded by Greek philosophy, this ecstatic relation to temporality was lost. God came to be seen not as the mysterious, absent godhead, but as the fully present God comprehensible in thought as were the Greek ideas. Now one contemplated the eternally, unchangeably present God in a detached quiet. Our primordial tense and anxious relation to past and future was replaced by a form of tranquility. In the process our ecstatic relation to temporality was lost. Time as the presence of a concernful absorption in things that are near and those longed for that are absent was lost in favor of the contemplation of the timelessly, eternal present.

The past is exemplified by the tradition into which we are "thrown" with distinct others. We are always already pre-articulately engaged in doing and making with distinct others as determined by the distinctive world we have inherited. Hence, even inarticulately we "are" our past. Further, since our doing and making are always determined by the end (*telos*) of the action, we are also always concernfully related to the future. We are always, in our doing and making, projected understandingly toward the outcome we wish to effect, which is in turn determined by the world into which we are thrown. Because of this thrownness, we can never bring about every conceivable utopian outcome; we are in our very being determined by our thrown co-determination with others, our past. In the present, we are always, pre-articulately, binding together past and future. We usually do this in a fashion in which we just go along with the crowd ("they-self") determined by a kind of majority tyranny, which in the technological age of mass societies can be very tyrannous precisely because it operates so softly and pleasantly, and on such an altogether inarticulate level.

When we are dragged along inarticulately, locked in a uniform present, which we take as endless and inevitable, we fail to see the precariousness of our situation. We can experience a life filled with significance and meaning only because of the background phenomenon "world." But the world is the product of past acts that were ecstatic and stood in the present, openly related to the past, while concernfully opening a future. If we cease to act with this kind of ecstatic concern, we will eventually lose our shared world; at the very least we would not open anything of value for those of the future. More to the point, if we fall out of a concernful, ecstatic relation to the world, things and others like ourselves, we run the risk of adopting the derivative, theoretical attitude that disinters and deconstructs the necessary background phenomenon "world," rendering it inoperative. We must articulate the phenomena without destroying their very basis.

Without a shared world, things would cease to come near for us, nothing would be truly present in any interesting sense. Absence would reign, we would be projected into the Nothing. Since Being presupposes presence— albeit not complete and eternal presence—to lose the world which is the prior condition for anything being present for us in our concern, would be to lose Being. To avoid this, one must thematically come to see the precariousness of the world, and presence more generally, and become responsible for its continuance. One must come to take conscious responsibility for opening a world for those to come which is linked to that which came to us from the past.

In experiencing thereby the precariousness of the world, one gains the detachment to see the need to act in the world to maintain ongoing worldhood. One comes back into one's shared world and sees the need to fully and completely assimilate the thrown tradition of one's destiny in an articulate remembering (*Andenken*). Only then can one grasp the actual future possibilities that can be opened out of the present and the past. Herein one accomplishes ecstatic temporality in an articulately concerned, loving, remembering re-appropriation of the past out of which one takes responsibility for the future.

In this fashion, the past of one's thrownness and the future of one's concern become co-present in the present. According to Heidegger, it is the acts of such ecstatically temporal persons that "throw forward" future worlds. This could be the act of anyone from the great statesman/founder (who never creates *ex nihilo*) to the great poet who in bringing a shared understanding to word reveals and makes present future possibilities beyond the endless, uniform repetition of present realities. And it could be the great political philosopher. The avoidance of the endless, uniform, repetition of the present—the End of History—is accomplished in ecstatic temporality.

My argument is that if political philosophy is not seen as an open, ecstatic relation to both the past and the future, all it can do is produce an endless repetition of the present, or some attempted eternal return of the same. If political philosophy is to be **an ongoing repeatable possibility**, it must adopt the stance of ecstatic temporality. Likewise, that we are ecstatically temporal, capable of making both the past and future present for us, is what differentiates us from all other species. It is what makes it possible for us to be historical beings. It is what makes it possible for us to be a "who," albeit not in some preposterous act of renouncing our whatness. I have already indicated that I do not think we can be a "who" in abstraction from being a "what," but our capacity to be historical beings presupposes that on some level we can be a "who." No pure "what" can make history.

Political philosophy must be phenomenological, explicating the pre-theoretical, shared articulation of reality. It must have a penetrating component of remembrance (*Andenken*) and a deep futural concern and care. It must have the analytic acumen to see what others only inarticulately live, have a penetrating understanding of its past, and the poetic capacity to articulate both so that a future different from the present can open itself up in some more or less predictable fashion. Any one of the elements is difficult; their fusion is rare. That forms the difference between greatness and mediocrity. If one cannot see the difference between Plato and Isocrates, or Hegel and Feuerbach, then one is not entitled to enter the environs of political philosophy.

Beyond that, in our time, at the very least, we need a philosophical propaedeutic that grounds poetry as truth, grounds the primacy of the pre-theoretical, opens us to a loving reappropriation of the past and frees us from modern constructivism. Heidegger helps us do all of these things. That he does not pass through the door to political philosophy is due to his refusal to see that man is both a "who" **and** a "what." He is also held back by his theoretically derivative preoccupation with post-metaphysical thinking—which is at best bad poetry—and his inability to adequately account for the phenomenon of transcendence—which phenomenally exists, even if not as perfect, a-temporal transcendence.

Strauss certainly co-opts a strong element of *Andenken* in his thinking. He sees the importance of making the past present and in his own phrase lovingly reappropriating it. But because he cannot ground the poetic element as does Heidegger, the concern for the past does not adequately link with a concern for opening future possibilities. Strauss never gets beyond anxiety about the present, and perhaps, longing for the past. In his desire to withdraw to a future epicurean garden, there seems to be a resigned acceptance of the End of History lurking in Strauss, even though he is clear that its arrival would predictably bring universal tyranny. Strauss's public depiction of philosophy seems to be a way to defend it qua private, withdrawn activity through a long, dark future he predicted was coming. That is of course speculation. But there is no sign that Strauss grounds political philosophy as an ongoing opening of future possibilities.[13] Ultimately, that depiction of political philosophy as a concerned opening of the future, would be the best defense against the End of History and any threat to philosophy. If one wanted to look at the matter only in this light, would that not now be philosophy's best public face, as caring political philosophy?

That the End of History is not possible can only be grounded in a philosophical showing of why man is a historical being capable of the ongoing possibility of political philosophy. As far as I am concerned, that effort does not culminate in historicism. Man can be an eternally historical being, and we can know this trans-historically. Ultimately Heidegger cannot deal with the latter adequately (the trans-historical); Strauss cannot adequately deal with the historical, especially as an ongoing possibility. Heidegger's deconstruction of the theoretical tradition of philosophy shows the extent to which political philosophy cannot be an activity that deduces prescriptions from theoretical premises—thought to be autonomous, whether as completed ontology or modern constructivism. But this is not telling for an ecstatic, phenomenological, non-constructivist, poetic political philosophy. One last thought: to the extent that political philosophy cannot henceforth dispense with poetry, I would argue that it cannot dispense with religion which has both a phenomenological basis and need for poetic speech. Here is where a truly fascinating dialogue can be constructed between Heidegger and Strauss. This is a subject that deserves a significant treatment of its own. At present all we can afford is a few intimations within the perspective of our present concern regarding the presuppositions of a future for political philosophy.

In his discussion of the "Fourfold," Heidegger asserts the necessity of keeping the divine "in things"—on the Earth and under the Sky. With this statement, Heidegger is asserting the need to keep religion phenomenologically grounded so that it does not fly off entirely to contemplation of a supra-temporal realm. In effect, Heidegger is criticizing various versions of scriptural religions for abstracting the element of the divine from the phenomenal world around us. A world of things that has been cast off by the divine to meaninglessness is ripe for endless technological manipulation, as there can be no sacred limitation on the manipulation of fallen things cut off from the godhead. Heidegger hopes for the divine to reign "in things."

Heidegger is in one respect decidedly post-Christian in his longings, especially as regards that version of Christianity he saw as infected with Greek philosophy. But he does make it clear that he thinks that in all pre-theoretical awareness there is always an element of the holy and the divine. Only a derivative theoretical staring can detach us from this phenomenological given. But he would presumably be open to elements of thought based on the notion of "Christ in the world," or various interpretations of the status of the Holy Spirit after the resurrection.

Strauss too arrives at the unavoidability of religion. In his interpretations of the Greek authors, especially Thucydides, he too lodges our openness to the divine in pre-theoretical awareness. Further, in his comparison of the Old Testament and Plato's *Laws* the primacy of pre-theoretical, religious experience seems to be reinforced which allows Strauss to note that there is a significant moral overlap between Scripture and Plato's *Laws*. The difference, Strauss stresses, is that the Old Testament sees the beginning of wisdom in fear of the Lord, whereas the Greeks see the beginning of wisdom in wonder. In a surprisingly Heideggerian vein, Strauss roots the difference between the pre-theoretical understandings of Scripture and the Greeks in a distinctive mood. For Heidegger, all pre-theoretical understanding is dominated by moods, along with there always being in every age a dominant background mood and its particular "understanding" and "interpretation."

Like Strauss, Heidegger sees the mood that dominated the Greeks as wonder. But in the *Beitrage*, Heidegger asserts that the dominant mood of our time is and should be anxiety. In a number of his Hölderlin lectures Heidegger also asserts that the mood for our time is mournful anticipation. Neither is to be confused with fear of the Lord. If we are to conclude that pre-theoretical experience is dominated by moods that cannot be theoretically mastered, one wonders what the move away from the dominance of fear of the Lord might mean for religion. We might keep in mind that in his concerns about the Decline of the West and the End of History, Strauss seems to project the dominance of anxiety in our time the same as Heidegger. And it is by no means clear that Strauss chooses fear of the Lord over wonder in his own doings. Where might all of this lead?

Heidegger would have religion eschew the flight to a totally a-temporal, transcendent godhead. Strauss does something curiously similar. Strauss frequently observes that the difference between Judaism and Islam on the one hand and Christianity on the other is that Christianity is based on a limited set of articles of faith that have no explicit political ramifications, lending itself to the distinction between the demands of faith—e.g., that deal with virgin birth, resurrection, the immortality of the individual soul and the mystery of the Trinity—on the one hand and political order on the other—the "two cities." Revelation in Islam and Judaism is the revelation of the law, complete with very minute prescriptions. Hence, Strauss makes it clear that the prophet in Judaism and Islam is a lawgiver, and can be associated with the political founder of the laws. The prophet is a very this worldly phenomenon. And politics and religion are one in a way they never are in Christianity.

Christianity, on the other hand, opened the door to political philosophy as Judaism and Islam could not because the actual, everyday political prescriptions were left open. We have a complicated set of crosscurrents here. Strauss clearly prefers the Old Testament to the *New*, and the prophets being seen as concrete lawgivers rather than as doctrinal spokespersons for the mysterious, transcendent Trinity. Strauss's Old Testament underplays mystery—even though who God is, is explicitly prohibited from being brought to presence in speech or image. Christianity plays up the mystery at the core of things and, through Christ coming into the world and promising his return, brings the divine into the vicinity of things. Christianity makes political philosophy not only possible but necessary because it separates religion and politics. And Christianity is open to the possibility of historicality.

Strauss and Heidegger, in different ways, seem to prefer to keep the divine close to everyday existence—either through the centrality of the prophet qua lawgiver or the Fourfold notion of the divine in things. But Strauss harkens back to the old God of tradition, whereas Heidegger waits for altogether new gods. In this, Strauss seems far more faithful to the ecstatic element of *Andenken* than does Heidegger. Heidegger betrays his own argument about the ecstatic fusion of temporality by longing for a future severed from the past. For Heidegger there remains an unavoidable question: being thrown into one religious tradition can we poetically project an entirely different one? But Strauss's stress on the past undoubtedly goes hand in hand with the limited place of poetry in his teaching. Strauss cannot open the future or deal with historicality more generally as can Christianity. I am suggesting that Christianity may have more philosophical resources for political philosophy than either Strauss or Heidegger would accept. It alone makes political philosophy necessary. It opens the possibility of historicality. And it is the tradition into which we are thrown far more than that of the Old Testament alone. It is open to the mystery at the core of Being—in the Trinity—but also of the divine in the world. And I would suggest that the prophet is no longer the best public mask for the political philosopher as Strauss seems to suggest.[14] And wonder and anxiety may be more productive moods than fear. But these are at best intimations to be explored.

Presumably, political philosophy in its poetic articulations of the phenomena always has multiple resources into which it is thrown from which to draw. Looking to the past, it is probable that political philosophy could only have continued, after pagan antiquity, in a Christian context, which is also, in its primal form, one of the quintessential examples of ecstatic temporality.[15] For Strauss, religion and the very possibility of political philosophy have to be dealt with together. There is much to ponder here as one thinks forward. At the present I want to leave matters at the following: If political philosophy is intrinsically both phenomenological and poetic, it cannot dispense with the issue of the divine, which is an issue that shows itself. The attempt to make the divine go away can only happen from a derivative theoretical stance, and probably only from the modern, constructivist, theoretical stance. Political philosophy and religion cannot part ways. It is important, however, which takes priority.

Strauss is clear that ours is a "moment," like that experienced by the Greeks, when all traditions are shattered and there is not yet an **ongoing** tradition of political philosophy. In this regard, we stand in a position similar to the classics, with one important exception. We live in a mass society, armed with technology, divorced from a variety of primary experiences, determined by hundreds of years of conscious theoretical constructivism that has passed through a long tradition included within which is Christianity. All of this is, for us, the deferred ramification of the past tradition. That means that we in principle start from a different phenomenological position than our Greek predecessors. Only we can figure out where we go from here; and in no interesting sense can it be back to a past moment. On the other hand, in no interesting sense can it be forward to some discontinuous utopia, or totally "new beginning." If, in the end, Heidegger longed for a radical new beginning, discontinuous with the past, and Strauss for a repetition of the past, then both must be wrong.

In an important respect, I believe Strauss is absolutely correct. I believe he is correct that pre-theoretical experience is primarily ordered toward the issue of the Good. Contrary to Heidegger, the question concerning the Good takes priority over the question concerning Being. The ontological question is not primary as I have argued in chapter 3. Pre-theoretical awareness contains inarticulate understandings of the best life and the best collective arrangements for our being-with, i.e., a conception of the best regime. If all "theory" is derivative, we have no place to stand to criticize the perceptions embedded in life itself, or to say, for example, that all "values" are either relative or equal. They are never equal in everyday life, and after Heidegger it will be hard to construct the unsullied standpoint by which theory can simply dismiss the everyday understandings upon which we act and make. We have to take pre-articulate perceptions seriously. We cannot start by theoretically dismissing them.

I think Strauss has upped the phenomenological ante on Heidegger. If the question of the Good is primary, then the ontological question about the nature of the whole, or the nature of Being is to some extent derivative. Heidegger goes astray when he makes the ontological question primary rather than the question of the Good. As I argued in chapter 3, only after passing through a series of phenomenologically prior questions does one get to the ontological question. First, what is the best life, then what is the best regime? As the individual and collective goods are dependent on the essence of man's humanity, next comes the question about who is man or what is the *psyche*; only then do we get to the question of how human beings are integrated into the larger whole. The ontological question is next to last in priority phenomenologically, followed by the most derivative question, "how do we know," the epistemological question.

Only from a theoretically derivative stance, the stance of constructivism—and deconstructivism is just the inversion of constructivism—can one make the primary phenomenological questions go away. On the phenomenological level, Strauss correctly takes the question of the Good as primary. But then he turns around and takes the question of the nature of the whole as primary when he discusses philosophy in its "original sense" and then posits political philosophy as but a branch of philosophy understood as ontology. Strauss thereby posits the question regarding Being as prior to the question of Good. He circles back to Heidegger's position. And in the process he contradicts himself.

Heidegger in effect abstracts from the question of the Good by making Being the primary question, and then asserts that every ethic presupposes a doctrine of Being thereby making ethics derivative. I would argue that the opposite is the case: Every understanding of the Good, as primary, presupposes an understanding of Being. For Heidegger, everything descends from a pre-scientific understanding of Being. But therein, Heidegger becomes a very poor phenomenologist. I would argue for the phenomenological priority of the Good and then, contrary to both Strauss and Heidegger, the derivative status of ontology. Hence philosophy cannot be primarily ontological nor contemplative of the nature of the whole.[16]

It is odd that both Heidegger and Strauss should give priority to the onto-logical in that they both go a long way toward incorporating the "phenome-nological move" and with it the practical insights of Aristotle. At the begin-nings of both the *Ethics* and the *Politics*, Aristotle clearly posits the question of the Good as primary: All individual action, and all group action, aims at the good. There are different conceptions of the good both for the individual and the collective. And in everyday experience those different conceptions are always hierarchically ranked. One intrinsically always seeks what is seen as the highest good. Heidegger fails to see this phenomenological priority of the Good and instead posits **a theoretical issue** as primary despite showing the derivative nature of the theoretical from the practical. Strauss ultimately does something similar and it leads him to make political philosophy either a branch of real, theoretical philosophy or a merely politic defense of philoso-phy understood theoretically as a form of ontology.

Heidegger is correct in positing the priority of the practical to the theoret-ical. But he does not consistently maintain what follows from that insight. In the end, he slips back into being a theoretician of a unique kind, as does Strauss. Strauss takes off from Heidegger's showing of the priority of pre-theoretical awareness, but in his own way circles around to the primacy of the theoretical as well. If the pre-theoretical is primary, and the question of the Good is primary in the pre-theoretical, then we have the basis for saying that political philosophy as a phenomenological interrogation of the pre-theoreti-cal, where the Good takes priority to ontology, **is proto-philosophy.** If all public speech is first and foremost shared, and it is poetic rather than repre-sentational, then ontology itself is poetry because we get to the questions con-cerning Being only by passing through other prior questions, the answers to which always remain presupposed in any ontology. I return to this issue of on-tology in chapter 20 on theoretical physics.

Ontology must always remain **explicitly** subservient to phenomenological political philosophy, the same as religion, because intrinsically it always al-ready is at a derivative remove from the question of the Good. In this regard, we are reminded that even in Plato, in the "divided line" and the allegory of the cave, Being itself "is" only because it is lit up by the higher and prior pri-macy of the Good as the highest cause. And as with the *Republic*, to the ex-tent that the Good is beyond Being—the multiplicity of the ideas determines the Being of things—it is in principle Not-Being. Hence the ground of all presence is absence. This is the basis of Platonic poetry, and it does not sound much like metaphysics understood as a doctrine of Being qua presence. Po-litical philosophy as I have tried to articulate it, as an ongoing activity, is not metaphysical. It is holistic, phenomenological proto-philosophy. And as I will try to show in the next section, Plato was already on this same path.

NOTES

1. The quotations here are all from Leo Strauss. See his *Studies in Platonic Political Philosophy* (Chicago: University of Chicago Press, 1983), (abbreviated SPPP); *Political Philosophy: Six Essays* by Leo Strauss, edited by Hilail Gildin (Indianapolis: Pegasus, 1975) (PP); *The City and Man* (Chicago: Rand McNally & Co., 1964) (CM); *Persecution and the Art of Writing* (Glencoe: The Free Press, 1952) (PAW).

2. For the sake of a formula, philosophy grows out of "community." Those who talk about philosophically "constructing" community, have the cart and the horse in the wrong order.

3. See "On a Possible Epicurean Garden for Philosophy: Philosophy and the City in the Thought of Leo Strauss," chapter 10.

4. This distinction originates in Nietzsche's "The Advantages and Disadvantages of History for Life," and determines much of twentieth century thought. Arendt, for example, departs from the same distinction and chooses *praxis*.

5. Heidegger is the one who grounds this notion in such works as *Being and Time*, and especially "Origin of the work of Art." Strauss ultimately rejects the primacy of this notion of ecstatic temporality by assigning it to modern political philosophy, showing modern political philosophy moving by "three waves" toward a dead end, and then seemingly rejecting modern political philosophy *in toto*.

6. I deal with this in my *Martin Heidegger: Paths Taken, Paths Opened* (Lanham: Rowman & Littlefield, 2007).

7. See my *Martin Heidegger: Paths Taken, Paths Opened*.

8. Those who think this is an either or choice will have an impossible time explaining where they stand to make the choice. Those self-styled "postmoderns" who believe that it is obvious that man is a "who" simply give straightforward manifestation to the modern, all too modern anti-nature animus that has ruled for five hundred years. They too cannot explain where they stand. And they inevitably contradict themselves, one manifestation of which I will deal with in the environmentalism chapter in Part 4.

9. I do not at present have the space to deal thematically with Heidegger's discussions of poetry as a form of Truth. It is not without its own problems. I deal with this issue thematically in *Martin Heidegger: Paths Taken, Paths Opened* (Lanham: Rowman & Littlefield, 2007).

10. To make a start, it is far more important to recover and ground ourselves in the phenomena than to recover some prior manifestation of "nature."

11. See my *Martin Heidegger: Paths Taken, Paths Opened*.

12. Heidegger does not want to admit this, but the reason for our necessary concern with and openness to the world and others rests on the fact that we are beings who must labor to live—scarcity rules—and must create the distinctive nature of our living together if we are to engage in any doing. We are beings that must do and make because of various needs. We must also procreate, raise children, educate and defend them and ourselves. All of this implies that while Heidegger is correct that we are not entirely a "what" in the way other species are, determined entirely by nature and instinct, we "are" a "what" to some extent. What we are is also determined by our ac-

tions, perceptions, aspirations, associations, thrown tradition, social setting and so on. On that level we "are" a "who." But we are not entirely either a what or a who. This is not, Heidegger to the contrary, an either/or choice. The two mysteriously interpenetrate each other.

13. We see more of this from Cropsey as I noted above. But it is not clear that he gets beyond a poetry that re-works past elements in the tradition. There does not seem to be the basis for novelty.

14. Strauss at one point asserts that Hegel was the last Christian philosopher announcing thereby his understanding that Christian philosophical options had been exhausted. If so, I am of a different opinion as I argue below.

15. Granted, at the dawn of the modern age, political philosophy had to emancipate itself from the stranglehold of theology. But that does not mean that political philosophy cannot now plumb Christian possibilities rather than long for an altogether new religion and new gods or return to pre-Christian scripture which is not what "we" are primarily thrown into. If the West is a tension between Reason and Revelation as Strauss argues, it is also what was until the WW II still referred to by Churchill and Roosevelt as Christendom. That is what is distinctive about the West and not the more ambiguous, if not in some ways contradictory, Judeo-Christendom. We can in the present only pick and choose from the past up to a certain point. Zoroastrianism may be in our past, and even inform early Christianity, but it is not a serious resource from which we can ecstatically draw in our own *Andenken*.

16. Herein Cropsey is clearer than Strauss in seeing philosophy as a form of "caring" and the ontological as posited by mind. I would only question the word "posit" with its Cartesian ring and implications. One can only "posit" what the phenomena allow.

Part Three

THE NON-METAPHYSICAL PLATO: SECOND BEGINNINGS?

Preface to Part 3:
Plato, Platonism, and a
Second Beginning

Will the real Plato please stand. Is it at all possible to bring the "real" Plato to stand out in the open after 2,400 years of layered sedimentation? And if we did succeed in bringing him into the light of day, what then? Would that unencumbered Plato have anything to say to us?

As a purely historical matter, Plato's dialogues have never really had a chance to stand on their own. His work was almost immediately passed through the lens of Aristotle and then neo-Platonism, other variants of Hellenism, the transformative influence of Cicero at Rome, and so on. By a series of what can only be described as accidents, Plato's texts became the primary property of Islam. There was then more than a millennium during which Plato's dialogues were lost to what became known as Western Civilization. By the time the dialogues were recovered in the West, there was more than a millennium of Aristotelian and Christian influence.

When Plato became available again in the West, it was, until very recently, only as passed through the lens of a well-entrenched Christian-Aristotelian juggernaut and not long thereafter the critical, anti-classical lens of Modernity. The reality is that Western Civilization has been predominantly Christian and Aristotelian. The extent to which the West is "Platonic" is both historically and philosophically problematic. It is only because of philosophical developments in the nineteenth and twentieth centuries that we have opened ourselves to Plato in anything resembling an originary fashion, and I would argue, for the first time.

We in the West have never really been open to a genuine Plato, and he to us, before very recently. Despite what has been the history of the Platonic dialogues in the West, it is a powerful orthodoxy in some circles that Plato (and, through his dialogues, Socrates) is the father of Western Civilization. It is also accepted by an increasing number in our post-Heideggerian time, without argument, that a more or less seamless history links Plato with modernity and our present. In each of these contemporary understandings there is a linear, one-directional view of history that leads on the one hand **upward** toward the perfection of philosophy and on the other **downward** toward nihilism. In each case, the movement is conceptualized as seamless and linear. In a rough and ready fashion, those two understandings respectively represent the two reigning orthodoxies in Platonic scholarship, one Anglo-American, one Continental.

The Anglo-American or "Oxbridge" understanding sees Plato as the brightest among the infants at the origin of philosophy. It sees Plato as offering the rudimentary first stumbling attempts to get to what we now view as genuine philosophy. The Anglo-American understanding views philosophy as primarily a logical and analytical undertaking that finds its highest manifestation in twentieth century Anglo-American analytic philosophy in any of its permutations. This view comes complete with an understanding of the order in which the Platonic dialogues were written and therewith an understanding of how Plato's thought developed over time.[1]

The Continental approach springs from the thought of Nietzsche and Heidegger, passes through authors like Derrida, and then into various permutations of deconstructionism, postmodernism, feminism and a seeming profusion of other –isms. This view, in the thought of both Nietzsche and Heidegger, sees the pre-philosophic beginnings as pure and fecund with the origins of the philosophic tradition causing a break with what was healthy and life-giving. After Plato everything is a uniform, seamless intensifying march to nihilism and a total moribund collapse of the West. This is all to be blamed on the initial outbreak of philosophy as "metaphysical" in the work of Plato. Philosophy is presented as a disease that is ultimately fatal.

In the chapters that follow in this section I want to offer a series of alternate suggestions on how to approach Plato. First, as already mentioned above, I will suggest that there are greater breaks within antiquity than we see elsewhere in the tradition. For example, there is less of a break between Aristotelian antiquity and the medieval thought it informed than there is between Socrates and Plato, between Plato and Aristotle, Plato and Neoplatonism, Plato and Cicero, Plato and Epicureanism. And there is greater continuity between medieval thought and modernity than is customarily accepted in many circles.

Second, over a number of years I have been led to question the whole notion of a seamless tradition where a central idea or set of ideas is developed in a one-directional, linear fashion. The Western tradition, indeed any tradition, has to be seen as discontinuous, with breaks and leaps that occur unpredictably and, as with the fate of Plato's texts, accidentally. With these leaps and breaks come unpredictable irruptions and zigzags, and unavoidable occlusions of one kind or another. This leads to a "happening" or "event" understanding of the nature of history and of Western history particularly. I will consider this idea in the next section.

Third, I will suggest that the break between Plato and Socrates has been largely occluded in the tradition and the break between Plato and Aristotle has been largely mis-conceptualized. The Platonic-Socratic break is the most massive. Fourth, there is the possibility that we can now return to an originary Plato in a way that, for a variety of reasons, has never yet been available. Fifth, this return can be seen as a "second beginning." We return to the core of Plato's teaching, not its surface rhetoric or poetry—and certainly not to what are seen as the textbook doctrines of Platonism—and then strike off from that originary core toward the future. This is a version of the ecstatic standing in the present and holding together past and future about which I have spoken above.

Finally, I will suggest that Plato had already grasped many of the core thoughts that later thinkers presented as novel and at times as alternatives to an allegedly Platonic, metaphysical understanding. Surprisingly, I have in mind here specifically that Plato understood notions customarily attributed to Nietzsche and Heidegger, which were thought by those later authors to be original to them. I will suggest that in Plato we confront an example of my central premise, that political philosophy is proto-philosophy. **I want to suggest the ways in which Plato himself understood political philosophy as architectonic proto-philosophy.**

As I argued above in "What is Political Philosophy," the reduction of philosophy to one of its parts is a mistake. It is especially a mistake when that reduction transforms philosophy into another manifestation of analyzing *logoi*. A version of that mistake originates in Socrates, is picked up by Aristotle and accelerates throughout the tradition of philosophy until philosophy is reduced to a form of autonomous logical analysis, eventually parasitically living off what are seen as more primary activities. I will argue that Plato had already seen the problem with that kind of reductionism and what would come to be called "logocentrism." Within the present environment of our time, what I see as the primary Platonic understanding can be very fecund and help us recapture a more comprehensive, architectonic understanding of the nature of philosophy than we have at present and have had for a very long time.

According to my understanding, philosophy in its highest and most comprehensive manifestation is not a detached, pure, theoretical undertaking, a mode of logical analysis, a form of metaphysics as presently understood, or a variety of other mistaken understandings. Many of those doors were opened by Aristotle's both epic-making and mistaken severing of theory and practice. More to the point, Aristotle opened the door to the severing of theoretical philosophy from a phenomenological basis even if he did not completely do that himself. Yet this is something he did not do in his practical works, which remain marvelous phenomenological exercises in my sense.

Throughout *Between Eternities*, my argument has been that a comprehensive proto-philosophy has to be phenomenological as I have posed the matter above. It must start from phenomena that present themselves. As conceptualized by Plato, these "phenomena" are the multiple *eidē*, the commonly shared "looks" of things that appear publicly for all together with the everyday opinions about them. A truly phenomenological philosophy can incorporate both theoretical and practical elements, both *logoi* and *poiesis*. But they all have to be generated out of the phenomena.

The opening moves in transforming philosophy into a form of autonomous *logos*, with its corresponding transformation of the locus of Truth from appearing *eidē* to statements, began, paradoxically with Socrates and then was accentuated and exacerbated by Aristotle. In between, Plato tried to transcend the problems to which this approach pointed. And this is only one example where he attempted to transcend a variety of problems, before the fact. He did this by trying to emend the teaching of Socrates, while retaining dialectical and phenomenological elements taken from the fundamentally a-poetic and un-erotic Socrates.

Plato's emendation of Socratism was almost immediately diverted and indeed reversed by Aristotle. And yet again paradoxically, the Aristotle of the practical works remained an unrivaled phenomenologist. Hence there were always two competing elements in Aristotle's thought. In time, the phenomenological element was defeated. The practical Aristotle was a phenomenologist; the theoretical Aristotle opened the door to Constructivism, and hence modernity, and the logical analysis that dominates contemporary Anglo-American philosophy. A second beginning is only possible from a phenomenological basis. Plato can teach us what this means.

The phenomenological Plato tried to transcend Socrates's longing for a fully present *logos* about the whole, which Aristotle codified in his theoretical works. In the process, Plato presented a basis upon which the locus of Truth could be in *aesthesis* (in the publicly appearing *eidē*) and hence a way in which Being and appearing are not radically severed, with Truth going to the side of the non-appearing. **Plato did not have a doctrine of Being as presence, and was not "logocentric."** Nor did he have a doctrine that radically separated Being and Not-Being, as becomes clear in the *Sophist*. Likewise, he did not juxtapose *logos* and *poiesis* in such a way that a choice was required; in fact, he tried to show why they had to be balanced and woven together. For Plato, absolutely contrary to Derrida, *logos* and *poiesis* interpenetrate each other.

I will suggest that Plato is the author who can show us how to bind together into a whole, appearing and non-appearing, Being and Not-Being, *logos* and *poiesis*, as well as ethics, politics, psychology, ontology and epistemology. That whole woven out of parts is, as I have argued above, the work of political philosophy understood as proto-philosophy.

NOTE

1. This assumed "knowledge" regarding the chronology of Plato's dialogues is based on a faith in what to my mind is a questionable, pseudo-scientific discipline. But even if we did know the order in which the dialogues were written, we would still have to have a penetrating, close internal analysis of each text individually to have any idea of how Plato's thought evolves from one text to the next. This close textual analysis is almost always lacking in the work of those who presume to know the order in which the dialogues were written.

Chapter Thirteen

Dialogue and Dialectic in Plato's *Phaedo*: Plato as Metaphysician, Epistemologist, Ontologist and Political Philosopher

I have, over a number of years, put forward the question of whether ours is a "post"-era. It is an open question despite the prevalence of terms like post-modernity, post-structuralism, post-philosophy, post-metaphysics. These terms set the parameters of much recent thought. At present I am particularly interested in the last term, post-metaphysics. For example, Heidegger and Derrida, among others, argue that we are at the end of the age of metaphysics, and by extension, at the dawn of a new post-metaphysical form of thought. For Heidegger the last metaphysician was Nietzsche, for Derrida it was Heidegger. There are no doubt still unplayed moves in this game of non-metaphysical one-upmanship. But there is agreement that Plato is the father of the metaphysical mode of thinking. There is further agreement that transcending that mode of thinking is a good thing. I will argue that the claim that Plato is the first metaphysician is wrong. It is based on a mistaken reading of Plato's dialogues. I will argue that it incorrectly reads later developments in the tradition backwards into Plato. Whether metaphysics as presently defined is good or bad is a question for another time.

Ultimately, demonstration of my thesis would require an analysis of the entire Platonic corpus. At present I will use a discussion of Plato's *Phaedo* as an indication of the argument.[1] The *Phaedo* gives us unique access to this issue. It contains a variety of the doctrines that could be seen as indicative of the fact that Plato has an "epistemological," "ontological" and "metaphysical" teaching. The *Phaedo* seems to assert the body/soul duality, the doctrine of the ideas, the immortality and transmigration of souls, the thesis that knowledge is remembering, a thesis about the cosmic support for justice, and so on. I will argue that when seen in the context of both the drama of the dialogue, and Socrates's explicit methodological statement at 96b–102a, there are no metaphysical, epistemological or ontological doctrines in the way we now use and understand those terms.

The *Phaedo* is one of those dialogues that presents itself as a flashback. It takes place a considerable time after Socrates's death when Phaedo and Echecrates meet to go over what Socrates's had discussed on his last day. Our knowledge of the discussion is dependent upon the memory/remembering of Phaedo. We are told specifically that Plato was not present (59c), so we need not conclude that the dialogue represents a mere act of stenography. Plato's "absence" is significant, as is the issue of "remembering." These issues become thematically important. Reliance on the intellectually limited Phaedo shows the account is only partially present.

Phaedo recounts that in watching Socrates on his last day he simultaneously felt pleasure because they were occupied with philosophy and pain because Socrates was presently to die. (59a–b) Likewise, we learn that as Socrates was released from his fetters on that last day, he reflected as well on the interpenetration of pleasure and pain. (60b1) This issue of opposition also returns thematically in the explicit discussion of the text. For example, later we are told that opposite ideas cannot approach each other and be co-causal. Dramatically we see that pleasure and pain interpenetrate and are implicated in each other's existence. The two "opposites" are in some way responsible for each other, which is to say, co-causal.

Furthermore, before the thematic discussion begins Socrates's wife has just left with his young son. Making all the best assumptions, fatherhood is an impressive feat for a man of his age. And "as he spoke he put his feet down on the ground and remained sitting in this way through the rest of the conversation." (61d) As Socrates discusses the relation between body and soul, dramatically issues of the body are intruded upon us to the point where the soon to be dead Socrates is determined to have his feet firmly planted on the ground. There is a significant materialism implied in this act. Perhaps what Plato gives dialectically, he mitigates dramatically. Surely one cannot understand the argument of the dialogue without taking the drama into account, especially when the drama and the argument involve the same issues and seem to move in different directions. We will return to this issue in chapter 16.

Before the thematic discussion is enjoined, Socrates is drawn into a discussion of poetry, or more generally, music. Socrates claims he has had certain dreams. Unlike his no-saying, negative *daimon,* his dreams actually tell him to do something positive—"make music and work at it." (60e6) He had had the dream before but now it had apparently acquired a certain urgency. During his incarceration he had responded by composing metrical versions of, for example, Aesop. On the surface this would seem to be a rather lame effort at being musical. Surely no powerful Muse was operating here. Is Plato signaling that Socrates is musically and poetically poetically defective?

Previously, Socrates had been convinced that in doing philosophy in the Socratic, dialectical fashion he was already making music. (61a2) But he worried that now that he was about to die the god of his dream had something else in mind and that in effect he had better hedge his bets. While in jail, Socrates concluded that a real poet "must compose myths and not speeches (*poiein muthous, all' ou logous* . . .)." The *Phaedo* explicitly enjoins the issue of the relation between the Socratic understanding of philosophy and poetry. We must wonder which of the two is manifest in the remainder of the dialogue and how we are to differentiate them. Like Nietzsche, Plato raises the question of whether Socrates's philosophical activity is musical or a-musical, or perhaps anti-musical.

Shortly, in discussing the premise that philosophy is a form of "preparing to die," Socrates says, "it is perhaps especially fitting, as I am going to the other world, to tell stories *(muthologein)* about the life there and consider what we think about it." (61e4) Later Plato has Socrates tell a *muthos* about "the things on the earth that is below the heaven." (110b) We must be alert to the question of whether the dialogue as a whole is consciously intended to be more like a *muthos* than a *logos,* or some complicated hybrid *(muthologein).*[2] Why does Plato have Socrates fiddle with poetry on his last day? Is this part of the way in which Plato makes the Platonic Socrates "young and beautiful/noble"?[3] Or, contrary to Nietzsche, Heidegger and Derrida, is it possible that **Platonic** writing in its entirety is some complicated synthesis of poetry and dialectic rather than the attempt to generate a logocentric epistemology, ontology or form of metaphysics? The elementary *muthos* would be necessary because the whole is not entirely present to thought.

We frequently conclude after reading the *Republic* that in the great confrontation between poetry and philosophy the victor is dialectical philosophy — a form of *logos* — and the vanquished is poetry. Having reached a similar conclusion, Nietzsche calls for a new Dionysian philosophy, a **philosophy** that is closer to poetry. Seeing Plato as the source of the modern hegemony of logic, Heidegger calls for an even more complete reversal, the return to the hegemony of autonomous poetry. Derrida argues that *muthos* and *logos* are simple opposites in the Platonic understanding while arguing in his own name that such an opposition never exists. Our question is, is the philosophy presented by Plato truly the opposite of poetry as is asserted by the post-metaphysicians who trace the foundation of metaphysics to Plato? Is Plato the ultimate father of logic, modern science, technology and nihilism, or the inventor of a new form of poetry or a novel hybrid of *logos* and *muthos*? And what would the aim of that new form of poetry or novel synthesis be?

The *Phaedo* consists of a series of proofs/stories. They are divided into two groups, separated by Socrates's methodological account, the discussion of how he was led to his "second sailing." Simmias and Cebes alternate as Socrates's interlocutor. Simmias is much easier to satisfy than Cebes who at times pushes the argument with ungentlemanly vigor even though it regards a subject—death—about which Socrates is no disinterested bystander. We might be inclined to think, therefore, that the exercises undertaken with Cebes have more weight than those performed for Simmias.

The doctrine that Socrates professes on this occasion is that philosophers wish to die and spend their lives preparing for it. The body is a burden for philosophers. Hence, Socrates's impending death should not be a cause for lamentation. At the end of the dialogue Socrates says to Crito, "We owe a cock to Aesculapius." (118a5) The doctor has finally cured Socrates of the sickness life and payment is due.[4]

Socrates bids all those who are wise to follow him as quickly as possible, for philosophy understood as preparing to die is a wishing to emancipate the soul/mind from the limitations and constraints of the body. Philosophers are of good cheer as death approaches for they have prepared (wished?) for death all their lives. With this argument the dialogue is thematically launched. Dramatically it is launched with observations about the agony Socrates's friends feel at his impending death. How are the two connected? Are Socrates's "arguments" primarily intended to minister to the pain of his friends, i.e., are they an act of concern and justice on his part?

Whatever the reason, Socrates opens by arguing that philosophy turns away from the body and loves the soul and the things that are the object of the soul alone. The senses, which are part of the body, have no part in truth. (65c) Only pure soul can get in touch with pure reality (*ton onton*). "In thought then, if at all, something of the realities becomes clear to [the soul]." (61c) "If pure knowledge (*phroneseos*) is impossible while the body is with us, one of two things must follow, **either** it cannot be acquired at all **or** only when we are dead." (66e5)

In beginning the discussion with Cebes, Socrates says he will speak of things that he grounds "only on hearsay." (61e) The "proof" of the body/soul distinction is that it is already accepted by common opinion. Further, "it is perhaps especially fitting, as I am going to the other world, to tell stories (*mythologein*) about the life there [where souls are separated from bodies] and consider what we think about it; for what else could one do in the time between now and sunset?" (61e) Perhaps true philosophy is something that takes a great deal of time, time which is presently not available. There is no reason to expect that the *Phaedo* represents Socrates's last word on any topic. The same would clearly have to be true for Plato. And how Socrates and Plato are related is the question that will never quite go away.

Socrates's "hearsay" turns out to be based on a story taken from the Orphic tradition, a story told by the Orphics only in secret to the initiates.[5] (62b2) Life is a kind of prison; the gods are our guardians; we mortals are the chattels of the gods. Socrates asks if Cebes believes this. He asserts that he does. This allows Socrates to proceed. Without this agreement, Socrates would have no place to begin. Socrates begins from *logoi* that already exist and continually asks if his interlocutor believes the asserted premise from which he begins. "We believe, do we not, that death is the separation of the soul from the body?" (64c) In this instance Simmias emphatically agrees. The *archai* for Socrates' various proofs are always the premises already accepted by his interlocutor(s). No further proof than that "we" agree is ever sought. What follows is always Socrates's attempt to show what follows from the agreed upon premise. Socrates starts from already extant phenomena visible to all. He does not start from things "beyond" the already available phenomena. This is phenomenology in my sense and not metaphysics.

The Orphic "story" gets Socrates into trouble. If we are the chattel of the gods it is impious to run away from them and deprive them of their property. Cebes observes that the wise ought to be troubled therefore about dying. Socrates shows pleasure that Cebes is unwilling to accept things too easily, unlike Simmias. Cebes will not be easily convinced. (63a) Socrates is forced beyond mere hearsay.[6] Hence, Socrates is forced to defend himself as if he was in a court of law. The frequently encountered metaphor that Socrates is being tried comes to the forefront. "If you convince us by what you say, that will serve as your defense." (63d) Socrates makes his "defense"; a defense and a "proof" are not the same. Of more interest, is there a **Platonic** trial of Socrates underway in the *Phaedo*? Put another way, is it possible that Plato is modifying and amending the Socratic influence?

In the first "proof" Socrates begins by getting Simmias's acceptance that death is nothing but the separation of the body from the soul. (64c) Further, Simmias accepts that the soul can exist alone by itself. He accepts that the true philosopher despises the things of the body, loves the soul and the objects available only to the soul. Simmias believes that the philosopher longs for unsullied knowledge. By contrast, the body and its desires are the cause of the love of money which is necessary for the needs of the body. The love of money is in turn the cause of factions, battles and war. (66c–d) **The body is the cause of politics**. Apparently, the philosopher, as Simmias understands him, is indifferent to politics. Yet in the *Republic,* the philosopher necessarily re-enters the cave, immerses himself in the ordinary experience of a particular political community. How does this relate to the alleged longing for the unsullied and eternal?

When questioned, Simmias emphatically accepts that there are such pure, unsullied "essences" as justice, beauty and goodness "in themselves" (*auto kath auto*). Since no such things are ever grasped with the senses, Socrates argues, they must be grasped directly by the soul/mind. This is true of the "essence" (*ousias*) of everything. (65e) "Of course," Simmias responds. Hence Socrates concludes that soul grasps *ousias* directly.

The philosopher spends his life trying to emancipate the soul from the body so he can be in touch with the pure essences. Asked if he agrees, Simmias says, "Most assuredly." The body makes slaves of us and necessitates political relations with other individuals—and Simmias is not a political man. (66d) It follows, therefore, according to Socrates, that only when we are dead will we possess pure knowledge (*phroneseos*). While we live we must be political and more or less ignorant.

The yield of this first "proof" is that true virtue consists only in possessing pure wisdom and this wisdom is only available in another world. Any virtue other than the intellectual virtue aimed at by the philosopher is either a chimera or at best an imitation of virtue. There are no independent moral virtues as with Aristotle. The only true "purification" requires the philosophic quitting of the things of the body and the things of this world. "This then, Simmias and Cebes, is the defense I offer to show that it is reasonable for me not to be grieved or troubled at leaving you and the rulers." (69e) It is a defense that shows that the philosopher is entirely unpolitical.

This ends Socrates's first "proof." Cebes is not persuaded. Cebes will not be persuaded until it is proved that the soul can exist without the body. That the body keeps the soul from pure knowledge may be true. But it does not prove that the soul is not scattered like smoke when it flies away from the body.

Socrates's second proof proceeds from an "ancient tradition" not unlike that related in the myth of Er in the *Republic*. The ancient tradition says that the living are born from the dead and hence that souls must exist somewhere else before they come here. (70c–d) Again, the *arche* is common opinion. Further, everything that is born—i.e., the living—must have been born from what is not yet living—i.e., the dead. Socrates extrapolates and claims that all things are born or generated from their opposites. He gives examples such as the greater being "born" of the smaller, the weaker from the stronger, the slower from the quicker etc. He then asks if this point is sufficiently proved. Cebes responds, "Certainly." (71a5)

Since living is accepted as the opposite of dead, the living must be generated from the dead. Therefore, our souls **exist** in some other world before they come into this world. Paradoxically, death and existence somehow go together. Furthermore, if generation were not always from opposites and back again all of existence would be reduced eventually to oneness. "All things would have the same form and be acted upon in the same way and stop being generated at all." (72b5) The interpenetration of opposites is necessary for there to be Being. Generation requires multiplicity and opposition. Otherwise, all life would be reduced to death, just as all falling asleep would lead to the absence of wakefulness. Leaving aside here the issue of whether there is in fact such a thing as opposites—and in the *Protagoras* that possibility is called into question—as well as the issue of whether all things have an opposite (mud?), it is clear that this "proof" rests on no more than Cebes's acceptance of the "ancient story," and his belief in simple opposition. What Socrates has proved is that certain things follow from opinions Cebes already holds.

Cebes is satisfied. He is especially pleased to see that this outcome also is consistent with the doctrine that learning is nothing but recollection. This is apparently a doctrine to which Cebes is already attached. This opinion implies that we first encounter certain pure truths in a previous time and another place. We then recollect those truths here and now. (73a) This ends the second proof as Simmias now steps in to ask for the proof of the doctrine of recollection.

Initially Cebes responds and gives a proof like that given in the *Meno*. (72b) But in that dialogue it is clear that no more is involved than Socrates's leading questions extracting the desired outcome from an untutored slave boy. Perhaps this is why Socrates immediately takes the argument away from Cebes who was apparently convinced by the logic of the *Meno*. Socrates takes a different tack. He observes that recollection is caused by both like and unlike things. A facsimile or picture of Simmias can remind one of the real Simmias. Seeing Simmias can remind one of Cebes who is his constant companion. Both what is like and unlike can be the cause of recollection. By analogy, equal objects available to the senses can remind us of pure equality (*auto to ison*) which is available only to the mind.

When one thing reminds someone of another that is recollection. In the case of things that never "appear" to the senses, the other thing must have originally been "seen" without the senses. Only when the soul is separate from the body is it possible to grasp such pure things. "He who thinks thus must of necessity have previous knowledge of the thing which he says the other resembles but falls short of." (74e) The theory of recollection has now been proved on the basis of taking the pure realities for granted. Their existence was previously based on acceptance of a story.

The assembly accepts that all the objects of the senses strive after the perfection of the pure thing to which they are "akin." Since the pure thing is not an object of sense we must have known it before we were born when the soul was not yet burdened by the body. The senses help us recall and recover a likeness of the pure knowledge we possessed at another time in another place. "If the essences (*ousia*) exist, and if we refer all our sensations to these . . . and compare our sensations with these, is it not a necessary inference that just as these abstractions exist, so our souls existed before we were born; and if these abstractions do not exist, our argument is of no force." (76d5–e4) It is significant that it is the easygoing Simmias who is the interlocutor for this part of the "proof." Simmias responds, "There is nothing so clear to me as this, that all such things, the beautiful, the good and all the others of which you were speaking just now, have a most real existence." (77a4) Socrates asks if Cebes agrees. Simmias responds, without Socrates asking, that he does.

Simmias and Cebes now accept that there is such a thing as the soul; death is the separation of the soul from the body; the soul existed before coming into the body; in its prior existence the soul was in touch with pure realities which are in some way the cause of what the senses grasp. But they both remain skeptical about the continued existence of the soul after death. The soul could still scatter with the wind after death. The fear of death still exists. Socrates is called on to ease Simmias's fear. His response? "You must sing charms to him every day until you charm away his fear." (77e5) Music, not *logos,* is the means beyond such fear.

But this is not adequate to silence Cebes. Hence the fourth "proof" is called into being. This proof has much more of the veneer of a *logos.* Since we are worried that the soul disperses after it is separated from the body, we inquire about what kind of things can suffer dispersal. Things that are wholes or ones cannot be decomposed. Things that are composed of parts can decompose and disperse. However, Socrates will only assert that this distinction is "probable." (78d)

That which is absolute (*auto kath auto*)— "absolute equality, absolute beauty, any absolute existence, true being (*auto to ison, auto to kalon, auto ekaston ho estin, to on*)"—admit of no change. Men, horses, cloaks and so on are constantly changing and are never the same. They are composed of parts. The absolute things are wholes qua one or unitary. Secondly, the absolute things are invisible. The things with parts are visible. (78d–79b) Socrates jumps to the conclusion that the invisible things are one and never change, the visible things are many and do change/decompose. The body is akin to the visible, the soul is akin to the invisible. "Then the soul is more like the invisible than the body is, and the body more like the visible." (79c) Hence the soul must be one and thereby cannot decompose. Therefore, the soul is eternal and lives on after separation from the body.

How strong is this argument? It is disquieting that in the *Republic* and the *Phaedrus* the soul is depicted as having parts. That which has parts can decompose and is therefore not eternal. Further, Socrates never does more than assert that the soul is "like" the divine and immortal. (79b5) But in the third proof we have already seen that what is "like" the pure things need not itself be pure. Also, the mere fact that we cannot see the soul does not prove that it exists. Finally, in trying to support the opinion that those who spend their lives in the pursuit of philosophy are most likely to go unsullied to the realm of pure being, Socrates mitigates his own point when he observes that the soul that has succumbed to the pleasures of the body "will be interpenetrated, I suppose, with the corporeal which intercourse and communion with the body have made a part of its nature because the body has been its constant companion and the object of its care." (81c)

In the process of making the initial proofs, Socrates denigrates mere political and moral virtue based only on habit and practice without the addition of philosophy and *nous*. (81b) Habitually virtuous souls, he says, come back into the world again. The souls of real philosophers do not. Therefore, Socrates advises that one should entirely quit the things of the body and pursue only the pure thought of the pure things. It is not clear how the Socrates of the *Phaedo* could have become known as the father of **political** philosophy. The philosopher here described would never re-enter the cave.

After this fourth "proof" Socrates is silent while Simmias and Cebes continue to converse. Finally Socrates asks, "Do you think there is any incompleteness in what has been said? There are still many subjects for doubt and many points open to attack, if anyone cares to discuss the matter thoroughly." (84c3) Both Simmias and Cebes remain in doubt. Each has a new question.

Simmias observes that the soul could be like a form of harmony, a harmony of bodily parts. This difficulty will be dispensed with quite easily. Simmias, like Cebes, accepts that learning is recollection. Hence he accepts that the soul exists before it enters the body. Therefore, the soul cannot be a harmony of bodily parts. The soul cannot be a harmony of parts if it existed before its parts. (91b) Socrates has shown Simmias he cannot hold these two opinions at the same time. Simmias is more committed to the recollection thesis than his present hypothesis. (92c6)

To drive home his refutation of the harmony thesis, Socrates takes off from a series of other opinions Simmias holds. Simmias hypothesizes that the soul is a harmony of the parts of the body. By this harmony thesis one could not account for virtue and vice. Soul cannot lead that of which it is composed. The **common experience** of moral virtue is destroyed if we accept the harmony premise. Simmias is unwilling to do that. Simmias drops the hypothesis to save the phenomena of ordinary moral experience. Socrates deals with Simmias simply by showing him that he cannot consistently hold this latest position and still accept other positions in some random fashion.

Socrates then calls on Cebes. The rejoinder to Cebes involves Socrates in explaining the methodological premise that came to dominate his later thinking. Cebes accepts that the soul existed before it entered into bodily form, "but it does not seem to me proved that it will still exist when we are dead." (87a2) Each soul may exist longer than the body, it may wear out many bodies, yet eventually perish. No one can know that the soul is not in its last life unless it can be shown that the soul is altogether immortal and imperishable. Clearly, Cebes has not been convinced by the previous proofs that all things are necessarily born of their opposites, or that the soul is "like" the pure and imperishable things. Hence Socrates is forced to try something new.

Before that new demonstration commences, prefaced by Socrates's famous methodological statement, there is an interlude where we are thrust forward in time again to Phaedo and Echecrates. We are forced to recall that our access to the discussion is based on the memory and recollection of Phaedo. This break, dramatically presenting the issue of recollection, is almost precisely in the middle of the dialogue.

During this interlude, Phaedo observes that everyone was disquieted by the two objections raised by Simmias and Cebes. The generality of the assembly had been convinced by the previous arguments. Then they became convinced by the two objections. (87c) This tells us a great deal about Socrates's audience. Socrates immediately sensed the effect of the two objections on the less philosophic of the participants. Phaedo says that Socrates moved immediately to "cure" the audience and recall them from their sense of "defeat." Thereby he saved them from becoming misologists. Those who have opinions in which they deeply believe, who then have them stolen, become haters of speech, and by extension, haters of philosophy.

We must ask the question whether Socrates cures his companions primarily with *music* or with what deserves to be called *logic*. Indeed Socrates says, "I fear that I am not just now in a philosophical frame of mind as regards this particular question, but am contentious." (91a) Is Socrates "eager only to make [his] own view seem true to the hearer"? (91a5) By the drama of the *Phaedo* we are led to see how easily the majority of Socrates's followers can be swayed. In the final analysis, only Cebes seems to some degree intellectually robust. He pushes for further proofs when others, including Simmias, are satisfied. As we will see, when Socrates finishes addressing Cebes's last objection, Cebes gets no chance to respond. Cebes is finally silenced by political necessities, i.e., Socrates's execution.

Before confronting the objection raised by Cebes, "Socrates paused for some time and was absorbed in thought." (95e5) Apparently he saw that the way was long if he was to truly convince Cebes. To do so Socrates describes his own early experience in trying to understand the first things and the causes of the "concrete" things that appear. When he was young he tried to study "nature" and, more importantly, the ground of nature **directly**. He sought the ultimate cause of all things—why they come into being, why they perish, why they exist. In the process he came to doubt all the things he formerly believed he knew. All of the knowledge of the senses and of common sense and ordinary experience became as nothing. Following his **direct** method, Socrates had arrived at explanations that were no longer comprehensible in light of the everyday phenomena from which he had started. (98e–99b) Forgetting the phenomena (the things that come forth into appearance for all collectively) and trying to look directly at the ground of Being, Socrates likens to being "completely blinded" (96c2), much as looking directly at the cause of Being (the Idea of the Good) is like looking directly at the sun in the parallel account in the *Republic*.

Then Socrates says he came into contact with the teaching of Anaxagoras that mind (*nous*) arranges and causes all things. Socrates interpreted this teaching teleologically. If mind were a cause it would surely cause only that which is best. If one could find what is best for everything, that would explain generation and decay, all change and stasis, all existing. We could then assume that the good holds together and causes all things. If mind rules the cosmos we could assume that all things strive after the state that represents their perfection, which is the ultimate cause of the generation and existence of all things. The world would be ruled by *final* causality. This was the younger Socrates's rather surprising interpretation of Anaxagoras.

Socrates was disappointed, however, to find that Anaxagoras did not follow this method when he turned to actual explanation. Anaxagoras fell back on a simple materialism in which air, earth, water "and many other absurdities" acted as causes. (98c2) Anaxagoras relied on *material* and *efficient* causality. So Socrates turned away from the teaching of Anaxagoras and "conducted [his] second voyage in quest of the cause." (99d2) While Socrates is not explicit about this, it appears that in the process he rejected not only Anaxagoras's materialism, but also the teleology he originally attributed to him. Does this mean that he also rejected that the cosmos is ruled by mind? It certainly seems to suggest that Socrates ceased trying to grasp the first cause directly. It was this rejection that led Socrates to the "Socratic" method.

> After this, then, since I had given up investigating *ta onta*, I decided that I must be careful not to suffer the misfortune which happens to people who look at the sun and watch it during an eclipse. For some of them ruin their eyes unless they look at its image in water or something of the sort. . . . So I thought I must have recourse to speeches and examine in them the truth of realities (*tous logous kataphugonta en ekeinois skopein ton onton ten aletheian*). (99e–100a)

Socrates's mature method led him to begin with everyday speeches (*logoi*), interrogating them attempting to find what is implied in them. The implication is that there is access to reality through these speeches, i.e., that some truth is contained in each speech, even if that element of truth must be culled and gleaned. This method eschews both the immediate data of the senses and direct apprehension (*nous*), and puts all faith in the interrogation of already existing *logoi*. This raises a question about the various origins of those *logoi*, an issue to which we will return shortly.

This new method, the "second sailing," is absolutely neutral as regards teleology.[7] This method is also metaphysically and ontologically neutral. As regards epistemology, Socrates adopts this method because he is convinced that all other methods lead to blindness and eventually misology and hatred of philosophy among the uninitiated, even the generality of his own followers. It assumes there is truth in everyday perceptions as they are presented in everyday *logoi*. This move is on the way to Aristotle's doctrinal statement that the locus of truth is statements. Hence it is on the way to establishing logic as our means to truth. In contemporary terms that makes Socrates logocentric and a metaphysician. But where does it leave Plato? Does Plato accept the hegemony of the interrogation of *logoi* as of the essence of philosophy? What becomes of the interpenetration of *logoi* and *mythoi* depicted in the drama of the *Phaedo*?

By adopting his "second sailing," Socrates could insure that his point of departure was always that which is publicly familiar. By extension, his point of arrival will likewise always retain an element of the familiar. With this method there is no danger of radically transcending the familiar and causing blindness. This explains why, throughout the Platonic dialogues, Socrates is frequently dealing with commonplace issues as they evolve in common discourse. Socrates tries to ascend beyond the commonplace through discussion, and attempts to discover what is implied and imbedded in *logoi*, but never flies beyond the *logoi* as is true of the materialists who give reductionist accounts of reality, or the teleologists who talk about realities that have no real element of appearing.

The new, Socratic method is in tension with the argument that pure soul can gain *direct* access to pure essences or the first cause. The Socratic method is based on a mediated approach to reality. How far it can go in its mediated efforts is not clear. Are there steps all the way to the *arche?* We are not told. Whether Socrates believed in the possibility of the direct apprehension of the first things—using the faculty *nous*—in his private investigations remains a matter for conjecture.[8] Whether that study would have been teleological or materialistic is likewise a matter for conjecture at another time.[9] For our purposes the important point is that in the *Phaedo,* there is no indication of the possibility of starting directly from the *arche* and working "down" to the visible world.

Having laid out his mature method, Socrates asserts that this new method forces one to believe in the existence of the pure realities: beauty, goodness, equality and the like. "If you grant this and agree that these exist, I believe I shall explain cause to you and shall prove that the soul is immortal." (100c) Cebes says equivocally, "**assume** that I do and go on." (100c2)

Socrates does not argue the matter here, but it could be asserted that the existence of the pure things is the **logical extension** of taking seriously what is imbedded in everyday *logoi*; they are not a directly grasped reality. Those *logoi* grow out of ordinary experience. In contemporary, and somewhat misleading terminology, common speech is impossible without assuming the existence of "universals." Put another way, common experience, as expressed in speech, points beyond itself. Our senses present us with a variety of sense data. Nonetheless, we perceive "things," that is, ensembles of such data. Ordinary experience points us toward the need for a principle or cause of unity.

What follows from his mature method, Socrates argues, is that the only cause of anything in the visible realm that we will admit is the pure thing that is akin to the visible one. Each sensible thing is what it is by "participating" in the pure thing it is like. The method of Socrates' "second sailing" involves: 1) *logoi* as the only "safe" point of departure, and 2) the "participation thesis" as the basis of causality, i.e., Socrates will rely on *formal* causality. It would appear that formal and final causality can be separated and operate independently.[10]

Armed with his methodological statement, accepted only equivocally by Cebes, Socrates proceeds to quiet the fears of his auditors caused by the objection raised by Cebes. Socrates will cure the disquiet of the audience in two ways: 1) an argument based on the participation thesis, and 2) an edifying *muthos*. Apparently, the argument based on the participation thesis is inadequate by itself. In the process, we witness the origins of **political** philosophy.

Socrates begins by asking if Cebes accepts the participation thesis. He says that he does. Socrates stresses that it is important that Cebes agree with him before they begin. (102d5) Agreement is the *arche* for this proof. An **unnamed** participant does not agree, observing that the participation thesis contradicts a previous argument that things grow out of or are caused by their opposites. Socrates' response is that the previous thesis only applies to "concrete" or visible things (*pragmata*). (103b2) This response raises all manner of difficulties for a theory of causation. Nonetheless, agreement seems to be restored. Socrates looked at Cebes and said: "and you—are you troubled by any of our friends' objections?" He responds: "no, not this time." (103c2) The matter is pursued no further.

Proceeding from the participation thesis as a given, Socrates argues that each "concrete thing" is caused by the pure thing which it is like. The complication is that almost all things participate in more than one pure cause or "idea." For example, that which participates in the idea five can also participate in the idea odd or the idea hand. But five "refuses the approach" of the idea even, despite the fact that five and even are themselves not opposites. "All things which, although not opposites one to another, always contain opposites; these exclude the idea which is opposed to the idea contained in them and when it approaches they either perish or withdraw." (104c) Hence nothing can participate in two such ideas simultaneously.

With Cebes's acceptance, Socrates moves to his conclusion, to his last "proof." Cebes accepts that it is the soul that causes the body to be alive. The idea of the soul accepts the approach of the idea life. Socrates does not explain the relation between the "idea" of the soul and the "actual" soul in concrete bodies. This difficulty aside, Socrates concludes that the idea of the soul will not admit the approach of the idea death. Therefore, he concludes, the soul is deathless. (105e) That which is deathless is immortal and imperishable. The soul continues on indefinitely after it leaves the body.

We cannot help but recall the previous proof of the prior existence of the soul. Death is born of life, and life in turn is born of death. The soul exists before it enters the body. That means the soul exists and is dead. Soul seems to admit the approach of the idea death. We must recall that belief in the prior existence of the soul is the basis in turn of many of the later "proofs." If that link collapses so does the entire chain. The murky distinction between what is "concrete" and what is a pure idea does not seem to offer any means of avoiding contradiction between a previous, necessary "proof" and this last one. Surely the soul—understood as the opposite of the body—is not "concrete." The earlier objection of the unnamed man signals a difficulty. And it is not accidental that he is "unnamed." The unnamed cannot enter everyday discourse.

Furthermore, in the *Apology,* Socrates argues that death could either be the continuation of consciousness or simple oblivion and nothingness. In that dialogue he argues that either way there is no need for fear. Here there seems to be considerable fear among members of the audience at the thought of nothingness. No doubt the different addressees of the respective dialogues account for the different arguments. But this hardly helps relieve our present confusion, especially if we assume that Plato is primarily engaged in logical proofs, or at least proto-attempts at such proofs. Our difficulty is removed if the *Phaedo* is primarily a depiction, qua exaggeration, of the operation of the pure Socratic method. But in the *Phaedo* we see the Socratic method conjoined with poetry, *muthos,* a conjunction Socrates probably never made himself. Plato is trying to demonstrate that the two cannot be separated without a descent into the contradiction the *Phaedo* depicts. Pure Socratic dialectic leads to confusion.

Whether Cebes, or anyone else, is confused, or if agreement has been reached is not altogether clear. There is equivocal assent on Cebes's part. But, we should recall that his previous reservations did not emerge until after a pause during which he and Simmias engaged in discussion. Simmias does say, however, "The subject is so great, and I have such a poor opinion of human weakness, that I cannot help having some doubt in my own mind about what has been said." (107b) Socrates also observes that "our first assumptions ought to be more carefully examined, even though they seem to you to be certain." (107b5) This would seem to represent a candid retrospective glance at the prior "proofs." Nothing apodictic has been demonstrated.

Cebes is precluded from pursuing the argument further because: 1) Socrates immediately launches into a long edifying story (107c–115a); and 2) at the culmination of the myth, Socrates rises abruptly to go and bathe, a process that takes a long time. When Socrates returns, it is time to take the poison. Hence the inquisitive Cebes never gets an opportunity to respond. Can we conclude that Socrates has gone a long way toward "curing" the distress of many of his friends due to their anguish about his, and their, death?

We need not retell the Socratic myth in detail. Suffice it to say, as his last act in life Plato has the dramatic Socrates do what the voice of his dream urged, make music. There is ample reason to believe that it is only **Plato's** Socrates who makes music. Socrates's story is used to buttress the preceding "proofs." It supports the belief that one should desire to separate the soul from the body and not fear death. It also grounds the idea that moral virtue has a cosmic support. Like the myth of Er that ends the *Republic,* which likewise cuts off any response by Glaucon, the need for this myth seems to be an admission of the unsatisfactory nature of the preceding "proofs."

As his last act, Plato's Socrates does poetry. Plato uses *muthos* to fill in the gaps at the point where *logoi* fail. Plato seems to imply the necessity of both *muthos* and *logos,* and their interdependence. It would be simply wrong, on the basis of this dialogue, to conclude, as does Derrida, that *logos* or logic takes priority over *muthos* or poetry. That would be to assume that Plato believes the proofs of the *Phaedo* are in fact conclusive. Given the status of the "proofs," that would in turn be to depict Plato as the brightest child in an age of the infancy of the intellect and the infancy of logic. But Plato is not engaged in a proto act of launching logic as is the conclusion of Anglo-American Platonic scholarship.

The proofs are clearly not conclusive. The *Phaedo* is not a manifestation of the autonomy of logic or the striving after a perfect metaphysical knowledge, but an indication of the mutual dependency of *muthos* and *logos*. We will return shortly to a discussion of how we can differentiate the two. It has also become incumbent upon us to discuss thematically the relation between philosophy and poetry. In the *Republic*, Socrates may vanquish poetry in the name of philosophy; Plato does no such thing.

We have argued that the *Phaedo* is not intended to represent logical proofs based on or leading to metaphysical, epistemological or ontological teachings. To reiterate, this point is further supported by observing that while the argument of the dialogue advances, there are dramatic elements that bear directly on the thematic discussion: 1) As he is unchained from his fetters in the early morning of his last day, Socrates rubs his arms and contemplates the relation between pleasure and pain. 2) Socrates's wife and children parade across the stage and depart. 3) Socrates sits upright throughout his last day with his feet firmly planted on the ground. As the position would be a demanding and uncomfortable one over a long period of time, Socrates must find being in touch with the earth very important. 4) There is a digression when information is relayed to Socrates that his jailer advises less animated discussion. Too much speech inflames the body occasioning the need for larger doses of poison. The activity of the soul affects the body. This would only be true if the body and soul interpenetrate each other. 5) Socrates plays affectionately with Phaedo's hair. 6) Having concluded a lengthy discussion of death—understood as the separation of the pure soul from the body— Socrates goes off to an equally lengthy bath. His explanation of this behavior is that he wishes to spare the women of his family the need to attend to this task. But there are few examples in the Platonic corpus of Socrates being concerned with mundane matters such as this –other than the *Symposium*. The episode seems to show that the care of the body is important to him. 7) At the very end of the dialogue, just before he dies, Socrates covers his face. Is this to hide something from his friends? The eyes are the window to the soul. Perhaps he covers up a tear. Less likely, perhaps he prays. Who could know?

The drama of the *Phaedo* all implicates the body, the importance Socrates attaches to it and its close relation to the soul. The drama of the dialogue moves in a direction of materialism, a direction opposed to the explicit teaching. We are forced, therefore, to reflect on the intention of the *Phaedo*. In light of the drama—to say nothing of the way the "proofs" themselves develop—we are forced to conclude that the "proofs" presented in the *Phaedo* are not Socrates's—or Plato's—last word on metaphysics, epistemology or ontology.

Literally the final word of the dialogue is *dikaiotatou*. Socrates is the "most righteous." No doubt Socrates's speeches are a sign of his justice toward his grieving friends. More to the point, the *Phaedo* represents a Platonic act of justice that makes the historical Socrates "young and noble."[11] In this way the *Phaedo* is part of Plato's defense together with necessary modification of the Socratic method. As such it is an addendum to the *Apology*, showing the most serious defense of Socrates against his accusers. In this way, the *Phaedo* becomes part of the serious defense of Socrates by Plato, as compared to the taunting defense Socrates gave on the day of his trial, for reasons only he could know for sure.

I am suggesting that in the *Phaedo* we are seeing a Platonic defense of Socrates together with a transformation of what would otherwise have been the unmediated and problematic Socratic influence. As we learn from the speech Socrates retells in the *Symposium*,[12] the philosophic longing leads one toward oneness with the eternal cause of all causes. That oneness would occur in silence. That silent oneness is what the Platonic dialogues equate with "blindness."

The **Platonic** method aims to moderate the pure philosophic *eros* that longs for the one and mitigate its dangers. This mitigation and moderation is not based entirely on a public prudence by which the philosophers defend themselves before the political community.[13] It is for the sake of philosophy as well. Noble as it is, the pure, erotic philosophic longing threatens not just the city but philosophy itself. Political philosophy is a moderate and moderating alternative. It descends into the cave to interrogate the *logoi*. It does so to avoid silence. On this Plato and Socrates agree. Outside the cave are the ideas—i.e. "Being"—and beyond Being is the Idea of the Good, the first cause. Being beyond the ideas, the Idea of the Good is technically Not-Being. One cannot speak or say Not-Being. The ultimate cause or ground is ungraspable and "absent," as is Plato in the *Phaedo*. Oneness with the cause of all causes can only occur in silence and threatens blindness.

Political philosophy is that philosophy that understands the danger of silence. It is not merely or even primarily prudent rhetoric that dissembles about the fully known first things before the public. That assumes one can grasp and speak about the first things. Platonic political philosophy is that form of philosophy that limits itself to the interrogation of *logoi* generated elsewhere. The pure philosophic longing generates nothing; it culminates in silence and potential madness. *Logoi* are generated out of ordinary experience by: 1) the political community and its traditions; 2) the poets and their creative, imitative embellishment; and 3) creative rearrangement and cosmetizing of ordinary experience. Philosophic reflection on philosophical *logoi* adds further speeches at one remove. Only Revelation could offer a third primary source for *logoi.* Strictly speaking, pure, erotic philosophy generates nothing. *Political* philosophy is closer to poetry than the pure philosophic longing for a direct, immediate grasp of the ultimate cause which remains absent.

In the *Phaedo* Plato gives an extended demonstration of the use of the Socratic method. That method is to start from *logoi* that already exist and interrogate them to see what is implied. Likewise, the new method involves comparing the implications of different *logoi.* It is assumed that people are uneasy when it is shown that their opinions contradict each other. The principle of non-contradiction, or internal consistency, is central to this new method. The new method eschews the attempt to grasp Being directly. It respects ordinary experience as a natural given. Even the poetry linked with Plato's use of the method is limited to being an extrapolation from ordinary experience.

The *Phaedo* never attempts to prove or refute the opinions interlocutors already hold. Nothing is ever proven except what follows from initial opinions and agreements. It could be argued that the opinions from which the proofs take off are demonstrated in the other dialogues. For example, it might be claimed that the *Meno* has proven the thesis that knowledge is recollection. One would have to go to each of the other dialogues and see if the "proofs" undertaken there are more apodictic than the ones presented in the *Phaedo.* My contention is that the same method is demonstrated in all the other Platonic dialogues along with the same Platonic modification of Socrates. That modification involves a synthesis of Socratic method and poetry. What might look like metaphysical, epistemological or ontological teachings are in fact no more than the yield from the application of this new Platonic method to common experience and commonly held opinions. We are only left to wonder about the cause of great poetic articulation of the whole. Are they backed by an element of *nous*?

Plato draws out what is implied in common experience. The way in which that common experience is a complex phenomenon of natural experiences together with a conventional political overlay—mediated as well by poetic and philosophic *logoi.* The dialectical interrogation of already extant logoi leads either to **agreement** or it leads those capable of it **toward** a mediated ascent to the clarity of a fully self-conscious political philosophy that "weaves" together all the human possibilities—purely philosophic, religious, political, unconsciously poetic, etc.—in a way that makes peace and preserves them all.[14] We will see this below in my treatment of Plato's Trilogy.

The pure, erotic philosophic longing may culminate in a kind of "seeing" (*nous*) comparable to a staring at the sun. Of course, that can only be known by those who have accomplished it. The fact of erotic longing does not assure one of the existence of the object of that longing—any more than physical desire assures one of a mate. We may simply be dealing with a paradoxical natural fact of human existence. But even if there is an object that corresponds with our natural longing to grasp the ground of all grounds, it is depicted by Plato as beyond speech. One must still get from that silence to speech. Given the blindness/madness such "seeing" risks, it would be a rare individual who could both "see" and speak. And it would be an even rarer individual who could speak beautifully, persuasively, prudently and moderately as well. *Logos* and *poiesis* rarely come together. They do in Plato in a way they did not in Socrates.

If Platonic philosophy, by which I mean political philosophy, is close to poetry, and Socrates is poetically defective as the *Phaedo* intimates, then Socrates cannot be the father of political philosophy. That honor is reserved for Plato. If Platonic political philosophy is a form of poetry, how can it be differentiated from other forms of poetry? In the *Republic* Plato gives different indications of an answer. First, the older poets were morally irresponsible. Second, they merely imitated the world of ordinary experience. Third, their speeches were entirely contradictory.

This issue can be approached from a different direction. Nietzsche opposes Dionysian poetry to an amusical philosophy. Dionysus is presented as the ground of inspired, intoxicated, unself-conscious creation *ex nihilo*. Dionysus is blind to the political and moral ramifications of what is created. Platonic poetry is a sober, moderate articulation of common natural experience, and a weaving together of natural types that would, if left entirely as they come from the hand of nature, be destructively in opposition to each other. Platonic poetry limits itself to moving within the confines of common experience and the natural world; it does not try to simply remake either. How the Platonic account of poetry relates to pre-Socratic poetry can be dealt with here only by way of an assertion. Homer, Hesiod, Pindar, the tragedians and comedic poets, also move within the orbit of ordinary experience. In depicting that experience, however, they provided no place for philosophy. In that respect, they had not grasped the whole. They were, therefore, incapable of adequately articulating and weaving together the whole in an appropriate way that could avoid being destructive of some of the parts.

Given the indication of Socrates's poetic inadequacy at the beginning of the *Phaedo*—we get other indications of this in the *Symposium*—we can conjecture that the Socrates of Plato's dialogues, who generates myths, is not the historical Socrates. The myth making Socrates is, again, a manifestation of Socrates "made young and beautiful." Further, the Socratic interrogation of *logoi* is potentially corrosive of common life—it destroys commitment to opinions without being able to replace them with anything. In this regard we must consider the large number of Socratic dialogues that end in *aporia*. Unless the Socratic method is moderated by the addition of a poetic element it remains problematic. It is Plato who makes that addition. Dialectic without poetry is corrosive; poetry without dialectical clarity is blind, limiting and contradictory. The Platonic addition of a poetic element to Socratic dialectic yields Platonic political philosophy, the architectonic science.[15]

In the *Phaedo* Socrates argues that philosophers love the soul and the objects that the soul alone can grasp. At one point he implies that the soul grasps these things directly, with Anaxagorean *nous*. We can speculate that there is another Platonic modification of Socratism at work. Socrates may have really thought that his dialectical method supplies all the steps of a ladder that leads all the way to the first things, without the need for an initial leap of "seeing." Plato sees many of the rungs missing, in need of being supplied by poetry.

The *Phaedrus* offers some support for this last speculation. In that dialogue, Plato's Socrates argues that writing is always a defective tool and backs up this understanding by never writing. Yet Plato wrote some of the most beautiful, philosophic poetry ever seen. Perhaps the refusal to write indicates that Socrates believed that the mediated, dialectical interrogation of *logoi* could lead all the way to the *arche*. Perhaps Plato believed that either a noetic leap was required at some point—a leap out of the speechless—or that poetry must provide surrogates for some of the rungs of the ladder.

The alleged Platonic "doctrine of the ideas" might be seen as one of those mythic rungs. Nonetheless it is also an elaboration of common experience. Our senses give us a multiplicity of data, yet what we perceive is "things," wholes qua ensembles. The hanging together of the separate qualities of sense data has to be explained. The doctrine of the ideas gives a poetic account plausible to common sense. As an apodictic doctrine, the doctrine of the ideas is easily assailable. But that is not its primary *raison d'etre*. Things as they present themselves in everyday perception point beyond themselves. So do speeches that attempt to articulate everyday experience. The Platonic dialogues demonstrate this. In the process, those dialogues with their interrogation of everyday perceptions show the way in which Plato still sees the locus of truth in everyday experience and not in statements alone. Socrates opened the door to this latter conclusion; Aristotle codified it. It is Heidegger who will again break open the obviousness of this conclusion. The important point is that it was no more obvious to Plato than to Heidegger.

In a sense the Platonic dialogues are rites of initiation. They can stimulate wonder and an ascent toward greater clarity of what is possible in the world and what is always at stake in our public doings—and for Plato that is the ground of political philosophy—but they cannot, nor do they intend to, demonstrate metaphysical, ontological or epistemological dogmas. Such dogmas would only be possible if an apodictic *logos* (logic) about the *arche* or first cause was possible. Even though philosophic *eros* points in that direction Plato questions whether such an apodictic *logos* is possible.

If the conclusion we have reached has merit, Plato cannot be the father of the history of metaphysics. That must be accomplished by someone else taking off from the Platonic dialogues with different assumptions, thereby radically transforming the Platonic understanding which informs the writing of dialogues and the synthesizing of the Socratic dialectic and poetry. If the metaphysical tradition of the West culminates in nihilism by dialectically destroying all traditions and values, as thinkers like Nietzsche, Heidegger and Derrida claim—a claim that is far from easy to state clearly, let alone prove— Plato cannot be seen as the cause. The cause must be traced to those who transformed Plato's **political philosophy** into a metaphysical, ontological or epistemological form of philosophy.

We should recall that it is Aristotle who is the father of the independence of logic. It is Aristotle who coins the term metaphysics. It is Aristotle who is the father of the separate sciences. It is Aristotle who radically differentiates theoretical from practical wisdom. Likewise, it is neo-Platonism that takes the discussions that form the initiatory rites of the Platonic dialogues and abstracts from them metaphysical and ontological teachings. It is the philosophers operating under the three great monotheistic religions that develop that tendency even more completely.

These were potential paths away from Plato, if one reads the dialogues in a certain way. They were not the only paths that could have been taken away from Plato. If the development of these metaphysical, ontological and epistemological readings of Plato leads to an impasse, it is still open to Western thought to return to Plato and strike off in a different direction. We can return to the point from which the questionable path originated. Plato is not proto-Aristotle, or proto-neo-Platonism, or proto-monotheistic *theo-logos.* Plato is the philosophic-poet who understands the necessary interdependence of pure philosophic *eros,* dialectic and poetry in a way the metaphysical tradition bent on the hegemony of an apodictic science of *logoi* never could. Plato is the founder of **political philosophy**. That foundation was accomplished by both borrowing from and transforming the legacy of Socrates.

Platonic political philosophy understands the necessity of the political horizon of human existence. And it is not just the human body that weds philosophy to the political horizon. That wedding is necessitated by the need to be grounded in *logoi* rather than risk silence. It proceeds from the recognition that autonomous thought cannot, ex *nihilo,* generate *logoi.* Political philosophy is not just the onerous, rhetorical necessity born of the need to defend oneself before the unphilosophic many. "Theory" and "practice" are inextricably linked.

There can be the continuity of a return to the origins that strikes off in novel directions. There is no need for the radical willing *ex nihilo* of Nietzsche, or the contentless, hopeful waiting in silence of the later Heidegger, or the dissolution of everything into the groundless, endless, aimless interpretation and reinterpretation of Derrida. The Platonic method of **political philosophy** can apply itself to the *logoi* of any time or place as long as those *logoi* retain a relation to a common shared experience. Only the explicit nature of the poetic articulation of the Platonic method needs to change over time.

NOTES

1. I will cite the Loeb translation by Harold North Fowler, occasionally amended: Plato, *Euthyphro, Apology, Crito, Phaedo, Phaedrus* (Cambridge: Harvard University Press, 1966).

2. If the latter, then Derrida is clearly wrong in thinking *muthos* and *logos* are simple opposites in the Platonic understanding. Cf. Jacques Derrida, "Plato's Pharmacy," in *Dissemination,* trans. Barbara Johnson (Chicago: University of Chicago Press, 1981), pp. 63–171. They may have been seen as opposites by the historical Socrates. For an extended discussion of Derrida on this topic see my "Cacophony or Silence: Derrida's Deconstructionism and the Possibility of Political Science."

3. Cf. Plato's "Epistle II," 314b4–314d, in *Timaeus, Critias, Cleitophon, Menexenus, Epistles,* trans. R. G. Bury (Cambridge: Harvard University Press, 1966).

4. Cf. Friedrich Nietzsche, "Twilight of the Idols," in *The Portable Nietzsche,* trans. Walter Kaufmann (New York: Penguin Books, 1980), esp. pp. 473–77.

5. Cf. W. K. C. Guthrie, *A History of Greek Philosophy* (Cambridge: Cambridge University Press, 1987), vol. IV, pp. 388–40.

6. Cf. Strauss's discussion of the origin of the idea of nature from reflections upon ordinary experience. Leo Strauss, *Natural Right and History* (Chicago: University of Chicago Press, 1968), pp. 81–119, esp. pp. 82–88.

7. Seth Benardete reaches the same conclusion in *Socrates' Second Sailing* (Chicago: University of Chicago Press, 1989), esp. pp. 1–5. See also Leo Strauss, *Xenophon's Socratic Discourse* (Ithaca: Cornell University Press, 1970), p. 149.

8. Cf. Leo Strauss, *Xenophon's Socrates* (Ithaca: Cornell University Press, 1972), pp. 116–26, esp. pp. 116–7, and also *Xenophon's Socratic Discourse,* 150.

9. Also a matter for conjecture is Plato's "unwritten doctrine." For our purposes we can observe that not only does it rely on hearsay to be established, but in its customary contemporary formulation it eschews in principle the explicitly stated method of interrogating *logoi.* Cf. Guthrie, *A History of Greek Philosophy*, vol. V, pp. 418–42.

10. Cf. Guthrie, *A History of Greek Philosophy*, vol. IV, pp. 350–52, and Aristotle, *Metaphysics*, 991a8–11.

11. Cf. note 3 above.

12. Cf. chapter 14 on the *Symposium.*

13. Cf. Leo Strauss, "On Classical Political Philosophy," in *What Is Political Philosophy* (Chicago: University of Chicago Press, 1988), p. 93. Strauss sees political philosophy as primarily a rhetorical defense of the philosophers and their purely philosophic doings before the political community. He also defines political philosophy as a subset of philosophy. Cf. "What Is Political Philosophy," pp. 10–11.

14. Consider here the implications of the weaving metaphor in the *Statesman.* One should also take into account that it is not put by Plato into the mouth of Socrates but rather an unnamed Eleatic Stranger.

15. Compare this with Aristotle's conclusion that **political science** is the architectonic science. *Nichomachean Ethics* 1094a15–109d–12. See also Leo Strauss, *City and Man* (Chicago: Rand McNally, 1964), esp. pp. 15–49 on who invented political philosophy and political science respectively.

Chapter Fourteen

Political Philosophy and Eros: Plato's Socrates in the *Symposium*

It is a commonplace to observe that Plato understood philosophy to be "erotic." For those looking for an understanding of philosophy that is neither analytic nor linguistic nor deconstructionist, and not "metaphysical" as that concept is now used in some circles as a term of opprobrium, erotic philosophy seems to offer an "existential" alternative. Regarding the primary textual document that must be confronted, the *Symposium*, Leo Strauss has asserted that the *Symposium* is not really about Eros, it is primarily about Socratic hubris.[1] I agree that Socrates and Socratism are primary issues. But I will argue that the *Symposium* **is** about Eros. It is a showing of the extent to which Socrates is no more erotic than he is poetic or Dionysian. When supplemented by evidence drawn from the *Phaedrus*, the parallel dialogue to the *Symposium* on the subject of Eros, we see that we have a subtle critique of Socrates and his conception of philosophy.[2] And we see Plato offering a different conception of philosophy than Socrates, which in fact does have elements of the erotic—even if philosophy is not simply reducible to Eros.

Throughout the Platonic corpus we are presented with a variety of metaphors for the nature of philosophy. We are told that philosophy **originates** in wonder (*thaumazein*). The dramatic Socrates likens philosophy to a form of midwifery. We also see philosophy described as a form of divinely inspired *mania*, a preparing to die, an ascent from the visible to the grasping of a pre-given set of intelligibles, a high level form of political rule by philosopher-kings, the action of a stinging fish (who awakens the morally somnambulant), the related image of the gadfly, a longing to know the first cause qua One (Idea of the Good), a form of Eros, a form of creation or *poiesis*, a form of "weaving." The list may not be exhaustive, but it is indicative of the variety of poetic intimations of the nature of philosophy offered in the Platonic dialogues. These intimations are **almost** always put in the mouth of Plato's dramatic character Socrates, occur at a specific point in a distinct dialogue, and serve a distinct dramatic purpose. We have no way of knowing whether the historical Socrates ever said any of these things. But when we look at the dramatic Socrates, we see that some of these intimations regarding philosophy fit his depicted behavior, others do not. And we suspect that upon reflection, these intimations cannot all be true simultaneously and cannot be synthesized into a coherent whole.

We have no other way to understand the ultimate status of these various intimations regarding the nature of philosophy than to take them one by one and see how they are informed by the surrounding drama and arguments in the particular dialogues in which they occur. But eventually we must compare the individual dialogues with others where different intimations occur. That said, we can nonetheless begin with some explicit hypotheses regarding how to sort out the various intimations and understandings.

A now traditional hypothesis—actually, in most instances it is merely an assertion or article of faith[3]—is that Socrates was primarily concerned with moral and political issues and that Plato was more "philosophical," understood as more theoretical, "metaphysical," ontological or cosmological. I do not accept this understanding and do not think it will stand up to scrutiny. My hypothesis is that both Plato and Socrates longed to be philosophers in the full sense. Among other things, that means that they were both questioning regarding the nature of philosophy itself at a time when its nature, and even whether it was good, was still very much an open question. I will hypothesize that Plato considered Socrates's reflections an advance over previous understandings of philosophy, most of which had not been explicitly articulated. But Plato also considered Socrates problematic. Others have reflected on the ways in which Socrates was morally and politically problematic. But I want to reflect on the ways in which he was philosophically problematic. I believe the *Symposium* is one of those dialogues where Plato is conducting that inspection.

But as we explore this hypothesis, we are quickly forced to confront the most difficult hermeneutic task when approaching Plato. Where do we find Plato, the author who says nothing in his own name; indeed, he only mentions his own name twice in all of the dialogues? What we most frequently have present for inspection is the **character** Socrates. It is, therefore, fairly enticing to simply take Socrates as Plato's spokesman.

But my hypothesis is that the two can be disentangled. Elsewhere,[4] I have more elaborately made the following argument, upon which I intend to build here. Plato once observed that his dramatic Socrates is a Socrates made young and beautiful.[5] Plato, in short, cleaned up the historical Socrates for dramatic purposes. But in the trilogy *Theaetetus, Sophist, Statesman*—which is intertwined in dramatic temporality with *Euthyphro, Apology, Crito,*

Phaedo—we get a depiction of the oldest Socrates. At the beginning of the *Theaetetus* Plato goes out his way to note that Socrates was ugly. If there were no deeper purpose, this would be a mean and gratuitous throwaway line. My suggestion is that this old and ugly Socrates of the Trilogy, and the temporally related dialogues, is the closest to the real Socrates that we ever see in the Platonic corpus.

I also suggest that very little of consequence changes between the philosophic aspirations of the dramatically youngest Socrates presented in the *Parmenides* and the old and ugly Socrates of the Trilogy.[6] Therefore, I conjecture that the earliest and latest dramatic Socrates more or less depict the real Socrates and actual Socratism. Elsewhere, in the dramatically middle aged Socrates, we have Socrates made young and beautiful.

It is in these dramatically "middle" dialogues that we get Plato's cosmetized Socrates. That beautified Socrates comes **closer** to carrying the dramatic burden of announcing Plato himself. In the *Symposium* we have the Socrates who consciously beautifies himself the most of any dialogue. But even in the "middle" dialogues one should not conclude that the dramatic Socrates is a simple spokesperson for Plato. In the middle dialogues Plato continues to carry out his critique of Socrates and Socratism. Finally, I want to argue that there remains **an element** of Socratism in Plato's final understanding of philosophy. But that element, which was for Plato **a part of the whole** that was philosophy, was the whole for Socrates. Socratism was narrow and limited. It needed to be emended and expanded.

PROLOGUE

The *Symposium* begins with a dramatic device that Plato uses with some frequency. The prologue to the dialogue takes place years after the event in question. Agathon has long since been forced to leave Athens and Alcibiades is dead. A dinner party had taken place shortly before the ill-fated Sicilian expedition and the associated profanation of the mysteries—in which Agathon-like Alcibiades was unfairly implicated. This flash forward prologue is a device also used in the Trilogy, and I believe it serves the same function in both cases. We get a chance to see what philosophy could have become after Socrates without the intervention of Plato.

The *Symposium* is related in the third person, and is traced to the memory of a certain Apollodoros. He announces that at the time of the event in question he was young and had been a follower of Socrates for only about three years. At the time of the retelling, he must be approaching middle to old age. As regards philosophy, Apollodoros shows himself to be a pedantic crank—he even somewhat proudly reports that two days before, Glaucon had called him "crazy" (*mantikos*). Apollodoros is openly disdainful of everyone who does not devote himself to philosophy in complete abstraction from any concern for reputation, wealth or political power. In this he appears to believe that he follows in the spirit of Socrates. Alcibiades will openly accuse Socrates of being disdainful in precisely this fashion. To what extent is Socrates responsible for followers like Apollodoros?

Apollodoros seems to have devoted his life to memorizing the speeches of Socrates and retelling the interactions he had with others. To put it mildly, this is a poor facsimile of philosophy. Without the **writings** of Plato, this is precisely what we would have to rely on for knowledge of Socrates. We will return below to the issue of writing and Eros, which is thematic in the *Phaedrus*. Socrates seems to have been responsible for this puppy like adoration on the part of more or less insubstantial human beings. Philosophy after Socrates could have turned into the wooden acts of memorization exemplified by "crazies" like Apollodoros, or remained dependent on the various "inspired," pre-articulate visions of the pre-Socratics which could not be defended or articulated in speech.

At the beginning of the *Symposium*, Apollodoros also mimics the beginning of the *Republic*. Just two days before the day that Apollodoros relates the events of the *Symposium* to an unnamed group of individuals, he states that he was going "up" to town when Glaucon, from behind, challenged him to wait.[7] Glaucon wanted to hear of the discussion that makes up the *Symposium*, albeit he mentions primarily wanting to hear the speeches of Agathon, Socrates and Alcibiades. (172a–b)[8] Years after the *Republic* took place, Glaucon was still interested in Socrates and his doings and speeches. Whether this is simultaneously a sign of continued interest in philosophy itself is hard to know. Glaucon had tried to get a retelling of events from a certain Phoenix, but Phoenix could not give a clear account. Glaucon apparently knew what Apollodoros asserts, that he, Apollodoros, had memorized the account by heart and had even gone to Socrates himself to fill in the details—the same thing happens in the Trilogy and forms the basis of the transmission of the account. Hence we assume Socrates could have challenged any details he thought were incorrect. The retelling is apparently correct from Socrates's perspective.[9]

Despite Apollodoros's apparently assiduous determination to get and memorize the speeches of the *Symposium*, his account is nonetheless made questionable by the fact that he got a good bit of it from another of Socrates's inconsequential followers, Aristodemus. Aristodemus is an unassuming man who also mimics Socrates by almost always going about barefooted. No one wishes to hear a speech by him and he seems to find this precisely as it should be. He was a silent auditor who hadn't been invited in the first place. Beyond his apparently limited acumen, his memory is anything but good. He forgot several speeches between the speeches of Phaedrus and Pausanias and he nodded off after the speech of Alcibiades, awakening only to see the last two participants fall asleep and Socrates head off to his daily regimen of interrogating individuals. Aristodemus is also one of the poorest drinkers. Aristodemus tells Apollodoros, who tells anyone who will listen. This could have been the history of philosophy, an oral history transmitted by cranks and groupies.

We have no clear example in the Platonic dialogues of anyone who followed Socrates who become philosophic: Plato himself is never a character in his dialogues. In the Platonic dialogues Socrates' avowed followers and admirers were limited individuals like Aristodemus and Apollodoros and well-intentioned yet hardly deep philosophers like Crito and Phaedo. His most interesting followers are men like Glaucon and Alcibiades. But there is no sign they became philosophers. For all his gifts, Alcibiades was politically problematic. More characteristic of Socrates's youthful followers perhaps is Glaucon's brother Antiphon who, we are told, turned to a preoccupation with horsemanship. Alcibiades turned to the pursuit of immortal fame but was ultimately a disaster for Athens.

As regards philosophy, the dramatic Socrates of the *Phaedrus* even points to Isocrates as his most promising student rather than Plato. Perhaps this is modesty on Plato's part. But then again he could have simply left out the reference to Isocrates unless he was in fact questioning Socrates's judgment. In the *Phaedrus* we also see Socrates actively seeking out Phaedrus and then uncharacteristically leading him out of town to a bucolic spot in the country to discuss Eros. How could Socrates possibly think he could learn anything of philosophic interest from Phaedrus, anymore than Euthyphro, Callicles, etc. etc.?[10]

What are we to make of Socrates' philosophic legacy as presented dramatically in the Platonic corpus? Are we to assume that he is merely a lover of speeches and, like Apollodoros, takes "immense delight in any . . . discourses, whether I speak them myself or hear them from others." (173c9–11) Is this really the wonder driven activity we are told is of the essence of philosophy (or erotic, or mantic, or inspired), or idle curiosity? Or is Nietzsche correct that Socrates invented a new form of *agon* that he could win because in the end, what he really wanted was honor and victories like most individuals? The dramatic Socrates is so enigmatic that we cannot answer these questions without looking very closely at the dialogues.

THE ORGANIZATION OF THE *SYMPOSIUM*

After the Prologue, there are some brief remarks that lead us to the various speeches. We will return to those remarks in a second. The speeches can be divided in a variety of ways. By my method, the first group includes Phaedrus,

Pausanias and Eryximachus. The second group includes the poets Aristophanes and Agathon. The third group includes Socrates and Alcibiades.[11] To divide in this fashion captures the importance of several interesting issues regarding the seating arrangements and the fluidity in the order of the speeches. First, there were several nameless individuals sitting between Phaedrus and Pausanias who spoke but whose speeches are not reported because those speeches were not remembered by Aristodemus and are not recorded even though Apollodoros went to Socrates to fill in his transcript—whether written or entirely memorized. Second, we have Aristodemus, who unlike the forgotten group of nameless speakers, is named but does not speak. He is apparently seated next to Eryximachus. Third, by following the seating order, Aristophanes was to have spoken after Pausanias except that Plato forces him to have hiccups and to delay until after Eryximachus. Finally, Alcibiades enters and sits between Socrates and Agathon even though he gives the last speech.

As regards the change of speaking position of Aristophanes, Leo Strauss has argued that this dramatic device signals that Plato believes that the two speeches are interchangeable.[12] I do not accept that reading. Once we add the unexpected speech of Alcibiades, and delete the forgotten speakers and Aristodemus, Aristophanes is moved to the **central** position with three speeches preceding his own and three after. I think it is precisely this centrality that Plato is emphasizing, while simultaneously having some fun at Aristophanes's expense getting even for the *Clouds* by rendering him laughable and the pawn of natural forces. I am going to suggest, again contrary to Strauss's reading, that Plato's Aristophanes stands for the necessity of piety based on fear as the foundation of the city and the family—positions that are also espoused in the *Clouds*.

Aristophanes is also the first speaker to give any legitimate status to heterosexuality, leaving it equal with homosexuality and lesbianism. In Socrates's retelling of the wisdom of Diotima, by comparison, heterosexuality and procreation, hence the family, are raised to an even more important position. Heterosexuality as the basis of the family is intimately related to the existence and well being of the *polis*. I will accept that Plato also shows how Aristophanes' ultimate understanding goes beyond piety and the primacy of heterosexuality and the family, showing thereby his views as in some ways pious frauds on Aristophanes' part. Still, his speech is central for the importance it gives to the family, religion and the *polis*.

Aristophanes's speech is central but, I will argue, not the highest. Following a hypothesis shared by others, I will argue that the speeches represent an ascent. But what this means is that in some fashion the speech of Alcibiades, being last, is highest, or at the very least, a necessary part of the whole. That leads us to a fourth issue. Like Aristophanes, Alcibiades's seating position and order in speaking are not identical. This calls attention to the importance of Alcibiades as it does to the centrality of Aristophanes. Alcibiades speaks last but sits between Socrates and Agathon. The speaking position points to Alcibiades being highest in some respect; his seating position in some fashion mitigates that. We will have to see what this means.

The various speeches are followed by a dramatic descent into chaos as the drunken mob breaks in from the street. At the end, the first speakers, and worst drinkers, have left, the chaos has died down, Alcibiades has presumably passed out, and Agathon, Aristophanes and Socrates are left discussing whether the same poet can do tragedy and comedy.[13] That Alcibiades has apparently succumbed to drink is perhaps another mitigation of his being simply highest—even though he has consumed a super-human amount of wine—the last doses of which are quaffed by the pitcher-full. The dignity of the Dionysian aside, self-consciousness has its virtues.

The dialogue as a whole is surrounded by indications of the breakdown of order and ultimate chaos. Aristodemus arrives uninvited. Agathon tells the servants to act as if they were the hosts and serve in any order they wish—an inversion of the aristocratic relation between servant and master. There is a democratic, consensual arrangement on the subject matter of the speeches and their order—together with an agreement to drink moderately—that Socrates ignores and Alcibiades tyrannically overthrows when he arrives uninvited.

Dramatic elements of the Dionysian overcoming of individual selfhood surround the dialogue from the flute girl that the anti-Dionysian Eryximachus[14] bids to leave, to Alcibiades's wreath that he eventually shares with Socrates and Agathon.[15] Then total chaos breaks out when the mob breaks through the door. We see a dramatic movement from moderation to excess, from hierarchical aristocratic order to democratic consensus to tyranny to chaos that parallels the descent of regimes depicted toward the end of the *Republic*. The speeches **ascend**, the political and moral order **descends**. Assuming this tells us more than that the Owl of Minerva takes flight at dusk, we will need to reflect on the ramifications of this inverse relation between intellectual and moral/political virtue.

Finally, we are told that when Socrates inadvertently runs into Aristodemus, he was fresh from the bath and wearing his best pair of slippers. This is very rare for Socrates. He has beautified himself and has even donned footwear. This is the beautiful and younger Socrates of my premise. When Socrates was tutored by Diotima, he was roughly as young as the Socrates of the *Parmenides*. In the *Symposium*, we see a Socrates who was still relatively young to middle aged and one who beautified himself. But dramatically we never see a Socrates who is simultaneously simply young and beautiful. Finally,

Socrates states that he beautified himself "to be a match for my handsome host." (174b2) Socrates is going to the house of Agathon with relish and open anticipation. It is Agathon, the recent victor who most interests him.

The evening depicted in the *Symposium* takes place out of the public arena, a private engagement, after dark. Socrates had purposely eschewed the public celebrations the day before because he "feared the crowd." In the *Apology,* Socrates admits that he never learned to speak persuasively to large crowds. Socrates is not ideally suited to a democracy. Socrates does better indoors, with the accomplished few, after dark, one on one. We are reminded of the difference between indoor and outdoor teachings in the *Clouds*. Even Aristophanes knew that Socrates's indoor teaching was different than the outdoor perception of philosophy that he, Aristophanes, both fostered and derided.

PHAEDRUS, PAUSANIAS AND ERYXIMACHUS: THE COSMOLOGY OF SELF-INTEREST

Each of the first three speakers fashions his speech to foster his personal interest. Phaedrus is young, attractive and an aspirant to being beloved. (See 178a–180b) He is not himself passionate, Dionysian or erotic. He wants to set the parameters for his courtship for the sake of a calculating self-interest. Pausanias is an older, not altogether attractive lover who is neither wealthy nor politically powerful. Hence he argues the case for a gentlemanly and virtuous lover. Eryximachus is an older lover and a doctor. He argues for the centrality of his art in the possibility of happiness. In the process, all three reduce Eros to a natural or cosmological principle rather than a personal or divine force. The cosmological accounts ascend in sophistication culminating in Erxyimachus's version of the teaching of Empendocles.[16]

Citing Hesiod, Acusilaus and Parmenides, Phaedrus argues that Eros is one of the oldest cosmic principles and probably ungenerated. As such, Eros is a first cause or first principle (*arche*), one of the very first things to emerge from Chaos—i.e., it emerged *ex nihilo* in the literal sense, Chaos being a form of no-thinged-ness. As such Eros is associated with order and beauty—i.e., the emergence of a Cosmos. With the emergence of Eros *ex nihilo*, Cosmos replaces Chaos. Hence Phaedrus argues that Eros is the cause of the greatest good—unsullied by any evil. Eros is for Phaedrus an all-encompassing monistic force that brings the good to mankind more than conventional goods like kinship, the glory of office or wealth. Hence, sensible persons should follow their erotic longings (a form of "inspiration") and find a beloved. Phaedrus presents himself as such a candidate. He wants lovers. But as an aspiring beloved, he has to admit that he is not himself a lover, and hence not inspired by Eros. He is simply calculating.[17] Phaedrus wants lovers to compete to give good things to him.[18]

Phaedrus is calculating, but also prudent and a conventional lover of virtue, especially courage and manliness. Hence Phaedrus links Eros with shame and ambition for the noble. He argues that both individuals and cities need these qualities. Manly and courageous lovers make the best citizens. An army made of lovers would never run in the face of the enemy because of the shame they would feel before their beloveds. Lovers engage in a mutual rivalry for honor—honor as an erotic good is something to which we return later in the dialogue, but it will eventually be divorced from the political in the everyday sense in which Phaedrus is concerned.

Many of the speakers in the *Symposium* are effete, dilettantish and largely apolitical. The first and the last, Phaedrus and Alcibiades are the exceptions to the rule. Socrates, we learn from the remarks of Alcibiades, has a certain toughness in battle and in enduring the natural elements. But that toughness appears to emanate from a kind of numbness rather than manliness *per se*. But Phaedrus openly admires toughness, manliness and courage. Phaedrus presents Eros as the cause of the "fury inspired" in the heroes who would consent to die for each other bringing honor and praise from the gods. This gives Phaedrus the opportunity to link up with and incorporate arguments from traditional Greek poetry. Still, Phaedrus is not himself a poetic innovator. And as one of the worst drinkers, Phaedrus is about the least Dionysian of the speakers.[19] The quintessential erotician and Dionysian is the last speaker, Alcibiades. Interestingly, Alcibiades gives no theoretical account of the whole whatsoever. As the calculating beloved, Phaedrus is the least inspired and erotic of the speakers. Likewise, his monistic cosmology is the least successful theoretical account of any of the speakers, as Pausanias immediately makes clear.

There were several speakers between Phaedrus and Pausanias, so it is significant that Pausanias wants to go back and specifically address Phaedrus. (See 180b–185e) Pausanias is a lover, and Phaedrus, along with Agathon, is an object of his interest. As a lover, Pausanias counts among those who are, unlike Phaedrus, inspired by Eros. But he is an extremely conventional man lacking in daring. Like Phaedrus who appeals to traditional Greek poetry and myth for what passes for the foundation of his account—and that is a form of *nomos* qua Greek custom—Pausanias appeals to actual law and customary practice in present Athens to ground his discussion. Pausanias is an overt conventionalist.

As a fellow cosmologist, Pausanias sees that Phaedrus's version of monism cannot explain the whole because it cannot explain the shameful and ignoble. Hence Pausanias posits that there are two forces that operate, both of them forms of Eros, one praiseworthy and one not. The praiseworthy form of Eros is the older. Like Phaedrus, in traditional fashion, Pausanias associates the old and the good. The ignoble form of Eros is younger and popular—the preserve of the *demos*. Pausanias draws the distinction between aristocracy and democracy, and as a gentleman, argues for the former and that it has a cosmic support. For Phaedrus the whole/nature was one and uniform. For Pausanias, the whole is twofold and hierarchical. Aristocracy requires a cosmological support in a hierarchical given.

Pausanias introduces hierarchical considerations into the distinction between Eros as it operates between women and men, and men and men, as well as between the body and the soul and between those individuals with and without *nous*—i.e., mind or intellect. Other than Socrates/Diotima, Pausanias is the only speaker explicitly to introduce mind into the equation—Agathon will do so implicitly. Yet ultimately, rather than following through and grounding his various hierarchies entirely in a cosmology, he grounds them in law and custom without discussing the relationship between cosmology and law.

Pausanias tries to argue that love of men, the soul and the mind are the higher forms of Eros and in fact this is what the Athenians believe, if they only knew it. But the fact that what he really wants is the attractive bodies of aristocratic young men is all too clear. Pausanias is a calculating man who tries to mask his true desire under a gentlemanly subterfuge. He tries to link his claim for being chosen by a beloved to higher phenomena like friendship, philosophy and "lofty notions." He is trying to play his only card—his gentlemanliness—because he is not young, attractive, rich, politically connected in the democracy, poetic or philosophical. Hence he argues that a thoughtful beloved will choose a virtuous gentleman over a well-connected, rich, powerful democrat, or any other claimant. (184e–185b)

While his cosmological dualism is a theoretical improvement over Phaedrus's monism, his account has all manner contradictions. And while he specifically raises the issue of law and convention—and hence of the relation between nature and convention—which Phaedrus does not, he can in no way integrate his cosmology and his conventionalism. The speech of Aristophanes will attempt to integrate nature and convention. Pausanias moves back and forth between cosmology and the law as his foundation in contradictory ways. And in the end he makes it clear that neither works completely in supporting his self-interest as a lover. He even makes it clear that he wants some emendations to custom, especially as regards the suspicions of the fathers as regards the lovers of their sons.[20] But he can in no way ground those innovations in anything but his self-interested desire. He has no poetic creativity.

In the end, Pausanias's appeals to cosmology, law, philosophy and hierarchy all collapse. And unlike Phaedrus, Pausanias is utterly effete and unmanly. Like Phaedrus, as one of the poorest drinkers, he is un-Dionysian. Despite trying to present himself as a virtuous man, he points out the lengths to which Eros can push even the only moderately erotic in the direction of immorality and vulgar calculations. It is perhaps not surprising therefore that while Eryximachus adopts the cosmological dualism of Pausanias, he drops the noble/base, higher/lower distinctions. He will base his claims on such things as "harmony" and happiness, not nobility or virtue. The doctor is no gentleman.

Eryximachus presents a dualistic, mechanistic, naturalistic, cosmological argument. (See 186a–189b) Like Pausanias he is a lover trying to make his case. He argues that he deserves preference because only a doctor can bring happiness. For Eryximachus, Eros is not a god and is not an impulse found in souls but is a force that operates entirely in bodies. In fact it operates in everything that is, implying that the doctor believes that everything is body. But Eros, as bodily drive, is in fact two separate drives. Medicine, "our great mystery," knows how to foster the one drive and hinder the other. The result is harmony or health. Without the intervention of the doctor, there would be no cosmic harmony. Nature is at odds with itself. The doctor creates agreement among things that are by nature at variance thereby creating mutual love and unanimity—the greatest good. It is art, not nature that is responsible for the good—a position that will be shared in different ways by the two poets.

Since love in its two manifestations operates in all things, without doctors there would be no good anywhere in the morally indifferent cosmos which is in fact at odds with itself as well as with the human good. Hence one should seek the company of doctors, not gentlemen, if one wants the good. Therein Eryximachus makes his case as a lover. If one wants to be happy one must be well ordered and the doctor brings order. And by consorting with the already well-ordered one avoids the emergence of disorder. One should therefore indulge well-ordered men as a means to one's own self-interest. We do not need myth, law, religion, music or philosophy to become well ordered. It is the doctor who is the god-like creature who completes and harmonizes what is by nature disorderly, not to say cosmically blind, dumb and immoral. Doctors take the place of gods. Eros is not a god, it is a blind, disorderly set of forces.

Eryximachus has announced the importance of art. Art, not nature, brings the good. For the sake of a formula, we can say that Phaedrus takes his stand on nature, Pausanias on law and custom, Eryximachus on art. We can assume that this movement represents an assent in Plato's eyes. But Eryximachus's account suffers from all manner of difficulties, especially from the perspective of self-interest. It is not at all clear how his cosmological account preferences pederasty as he desires. If harmony is produced by a doctor out of an original natural opposition, this seems to point to heterosexuality. Bringing harmony to opposites is what brings order. If all of nature were moved by the love of similars for each other (homosexuality) there would be no natural disorder for art to overcome. Indeed, if only similars congregated together, the cosmos, which presumably requires opposition, would collapse. That would be a collapse into nothingness or chaos. Only a harmony constructed out of opposites would lead to a Cosmos. Eryximachus unwittingly leads us to the doorstep of the conclusion that pederasty while perhaps good is unnatural and its victory would lead to chaos. The confirmed pederast would need to support heterosexuality out of self-interest.[21] Eryximachus's cosmology and self-interest are not altogether consistent.

Eryximachus could perhaps fall back on the argument that if nature is inadequate for happiness, then art is forced to supply the good entirely out of itself. His thoroughgoing naturalism seems to foreclose that possibility. And then he would have to explain the good on the basis of some other premise than harmony. Eryximachus has provided us with a more cosmologically sophisticated teaching than Phaedrus, but he comes close to making the human things dissolve. The total reign of Necessity—as Agathon will make clear—leaves no room for the human. For our purposes, we can leave matters at the conclusion that ultimately cosmology, especially of a purely naturalistic form, points beyond itself. The same can be said for the principle of calculating self-interest.

THE CENTRALITY OF ARISTOPHANES

Plato accentuates Aristophanes's centrality by a comic device that has him overcome by a violent force over which he has no control. But there is more going on with this dramatic device than accentuating Aristophanes's centrality or a payback for the *Clouds*. Following the advice of Eryximachus, Aristophanes cures his hiccups by opposing their violent motion with another violent motion, sneezing. This success occurs only after none of the less violent measures suggested by Eryximachus worked. This represents an admission that there is something to the doctor's purely materialistic art. And it is a concession to the cosmic importance of motion. It is a further concession to the efficacy of the conjunction of like things bringing harmony, in this case two violent motions opposed to each other. Plato seems to be silently indicating that a better man than Eryximachus might have been able to make more out of his cosmological position that he did.

Be that as it may, with the speech of Aristophanes we get something altogether different, as Aristophanes asserts. (See 189c–194e) We begin not with nature, law or cosmological principles, but the fallen nature of man—a religious premise. Aristophanes does not try to link this fallen nature with any cosmic principle. He relates it to our own hubris and desire to rival the gods. It is precisely such an attempt to rival the gods that is manifested in Eryximachus's aspirations for medicine. Piety, based on self-interested fear, dictates that we not move in this direction.

The advice resulting from Aristophanes's story seems to be straightforward—do not attempt to rival the traditional gods. Piety, based on fear, **not love**, is required for us to achieve the most happiness of which we are capable. Furthermore, Eros is not a god or cosmological principle, it is a sign of our fallen state, of our **longing** for a lost oneness—in this there is some, at least superficial, overlap with the forthcoming speech Socrates attributes to Diotima. The good is to be found in a longed for, if impossible, return to a lost golden age and a lost unity. Aristophanes seems to be counseling that one should not try to raise man, Eros or cosmic principles above the status of personal, providential gods. This appears to be a very conservative teaching—do not innovate regarding religion, nor attempt to replace religion with science. Art should be in the service of religion and religion should know the proper place of fear and piety. Plato's Aristophanes appears to arrive at the same conclusion we reach in the *Clouds* where one of the traditional gods arrives at the end to restore order after Socrates's hubristic, rationalist, atheistic house of philosophy is destroyed.

Further, Aristophanes seems to make all forms of Eros, including heterosexuality, equal. He admits that in our fallen state we no longer beget upon the Earth and therefore heterosexual Eros is solely responsible for the continuation of the race. This gives heterosexuality a certain pride of place it did not have in the first three speeches. The other forms of Eros are justified by the fact that they bring satiety to longing such that individuals can get on with ordinary life. For Aristophanes, that ordinary life seems to have its locus primarily in domestic life (*oikos*) rather than political life (*polis*). There seems to be a praise of the domestic over the political, especially if the political involves the search for personal greatness and glory or collective empire. Happiness is found in finding a mate and achieving as much domestic oneness as possible. At its peak, the political strives for immortal glory and, in that attempt, tries to rival the gods.

But for all its surface piety, there is much that might be considered impious in Aristophanes's "theology," were it not for the fact that he remains committed to the traditional depiction of the gods, especially as personally involved gods. This is true despite the fact that the traditional depiction is the invention of the older poets, as Agathon will make clear. But Aristophanes apparently believes that it is better to venerate the old rather than challenge it through innovation. This is part of his lowering of the status of honor and the longing for glory, e.g., the poetic kind Agathon will espouse. That longing, presented as a form of Eros by Diotima, leads either to a more creative, innovative poetry, the political or philosophy. Aristophanes lowers the status of all three as being at odds with **human** happiness.

The conservative Aristophanes accepts the gods as traditionally presented even though they are not beautiful, just or intrinsically loveable. They are jealous and fractious to say nothing of fearful and resentful of rivals. And they are dependent—they do not abolish the primordial, hubristic humans because they need observances and honors from them. Aristophanes will not censor the traditional depictions as would the Socrates of the *Republic*, nor emend traditional theology as the more daring Agathon attempts by giving us a personal god of love rather than fear. What Aristophanes wants of his gods is a source of fear to uphold the law and impose limits. But he does not really want the law of imperial Athens. He longs for pre-imperial virtue, the virtue of the rustic fighters of Marathon.

Aristophanes does not want to use art to cure the natural situation. He wants to use his art to accommodate human beings to their natural situation. That situation is one of alienation and lack of wholeness. It is a situation moved inarticulately—Aristophanes's lovers do not even know precisely what it is they want, primarily the desire to attain wholeness. But that desire is a tragic longing. It is rarely accomplished and then only for brief periods. Eros longs for unity and completeness, not honor or glory, or even primarily other bodies. Were Eros successful, it would lead to the loss of self, the same as the victory of the Dionysian. The good is the overcoming of the self, and of the individuation it implies, not the heightening of individual consciousness as is true for both philosophy and the longing for glory.

Aristophanes asserts that it is primarily those who were originally whole males who go into public careers. They are the sources of the political. As to heterosexuality, he observes that it leads to various forms of vice, from adultery to incest. But in the end, all Eros is the same, understood as a longing for unity on the part of the soul. Any hierarchical differences between souls are conventional. The *polis* should at most represent a minimal extension of the domestic, which is grounded in the natural longing for the **private** pursuit of wholeness. Hence just as we should not innovate in theology but accept the traditional gods, in politics we should not innovate and turn the political into a stage to pursue glory equal to the gods. Eros points toward the love of one's own, but understood primarily as the private pursuit of wholeness. Wholeness is not possible in the *polis*. The old primordial state is the good, but the private, not the public, is the primary arena of the good.

Nowhere does Aristophanes extol or even add mind (*nous*) to the equation. Thought is not the path to wholeness, it is based on something inarticulate that prospers in the domestic arena. Eros is not a cosmic principle in all things. Eros is merely a human phenomenon, not even part of the animal kingdom as it will be for Agathon. Aristophanes eschews cosmology, it smacks of mind. He encourages human beings to accept their natural condition and attend to human affairs. But the human affairs that are pertinent do not include philosophy, or a politics of personal or imperial glory. Aristophanes has raised the bar by opening the door to discussion of the relation between the *oikos* and the *polis*. But in the end, despite his praise of piety and convention, he shows that the private, domestic pursuits are the means to as much happiness as is possible, albeit rarely. The comic poet presents a tragic picture. Human happiness is rarely possible. To shoot higher than that rare happiness is to miss out on the limited possibilities available to human beings. Man is not by nature a political or philosophic being, or a being capable of satisfaction.

AGATHON: POETRY AND INNOVATION

We know that the historical Agathon was a minor figure. He was a tragic poet at the moment of the decay and dissolution of that art form. And on first inspection, Plato's dramatic Agathon **seems** to present a light and merely pleasing speech that is somewhat frivolous and fatuous. It is tempting therefore to put our first impression of the dramatic Agathon together with what we know of the historical Agathon and dismiss his speech as that of a lightweight. But what the dramatic Agathon suggests is very daring and in many different ways a movement in the direction of Socrates. That is what makes his speech higher than that of his fellow poet Aristophanes. (194e–201c)

Agathon possesses a higher, more expansive and more profound understanding of the place of poetry in the whole. Diotima's account integrates into a whole more of the parts intimated by previous speakers than anyone else—homosexuality, heterosexuality, the *polis*, love of honor and mind. **But the dramatic Socrates who is the mouthpiece for her wisdom is not erotic and is incapable of poetry. He too is simply incapable of grasping important parts of the human situation or of how to integrate them.** Since the human is part of the larger whole, Socrates cannot therefore adequately grasp/fashion the whole. Hence Socrates does simply stand at the peak. To grasp the human as part of the whole, one must descend from the lofty height of self-forgetting, motionless contemplation, for which Socrates longs, and understand the place of poetry.

Agathon is the most daring and innovative speaker yet. He alone gives manifestation to the older (and highest) meaning of poetry (*poiesis*) as a form of creation or making. And other than the existentially impervious and numb Socrates, he is the best drinker, the last to nod off. Hence he is the most Dionysian—seemingly more so than the dramatic embodiment of the Dionysian, Alcibiades, who drops off before him. And despite being a tragic poet, he will offer a very optimistic vision, a beautiful illusion. Nietzsche to the contrary notwithstanding, Agathon's vision is more optimistic than that of the dramatic Socrates. That said, Agathon is also the most Socratic of the speakers. Agathon is the first to argue that one should begin with what Eros itself is and only then proceed to its effects. What is Eros? Agathon adopts a version of the Socratic "what is" question.[22]

Contrary to the assertions of previous speakers that Eros is the oldest of gods/principles, Agathon asserts that he is the youngest. He comes into being after the cosmic gods and the Olympians. Coming last, Eros rules the Olympians and the cosmic gods/principles. Yet he has no parents, he is un-generated. Since he has no parents, yet did not exist before the Olympians came to power, he springs forth *ex nihilo*. Oldness is not for Agathon a basis for ruling. The old is not the good, Agathon rejects the conservative premise of Aristophanes. The newest represents the good.

The good, it will turn out, is the most beautiful and civilizing. Agathon questions the old, e.g., Hesiod and Parmenides. They both confused Eros and Necessity, as did the first three cosmologists. Eros comes after and replaces Necessity. Necessity is the basis of violence and disorder. Eros brings order, beauty and civility even to the Olympian gods. To that extent, Eros as brought forth by Agathon replaces and rules the Olympian gods. The older state of man, like Hobbes's state of nature, is unfit for the pursuit of the human good. Art must overcome that prior disorder and violence.

Agathon asserts that Eros **is**, as well as stands for, beauty, delicacy, pliancy, youth, softness, etc. Agathon also asserts that Eros would need a poet such as Homer to properly set forth his qualities. Agathon sees himself as that poet. Despite the piety he shows toward him, Homer is a poet implicated in the ear-lier depiction of the gods as violent. Homer, and the other traditional poets, depicted the Olympians gelding and imprisoning their parents and behaving violently and unjustly toward each other. "Aforetime . . . there were many strange doings among the gods, as legend tells, because of the dominion of Necessity. But since [Eros] arose, the loving of beautiful things has brought all kinds of benefits both to gods and to men." (197b5-8)

Agathon's poetry replaces Homer's with a new depiction of the gods. The new poetry gives us a god of love, beauty and civility. That a newer god can rule the older gods, and move us from fear and violence to love and civility, is the sign of possible progress and the need for creative innovation not pious veneration of the past. Aristophanes limits himself and his art to venerating the past despite seeing the problematic nature of the traditional gods. For Agathon, neither Necessity nor Tradition should rule. Agathon, like the Socrates of the *Republic,* sees that the good requires the renovation of the tra-ditional picture of the gods. Love and beauty are to take the place of violence and fear as the foundations of human order. These foundations, like the god

Eros, spring forth *ex nihilo* from the creativity of an Agathon. As with Eryximachus, art corrects what is given and brings the good. But it is a different art, one that works on the soul not the body.

That the poets create the gods out of nothing is due to their love of beauty and civility. At least this will be true of those poets who come after the birth of Eros—after Agathon. Homer, and previous poets as well, were not clear-sighted devotees of Eros. Agathon is a clear-sighted and self-conscious actor/creator—again bringing him closer to philosophy, if not closer to the ultimate philosophic longing of Socrates for contemplative self-immolation. Agathon argues that it is primarily the love of the beautiful that is indicative of Eros, a premise to which Socrates/Diotima will return. But Agathon also argues that Eros is a love of glory and fame—likewise a premise to which Socrates/Diotima will return, albeit to recast Agathon's understanding of immortal glory as the love of immortality as pointing ultimately to a love of eternality.[23]

Socrates does not pursue immortal **fame**—which Agathon makes clear requires written works—through a poetic bringing of order. Socrates is more given to motionless, passive staring at what is posited as an **eternal** order that is already existent by nature. Socrates feels no need to bring order and abstracts from the very undertaking. But if that order needs to be created first, Socrates becomes dependent upon a prior poet.

Agathon argues that Eros—and by extension the truly artful poet—never uses nor is the victim of violence. Eros has no need to give or take injury because he/it operates entirely on souls not bodies. Eros—as well as the erotic poet—is by nature pliant, which means capable of moving quietly and secretly in and out of the souls of men without being noticed. The erotic poet, while more self-conscious than previous poets, operates on an inarticulate, subconscious level to move men's souls. He does not operate on the level of self-conscious mind. Love always operates to bring willing service without reliance on fear.[24] Given that no pleasure is stronger than love, it can allegedly rule all the other pleasures and drives, limiting them and bringing temperate control. As a purely physical love it makes little sense to present the strongest desire as the basis of self-control. As the love of beauty and honor this makes sense. Agathon seems to abstract from bodily desire just as he abstracts from self-conscious mind. He wishes to operate entirely on the sub-conscious **soul**.

Like Eryximachus, Agathon praises his art. But Agathon makes a far more comprehensive claim for his art. He claims that it creates all forms of life—by which he means all forms of truly human life. (197a3) Nature is formless, only poetry brings form. Hence everyone is dependent on the making of the poet and ruled by him. But as Agathon makes clear there are always competing poets. There are the older poets with their gods and the newer poets and their gods. The poets contest with each other like gods to rule the human realm. And for Agathon, Eros is a principle that rules primarily in the human realm—albeit also among animals—but not in the larger cosmic realm where Necessity rules. Agathon introduces a distinction between a creative human realm of Freedom ruled by poets and the realm of Necessity.

Agathon proves Aristophanes's suggestion that some men aspire to be gods. But he implies that to refuse to do so locks us into the realm of Necessity and leads to ugliness and violence. In Agathon's vision, the ugliness and violence of Necessity cannot be subdued by any merely bodily regimen or restraint based on piety and fear. One needs a god of love. Even Aristophanes sees that the originators of the Olympian gods are the traditional poets. He does not want to see them overthrown because they are a source of order. Aristophanes is unwilling to innovate in the hopes of a better principle of order. He is the quintessential conservative. Innovation always makes things worse.

Agathon is an innovator. He does not see the past as a golden age. The past, the natural condition, is one of savage Necessity. Order comes later and is of poetic origin. Higher forms of order come last. The good is associated more with the end of the process than the beginning. The good is not the old, it is a *telos*, which does not, however, actualize itself. We can construct order, rather than simply manipulate Necessity, because it is possible to operate on the soul independently. Hence Eros alone can cast out alienation. But for Agathon, unlike Aristophanes, it is alienation from others, not self-alienation that takes precedence. But this overcoming is possible only by significantly abstracting from bodily love in the name of the love of beauty, honor and glory. Yet Agathon's account is severed from courage and manliness, just as it is severed from the collective pursuit of glory. Agathon's position, while it could ultimately be the ground of the political, is nonetheless almost largely apolitical. Agathon abstracts from the political because he tries to abstract from Necessity and fear. In the process, bodily *eros*, as the basis of the family, is ignored.

SOCRATES'S REPETITION OF DIOTIMA'S WISDOM

Before Socrates begins to relate his youthful exchanges with Diotima there is an interlude in which he engages Agathon in a dialectical exchange. Socrates gets Agathon to admit a premise of Diotima's teaching that Eros himself is different from the object(s) of his longing. This means that Eros is not himself a god and does not possess any of the qualities he longs for or fosters. Eros is precisely a sign of deficiency and lack, a premise reminiscent of Aristophanes's presentation albeit as we will see, not the same. We have gone from Eros being the oldest and all-encompassing **force**, to the oldest **god**, to the youngest god, to **no** god at all.

Apparently, given his seeming acceptance of Diotima's teaching, Socrates is altogether comfortable with this progression. This lowering of the status of Eros is part of Diotima's theological innovation in which the highest gods become perfect possessors of the objects for which Eros longs. As such, the gods cease to have any incentive to act toward each other or man. They become eternal, but also inert. The perfection of the gods goes hand in hand with their inertia and indifference. They become at best objects of contemplation.

Socrates gets Agathon to confess that he didn't know what he was talking about in attributing the various grand qualities to Eros. But Agathon gives up too quickly, and fails to recognize just how significant his position really is. Diotima's teaching will reinforce its significance, which rests on the centrality of poetry. With his all too quick capitulation, Socrates dramatically secures a victory over Agathon before even offering his required presentation. (201b–c) Philosophy seems, thereby, to defeat poetry. But how substantial is this victory?

Before he makes his presentation, Plato shows Socrates's determination to win a quick victory over Agathon and therewith his attempt to reverse the popular victories Agathon had scored both before the *demos*, and on the evening in question before the few. Socrates cannot sway the many, he is no gentleman, and he demonstrates both his pugnacity and bad form. He is willing to admit only that Agathon's presentation was "pleasing." Of Agathon's speech Socrates says that substantively the greater part of it was not very astounding. Socrates ignores the other speakers and goes after his host, reducing the evening to a one on one *agon*. This is more than a dramatic confrontation between philosophy and poetry, it is a sign that Socrates is **resentful** of Agathon's success. Socrates proceeds from *ressentiment*.

At the end of his rendering of Diotima's teaching (201d–212b), Socrates does not receive the same uproarious applause afforded to Agathon by everyone assembled. Agathon knows how to move both gentlemen and the *demos*. Socrates receives polite applause from everyone except Aristophanes who wishes to raise an objection but is cut off by the riotous entrance of Alcibiades and his entourage. Plato will not allow Aristophanes to offer an objection to Socrates's effort. Plato limits his objections to Socrates to those that can be gleaned from the drama.

Socrates asserts that at the beginning of the evening he believed that he would have success in giving his speech because he knew he would speak the truth. With cranky bad form he observes that it now appears that the form of the presentation takes precedence over its truth in the eyes of those assembled. Socrates is openly miffed that Agathon got such a strong reception. Hence he refuses to play the game by the rules previously established. He engages Agathon in dialectic rather than giving a speech as previously agreed.

He tries to shift the playing field to one where he usually wins. There seems to be a contest afoot and it is primarily between Agathon and Socrates, innovative poetry and static, contemplative philosophy. (222c–223b) Socrates enjoined the contest between poetry and philosophy in the *Republic* as well. But in the *Symposium*, Plato will not allow Socrates to be such a clear-cut winner. Poetry remains standing at the end of the day, perhaps victorious.

We are struck by the extent to which Plato's Socrates does not even pretend to create (*poiesis*) a speech of his own. He simply reports, and at times summarizes, a series of discussions he had with a Mantinean women named Diotima when he was a young man. (201d–212b) Thereby, Diotima becomes, as it were, the only woman (the flute girl is thrown out at the beginning) and the only foreigner at the discussion. Socrates praises her daimonic (not godlike) capacities for having helped delay the plague at Athens for ten years. Unfortunately, that delay caused the outbreak of the plague to occur at a crucial moment during the Peloponnesian War. In short, the delay was of dubious value. Later Socrates will, more than once, call Diotima one of "our perfect professors" (*sophistai*). To call her a sophist is a dubious form of praise. It is not clear how highly Socrates regards her.

Socrates reports that Diotima was skeptical that he could become a devotee of Eros. Socrates reports that she offered him initiation rites which she doubted he could follow. It is an odd relationship that Plato has dramatically constructed between Socrates and Diotima. Yet her teaching, initially delivered in dialectical form—switching over to long, assertive speeches—passes for Socrates's presentation. Why doesn't Plato allow Socrates to simply speak in his own name? Does this not indicate that Socrates is utterly devoid of poetic ability, just as he has no personal knowledge of erotic longing, and is in no way moved by Dionysus? And to top it all off, he is resentful of his host and goes for trivial and superficial victories.

In separate dialogues, Plato presents Diotima and Parmenides as the teachers of the young Socrates. It is not clear what he actually learned from either.[25] In the *Symposium* we are told by Socrates that it is from Diotima that he learned all he now knows of love-matters. Apparently he has no other access to the subject, including his own experience, as Alcibiades's presentation makes clear. Socrates does assert that Diotima cured him of belief in opinions like those of Agathon, i.e., that Eros was a god. This is an opinion Socrates claims he held as a young man but has now grown out of, unlike Agathon.

One of the first things we learn is that the young Socrates not only believed, as did Agathon, that Eros was a god, he also believed in the existence of opposites[26] He claims Diotima talked him out of both commitments. But one would presume that the dialectical method as deployed by Socrates would have as one of its central premises the principle of non-contradiction. The old Socrates of the Trilogy[27] still appears to believe in the existence of opposites so it is not clear that Diotima's teaching had any lasting effect. The old Socrates of the *Phaedo* uses the existence of opposites as the basis of one of his "proofs." Diotima argues that there are, however, possibilities that exist between apparent opposites. If one is not beautiful, for example, one is not thereby ugly. Likewise, between knowledge and ignorance exists "right opinion"—the possible existence of which Socrates "refutes" in the *Theaetetus*. And there is the possibility of something between mortals and gods, a *daimon* like Eros.

Throughout the *Phaedrus*, but especially in the palinode, it is stressed that Socrates sits under and is subservient to the inspiration of Plato—i.e., the tree that overarches the discussants. In several senses to which we will return, without Plato's *poiesis*, Socrates cannot exist. Plato suggests that a Socrates tutored by Plato might succeed where a Socrates tutored by Parmenides and Diotima did not. Such a Socrates would not have to be replaced as he is by the Eleatic Stranger in the Trilogy. In the end, Socrates has to be subservient to someone else because he possesses no Eros, poetry, inspiration or capacity for the Dionysian. Socrates does not represent an autonomous possibility. The same is true of dialectic by itself.

According to Diotima, Eros was generated. He is the progeny of Resource (plentiful and wise) and Poverty (unwise and resourceless but cunning).[28] He was conceived during a celebration put on by the gods to honor Aphrodite's birth.[29] In effect, Poverty raped Resource and gave birth to Eros. Since Eros is generated, bodily desire and intercourse clearly antedate his birth. Perhaps Aphrodite is associated with bodily longing, with Eros more associated with spiritual longing—albeit this is not entirely clear. What Eros becomes is a longing for what is desirable but is lacking—the good. Eros is responsible for Diotima's famous ladder of love, presumably all of its rungs. Eros is desirous of many but not all good things—not things like wealth. Diotima argues that Eros is "desirous and competent of wisdom" as well as "artful speech." (203d5) Eros is a philosopher and rhetorician. Neither gods nor the ignorant pursue wisdom. Neither feels defective or lacking. The philosopher is neither a god nor ignorant. Socrates is surely shown to be defective as a rhetorician.[30]

While Eros is the love of the good—a longing Diotima says is common to all human beings—it is, according to Diotima, catalyzed by beauty. Hence Agathon is partly correct in linking Eros and beauty. Eros longs for beauty and the good in the hopes of gaining happiness, understood as the cessation of want and longing. But we long to have these things be ours forever, hence we long for immortality. Eros is a longing for the good, the beautiful and the immortal. Hence we long for wisdom only to the extent that it is perceived to bring us the good, the beautiful and immortality. Wisdom is not an end in itself.

Diotima then makes a jump to the issue of poetry. She says that like Eros, *poiesis* refers to many phenomena, many forms of making. But poetry is customarily applied only to the making that employs music. And Eros is usually linked with physical desire and longing. On the level of the body one can gain a semblance of immortality through one's offspring and the continuation of one's bloodline after death. But this is not the only way to pursue immortality. On the level of noble pursuits/deeds and beautiful *logoi* one can gain a reputation and glory that lives on beyond one's death. In glory one gains immortality. Socrates cared for neither children nor public glory, at least not in any conventional sense. And he left no *logos* of his own in writing.

Of poetry Diotima says: "[P]oetry is more than a single thing. For of anything whatever that passes from not being into being the whole cause is composing or poetry." (205b8) Poetry is the cause of things coming into being from out of nothing. Eros on the other hand, by being generated does not spring forth *ex nihilo*. The linkage between Eros and poetry is to be found in Diotima's claim that Eros is a form of begetting on beautiful bodies and souls. Procreating deals with the bodies, poetry with the souls. Eros is the cause of poetry's longing for the good, the beautiful and the immortal by acting on souls using beautiful creations. Diotima approaches the centrality of poetry that Agathon had already presented. Poetry is a creating and forming *ex nihilo* driven by a longing for beauty and immortality.

While it is not her highest concern, Diotima gives a centrality to bodily procreation that no one so far has, not even Aristophanes. With that centrality she grounds the importance of the family—not as the prerequisite for the *polis*, but for the immortality of the species. The *polis*, she asserts, has its foundation in poetry and a different form of longing for immortality. Diotima asserts that all mortal men seek to be immortal. Mortals will sacrifice their lives in the name of their progeny, especially their poetic progeny.[31] As regards all of this, Plato forces his dramatic Socrates to admit that he just does not get it. (206b8) Socrates does not understand this longing for **immortality**. He understands only the desire for the **eternal**, something entirely different. One must grant that longing for immortality will not capture the eternal. One's bloodline can come to an end. One's civilization can end and with it memory of its greatest political and poetic deeds. The Eros for the eternally true seems to offer less contingency than the longing for immortality. However, it can be sustained only as long as the mortal being remains alive.

By gaining oneness with the eternal, one achieves eternality in one's lifetime. But with death comes the cessation of consciousness and the cessation of oneness—unless, of course, the individual soul is eternal, and Diotima makes no such claim. Aristophanes had argued that Eros was a longing for wholeness to be accomplished on a primarily bodily level. It was a tragic longing. Success would bring with it the cessation of individual self-consciousness. By attempting oneness on the level of body, Aristophanes had no need to implicate mind. In the longing for the eternal, Eros is a longing for oneness, albeit with the eternal truths in oneness with individual mind. Were one to accomplish that oneness with the eternal through mind, one would likewise bring about the cessation of self-consciousness. If wisdom is self-understanding—Know thy**self**—then it is only possible by remaining a self. Aristophanes and Socrates long for self-immolation.

What Socrates seems to like most about Diotima's presentation is that it culminates in postulating the motionless overcoming of self in the oneness of individual mind and the eternal. But this conclusion is not central to her main teaching. It comes as part of a final "initiation rite" which she is clear she doubts Socrates will understand. Diotima's primary teaching focuses on pro-creation and poetry. Socrates cares nothing for the Eros that leads to honor and glory or children. His longing would undermine the forms of Eros that bring one back to oneself in the *oikos* and *polis*.

Hegel argued that the origin of individual self-consciousness is to be found in desire, which brings one back from contemplating external objects. Only those forms of Eros that rest on **personal** desire bring one back to oneself. As we see in the Trilogy, Socrates, the midwife, aborts but cannot beget. He negates poetic creativity, which both Agathon and Diotima make clear is the basis of the beautiful things, including those with which Socrates longs to gain contemplative oneness. In undermining the family and honor, and therewith the *polis*,[32] Socrates undermines attachment to one's own but also undermines the generation of the objects he longs to contemplate.

Given the disdain of Socrates for the concerns of the world that Alcibiades discusses and the resentment he shows toward Agathon, he undermines the creativity that is necessary even for the contemplative.[33] Socrates's one-dimensional longing is tragic and world denying. Unfortunately, without an Eros that implicates mind, the other forms of Eros can be blind. To be sanguine, Eros must not exist only in one of its forms; all of its manifestations must be integrated. That task can only be performed by a poetry informed by mind.

Somehow the unity that is needed is to integrate passionate loving and mind without losing self. It would require an integration of the poetic longing of Agathon and the theoretical longing of Socrates and an intimate actual knowledge of the erotic as contained in Alcibiades. **The high must inform the low without replacing or obliterating it.** Alcibiades is the speaker who forces us to remember this. Even as the quintessential devotee of Eros and Dionysus, he is highly self-conscious, even when extremely drunk. He makes it clear that he is ruled by an element of mind. But his love of the opinion of the demos ultimately makes an appropriate unity of drives impossible for him. Somehow mind (philosophy) and passion (Eros) and creativity (poetry) must be bound together. No one in the dialogue achieves that unity and integration. The mistake is to believe that Socrates comes closest. In many ways it is in fact Alcibiades—hence his speech is last.

Socrates is so moved by Diotima's Eros of mind that he does not write/create, he does not love procreation, other bodies, or his own *polis*. This is not because of the purity of his Eros, but because of his lack of desire and *poiesis*. Yet his competitiveness shows he has *thumos*. Socrates also has wonder (*thaumazein*). Throughout the Diotima section Socrates keeps saying that he "wonders" regarding this and that. Diotima keeps telling him to quit wondering.[34] To make wonder the basis of wisdom rather than Eros is to make a passive emotion take the place of an active one. Wonder seems to inevitably point toward a passive, static staring and contemplation directed at what are alleged to be eternal, self-standing objects. To the extent that those objects are the creations of the poets they are anything but self-standing and the wonder driven contemplative philosopher is anything but self-sufficient.

Diotima argues that both the body and the soul are in constant flux throughout our lives. Even what passes for knowledge is never the same from moment to moment due to forgetting and relearning. All mortal things are involved in this constant replacement. It is this that makes us long for immortality, the only cessation of the flux possible. A soul in constant flux could never incorporate eternal self-standing entities even if they existed. If Diotima is correct, such a oneness is a chimera. Hence we must all beget, including the creation of beautiful conceptions. And this forms a link that binds mankind into a possible community of friends. Diotima appears to have in mind here a community of philosophic and poetic friends in one's lifetime, and a community with those in the future made possible by what is left behind by poets and philosophers, both of whom are likened to legislators like Lycurgus, but on a very comprehensive plane. Such friendship presupposes writing. Socrates does not write. Oneness with the eternal can be achieved without writing; immortality cannot.

Diotima concludes with her initiation rites aimed at Socrates. It represents a last ditch attempt to see if Socrates can be saved. Diotima doubts it. There are eight steps on her initiatory ladder of Eros. 1. Longing for the beautiful body of one particular person. 2. A longing for and love of all beautiful bodies. 3. The longing for and love of beautiful souls. 4. The longing for and love of beautiful observances and laws. 5. The longing for and love of beautiful forms of knowledge. 6. Philosophic contemplation of pure conceptions. 7. The longing for and love of a single form of pure beauty. 8. The longing for and love of every beautiful form independent and by itself. (210a–c)

Socrates already longs for the top rungs. The initiation is to be found in the lower rungs and the realization that **there is no ladder without all of the**

rungs. Socrates wishes to leap to the top of the ladder. Socratic dialectic to the contrary notwithstanding, Plato makes it clear that he thinks Socrates longed to leap directly to the contemplation of the things at the top of this ladder. Socrates assumed they existed and did not need to be created. Dialectic could never get there by slow steps, a leap was always implied. So why did Socrates really turn to dialectic, or his "second sailing"? Was dialectic just a tool for gaining victories and assuaging his resentment?

Socrates ends by saying that "I am persuaded by this." He claims he honors all love matters. Alcibiades puts the lie to the fact that he honors **all** love matters. One must assume that the only things to which Socrates is actually persuaded are the higher rungs of Diotima's initiatory ladder. In the end, Diotima was no more successful with Socrates than Parmenides. At the end of Socrates's life, when the issues of the place of politics, and of the nature of philosophy, are at stake, Plato replaces the old and ugly Socrates with the Eleatic Stranger. That speaks volumes.

ALCIBIADES: THE EROTIC, POLITICAL AND DIONYSIAN MAN

Alcibiades's speech (214e–222b) lets us see what is defective and missing in Socrates. The *Symposium* would be incomplete without his arrival and his speech. In short, Socrates does not understand the strictly human because he has no first-hand experience of it. Socrates is not a whole human being. By sitting between Agathon and Socrates, Alcibiades reinforces what is implied in his speech. Agathon and Socrates are the two phenomena that have to be synthesized—the passionate and the detached, *poiesis* and individual mind. That synthesis, may look more like a reformed Alcibiades than either Socrates or Agathon.

When Alcibiades arrives, Agathon bids him to come and sit near him "as a third." Besides himself and Alcibiades, the third is Socrates whom Alcibiades initially does not see. Agathon is clear that the three of them are the only ones who count. After overturning the previous consensual arrangements, Alcibiades proposes to praise Socrates instead of Eros. He says specifically that he will use images in the service of conveying the truth—i.e., a form of poetry. He uses the images of the Silenus and the satyr Marsyas. His account is inspired by wine, with his inebriation vouching for his being forthcoming. And Socrates is bid to speak up if Alcibiades says anything that isn't true. Socrates will speak only at the end to mitigate Alcibiades's advice to Agathon to stay away from Socrates. As to Alcibiades' speech itself, Socrates's silence appears to endorse its truthfulness. And there is no indication that Socrates is in any fashion embarrassed by it.

The "speech" of Alcibiades is the only presentation that has no theoretical component. As the last, and in some fashion, highest speech it points to the fact that detached theoretical contemplation is not the highest activity.[35] Alcibiades gives us one of the keenest looks at the real Socrates we ever get. The Trilogy may give us a closer look at his principles, but Socrates himself is revealed most intimately in the *Symposium.* We see a Socrates who claims to be erotic but is not; just as in the *Phaedrus* we see a Socrates who claims to be inspired, possessed of *mania*, but is not. In the *Phaedo* we see a Socrates who is apoetic.

Alcibiades observes that Socrates produces a frenzy in others but is all coolness and moderation himself. Even what appears to be courage, endurance and manliness is no more than lack of strong emotions. Socrates is disdainful of those who experience the strong passions and emotions that he does not. He is disdainful and that is what should bring him to trial, not that he corrupts anyone. In the words of Alcibiades, "gentlemen of the jury . . . you are here to try Socrates for his lofty disdain." (219c6) Alcibiades is passionately drawn to Socrates, but like Phaedrus, Socrates is the unmoved beloved. In a variety of ways, the *Symposium*, and the Platonic corpus as a whole, show Socrates to be, like Phaedrus, a cool, calculating utilitarian.

Alcibiades reports that in response to his sexual advances, Socrates coldly responded that his (Socrates's) inner beauty was greater than Alcibiades's external beauty of form (*eidos*) and hence to trade his goods for those of Alcibiades would be a bad trade. Socrates discussed the matter as if it was a business transaction. On Alcibiades's behalf, we can observe that what he really wanted from Socrates was wisdom and truth, not sexual gratification. His love of Socrates is a sign of his love of wisdom, of his philosophic nature. Alcibiades was prepared to trade the good of the body for the good of the soul.

But eventually Alcibiades's erotic and Dionysian traits prevailed and he gave up on Socrates and pursued a political life.[36] One wonders what would have happened if Socrates had taken him into his philosophic confidence—if Socrates was capable of that. Alcibiades needed Socrates to complete himself. But Socrates likewise needs the erotic traits of Alcibiades to complete himself. Alcibiades and Socrates needed each other to supply their missing half. But contrary to Aristophanes, it is unlike halves that need to be brought together. Likewise, Socrates and Agathon need each other to supply mind and poetic ability respectively.

Alcibiades is not only embarrassingly forthcoming, given his advanced inebriation, but he may actually grasp the true Socrates more clearly than even he consciously knew. In likening Socrates to a Silenus—ugly on the outside, divine and beautiful on the inside—he makes it clear that whatever one sees on the outside (*eidos*) is not the truth. One cannot proceed from or through the *eidē* (or speeches about *eidē*) to the truth as Socrates presumes to do with his dialectical method. In Alcibiades's eyes, like the Silenus, Socrates is mock erotic on the outside but all moderation (*sophrosyne*) on the inside.[37]

Throughout Alcibiades's discussion, as is true of the Socrates/Diotima section, words related to *thaumazein* like wondrous, amazing, astonishing keep coming up until it forms a steady drumbeat. Alcibiades reports that in both his deeds and his speeches Socrates has no comparison, ancient or modern. In this he is amazing and astonishing. As regards his speeches, their mundane exterior makes Socrates laughable—ungentlemanly. He starts with dreary and insignificant things and tries to ascend to the truth. Diotima advised him to start from beautiful bodies and ascend from there. Socrates appears not to have gotten the point that you cannot ascend from the ugly to the beautiful. And there is no incentive to contemplation if the ultimate object is not beautiful. And yet for all the banality of the subjects he discusses, Alcibiades admits that the speeches of Socrates intoxicate precisely for their uniqueness. They do not intoxicate for their wisdom. Like Agathon, Alcibiades reveres novelty.

As regards deeds, Socrates amazed Alcibiades in battle. He once saved Alcibiades's life and eschewed the honor that was due. More amazing in the eyes of Alcibiades were Socrates's actions during retreat when the army had been routed. He moved like a proud strutting goose looking lazily in all directions. But it turned out that this had a utilitarian purpose, a man adopting such an attitude is, according to the general Alcibiades, the last to be attacked. But the most wondrous and amazing deed in Alcibiades's eyes happened on one campaign when Socrates stood motionless, contemplating from dawn one day to dawn the next.[38] This reproduces Socrates' motionless contemplation on the way to Agathon's house. There is little motion in his soul to begin with, and then he ascends to motionless contemplation at a time of war with violent motion all around him. This is amazing for it is without precedent. Again, it is not Socrates's wisdom that intoxicated spectators and caused wonder and awe, but his utter uniqueness. It is not that he was divine, it was that he was unlike any other human being.

If it is true that Alcibiades and Socrates need each other to be complete, the fact that Alcibiades is more open to the things Socrates represents than vice versa may well show that an Alcibiades is a better subject upon which to work an ultimate synthesis. Which is more likely as a point of departure, an Alcibiades made wise and self-controlled or a Socrates made young and beautiful?

In the end, the intrusion of the unruly crowd brings us back to the importance of the poets and legislators and the need to create a basis for order to hold off chaos. Like the flute-playing Marsyas, Socrates can intoxicate the few but he can have no effect on the many. As regards Marsyas, Strauss makes the tantalizing observation that he was defeated and flayed by Apollo.[39] As is Marsyas, Socrates is in his own way defeated by Apollo. Socrates has to be supplemented by someone who can bring order and beauty, thus fashioning a cosmos out of chaos. Socrates is neither Dionysian nor Apollonian. That he can cause frenzy in his listeners, even with the mere use of prose exercised on mundane subjects, shows that Socrates can at least have an effect on others, but it is a problematic effect. Perhaps, therefore, Alcibiades was wise in turning away from the Siren-like speeches of Socrates that pulled him away from concern for the affairs of the *polis*, making him feel guilty for even thinking about political engagement. Lofty disdain for beauty, wealth and honor are not unmitigated virtues if they are the grounds of order, a dam against the intrusion of chaos.

CONCLUSION

Viewed in light of what we have discovered in the *Symposium*, the *Phaedrus* offers a perfect sequel. It is a **sequel** to the extent that the Socrates of the *Phaedrus* is older than in the *Symposium*—older than both the young Socrates who met Diotima and the Socrates who actually attended the diner. The *Phaedrus* thematically addresses the relation between Eros and Writing. The *Symposium* makes clear why these seemingly heterogeneous subjects in fact necessarily go together. Eros points to the centrality of *poiesis* which when linked to the issue of immortality points toward the necessity of writing. Socrates does not write and in the *Phaedrus* he tries to make a virtue of the fact. Plato does not agree as is shown by the simple fact that this is related in a written text. The *Phaedrus* even shares the character Phaedrus with the *Symposium*, highlighting him by naming the dialogue after him.

The *Phaedrus* also makes clear Socrates's ultimate dependence. Socrates claims to be "inspired" in his first speech. But it is pedestrian and even he admits it. Throughout that first speech, Socrates covers his head both out of shame and to block out his surroundings. With his eyes open in the palinode, now under the inspiration of his surroundings, which includes the spreading arms of Plato represented by the tree under which they sit (*platanos*), **shielded from the sun**, Socrates actually offers a beautiful speech. That he could give a beautiful speech was entirely the doing of Plato. But that he is there in the first place is the doing of Phaedrus. Socrates almost never left the city, and when he did, as in the *Republic*, it was never to go out into nature as is the case in the *Phaedrus*. Socrates was an urban intellectual, not an aficionado of the rustic and natural.

From the *Symposium* we know that Phaedrus is a fairly superficial, calculating, unpoetic, unerotic, un-Dionysian man. He is most assuredly not wise nor does he posses or praise mind. It is utterly perplexing why Socrates should seek out such a man and then follow him out of the city and into the natural surroundings in such uncharacteristic fashion. The answer is found in Phaedrus's statement that he (Phaedrus) is a lover of speeches. So is Socrates. He knows that Phaedrus has with him a speech by Lysias. Lysias's speech turns out to be right up the pedestrian and calculating Phaedrus's alley. It self-interestedly tries to argue that a potential beloved should choose a non-lover—someone without passion—over a true lover. But clearly, Lysias's alleged non-lover wants the same things as any other lover. The speech manifests a trivial cleverness. Phaedrus' speech in the *Symposium* shows us he is prone to admire just that kind of calculating cleverness. After listening to Lysias's speech, Socrates moves immediately to "refute" it with an equally banal speech of his own. And as is predictable given his nature, Phaedrus likes it and Socrates achieves an easy victory. Even more than being a lover of speeches, Socrates is a lover of winning victories in speech. That is the only effect of the speech of Socrates not under the influence of Plato.

Plato goes beyond that speech to force his dramatic Socrates to negate it with a poetic speech inspired by Plato. In that speech, Plato poetically vindicates Diotima's main teaching. He poetically supplies the beautiful and eternal objects outside the cosmos as an object of erotic longing. But in the chariot image in the Platonically inspired palinode, Plato shows the importance of integrating pure physical desire—it is the horse that does most of the heavy lifting in the ascent to the vault of heaven—poetic Eros—the other horse—and mind, represented by the charioteer. Only as a team, with the three elements synthesized, is an ascent possible. Plato likewise shows the tragic extent to which the strenuous longing to rise can yield but the briefest and most fleeting visions. The active ascent is not allowed to yield a static staring as Socrates wishes. There is no Socratic motionlessness in palinode. There is much motion, longing and striving. That is the difference between Plato's understanding and that of Socrates.

In the *Phaedrus*, Plato simultaneously completes, amends and extends his picture of what Socrates represented. What Socrates represented was in some respects vulgar—his *resentiment* and longing for shallow victories. In other respects what he represented was an advance over pre-Socratic thought especially the discursive elements represented by his commitment to dialectic. That discursive element is important as part of a whole even if it may have been largely no more than a combative tool for Socrates himself. And Socrates's longing to jump to motionless oneness with unchangeable eternals—a longing that could not be squared with his dialectical method—provided Plato with a serviceable **public** image for philosophy as part of his Platonic defense of philosophy.

But Plato also supplies an understanding of the things that are lacking in Socrates. That includes a passionate understanding of the human things, the *poiesis* necessary to supply objects of longing for humanity, and the wisdom and mind to know how to fashion into a whole the parts which—some having to be invented—do not automatically fashion themselves into a whole even if they exist independently.[40] In short, Plato supplies us with the basis for a cosmos where otherwise there would only be a chaos. **This creating and synthesizing is political philosophy understood as proto-philosophy.** Plato invented it. Socrates could not. Political philosophy so understood stands higher and is more comprehensive than philosophy understood as motionless static staring at indifferent, unchanging realities. Plato as political philosopher and textbook Platonism are two entirely different things. As synthesizing, poetic pro-philosophy, political philosophy is as possible now as it was in the time of Plato.

NOTES

1. Leo Strauss, *Leo Strauss on Plato's Symposium*, edited with a foreword by Seth Benardete (Chicago: University of Chicago Press, 2001).

2. The *Phaedrus* can be treated as a sequel to the *Symposium* given that the dramatic Socrates of the *Symposium*—especially at the time he received his instruction from Diotima—is younger than the dramatic Socrates of the *Phaedrus*.

3. To believe that we can arrive at final assertions about Plato that are the truth, the whole truth and nothing but the truth is a mistake when dealing with a literary form like the dialogue. One of my hypotheses is that Plato absolutely did not want to reduce philosophy to a set of pure assertions. Put another way, for Plato philosophy cannot be reduced to logic, analysis or linguistic exposition—albeit they may have their place to play in a larger whole. Philosophy is an ongoing doing and questioning, as is depicted in the Platonic dialogues.

4. See chapter 16: "Between Platonism and Postmodernism: Plato's Emendation of Socratism in the Trilogy."

5. See Plato's Second letter.

6. See the next chapter: "Plato's *Parmenides*: Socratism and the Origins of Platonic Political Philosophy."

7. For what it is worth, the retelling took place while Apollodoros and others **walked** up to town. That is to say, unlike the *Phaedrus* that is rendered while sitting and at rest, here we have motion. Dramatically, and reinforced by the speech of Alcibiades, we find that Socrates was much given to moments of motionlessness and rest. Thinking and the cessation of motion are conjoined in Socrates. Being and motion are thematically conjoined in the Trilogy. *Eros*, assuredly, is a form of motion.

8. Plato, *The Symposium*, trans. by W. R. M. Lamb (Cambridge, MA: Harvard University Press, 1925). Glaucon demonstrates thereby the same discrimination regarding the most important speeches that most readers come to accept.

9. Alcibiades also challenges Socrates to speak up if anything he says is incorrect. Socrates remains silent.

10. The dialogues that Plato has Socrates actively initiate—unlike dialogues such as the *Republic* that are dramatically forced upon him—raise questions regarding why Socrates would seek out such individuals. His only encounter with a fellow philosopher is his youthful encounter with Parmenides who quite uncharacteristically defeats and silences him.

11. This division can be made on the basis of shared premises. The first three attempt cosmological accounts in the service of calculating self-interest. The second two are poets. Socrates and Alcibiades in effect have the subject of Socrates as their shared premise. Strauss divides the speeches into three groups with Phaedrus in a group by himself, then Pausanias, Eryximachus, and Aristophanes, and finally, Agathon, Socrates and Alcibiades. Ultimately, I do not think either of these distinctions gets to the heart of the matter. See *Leo Strauss on Plato's Symposium.*

12. See *Leo Strauss on Plato's Symposium.*

13. The interpretation of tragedy and comedy can no doubt be said of the speech of Aristophanes, but on a higher level it is undoubtedly true of Plato as well. Whether Socrates is depicted as the anti-tragic, rationalist, optimist, what Nietzsche would make of him is an open question.

14. Eryximachus not only sends the Dionysian flute girl away, but gives a particularly anti-Dionysian account of drinking as harmful to man.

15. There is an exchange between Agathon and Socrates where Socrates chides Agathon that wisdom cannot be obtained by osmosis—i.e., by merely sitting next to him. Agathon responds that at another time they will have to go to court on this—invoking the eventual trial and death of Socrates—with Dionysus as judge, not the democratic majority. Socrates does assert that he tries to understand nothing but love matters but there is no dramatic indication of this any more than that he is Dionysian. Socrates is never affected by drink. Plato's Socrates does assert that it is Aristophanes who divides his allegiance between Dionysos and Aphrodite. But it is Alcibiades who gives manifestation to both.

16. The linkage of mechanistic cosmological accounts with the centrality of self-interest in moral and political matters is indicative of a variety of modern authors, e.g., Spinoza and Hobbes. That the first three speeches in the *Symposium* are followed in ascending order by those of the poets Aristophanes and Agathon and those of Socrates and Alcibiades is indicative of a Platonic rejection of the modern approach. By that I mean that Plato rejects both the political and moral primacy of self-interest and the reduction of philosophy to cosmology whether monistic, dualistic or pluralistic.

17. We see the same thing in the *Phaedrus* where Phaedrus praises to Socrates a vulgar and calculating speech on Eros by Lysias. All the other speakers—with Socrates remaining somewhat problematic—appear to be lovers in one sense or another. Even Aristedemos and Apollodoros love Socrates.

18. A similar picture of Phaedrus emerges in the *Phaedrus.* He is greatly taken by a calculating speech of Lysias, to the effect that one should choose as a lover a non-lover. Of course this is the calculating of an actual lover trying to present himself as a non-lover. Phaedrus admires this kind of self-interested speech. It is not clear that this calculating self-interest goes together with Phaedrus's admiration for manliness and courage. Hobbes is undoubtedly clearer in this respect.

19. Given that Phaedrus is a young and attractive, yet unerotic, calculating, un-Dionysian dilettante, all manner of questions are raised as to why in the *Phaedrus* Socrates specifically seeks him out and leads him off into the country for a *tête-à-tête*. What is Socrates's incentive? If Socrates is not physically moved by the vastly more substantial and equally attractive Alcibiades, how could he be moved by an insubstantial, pretty-boy airhead?

20. Pausanias is by **nature** inclined toward youngsters even though the *nomos* forbids it. He will not completely follow nature because of his fear of the fathers and his fear of conventional opprobrium. Pausanias is in no way daring. But he ultimately understands that nature, not law, signals the good.

21. We have in no way exhausted the cosmological issue in the first three speeches. But the cosmological difficulties need not detain us at this point for they are not central to our present interests.

22. He also sees goodness in the same four virtues Socrates presents in the *Republic*: justice, moderation, courage and wisdom (*sophia*).

23. Hannah Arendt has argued that the longing for immortality and the longing to grasp the eternal are two different things, inappropriately merged by Socrates. The one presupposes action, the other detached contemplation. We will have to see how this fits in at the appropriate moment. But there seems to be something to this distinction in the *Symposium*. Agathon is concerned only with immortal glory. Contemplative oneness with the eternal does not interest him.

24. One suspects that on some level Aristophanes is correct that the total elimination of fear would not be sanguine. But total reliance on it is not sanguine either. That fear and love must be balanced is why poetry must be supplemented by politics.

25. See chapter 15 on the *Parmenides* below.

26. It seems impossible that there could be something between mortality and immortality. Yet the poetic position of Diotima requires this element. Like Socrates, Diotima uses dialectic, but she supplements it with poetic long speeches, which Socrates does not. This points to Socrates's deficiency and is part of what is needed to cosmetize Socrates to make him young and beautiful. The young Socrates believed in things like Agathon. Diotima weaned him of those, but the poetic element apparently never took.

27. See chapter 16 on Plato's Trilogy below.

28. Descent from Poverty makes Eros hard, poor, parched, homeless and shoeless. We recall that Aristodemus, as is usually true of Socrates, arrives shoeless. In many ways all of the above characteristics, especially the oddly included shoelessness, seem to refer to Socrates, and the man who mimics him.

29. We are told that there was no wine at the celebration for Aphrodite—only nectar—hence there was no Dionysus. Eros precedes Dionysus.

30. One should consider here the *Apology,* where Socrates admits as much, but especially the *Gorgias*. While Socrates has some success with Polus, he fails with Callicles.

31. Agreeing to some extent with Nietzsche, against Locke and Hobbes, Diotima asserts that the most comprehensive drive in human beings is not self-preservation—or for that matter, wisdom or justice.

32. In Socrates's report of Diotima's position, there is only the vaguest feint in the direction of the *polis*. It comes simultaneously with a bow to homosexuality. Socrates reports that Diotima observed that it is men who go into the public arena. It is the love of the beautiful bodies of other men that leads them to the love of beautiful pursuits and honor. It makes it sound as if the *polis* is dependent upon homosexuals and that all poets and founders are homosexual. Whether Diotima had a more complete teaching regarding the political or not, Socrates chose not to report it and it is a subject from which his presentation largely abstracts. Socrates is not moved by the forms of *eros* that lead to love of one's own—linking with the body, the procreation of children and the love of honor and the *polis*. He cares about the good and the beautiful, but only if they are eternal. He leaves no place for familial love or justice except, perhaps, as inert ideas.

33. Is it Diotima's teaching that the "eternal" ideas, like the gods, are created by the poetic Eros that longs for the beautiful and immortal glory? Apparently.

34. He especially wonders if the argument about the longing for immortality via procreation and poetry can be true, as opposed to the longing for oneness with the eternal. See (208a–209d).

35. Put another way, it is not self-sufficient. It is dependent on prior activities.

36. In the two short dialogues Alcibiades I and II we see Socrates actively following and seeking out Alcibiades with the plan of dissuading him from going into political life. But it is not clear what his motivation was—to save Alcibiades, to save Athens, or to divert Alcibiades to philosophy. In those two dialogues, the latter seems to be the least persuasive motivation.

37. One might note Aristotle's distinction between "moderation" as discussed in Book III of the *Nichomachean Ethics* and "self-control" as discussed in Book VII. The self-controlled person has strong desires but still controls them. The moderate person has weak desires. Socrates appears to have no desires. Being moderate under the circumstances is not a sign of virtue but of existential numbness. In that vein, Alcibiades asserts that no matter how much he drinks, Socrates has never been seen drunk, and the ending of the *Symposium* bears this out dramatically.

38. We are told that he then said a prayer to the sun and went about his business. If this is the sun as depicted in the allegory of the cave in the *Republic*, we have an intimation of the object of Socrates' contemplation.

39. See *Leo Strauss on Plato's Symposium.*

40. We reach a similar outcome with the active "weaving" metaphor of the Eleatic Stranger in the Trilogy.

Chapter Fifteen

Plato's *Parmenides*: Socratism and the Origins of Platonic Political Philosophy

There is something in . . . Plato that does not really belong to Plato but is merely encountered in his philosophy . . . namely, the Socratism for which he was really too noble. . . . Plato did everything he could in order to read something refined and noble into the proposition of his teacher—above all himself. He was the most audacious of all interpreters and took the whole Socrates only the way one picks a popular tune and folk song from the streets in order to vary it into the infinite and impossible.[1]

Hegel asserted that Plato's *Parmenides* was the single greatest example of ancient dialectic. Of course, his implication was that ancient dialectic, even at its best, was limited vis-à-vis modern or Hegelian dialectic in that it did not rise beyond the display of mere opposition or negation. Indeed, it has frequently been concluded that the *Parmenides* has a yield that is primarily negative, ending in the *aporia* of a series of either/or conundrums beyond which thought cannot travel. If this were the case, it would demonstrate why a pure, autonomous theoretical understanding was ultimately incapable of rising to wisdom. But is Plato's *Parmenides* only, or even primarily, a theoretical dialogue about the limits of theoretical understanding? And is there no positive yield from the dialogue, no rising above merely conflicting positions toward wisdom?

The second and larger of the two distinct parts of the *Parmenides* appears to be a series of either/or propositions, all of which can be shown to be both true and false. But the other part of the dialogue has a different form. More than a few have argued that the two parts were either pasted together after the fact—perhaps by someone other than Plato himself—or were written at such disparate times that no significant synthesis is possible. I will argue that the two parts form a complete whole and that by using this literary device Plato was precisely trying to point to the ways in which the whole is and must be a whole fashioned out of heterogeneous parts.

Abstracting for a moment from the substance of the initial narrated part of the dialogue, the central feature of the first part is the introduction of two young men for whom, we may hypothesize, the presentation is intended. In each case we know what happened to the young men in their later lives. Hence we are invited to speculate on the ways in which the theoretical presentation by Parmenides that they witnessed affected them, or perhaps left them largely untouched and unmoved. Either way, we are brought to confront the question of the public effect of philosophy, especially when conducted in the specific theoretical fashion of Plato's Parmenides.

The central young man for our purposes is Socrates when he was quite young. Limiting ourselves to the evidence internal to the Platonic dialogues alone, we know a number of things about the course of Socrates's life.[2] We know, for example, about his "second sailing" or turn toward being "Socratic" asserted in the *Phaedo*.[3] We know of his interactions with a number of non-philosophic individuals, some of them friends and supporters, most of them cordial, but some approaching threatening and a few actually successful in ending Socrates's life. Dramatically we know a great deal about Socrates's end—both philosophically and in regard to his indictment and execution by the city. The last days of Socrates, both as a citizen and as a philosopher, are presented to us dramatically by Plato through his temporal intertwining of the "trial and death" dialogues *Euthyphro*, *Apology*, *Crito*, *Phaedo* and the trilogy *Theaetetus*, *Sophist*, *Statesman*.[4] When we take into account the *Parmenides*, we are in a position to compare the early, middle and late Socrates as presented dramatically by Plato.[5]

But we should not overlook the presence in the dialogue of the young Aristoteles.[6] From information internal to the dialogue we know roughly three things about him. He is the principal interlocutor of the second half of the dialogue. He does not push Parmenides philosophically in the slightest. In the Platonic cosmos of interlocutors, he as is passive as it gets. The third and most important thing we know is that while he consorted with philosophers in his youth, in his maturity he became one of the thirty tyrants in Athens after its defeat in the Peloponnesian War. Hence we assume he did not pursue philosophy in his maturity any more than Antiphon, who is the conduit for the presentation of the dialogue. But there is no sign that he ever became hostile to philosophy as did some of those who came into contact with Socrates.

I suggest that Plato has forced us to reflect upon the two central young men in the dialogue, how Parmenides's public showing of philosophy affected them, and how that showing affected their eventual life histories. I would further suggest that this is part of Plato's reflections upon the public nature and, at the time, the precarious public future of philosophy. I will argue that one of the keys to unlocking the *Parmenides* is understanding the relation between the theoretical showing of philosophy presented by Parmenides in the second part of the dialogue and how if affected the two young men present. This is an extension of the understanding that the *Parmenides* is one of those Platonic dialogues, along with the Trilogy and the trial and death dialogues and several others, which have as their central concern the nature of philosophy and its future.

None of what I have just said, however, should be taken to indicate that we should not reflect upon the purely theoretical import of the dialogue. Nor should it be taken to foreclose the issue of whether or not the second part of the dialogue rises above a mere negative aporetic confrontation of mutually contradictory *logoi* to the presentation of a positive teaching. I want to argue that it is precisely because of the theoretical yield of the second part of the dialogue that Plato is suggesting that a different public manifestation of philosophy than that theoretically presented by either Socrates or Parmenides is required. I will designate that different presentation Platonism. But I will use that term as interchangeable with political philosophy in the sense I have been trying to articulate above.

To give something of a formulaic presentiment of the argument to come, on the one hand Plato is engaged in a form of one-upsmanship with both Socrates and Parmenides. On the other hand, Plato is demonstrating why Aristotele's sundering of theoretical and practical wisdom, making each autonomous, is a mistake. More to the point, Plato is attempting to show why none of the branches of philosophy we now separate—from ethics and political philosophy to epistemology and ontology—are capable of being separated.

The beginning of the *Parmenides* introduces us to the names of characters with which we are familiar. We have Adeimantus, Glaucon, Cephalus (from Clazomenae, home of Anaxagoras), and Socrates. Their conjunction reminds us of the *Republic* and at some point we must reflect upon that link even if we cannot prove that these are the same individuals. They are nonetheless the same names. But other than the young Socrates, they play no real part in the dialogue, the actual events of which take place roughly 50 years before the time when it is narrated. The Cephalus of the *Parmenides* attempts to get a report from Antiphon—the half brother of Glaucon and Adeimantus—regarding long past events. Antiphon, we learn, in turn received his information from a Pythodoros, a general who was a friend of Zeno's and was present during the actual discussion between the young Socrates and old Parmenides.[7]

Cephalus shows that his memory is none too good by failing to remember the name of Antiphon, even though he knows his brothers Glaucon and

Adeimantus. Further, as a young man, Antiphon had memorized an account of the discussion he had gotten from Pythodoros—which may imply that there was a transcript of some kind that had been prepared. Cephalus wanted Antiphon to repeat what he had memorized. But by this time, Antiphon himself had long since given up any interest in philosophy. His life was now devoted to the love of horses. Given the time interval, the fourth-hand nature of the account—Cephalus is retelling it to unknown hearers—the questionable nature of Cephalus's memory and lack of interest in philosophy on the part of the principal conduit Antiphon, our confidence level in the quality of the narrated report should be very low even if there was in fact a reliable written transcript extant. In light of the passage of time and Antiphon's philosophical disinterest, the intricacy and detail of the account Antiphon gave, and that Cephalus repeats, especially of the second part of the dialogue, is stunning. How many could reproduce such a thing? Why has Plato proffered this elaborate prologue to his dialogue? It is very obtrusive and extremely odd.

This flashback approach is a device that Plato uses elsewhere, notably in the Trilogy of *Theaetetus, Sophist, Statesman*. I would suggest that it is a device that seems to be used whenever the nature of philosophy is a central or the primary issue of the dialogue. It is my speculation that it is a device that Plato uses to show, among other things, what philosophy can devolve into over time. Rather than remaining the actively engaged undertaking of a flexible and energetic mind strenuously confronting the phenomena themselves directly, philosophy always runs the risk of devolving into a passive memorization and recitation of sacrosanct deeds and officially recognized dogmas. At that point the active engagement of mind has ceased.

This passivity and devolution into orthodoxy is a manifestation of philosophy that I believe Plato explicitly attempts to counteract—especially with the *Parmenides*, as well as in the Trilogy.[8] The Zeno of the *Parmenides*—from the *Phaedrus* we know that Plato held him in minimal regard as a mere rhetorician—is so complete a proponent of this model of philosophy that Plato presents him as performing philosophically by reading from a written text—from which we are told he has repeatedly read before. He was just finishing such a reading when Pythodoros, Aristoteles and Parmenides arrive in the *Parmenides*.

Further, unlike the Socrates of the Trilogy, who is old and, we are repeatedly and obtrusively told, ugly, the character Parmenides is explicitly said to be handsome and of noble countenance.[9] Even Zeno is said to be tall and good looking, and perhaps Parmenides's lover. It is not necessary for Plato to make Parmenides young and beautiful as he says he must do for Socrates. One final prefatory remark: the original meeting took place outside the walls of Athens and hence we may assume that this granted Parmenides and

Socrates a freedom and latitude that might otherwise be mitigated by moral and political circumspection if the venue had been within the walls of Athens.

As the substantive part of the dialogue begins, Socrates is questioning Zeno. In effect, Socrates questions whether concepts such as like and unlike can intermingle or partake of each other. He asserts that they cannot. Zeno seems to have agreed with this premise. In his youthful version of the "doctrine of the *eidē*"—*eidē* understood as visible, surface "looks"—Socrates accepts that "concrete" things can partake of multiple and contradictory *eidē*, but the *eidē* themselves, when separated from concrete things in some mysterious fashion, cannot partake of each other.[10] Socrates concludes his remarks to Zeno by asserting: "then if it is impossible for the unlike to be like and the like unlike, it is impossible for being to be many . . . Is that the purpose of your treatises, to maintain against all arguments that being is not many?"[11] (127e3)

Socrates then confidently, if nonetheless impudently, goes on to tweak Parmenides about Zeno being his lover and tweak Zeno about a lack of originality—Parmenides says that the All is One, Zeno that the All is not many. Zeno responds defensively that his work has no other intention than to defend Parmenides's position and further was written when he was young, in a spirit of controversy. And it was stolen so that he had no control over whether it would be published, an unpersuasive argument given that Zeno apparently reused it over and over again anyway.[12] After accepting this response Socrates launches into a presentation of his youthful doctrine of the *eidē*.

In the young Socrates's doctrine there are "*eidē* in themselves" and the many things in the sensible world "partake" of or "participate" (*metechein*) in them. The many things can participate in opposites, but the *eidē* themselves do not so participate. Hence things in the sensible world can participate in both oneness and multiplicity, thereby solving the problem of the relation between the one and the many. As regards each other, Socrates's *eidē* remain pure and indifferent to each other. What is the ontological status of the *eidē*? Even though they are "looks"—and the young Socrates also likens them to *genē* (129c2)—they seem necessarily to be "intelligibles" that are pure, "in themselves," eternal, "abstracted" from the visible, etc.—they are also frequently likened to *idea*. But their purity raises the paradox of the "participation thesis," how does one bridge the gap between the *eidē* as pure intelligibles and as the cause of the many concrete things in the sensible world that have visible looks? Either one reifies the *eidē* qua detached ideas—or one makes them so pure that they seemingly cannot be causes at all, and perhaps are incapable of even being grasped by a finite mind.

Socrates says that he would be amazed (*thaumastos*) if anyone could show that the intelligibles themselves intermingled. Parmenides takes up the challenge: "Socrates what an admirable talent for argument (*logos*) you have."[13] (130b3) He gets Socrates to admit that there are pure *eidē* in themselves for relational qualities such as like/unlike, same/other, one/many, motion/rest and also of ethical qualities like just, beautiful, and good. But a sophomoric inconsistency by Socrates allows Parmenides his initial opening. Socrates is unsure if there are *eidē* of concrete things like man, fire and water. And he rejects that there are pure *eidē* of things like hair, mud and dirt. Parmenides attributes this confusion to Socrates's youth and the fact that philosophy has yet to take hold of him and because "you still consider people's opinions."[14]

Then Parmenides shows another confusion on Socrates's part. While Socrates sees the *eidē* as pure intelligibles, he also appears to see them as extended things in time and space. Parmenides asks if the many things partake of a part or the whole of the operative *eidē*. Socrates accepts that these are the only two possible manifestations of participation (*metechein*). When Socrates accepts that the whole *eidē* is in each thing he is stuck with the conclusion that each *eidos* by being in many things is many and hence separate from itself as a One or unity. (131c6) But that difficulty in turn points toward an alternate difficulty that each participating thing participates only in a part of each *eidē*. Hence, for example, the *eidē* small would be larger than each thing that participates in it, and other such absurdities. Socrates will not accept that the One can have parts and still be One for that would mean that unity partakes of multiplicity, which requires the mingling of *eidē* which Socrates rejects. By reifying the *eidē* Socrates seems incapable of explaining the idea of participation.

Next Parmenides launches into what has come to be known as the "third man" argument.[15] If the many things are what they are by partaking of a one, both that one and those things that participate in it manifest the same quality. But this could only be true if they both participate in yet another *eidos*. But then those three too would all exhibit the same quality only by participating in yet another *eidos* and so on infinitely. An infinite multiplication of *eidē* seemingly becomes inevitable. To get out of this bind, Socrates makes a proto-Kantian move (minus the *ding-an-sich*) and conjectures that the *eidē* may be mere thoughts. Presumably they would exist in the mind of the thinker. At least this maneuver counteracts reifying the *eidē*. Parmenides responds by noting that every thought is a thought of some specific thing. If the *eidē* have the status of thoughts, all things that participate in them must themselves be thoughts and hence everything dissolves into thoughts. To push this line of argument to an extreme, Parmenides then draws the unnecessary, if not silly, conclusion that all things must think (for how could they be thoughts if they did not think).

At this point in the argument, Socrates is as silent as many of his future interlocutors will be. Eventually he makes a proto-Aristotelian move: "I think the most likely view is that these *eidē* exist in nature as patterns (*paradeigmata*)." (132c6) Things merely "imitate" these patterns. Hence the *eidē* are like the things that imitate them. But to be like each other they must participate in the same *eidē*, and hence the infinite regress of the Third Man reappears.

Explaining the *eidē* presents problems that Socrates seems incapable of overcoming. For example, there are problems if we conceive of them as either in nature or as purely transcendent. Parmenides summarizes where the discussion has arrived: "Then it is not by likeness that other things partake of the *eidē*; we must seek some other method of participation," and "do you see, then Socrates, how great the difficulty is if we maintain that ideas are separate things in themselves?" (133a2–7)[16] "Now we come to a still more fearful consequence." (134c2) If the *eidē* are intelligibles that are pure, perfect and transcendent, only God can know them. We will not know of them or of God, God will be occupied only with the intelligibles and will not know human things. God would neither rule us nor know anything about us or our world. Hence God could in no way be the cause of our world. We would only have knowledge of things in the sensible world of which God would have no knowledge. Socrates responds: "[S]urely this is a most amazing argument if it makes us deprive God of knowledge." (134d8) Socrates seems little concerned with whether or not God rules us.

Socrates has been silenced, a rare occurrence. Apparently, the *eidē* can be neither pure, absolute realities in themselves nor patterns nor "paradigms" **in** things, nor mere thoughts either. Parmenides seems to have destroyed the doctrine of the *eidē*. Nonetheless, he asserts, seemingly categorically, perhaps with the imprimatur of Plato himself lurking in the background, that: "[I]f anyone, with his mind fixed on all these objections and others like them denies the existence of the *eidē* of things and does not assume an *eidos* under which each individual thing is classed, he will be quite at a loss since he denies that the *eidē* of each thing is always the same, and **in this way he will utterly destroy the power of carrying on discussion**." [my emphasis] (134b3–134c2) **Hence philosophy itself would be destroyed**.

Conventional scholarship has seen the *Parmenides*, and the Trilogy, as signs of the late or mature Plato either rethinking or jettisoning "the doctrine of the ideas." But to my mind this focus on the evolution of Plato's thought forces these scholars to ask the wrong questions. What is at stake is not the evolution of Plato's doctrine of the ideas, but the status of **Socrates's** doctrine of the *eidē*. In the *Parmenides* we have the young Socrates articulate the doctrine. He is silenced. In the Trilogy, and the dramatically related *Phaedo*—frequently seen as the fullest manifestation of the defense of the doctrine of the ideas—we have the oldest Socrates. How does this fact help us?

We can add to the earliest and oldest Socrates, the Socrates of a "middle" dialogue like the *Republic, Symposium, Phaedrus, Meno, Gorgias*, etc.— middle in the sense of Socrates being dramatically middle-aged. In the *Republic*, Plato's Socrates also trots out the doctrine of the *eidē*. The *Parmenides* dramatically points to the *Republic* given the overlapping names of characters who appear in the *Republic*. The question is: in what ways does Socrates's thinking evolve from his youngest presentation of the doctrine of the *eidē* to his oldest philosophical undertakings? Put another way, in what way did Parmenides' philosophic demonstration change his understanding?

The answer is that there is almost no real change and Parmenides apparently had no effect other perhaps than teaching Socrates to raise matters to the level of the open and manifest *aporia* of irresolvable antinomies that he does repeatedly with other interlocutors. I suggest that this is precisely what was for Plato most problematic about Socrates—as a **philosopher**—rather than in his relation to the *polis*. But we also need to see the ways in which Plato saw Socrates as an advance over his predecessors just as he saw Parmenides as superior to all previous pre-Socratic philosophers. We will return to this issue in conclusion.

In concluding the first part of the dialogue, Parmenides tells Socrates he must, before trying to save the doctrine of *eidē*, gain intellectual rigor. To do so he must first take his mind on a tour of as many dialectical exercises as possible, in speech. Only this rigorous training might lead Socrates to know how and why to transform his position. Parmenides is eventually talked into giving Socrates an example of what he means and this leads us to the second part of the dialogue. That does not occur until Zeno notes that having Parmenides do so in public would be inappropriate if performed before the many (*hoi polloi*) rather than the small select group present: "[F]or the many do not realize that except by this wandering path through all things the mind (*nous*) cannot attain truth (*alētheia*)." Our question is, is the mature Socratic showing of philosophy one that is appropriate to show in public before the *demos*?

Aristoteles, the future co-tyrant, is chosen as interlocutor because he will not be overly curious and hence Parmenides will be given ample opportunity to **rest**. A certain bias **toward** rest will manifest itself in the second half of the dialogue. Parmenides is quite clear in his own mind that unlike Socrates, Aristoteles has no philosophical promise. What must Aristoteles have made of the undertaking in which he participated? Did he get any more out of it than Socrates?

Before proceeding to the second part of the *Parmenides,* which is an intellectual gymnastic performed allegedly for the sake of helping the young Socrates amend the doctrine of the *eidē,* we need to give some thought to what we know about the historical Parmenides and his teaching. I will argue that Plato's Parmenides is by no means a simple historical representation of the actual Parmenides. While we have limited evidence to go on, Plato's Parmenides seems to present an emendation of the teaching of the historical Parmenides. From what can be gathered from the extant fragments and other second hand information generated in antiquity, the real Parmenides made a sharp distinction between the intelligible realm and the realm of opinion and the senses. Only the intelligible realm was granted full reality or Being. That not only made it difficult, but perhaps impossible, to explain the realm of opinion. In the process it threatened to make speech or discourse impossible and the openness to the intelligible only available in silence, i.e., in motionless, contemplative unity.

The Socratic method, in its "second voyage" permutation, moves toward a resolution of this problem by explicitly making everyday speech or opinion (*doxa*) the point of access to the *eidē* and the larger intelligible realm in general. But with the Socratic method there is the question of whether one can actually get to the pure intelligibles. Without establishing the existence of an intelligible realm, explaining its status, and how we link up with it, there is the danger of speech becoming meaningless. The issue between the historical Parmenides and the Socrates of the "second sailing" coalesces around the possibility of meaningful speech. As Plato's Parmenides asserts, without some doctrine of the intelligibles, discourse or philosophy becomes impossible. To that end, Plato's Parmenides seems to fall between the Socrates of the second voyage and the historical Parmenides. He has something to say about the realm of opinion. In that regard he represents a half-way house.[17] Beyond that, Plato's Parmenides seems to ignore the famous Parmenidean doctrine that one should never say that Not Being is.

In the *Phaedo*, Socrates relates how he moved from being pre-Socratic to being Socratic. He continued to believe, as he had when he was young, that to understand a thing it was necessary to articulate it in relation to its cause, the cause being responsible for each thing being what it truly is. He had previously tried to think cause teleologically—he understood that to mean that the ultimate cause was the good. Having jettisoned these attempts he turned to the *eidē* as the primary causes—thought neither teleologically nor as active Mind. This new attempt turned him toward interrogating common perceptions and opinions about things as the means of access to the *eidē*. But the ontological status of the *eidē* remained ambiguous as well as their relation to other intelligibles. Right up to the end of his life, Socrates simply finessed the issue of whether the *eidē* were pure and transcendent or in the things, or mere presuppositions of everday speech. And he had no doctrine of Being.

My suggestion is that Socrates's solution to the problems presented to him by Parmenides when he was young was to run away from confronting the ontological question. In short, Socrates could speak — and to some it seemed that he did so endlessly — but he had no doctrine of Being, and hence no standard of meaning other than accepting what was embedded in common speech.[18] The **historical** Parmenides had a doctrine of Being, but ultimately could not speak meaningfully about the realm of visible things and everyday opinions even though he had made the very real advance of associating the real with the intelligible. Plato tried to bridge both gaps, that of the historical Parmenides and the Socratic Socrates.

But the mature Socrates was always at the borderline of endless, meaningless chatter, which of course was precisely his reputation among the many. The mature Socrates never truly confronted the problem of ultimate intelligibility. By his own admission this pointed toward the further problem of the link between intelligibility and teleology and between intelligibility and Mind. What happened to Socrates between his youth and maturity? The Socratic method points toward the centrality of the *eidē* that Socrates already accepted in his youth, at least as presented in the *Parmenides*. But he ceased trying to reflect on their ontological status. Parmenides apparently convinced him that he needed the *eidē* **but also** that he could not ground them in a doctrine of Being.

There is one other preliminary issue that we must deal with before turning to the second part of the *Parmenides*. How many in number are there and what is the order of the propositions upon which Parmenides reflects. For example, commentators like Sinaiko and Brumbaugh conclude that there are eight divisions.[19] The first four deal with what is true for the One itself if the One "is" (first pair) or "is not" (second pair). The last four deal with what is true for the others (whatever that ends up meaning) if the One "is" (third pair) or if the One "is not" (final pair). I suggest that this imposes far more symmetry and order than actually exists in the text itself. In fact, I suggest that Plato purposely creates a more fluid, disorderly arrangement in which seeming sections merge from two to one, or where the borderlines are purposely obscure. This parallels the substantive point being made and goes hand in hand with the fact that the dialogue as a whole is composed of two distinctly different and both quantitatively and qualitatively unequal parts. But I will allow what I mean as regards the order and arrangement of the second part to emerge as the discussion unfolds.

FIRST DIVISION (137a–142a). "If the One exists, the One cannot be Many." (137c3) In his first attempt or "cut," Parmenides proceeds to articulate what must be true of the One itself on the basis of the premise that the One both "is," and is a Unity. The One cannot be a Whole (*holon*) for a Whole is that which has no parts (*meros*) missing. Hence it would have parts. If the

One is truly One, it is unlimited, has no form, no beginning or end. It exists nowhere spatially, for then it would be in something (or "in itself" which would make it two) and be limited. Therefore, since it is nowhere, the One has no Other. Since it is nowhere, it cannot go anywhere, hence it is neither in motion nor at rest. It is not like or unlike itself or anything else. It is not the Same as itself or anything else. The One does not relate to itself or anything Other in any way. It is not in time for then it would have a beginning and end and be growing both older and younger than itself.

The inevitable upshot of all this is that if what has been asserted is true, then in a very real sense the One is not. "Can the One partake of Being (*ousia*) at all? Apparently not. Then the One is not at all. Evidently not. Then it has no Being even so as to be One, for if it were One it would be and would partake of Being." (142a) As Not-Being or No-thing, there can be no name for the One, no discourse about it, no knowledge or opinion about it. As a One that has no attributes, predicates, qualities or relations, it is in principle a totally transcendent No-thing-ness. We have been pushed into silence, philosophy is impossible. At best we have pushed into the mystical realm of the ineffable One of neo-Platonism.

SECOND DIVISION (142b–143a). "Shall we then return to our hypothesis and see if a review of our argument discloses any new point of view?" In this second cut Parmenides takes seriously, as he did not in the first, his actual statement, "if the One **is**." The previous cut had largely abstracted from the actual issue of Being, in fact concluding ultimately that the One is Not-Being. But now Parmenides hypothetically accepts that Being and Unity/Oneness are two, otherwise one could only say, "the One is One." Now the One is taken as the Whole—a premise that was rejected the first time. The One qua Whole has twoness, Unity and Being. The conundrum in the first cut comes from failing to deal specifically with Being. The conundrum in the second cut comes from treating the One as the Whole—i.e., as not One. Since the Whole is two, it is a Whole/One that has parts. Thereby a version of the infinite regress of the "Third Man" immediately appears. Unity/Oneness must have Being, and Being must have Unity/Oneness; hence, each is a two that is then infinitely reproduced. Hence the Whole is infinite in number or Many. Oneness has dissolved. Taking the One as **totally transcendent** of Otherness leads into mystical Nothingness or infinite regression. May we conclude, therefore, that the One cannot be totally transcendent?

THIRD DIVISION (143A–155E). The third division is by far the longest. "Let us make **another** fresh start." Now it is posited that Being and One are Other (*heteron*) or Different than each other. Parmenides adds the suggestive observation "if the One is not [identical to] Being." (143b2) As Other, Being and One are not the Same. At this point we get some fancy footwork, or to use a different metaphor, the hand may be quicker than the eye. Parmenides concludes that on this third premise there must be three pairs: Being and One, One and Other, Other and Being. Since each term itself is One, when all is said and done we have three independent terms. Obviously, the "Third Man" regression now becomes a multiplication contest. Parmenides concludes that if the One exists, all number exists and hence existences are infinite. We have now laid the foundation for conceiving of the One as including Manyness, which is to say, all Others. Does this mean that according to this cut the One would be totally "immanent"?

This conclusion would seem to follow given that if the parts of Being are infinite, Being is distributed over all things and that must include the things in the sensible world. But each thing is a distinct thing only by being a One. Being and Oneness must both be distributed infinitely over all things. Thus all things that have Being and Unity are now conceived of as making up the One that is a Whole. Are we not now in fact about to explore the ramifications of the One not as totally transcendent and by itself—whether as Nothing-ness, as all attributes and ideas without concrete manifestation[20]—but as totally immanent and overlapping with all things.

Parmenides stresses that to be an individual thing—"concrete" things included—each thing must be a One itself. All Ones are divided qua Wholes that have unity and Being, and to the extent that they "are" are the Same—without unity no-thing would be. Therefore, both Being and One are both Many while being the Same. If the Whole **is** both One and Many the Whole would have a beginning, middle and end, spatially understood. Hence the One would have a shape and be in space. It would be both in itself and Other—it must be somewhere or it would be No-thing. As a result, the One must be both in motion and at rest. And by a movement that is reasonably straightforward, Parmenides pushes to his first provisional conclusion in the third cut that the One is the Same with itself and Other than itself, and the Same and Other as all others that are not itself.

Then Parmenides turns the premises around and says that the One is not the Same as the Whole but Other than the Whole. But by the same token, all the others are the Other of the One. But since they are all identical in being Other they are thereby the Same. We are projected into the issue of whether the One and the others can each participate in both Identity and Difference simultaneously. By this latest approach the One eventually comes to be both like and unlike the others and both like and unlike itself.

Parmenides continues to explore the **spatial** aspect of his present line of attack. He hypothetically assumes that along the present cut the One is in itself and in all other things. Hence the one must "touch" itself and others. (The conventional spatial metaphor "touching" is substituted for the more ambiguous "partaking" or "participating" used by Socrates.) If only the One exists there is no touching or contact. Hence there is no number, all number being built up from ones. But by being ones, the others participate in Being and thereby the One "touches" them if it is. Yet to be distinctive and itself the One must also be Other than all the others. Hence we are now driven to the conclusion that the One touches and does not touch the others.

Further, if both the One and the others exist and there is nothing apart from the One and the others, they must be in each other or nowhere. If the One is in the others they are greater than the One. If the others are in the One, it is greater than they are. And so on, to the conclusion that the One is equal to, greater than and smaller than, itself and the others. If we think the One as existing and as forming a Whole with all the others, the One and the others have all possible attributes—the exact opposite of the first cut where the One is so transcendent that it has no attributes. The One is either No-thing or Everything/All (*pan*). There are conundrums lurking whether we take the One as totally transcendent or as spatial and totally immanent, as everything or No-thing. Is there a "middle" position or a synthetic possibility lurking here?

Now Parmenides moves from his spatial reflections to temporal ones. Again, this is either by far longest of all the cuts, or multiple cuts. Once again Parmenides posits that the One has Being. "But is 'to be' anything else than participation in existence together with present time." (152a) Here we are thrust into an issue that is central for Heidegger. Are Being and Time linked necessarily around the idea of the present moment or **presence** more generally? In support of Heidegger's thesis, we can say no more at present than that one character in one Platonic dialogue in one hypothetical cut links Being and temporality. Heidegger of course would like to disentangle the idea of presence from the uniform passing of present moments that move inexorably from past to future. Instead, Heidegger pairs presence with absence or Not-Being/No-thing-ness. For Heidegger, the Other of presence is absence, not past and future which as past or future present moments are identical. Interestingly, the pairing of presence/No-thing-ness is precisely what is implied in Parmenides' first cut where the One collapses into Not-Being or total absence. Not-Being can **be** Nothing but absent and mysterious.[21]

Parmenides' point appears to be that by partaking of Being, the One necessarily partakes of Time. But the temporal discussion quite rightly arises only in conjunction with the thought experiment that takes the One as the All. If the One is the All, that implies both temporal and spatial components. Further, since time always moves forward—as a succession of present nows— Parmenides concludes that the One is always growing older and younger than itself. Hence the One truly "is" only in the present when it ceases "becoming" older and/or younger than itself. But then Parmenides turns the hypothesis around and also shows that the One is always the same age as itself and hence equal to itself. In that case the One neither is nor becomes older or younger than itself. **Thinking the One temporally presents as many problems as thinking the One spatially, or thinking it as absent and hence as Nothing.**

Next Parmenides explores premises which amount to raising the question of whether the One has existed for all time or came into Being. He starts by asserting that the smaller numbers, starting with One, come into Being first. Hence the One must come into Being first of all. Hence all other things are younger.[22] But, Parmenides asks, is the One really One qua Whole or All until all the parts arrive? If not, then the One becomes truly One only at the end. In that case most of the other things are older than the One. But since the parts are parts only by themselves being Ones, the One and the others also must come into Being at the same time. Hence the One would be wanting in its essence at no time. It would never become older or younger than itself or the other things. It never came into Being, either before or after the others.

Hence the One and the others exist simultaneously for all time. We arrive at the same point we did with the spatial exploration. Temporally, all conceivable permutations can be predicated of the One. It is eternal. It comes into Being. It comes into Being before the others and after. And so on. Since everything can be said of the One that is the Whole and has Being, including all conceivable contradictory pairs, in effect nothing distinctive can be said about it. Once again it moves in the direction of No-thing-ness or Not-Being. The One cannot be spoken. And between Parmenides and Socrates the main issue is the possibility of meaningful speech.

Parmenides ends the third cut with a stunning assertion. If the One is *not* in time or space, "there would be no knowledge (*episteme*) and opinion (*doxa*) and perception (*aisthesis*) of it." On the other hand, "there must be [knowledge, opinion and perception of the One] if we are now carrying on all this discussion about it. You are right. And it has a name and definition, is named and defined, and all the similar attributes which pertain to other things pertain also to the One." In that case we would seem to have defended the possibility of discourse and philosophy. Should, therefore, the premise of the One being the Whole, in space and time, be chosen over the premise of the One as totally transcendent precisely on this basis, regardless of all the attendant conundrums, **for the sake of saving philosophy**?

Would, for example, someone like Hegel be a thinker who had handled the ontological issue somewhat successfully precisely because he linked the One with speech/speeches in the world? If there are competing conundrums, should we not choose the premise that, even if far from ontologically apodictic, at least saves meaningful speech and philosophy? Or should the yardstick be political philosophy, which ultimately, as I will argue, takes its bearings by the good for the soul?

Or, would it make more strategic sense to try to fashion some kind of synthesis between transcendent and immanent, temporal and atemporal, spatial and "beyond" all spatiality? For example, might we not say that Christianity accomplishes a fairly adept synthesis? We have the transcendent God the father who creates all others while remaining transcendent. We have Christ in the world as well as the Holy Spirit as manifestations of the Three in One.[23] Of course this brings us to the borderline of the perhaps preposterous, and certainly blasphemous thought that Christianity is the invention of philosophers because it solves a series of philosophical conundrums in a useful fashion.

Be that as it may, Plato's *Parmenides* eventually experiments with its own attempt at a synthesis. We will come to this shortly. For now we must be ever mindful of the question regarding the best theoretical stance for philosophy to assume given that the *Parmenides* is demonstrating that none can ever be ontologically perfect, albeit some have worse problems than others. If it can be shown that all pure theoretical/ontological positions necessarily lead to conundrums that cannot be transcended, what becomes the basis or ground for choosing among the various possibilities or trying to synthesize them? That is the ultimate question to which we must return. I believe it is answered most clearly in the Trilogy.

FOURTH DIVISION (155e–157b). "Let us discuss the matter once more and for the **third** time."[24] This leads us again into the question of the ordering of the parts of Parmenides's presentation that I mentioned above. This might be the **fourth** cut, if not the eighth, given the length of cut three. By explicitly making it the third Parmenides forces us to go back and combine two previous cuts into one. The most feasible solution is to combine the first two dealing with the issue of the One as transcendent. What happens is that we then end up with a discussion of the One that is constructed out of a two, just as we do with the dialogue as a whole. I suggest that Plato is, through the structure of the dialogue, reinforcing a substantive point regarding the complicated if not contradictory or irrational nature of the Whole he has Parmenides fleshing out for us theoretically.

Parmenides begins the newly announced third cut in the following way: "If the One is such as we have described it, being both One and Many and neither One nor Many, and partakes of time,[25] must it not, because One is, sometimes partake of Being, and again because One is not, sometime not partake of Being." In this latest cut, Parmenides will paint a picture where the One, by gaining and losing Being, is generated and destroyed. We have a constant process of coming to be and passing away, not the one directional coming to be for all time flirted with in the last cut. The One is both Being and Not-Being, both in motion and rest, **but not simultaneously**. But must it not also be both in time **and out of it**? Apparently not, for the premise only includes "and partakes of time." Parmenides is experimenting with synthesizing motion and rest, Being and Nothing, One and Many and so on. What he does not attempt is to synthesize is Time and whatever its opposite might be—"eternity"?

Parmenides accomplishes his experimental synthesis by positing the concept of the "instant" or "moment." This notion allows him to posit that the One is both of all possible pairs, **but not simultaneously**. It passes back and forth from one state to another. Hence there is a "moment" (*Augenblick*?) of transition when it is **neither** of the pairs. It **endures** a process of going back and forth through the moment. (This may imply that it is passive and acted upon by some other force.) But the One cannot be "becoming" when it is on the Nothing side of the instant moving from Nothing toward the moment. Hence "it" is enduring "becoming" only in the instant on the other side of the moment. But when it is becoming, it is Not-Being. Apparently the One, by this hypothesis, has Being only after the Moment. Otherwise Being would have to be associated with either Becoming or No-thing. Then at the instant, moment or intermediate between Nothing and Being the One would not be in Space and would truly **be** neither Nothing or Being for only the conceptual blink of an eye. Needless to say, Parmenides's experiment with this synthesis arrives at conundrums as well. My allusions to Heidegger and Christianity above at least serve to show that other similar attempts are possible and in fact have been attempted. What will not be attempted by Parmenides is an actual reduction of the One to an Identity containing both Being and Not-Being, which might perhaps point toward something like Heidegger's discussion of the interpenetration of absence and presence. Parmenides has not proved that other synthetic attempts might not work better than his flirtation with the idea of the instant. But in the end perhaps he will have demonstrated that no experiment can ever be completely free from problems.

DIVISION FIVE (157b–159a). From here to the end, Parmenides proposes to change his approach and look at matters from the side of the "other things."[26] In the first cut in this new approach he asks: "What will happen to the other things if the One exists?" Of course we have already dealt with the One as the Other of all the others. It remains to be seen what the reversal of perspective yields. If the One exists, the others as Other would seem not to be One and not to have Being. But the others partake of the One in a certain necessary fashion, otherwise they could not be separate from each other. The others as One have parts that are parts of a whole only by partaking of the One. But each of the parts is also a One, or it would not be a distinct part, in a regress that moves **toward** an indivisible One that has no parts, which in fact can never arrive. We will return to this issue in chapter 20 on theoretical physics.

Nevertheless, Parmenides leaves it ambiguous whether or not this is an infinite regress. Needless to say, this would have ramifications for sub-atomic physics. Conceptualization, after all, must always precede experiment. At the very least as we move down toward the smallest One that is indivisible, we get caught in certain necessary conceptual difficulties. Were we to arrive at an ultimate One qua smallest—as opposed to a One qua comprehensive—we would find that we encounter the same issues we do in talking about the comprehensive One. For example, the One might be Nothing, in or out of time and space.

Parmenides asserts that in their own "nature" as separate things the others must each be One, but qua parts of a Whole they are unlimited in number. Hence the others are both limited and unlimited. Consequently, all the others are both like and unlike one another and themselves (all things are like qua ones made of parts, unlike qua different). In this way the others are like the One itself in relation to itself and others in a previous cut. To jump to his ultimate conclusion, Parmenides proceeds to show that the others are Same and Other than each other, in motion and at rest, and "we can easily show that the things that are other than One experience all opposite **affections** (*pathē*)." This latter metaphor points toward passive suffering at the hands of some external force. By this cut all attributes can be predicated of the others, just as in a previous cut all attributes could be predicated of the One. On that level the One and the others would be Same without being Identical.

DIVISION SIX (159b–160b). "Then what if we drop these matters as evident and again consider whether, if One is, the things other than One are as we have said." "Let us then begin at the beginning (*arches*)."[27] Parmenides now starts by positing that the One and the others are separate from each other. Nonetheless, the One + the others = All things (*pan*). As separate from each other, the One and the others are **not** the Same. What is truly One/Unity has no parts. Hence the One as separate cannot be in the others as a whole or as a part. Then the others cannot partake of the One in any way since they cannot partake of it as a whole or a part. Therefore, the others are not One in any sense. Nor are the others many for many is number and all number is built up out of initial Ones. Thus the others are deprived of all number, cannot be like or unlike the One; hence likeness and unlikeness are not in them. Therefore they are not Same or Other. In other words, the others are not Other or the Same as each other or the One, neither Become nor are destroyed or "are" and so on to the inevitable conclusion that the others have no attributes. Summarizing the first two cuts in this second approach, Parmenides says, "therefore if the One exists, the One is all things and Nothing at all in relation both to itself and all others." We will shortly reach the same conclusion starting from the premise that the One is not. We are reproducing, vis-à-vis the others, the same series of conclusions we applied previously to the One. Either the One and the others have all attributes/predicates or no attributes/predicates. They are related as Identical or totally separate qua indifferent Difference.

DIVISION SEVEN (160b–163b). Now we move to the longest of the cuts in the final six. "Now consider if the One does not exist." Parmenides begins by extracting from Aristoteles the admission that there are such things as "complete opposites."[28] We should by now have ample evidence that Plato's Parmenides is very skeptical about the existence of pure opposites, and by extension he must be skeptical about the principal of non-contradiction.[29] It may be useful in speech and still have no ontological foundation. Parmenides also extracts from the young tyrant to be the conclusion that if the One is not, the statement alone implies that it is different than the others, for they surely "are." Without belaboring matters, Parmenides is headed toward showing that whether the One is or is not, we arrive at the same either/or situation that both the One and the others either have all attributes or none, either are or are not. From the perspective of discourse and philosophy we either have silence or speech without limits unless we fashion some synthetic position. All ontological positions will be more or less jury-rigged, but somehow meaningful speech still needs a basis. We have had one flirtation with a synthetic cut with the thought experiment regarding the "instant."[30]

But to return, if the One is not, two things are implied: 1) since we are speaking of it, it is therefore known; 2) it is something Other than the other things and hence different. As different, Difference or Otherness resides in the Not-One itself. Even Nothingness has attributes. And from there, as we have seen before, Parmenides moves to showing that the Not-One possesses **all** attributes. The only attribute it does not partake of is Being. Not-Being, like Being and all the others, has all attributes or none. The good news would be that since Not-Being has all attributes except Being we can talk about it. We can only talk about that which has attributes or relationships. Otherwise, silence, or as Parmenides puts it "there is no use saying anything at all." (161a4) If we are to speak, the One, Being, Not-Being, the others, whatever, must have some attributes or relations. But if they all have all attributes we will be left with babble. All difference cannot be allowed to dissolve into differenceless Identity.

The stunning final conclusion to this cut is that Not-Being even participates in Being. "Then if it does not exist and is to continue to be non-existent, it must have the existence of Not-Being as a bond in order to attain its perfect existence." (162a4) Likewise Being must participate in Not-Being. **This seems to be a central point to which we keep returning**. It is precisely the point that the Eleatic Stranger will make in the *Sophist*. But the historical Parmenides's position was that we should never say that Not-Being is. We have the Eleatic Stranger's corroboration of this doctrinal position on behalf of

Parmenides in the *Sophist.* So why does Plato make his Parmenides seem to hold a position the historical Parmenides apparently did not? Perhaps this serves to accentuate Plato's own position. Perhaps it shows Plato's belief that Parmenides's own logic should have led him in a different direction than it did. Perhaps Parmenides should have strategically chosen a public teaching that stressed synthesizing Not-Being and Being and the One and the Many, or used other synthetic devices like the "instant." A responsible speculation might also be that Plato concluded that one should not choose to adopt a public stance that expelled Not-Being from Being. Put another way, Being always contains an element of absence, contrary to the comforting teaching of textbook Platonism.[31] And this conclusion did not await Heidegger coming on the scene.

DIVISION EIGHT (163b–164b). "Let us now go back again to the beginning (*archen*)." We must notice that despite what we expected, and what appeared to be announced, we have slipped over into again considering what is true for the One rather than what is true of the others. This means, rather than the seeming symmetry of dealing with what is true for the One if it is and is not, and of the others if the One is and is not we have a more random and complicated procedure in which we are now involved in some seeming redundancy. Division eight again considers what is true for the One if it is not. Parmenides quickly, peremptorily and assertively states that the Not-One or Not-Being cannot exist, perish or come into Being, cannot change, move, be in motion or at rest, in short, no attribute can pertain to it. This point has already been established and is entirely redundant and breaks with the announced order. Why? Does it accentuate that to talk of the One at all it must be done in relation to the others? That is in a way the point of Socrates's "second sailing" which starts with speeches about the others.

DIVISION NINE (164b–165e). With the ninth cut we return to the issue of what the consequences are for the others if the One does not exist. It is asserted that the others at least exist. This will be refuted by both divisions nine and ten. If the One did not exist, the others would be the other of each other only, otherwise they would be the others of Nothing. But if they do not partake of the One, the others are not ones and hence can ultimately have no others. They would at best be "seeming" ones and "seeming" others. On closer inspection they will in fact transform themselves into mere dreams. The others will be transient multitudes masquerading as Unities. But without participating in the One, none of the others will have a limit (*peras*). Parmenides repeatedly uses words like *ekaston, doxei, phainetai, phantasma*. If the One is not, everything will dissolve into seeming, appearing, phantoms, mere opinions and so on. Nothing will be, neither the One nor the others. This is clearly unacceptable, especially if saving philosophy is the central issue.

DIVISION TEN (165e–end). "Let us go back one more time to the be-ginning and tell the consequences if the others exist and the One does not." The others will be neither One nor Many (to be ones themselves requires that they participate in the One. They cannot be many unless they are first indi-vidually One). The others do not even **appear** to be One or Many. Hence the All is Nothing, nothing "is" or appears. The others would neither be nor be perceived. If the One does not exist Nothing is and "it" has no Other.

The last two divisions make a unified front. Our problem is not just that if the One does not exist we are incapable of philosophy, but speaking and even perceiving would be impossible. **The One simply must "be" in some fash-ion, despite the conundrums to which this leads.** Here is an outcome that at last seems definitive. Hence it is clear by the end of Parmenides' efforts that whatever synthesis or other solution one pursues ontologically, on some level the One must be even if it forms a complicated unity with Not-Being and is ambiguously related to the Whole with its otherness and difference. Of course, Not-Being in turn must also be. We have arrived at the position of the Eleatic Stranger in the Trilogy.

The *Parmenides* ends with what seems to be a summary of the entire un-dertaking and not just of the tenth cut. "[W]hether the One is or is not the One and the others in relation to themselves and to each other all in every way are and are not and appear and do not appear (*phainetai*)." Literally the last word of the text is *alethestata*, "truly so," or perhaps "most truly." That word is pre-sumably uttered by Aristoteles. Yet it is in fact Plato's last word.

As at the end of the *Sophist* and *Statesman*, in the *Parmenides* Socrates gets no chance to respond. In line with what I have argued above, we are left to wonder what he got out of the exercise. We have to turn to the dialogues where Socrates is dramatically older to try to get an answer to that question, specifically those seven intertwined dialogues that deal with his final days. They too bring together the issues of knowing and Being. But they intertwine epistemic and ontological issues with ethical and political ones in a way that is only tangentially raised in the *Parmenides* by the presence of Aristoteles. I believe this points to the fact that for Plato epistemology and/or ontology can-not be foundational and certainly not autonomous. Only the good for the soul can ultimately be foundational.[32] It alone informs our choices regarding plau-sible ontological syntheses.

The *Parmenides* is primarily about the fundamental nature of philosophy, its possible foundation and its necessary public face. Given that philosophy must be able to both speak and speak in public, certain things **must** be as-sumed. **If those assumptions must be then they are.** The *Parmenides* is part of a larger Platonic showing that the theoretical manifestation of philosophy can never be autonomous. We are forced beyond the ontological to understand what theoretical synthesis must be constructed. The question is, is there an advantage to offering a **theoretical/ontological** showing of philosophy as the main part of its public face? I have the following in mind. Parmenides gives a technical and theoretical showing of philosophy that does not link up with the language or issues of everyday life. It is not phenomenological. Socrates's showing of philosophy does link up with the language and issues of everyday life in hopes of using that interrogation as a means of access to theoretical questions and ontological foundations. But Socrates never really gets to the ultimate theoretical foundations, he has no doctrine of Being. By not having a technical face to his teaching, Socrates also ultimately failed to generate the kind of awe that Parmenides did, which may have sheltered Parmenides from Socrates's fate. Indeed, Parmenides, while not converting Aristoteles to philosophy, or moderating his tendency to tyranny, apparently never provoked contempt for philosophy, a contempt Socrates provoked in more than a few.

I am suggesting that the *Parmenides*, like other Platonic dialogues, is part of an ongoing interrogation of Socratism by Plato. But I am not implying that Parmenides, whether in his historical or Platonic incarnation, is without limitations. **On some level, a doctrine of Being is needed and a technical showing of philosophy is publicly salutary**. But Parmenides seems incapable of getting past the merely theoretical showing of philosophy, which I am suggesting cannot be foundational because it can arrive at no apodictic point of departure (*arche*). The highest and most comprehensive manifestation of philosophy is an undertaking that must include self-conscious reflections on the public face of philosophy and especially on where one goes after seeing the limitations of a simply theoretical or technical manifestation of philosophy.

The historical Parmenides represented a great advance over his predecessors by making the intelligible the source of the real. But Socrates represented an advance in his own right by being able to incorporate everyday speech into philosophy, giving it a means to avoid mystical silence or paradoxical oracularism. The one thing that is ultimately missing from both the Parmenidean and Socratic showings of philosophy is the poetic element that is necessary to weave the parts into a whole. We have ample evidence from the Trilogy that "weaving" is at the heart of philosophy in its most comprehensive manifestation.[33] That weaving is the ultimate foundational activity. That activity must be theoretically informed. But perhaps even more importantly it must be phenomenologically informed. The weaving activity that binds together the theoretical and the everyday—e.g. the Parmenidean technical showing and Socratic everyday discursivity among other things—is political philosophy as I am designating it. It is philosophy in its most comprehensive manifestation and Plato is its founder, not Socrates. It is a possibility that can always be deployed now and into the future.[34]

Even Socrates at his dramatically most mature—as seen for example in the *Theaetetus*—doesn't adequately synthesize (or even attempt to) the many theoretical conundrums raised by Parmenides. Socrates is theoretically inadequate—and that leaves aside the extent to which he was politically and morally questionable, and utterly incapable of *poiesis* as the *Phaedo* makes amply clear.[35] In the end, discursivity must point to ontology while ontology itself has to rest on synthetic, poetic experiments. And those experiments will have to change over time. The need to do so and the parameters within which it should be undertaken will not change. That is the positive yield of the *Parmenides*.

There are certain theoretical necessities that simply cannot be overlooked without hopeless confusions and contradictions. But the massive fact that Plato's Parmenides seems to overlook is that the Whole also includes the human as a distinctive part. In other words, the ethical and the political also must be blended into any complete account of the Whole. Parmenides can only give us a purely theoretical manifestation of philosophy. But to take into account the many, understood politically (here meaning the non-philosophers), requires a poetic manifestation to any plausible ontological synthesis. Parmenides does not even try. Socrates is also incapable of it as well. The oldest dramatic Socrates presented to us by Plato still does not seem to understand what is theoretically and poetically needed. Socrates can speak the language of the street. He runs no risk of falling into silence. But theoretically he can never overcome **openly** displaying *aporia*. Parmenides can speak theoretically/technically but always at the border of silence. Only Plato binds the parts into a Whole.

NOTES

1. Friedrich Nietzsche, *Beyond Good and Evil*, #190, trans. Kaufmann (New York: Vintage Books, 1966).

2. In this regard see chapter 16, "Between Platonism and Postmodernism: Plato's Emendation of Socratism in the Trilogy."

3. In this regard, see chapter 13 on the Phaedo, and also Seth Benardete, *Socrates' Second Sailing: On Plato's Republic* (Chicago: University of Chicago Press, 1989).

4. While there is also the Trilogy of *Republic, Timaeus, Critias*, henceforth I will use the term "Trilogy" to refer to the *Theaetetus, Sophist, Statesman*.

5. This seems to me to be a far more fruitful undertaking than those speculative reflections that assume to know the order in which the dialogues are written. At best,

that focus deflects our attention away from the substance of the texts themselves and toward issues that are not the ones that Plato specifically raises. Beyond that, the "stylometrics" upon which contemporary opinions about Plato's growth and development are based, is at best a "science" that while probably superior to alchemy and astrology, hardly rises to the epistemic level of something as substantial as the science of voter studies. To be generous, stylometrics is not an exact science. But even if it were, we would still need to know precisely what the substantive point of the various dialogues was before we could proceed. The substantive analysis takes priority. Focusing on the order in which the dialogues were written seems to divert most commentators away from a thoroughgoing substantive confrontation.

6. I have concluded, for example, contrary to Heidegger, that Aristoteles' presence does not primarily signal a subtle confrontation by Plato with his student Aristotle, who may or may not have been on Plato's mind when the *Parmenides* was written. See Heidegger's *Sophist* (Bloomington: Indiana University Press, 1998).

7. The mingling of philosophers and men of affairs makes an important point. Long after his death, non-philosophers including the fellow citizens brought by Cephalus were still interested in Socrates and philosophy. What had been unleashed was now a public phenomenon that could not be returned to Pandora's box.

8. See "Between Platonism and Postmodernism."

9. Plato tells us that the Socrates he presents is a Socrates made "young and beautiful," not the real Socrates. But in the Trilogy, and by extension the trial and death dialogues, Socrates is old and explicitly said to be ugly. It is in those seven dialogues that we see the real Socrates, at least as closely as we ever approach him in the Platonic dialogues. For an elaboration of this argument see the chapter "Between Platonism and Postmodernism" below. In the *Parmenides* we get the youngest Socrates. He is young and ugly. When compared with the Socrates of the Trilogy we can ask the question of how he changed.

10. The Socrates of the *Theaetetus* and *Phaedo* seems still to hold this position. The Eleatic Stranger, however, holds that some *eidē* can partake of other *eidē*, albeit not of all *eidē*.

11. Plato, *Parmenides*. I have worked from the Loeb edition translated by H. N. Fowler with my own occasional emendations (Cambridge: Harvard University Press, 1926).

12. While unpersuasive in the present dialogue, this does point us toward the issue of the virtue of writing discussed in the *Phaedrus*.

13. The ambiguity of the word *logos* masks whether Parmenides is praising Socrates for his ability to pursue the inner reason operating in all things or for his agonistic and eristic abilities.

14. I will argue that the Socratic method, the second sailing discussed in the *Phaedo*, requires precisely that one begin from common opinions, and it is not clear from any of the Platonic dialogues that Socrates can ascend much beyond them, and certainly not all the way "up' to the intelligibles themselves.

15. The designation comes from Aristotle, albeit in recent scholarship the issue has been associated with an article by Professor Vlastos. See "The Third Man Argument in the *Parmenides*," in *Philosophical Review* 63 (1954), 289–301.

16. In the second half of the dialogue we will learn that if the One is entirely transcendent we are forced into utter silence. So Parmenides will not totally dismiss the immanence of the One as a possibility—albeit fraught with its own problems.

17. That half-way house may be close to the position of Plato whereas the doctrine of the *eidē* is something that follows by extension from the Socratic method or second sailing.

18. The Socrates of the *Phaedo* does observe that his new method saved him from trying to look directly at intelligible reality—likened in the *Republic* to looking directly at the sun. The sun is a metaphor for the first cause that exists in the intelligible realm beyond the sensible realm of the cave.

19. See Herman L. Sinaiko, *Love, Knowledge, and Discourse in Plato: Dialogue and Dialectic in Phaedrus, Republic, Parmenides* (Chicago: University of Chicago Press, 1965), pp. 227–31.

20. In that case we would be in the vicinity of the pre-incarnate One of Hegel's *Logic*. Therein, Hegel equates the One as implying both Not-Being and the totality of all concepts.

21. This is not the place to pursue the matter further, but the *Parmenides* is a perfect dialogue to use to set up a discussion with Heidegger; perhaps it even represents a response. In it Plato seems to be perfectly cognizant of the issue of presence and absence and the necessity that they may in some sense be co-present in each other. If so, Heidegger in no way thought a thought unavailable to Plato.

22. Parmenides introduces another complication that opens an entirely different can of worms. He asks if the One can come into Being contrary to its own "nature." (153c) If the One has a "nature" or "essence" is there a higher principle than the One, something that supervenes over it and determines it? If so, the discussion would simply have to begin again, taking into account "natures" and "essences." To a certain extent, this is what Socrates's doctrine of the *eidē* does. At present I would merely suggest that these reflections would lead us toward the *Timaeus*.

23. Or again, has Hegel offered the best solution? Once the Hegelian One becomes a Whole with all other things, nothing transcendent remains. Again, is the best theoretical position the one **that best saves philosophy as an antonomous ontological activity,** or that takes its bearings by something else like the human soul?

24. An alternate translation might read: "Let us now take up a **third** thing." Either way will make my point.

25. It should be noticed that Parmenides does not add "and does **not** partake of time." Does this signal something we have just raised, that Being **should** be conceptualized as in time for purposes of saving philosophy?

26. It appears that for Parmenides the "other things" is a category that includes both the many things in the sensible world and the multiplicity of *eidē* in their variety of forms including pure concepts such as Other and Same. We should note that, once we collapse cuts one and two, we have three cuts on what is true for the One if it is or is not, and we appear to have twice as many, six, on the subject of what follows for the others if the One is or is not. Does this indicate that there is a quantitative preponderance of arguments that favor approaching the central ontological questions from the "other things" rather than trying to directly grasp the One or Being?

If so, it would be an argument against Heidegger and for Socrates, at least in this one regard.

27. This term could be taken in the sense of "first principles" or "first cause" as well as "beginning."

28. This is not to imply that this is the first time that Parmenides has extracted something questionable from Aristoteles. He does it frequently. He also uses implausible examples and tortured logic. I have chosen not to make this my focus, for in the end it would add nothing to the point I am trying to make, either pro or con. It is what Parmenides shows *in toto* that interests me.

29. I would suggest that the Socratic method positively requires commitment to the principle of non-contradiction.

30. We shall get another such experiment from the Eleatic Stranger in the trilogy in what I call the "commingling doctrine." In the *Theaetetus* and the *Phaedo*, Socrates remains explicitly committed to the existence of opposites and the principal of non-contradiction. He cannot get to any such synthetic position. This is due to his deficiency in *poiesis* that is made explicitly evident in several Platonic dialogues.

31. That customary understanding is still held by as radical a thinker as Heidegger.

32. See chapters 13 (on the *Phaedo*) and 16 (on the Trilogy).

33. See especially "Between Platonism and Postmodernism."

34. The contemporary pessimism that ensues from the clash between a moribund modern rationalism and irrationalism is due to overestimating the theoretical claims of modern rationalism. We have reached no end of the philosophic tradition because the truly Platonic can always be reappropriated anew. All manner of "beginnings" are possible.

35. When called upon by a daimonic voice to make music or poetry, Socrates, who has very little time left to comply, makes Aesop's fable rhyme. The *Symposium*, which demonstrates Socrates's unerotic nature, points in the same direction.

Chapter Sixteen

Between Platonism and Postmodernism: Plato's Emendation of Socratism in the Trilogy

Accordingly, *politike episteme* is genuine *sophia*, and the *politikos* is the true *philosophos*; that is the conception of Plato.[1]

The fundamental difference between Plato and Aristotle shows itself solely in the way in which they **stand toward** theory . . . Plato **does not permit** the philosophers . . . the life in philosophizing or **lingering** in [theoretical] contemplation of truth.[2]

Plato's Trilogy *Theaetetus, Sophist* and *Statesman*, begins with a dialogue devoted to a discussion of knowledge which ends in *aporia*. It culminates in a dialogue that assigns to mortal "statesmen" the godlike task of filling in for the absent gods and/or the non-existence of any supportive cosmic or natural order. How can those godlike tasks be accomplished in the absence of knowledge? One of the boldest conclusions regarding how this seeming difficulty can be overcome is found in Stanley Rosen's assertion that "Plato presents us with a striking anticipation of the modern problematic of theory and practice . . . he is much closer in thought and spirit to the moderns."[3] By that observation he means, I take it, that in Nietzschean fashion one confronts the epistemic abyss with an act of creation or *poiesis* understood as ungrounded will.[4] One "constructs" order where it does not already exist. Plato, far from being an "essentialist," or "foundationalist" is actually a "constructivist," or even "postmodernist."

But must we conclude that Plato's Trilogy Thrusts us into the middle of a situation very like that in one fairly popular reading of Nietzsche wherein everything rests on philosopher-kings who stand nowhere—i.e., over an abyss—and will the human world *ex nihilo*.[5] Such a position is of course scandalous from the perspective of the traditional Anglo-American scholarship that presents a Plato who comes complete with early, middle and late periods and whose thought is based on a "doctrine of ideas"—understood as transcendent metaphysical realities or directly accessible "intelligibles"—that gives the world certainty and security, allowing us to deduce moral and political imperatives in an absolutist fashion.

For present purposes I will call this latter, conventional understanding **Platonism**. I will designate as **Postmodernism** that position which posits the need for and primacy of groundless poetry and creativity in the face of the absence of divine, cosmic, natural or metaphysical support for human existence. My argument will be that, so understood, Plato is neither a Platonist nor a Postmodernist. Further, both the Platonists and the Postmodernists—whether Nietzsche, Heidegger or their epigoni—conclude that Plato is a "metaphysician." I will argue that he is not a metaphysician in either the traditional sense—believing in self-standing transcendent realities—or in Heidegger's unique deployment of the term that has gained hegemony in contemporary discourse—possessing a doctrine of Being as presence.

There is a second prong to my thesis. In a famous observation, Leo Strauss observed that without intending to Heidegger had opened a door back to the recovery of an authentic Plato who had perhaps not been open and available for a very long time, if ever.[6] I agree that Heidegger's radical questioning of the presuppositions of the philosophic tradition both allows and forces us to take a fresh look at Plato. But Heidegger's own reading of Plato circles back into a fairly conventional understanding wherein Plato is a rudimentary moment on the way to Aristotle. My argument is that Aristotle represents a radical break from Plato, an almost immediate covering over of Plato's actual position. It is from Aristotle that most of the traditional maneuvers that Heidegger analyzes and rejects descend.

For my purposes, far more radical is the questioning of Nietzsche who specifically construed the cultural icon Socrates as a "problem." My argument will be that Plato already saw the problem and his own teaching represents the attempt to supply the corrective **before the fact**. This is one of the keys to unlocking the intention of Plato's Trilogy.[7] To put the matter in a formula: Plato's actual teaching is a corrective for Socratism, not just politically and morally but theoretically as well.

Socrates presented Plato with a problem.[8] Yet he represented an advance over pre-Socratic thought. That advance is to be found in the move from the vague and ambiguous, "inspired" poetic language and images of the pre-Socratics. The Socratic undertaking represented an attempt to get beyond that inspired *mania* that passed for philosophy toward the sanity of discursive rigor, in Socrates's case through the deployment of dialectic. This is all part of what is usually meant by the "Socratic turn."

Pre-Socratic philosophy had seemed mad to the citizens of the ancient cities in which it emerged as well as threatening to the everyday perceptions and the accounts of the first things contained in the laws. With the Socratic transformation philosophy at least came to speak in the language of the marketplace, eschewed direct discussion of the first things that were already dealt with in the laws and focused on issues that emerged in everyday, pre-theoretical or "natural" experience and what is implied in it.[9] Philosophy thereby became more self-consciously prudent and moderate.[10]

In what follows, I will argue that the Socratic turn was at least, if not more, an **epistemic turn** rather than a primarily defensive or prudential transformation of philosophy. But I also want to point to the ways in which much of what has come to be called the Socratic turn was precisely **not** Socratic. What has come down to us as the Socratic turn was in fact the Platonic emendation of Socratism. The "Platonic Turn" takes place in the making of the real Socrates "young and beautiful." The initiator of this new form of philosophy, political philosophy in the sense I articulate, is Plato. Plato presents us with what pass for Socratic, doctrinal statements. But he also depicts for us, more quietly, the curious and problematic nature of Socrates as a philosopher. In the process, a new form of philosophy, political philosophy, comes into existence, of which Plato is the founder. I am going to argue that Plato saw political philosophy as proto-philosophy.

Political philosophy as I will articulate it is not to be understood as one subsection of philosophy among many. Indeed the various subsections of philosophy from aesthetics to epistemology have been spun off by political philosophy itself, as have the social sciences and the natural sciences, on occasion with full self-conscious clarity of purpose, but to my mind in all cases mistakenly. For a variety of reasons, only now is the recovery of unity faintly visible as a future possibility.[11] If correctly understood, political philosophy is precisely proto-philosophy. It is the most fully awake and self-conscious manifestation of philosophy,[12] unlike its mad and intoxicated, pre-Socratic predecessor, which longed for a non-discursive contemplative oneness with the first things in which the thinker loses himself. Philosophy, so understood, sinks to a lower level of awakeness than what I believe Plato is offering. True philosophy longs for full, **self-conscious** clarity.[13]

There is no reason to believe that the first manifestations of philosophy— pre-Socratic or Socratic—represent its essential manifestation. I will argue that that is to be found in political philosophy and not the divine madness Plato attributes to pre-Socratic philosophy, to which his Socrates pays some lip service, without any evidence of his *mania* or *eros* ever manifesting itself dramatically. Furthermore, what I am claiming on behalf of Plato must be differentiated from that pure theoretical staring valorized by Aristotle. The detached, contemplative theoretical understanding of philosophy originated in the tradition thanks to Aristotle. It gained momentum for reasons that in many ways had to do with the philosophic confrontation with Scripture and the resultant need for the philosophers to carve out a place for themselves in a world that already had the Law. I will argue that Plato was presenting an entirely different understanding of philosophy. That understanding was neither "metaphysical" (in either the traditional or post-Heideggerian sense) nor voluntarist in the Nietzschean sense.

Plato's teaching represents an emendation of Socratism. Socrates represented an advance over pre-Socratic thought, but still represented a problem. Socratism was discursive in a way pre-Socratic thought was not, hence in less danger of the unself-conscious *mania* implied in the pre-Socratic longing for a direct, non-discursive relation to Being. Finally, while Socratism and its deployment of dialectic pointed **toward** "intelligibles"—it did not presuppose them as directly accessible autonomous metaphysical realities—in fact, Socratic dialectic could never get to the things it pointed toward nor discursively articulate them. Therein lay a problem in Socratism regarding of which, I will argue, Socrates was unaware.

SOCRATISM

Plato's Trilogy *Theaetetus, Sophist, Statesman* is about the nature of philosophy. Dramatically the Trilogy is set at the end of Socrates's life and explicitly intertwined with the trial and death dialogues *Euthyphro, Apology, Crito* and *Phaedo*. Those dialogues force upon us the issue of whether Socrates was a morally and politically questionable phenomenon. For example, the *Apology* is an extremely curious effort if in fact Socrates was actually trying to defend himself. It is at best artless; at worst it has elements that are positively arrogant and taunting. Socrates was an unusual man. And even when his heart seems to be in the right place, by which I mean engaged in an action of which ordinary citizens would approve—as in the *Euthyphro* where he tries to moderate a rash young man—there is no evidence that he is efficacious.[14] There is no evidence in any Platonic dialogue that Socrates made a single individual better, while in the *Meno* we see that he so irritates some that among the auditors are future indicters.[15] I take Socrates' political and moral questionableness as a given, as well as the issue of his practical efficacy. These issues arise throughout the Platonic corpus. But they are not my present focus.

It is an interrogation of Socrates as a philosopher that I presently want to take as the key to Plato's Trilogy. In the Trilogy, we have dueling philosophers, an old Socrates, a citizen that Athens put to death, and an unnamed Eleatic who escaped similar opprobrium. More to the point, having spent the first of the two days covered by the Trilogy under the leadership of Socrates, Theodoros and the other participants and auditors seem to have gone out of their way to bring another philosopher to lead their discussion the second day, one they specifically designate as a "manly philosopher."[16] They have no interest in spending another day in the clutches of Socrates.

Both Socrates and the Eleatic Stranger have what we can call a discursive method. Socrates primarily deploys "dialectic," a method by which common opinions are solicited and interrogated. In the *Theaetetus*, all such opinions are dismissed and everyone goes away in confusion. The Stranger uses a related but nonetheless different method, *diaeresis*, to which we will return in the next section. Unlike Socrates, when the Stranger is finished we have at least the dramatic appearance of having reached a positive yield, at the very least the discussants reach seeming agreement.

Socrates's unique undertaking has several distinctive features and presuppositions. The opening gambit in its deployment is almost always the question "what is ___?" By this gambit Socrates tries to elicit a cognitive, intelligible "one," *eidos* or "essence" rather than a concrete list of examples. But far from these "essences" positing the existence of some kind of self-standing metaphysical entities, what is implied in the dialectical method is the epistemic priority of "everyday" experience.[17] This is a "phenomenological" point of departure in my sense. This interrogation of shared, common experience points us **toward** the possible existence of an ensemble of cognitive ones or essences that are implied in everyday *aisthesis* and *doxa*.

The dialectical part of the Socratic undertaking comes from the fact that those everyday opinions that are solicited by the Socratic method are always shown to be either internally contradictory or to contradict other opinions held simultaneously. We are forced to conclude that the removal of contradiction is a primary end of the Socratic method. Hence the principle of non-contradiction is a primary **commitment** of the Socratic method. Further, Socrates attempted to get all of those who had a reputation for wisdom, and more than a few who did not, to give a complete and consistent articulation or *logos* regarding their opinions and actions. The assumption has to have been that if one could develop an ensemble of *logoi* that were internally consistent and consistent with each other, then one would have reached the goal, a discursive treatment of the ensemble of ones, essences, *eidē* or "ideas" as they relate to each other. That would be wisdom. Such wisdom would, presumably, allow one to lead the best life. In this fashion, Socrates prepared the way for the transference of the locus of truth to *logoi* or statements, as Aristotle would shortly assert. There is no indication it would lead to apodictic knowledge about the nature of the whole—whether understood as cosmology, ontology or metaphysics.

There are many more presuppositions embedded in the Socratic undertaking, if we are to see it as something more than just a unique form of *agon*, as Nietzsche asserted.[18] For example, it simply must proceed on the assumption that the unexamined life is not worth living. Socrates attempts to raise the level of self-consciousness in the thinking, doing and making of his interlocutors and hearers. Perhaps the last of the true Socratics, Hegel, grasped this presupposition most clearly, making the highest level of self-consciousness the final *telos* of Spirit.[19] For Hegel, fully transparent self-consciousness was the very heart and soul of philosophy. Socrates does not prove that the most self-conscious life is best, but no other premise accounts for his behavior on any principled level. That said, the repeated intrusion by Plato of Socrates's "little voice" or *daimon* shows that on some level Socrates either was unsuccessful in the pursuit of full self-consciousness or he simply contradicted himself. Socrates never interrogates his little voice. It is in principle an unconscious force that he obeys without hesitation.[20]

The *aporia* that Socrates repeatedly creates—through what can be called his deconstruction of everyday perceptions and opinions—is due to his paradoxically unreflective commitment to a fully self-conscious life as the best life. Socrates aims at, but does not achieve, a life in which all acts are voluntary and intentional. For Socrates, nothing counted as "knowing" unless it was fully, self-consciously articulated in speech prior to any doing or making so as to avoid both internal contradiction and contradiction with other speeches. But Socrates could never get to such a perfect speech. And he simply would not accept that there was already "knowing" embedded in our everyday doing and making. But the distinctively Socratic undertaking made no sense unless there was some knowing contained in the speeches, opinions and actions he interrogated. Socrates's undertaking simply had to proceed on the assumption that some truth is already, inarticulately contained in life itself. If not, why interrogate speeches as a means to knowledge and truth?

In places the dramatic Socrates in fact does presuppose that such knowledge exists on a pre-articulate level. He should be openly led to reflecting on how it got there. In the *Meno*, for example, he sees that his undertaking raises the possibility of "innate ideas." Socrates supports this possibility by an appeal to Greek language. Such words as *anamnesis* and *alētheia* pointed toward a theory of "remembrance" that could also tap into the already given Pythagorean doctrine of the transmigration of souls. And Socrates makes moves like this in more than one place.

That said, the Socratic undertaking positively implied that the locus of truth was to be found in speech, and not in things or actions. That opened the door to Aristotle's assertion that the locus of truth is in statements. Furthermore, the "what is" questions, in asking for an *eidos* rather than a list of visible things, posited the existence of something available only to thought but not the senses. The cause of visible things being what they are would thereby be something invisible, hence "intelligible" only to a faculty other than the senses. The distinction between thought and appearance lurks in the Socratic method because it lurks in everyday experience. But in the end, the Socratic method moves in epistemological directions that ultimately make the dialectical method problematic. We will return to this shortly.

On an ethical level, if only fully self-conscious acts count as ones performed with knowledge, we are pointed toward the hegemony of a rational ethics where virtue must, in its entirety, "be" knowledge. If one also posits, as Socrates does, the premise that all fully self-conscious individuals desire the good, then one is forced into the paradoxical conclusion that no one does evil voluntarily. All of this leads to positing the difference between knowledge and opinion, with opinion (for example in the form of habit) providing no basis for virtue. All those without full self-conscious clarity are without knowledge and hence by extension cannot be virtuous. Hence out goes the authority of everyone from fathers and elders to prominent citizens, tradition and the laws. In the end "Reason" replaces everything and everybody as the only source of authority and virtue. Reason becomes intrinsically deconstructive and potentially nihilistic.

There is nonetheless substantial evidence that Socrates deployed the method of interrogating individuals and their opinions and perceptions primarily for his **own sake**, more than for the sake of his interlocutor or the well being of the larger community. Socrates wanted to arrive at full self-conscious clarity for himself. He needed clarity about all the individual things that were potential targets of the "what is" questions, from the nature of various visible things, to the nature of the virtues, to the nature of concepts such as sameness, like, oneness, and so on. He interrogated others to see if in fact any of them had this knowledge and if he could tease it out of them. Again, the paradox is that this undertaking presumes that in some pre-articulate fashion those interrogated already possessed something that deserved to be called knowledge. If the task was to tease out knowledge that was already implicit, this leaves the question of why we are better off, in our everyday existence, by making it explicit. Socrates never explicitly enjoins this question. And even if one arrived at knowledge of the multiplicity of *eidē* of the individual things, there was absolutely no assurance they could be synthesized into a whole. The weaving of the whole implies a *poiesis* Socrates did not possess. I would go so far as to say that Socrates' undertaking could never deliver what he most wanted, which is to say that he was ultimately confused and less than fully self-conscious. In the *Lesser Hippias* (376c), Plato makes Socrates admit that even he in fact vacillated regarding some of his core premises or presuppositions, such as that it is better to do injustice voluntarily than involuntarily. In the end, was not Socrates himself incapable of self-conscious clarity while publicly destroying perfectly serviceable opinions? We should keep in mind that the history of post-Hegelian philosophy is the history of various doubts about the possibility and even the value of fully transparent self-consciousness. Was Plato already reflecting upon that issue?

In the *Theaetetus*, Socratic questioning is deployed in such a way that all the opinions solicited are rejected and the dialogue ends with no positive statement or position offered. Socratic questioning seems almost always to have an utterly negative yield—i.e., it is deconstructive without being constructive.[21] But as we have seen in previous chapters, that outcome is avoided only in the dialogues to which an element of *poiesis* is added. But Plato is at pains to show that Socrates is not poetic, erotic, manic, Dionysian, or anything of the kind. Those elements are added by Plato in his attempt to make Socrates young and beautiful.

Socrates does end the *Theaetetus* by saying that he has deployed his questioning with the **moral** intention of making Theaetetus more gentle, but this seems an altogether pointless exercise given that we are specifically told that Theaetetus was gentle before Socrates met him. Since there appears to be no ultimate epistemic yield from the *Theaetetus,* or a useful moral yield, we are led to wonder what the point of Socrates's undertaking is. Maybe the better question is, why did Plato show his dramatic Socrates in such a negative light?

The negativity of dialectic seems to be driven home to us as well by the odd metaphor for philosophy that Plato has the Socrates of the *Theaetetus* deploy, a metaphor which is exclusive to the *Theaetetus*. Socrates asserts that the **origin** of philosophy is to be found in wonder (*thaumazein*), but its **end** is asserted to be "midwifery." In the *Symposium*, by contrast, philosophy is associated with *eros*, in the *Phaedrus* the foundation of philosophy is said to be *mania* or divine inspiration, in the *Phaedo* it is "preparing to die," in the *Meno* it is likened to the effect of a stinging fish, in the *Apology* to that of a gadfly. Plato puts various metaphors in the mouth of his Socrates in different dialogues and they have entirely different ramifications. Each has to be considered in light of the specific dialogue in which it appears. We need to realize that in the end, these various possibilities—wonder, *eros*, *mania*, midwifery, preparing to die, fully self-conscious clarity, stinging fish, gadfly—cannot be synthesized.[22] They do not present a consistent picture of philosophy, certainly not of political philosophy as proto-philosophy.

For the moment all I want to assert is that the midwife metaphor in the *Theaetetus* is by far the most limiting vision of philosophy in the Platonic dialogues. In the midwife metaphor, Socrates in effect says that he is barren of positive doctrines and hence has limited himself to inducing the birth of positive doctrines in others. Socrates then proceeds to **abort all of those positive positions** that he inseminates. Theaetetus does remark toward the end of the dialogue that Socrates in fact has induced in him more ideas then he actually knew that he had. But they are all aborted. So in the end we see that Socrates actually engages in artificial insemination, artificially induced labor and abortion. It is not at all clear why it is decent to put a person through this regime of insemination, labor and abortion except in the service of heightening self-consciousness. But having arrived there, where has one been left, self-conscious of knowing nothing and being unable to commence action with a good conscience?

Again, since Theaetetus is already gentle before he meets Socrates—and Euthyphro, upon whom Socrates deploys the same tactics later in the same day, is a man who actually needs to be aborted, but apparently goes on his merry way impervious to Socrates's efforts—there appears to be no substantial moral yield of any consequence from Socrates's efforts.[23] Actually, if one adds to this that there are all manner of moral and political opinions that every decent society needs that should not be gratuitously undermined, we cannot help but question the moral value of dialectic—it can become a mindless, nihilistic deconstructionism. Everything therefore seems to stand or fall on dialectic's philosophic or epistemic virtuosity. Can dialectic, **autonomously deployed** as it is in the *Theaetetus*, in any way be the basis of a sound theoretical position? We know that none was ever inseminated in Theaetetus.

But perhaps this is due to Theaetetus's limitations. It seems, does it not, that unlike the "late" Trilogy, there are positive yields from the "middle" Socratic dialogues. By middle I here mean dialogues in which Socrates is **dramatically** younger than in the Trilogy and dramatically older than in the *Parmenides*. For present purposes this especially includes the *Republic*, *Phaedrus* and *Symposium*, but also the *Gorgias, Philebus* and *Protagoras* among others. In the dramatically "middle" dialogues, Socrates seems to produce substantive outcomes. Furthermore, in all those dialogues Socrates's philosophical quiver contains more arrows than just dialectic deployed autonomously, including "long" speeches—that assert various positions—plus the use of models (*paradeigma*), images (*eikon, eidolon*) and stories (*muthos*).[24]

There is one dramatically "early" dialogue—*Parmenides*—in which Socrates is very young. As we have seen, Plato's character Parmenides utterly destroys the "doctrine of ideas" that might seem to be the central positive doctrine asserted in the *Republic* and more or less supported at least on the surface in the palinode of the *Phaedrus* and to some extent in the speech of Diotima in the *Symposium*. The epistemic criticism of Socratism in the *Parmenides* is perfectly applicable to doings of Socrates in all of the dialogues, which still seem to point toward a doctrine of the *eidē*.[25] The youngest Socrates cannot defend what so many see as his central epistemological doctrine. The oldest Socrates admits he has no positive doctrines, he is just a midwife. Both the youngest and the oldest Socrates are presented in different ways as impotent. Is it not the autonomous application of the Socratic method of dialectic that is impotent?

If we had only the *Parmenides* and the *Theaetetus* to go on—one depicting the youngest, the other the oldest Socrates—we would have to conclude that Socrates traversed his entire life without gaining in philosophical efficacy. Further we would conclude that at the end of his life, his dialectical method still presupposed, or at least implied, that which was refuted when he was young. But in the dramatically "middle" dialogues Socrates seems to be more efficacious. How are we to account for the "middle" Socrates who has other philosophical tools at his disposal beyond dialectic and seems to be more than an impotent midwife?

As I have repeatedly observed, Plato tells us that the Socrates he presents in his dialogues is a Socrates made "young and beautiful."[26] But in the trilogy we have a Socrates who is at his oldest and is explicitly depicted as ugly. In fact Plato hammers home to us Socrates's ugliness in a way that would be gratuitously vulgar if there were not some reason for it. The hypothesis I continue to explore is that the Socrates of the dramatically "middle" dialogues is Plato's beautiful and cosmetized Socrates.[27] The Socrates of the *Theaetetus* and related dialogues is the closest glimpse we ever get of the real Socrates except perhaps for the *Parmenides* when he still had a few lingering metaphysical pretensions. Socrates became more modest in old age, but his dialectical method still pointed toward what he actually asserted as metaphysically existing when he was young.

In the Trilogy, the Eleatic Stranger carries the burden of mounting the critique of the limitations of real Socratism. To the Eleatic Stranger's position we would have to add the critique of that other major Eleatic character we confront in the Platonic dialogues, Plato's Parmenides.[28] But the Eleatic Stranger's position should not be taken as identical to Plato's. Before any conclusion in that regard is possible, one must compare the Eleaticism—for want of a better term—of the *Sophist*, *Statesman* and *Parmenides* with the vision of philosophy carried by the cosmetized Socrates of the middle dialogues. That latter task will have to be a project for the future; at present I want to explore the ramifications of the Eleatic Stranger's confrontation with Socratism.

The *Theaetetus* launches the Trilogy with a distinctive dramatic device we have seen before—there is an elaborate prologue. We are dramatically thrown forward roughly thirty years from when the actual discussion that is reported takes place. Socrates is in his grave and Theaetetus has lived an illustrious life that appears about to end. To the end, Theaetetus has remained a brave and patriotic citizen despite his intellectual accomplishments.[29] The Trilogy is made present to us through a text developed by Euclides largely by repeatedly going to Socrates, apparently while he was in his jail cell awaiting execution.[30] Terpsion has heard of the text and wishes to have it read. They render themselves **in a position of rest** and it is read to them while they passively listen.[31] Socrates and the rest go together: his motionless in the *Symposium*, his reumbant position in the *Phaedrus*, etc. What are we to make of this prologue qua flash-forward?[32]

I want to point to three issues as they relate to this prologue. Other than giving us a look at the future of one of the central characters in the Trilogy, Theaetetus, thirty years after he met Socrates, we also get a glimpse of the future of Socratism. His fame and influence were destined to spread far and wide. The fact that Socrates did not write anything was not going to check that influence. For better or worse Socratism was destined to be a part of the human cosmos. If there was anything potentially deleterious about that influence it was doubly important for Plato to check it. Second, the prologue to the Trilogy shows us what philosophy could become at the hands of men like Terpsion and Euclides. It could become a static enterprise of repeating formulas and exercises. Even the doings of the Socrates who allegedly had no doctrines could be reduced to a kind of learning by rote.

Both Terpsion and Euclides sit passively while a slave boy reads to them. In stark contrast to this cessation of motion—and the *Symposium* shows us that Socrates himself was prone to this motionlessness—is the dynamic vision of philosophy I believe Plato is juxtaposing. For Plato, philosophy was not about doctrines and passive theoretical staring. Philosophy was to be an ongoing way of life and confrontation with the issues that arise from within it. And it was to be an ongoing creative synthesis of different elements, which required active interpretation.

Finally, the prologue points to the issue of memory. On the surface level we have the issue of keeping alive a record of the past—which is thematic throughout the Platonic corpus. I am not, however, primarily interested at present in thematically interrogating the so-called *anamnesis* thesis which we have already confronted in the *Phaedo*. As the issue of memory comes up in the Trilogy, it signals the possibility of something being present before the mind that, at least at the moment in question, is not present through perception, *aisthesis*. This opens us ultimately to the possibility of a form of knowing that is not dependent on *aisthesis* and is thereby "direct." The issue of the existence of a faculty that can directly access "intelligibles" not present to the mind through perception is lurking in the background throughout the Trilogy, a noetic, *alogon* grasping the possibility of which neither Socrates nor the Eleatic Stranger explicitly acknowledges.

After the prologue, the Trilogy proper begins with Socrates and Theodoros discussing a promising young Athenian. (143e4–144b8) As they do so, he and two other boys approach from the direction of the gymnasium—the quintessential house of motion. Eventually we discover (in the *Sophist*) that there is one boy with the same name as Socrates, one who looks like him—Theaetetus—and one who has no name and no look that is given us, yet he nonetheless exists. This dramatic device parallels the unavoidable conclusion we reach at the end of the Trilogy that there is no one to one relationship between names and looks (*eidē*) or between looks and cognitive entities or "intelligibles." It further raises the possibility that there can be things that exist that have neither a look—hence no connection with *aisthesis*—nor a name and hence cannot easily be discursively articulated, if at all.

Consequently, we are forced to consider the issue of the unavoidable limitation of any discursivity whether dialectical in form, through *diaeresis/ synagoge,* or the Aristotelian "logic" of categories and predication. **Let us assume that for Plato, philosophy cannot be reduced to a discursive method.** Nonetheless, discursivity, speech, *logos*, etc., are required if one is to avoid the *alogon mania* of pre-Socratic thought. Socrates, however, cannot get beyond dialectically culling everyday speeches and perceptions. We need discursivity, but it cannot be the entirety of philosophy. Thus, speech and/or statements, hence logical analysis, cannot be the only locus of truth.

After Socrates induces Theaetetus to give the definition that knowledge is perception (*aisthesis*) he moves to conflate this with what the sophist Protagoras meant by "man is the measure" of all things. That position is then asserted to be the core understanding of all of the poets and thinkers since Homer other than the Eleatics. Everyone in this "flux crowd" is alleged to believe that all is motion and becoming, nothing is at rest. Socrates begs off confronting the Eleatic position that all is one and rest by stating his extreme veneration for Parmenides. (145c8–153d11) The Eleatic Stranger, showing no such veneration, takes on this allegedly Eleatic position in the *Sophist* and shows why the "rest crowd" is defective.

Socrates's grand conflation of Theaetetus, Protagoras, Homer *et al.* is anything but obvious. But by moving in and out of the different components of this conflation Socrates can "demonstrate" that unless there is something at rest it is impossible to assign names to anything. If that is true, without something existing that is at rest it would be impossible to engage in speech, or more generally to live a life, which requires that we make future predictions based on past precedents. Those predictions require that things stand still long enough for prediction to be feasible. After showing the contradictions one is driven into in trying to maintain the position of the flux crowd—and more generally the position that associates knowledge entirely with *aisthesis*—Socrates goes on to do the same with two further definitions he artificially inseminates in *Theaetetus*: knowledge is right opinion and knowledge is right opinion plus a discursive explication (*logos*).[33]

In the middle of the *Theaetetus* we confront what looks like a very contrived digression conducted with Theodoros in which Socrates offers **assertions** about the nature of philosophy.[34] In that digression (172c6–177c1) Socrates rehearses an argument he will shortly use in his defense in the *Apology*: True philosophy will always appear ridiculous in courts of law or public assemblies. Philosophers are foreign to the ways of the *polis*.[35] But only the philosophers have true leisure and are free men precisely because they are indifferent to everyday concerns, whereas everyday citizens can never allow their activities and thoughts to take an independent course. Then in an extraordinary statement, Socrates simply confesses to what he will shortly in the *Apology* call the "older charges" brought against him by Aristophanes:

> It is only his body that has its place and home in the city; his mind, considering all these things petty and of no account, disdains them and is borne in all directions, as Pindar says, "both below the earth," and measuring the surface of the earth, . . . studying the stars, and investigating the universal nature of everything that is, each in its entirety, never lowering itself to anything close at hand. (173e2–174a2)[36]

Socrates further asserts that, like Thales, philosophers will always be held in contempt for studying the intelligible things in themselves and how they differ from each other, appearing to hang at a dizzying height, at least to those below. The picture of Socrates suspended in a basket toward the beginning of the *Clouds* is the clear allusion. Socrates ends his digression with an observation that almost totally reproduces his argument in the *Phaedo* that philosophy is a form of "preparing to die": "We ought to try to escape from earth to the dwelling of the gods as quickly as we can; and to escape is to become like God, so far as this is possible." (176b1–3)

If I am correct that the *Theaetetus* represents an inspection of Socratism, and that means of the real Socrates—"old and ugly"—it is simultaneously an inspection of Socratic dialectic as central to the genuine Socratism. If so, the digression on philosophy, like the midwife metaphor, must shed light on Socrates's deployment of dialectic. If the use of dialectic is consistent with Socrates's understanding of the nature of philosophy, then it seems that the real Socrates must have thought that dialectic was not primarily a moral tool, as he indicates at the end of the *Theaetetus*, but a tool that would get him to detached theoretical staring—i.e., *alogon* contemplation of pure intelligibles. That is supported by Socrates's analysis of what he learned from Diotima. If, on the surface at least, and probably at a deeper level, dialectic really yields only unavoidable antinomies, and yields a form of deconstructionism, apparently it cannot accomplish what the real Socrates hoped.[37]

Projecting this line of thought further, what one begins to see is that a fully autonomous operation of dialectic does **not presuppose** the need for anything like *noesis* or direct theoretical grasping of *archai* as **a point of departure**. Dialectic presupposes that there must be some knowledge in everyday perception, and it primarily **points toward** cognitive entities or "intelligibles" as its **end**. But it can never get there and is therefore deceived. In the "middle" Platonic dialogues led by the cosmetized Platonic Socrates, **dialectic is never deployed autonomously**. It is always supplemented by images, stories, models and what I will shortly call the normative. While it is true that in the *Theaetetus* we have the metaphors of the aviary and signet ring, they are used by Socrates not to supplement or add a positive element to dialectic, but in effect as part of his process of artificial insemination, to draw refutable opinions out of Theaetetus. I will return shortly to this issue of the possible autonomy of dialectic.

Socrates the abortionist midwife has nothing positive of his own to bring forth as a doctrine to supplement the deployment of his dialectical method. Strikingly, even Protagoras—admittedly through the mouth of Socrates—like the Eleatic Stranger, supplements his deployment of a discursive method with an appeal to "better and worse," i.e., the normative. In the *Theaetetus*, Socrates does not. What I am suggesting is that Plato is showing Socrates as pursuing a narrow, discursive deployment of philosophy, which can abort but produce nothing positive, implies no *noesis* or creativity (*poiesis*), and is incapable of reaching its desired goal of pure detached theoretical staring, except at antinomies.[38]

The starting point for dialectic, at least as the old and ugly Socrates deploys it, is not *alogon archai* but everyday experience, common sense and shared perceptions. The public showing of reality is simply taken as a given. Indeed many of Socrates's "refutations" are built on showing how a particular theoretical hypothesis contradicts commonly held perceptions or opinions.[39] It is clear that the interrogation of everyday opinions and experience is central to Socrates's deployment of dialectic. It inevitably directs its deployer toward a world of multiple species (*gene*) parts (*mere*) or looks (*eidē*)—and Socrates seems to use these terms interchangeably. The question is always how dialectic leads us beyond the perceptible looks to something cognitive or intelligible that has no aesthetic component. The seemingly interchangeable use of *eidos*—along with *meros* and *genos*—and *idea* points to a conundrum that dialectic by itself cannot solve. It does not appear that one can move seamlessly from interrogating the *eidē* to grasping intelligibles that can be contemplated in a pure staring. One must already pre-discursively grasp or "know" the *eidē* that condition everyday experience prior to any discursive culling of them. But the fact that they are presupposed does not prove they exist as autonomous intelligibles. In short, one might be doing no more than interrogating everyday speech.[40]

Contrary to Socrates, given what is shown in the *Theaetetus*, it seems to follow that one cannot link the term "knowledge" with anything that comes to presence primarily in discursivity. As a term it must be assigned to the **pre-discursive**, by which I mean, something already grasped that becomes manifest in everyday perception and speech. Discursivity of one kind or another (dialectic, *diaeresis*, "logic") can tease out what is embedded and implied in common understanding and point **toward** the purely cognitive, but only because it rests on a "phenomenology" of everyday experience. Again, it is in no way clear that the pre-discursive is grounded in transcendent intelligibles.

Further, only by differentiating "knowledge" (a something pre-articulate) from "truth," and moving truth to the side of discursivity (as Aristotle will by saying that true and false are terms that only apply to statements) might it be possible to avoid some of the conundrums Socrates points to in his various abortions. But that finesses the real issue of the relation of discursivity to something pre-discursive, on the one hand, or to something that is a self-standing intelligible, on the other. By trying to make discursivity autonomous we run into all of the difficulties sketched out for us in the Trilogy. Discursivity stands **between** everyday perception (and the knowledge it presupposes) and any possible independent intelligibles.

I am headed in the following direction: Dialectic starts from the various *eidē* displayed in everyday living and points toward various intelligibles or cognitive forms—Being, Same, Other, etc. The **autonomous** deployment of any form of discursivity leads at best to the showing of antinomies, at worst to the questionable practice of deconstructively undermining shared opinions without being able to put anything in their place. Dialectic must always be supplemented by something other than itself. There is no doubt that the relation between perception and thought/cognition is thematic in the *Theaetetus*. But there is no resolution of the nature of their relationship other than the vague intimations we get that apparently there would be no Being without motion, and no possibility of speech without something at rest. But Socrates never pushes on to any kind of positive resolution of the relation between motion/rest, perception/cognition, Being/Not-Being. It is the Eleatic Stranger who does that. The implicit commitment of Socratism to the principle of non-contradiction makes it impossible for him to push toward the kind of synthetic position the Stranger will assert. Hence he cannot get to an understanding of how everyday experience—which dialectic can interrogate—and cognition of intelligibles are linked.

Finally, we should note that nowhere in the Trilogy are *eros* or *mania* displayed either thematically or dramatically. Neither Socrates nor the Stranger thematically presents philosophy as erotic, manic or "inspired" in any sense. Socrates, the abortionist midwife, would appear to be particularly unerotic, a conclusion we also reach in the *Symposium*.[41] Again, the Socrates of the Trilogy asserts that the origin of philosophy is to be found in wonder (*thaumazein*), not in *eros* or *mania*. Wonder and *eros/mania* are two different things—wonder points toward detached theoretical staring (rest), *eros* toward ongoing active longing (motion). Also different are *eros* on the on hand, and preparing to die and midwifery on the other. Throughout the Platonic corpus there are competing visions of and metaphors for philosophy. They are not the same and they cannot be synthesized. One must sort through them with an eye to which belong to the presentation of the "middle" Socrates and which to the presentation of the "late" or "old" Socrates.

ELEATICISM

As opposed to Socrates, and presumably as a straightforward jab, Theodoros introduces the Eleatic Stranger as a manly or courageous philosopher.[42] Socrates, the self-proclaimed midwife, with his seemingly incessant quibbling that never courageously pushes through to a positive position, apparently did not present a manly **look** or *eidos* to Theodoros and the others during the action of the *Theaetetus*. On the surface at least, the Stranger will reach a positive outcome in both the *Sophist* and *Statesman* and bring about "agreement" which he states at the beginning of the *sophist* is his intention and the aim of his method (218c3).[43] By comparison, we are never really sure what Socrates's aim is. For example, does he deploy dialectic to produce a moral or epistemic outcome, or as part of his personal efforts to gain clarity? Or did he simply like to win battles?[44] There is ample evidence that dialectic alone can accomplish none of these ends if deployed autonomously other than to merely win battles.

Socrates gets even with his companions by imposing the issue for the day upon the Stranger, with the subject of names and naming providing the opening gambit. (216c3–217a9) Is there a possible linkage of *onoma* with *eidos, meros* and *genos*? This makes for a somewhat plausible segue from the *Theaetetus*. If the various looks are the point of departure for philosophy, as they are for Socrates, and if common language and understanding are unavoidable givens, as least as a point of departure, as they are in the *Theaetetus*, then names and naming become very important in philosophic reflection. We would want to know if there is a one to one correspondence, or any correspondence, between the looks and the names and between either of those and intelligible realities.[45]

Once the subject is agreed upon—whether the names Sophist, Statesman, Philosopher represent one two or three "looks," and thereby a consideration of what each "is"—Theodoros announces that the Stranger has heard and re-members a discussion of the subject that he can repeat. While this invocation of memorization and recollection harkens back to the prologue—and is reminiscent of Zeno in the *Parmenides*—it is hard to know what to make of it. Is Plato really intending that we conclude that the Stranger is to give a performance by rote? Apparently. I take this as one of many clues that the Stranger is not simply the spokesman for Plato.[46]

The Stranger deploys a seemingly rigorous, technical, discursive method of division or *diaeresis*. Usually there is a recombination, *synagoge*, that follows the division, by way of a summary. As we watch the deployment of this *diaeresis/synagoge*, several things become clear. 1) Before he starts, the Stranger obviously knows where he is heading. This is already implied in the fact that he is apparently giving a presentation by rote. 2) The knowledge that allows him to know where he is going is not generated by *diaeresis* itself, but supplements it from the outside. 3) His discursive method, while giving the impression of precision and producing at least plausible moves at each cut, produces outcomes that at times can be preposterous—i.e., they are an affront to everyday experience as in the conclusion that man is the "featherless biped." 4) The various cuts in search of the Sophist proceed in multiple directions, at times starting from different sides of the same cut, at other times finding the same category on opposite sides of the cuts. One is forced to reach one of several conclusions: either the looks that constitute reality are very fluid and the method parallels this fluidity; or the slippage between looks and names makes any discursive undertaking less than apodictic; or the Stranger is imposing his will on the phenomena and engaging in an almost Nietzschean form of willfulness. 5) The neutral application of *diaeresis* clearly has to be supplemented by the introduction of what I have called the normative element—"better and worse"—and various other seeming digressions to provide images (*eikon*), models (*paradeigma*) and stories (*muthos*) which supplement the undertaking. This is consistent with what the "middle," cosmetized Socrates does. 6) Finally, and significantly given the dramatic interweaving of the trilogy with the trial and death dialogues, we should note that the thematically political dialogue is assigned to the Stranger, not Socrates. Socrates is forced to suffer in silence.

The method of *diaeresis* is in some ways similar to dialectic but is not identical. Both methods start from the premise that the point of departure is an interrogation of the publicly shared looks (*eidē*). Both share the premise that the pre-discursive "phenomena" must be passed through and into some form of discursivity, some rigorous form of *logos*. Neither seems adequate if applied autonomously. Dialectic, as Socrates deploys it, culls common looks by searching for the contradiction free opinion about the nature or essence of the individual *eidē* and then from there to a search for a comprehensive, contradiction free comprehensive *logos*. *Diaeresis*, while dealing with the kinds of things that would fit within the form "What is a ____?" starts by **positing** a category to which the thing belongs—e.g., knowledge (*episteme*) or art (*technē*)—and proceeds to divide that posited category by choosing one of two **posited** possibilities. The division that takes place in *diaeresis* also seems necessarily to point toward a subsequent re-combining or *synagoge*. While the posited opening categories are themselves based on everyday experience, positing them points to a degree of imaginative creativity (*poiesis*).

In the Stranger's application, the *synagoge* takes the form of a summary, which does not always culminate in a mere inverted *diaeresis*—something is usually added, deleted or both. Both the initial positing and the recombining point to an external understanding that is not contained within the technical application of the discursive method itself. In the *Theaetetus*, while Socratic dialectic may vaguely point beyond itself, it is deployed autonomously and is not used in conjunction with any supplements of which we are made aware or can easily infer.

The opening move in most of the Stranger's divisions is instructive. For example, sophistry is said to be an understanding, which can fit one of two *eidē*, knowledge or art. Sophistry is assigned to the division art without further argument. Art is then divided into "productive" (*poietike*) and "acquisitive" (*ktetike*). In all but the last division in the *Sophist*—and it is a grand summary as much as anything else—sophistry is assigned to the category acquisitive. The change in the last, summary division sends up a red flare. The category production is said to include the production of that which did not previously exist and does not produce itself. By contrast, *physis* would designate the category of those things that produce themselves. Everything from agriculture to moneymaking and learning (*mathesis*) is made to fit under the category of acquisition.

We are immediately forced to wonder if philosophy is the "other" of sophistry and hence if it is primarily productive—the other of acquisitive—at least in the mind of the Stranger. For example, **is philosophy productive in the sense of imposing categories on phenomena that already have a preexisting, public look?** Is this what the Stranger is doing? So understood, the philosopher would not construct the looks themselves which are publicly displayed before the fact, he would merely categorize them, i.e., interpret them as part of his making them intelligibly present in speech. Does philosophy **always** presuppose a prior, publicly displayed, pre-discursive understanding, to which is applied a discursive "productivity?"[47]

By placing the sophist primarily on the acquisitive side of his cuts, the Stranger asserts that the Sophist does not create the categories, arguments and theories he uses. He simply moves within the interstices of categories, arguments and theories that already publicly exist. It appears that neither the Sophists nor Socrates are productive, or more generally poetic.[48] Socrates refutes or aborts positions that already exist; the Sophist manipulates already existing positions to some useful advantage—e.g., his wage earning.

After a series of deployments of the method of division—proving that the subject matter presents a degree of fluidity open to interpretation—the Stranger admits that **his use of the method of division up to that point was defective.** These first divisions tried to sort into one *eidos* or *genos* things that were alike in some essential respect, separating them from all others that were different in some essential respect. Each *eidos/genos* had individuals that were simultaneously **like** each other, without being the **same**, and different from every other **individual** *genos*, albeit not in every respect. Having offered his admission, the Stranger asserts that it is necessary to make divisions using an entirely different criteria, separating "better from worse." He introduces what I want to call the normative element. It depends on the primacy of the good.

A great deal is implied in this move. The origin of the knowledge by which the Stranger chooses one criteria of separation—what we might call purely technical from the normative—from the other is not discussed. But he shows that the pure, autonomous application of the merely technical art of division needs to be supplemented by something external to the method itself. When we pursue the method of division informed by "better and worse" we arrive at the conclusion that sophistry is **the art of separating better from worse as it pertains to the soul through the removal of ignorance by a process of education that involves cross-examining the conceit of wisdom.** This definition seems to apply to the Socrates of the *Theaetetus*— less so than to the dramatically "middle" Socrates. I want to argue that with this move we jump from an autonomous epistemic realm to the realm of concern for the good of the soul. In the process, we begin to see the architectonic priority of the Good to any autonomous technical method. More generally, there can be no pure theoretical knowledge divorced from knowledge of the good for the soul.

After the move to the "normative" form of division, we arrive at the central part of the *Sophist,* which completely abstracts from *diaeresis.* We get a thematic discussion of the nature of images versus originals, the raising of the issue of Not-Being and the assertion of a positive "theoretical" doctrine of the commingling and non-commingling of intelligible forms (as opposed to those *eidē* grasped by *aesthesis).* The Stranger asserts that the necessity of his "commingling doctrine," to which everything seems to lead, is for the **primary purpose of preserving the possibility of discourse.** Without this less than apodictically satisfying doctrine, intelligible speech would not be possible.

The Stranger asserts that the possibility of meaningful discourse is linked with the absolute necessity of grounding the possibility of falsehood. Obviously alluding to Socrates the midwife, the Stranger eventually observes that every "newborn offspring" (259e2) should not be attacked. The Stranger observes that it offends both good taste (gentlemanly morality) and philosophy to attack all doctrines indiscriminately. We assume that he has in mind that this is especially true of very vulnerable offspring like his commingling doctrine. Undermining that doctrine, or some comparable synthesis, would have as its yield the obliteration of all rational discourse and thereby the basis for arguing the superiority of philosophy to sophistry. Some doctrines should not be subjected to dialectical dismemberment nor diaeretic division. This is as much as to say that the commingling doctrine cannot be proved apodictically, but can be seen, from the perspective of the good, to be necessary.

The commingling doctrine, or a better replacement provided by someone else—perhaps by Plato through the young and beautiful Socrates—is needed if we are to establish the possibility of falsity and hence of the distinction between true and false speeches and true and false images. Allegedly, only such a doctrine can in turn help pin down the sophist and differentiate him from the philosopher. Ultimately, the Stranger observes, the sophist eludes the grasp of those who approach by running into the thicket of Being and Not-Being. Only by dealing adequately with those two "intelligible forms" can we pin down the sophist. Treating both Being and Not-Being as intelligible forms and allowing them to commingle cannot be done by anyone who presupposes the principle of non-contradiction.[49] Sound discourse, we should keep in mind, and its distinction between true and false, is needed for not only philosophy, but for healthy moral and political existence, which are in turn needed for the good of the soul. Everything ultimately points in the direction of the architectonic status of the good of the soul—"better and worse," the normative. All things are judged in its light. If so, a combination of ethics and psychology takes priority over epistemology, metaphysics, ontology, cosmology, pure autonomous theory in any form.

I intend only a brief word about what we might call the Stranger's metaphysical or ontological commingling doctrine. The primary thing to keep in mind is its purpose. Put another way, metaphysical doctrines can be no more autonomous than discursive methods. In effect, the Stranger starts from previously existing theoretical positions already presented by others, such as that Being is Rest, Being is Motion, Being is One, Being is more than One, etc. Even here the Stranger is beginning from publicly extant opinion. He dispenses with the historical Parmenides expeditiously.[50] The moment one says Being **is** X—even if the X is filled in with "One"—one immediately has more than one, in this instance Being and One which are two. By a process we need not presently follow, the Stranger ends up **positing** three cognitive or intelligible forms, Being, Motion and Rest. From them he then **generates** two more, Other and Same. We are in the vicinity of the Hegel of the *Logic* who posits the pre-incarnate One as Concept (*Begriff*) and then shows concepts generating out of each other.

The Stranger goes on to argue that Motion and Rest both "are" but are not the Same as Being because by both being the Same, Motion would be Rest and Rest would be Motion. Hence they both "are" but they are not the Same, so they are Other than Being. In fact, everything but Being is Other than Being. To the extent that both Motion and Rest are Other than Being, they are both Not-Being. Therefore, Not-Being "is" because Motion and Rest are. Hence, Not-Being has Being. Each thing that is, is Other than all the others, but Being is not the Same as Other. Both Motion and Rest are Other than each other, so both Same and Other are Not-Being. A being is what it is **by not being all the other beings**. So, Not-Being is intimately related to the Being of every being. Being, by its being Other than everything else, therefore, is Not-Being. **Being is what it is not, more than what it is.** Both Being and Not-Being are, co-mingle with each other, and are mysterious in the extreme. (255a4–260b3) We are now in the vicinity of Heidegger. That Plato could think the thoughts attributed to later thinkers as novelties should be left open for consideration. Maybe Heidegger is right in one assertion, that the beginning is always purer than what follows.

In brief form, this is the exercise that "grounds" the Stranger's doctrine of the co-mingling (*summignusthai*) of the cognitive or intelligible forms or ideas.[51] We must recall that the purpose of this exercise is to support the Stranger's assertion that the very possibility of discourse requires the interweaving of the intelligible forms (259e). While not all forms can interweave, Being and Not-Being must. And Motion and Rest must both "participate" (*metachein*) in Being. And each thing "is" as much by being Other than all the others as by being distinctly itself (*auto kath auto*). Hence the Being of each thing is massively determined by Not-Being and Otherness. This is the reality that the Sophists exploit to their advantage. The "intelligible whole" must be woven together of contradictory parts. This "weaving" may be true of all wholes. If so, in the very interstices of any whole lies a necessary and unavoidable opacity. **In response to Heidegger, this is most assuredly not a doctrine of Being qua full presence.** This doctrine implies very considerable absence. Again, the thought did not await Heidegger. The need to hold together complex if not contradictory parts will recur in the *Statesman* on a political plane with its own "weaving" and its own cosmos filled with Not-Being. Hence we have a parallel between the political and the "ontological"; both must be woven together with an eye to the possibility of meaningful discourse and an understanding of the priority of the Good.

I have suggested that the Socrates of the *Theaetetus* actually hoped that dialectic could lead him toward a contradiction free theory as well as the contemplation of purely present intelligibles. But he was unable to give birth to that theory himself, and we have ample evidence that his method by itself can get one no further than the contemplation of antinomies **but not to the weaving of antinomous intelligibles.** This is the most rarefied level upon which Socrates lacked *poiesis*. In response to Socrates, the message of the Stranger is, do not destroy positions you cannot replace even if they imply contradiction because discourse, and Being itself, both rest on contradiction, or put differently, their articulation in speech rests on poetic syntheses.

There seems to be an implication lurking in the trilogy that knowledge of the good of the soul is more available than ontological knowledge of the whole or a discursive articulation of it. The theoretical, metaphysical or ontological manifestations of philosophy—other than as the contemplation of the ever-recurrent antinomies, i.e., "fundamental questions"—can be no more autonomous than the merely technical, discursive manifestations of philosophy. Everything points to a knowing and understanding that stands outside anything explicitly discussed in the Trilogy, albeit indirectly intimated. Ultimately, it points toward the Good of the *psyche* as architectonic. And it points toward the necessity of a high level *poiesis*.

In the *Statesman*, the Stranger points to our need not only for a doctrine of the mingling of the intelligibles, but by his actions indicates even more clearly the need for a mingling of techniques and methods. I want to argue that it is precisely this mingling that is philosophy in its highest Platonic manifestation. Philosophy must weave together discursivity, *alogon* grasping, pre-theoretical "acquisition," and poetic "production. It stands on the ground of knowledge of the good for the human soul to construct this "weaving." Socrates, the sterile midwife, is incapable of many of these elements. **This weaving is political philosophy as proto-philosophy.**

In the *Statesman*, we confront the explicit deployment of the term "weaving." While *diaeresis* is again deployed, it does not play as prominent a role in the *Statesman* as in the *Sophist*. In the *Statesman,* the Stranger relies more heavily on images, models, stories and again the irruption of "the normative," this time in the form of the doctrine of "the mean" or "due measure" (*pros to metriou*).[52] The Stranger deploys an entire arsenal of tools and approaches, each supplying a part of his final positive doctrine. None of the parts can stand alone. The blending of the parts again points beyond itself to the understanding or ground that informs the Stranger's deeds. This can be nothing other than the good for the soul.

It is clear that the discussion in the *Statesman* is every bit as much about the clarification of the nature of philosophy and its noetic basis as it is about statesmanship *per se*. It is my argument that the "weaving" metaphor of the Statesman fits the philosopher as much as it does any mere political functionary. In fact, the statesman who emerges in the *Statesman* is anything but a mere political functionary. To properly conduct **his** political task, his mind must have spanned the cosmos, grasping as a result how the human part fits into the larger cosmic whole. Only then can he know how to conduct his necessary political weaving. He must be a philosopher. He must know as well how to weave the intelligible elements together and when to use discursive techniques and when to use productive (poetic) and acquisitive (phenomenological/discursive) ones.

What we learn from the *Sophist* points toward the fluidity of the pre-given looks of the phenomena that present themselves in everyday experience. Those looks lend themselves to multiple discursive divisions and presentations. The philosopher tries to ascend above the visible looks in the direction of intelligibles but can never achieve any complete purchase in that realm anymore than the chariot driver of the *Phaedrus* who accomplishes at most a fleeting glance. Hence the philosopher is bound to a "middle" realm. That middle realm is between the realm of the everyday looks and a never altogether present intelligible realm. For **epistemic** reasons the philosopher cannot stand outside the everyday *eidē* in autonomous, theoretical, contemplative detachment. He weaves the everyday and the intelligible together. While there may come and go many "philosophies," like the commingling doctrine of the Stranger, the highest wisdom of philosophy at its most awake, is a mixing of and weaving together of the whole. The philosopher must hold together discursivity and intelligibility for the sake of the human good. In this fashion, he cares for his fellow humans and becomes a citizen in the highest sense.

It is the philosopher qua statesman in the highest sense—henceforth designated *politikos*—who is responsible for blending the parts into a whole, a whole that apparently would not produce itself. **This is neither the simple acquisition of intelligible givens to stare at valorized in Platonism nor the pure, ungrounded *poiesis* of Postmodernism.** Philosophy is both productive and acquisitive and neither simply productive nor simply acquisitive. It is political to the extent it takes its bearings by the good for the soul. The *politikos* engages in both production and acquisition. But a central issue is finessed by the Stranger by positing "knowledge" not "art" as the starting point of his opening *diaeresis* regarding the *politikos*. Unlike the sophist, the *politikos* allegedly has knowledge. In his initial diaeretic attempt to grasp the *politikos*, the Stranger presents him as a being with the knowledge of "human care taking" offered and exercised voluntarily over allegedly tame herd animals.

Then the Stranger moves quickly to his cosmic story (*muthos*). The point of the story is that the human things are massively affected by the situation in the larger cosmic whole of which they form a part. **The cosmos is not presented as stable or static**, over time there have been radical transformations in its nature.[53] We have no way of knowing if our age is now permanent or if another epochal cosmic transformation of some kind is inevitable.[54] In the age in which we live the gods have left and we do not receive everything directly from the hand of nature as we did in the Eden-like age of Cronos.[55] Far from being a statement of sugar-coated optimism, this is a sobering picture very Heideggerian in its depiction of the flight of the gods. We are on our own and must to some extent produce our existence and that means especially our political and moral existence.

If we follow the logic of the story, we are not naturally political. Hence the shaping/caring hand of the *politikos* is most essential in our age. After his story, the Stranger undertakes an elaborate *diaeresis* regarding the everyday art of weaving and its nature but also the arts and knowledges that, while different, are nonetheless related to and most importantly, subservient to the master art that dictates its needs to them. In like fashion, *politike* is a form of weaving. It has subservient arts and knowledges. In fact, all the arts and knowledges are subservient to the needs of the *politikos*.[56] Political philosophy is the architectonic activity.

While impressed with the Stranger's virtuosity, we remain perplexed how he can possibly presume to know the nature of the cosmos and the transformations it has gone through over what must be extraordinary stretches of time. Have we followed the tortuous path in the *Sophist* and *Statesman* only to arrive at a whopper swallowed whole by an all too easy going young Socrates? In the end, is the Stranger merely a super-sophist? Or does he have a clearer understanding of what is at stake than the sophists together with a more benevolent heart that is concerned for the greater good rather than the momentary utility of a small-minded wage earner? If so, again, that would ultimately imply that what he really possesses is knowledge of what is good for the human soul. I return to my prior suggestion, must not ethics and psychology rather than cosmology or ontology be the foundation upon which the Stranger, and perhaps Plato as well, builds his stories, shapes his use of discursivity and blends together the other elements of his arsenal? The human condition, in all its diversity, together with a grasping of the enduring needs and desires of the human soul, is the knowledge that is presupposed. What passes for cosmology, ontology or metaphysics represents an extrapolation from the one thing we can know to some extent, the human condition.

We are forced to conclude that like discursivity (logic), cosmology, ontology or metaphysics can never be autonomous, theoretical possibilities. Plato is no ontologist or metaphysician as Heidegger, Derrida and others have asserted. He is a psychologist with clarity about our unavoidable phenomenological dependence of philosophy on a shared public world as a point of departure. That means he understands the dominance of *aisthesis* in our existence while pointing toward the necessity of positing certain cognitive forms if we are to explain the common experience of the world in which the human soul exists. To let go of certain necessities is literally to be cast out into speechlessness. Ultimately the status and even existence of the cognitive forms, "knowable" only in some extra-discursive fashion, appears to be an extrapolation from ethics and psychology. Put another way, "if they must be then they are." While there are intimations, there is no clear assertion of a direct noetic "grasping" faculty ("intuition") in the Trilogy, although it is not ruled out. While the existence of the noetic things is posited, that positing is **not** the work of a contemplative consciousness that is in touch with some pure presence as Heidegger claims. But there is no reason to call the extrapolative effort of the *politikos* a free-floating, autonomous act of Will either, which would be to ignore the importance of phenomenological roots.

Casting our glance back at the *Sophist* from the vantage of the *Statesman,* we recall that it was argued that the doctrine of cognitive mingling was needed to make philosophy, or for that matter any discourse, possible. And the cognitive doctrine of mingling was necessary as a propaedeutic to the weaving of the *Statesman* that culminates in the weaving together of the different types of human souls. The implication of the Stranger's weaving metaphor is that there is a natural fabric to the human condition and it centers on the ensemble of human soul types. Nonetheless, even the natural types must be educated with an eye to weaving them into a whole just as the different elements of a philosophical arsenal must be presented in such a way as to make them amenable to being blended together into a whole as well.

In the weaving together of souls the same mingling of what might appear to be opposites is stressed that we get epistemically in the *Sophist*'s mingling doctrine. The city needs the "hard" (manliness) and the "soft" (moderation).[57] Both are parts of virtue. Neither is simply desirable by itself. Apart, each can in fact be a vice. Much the same conclusion could be applied to the epistemic weaving of the *Sophist*. Things that are useful and virtuous together may not be useful when found apart—e.g., autonomous "logic." In the pre-philosophic, poetic language of pre-Socratic thought (which lacked anything resembling *apodeixis* or demonstration qua dialectic or *diaeresis*) strife is the mother of all order. But strife can yield order only with the proper intervention of *nous*. Plato appears to end up in some important ways close to Heraclites, with, however, a major bow to Parmenides in his recognition that somewhere something must not only be posited as at rest, but also **be** at rest. But that which is at rest can be brought to speech in a variety of ways.

To conclude, the primary weaving to which the Stranger points can only be accomplished by giving men proper opinions. And hence we circle back to what the Stranger posited as the primary reason for choosing any philosophic method, to bring **agreement**. And agreement is what we get at the end of the *Statesman* unlike the *aporia* at the end of the *Theaetetus*. The easygoing and pliant young Socrates happily assents to the doctrine the Stranger finally weaves together for him. Yet he shows that he really has not understood what has happened. Young Socrates is allowed by Plato to have the last word and hence gives the Trilogy its valedictory: "You have given us, Stranger, a most complete and admirable treatment of the king and the statesman." (311c9–10) He has missed entirely that we have been discussing the statesman and the philosopher, or more to the point, the *politikos* as philosopher. Socrates is given no more chance for a rejoinder than was Glaucon at the end of the *Republic*. Plato will draw no explicit conclusions for us. But in a matter of days Socrates stands before the Athenian jury. Shortly thereafter he meets his fate. It is hard not to draw conclusions from that fact.

CONCLUSION

During the twentieth century, we have repeatedly been told that we have arrived at the end of the philosophical/metaphysical tradition that originated with Plato. Far from it. In one respect, the Platonic tradition has yet to begin. The metaphysical tradition, if we borrow from Heidegger, presumes that it is possible to stare theoretically at cognitively present entities. Metaphysics so understood rests on an understanding that is precisely what Plato was **not** attempting to set in motion.[58] If there was a single origin of the metaphysical tradition as Heidegger depicted it, it emanated from Aristotle. **That tradition** may have reached its end, or for a variety of reasons lost persuasiveness, but any tradition that might emanate from Plato is not at an end, for it has hardly been opened, let alone plumbed. To borrow from Heidegger, perhaps now a return to Plato is possible for the first time and then a new striking off, a "second beginning." A second beginning from Plato, not the pre-Socratics as Heidegger seems to suggest.

Plato was a "phenomenologist," before the fact. He takes the pre-given, public "looks" as the point of departure for philosophy. Philosophy must give those phenomena a discursive articulation. But more than one is always possible. That discursive articulation of the phenomena, or as Strauss will call them, "natural experience," sets the stage for the generation of "scientific" categories. Plato consciously remains positioned between natural experience and the kind of scientific categories Aristotle launches. In fact, he will allow neither of the two basic moves that Aristotle makes. He will not allow the existence of an autonomous theory, and he will not allow the existence of an autonomous political science. Those Aristotelian moves are precisely the negation of the inner truth of Plato's position.

Contrary to the Plato of Plato**nism**, Plato offers us an understanding of philosophy that has theoretical and discursive **components** while not eventuating in an autonomous ontology or metaphysic as the end toward which philosophy aims or as the foundation upon which it is built. Plato also offers us an understanding of the poetic elements that can never be expunged from philosophy, but he does it in a way that does not end in the hegemony of the groundless Will. Plato offers for our consideration an integrative vision of philosophy. That is especially useful for us at a time of the disintegration of thought into competing parallel paradigms or language games, and the general fragmentation of postmodernism.[59]

Plato concluded that philosophy qua discursive can get no further on its own than a series of antinomies that cannot be transcended. The response to that theoretical conclusion is political philosophy, a philosophy that sees the shared, public display of the ensemble of looks that constitute reality—i.e., the political in the widest sense—as the ground of philosophy. It grasps that philosophy can never theoretically emancipate itself from that beginning in any complete fashion. It also grasps that the only place that stands still, the only position of rest in what might otherwise be an unremitting reign of flux, is the human soul, its diversity, its desires and needs. Everything else may have to be extrapolated from the phenomenological and the psychological in weaving together a whole.

Socrates is not the father of political philosophy because he is the problem that causes it to come into existence. Socrates longed for a basis for pure theory. Socrates hoped that dialectic would get him to pure theoretical staring. It is precisely a critique of this longing that Plato provides for all times without falling into the constructivism of modern thought that inevitably leads to the groundless, willful subjectivism of Nietzsche. Plato is not the ultimate cause of Nietzsche. The philosophic "tradition" does not begin with Plato and end with Nietzsche. **Heidegger is wrong**. Nietzsche is correct to this extent. Socrates was a problem. But Plato moved before the fact to correct the problem. Socrates, Cicero to the contrary notwithstanding, never broke through to political philosophy, and hence never really brought philosophy "down from the heavens." It is precisely the heavens to which he hoped to ascend. What is political philosophy? **It is not primarily the politic defense of the philosophers before the city**. It is the highest and most awake form of philosophy. It stands beyond the chimera of autonomous theory. It is both acquisitive and productive, grasping and creative qua blending and weaving. It is, as I have argued, architectonic and holistic.

From the Trilogy we get a vision of "knowledge" residing in pre-scientific awareness that is present to all. In the *Theaetetus* Socrates shows the problems with trying to associate the term "knowledge" with anything beyond this immediate awareness. Plato has both Socrates and the Stranger demonstrate the ways in which the **autonomous** discursive culling of immediate knowledge leads to antinomies, or fatuousness. But accepting, as Plato did, the superiority of discursivity to the *mania* and inspired poetic dreaming of pre-Socratic thought, the question became how to respond. Plato's response was political philosophy in the dynamic sense of architectonic weaving we have considered. The systematic and theoretico-deductive tradition of political philosophy—for example, Hobbes—is at odds with the original understanding of political philosophy as first philosophy. That modern manifestation of political philosophy is probably at an end. The Platonic version is perfectly deployable in our time.

The greatest thinkers of our time—Nietzsche and Heidegger, as well as those who descend from them—do not push through to political philosophy. Heidegger, for example, remains oddly determined by the traditional belief that philosophy must be scientific/theoretical and ultimately reduced to a form of discursivity. He simply wishes to overcome philosophy so understood. Hence he sees where Aristotle arrived as where Plato was headed. Seeing the theoretical tradition of philosophy as leading to the oblivion of Being—or nihilism—Heidegger opts for a taking apart of the tradition that has parallels in autonomous *diaeresis*. Nietzsche also takes theoretical discursivity as at the heart of past philosophy. He criticizes it as "prejudiced," and publicly opts for an autonomous, "inspired"—which is to say non-discursive—Dionysian poetry and even religiosity.

Derrida's "deconstructionism" for all intents and purposes transforms philosophy into a diaeretic taking apart. Deconstructionism is presented as an autonomous technical method. But all manner of things are brought in through the back door when we are not looking—making us wonder if Derrida's is consciously or unconsciously weaving and blending. **Either way, he is a terrible psychologist and poet.** We are told by Derrida—it is basically asserted with an added nod to Heidegger—that there is no possibility of full presence. The non-presence of texts and authors, for example, is then said to mean that every reading of a text is an interpretation or re-writing of the text. But how can anyone know a text has been re-written except in comparison with the original. Further, the underlying premise of deconstructionism is the **moral premise** that we ought to deconstruct. In other words, the good requires that we not allow any manifestation of presence to ossify. To take apart all ossifications produces the good—or at least a better situation than if we had left things alone.[60] But this conclusion is only possible on the basis of knowledge of the human soul and its needs and desires, which deconstructionism cannot admit exists, for the human soul has no more presence than anything else. **Deconstructionism is not a fully awake form of philosophy**. Deconstructionism cannot push through to political philosophy any more than Nietzsche and Heidegger can.

By contrast, Platonic political philosophy, as far as it is deployed in the Trilogy, takes its stand in two places. First, there is the ensemble of the pre-discursive looks. For want of a better term, I will call this a phenomenological basis.[61] Second, it takes a stand on the human soul and its multiple needs and desires, the normative, with the primacy of the Good. Political philosophy also sees the need for self-conscious, articulate discursivity. One cannot allow the simple hegemony of "inspiration," the unconscious or *mania*, divine or otherwise. But simultaneously it must be realized that discursivity itself cannot be autonomous. Philosophy cannot be reduced to "logic" any more than it can be reduced to pre-discursive phenomenological "seeing." Philosophy either points toward rather noetically intuits—and I see no explicit indication of the latter noetic grasping in Plato—supra-discursive, cognitive forms that must be.[62] Philosophy does not, in the manner of Platonism, deduce moral and political norms from forms that are fully present to detached theoretical staring.

Political philosophy is an active weaving and blending of pre-discursive vision, technical discursive method, psychology, and a supra-discursive grasping/positing of cognitive forms all undertaken with fully awake clarity regarding the primacy of the Good. As such political philosophy is a dynamic ongoing doing and discussing that cannot come to an end. It is not reducible to any of its parts nor can it devolve into a detached theoretical staring. It is a possibility perfectly available to us at present and into the future.

NOTES

1. Martin Heidegger, *Plato's Sophist* (Bloomington: Indiana University Press, 1997), p. 93.
2. Leo Strauss, *Philosophy and Law* (Philadelphia: Jewish Publication Society, 1987), p. 109.
3. Stanley Rosen, *Plato's Statesman* (New Haven: Yale University Press, 1995), pp. viii–ix.
4. Rosen first developed this position in his interpretation of the *Sophist* in *Plato's Sophist: The Drama of Original and Image* (New Haven: Yale University Press, 1983), and then carried it forward in his 1995 interpretation of the *Statesman*. I am not altogether certain that this is Rosen's final position, although I think that at the very least he ultimately comes perilously close to it. Consider in this regard the following; "It is in no sense an anachronism to suggest that the Stranger is a Platonic anticipation of certain aspects of the Cartesian attempt to master nature by *technē*, including the *technē* of a *mathesis universalis*" (*Plato's Statesman*, p. 15).
5. I use the phrase "popular reading" because it is a reading I do not accept. For my understanding of Nietzsche the reader is referred to my *Nietzsche, Heidegger and the Transition to Postmodernity* (Chicago: University of Chicago Press, 1996) and *Martin Heidegger: Paths Taken, Paths Opened* (Lanham, MD: Rowman & Littlefield, 2007).

6. Leo Strauss, "An Unspoken Prologue," *Interpretation*, Vol. 7, no. 3, September 1978.

7. It is not altogether novel to read Plato's Trilogy as representing a critique of Socrates by the Eleatic Stranger, with Plato siding with the Stranger. Traditional scholarship sees the "later" Plato as having outgrown his Socratic moment, with his own thought having developed in the direction of the Stranger's position. But that is not my primary point. I believe Socrates was always a problem for Plato.

8. That problem is pointed out in its political and moral components by Plato's dramatically intertwining of the Trilogy with the trial and death dialogues. That intertwining, while mentioned by several scholars, is most exhaustively explored by Joseph Cropsey in *Plato's World, Man's Place in the Cosmos* (Chicago: University of Chicago Press, 1995). Unlike Cropsey, I want to stress the ways in which Socrates represented something that was **epistemically** problematic for philosophy, not just politically and morally dangerous.

9. This terminology points toward the path-breaking and door-opening distinction that is at the core of Heidegger's analysis of the facticity that underlies all theory. It is a terminology that is also adopted and adapted by Strauss. See chapter 10 "On a Possible Epicurean Garden for Philosophy." For Heidegger, see *Plato's Sophist*.

10. According to Strauss, with this prudence and moderation came the origins of political philosophy understood as the political face of philosophy or the politic presentation of philosophy before the city. Occasionally, Strauss mentions that political philosophy could also mean the philosophic treatment of the nature of the political and the things most important to political life, like justice. But this second possibility always seems to take a back seat for Strauss. According to Strauss, with Socrates philosophy turned from an attempt to grasp the "first things" or the "first cause" directly (which means extra-discursively) and adopted instead a mediated "Socratic" or "dialectical" approach to the first things. This led to an interrogation of the things that are "first for us," the visible world of things and the various opinions regarding the "nature" or "being" of those various things—including things as disparate as trees, dogs, man, friendship, justice, sameness and Being. In *What Is Political Philosophy* (Chicago: University of Chicago Press, 1988), p. 10, Strauss also argues that political philosophy is but a **branch** of pure, theoretical philosophy itself. This would seem to imply that philosophy itself is primarily metaphysical, cosmological or ontological. While I am not positive this is Strauss's last word on the subject, it is one of his most open and visible words. Contrary to this understanding, I continue to argue that political philosophy is itself proto-philosophy.

11. I have sketched this possibility of wholeness in chapter 3 "What Is Political Philosophy: A Phenomenological Approach," above. I will also suggest, although at present it can be no more than an assertion, that the Platonic discovery of political philosophy far from being deepened and expanded by Aristotle, or the rest of the tradition thereafter, was primarily occluded and covered up almost immediately. Although, as we will see in the next chapter, the Aristotle of the practical works retained the "phenomenological" perspective of Plato.

12. I see no reason to accept the self-invalidating, internally contradictory critiques of self-knowing and self-consciousness that form the basis of much post-

Heideggerian philosophy. One need not theoretically prove the possibility of full self-conscious transparency to take longing for self-knowledge and self-conscious clarity as intrinsic to philosophy. In principle, no disproof of the possibility can be given except by utterly rhetorical, Derridean-like sleights of hand.

13. While Socrates seems implicated in designating philosophy as erotic in the *Symposium* he does so only by reporting a discussion he allegedly had with a certain woman named Diotima. But of all of those present in the *Symposium*, Socrates merely reports a speech rather than creating (*poiesis*) one. And the drama of the *Symposium*, together with the "speech" of Alcibiades, shows that Socrates is anything but erotic. In the *Phaedrus* Socrates links philosophy with *mania*, but again the drama proves that **he** is anything but inspired, except by the auspices of the place he occupies and the "divine" tree (*platanos*) under which he sits. What he is is a lover of speeches, so much so that he will waste his time talking to the likes of Phaedrus, among many, from whom he can expect to learn nothing of interest. And the Socrates of the *Phaedrus* is so lacking in philosophical judgment that he asserts that Isocrates possesses greater philosophical promise than Plato.

14. At the end of the *Euthyphro*, Euthyphro has no further interest in talking with Socrates and flees his clutches. While he may not immediately go into the court as he had initially planned, there is no evidence whatsoever that he has had any change of heart. Quite the contrary, he simply had no further interest in engaging in discussion with Socrates.

15. In this regard, one might also consider the *Cleitophon*.

16. I will return to this issue shortly.

17. In the *Phaedo*, Socrates claims that when he was young he tried to study "nature" directly as did the pre-Socratics. But he gave up that approach and undertook his "second sailing"; he tried to access the whole indirectly through the interrogation of speeches—i.e., dialectic. In the *Parmenides*, the youngest depiction of Socrates, it appears that Socrates is already underway in that second sailing except he **starts** from pure *eidē* rather than finds them in everyday speeches. We appear to have no Platonic depiction of the pre-Socratic Socrates. See chapter 15 "Plato's Parmenides: Socratism and the Origins of Platonic Political Philosophy" above.

18. See the section "The Problem of Socrates" in Nietzsche's *Twilight of the Idols*.

19. "The essence of spirit, then, is self-consciousness." And also: "Man can only fulfill himself through education and discipline; his immediate existence contains merely the possibility of self-realization (i.e., of becoming rational and free)." And also: "[Man] ceases to be merely a natural being at the mercy of immediate intuitions and impulses which he must satisfy and perpetuate, . . . knowledge leads him to control his impulses; he places the ideal, the realm of thought, between the demands of the impulse and [its] satisfaction." G. W. F. Hegel, *Lectures on the Philosophy of World History: Introduction* (Cambridge: Cambridge University Press, 1984), pp 49–51.

20. The alternative is that the invocation of this voice is just a shabby canard and Socrates is just a theatrical faker.

21. Cleitophon in fact indicts Socrates for his inability to ever get anyone past the point of seeing that they are unclear. "For I shall maintain, Socrates, that while you

are of untold value to a man who has not been exhorted, to him who has been exhorted you are almost an actual hindrance in the way of his attaining the goal of virtue and becoming a happy man." Plato, *Cleitophon*, trans. by R. G. Bury (Cambridge, MA: Harvard University Press, 1929). (410e)

22. And this abstracts completely from what we are to make of philosophic kingship in the *Republic*. One might conclude that these represent an ongoing series of thought experiments by Socrates. If so, he never resolved the issue satisfactorily. But one can unravel Plato's point if one sees how these suggestions fit into each dialogue and into his larger emendation of Socratism.

23. There is some indication that Theaetetus may actually have suffered some harm at Socrates's hands. I grant that the following is speculative. It is said that the Theaetetus of thirty years later is not only suffering from wounds but from dysentery—a condition of flux. We may be led to wonder if Socrates induced an intellectual flux into Theaetetus's life. One way or the other we have to make something of Plato's intruding this issue of dysentery which would otherwise be a gratuitous and unseemly throw-away. This is especially true in a dialogue that thematically confronts the "flux crowd."

24. It might appear that the very oldest Socrates presented in the *Phaedo* does present a positive doctrine. He uses a variety of rhetorical devices and logic chopping to assert the immortality of the soul. Yet despite his *daimon* telling him to do poetry, he proves that he is incapable. Far from contradicting the thesis I am going to present in a moment, what Plato is doing is indicating Socrates's decency and good intentions on a day when his friends are grieving. Socrates tries to convince his friends that they should not mourn but be happy for him. See the discussion of the *Phaedo* in chapter 13.

25. See chapter 15 on the *Parmenides*.

26. *Epistle II*, 314c2 in Plato, *Timaeus, Critias, Cleitophan, Menexenus, Epistles*, trans. by R. G. Bury (Cambridge: Harvard University Press, 1929).

27. In the "middle" dialogue *Symposium*, Plato quite explicitly has his Socrates, in a very uncharacteristic fashion, beautify himself to go to the dinner party.

28. It should be noted that there appears to be a difference between the Platonic Parmenides and what we have come to take as historical Parmenideanism.

29. Cropsey focuses on Theaetetus's intellectual accomplishments as a mathematician. This is helpful in that it links up with the *Theaetetus'* thematic mathematical reflections regarding the irrationals. But if we stick strictly to what is thematically presented in the beginning of the text, it is Theaetetus's moral and political deeds that Plato is stressing through the discussion by Terpsion and Euclides. Cropsey, *Plato's World*, pp. 27–30.

30. Cropsey observes that this makes the Trilogy as close to a written text by Socrates as we have. One can deflect this observation in the direction of my thesis: Socrates had an opportunity to correct anything he wished and was satisfied that this was an accurate picture of his doings no matter how questionable.

31. Recall that those who make the text present for us in the *Symposium* are walking and in motion throughout. Motion and rest are important themes in the Platonic dialogues, both thematically and dramatically.

32. Klein offers the perplexing assertion that "there is hardly any doubt that this prologue was not part of the original dialogue." His reasons for this conclusion do not seem to me to be very compelling. See Jacob Klein, *Plato's Trilogy* (Chicago: University of Chicago Press, 1977), p. 75. Benardete offers several suggestions, all of which seem useful. One of his suggestions is that this literary device allows Plato to show Socrates entirely from the outside without Socrates being able to supply any of his inner thoughts and reasons as he does, for example, in the *Republic*. This seems to me to support my thesis that Plato is attempting to make us view Socratism from an external standpoint. See Seth Benardete, *The Being of the Beautiful* (Chicago: University of Chicago Press, 1984).

33. It is interesting how often Plato has Socrates use precisely these last two definitions of knowledge in crucial places throughout the Platonic dialogues, especially in the *Republic* and *Symposium*. Plato's "middle" Socrates frequently takes the existence of "right opinion," for example, as a given as part of his various "proofs" and "refutations."

34. I say contrived in that it highlights how Socrates repeatedly tries to draw Theodoros into the discussion while Theodoros repeatedly tries to avoid it. On one level this is part of the dramatic *agon* that goes on between the two. On another level, as a mathematician, Theodoros is a representative of an apodictic knowledge that Plato is intent on suggesting does not exist.

35. It might be said that the Socrates of the Trilogy does not completely fit his own picture of the alienation of the philosopher from the everyday world. He claims he cares about the promising youngsters from his own Athens, rather than promising foreigners, and as Theaetetus approaches Socrates recites minutia about his family background and resources. But this largely fits under the heading of gossip rather than intimate knowledge about the political ways of Athens.

36. I have used the H. N. Fowler translation, *Theaetetus/Sophist*, in the Loeb Library (Cambridge: Harvard University Press, 1977).

37. When we stand back and look at the *Theaetetus* as a whole, we note that not only does it end in *aporia*, but on a slightly more positive note it presents a series of antinomies that follow from adopting either of two allegedly exhaustive and opposed hypotheses. This adds some substantive grist to the Socratic mill regarding his ultimate wisdom being knowledge of his own ignorance. We are ignorant to the extent we know we are unable to give a discursive articulation of the whole because every attempt ends in an antinomy. The ensemble of those antinomies would be one's highest wisdom. As regards antinomies at least, it is possible that Socrates did learn something in his youth from Parmenides, at least from the Parmenides of Plato's *Parmenides*. But perhaps it was not the correct lesson that he learned.

38. I am fascinated by Strauss's speculation that the "second sailing" described in the *Phaedo*, or the "Socratic turn" toward the dialectical method, was adopted to replace the pre-Socratic attempt to approach the first things in a direct and unmediated fashion. But Strauss argues that ultimately this was, from the perspective of the real Socrates, primarily rhetorical. Under the façade of that politic, public presentation of philosophy, Strauss argues that Socrates continued not only to study "nature" but to approach it directly. **That means that Socrates continued to pursue philosophy as**

a detached theoretical undertaking that could directly grasp the first things. But even Strauss does not find support for this position in Platonic texts; he turns instead to Xenophon. As fascinating as this speculation is, I have not found it useful in interpreting Plato. It seems to me that Plato is showing the real Socrates as all too devoted to the dialectical method. However, in Strauss's position as in mine, Socrates ends up **aiming** at a direct, pure form of theoretical contemplation.

39. In this regard, Heidegger is very useful in opening a novel perspective upon the Platonic texts and Plato's presentation of Socrates. See, *Plato's Sophist*; see especially pp. 5–34. In effect, Heidegger's argument is that Socratic/Platonic philosophy grows out of "natural" or "pre-theoretical" experience and natural language and the sifting and culling of that pre-theoretical revelation of things leads to a halfway house between natural experience and "science." Heidegger sees the longing to be scientific as the appropriate longing of philosophy, albeit that longing has reached its end. To that extent Heidegger is closer in spirit to Aristotle than Plato. Aristotle is for Heidegger the first truly scientific thinker—working in categories that allegedly transcend natural experience and natural language, at least in the theoretical works. **Heidegger is critical of dialectic as at best a rudimentary attempt at scientific philosophy.** This brings us to the epigram from Heidegger, which began this chapter and which seems to me to be precisely on target but at odds with Heidegger's own understanding. In that quote, Heidegger is precisely pointing to the way in which Plato's position is distinctive as opposed to rudimentary. To the extent that Heidegger never differentiates between Plato and Socrates—as, for example, Nietzsche does—all Heidegger can say of Plato is that he is a rudimentary thinker and that the understanding that presents the *politikos* as *philosophos* is an unscientific position. I reject that conclusion in favor of the conclusion that Plato is not "on the way" to Aristotle, but has a position that is critical of Aristotle, before the fact, for the same reasons it is critical of Socrates. Of this more in a moment.

40. Socrates admits as much in the *Euthydemus*. (277e)

41. See chapter 14 on the *Symposium*.

42. Benardete translates *mala de andra philosophon* as "a man very much a philosopher." Benardete's translation seems to me not entirely to capture what I take to be the primary point. Fowler seems to me to be more on the scent with "a real philosopher." Yet that is far from literal. If one looks at Theaetetus 203e6, as one example, or at the use of *andra* for manly/courageous/hard (vs. *sophrosyne* as soft) in the weaving image in the *Statesman* one is forced to see that stressing **manly** is intended.

43. Notice also how the Stranger seems to take a shot at dialectic at 217e2.

44. Contrary to Nietzsche, it is hard to see how that could have so fascinated his contemporaries as opposed to annoying them. Yet Socrates picks fights he "wins" only rhetorically.

45. Again, as the drama of the *Theaetetus* shows—via the three boys who approach Socrates and Theodoros at the beginning—the same name can go with different looks, the same look can be given different names, and things with no look and no name can still be. Shortly, the Stranger will demonstrate, in a parallel fashion, the fluidity of the world of the looks and the multiplicity of plausible names that can be applied to them.

46. To repeat my earlier observation, to find the real Plato one ultimately needs to compare the performance of the Stranger with the performances of the young and beautiful Socrates of the dramatically "middle" dialogues. My speculation is that Plato himself is closest to the young and beautiful Socrates of the "middle" dialogues. Again, recall how the dramatic Socrates engages in the uncharacteristic act of fancying himself up to go to the meeting presented in the *Symposium*. He wants to be as cosmetized and beautiful as possible. And recall how the "inspired" speech of the *Phaedrus*, the palinode, takes place literally **under** the direct auspices of Plato himself.

47. In this vein, one might consider Heidegger's treatment of the relation between "interpretation" and "understanding" in *Being and Time* (New York: Harper and Row, 1962), pp. 188–203, 385–89.

48. In the *Phaedo*, Socrates reports that while he was in jail awaiting execution a voice came to him and told him to make music. His response was to make Aesop's fables rhyme, a rather lame effort at *poiesis*. This is, however, one of the rare occasions when his little voice told him something positive rather than holding him back and always saying "no." But the voice did not move him toward actual creativity.

49. We are reminded of the *Republic* where the Good is the first cause of all things and by being beyond the intelligible ideas (which grant the tribes of beings their Being) is in principle Not-Being.

50. I say the historical Parmenides because Plato's Parmenides is an apostate on many of the same things as the Eleatic Stranger.

51. Cropsey makes the following penetrating observation: "The youthful Socrates of the *Parmenides* could see easily enough that a particular entity would participate in many Ideas, but he did not admit the participation of any Idea in another. The Stranger argues otherwise." *Plato's World* (103). I believe this helps support my contention that the Stranger brings a critique against Socratism. But in the end, I think Cropsey sees the positions of Socrates and the Stranger as more mutually supportive than I do and dialectic and *diaeresis* as supplementary, which I do not think they are.

52. This latter device again highlights the intrusion of the centrality of the human soul in the Platonic understanding of the Good together with an understanding of its desires and needs. The Good of the good takes priority over rhetoric, logic, ontology and metaphysics. As the Good of the soul, *psyche*, this implies the priority of ethics and psychology. This should be compared with Nietzsche's assertion that we **again** need to see psychology as the queen of the sciences. *Beyond Good and Evil*, (New York: Vintage Books, 1989), pp. 31–32.

53. In this regard, see chapter 22 in this volume.

54. One might call such an epochal transformation an "event" or "happening" (*Ereignis*).

55. We should not lose sight of the very chaotic character of the *Statesman*. It jumps about in fits and starts, from subject to subject and method to method, only in the end weaving all the chaotic parts into a whole. In this, the dialogue exactly parallels the Eleatic Stranger's depiction of the cosmos in our age. What is needed is to weave together a whole out of disparate parts.

56. Obviously, both dialectic and *diaeresis* would be subservient to *politike*. *Politike* is the architectonic science as Aristotle **says**. But everything Aristotle does theoretically

negates the full implication of his statement regarding the *politike* of the *politikos*. For Aristotle accepts the possibility of theoretical staring at fixed intelligible entities.

57. These two elements seem to be woven together in the character Theaetetus. He is gentle even though he is militarily courageous and has a quick mind, which the *Statesman* also presents as a manly character trait.

58. While Plato's position is not in my opinion simply the same as that of his Eleatic Stranger, it is closer to the Eleatic Stranger's position than that of the Socrates of the *Theaetetus*, and hence for purposes of this conclusion I will treat them as the same.

59. This is the vision of postmodernism we get from Lyotard, Rorty and Vattimo to name only a few. It clearly also evokes the thinking of the later Wittgenstein. See especially, Jean-Francois Lyotard, *The Postmodern Condition: A Report on Knowledge*, trans. by G. Bennington and B. Massumi (Minneapolis: University of Minnesota Press, 1984).

60. There is also a furtive form of prediction taking place wherein we are led to believe that the future will be better than the present after one has responded to the **moral** imperative "thou shalt deconstruct." But that kind of prediction is only possible if the cosmos is far more stable—i.e. there is far more presence—than deconstructionism will admit with all its talk about traces, absence and alterity.

61. Incidentally, we are in no position to say that the present looks that confront us are conventional or unnatural as opposed to some prior "natural" ones. That would be a pure construct. It presumes more than we can know. What we can do is simply begin. Hence as phenomenological, political philosophy is always possible, now and into the future. It turns itself loose on the reigning looks.

62. In the *Statesman*, they are given the vague designation *asomata*.

Chapter Seventeen

Aristotle on Reason and Its Limits

As we saw above with Machiavelli, modernity was born of a faith that through a conscious application of a newly posited vision of reason it was possible to transform and regulate the natural whole—both human and non-human—thereby greatly improving the possibility of human freedom and happiness. Four hundred years later many in our time seem to have arrived at the conclusion that Western rationalism itself—not just its modern version—is the cause of nihilism. Having shaken the traditional bases of community and morality, it is now asserted that reason is impotent to provide a substitute; it is destructive without the possibility of being constructive. As an alternative we are offered a praise of various non-rational wellsprings for order and community in instinct, poetic "inspiration," a turn to the East, a hopeful waiting for a new dispensation of Being, *différance*, and undoubtedly with other permutations yet to come.

As markets become global, and as the modern, technological civilization that was raised on the proto-modern view of reason continues to destroy the last vestiges of age-old traditions and customs, a paradox emerges. Call it the rationalist faith, the modern project, the Enlightenment dream, or whatever, the core premises that support an increasingly global, modern, technological civilization have come under attack. Material benefits alone will not indefinitely sustain a rationalist civilization that has lost its faith in reason, no matter how global or technically efficient it becomes. This is equally true of the Enlightenment moral and political project, which is based on the same proto-modern, "constructivist" conception of reason that we confronted above.[1]

It could be argued that this modern and, I would argue, postmodernist, "constructivist"/"deconstructivist" conception of reason is responsible for the late modern collapse of faith in reason. Proto-modern reason set out to conquer chance, master, torture and put the question to nature. In opposing the Realm of Freedom to the Realm of Nature, Kant merely codified what was always present. Proto-modern reason has always seen itself as nature's "other," and eventually as the other of custom and tradition as well. That stance increasingly left reason without a foil. While nature, and its cousin tradition, remained as foils, reason could still take its bearings. **As the foil dissolved, reason could find only itself wherever it looked**, and retained no other end than aimless mastery and domination, as Heidegger argued.[2]

When we should have arrived at the modern eschaton we see ever more total warfare, genocide, devices of mass destruction, appalling new technologies—with the biologists offering even more frightening gifts than the physicists—overpopulation, pollution, dwindling resources, and so on. These ills—together with racism, sexism, classism—are increasingly laid at the door of the Western conception of reason. In this environment we will at best career from one pole of distinctively modern dichotomies to another. We will pursue a form of reason that has as its only end continual manipulation or repeatedly praise irreason, fate, spontaneity, creativity, will, instinct, *différance*. Unless the *modern* conception of reason can find a way to transform itself, it is predictable that this tendency will accelerate. But I see no basis upon which modern reason can transform itself.

With the collapse of faith in reason, philosophy increasingly transforms itself into hermeneutics; life itself becomes seen as a multiplicity of texts that are continually reinterpreted.[3] As a result, science becomes one among many forms of interpretation or poetry. Indeed as Nietzsche predicted, life becomes a fable.[4] Hence, with the modern prophet of Dionysos in the lead, armies of social scientists fan out to discover the irrational bases of everything from human consciousness to science, art, culture, civilization and reason itself. The greatest thinker of the twentieth century—Heidegger—becomes the ontologist of a postmodern traditionalism, the proponent of closed cultural wholes defined by either spontaneous resoluteness and authenticity or a newly autochthonous, inspired, native poetry with its own native gods.

Hoping to find an alternative to the choice between proto-modern reason and postmodern irreason we turn away in search of an alternate understanding of reason. We approach the pre-modern understanding of reason not to find premade recipes that are immediately applicable to our present situation, but to make an **initial** step out of the late modern reason/irreason dichotomy. In pursuit of that alternate understanding, I will focus on Aristotle's *Politics*, with special attention to Books 1 and 2. With the yield of that examination in hand I will return to the question of the contemporary predicament of reason. Despite my understanding that Aristotle's **theoretical** works pursue and develop the worst of the Socratic longing, the practical works represent some of the best phenomenology that has ever been done. Aristotle's attempt to make the theoretical autonomous was the prerequisite for the modern transformation of reason that unhinged it from phenomenological underpinnings. But in the practical works Aristotle gives us an understanding of reason that provides an alternative to modern constructivism and postmodern irreason.

It is customary to observe that Socrates is the father of Western rationalism. Following the Nietzschean variant of that understanding, with Socrates reason came to challenge ancestral custom and the spontaneous instinct of "natural" actors as the foundation for order in moral and political life. This view has some plausibility.[5] For example, in Aristophanes's *Clouds* Socratic philosophy is presented as symptomatic of the breakdown of filial piety and, more generally, traditional standards of virtue. This is clearly not the entire story, but it is disquieting to see the great number of dialogues led by Socrates that culminate in *aporia*.[6] For example, as we have seen, in the *Theaetetus* Socrates elicits commonly held opinions about knowledge and proceeds to show them all to be inadequate. At the end of the dialogue, having destroyed commitment to those opinions, he leaves the discussion to go to court to face charges of importing new gods and corrupting the young. When the same discussants return the next day, Plato turns leadership of the discussion over to an "Eleatic Stranger" who explicitly states that his method of division aims at "agreement." Indeed, he seems to secure agreement in the most thematically political of the dialogues of the Trilogy, the *Statesman*. That Plato is questioning the influence of Socrates seems clear not only by the change of discussion leaders but by the linking of the Trilogy in dramatic temporality with the four trial and death dialogues.[7]

Socrates' method, which elicits answers to "what is" questions, leads to *aporia*—and therewith to a politically and morally questionable outcome. Socrates's version of the dialectical method demands of actors that they provide a fully articulate, apodictic explanation of their behavior in a way that does not contradict other opinions they hold. Hence, both "clear and distinct" ideas and the principle of non-contradiction are demanded. Socrates' understanding that "virtue is knowledge" is a principle that cannot be lived up to by someone who is virtuous by nature or habit. Apparently, only the philosopher can be virtuous. If we compare this understanding with what we may assume is Plato's emendation, including the *Republic* which ends with the myth of Er, both *logos* and *muthos* are required. As Plato shows in the *Phaedo*, *Symposium* and elsewhere, Socrates is hopeless when it comes to *poiesis* and *muthos*. Called on by what he takes to be a divine voice to do poetry, all he can come up with is the effort to make Aesop's *Fables* rhyme.[8]

There is something questionable about Socratic rationalism. Plato already saw this as clearly as Nietzsche would twenty-four hundred years later.

Chapter Seventeen

Socrates always ran the risk of not so much moderating individuals who thought they knew more than they did, but of undermining the shared opinions without which life is impossible. And he was unable to replace those opinions with anything but *aporia*. Applied without the supplement of poetry and the "weaving" we confront in the Trilogy, Socratic rationalism is potentially nihilistic.[9] Throughout the dialogues, Plato interweaves *muthos* and *logos* with a respect for the phenomenology of the *eidē* as they already appear. Socrates the barren "midwife" did not write, and was not poetic. Socrates negates opinions, some of which—for example Polemarchus's—are perfectly serviceable as the basis of decent political and moral life, without substituting anything in their place. Socrates is daring, driven by a faith that was immoderate and could not be proved. That faith was the element in his longing that was irrational. The basis of Socratic rationalism was itself irrational. The Platonic position, as I have argued above, was far more self-consciously adopted and presented an understanding of the place of reason that was far more moderate and clear about its suppositions and possibilities.

Something similar can be found in Aristotle's **practical** works. Viewed with some care, it becomes clear that they are very circumspect. The determination not to let Athens sin a second time against philosophy no doubt partially accounts for Aristotle's reticence. But that kind of prudence is not the only explanation. Aristotle's frequently articulated practical method is equally significant. Like Socrates's "second sailing," Aristotle always *begins* from commonly held opinions. **But Aristotle never completely transcends them.** He juxtaposes different opinions. He articulates what is embedded in them. He usually finds some shred of an acceptable yield in almost every opinion that he has chosen to publicly reproduce. Those with whom he openly chooses to pick fights—like Socrates—are always engaged with an eye to defending common opinion against **theoretical attack.**

Aristotle acts "as-if" something true is embedded in the common experience of reality as that experience is articulated in commonly held opinions. This is the phenomenological element in Aristotle's approach. Common experience and commonly held opinions are more than just a *beginning point* for Aristotle. Aristotle begins from what Husserl and Heidegger would later call the "pre-scientific" awareness of everyday life. When he is finished, he leaves much of it intact. Aristotle's method is intimately related to his understanding of the role reason should play in political and moral affairs and within the natural whole more generally. Aristotle quietly makes clear the revolutionary potential of reason, but also articulates its necessary limits.[10] As I have already suggested, Socrates did not bring philosophy "down from the heavens" as Cicero suggested. While he did make philosophy inquire into the human things, it was as a means to an ascent to a contemplation of detached intelligibles. Socrates interrogated common opinions, but he found no wisdom in any of them. As he says in the *Apology*, he dismissed the wisdom of the priests, poets, statesmen, artisans and other claimants to wisdom. And he made their alleged deficiencies all too clear to them even on a day when he was supposed to be defending himself.

Socrates started from common opinions but only to transcend them. Socrates's doings can only be seen as a longing to start from the method he described in the *Phaedo* as his "second sailing" and then ascend **back** to the heavens. And what he longed for was an understanding of the whole that could be seen as rational and without contradiction. He could not find that in the realm of the *eidē*. He never really found it in the intelligible realm either. Unlike the moderns, he did not long to transform the realm of the *eidē* into a rational whole as a basis for *technē*. But his longing for a rationalized whole opened the door to that possibility as did Aristotle making the theoretical autonomous. **Unmediated, the Socratic longing leads in the direction of the proto-modern conception of reason, which tries to correct Being.** Without moderation that longing eventually leads to a choice between reason and irreason that is unnecessary. A moderation of that longing can be found in the work of Plato; another can be found in the practical works of Aristotle, a manifestation of which we are about to consider. A third form of that moderation is needed in our time, not a choice for irreason. We must not lose our hold on reason, but we must grasp its limits, its legitimate possibilities, its appropriate task, and its place in the whole.

Like Socrates and Plato, Aristotle accepts as an already given phenomenon the *nomos/physis* distinction, a distinction that had already emerged and been used prominently by the sophists.[11] It was already part of *common opinion*. As Strauss has shown, it arose in common opinion and was not a **theoretical construct**. According to this already existing opinion, that which is natural has a higher dignity than that which is merely conventional. Unlike the competing *nomoi* of the various cities, nature is the same everywhere and always. As Aristotle says, fire burns the same in Greece and Persia. Socrates' version of this understanding can, perhaps, be gleaned from the argument put in his mouth in the *Republic*. The nature of a thing is to be found in its essential Being, in its *eidos* or *idea*, which is there posited as graspable in a form of thought detached from *aesthesis* and common opinion. Matter always sullies the pure form. A thing is what it is only in relation to its "whatness" qua *eidos*, which started out as a "look" or "surface," and was transformed into a pure intelligible form with no element of *aesthesis*. That was the Socratic longing.

Aristotle accepts common opinion and does not try to transcend it except in the direction of "nature" which, I will argue, has a phenomenological status and is not intended as an intelligible. In the traditional version of the nature/convention distinction, the conventional *nomoi* oppose **themselves** to the natural. The merely conventional is based on custom or accident, or the unconscious action of human beings. On the surface, the opposition is between what produces itself and what requires human action to come into being. For Socrates the nature of a thing is to be found in the cause of the thing understood ultimately as an intelligible form. At least this is what Plato's dramatic Socrates seems to assert on particular days in front of certain particular audiences.[12]

Aristotle grounds his discussion of reason in his **phenomenological presentation of nature**.[13] The result is that we never get a stark opposition between reason on the one hand and everything from tradition and laws to material reality and the movement of the cosmos on the other. This fact begins to emerge at the very beginning of the *Politics*. Aristotle asserts that man is by nature a political animal and the political community is itself natural. This naturalness is arrived at by combining two separate arguments. First, Aristotle says, "It is by looking at how things develop *naturally* from the *beginning* that one may best study them."[14] (1252a25) [my emphasis] This is part of Aristotle's discussion of the naturalness of the family, which is one of the building blocks of the political community. Second, Aristotle says, "nature is an *end*: what each thing is—for example, a human being, a horse, or a household—when its coming into being is complete is, we assert, the nature of that thing." (1252b32) Nature is to be grasped in the complex way that things emerge into view in everyday life. Things emerge from a beginning, develop and **present themselves** on their own from their beginnings and in relation to that end toward which they are oriented.[15]

I want to approach this dichotomy in the way nature presents itself, and hence how the question of nature or Being more generally presents itself phenomenologically, in light of Aristotle's philosophical reflections on Being as a "power" (*dynamis*) that emerges, comes forth to the surface to be at "work," and moves toward its *telos*. All of these ideas are phenomenological, they simply articulate how things **show themselves**: they are manifestations of *alētheia* in Heidegger's sense, truth that emerges into presence and appears for all in everyday perceptions and speeches. When articulated in speech these presentations come forth as "to be" is "to be at work" (*energeia*) They come to presence and are at work in mind, matter, *polis*, tradition and many other manifestations.[16] These initial articulations point directly to Aristotle's discussion of "causality." Following this movement will be useful from the perspective of our task of discovering a function for reason in our time, a phenomenological function. By way of approaching these issues in a fashion freed from the encrustation of millennia of sedimented interpretation, consider the following from Heidegger:

For centuries philosophy has taught that there are four causes: (1) the *causa materialis*, the material, the matter out of which, for example, a silver chalice is made; (2) The *causa formalis*, the form, the shape into which the material enters; (3) the *causa finalis*, the end, for example, the sacrificial rite in relation to which the required chalice is determined as to its form and matter; (4) the *causa efficiens*, which brings about the effect that is the finished, actual chalice, in this instance, the silversmith. . . .

Silver is that out of which the silver chalice is made. As this matter (*hyle*), it is co-responsible for the chalice. The chalice is indebted to, i.e., owes thanks to, the silver for that of which it consists. But the sacrificial vessel is indebted not only to the silver. As a chalice, that which is indebted to the silver appears in the aspect of a chalice, and not in that of a brooch or a ring. Thus the sacred vessel is at the same time indebted to the aspect (*eidos*) of chaliceness. . . .

But there remains yet a third something that is above all responsible for the sacrificial vessel. It is that which in advance confines the chalice within the realm of consecration and bestowal. . . . That which gives bounds, that which completes, in this sense is called in Greek *telos*, which is all too often translated as "aim" or "purpose" and so misinterpreted. The *telos* is responsible for what as matter and what as aspect are together co-responsible for the sacrificial vessel.

Finally, there is a fourth participant in the responsibility for the finished sacrificial vessel's lying before us ready for use, i.e., the silversmith. . . .

The three previously mentioned ways of being responsible owe thanks to the pondering of the silversmith for the "that" and the "how" of their coming into appearance and into play for the production of the sacrificial vessel. . . .

In order to guard against misinterpretations of being responsible and being indebted, let us clarify the four ways of being responsible in terms of that for which they are responsible. According to our example, they are responsible for the silver chalice's lying ready before us . . . [which] characterize the presencing of something that is present. . . .

The modes of occasioning, the four causes, are at play, then, within bringing forth. Through bringing forth the growing things of nature as well as whatever is completed through the crafts and the arts come at any given time to their appearance.[17]

And further:

Now we know that Aristotle often also uses *aitia* and *arche,* which we translate as "cause." [the second as beginning or first principle] We gain from this the undeniable fact: *dynamis* is comprehended by Aristotle as a kind of cause . . . . What is at issue here is not at all a cause-and-effect relationship, where we immediately think of the transfer of force, the effect of distance, and so on, and then puzzle over the secret relationship between cause and effect. Much more, it is maintained clearly and simply: force is an origin, the from-out-of-which for a change, and this in such a way that the origin is different from that which changes.[18]

As Heidegger suggests, Aristotle proceeds on the assumption that the nature of a thing is to be understood in relation to that which is "responsible for" its being what it is. That which is responsible causes a thing to come forth, develop, and move toward an end. This is how things appear phenomenologically in everyday experience. Hence in approaching "nature," we are led to a discussion of causality, understanding that causality is fourfold and that the four causes can never be separated—e.g., in the manner attempted by modern philosophy which transforms the conception of and tries to give priority, indeed autonomy, to efficient causality.

Philosophically, so Heidegger suggests, the notion of causality in turn leads us to a discussion of Being, to reflect upon the means by which things come to presence, such that Being qua *energeia* is the efficient cause acting through man who binds together the four causes. This is an example of how a phenomenological philosophy moves from what is embedded in everyday experience to a consideration of many things including Being. **But to move beyond this as Aristotle did, to announce the autonomy of theory from its phenomenological base, was a mistake of the first order.**[19]

By the understanding Heidegger applies to Aristotle, the nature of a thing is that which is responsible for it being what it is—for its Being. That which is responsible for a thing is what causes it. Nature is to be grasped through an understanding of the fourfold causality of bringing forth into appearance. First, a thing is what it is because of the matter (*hyle*) that constitutes it, i.e., the material cause. Second, a thing is what it is because of the distinctive shape, look or form (*eidos*) that differentiates its determinant form from that of other things, i.e., the formal cause. The formal cause accounts for a thing being a determinate thing rather than indeterminate material. It accounts for the "whatness" of a thing and is linked to its facade, outer appearance or "look." Third, a thing is what it is on account of the end (*telos*) toward which it is oriented. That end is always co-present in anything that appears, i.e., the final cause. Finally, there is the more mysterious efficient cause that binds together the other three causes within itself. The artisan or person applying reason is the vehicle by which the four causes are bound together in things produced by man. The artificer is the efficient cause only as the vehicle for something else operating through him. This implies that the natural things are likewise the product of an artificer other than man. That is not a theoretical conclusion; it is implied in how the phenomena show themselves.

The four causes account for the power by which reality comes forth into appearance. Some things seem to come forth on their own, others seem to need the intervention of man. This seems to set up a distinction between that which presents **itself** and that which requires what common experience designates "conscious action." There is a tendency, therefore, to call only that which seems to present **itself** as natural, and everything else as conventional.

But that is a mistake. That is because the natural must be seen as **both** that which seemingly actualizes itself and as that which requires the "conscious" intervention of man to emerge and/or reach a *telos*. **Phenomenologically, nature is the totality of what comes forth in the complex totality of ways that presencing occurs.**

If we follow both the phenomenological basis or origin of this ultimate outcome, as well as the movement of articulation by which we arrive at it, human reason cannot be conceptualized as autonomous efficient causality as becomes the case in modernity and in all constructivism. Man is but a part of nature, albeit the distinctive part that binds together the whole. For example, when Aristotle says that the moral virtues are based on habits supplied by the laws and human education, he never reaches the conclusion that they are unnatural **or the other of nature** even though the laws do not, except in exceptional circumstances, simply bring themselves to presence. Quite the contrary, nature manifests itself in a variety of ways—e.g., as *nomos* or *ethos*, or as things that grow and seemingly present themselves, as the human acts that bring things to their *teloi*. To use another of Aristotle's examples, we may by nature be right handed, but by training we can become ambidextrous. Both are in their own ways natural. We cannot, in any serious sense, learn to write well with either a right or left foot or our mouths. Indeed, at any given moment we may not write at all until the appropriate prerequisites are available. But writing is still natural to man. This complicated and complex understanding provides us with Aristotle's depiction of nature, not just nature as the other of convention.

To return to Aristotle's distinction at the beginning of the *Politics*, the family is natural in the sense that male and female are driven into community by means other than what might at first sight appear to be "conscious choice." The sexual drive is the origin of the family, the rearing and teaching of the young, and potentially the friendship of its founding partners and progeny are its ends, and thereby the basis of its continuation. Both origin and end are natural and belong together **even if the end requires human intervention**. The conjunction of male and female is "of necessity" because of the inability of either to exist without the other. Instinct stands at the origin of the family, or in Aristotle's terms, the family exists not from "intentional choice" but by spontaneously emerging into presence as a kind of "natural striving." (1251a28–30) The family, on the initial, instinctive, material level is sufficient only for the reproduction of the species. Under the most ideal conditions it might be adequate for the continued preservation of the family members. Normally it is not, therefore, self-preservation which usually requires a larger partnership. The village comes into existence when a number of families are "driven" together. This coming together implies both the operation of the same kind of causality that founds the family but also what will look to everyday opinion like "conscious choice." The two operate together and form the natural.

Since human beings desire not mere life but the good life, the village is still not sufficient. We are inclined **toward** the *polis*. The *polis* is natural, but not in precisely the same way as the family or the village. Again, Aristotle says that the move from the village to the *polis* requires "conscious choice." "There is in everyone by nature a [spontaneous] impulse toward [the *polis*]. And yet the one who first constituted [a *polis*] is responsible for the greatest of goods." (1253a30) The *polis* is natural because the good life is a natural possibility. The highest human happiness requires more than the gratification of the pleasures implicated in self-preservation and the preservation of the species. The virtues that we encounter in the *Nicomachean Ethics* are prerequisites for happiness and they imply the highest end of education and habits only a *polis* can supply.[20] The *polis* and the virtues are as natural as the family even though they require the intervention of conscious choice. Everything that comes from human intervention is not thereby conventional.

As things appear in everyday perception, instinct alone does not drive us to be everything we can be. "Conscious reason" must intervene in the form of providing for habits and laws. As regards instinct, it could be said that human beings are "underdetermined." We are naturally political beings not because of material causality or efficient causality, but because unlike other species we have speech (*logos*). *Logos* makes its own demands upon us just as it operates through us. Movement toward an end requires the intervention of reason but that does not mean that it is the task of reason to root out "undesirable" manifestations of causality wherever they are found. The four components of causality must operate **in concert** if we are to be what we truly are by nature. We are neither wholly determined by "unconscious necessity" nor by conscious, "intentional choice." Both are part of a whole that deserves to be called natural.

All actions and all partnerships aim at a good. The highest good, that which is not a means to something else, is happiness. The most comprehensive partnership, the *polis*, aims at the happiness of its members. But our highest happiness ultimately turns out to require both *logos* and *praxis*—indeed, human doing and making is not *praxis* without an element of *logos*. Both are part of a complex whole, both presuppose the *polis*. But to remain for the moment within the perspective of *praxis* alone, the city must engage its citizens in certain forms of action that will become habitual, which requires repetition or practice. In that fashion an end is thereby built into even those actions that do not appear to proceed from conscious choice. How that end enters the equation remains crucial, as does its status. We will return to this below.

Aristotle says that what differentiates "political" relationships from "kingly" or "despotic" ones is the necessity that citizens be free and equal, and in position to rule and be ruled in turn. Indeed, citizens are defined as those who participate in deliberation and decision-making, not just potentially, but in fact, because participation is the educational tool that forms habits, a prerequisite for the satisfaction and happiness of its members.[21] Deliberation (*logos*) is at the beginning of the *polis*, part of its functioning and its end.

Following the line of argument we have adopted, our nature as human beings is found in the complex interplay of the four manifestations of causality in their totality. That interplay determines what comes forth ultimately as the reality that appears for and through us. There is no fixed, determinate, dogmatic way to strike a balance between the complex sources of our nature as a species or as individuals. What is required is a balancing of emergent beginning and end in a fashion that will require a different balance as circumstances change. Reason is the natural tool that performs this delicate balancing act. **Therefore the balancing act itself and its outcome are both natural.**

Having raised the issue of nature at the beginning of the *Politics*, and implied that it actualizes itself and comes to appearance in complex ways, Aristotle next indicates some potential applications of reason. Conceiving nature as a complex whole and reason as a balancing tool, Aristotle measures several conventional institutions as regards their reasonableness and naturalness: 1) slavery, 2) relations between husband and wife, and 3) the origin and management of material wealth. Despite following his customary method, beginning from commonly held opinions, and remaining within the orbit of the conventional *nomoi*, it becomes apparent how potentially revolutionary Aristotle's understanding of reason is from the perspective of Athenian manifestations of *nomoi*.

Aristotle's discussion of slavery is part of his discussion of household management, or more generally, economics. Slaves are part of the property of the household. It is just for the slave to belong to the master because by nature he "does not belong to himself." (1254a14) The slave does not belong to himself because he is incapable of *praxis*, i.e., moral and political action and deliberation. Aristotle asserts that "life is *praxis*, not *techne*," and *praxis* requires action in accordance with the rational part of the soul, and the slave does not have the rational part. Hence it is just to rule the slave despotically. By comparison, in political rule, both ruler and ruled participate in reason, virtue and *praxis*, and must relate as equals, sharing rule and being ruled in turn.

The discussion of the naturalness or reasonableness of slavery begins from what Aristotle calls the **commonly accepted opinion** that the soul is different than the body and is higher in dignity than the body. Aristotle does not posit or construct this distinction theoretically; he takes off from an opinion that already exists. He then joins that opinion with another that already exists, that the higher should rule the lower.[22] If these opinions did not already exist, Aristotle would have no place to begin.

Slaves by nature are those who have *no* participation in reason. Since their own soul cannot rule their bodies it is best that someone else's soul do it for them. If one thinks this through it becomes clear that this primarily benefits the natural slave. (1255a1) It is not entirely clear what the benefit to the master is of having a natural slave. At best, natural slaves have strong bodies and no reason, presumably making them useful for manual labor. But even in manual labor they would, because of their deficiency in reason, require close supervision. The investment in supervision would frequently outweigh the yield in labor. In our time such natural slaves probably would be judged appropriate candidates for institutionalization.[23] No doubt this is why Aristotle concludes that there is nothing noble or great about mastery; it would be so frustrating and time consuming that one should hire an overseer, thereby being freed to spend one's time on "philosophy" and "politics," the truly choice-worthy activities. (1255b32–37)

"Unnatural" slavery rests on war, or more generally, on force. Further, "the beginnings of wars are not always just, and no one would assert that someone not meriting enslavement ought ever to be a slave. Otherwise, the result will be that those held to be the best born will become slaves and the offspring of slaves if they happen to be captured and sold." (1255a25–29) Clearly, the kind of slavery prevalent in Aristotle's time was not "natural" since it was based on force, hence it was contrary to reason. The things that are contrary to reason are unnatural. Unnatural and unjust are commonly held to be words that mean the same thing. Aristotle does not openly advise overturning such unnatural institutions but makes it clear, from the perspective of the master, that self-interest alone will show how questionable the institution is. Be this as it may, Aristotle is clearly not rationalizing or justifying prevailing institutions of slavery, quite the contrary. Reason shows the injustice of this institution, even if it emerged out of other perfectly pre-conscious "natural" inclinations. We learn that Reason can take a critical stance to what is given and still remain a part of the natural whole rather than its other. Therein lies Aristotle's response to Kant.

The natural rule of master over slave is the rule of one who is complete and in possession of reason over one who is incomplete, without reason and incapable of ever developing reason. That is the model for despotic rule of any kind. By comparison, the model for kingly rule is that of parent over child, where authority is based on the rule of one who is complete and rational over one who is presently incomplete, but who with the correct efforts of education and some luck will eventually be complete—although no simple necessity operates here.

Political rule, the rule of free and equal individuals who rule and are ruled in turn, has as its model the rule of husband over wife. On the basis of Aristotle's definition of political rule, it seems straightforward that men and women are equals who should rule and be ruled in turn. But Aristotle does not seem willing to draw this conclusion. For example, he says "the relation of male to female is by nature a relation of superior to inferior and ruler to ruled." (1254b12) In a now infamous argument in *On the Generation of Animals*, Aristotle seems to assert the inferiority of the female in another way. In procreation women supply only the matter, men supply the form. Form is higher than matter. Aristotle therein implies, contrary to our argument, that one can somehow separate the forms of causality. But this flies in the face of the co-equal nature of the four causes and the fact that they can only work "naturally" as part of a unity. The latter is the doctrine to maintain.

Obviously Aristotle's biology is, in many of its empirical particulars, inadequate and superseded. But this need not concern us at present. Aristotle's biological discussions do not form the basis of his practical discussions of the relation between men and women, and as I have suggested are at odds with the theory that evolves phenomenologically. To be sure, the difference between men and women is partly determined by a bodily difference. But this is not the level on which Aristotle primarily carries the argument. The operative discussion is the following: "the free person rules the slave, the male the female, and the man the child in different ways. The parts of the soul are present in all, but they are present in a different way. The slave is wholly lacking the deliberative element; the female **has it but it lacks authority**; the child has it but it is incomplete." (1260a8–13) [my emphasis] In women the ruling element "lacks authority." Aristotle says no more than this. We must ask why the ruling element lacks authority in women. Since reason requires practice to develop, it seems plausible to conclude that reason is inoperative in women because the prevailing laws give them no opportunity to practice its use. Hence women are inferior to men not according to nature, but because of the laws. Those laws would, therefore, as in the case of slavery, clearly be unnatural and thereby unjust.

Yet matters are not quite as clear as this might lead us to believe. In his discussion of Socrates, Aristotle criticizes Socrates's attempt to make men and women identical by giving them the same virtues. Aristotle says that there are different virtues that apply to men and women. He mentions different forms of moderation, courage and justice. (1260a20–24) This list leaves out Socrates's fourth virtue, wisdom. Apparently, there is only one kind of wisdom, applicable equally to both men and women. If so then men and women are potentially equal as regards their reason, unequal as regards their bodies. If a *polis* could be constructed that could be indifferent to the body, men and women could be simply equal. In all those affairs of the city where the operation of reason is at stake they should, according to reason, be equal. But this would only be possible if the four manifestations of causality could be separated.

In all those affairs of the city that implicate the body, men and women may not be able to be simply equal because phenomenologically **nature presences**

through appearances and that fact must be given its due. Put another way, as regards *common opinion*, which accepts the distinction between body and soul, their souls are equal, but it is impossible to see the qualities of the soul as one can see the qualities of the body. This is part of the complexity of the natural. Cities must rely heavily on appearance. Formal causality exacts its demands. **It is impossible for the city to simply transcend appearance.**

Cities need leaders with unquestioned authority, which frequently must be based on factors that are not simply rational, so they need to rely on surface qualities like attractiveness, size and strength. A large build and deep voice project authority without elaborate proofs, and when life and death are at stake, that may be crucial. Consequently, Aristotle says that "the male, unless constituted in some respect contrary to nature, is by nature more expert at leading than the female. . . . In most political offices, it is true, there is an alternation of ruler and ruled, since they tend by their nature to be on an equal footing and to differ in nothing; all the same, when one rules and the other is ruled, [the ruler] seeks to establish differences **in external appearance, forms of address, and prerogatives**. . . ." (1259b1–10) [my emphasis] A tall, commanding, sonorous male simply has advantages in some instances, and this is by nature. Any political inequality that must exist between male and female is a matter of "appearance"—but this too is part of nature. Where "appearance" is essential, and its eradication would be difficult, impossible or unwise, reason should not take a stance against it. Where would reason as we are articulating it stand to accomplish that feat? Aristotle is not positing an autonomous ego that stands nowhere, as with Descartes.

Having admitted the importance of appearance, Aristotle is nonetheless clearly unwilling to reduce virtue only to qualities that line up with size, strength, natural courage, "virility." In the *Ethics* Aristotle clearly tries to moderate the Homeric reduction of virtue to courage and virility. This can be seen in a variety of ways. For example, courage is one of the lowest of the Aristotelian virtues as a result of being grouped with temperance as one of the virtues of the "irrational" part of the soul.[24] All of the other virtues come after this in a clear ascent. And as regards the relation between men and women, in the *Ethics* we also find that despite the importance of justice as the cement of a *polis*—and justice is asserted to have a natural basis—the most substantial foundation of community among individuals is ultimately friendship.

Justice inevitably has a coercive element; friendship rests on choice and points toward a potential basis in reason. While there are three bases of true friendship—utility, pleasure and what is ambiguously called shared virtue—virtue is clearly the most durable ground of friendship, with the highest virtue being the ground of the best friendship. Aristotle says that at its peak marriage culminates in friendship. (*Ethics* 1162a16–27) This means that marriage, at its peak, points beyond the factors that are the immediate cause of the family, to a community of equals based on virtue and ultimately the highest virtue, a perfected reason. Therein friendship points beyond the *polis* without negating the need for or naturalness of the *polis*.

Put another way, the relation between husband and wife, when reason is present, points beyond the pleasure and utility that are the immediate cause of the family, and in most instances even the *polis*, to a community of true equality. Only in the most extraordinary circumstances could the *polis* actualize the same kind of equality. But within a family, protected by the laws of a particular *polis*, surface appearance need not play the same role it does **naturally** in the *polis*. In the family, men and woman can be truly equal.[25]

Aristotle's account of the relation between husband and wife points far beyond the conventional arrangements in Athens while continuing to admit that there is always a natural element embedded in common opinion. Nonetheless, the implications of his account are potentially quite revolutionary. Yet Aristotle does not draw the most radical conclusions—e.g., that the *polis* should aim at the highest kind of friendship—for several reasons.[26] Aristotle refuses to radically transcend common opinion even when it points beyond present institutions because every *polis* has an element of the natural about it—contrary to the textbook renditions of the *nomos/physis* distinction. Aristotle recognizes that nature imposes limits on reason's ability to actualize final causes, to say nothing of utopian day dreams. Further, **given that appearance is a part of nature**, it is impossible for reason to ever presume to abolish the hegemony of appearance.

Finally, Aristotle applies his discussion of reason to economic institutions or household management. Material goods are needed for life. Leisure is required for the good life since the end of life is **action not production**. Therefore, there must be a surplus of material goods to support *praxis* and ultimately *theoria*. In some way the *polis* must produce wealth. But those who do the producing are not fit, as a result, for political participation, the highest friendship or *theoria*.

In the absolutely best society, the citizens would be neither laborers, merchants, farmers, nor engaged in commerce, even though the *polis* requires those activities. (*Politics* 1328b35–1329a5) Hence everyone will not be equally suited for *praxis* given the diversity the city requires for its mere existence. It is not the task of reason to rail against this aspect of nature. Nonetheless, as the discussion of the natural means for producing wealth shows, it is, despite the seeming paradox, **sometimes natural to go beyond the natural**.

Let us pursue that last, seemingly paradoxical statement in the following fashion. Aristotle presents a delicately drawn discussion of the relation between "business" and "household management." He says that in one sense business belongs to household management, in another sense it does not. The main concern of household management is managing the relations between individuals: i.e., masters ruling slaves, parents ruling children, husbands relating to wives. Household management is directed to producing the excellence and happiness of the members of the family to the extent possible. Since this presupposes means, some attention the creation of wealth is necessary. Hence some aspects of business belong to household management.

The part of business that belongs to household management is that which is concerned with the natural production of wealth. Aristotle says there are various natural bases of wealth: hunting, agriculture, herding, and piracy (seemingly a concession to the Homeric legacy). Likewise, there is a natural form of exchange: barter. Commerce and usury are unnatural. This is because everything natural has a limit. For example, the *polis* has a natural size, growth beyond which is unnatural. A tree, an animal, a man, all reach a certain terminus and stop growing. The natural limit for a *polis* is the size that allows more or less face to face deliberation to be a reality.

Likewise, a natural amount of wealth should have a limit. Commerce and usury are means of producing wealth that is limitless. (1257b25) The good life cannot be had while pursuing unlimited wealth—or unlimited *technē*, which can have no other end than unlimited wealth. Unlimited wealth only leads to the excesses that destroy virtue. (1258a1) The end of household management—as is also true of politics—is not to transform the natural situation of man for the sake of emancipation from the complex causal whole that is nature, but to acquire enough from nature to make natural possibilities like politics, *aretē* and *theoria* possible. Beyond that one is only creating tools of enslavement.

Aristotle's account is surely not a mere rationalization of the economic institutions of democratic, imperialistic **commercial** Athens. Nor is it a reactionary rationalization of the older, agrarian, aristocratic disdain of business, usury and commerce. Reason points to the need for leisure to achieve excellence and as the prerequisite for participation in politics understood as a deliberative activity. That requires either that the *polis* be very fortunate through fortuitous circumstances or shrewd dealings, or that some of its members work so that others may have leisure. It is unlikely that the natural means to wealth will supply enough equipment for very many to have leisure. Hence either slavery or commerce—the pursuit of unlimited wealth—is necessary. Both are unnatural.

Nature seems to force us in the direction of, by definition, "unnatural" institutions. **This goes to the heart of Aristotle's complex understanding of reason and nature.** In Book 1 of the *Politics*, Aristotle shows the unnaturalness of three institutions as they are constituted in contemporary Greek life. The potentially revolutionary character of reason becomes manifest. But Aristotle never goes on to call for the overthrow of those contemporary institutions. And unlike so many of Plato's dialogues that give us a picture of Socrates, we are not left by Aristotle with a sense of *aporia*. Yet we are made aware that through reason nature is complex and does offer options.

Book 2 of the *Politics* can be divided into three parts. First, Aristotle discusses three "conscious" applications of reason which led to theoretical attempts to fashion ideal cities in speech. Second, he discusses three actual constitutions that are reputed to be excellent and that emerged into presence over time with greater or lesser degrees of "conscious action." Finally, he discusses legislators who "consciously" created "both laws and regimes."

The most extended discussion is the first, centering primarily on Socrates' ideal community presented in the *Republic*. Surely Aristotle was aware of the place this discussion played dramatically in the dialogue as whole. He no doubt also understood its ironic nature, at least on Plato's part. Nonetheless, he chose to treat the ideal city depicted there as Socrates's last word on the matter. In fact, he treats the discussion as if it was Plato's last word.[27]

Aristotle accuses Socrates of the error of trying to unify his ideal city too much and in trying to achieve the unity that is needed in the wrong way. Socrates proposes to unify the city by making it impossible to love one's own more than the common good. Hence he abolishes private property and the family, the two most powerful objects of natural affection in most individuals. Aristotle counters that the appropriate ground of unity in the city is education, i.e., shared habits, opinions and laws. Consequently, regardless of how much "conscious" choice went into the habits, laws and opinions of a community, their existence is natural because they unify the city while leaving a needed, natural diversity of human types and natural longings, which Socrates does not.

Total unity is not possible on the level of the body, for the body necessarily requires that we show respect for our particularity. The natural diversity of attributes that display themselves between particular individuals is the basis of the division of labor that a self-sufficient *polis* requires. That necessary division of labor makes different kinds, degrees and amounts of property inevitable. Aristotle understood this as clearly as Madison. Further, following his discussion of distributive justice in Book V of the *Ethics*, Aristotle argues that to reward different degrees of effort or merit equally is as much a cause of disunity as to have unjustly unequal distributions of property. The only just principle is to give equal things to equals, not equal things to all.

Aristotle also enters into a string of quite minute objections to Socrates. They all have the same point in common: property held in common is never cared for like private property because the love of one's own is an ineradicable, self-emergent drive. And private property is the prerequisite for the exercise of many of the virtues, such as liberality. Hence the abolition of private property is unnatural.

The attempt to achieve unity through the abolition of the family likewise falters. Again, a prerequisite for virtue is destroyed. The incentive to sexual moderation is removed. Further, attempts by reason to abolish the family and natural affection cannot be successful because natural similarities between parents and children will assert themselves. Reason cannot ignore nature in its complex manifestations. Put formulaically, **reason cannot replace material, efficient or formal causality in its pursuit of final causality any more than it can invent final causes *ex nihilo*, or any more than it can act as an autonomous efficient cause.**

Aristotle goes on to observe that the family is the place where we learn affection, devotion, camaraderie and other necessary attachments that the *polis* eventually requires for its existence. In the family these things first emerge and become present. In the *polis* they would require such massive efforts at education and coercion that it is unlikely they would emerge if there were not preexistent manifestations of them. Public education must rest on an extension of an affection that has already been brought forth. The affection for the city can only be constructed as an extension of parental and familial affection. (1262b22) Eradicate the arena for the development of affection and no legislator will ever be able to construct a substitute on a basis that is entirely "conscious." The skillful legislator must shape naturally occurring drives and outcomes that come to presence before his efforts. Once again we see a paradigm for the use of reason that will not allow it to be autonomous or to advance *ex nihilo*.

Phaleas misused reason in a different fashion than Socrates. He hoped that the equalization of property would be sufficient to deal with all problems in political life. Therefore, he reduced the political problem to one amenable to mathematical treatment. He attempted one form—mathematical—of a theoretical application of reason to political life. Aristotle argues that such applications of reason merely create new problems. For example, given unequal birthrates for different families, no equalization of property would survive even one generation without equalization of births. Furthermore, if individual citizens' desires remain different and unequal, equal property will not eliminate strife. And conflict is occasioned by a variety of things other than property, e.g., the pursuit of honor. The equal distribution of honors causes animosity every bit as much as the equal distribution of property whenever inequality of merit remains.

Finally, Aristotle observes that natural longing and desire, in all its forms, is unlimited. And the pursuit of the comforts and pleasures of the body are what the majority of individuals primarily pursue. The equal distribution of property will not cure natural intemperance. That requires law and education. Aristotle advises, therefore, that individuals seek satisfaction through "philosophy," or more generally, education.[28] (1267a10–12) Human beings are moved by multiple, spontaneous drives. Proceeding as if only one drive operated, or as if all drives were mutually compatible, is a mistake. Phaleas misunderstood how complicated our natural drives really are.

Hippodamus engaged in an even more radical mathematicization of reason than Phaleas. Hippodamus proposed a society of 10,000 citizens. He then tried to divide everything in his society into threes, which will not yield a whole or "rational" number, as the Greeks understood these things. There were to be three classes—artisans, farmers and military; three divisions of land—sacred, public, private; three kinds of laws, etc. This "rationalization" of life will not work. Since the military will not farm and the farmers will farm only their own lands, it is not clear who farms the public land from which the military is to receive its subsistence. Likewise, if the farmers and the artisans have no arms how will they defend themselves against the designs of those who do have that monopoly? The objections to Hippodamus all have the same form: Hippodamus tried to dictate theoretical rules to reality **as it presents itself**. This attempt at rationalization will always fail. Theoretical reason cannot impose itself on political and moral reality in this fashion because the whole of nature or Being is too complex to admit it without paying an extreme price.

In Book 7 of the *Politics* we learn that Hippodamus was also a city planner. He had proposed a plan for laying out cities along purely rational lines with straight streets intersecting at right angles. (1330b20–27) But it becomes clear that cities that have developed "naturally"—that is, through a pattern of spontaneous development over an extended number of years, one which is not "consciously" planned—have significant advantages over Hippodamus's rational city. Other than the inherent charm and aesthetic qualities of cities developed by more or less "natural" growth, older Greek cities, with wandering streets laid out in unpredictable patterns were very valuable for defensive purposes because they made it difficult for attackers to find their way around, making defense much easier. This is an example of how things that grow and develop have advantages over those that emanate from the conscious application of theoretical reason.

Apparently Hippodamus had also proposed an institution that would reward with honor proposals for innovations in the laws. Aristotle observes that this institution is "not safe." (1268b24) This conclusion leads Aristotle into a discussion of whether it is harmful or advantageous to change traditional laws. He observes that change is advantageous in medicine, the arts and the sciences. But the situation is more complicated when it comes to politics. Aristotle grants that "early" laws were primitive and even simpleminded. They deserved to be consciously changed. Indeed, Aristotle says that no *written* law should remain simply unchanged. Nonetheless, in "later times" when the potential for improvement is small, laws should not be frequently changed: "Law has no strength with respect to obedience apart from habit, and this is not created except over a period of time." (1269a20)

The customs and habits (*ethoi*) that have developed slowly over a period of time are needed. While "in general, [we] seek not the traditional but the good," (1269a3) Aristotle makes it clear that the good seldom actualizes itself through "conscious" creation alone. Tradition cannot be autonomous, but neither can theoretical reason qua efficient cause presume to replace it. Hence while one should not venerate blind tradition, one must appreciate the limits of reason in supplying an alternative. Consequently, Hippodamus's institution of rewarding innovation is not a good idea. Like Socrates and Phaleas, Hippodamus overestimates what the conscious application of reason can do. This is because none of them properly understood the complexity of nature as the entirety of what emerges into presence through various conduits.

Next, Aristotle investigates three reputedly excellent regimes—Sparta, Crete and Carthage. As a preface to his discussion of Sparta (1269a29–1271b19), Aristotle reiterates that any good city, one that makes possible the good life, must provide for the possibility of leisure. The Spartans do so, to the extent that they do, through the unnatural institution of slavery. The trouble the Spartans have with their slaves is a clear sign that slavery is not the best way to deal with the need for leisure.

Aristotle admits that the institution of slavery emerged before the efforts of Sparta's great legislator Lycurgus. But, Aristotle says, Lycurgus did nothing to eliminate slavery nor to moderate or lessen its deleterious effects. This was unwise. Lycurgus made several other more egregious errors. He either confused martial virtue with the entirety of virtue, or he concluded that Spartan men could not be gentlemen. Hence Spartan education was aimed entirely at the virtues useful in war. No effort was made to create the virtues needed for peace and leisure. Lycurgus erred as well in his constitution of the famous Spartan common mess. Only those who contributed were allowed to participate. An institution aimed at unifying the city by giving it common bonds thereby divided it along class lines. Furthermore, the women did not participate in the common mess. This oversight is just part of Lycurgus's general failure with regard to the education of women. Half the populace was ignored as regards virtue and this proved to be the basis of many difficulties.

Aristotle says that Lycurgus failed with the Spartan women, and then gave up trying to have any effect on them. While the men were educated to be hearty, rugged, patriotic and courageous, the women were licentious and addicted to luxury. When the men were away at war, which was a great deal of the time, the women were left to administer many of the affairs of the city including the education of the young. And due to the idiosyncrasies of the poorly constructed inheritance laws the women came to own a significant amount of the property. The men had little time for leisure, and when they did, they had cultivated none of the leisured virtues that would make its exercise fruitful; hence all they could do was give themselves over to bouts of licentiousness. The softness, luxury, greed and inequality, which existed side by side with the famous Spartan virtue, led to a situation where the Spartans could no longer support as many troops as they had previously. A city organized with an eye to war became less and less able to prosecute it over time.

Many lessons can be gleaned from the discussion of Sparta. First, one cannot forget half the society and hope it will prosper. Women need education and virtue as well as the men. This supports the discussion of women in Book 1. Second, leisure is required for a society to be well ruled. Leisure requires education in the virtues that make its proper use possible. Martial virtues alone will not check the unlimited passions like greed and the desires for bodily comfort and pleasure. Martial virtue must be supplemented by gentlemanly virtue. Third, one should not attempt to establish leisure on the basis of slavery. One must look to the natural means of generating wealth, primarily herding, agriculture and the arts, or accept the necessity of "unnatural" commerce which in the end is better than accepting slavery. Of course, those engaged in herding, farming, labor, commerce, etc., have little time for leisure. Still, those engaged in these activities are not slaves, they can achieve some self-sufficiency. Finally, we learn that even a legislator with the reputation of a Lycurgus faces incredible difficulties in trying to base the *polis* almost entirely on consciously executed legislation.

In his discussion of Crete (1271b20–1272b22), the other Greek city, Aristotle stresses the close links with Sparta. Crete had had an ancient civilization with ancient laws. The Spartans sent colonists and turned the original inhabitants into their slaves. The colonists kept many of the ancient traditions of Crete but made some modifications by way of adding selected Spartan institutions. While far from ideal, it is clear that Aristotle believes that Crete is an improvement over Sparta. For example, Crete had a revised version of the Spartan common mess. The Cretan version paid for the undertaking out of public funds, hence helping to bridge the gap between rich and poor and binding the community together better than the Spartan version. Crete also admitted both males and females to the mess, thereby having some effect on the virtue of that half of the population that Lycurgus had ignored.

Like the Spartans, the Cretans still had the institution of slavery. Yet they did not have the same problems with rebellious slaves. Their good fortune in this regard seems, however, to be the fortuitous byproduct of being an island nation isolated from influences that elsewhere would likely fan the flames of rebellion. The improvement of the common mess can be traced to modifications that trial and error make possible. The improvement with regard to the slave population is due to fortuitous natural circumstances. Reason can come to presence in a variety of ways just as nature as a complex whole does. In none of the applications that Aristotle suggests is Reason to be seen as a mere autonomous efficient cause that operates *ex nihilo*.

Among the Spartans the office of "orderer" was filled from the ranks of prominent families. The Cretan version was elected from all the citizens, giving them all an incentive to wish for the regime to continue. But the Cretans introduce new problems. Their orderers were granted too much discretion. As a consequence the laws did not have the needed hegemony, and thereby, too much was done "in accordance with human wish." (1272b7) Reason operated more effectively when lodged in laws than in the conscious discretion of individuals. People resent being limited by the will of other individuals, but chafe far less under the limitations imposed by the invisible will of the law.

The Cretans also consciously introduced an institution that Aristotle thinks is very unwise. The Cretans could declare "lack of order," and thereby suspend the operation of the laws. The political partnership in effect dissolves and the regime changes into one that is more dynastic than political. Aristotle says that any other community would be in danger of external attack during these disruptions. Crete is once again saved by the fortuitous fact of being on an island. The political life of Crete is shaped by ancient tradition, invasion and occupation, conscious emendation of laws by occupying lawgivers, and its fortuitous natural setting. Where the lawgiver merely reforms a previously given institution, the outcome is better than in Sparta. Where the lawgiver innovates, the result is actually or potentially disastrous.

Aristotle's third example of an already existing, reputedly excellent *polis*, is the non-Greek city of Carthage. (1272b24–1273b26) Carthage turns out to be the best regime of the three despite the common Greek prejudice against "barbarians." Carthage is indicative of an excellent regime in that the people acquiesce to the laws voluntarily, there is no factional conflict and there has never been a tyrant. (1272b24–33) In other words, the existence of the tranquility that makes leisure both possible and valuable is the sign of a good regime. Further, Carthage is a prosperous society that provides for leisure without slavery.

Aristotle says that there are similarities with the Spartan regime but in every case affairs are "better handled" in Carthage. Carthage alone of the three regimes is said to have "aristocratic" institutions: e.g., offices are elected on the basis of desert and the kings are selected from outstanding families by election rather than merely serving due to superannuation. Carthage does deviate from aristocracy in the direction of both democracy and oligarchy. Legislative proposals must be submitted by the aristocratic elements of the society but may be discussed and criticized by the many. And many offices are distributed on the basis of wealth. Of this oligarchic element Aristotle says, "this is an error of the legislator." (1273a32) The ability to buy offices tends to make wealth more honored than virtue. And those who buy offices desire to profit from what costs them dearly, and this is not conducive of just decision-making. Under these arrangements the best situation would be where the virtuous are also well-off. But that requires the infrequent combination of natural endowment, good upbringing in a good regime, and incredible luck. It would also require institutions of inherited wealth and a more or less socially static society.

The potentially damaging influences of the oligarchic elements at Carthage are mitigated by the fact that Carthage has institutions through which the many are constantly becoming wealthy. Carthage has upward mobility, and that surely implies downward mobility as well. Carthage is a commercial city. It pursues and creates unnatural wealth. The unjust rule of the rich is mitigated by the unnatural accumulation of property available to the many. The two questionable institutions cancel each other out and lead to the desirable stability that Aristotle praises. Aristotle goes on to say that this balancing out "is really the work of chance." (1273b21–22) Chance, not conscious design, is responsible for Carthage's stability. The one time he talks about conscious legislation at Carthage, Aristotle attributes "an error" to the legislator. Herein we again see how Aristotle points to the limitations of the "conscious" application of reason to political and moral affairs. What evolves on its own frequently has more reason behind it than what is consciously constructed.

The ground of stability in the best actual regime discussed is Chance. It is primarily the product of an evolution, which eventuates in various institutions—which from the perspective of reason are unnatural—being balanced. It would be a mistake on the part of reason to try to replace these "unnatural" institutions. Aristotle has given every indication that conscious reason will replace it with something worse. Sparta, the regime that is most completely the work of conscious legislation, is by far the worst of Aristotle's three. Crete, the product of a complicated mélange of tradition, tinkering and auspicious location, is in the middle. The barbarian city Carthage is best. It comes close to a version of "polity."

The third part of Book 2 is the shortest. Aristotle discusses legislators who created both "laws and regimes." (1273b33) The discussion of Solon is especially interesting. It is reported that Solon was reputed to have reformed an oligarchy making it mixed and moderate. But Aristotle says "it would seem, though, that Solon found these things existing previously." (1273b42) Aristotle says further that Solon's best efforts appear "to have happened coincidentally rather than in accordance with the intention of Solon." (1274a12–14) In fact, at best, things did not go according to Solon's expectation. At worst, Solon over-legislated. Again, we are forced to reflect on the limits of the conscious exercise of reason. Of the remaining legislators, Aristotle observes that despite their repute none seem to have invented anything genuinely novel.

Nonetheless, several of them thought they had done novel things. Apparently, this is an indication of how few novelties there really are within the natural whole. Given the unlikelihood of improvement through conscious change, one should not fall prey to the promise of novelty.

Aristotle's observation that the *polis* has as its end the pursuit of the highest good might lead one to believe that the creation of a regime where everyone reaches a uniform, prescribed telic excellence is the task that reason is required to perform. But unlike the case with other species, human nature is complex and does not actualize itself by simple necessity. Left to our spontaneous "instincts" we would be the confused nexus of competing drives all of which are natural. Those drives must be given order. The various sources of order as well as the reason that balances ("weaves"?) them are all natural.

In the *Ethics* we confront Aristotle's understanding that thought does not originate action. Action originates in desire. Properly trained desire can become "deliberate desire," or "rational desire." This requires education and laws. Reason must intervene and work through trained desire—thereby accepting the originary force of desire. In a similar fashion, reason can reform the laws that are already given. Given this limitation, mass aristocracy is not feasible, and virtue based on autonomous reason is not possible. Beyond that, if everyone arrived at the same manifestation of virtue or excellence, it would seem that this would manifest itself politically in a universal, participatory aristocracy. But ultimately this is not Aristotle's best regime. Hence what are we to make of the political bearing of virtue?

In Aristotle's discussion of virtue, there are ten moral virtues, which find an initial peak in *megalopsychia*, the "great-souled" person. That peak occurs in Book 4 of the *Ethics*. In Book 5 we are presented with another peak, "complete" justice, which is said to presuppose the existence of the prior ten moral virtues. In Book 6 we are given the five intellectual virtues, one of which, *phronesis*, represents yet another moral peak. In the *Ethics* this list of virtues is followed by a discussion of such topics as "moral strength" and an extended discussion of friendship. The *Ethics* culminates in the assertion that friendship is a higher basis for community than the coercive elements implied in "partial" justice, and finally that the greatest happiness requires a friendship founded on "philosophy," which is presented as a form of *theoria* or contemplative life more or less in the Socratic fashion of detached, motionless staring. To say the least, there is much in this discussion that remains ambiguous. For the moment let me merely assert that there are a series of peaks to virtue that move in the following order: *megalopsychia*, complete justice, *phronesis*, *sophia*, culminating in *theoria*. I do not think that any of these peaks adequately describes the activity of Aristotle or the usage of reason we are discussing. It is far better captured by Plato's *politikos*.

The first peak of moral virtue is to be found in Aristotle's discussion of the "great-souled" person (*megalopsychia*) who thinks he is deserving of great honor and is. (1123a34–1125a36) He longs for the respect and honor that is due to someone of great intrinsic worth because he is the peak or summation of the other separate nine moral virtues. Leaving aside for the moment the status of "philosophy," the great-souled man seems, within a purely practical perspective, to be the peak of virtue, the *telos* toward which the city should point.

The problem with this conclusion is that the great-souled man refuses to compete or wrangle over small things, hence would be uninterested in day-to-day political participation. Small deeds, small honors, petty issues and efforts are things he disdains. It is inevitable, therefore, that the great-souled man adopts a stance of aloofness and detachment in a way mimicking *theoria*. He would never concern himself with the day-to-day administration of the petty things of everyday life or the ordinary participation that is part of the "political" rule whereby one rules and is ruled in turn. Ordinary political participation and deliberation would be beneath him. He would never associate with sophists, he would not be found in the *agora*, the courts, or the legislative assembly. But when great issues were at stake, great and monumental deeds needed, significant risks required, he would be the first to step forward. He would participate in the affairs of the city only when something of great importance, arduous and grand, was at stake.

It is the reticence of the honor-loving, great-souled man that makes his relation to the city politically ambiguous and uneasy. As a peak of virtue, the great-souled man shows the ambiguous relation of great virtue to the day-to-day affairs of political life. As Lincoln observed in his discussion of "the tribe of the eagle and the family of the lion," great virtue is frequently dangerous to the continued existence of the laws. The great-souled man's existence must be balanced carefully with needs of the whole. This is also true politically of the *phronimos*, the *sophos* and the being who like Heidegger's silversmith, binds together the four causes, who I have likened to Plato's *politikos*.

Despite the great-souled man being a peak of virtue, it is not possible to found a regime based on his day-to-day rule. At best his rule would be kingly rather than political, ruling out the participation required in a truly "political" situation where equals rule and are ruled in turn. That participation provides the practice and habits needed to establish virtue in some fair, broadly based way. Nevertheless, it is necessary that the great-souled man be a part of the political equation. He will be needed in emergencies. He also holds aloft the moral standard toward which action should be oriented (he fits in as a form of final causality for others).

He also provides the needed "pathos of distance" even higher peaks of virtue require. His virtue will be esteemed and looked up to but he will not be a ruler on a day-to-day basis. Having inherited or already made wealth, for he would disdain pursuing wealth, he would stand as a moral standard, and as a social standard. Those who aspired to social acceptance would moderate their political, moral and economic behavior in the hopes of achieving some kind of comparable social standing. In this indirect way, great virtue would serve a beneficial political, social, and moral function.

Consequently, Aristotle's discussion of the various peaks of virtue is consistent with his discussion of the **political need** for a "middling" virtue attainable by all citizens. Aristotle observes in the *Politics* that one must look for "what regime is best and what way of life is best for most cities and most human beings, judging with a view neither to virtue of the sort that is beyond private persons, nor to education, in respect to those things requiring [special advantages provided by] nature and an equipment dependent on chance, nor to the regime that one would pray for, but a way of life which is possible for most to participate in, and a regime in which most cities can share." (1295a25–30)

In the *Ethics* Aristotle observes that virtue is the prerequisite for happiness, but also that it is a mean. In the *Politics* he says that if "the happy life is one in accordance with virtue and unimpeded, and that virtue is a mean, then **the middling sort of life** is best—the mean that is capable of being attained by each sort of individual." [my emphasis] (1295a37) From this Aristotle reaches the conclusion that that regime is best which is ruled on a day-to-day basis by the middling, in short, the middle class that is middling in both virtue and wealth. That regime is called a polity.

The middling elements of a polity are most likely to act in a way consistent with reason, i.e., they are the most moderate. The underendowed are envious; the overly well endowed are arrogant. The completely leisured are prone to war and great contests in pursuit of honor. And the really excellent "neither wish to be ruled nor know how to be." (1295b14) Therefore, the rule of the middle class, and those of middling virtue, is most in accord with reason. Valuing their freedom, the middle class will not side with the rich in taking the freedom of the many. Having some property, the middle class will never side with the leveling instincts of the many. Having some virtue, and aspiring to social standing, the middle class will not resent the excellence—and occasional arrogance—of the class with great virtue and social standing. Having occasional leisure, the middle class will not destroy the complete leisure of the few.

Disdaining the pursuit of wealth in favor of virtue, any aristocratic class this society would have would not be the wealthiest, hence their political influence would be more limited than the wealthy. The truly wealthy will be restrained in their pursuit of unnatural wealth only by their own social aspirations. By its mere existence, an aristocratic class provides the best restraint on the unlimited pursuit of wealth that is available, social acceptability. The many would be mollified by the possibilities of freedom, political participation, and upward economic mobility. The best regime is a polity, ruled on a day-to-day basis by the middle class—a commercial class that generates the wealth necessary for leisure—with an aristocratic class that exists on the periphery of day-to-day affairs. Since nature presences in a variety of human types, balancing the parts is necessary. They are all natural, but so is the balance of them by reason, and so is the reason that does the balancing.

In the last analysis there is one paradox: aristocracy in the serious sense could only mean a class of great-souled individuals. Put in that fashion the problem is clear. As Aristotle defines this virtue, there is only room for one great-souled person at a time. And if the "completely" just person and the *phronimos* presuppose all the previous moral virtues, that implies *megalopsychia*, and the same problem reappears with them. Hence to say that the end of the *polis* is the good life, and that the good life requires virtue, and indeed the highest virtue, does not point to aristocratic rule. Again, Aristotle further complicates the matter by asserting that the highest virtue is to be attained by "philosophy." But I will argue that when he makes this assertion he does not mean either his autonomous theoretical reason—conceptualized in the *Ethics* as *episteme* + *nous* = *sophia*—or the exercise of a weaving or balancing Reason such as I am sketching.

To be a citizen of a regime one must be able to participate in deliberation, decision-making and administration. Citizenship is dependent, therefore, on the nature of the regime. To be a citizen is to participate in the affairs of a particular city. There is no possibility of living outside of **some particular regime**, even if there are virtues that seem to lie beyond moral and political virtue. Aristotle affirms this when he makes political science the "master science." Hence it is inevitable that a tension will emerge between being an excellent citizen and an excellent human being, and presumably that means "philosopher." (1276b33) The best regime must be so constituted that it points beyond itself to the types of individuals who cannot exist without the city and who can only exist at its fringes: the great-souled, the *sophos* the "philosophers," and those who exercise reason as we have been discussing it.

As both the *Ethics* and Books 7 and 8 of the *Politics* indicate, Aristotle is at some pains to leave ambiguous the nature of "philosophy," just as he is at pains to soften the potential tension between the few and the many on a purely economic level. For example, we must recognize that the education discussed in Book 8 of the *Politics* is predominately aimed at a leisured gentry, not the middling elements who of necessity will have to work. For the benefit of this gentry, in Book 7 Aristotle asks whether the most choice worthy way of life is politics or philosophy. In that discussion, philosophy is associated with the private life that transcends the public arena of deliberation. Philosophy, as depicted in Book 7, requires "some sort of study," i.e., the "liberal arts." (1324a28) Aristotle adds elliptically, "some assert [that this] is the only philosophic way of life." (1324a26–30) Philosophy so understood is not a form of inactivity; it involves actions that are "complete in themselves, and the sorts of study and ways of thinking that are for their own sake. **Acting well** is the end." [my emphasis] (1325b18–20)

Those who pursue these studies disdain labor and the pursuit of wealth. (1328b36–40) They will also disdain the deeds of the great-souled man. Their education consists of such things as music, poetry and gymnastic, an education reminiscent of the early stages of the curriculum presented in the *Republic*. It is clear that what is here called "philosophy" is a standard for an educated leisured gentry that has respect for and pretensions to great-souledness, but no willingness or capacity to perform great deeds. They will be a bookish gentry. They provide a cultured restraint on the potentially warlike spiritedness of the truly great-souled, and another step on the ladder between middling virtue and the souls in and through whom all existence is affirmed.

It could be asserted that this is what is meant by "philosophy" throughout Aristotle's practical works, including the discussion in Book 10 of the *Ethics*—i.e., contemplative *theoria*. The aim is to draw a link between philosophy as it was practiced by those from Anaxagoras to Socrates that the city scorned, and those who engage in the activities of noble leisure which prosper in privacy, friendship and the family, i.e., beyond the public arena. Even Thales, who in a popular story was ridiculed by a slave girl, is presented by Aristotle in an attractive public persona, as a man who could occasionally be shrewd in business. Aristotle is not trying to depict the truly highest perfection of reason so much as soften the public image of philosophy by presenting it in gentlemanly guise, offering a surrogate for non-philosophers.

But the picture to this point has left out several of the rungs of Aristotle's ladder. Since "complete" justice and *phronesis* are said to presuppose all the moral virtues, while going beyond them, they are presented as peaks beyond *megalopsychia*. Of complete justice almost nothing is said except to give the definition. Of the *phronimos* we learn that he deals entirely with the *means* to moral ends. The ends are not grasped by *phronesis*. Hence *phronesis* is entirely determined by something outside itself—and that means in practical terms the *ethos* of a specific moral and political regime that, through its laws and education, supplies the distinctive ends. *Sophia* or theoretical wisdom is defined as *nous*—the capacity to directly grasp the *arche* or first principles— plus *episteme*—the capacity to deduce what follows theoretically from those principles. As such, theoretical philosophy is reduced to a systematic, deductive enterprise. If what I have argued is persuasive, the philosopher in the highest sense is the one who, like Heidegger's silversmith, binds together the four causes, balancing the various aspects of emergent nature into a fully present whole, thereby becoming the completing and culminating part of Nature. Aristotle's *sophos* or person of contemplative *theoria* is a far lower phenomenon.

Only one individual truly approaches self-sufficiency. He sets the horizon in which *phronesis*, *sophia* and *theoria* can operate. To the extent that his undertaking is rarely needed in its highest manifestation, hence rarely exercised, such a person will be slow to act on most occasions. Being a part of the emergence process of nature (*physis*), this person will experience himself/herself at a height. In this regard, this person is substantially like the great-souled person. But such individuals must also have an understanding of the whole, including the human things, and the practical knowledge of the means to ends of the *phronimos*. Hence this will be a great-souledness of a very high magnitude—a phenomenon well above and beyond everyday affairs.

My suggestion is as follows: The first peak of virtue is the *megalopsychia*, which manifests itself in a relatively instinctive fashion. This is followed by *phronesis* (there is simply no data supplied by Aristotle that allows one to judge what to do with "complete" justice), which presupposes not only understanding of the ends, but leisure, considerable practice and natural gifts. Next is *sophia*, which manifests itself in a self-forgetting, apolitical, systematic, deductive enterprise that is far from self-sufficient because it is incapable of securing its own prerequisites. The final peak is the great balancer for whom there is no simple name in Aristotle, but we can borrow Plato's name *politikos*. He can be called a philosopher, but this is at best paradoxical given the literal meaning of the term, and likewise confusing if not separated from the gentrified manifestation of that term as I have already discussed. All of the self-emergent rungs of the ladder find their justification **and their place in the whole** through that exercise of reason that binds together the parts of emergent nature into a completed whole. Reason so conceived completes nature by being its final part. Being as *energeia* puts itself to work through all the parts, but especially in the culminating part wherein it becomes self-conscious as *nous* **in action** (which differs from the inert grasping capacity of the *nous* discussed in Book 6 of the *Ethics*).

Excellence is the end of the *polis*, but the higher manifestations of virtue and excellence flourish only on the fringes of day-to-day affairs. The best regime fosters true excellence but still grounds the legitimacy to rule of the middling elements. Their legitimate right to rule is grounded—somewhat ironically—in their collective virtue. The participation that actualizes this collective virtue implies some rough equality, hence "it is clear that legislation must necessarily have to do with those who are equal both in stock and capacity, and that for the other sort of person there is no law." (1284a11–14)

The multitude of equals have a claim to rule on the basis of virtue, but it is their cumulative virtue that grounds that claim, not individual excellence. For the truly outstanding there can be no law, hence "such persons can no longer be regarded as part of the city." (1284a7–8) Of course, therein we see a great potential danger. Virtue plays a role in the city, but hardly a dogmatic one. By integrating virtue into the city one limits the claims of the few based on wealth, the many based on mere numbers and of the strong on their intrepidity and daring. Hence virtue remains respected, even if in its highest manifestations it is not given immediate access to rule or even frequent public manifestation. But all the parts of nature must be respected, they must all be bound together in the final equation that is completed nature.

The best regime is one that makes possible a leisured, virtuous few within the midst of the moderate rule of the middling elements. It is not administered by the most virtuous in any of their manifestations. The education of Book 8 of the *Politics* is aimed at a group of individuals who eschew the expertise that the various public arts require and will not expend the time that day-to-day political participation implies. In the interstices of a genteel—bookish rather than militaristic—leisured class, shielded by the pathos of distance that that class legitimates, the true philosophers will be found, i.e., the true proponents of reason.

But this is at best always an uneasy balance. The best regime maximizes participation—and the educative function it serves—while protecting both property and achievement. This balancing is best accomplished by the rule of law rather than the rule of men. And the rule of old established laws is best for it is not good to give the passions the repeated example of changeable laws. Only thereby is law "intellect without appetite." (1287a32) Aristotle points toward the rule of law and not the rule of men, no matter how excellent. And for the same reason, laws based on long-established unwritten custom are preferable to written laws, whose human origin is all too clear. Laws consciously written at a certain time give the example that such can be repeated, breaking down the habit necessary to support the laws, and giving momentary passion greater chance of hegemony over reason.

The giving of laws might seem to be the task of Aristotle's prudent or practically wise individual (*phronimos*). But that cannot be. He merely operates **within a horizon already set for him**, calculating means to ends already established. He may engage in reform rather than originating new laws. Book 2 of the *Politics* gives various examples of how limited conscious attempts to originate the ends in political life are. The *phronimos* operates best within the parameters of established custom. Indeed, virtue in all its more rarefied manifestations presupposes an already existing *polis*. But any decent *polis* must point beyond itself. While the *polis* is necessary for virtue, it is not sufficient.

Indeed, the *polis* is the prerequisite for virtue, but also a limitation on its peak attainments and practice. But if virtue is disregarded there is no limit on the greed and arrogance of the few and the envy of the many, which can only tear apart a community. Reason must grasp both the *telos* and the limits to its actualization. In applying reason to political life one must be impressed with the need to limit one's efforts to a delicate balancing act that has to be continually restruck.

Proto-modernity, as we saw in Machiavelli, developed a view of reason in which its task was to emancipate itself from Chance, natural determination, tradition, in short, everything "other" than an autonomous reason, which was conceived as an efficient cause. Eventually, it became the task of autonomous reason to generate abstract, universal ends. Those abstract universal rules or laws became the only basis of rationality. In this understanding, we become moral only by adopting this abstract universal stance. Only as abstract, immaterial, universal selves are we moral, rational or human. In the process, the self-emergent complexity of nature is ignored. Reason so conceived was obliged to depict self-emergent custom, instinct, particularity in all its forms, as irrational and amoral. Later moderns took the proto-modern dichotomy at face value, opting instead for the opposite pole of the new modern dichotomies—praising the fecundity of irreason in all its forms.

For those who believe nihilism is the inevitable outcome of unleashing the modern understanding of reason, first there arose various proposals for reliance on or recovery of instinct—or other alleged, deep, unself-conscious sources of action. That was followed by various proposals for the recovery of religion and tradition. Hence, in opposition to the distinctively proto-modern dichotomy reason/nature, came the late modern dichotomies reason/will, reason/instinct, reason/tradition, reason/religion, etc. We are now left in a position where we seem forced to choose between an autonomous reason that aims at creating a universal *polis* for abstract individuals, and various forms of the spontaneity and immediacy that leave us locked within unmediated versions of the particular and the parochial. This latter option plunges us into a kind of blindness in which we are forced to rejoice in every chance occurrence or willful deed. In Nietzsche's terminology we are left with the "innocence and forgetting" by which we affirm Chance, i.e., we will "the eternal recurrence of the same." In Heidegger's terms, we await a new, mysterious, rooted dispensation of Being over which we can have no control.

Through Aristotle we can arrive at an understanding of reason that works in harmony with what **emerges into presence without the intervention of man** conceived as autonomous, efficient cause—a thoroughly modern transformation of the meaning of the *causa efficiens*. Reason becomes neither the autonomous activity that aims only at the universal—as in Kant, Hegel, Marx, et al.—nor a scapegoat that is sacrificed to the fecundity of the particular. Reason remains within the limits of complex, emergent nature accepting the value of custom and tradition while taking its bearings by potential ends, all of which are a part of nature. Reason sees itself as the final or culminating part of nature rather than as nature's other.

Grasping this vision of reason is not the same a proposing an immediate solution to a present predicament. First, Aristotle's account is not without its own difficulties. Aristotle's radical split between *phronimos* and *sophos*, which projected philosophy as an entirely theoretical activity that is divorced from practical reasoning, and a practical reason which in turn has no theoretical insight, opened a door to the modern projection of an autonomous, theoretical reason outside nature. Aristotle is, therefore, implicated in the late-modern problem we confront far more than Plato—contrary to various postmodern attempts to implicate Plato. An autonomous theory like that projected by Aristotle—if I am correct, at least as one of the lower rungs of an ascending ladder that gains significance as part of a whole—opened the possibility of that modern rationality that tries to emancipate itself from Nature.

Put another way, Aristotle's own balancing act generated a problem that must now be dealt with by a categorically different balancing act. Or approached from the Platonic metaphor, the Aristotelian philosopher, interpreted as practitioner of theoretical reason, has seemingly no incentive to reenter the cave, and his *phronimos* is without the theoretical insight to understand the present problem in its depths. Hence neither is of any use to us at present. But if I am correct, neither represented a final or self-sufficient phenomenon for Aristotle. What we see demonstrated here is the unpredictable, deferred ramifications of any balancing act, and hence why repeated rebalancings of nature are required. Nature as emergent *energeia* is not static. It continually reconstitutes itself. We humans are the culminating piece in that ongoing reconstitution.

Further, in an age in which tradition is being daily uprooted, and is in some places all but gone as a living thing, and in which instinct and habit have been morally delegitimized—i.e., in a post-Kantian environment—it may not be immediately possible to strike anything like the balance Aristotle aimed for even if we concluded it was desirable. But the metaphor of reason as the culminating part of nature used to balance the other self-emergent parts remains of value. In our time reason may have to undertake an activity, which for Aristotle would never have been necessary. Reason may have to address itself to the conditions under which genuine traditions and customs emerge, and under which that which **presents itself** can be relegitimized. It may also have to construct a new ladder out of different, already available materials that present themselves. Given the radical transformation of reality wrought by the modern application of reason, it will be new elements that need to be balanced into a new whole.

My suggestion is simple: We need an understanding of reason as part of nature, not that which negates what emerges (*physis*). Hence we must be willing to bind ourselves to presently emergent appearances and forms and presently possible ends. To follow the intimation above, reason must bind together the four forms of causality through which nature presences. It thereby becomes the means by which nature completes itself ever anew.[29]

One implication is that we must eschew the longstanding, and long since theoretical, nature/convention (*physis/nomos*) distinction as it has come down to us. Nature must be seen as the totality of emergent appearance, and that includes the products of human art and human living together collectively. We must eschew the conventional reading of Aristotle, and the ancients more generally, which remains tied to the dominant form of common opinion at the inception of Greek thought—the older *nomos/physis* distinction was adopted from already existent common opinion.[30]

Our now conventional hermeneutic traditions will eventually fare no better than the political and moral ones that modern reason has already destroyed. And it would be an error to believe that modern reason, which from the beginning longed to establish its autonomy and in the process transformed the world and gained thereby great inertial force, will easily yield the field. To oppose it will lead to the danger of seeming to side with the late modern proponents of irreason. But the alternative would be to rattle around indefinitely in various fruitless, modern dichotomies. And that is precisely where we cannot remain.

NOTES

1. Modern reason tries to construct theoretical **points of departure**, which it then uses as the means to escape traditional and natural determination. These theoretical constructs, whether in modern natural science or Kantian and post-Kantian moral theory, or wherever, dictate to nature what will be accepted as legitimate, indeed what will be accepted as having reality or Being. In Heidegger's terms, we are in the midst of "The Age of the World Picture," the age of total "Enframing." See Heidegger, "The Age of the World Picture," and "The Question Concerning Technology," in *The Question Concerning Technology and Other Essays*, trans. William Lovitt (New York: Harper and Row, 1977).

2. See my *Martin Heidegger: Paths Taken, Paths Opened* (Lanham, MD: Rowman & Littlefield, 2007).

3. See especially in this regard Jacques Derrida, *Of Grammatology* (Baltimore: Johns Hopkins University Press, 1976). For a different understanding that still sees

interpretation of texts as central to the philosophic enterprise, see Leo Strauss, *Persecution and the Art of Writing* (Glencoe: The Free Press, 1952). See also chapter 6 on Derrida.

4. See in this regard Gianni Vattimo, *The Transparent Society* (Baltimore: Johns Hopkins University Press, 1992), especially pp. 1–11, 62–75.

5. I discuss this subject in my *Nietzsche, Heidegger and the Transition to Postmodernity* (Chicago: University of Chicago Press, 1996), especially pp. 73–83, 269 note 10 and 302 note 8.

6. The *Clouds* also makes clear that traditional norms had already broken down prior to any influence traceable to Socrates. As the breakdown of the traditional order and piety antedates Socrates' influence, he primarily represents an alternative to the decaying order. How apt Socrates is in that regard remains an open question. See in this regard chapter 14 on *Symposium*.

7. For an elaboration of this issue see Joseph Cropsey's path breaking *Plato's World: Man's Place in the Cosmos* (Chicago: University of Chicago Press, 1995).

8. See the discussion of the *Phaedo* in chapter 13.

9. It must also be moderated by the "practical," which means "phenomenological" deployment we will see in Aristotle's practical works.

10. This is what clearly differentiates both Plato, and Aristotle in the practical works, from Socrates. Socrates is not the father of political philosophy. The invention of political philosophy required not only the discovery of reason—conjoined with the discovery of "nature"—but also knowledge of its limits.

11. See in this regard, Leo Strauss, *Natural Right and History* (Chicago: University of Chicago Press, 1971), pp. 81–103.

12. We should not underestimate the extent to which the so called "doctrine of the ideas," is a Socratic invention which is either merely reported by Plato, or in a variety of subtle ways, criticized.

13. In this regard see chapter 22 in this book.

14. I have relied on the Carnes Lord translation of Aristotle's *Politics* (Chicago: University of Chicago Press, 1984).

15. That some things emerge on their own without human intervention and tend, like an acorn, toward a finished state is not a theoretical construct, it is how things **present themselves** in everyday appearance. Teleology itself is not a theoretical construct, it is an articulation of how things present themselves. To make this everyday appearance go away requires a theoretical construct. **Only constructivism can destroy teleology**, and it must undermine the status of phenomenology to do it.

16. A useful treatment of Aristotle's ontology can be found in Jacob Klein, *Lectures and Essays*, ed. by Robert B. Williamson and Elliot Zuckerman (Annapolis: St. John's College Press, 1985).

17. See Martin Heidegger, "The Question Concerning Technology," in *Martin Heidegger: Basic Writings*, ed. by David Farrell Krell (San Francisco: HarperCollins, 1993), pp. 313–317. Only a few have seen the extent to which Heidegger's reflections are dependent on his penetrating interpretation of Aristotle which is based on a familiarity with the texts of Aristotle that few have ever possessed.

18. This comes from Heidegger in a section entitled "Meaning of *dynamis kata kinesin*," in *Aristotle's Metaphysics Theta 1–3*, trans. Walter Brogan and Peter Warnek (Bloomington: Indiana University Press, 1995), p. 70. Throughout this work, Heidegger is attempting to articulate Aristotle's conception of Being.

19. It has been argued that the presentation of philosophy as concerned with autonomous theoretical entities is a consciously adopted defensive stance. It makes some sense that philosophy self-consciously assumed this stance in its confrontation with revealed religion. It makes considerable sense when applied to an author like Farabi who was operating in an environment where the law was already given and hence ethics and politics were withdrawn from the arena philosophy could openly engage. One could not be openly Socratic in questioning in that environment without considerable risk. One could defend philosophy from the charge of meddling in the moral and political things that were already decided by claiming philosophy was a purely theoretical undertaking aimed at grasping pure intelligibles. But it is not at all clear that Aristotle argued for the sharp distinction between theory and practice, and hence the autonomy of theory, on these defensive grounds. Either way, this picture of philosophy as an autonomous theoretical activity was the prerequisite for the modern move to a new form of theory which was so autonomous from the phenomenological ground of philosophy that it could legitimately dictate to it and transform it.

20. I have used the Martin Ostwald translation of Aristotle's *Nicomachean Ethics* (Indianapolis: Bobbs-Merrill, 1962). Henceforth the title will be abbreviated as *Ethics*.

21. By nature the only individuals not fit for political participation are those incapable of achieving true happiness (slaves), those not yet capable of doing so (children), and gods, those who are self-sufficient as regards happiness.

22. Plato has Socrates make an identical beginning in the *Gorgias*. It is the acceptance simultaneously of the body/soul distinction and other opinions that bring his opponents in the *Gorgias* and elsewhere to ruin. (464a–b) That this beginning point is based primarily on commonly accepted opinion can be seen by comparing this account with the discussion of the soul in *De Anima*, where it is clear that the clean split between body and soul is not maintainable. Cf. 402a5–8, 404a25–31, 408b25–28, 412a15–21, 412b18–20.

23. For a similar conclusion see Harry V. Jaffa, "Aristotle," in Leo Strauss and Joseph Cropsey, eds., *History of Political Philosophy*, 2nd ed. (Chicago: Rand McNally, 1972), p. 76. Natural slaves are at best a mixed blessing. A certain affection might develop between a rational master and a natural slave, "but for those who do not merit [slavery] in this way but [who are slaves] according to law and by force, the opposite is the case." (*Politics*, 1255b13) Slavery based upon law or force is not only unnatural but, Aristotle makes clear, will inevitably lead to the kind of animosity that occasions revolts.

24. For a more complete discussion of this issue, see Stephen G. Salkever, "Gendered Virtue: Plato and Aristotle on the Politics of Virility," in *Finding the Mean: Theory and Practice in Aristotelian Political Philosophy* (Princeton: Princeton University Press, 1990), pp. 165–204.

25. The now customary, and almost instinctive, response is to accuse Aristotle of misogyny. Compare this with Saxonhouse's nuanced account. See Arlene Saxonhouse in *Women in the History of Political Thought* (New York: Praeger, 1985), pp. 63–69. Saxonhouse argues that Socrates had destroyed the private, making all virtue public— e.g., in the *Republic*. In doing so he required the total identity of men and women. She argues that Aristotle differentiates the private from the public, assigning women to the private sphere, leaving the public sphere for men. **I am suggesting that Aristotle's argument is potentially more radical than that.** What must be understood is the reason why, having granted the questionableness of conventional Athenian relations between men and women, Aristotle refused to radically reform the city on this score. It follows from the complexity of the natural whole, especially as articulated vis-à-vis the totality of the manifestations of causality and the necessity of their operating together.

26. It is left to someone like Marx to pursue this dream; and the extraordinary brutality and loss of life that that pursuit entailed is a testimony to the limits of reason by nature.

27. Part of the reason can be traced to the fact that Aristotle has concluded that it is both prudent and politic to publicly pick a fight with Socrates. Disagreeing with a man put to death for undermining the morals of the young and importing new gods into the city is not a dangerous undertaking, quite the contrary. But it also has to do with his complex understanding of nature.

28. I will argue shortly that this is a metaphorical usage of the term "philosophy" put forward for public consumption. So understood, philosophy is roughly comparable to an appreciation of what we call the humanities.

29. I will return to this understanding of nature in the discussion of environmentalism in chapter 22.

30. We will, initially at least, have to discard this distinction precisely to be able to recover a workable conception of the "phenomenon" of nature. It is a distinction that only marginally shows itself in our time.

Part Four

POLITICAL PHILOSOPHY
AFTER MODERNITY?

Preface to Part 4:
Openings Toward the Postmodern

The essays in part 4 engage in several thought experiments indicative of how we might begin to think forward toward a postmodern future. These essays are not intended to be the last word, just hopefully provocative first words that might make the phenomena of our time visible in a new way, and open new ways of thinking forward. These essays are attempts to open several doors and are intended as invitations to think about walking down the paths that exist on the other side; or to find still other doors altogether. They are invitations to keep the future open. It is predictable that for many these essays will have little to say; and that is probably just as well. But I hope they will be a spur to further future oriented thought for at least a few.

The genuinely *post*modern as I understand it, if it is to beyond the modern, will have to reflect on the core phenomena of modernity that are all around us, bring them into the light of day and rescue them from becoming the kind of background phenomena that are so occluded and forgotten that they quietly enslave us. One of the central background phenomena of modernity is an ongoing deep-seated anti-nature animus. For many reasons, some of which have entered into consideration above, it is now time to recover a relation to the phenomenon "nature." The postmodern will have to find a way to be related to "nature" in a stance that is not antagonistic. But in relating to nature as a phenomenon, rather than as an idea or concept, we will not relate to it as fixed and static but as both dynamic and as including man's history making ability as part of the whole that is "nature." I deal with this issue specifically in the final essay of this section but the idea of man's nature or essence being that of a history making being is something I have dealt with throughout *Between Eternities*.

Beyond a clear anti-nature animus, modernity has from the beginning also been antagonistic to revealed religion as well. Arguably, the primary impetus to the launching of modernity was a perceived need to emancipate both philosophy and political life from a theological stranglehold that had reached a point that had debilitating effects. It is necessary to rethink the unavoidable place of religion in human life and its relation to thought and practice.

Likewise, modernity is fundamentally associated with the launching of the new natural science. That science needs to be interrogated continually as to its nature and its philosophical status, as well as its advantages and disadvantages, if we are not to be enslaved yet again by a tool initially launched to help free us.

And morally and politically, deep within the interstices of modernity has always been a universalistic and cosmopolitan longing that ultimately has anti-political and anti-history making implications. We must again reflect upon the relation between the universal, the cosmopolitan and the good. At the very least, that has not been done for a very long time.

At a bare minimum one must question these core phenomena of modernity, making them present and bringing them into the open for inspection: 1) modernity's anti-nature animus, 2) modernity's anti-religion animus, 3) modernity's pro modern science inclination, 4) modernity's inherent abstract universalistic and cosmopolitan longings, and 5) modernity's anti-political bias, hence its End of History inclination.

While not exhaustive, these are some of the central and important phenomena of modernity, phenomena that determine our present way of life, and more generally, **the way life presents itself to us**. Questioning primary and fundamental phenomena at a deep level is the kind of questioning that could open the possibility of postmodernity as long as that questioning keeps in touch with the past tradition that led us to our present situation. We must understand not only the nature of our present, but the trajectory that brought us here if we are to find our way into a healthy future. This points toward another underlying phenomenon of modernity, the either/or decision it has posed between Constructivist Reason and Tradition (constructed as blind and malignant accident).

This kind of fundamental questioning needs to be brought forth for inspection in the full light of day, in the public arena, and undertaken in publicly accessible speech if we are to open the phenomena for ourselves and those who will come after us in a sanguine fashion. The more the phenomena that determine us remain absent, the more those phenomena will silently master us in a way that will deny us any future.

A significant number of modern premises, which in many cases in the past were openly and substantively defended, have sunk to the level of platitudes and become accepted as self-evident givens when they are anything but obvious. At that point, without a rational defense, those premises can be maintained only as forgotten presuppositions or as public myths. And that is not the Western way of doing things; we believe that the unexamined life is not worth living. As but one example of what I have in mind, I am going to suggest below that much of our public understanding of modern science, and the customary self-understanding of the sciences as well, has sunk to the level of myth.

I am especially interested in modern science as it displays itself at the theoretical cutting edge in cosmological and biological theory. I will try to raise the unavoidable question of whether either at the origins of the new science, or throughout its modern history, modern science was ever intended to be, or could ever become, ontological. I want to reflect upon the ramifications of cutting edge theorizing that increasingly divorces itself from the phenomena, and hence from even the possibility of empirical validation as that has been understood throughout the history of modern science from Bacon and Descartes until very recently.

Can there be a postmodern, phenomenological science that is true to the essence of modern science in its original deployment that does not land us in the lap of fatuous, relativist nonsense like that found in much lampooned longings for things like native-American or feminist biology and cosmology. I will merely suggest at present that modern science can continue to have a foundation in empirical validation without the need for mythical ontological pretensions. And in pursuing the necessary phenomenological link for future science we can avoid postmodernist, ideological idiocies of one kind or another.

Sticking with the theme of a possible descent into an all too possible new postmodern mythologizing, various central modern philosophical notions have lost credibility and thereby have already deconstructed themselves. On one level, that many unthinkingly still follow in the wake of these withdrawing notions is evidence of nothing of importance other than that not everyone leads an articulate life; or that at best there is a lag time necessary for actual clarity to find its way to the public arena. But to continue to defend many of those notions will only happen on a mythological level.

Among the notions that have lost philosophical credibility are the notions of historical linearity and individual and collective self-transparency. In what follows, I offer an alternative conception of history as determined by what I call "event horizons." I then explore what is involved for future political and moral life as it plays itself out on the forthcoming global stage without mythical belief in linearity and total transparency. This leads me to reflections on how morality must be discussed "vertically" rather than in light of the "horizontal" principle of abstract linear universality, which has come to dominate within modernity.

Neither the principles of linearity and transparency nor a historical notion requiring or presupposing the actualization of an abstract universal good retains the chance of any future philosophical plausibility. In a post-Heideggerian world, not only are many of these notions philosophically indefensible, but notions of universality (i.e. a world freed from thrownness), linearity, transparency and inevitability **are immense moral narcotics** that will destroy the possibility of resolute political and moral action across generations at a time when moral and political staying power are most needed.

Further, I want to suggest that what is implied as we lose faith in modern Constructivist models of Reason is a new credibility for revealed religion and Faith. The alternative of Faith will simply not go away in the future that is coming despite modern, all too modern, rooting interests. We are already shaped by a two-millennium history that descends from revealed religion and we cannot will it away. If we are honest, regardless of our rooting interests, we will be forced to admit that the postmodern world will require a new appreciation of the complicated relation between Reason and Faith. But despite the rise in status of Faith, it is imperative that political philosophy as I have conceptualized it retain hegemony as a holistic, dialectical, phenomenological undertaking. As architectonic, political philosophy retains hegemony over Theology, Physics, Biology and all other subsidiary undertakings. That means that none of those alternatives can presume to autonomy.

These observations will lead me to reflect briefly upon the philosophical resources already available in the three revealed, Scriptural traditions. I conclude not only that the West is and can only be Christian, but that the richest theological and philosophical resources still lie fallow within Christianity. For example only Christianity is ecstatically temporal and only Christianity has a positive need for political philosophy as it rests on articles of Faith, not on everyday law.

There is no need for giving ourselves over to Nietzsche's vague invocation of the Dionysian or Heidegger's even vaguer waiting for new gods. The West simply is Christian in one way or the other—and in either its present increasingly secular form or some original manifestation yet to come always will be. Postmodernity need not be post-Scriptural or post-Christian as Nietzsche and Heidegger wished any more than it needs to continue to have an anti-nature animus or set its sights on pursuing the abstract universal. We will have to prepare ourselves to quit many soothing myths that make us late moderns far less than we can be.

Chapter Eighteen

Legitimacy, International Morality and the Postmodern Global Future

The UN is the real source of legitimacy.

—German Foreign Minister Joschka Fischer
(*USA Today*, November 20, 2003, p. 13A)

More than a few, both outside as well as inside the United States, share the view of the German Foreign Minister. So widely held is this view that using the quote above as an exemplar of the issue from which I intend to depart dialectically might seem trivial.[1] Indeed in many circles this premise regarding the basis of moral legitimacy is an article of faith believed to have the immediate obviousness of a primary color: Either you see it or you don't. But it is an inarticulate faith that is almost always incapable of legitimizing itself.

Why do so many believe that the only basis for moral legitimacy in international action is a flawed, frequently impotent, corrupt institution like the United Nations? How can one take seriously an institution that will take as interesting the views of Syria or Iran on human rights by putting them on an international council to deal with human rights outrages? Can any interesting philosophical sense be made of seeing such an institution as the basis of morality or legitimacy? I will argue that there are all manner of questionable, inarticulately held, modern, philosophical premises underlying this understanding and it is time to unpack them and consider them in the light of day. I will go further; nothing of value is to be gained any longer by acting on the basis of any of these mythical premises.

Let there be no mistake, lurking here is primarily a philosophical issue. No list of practical considerations can get to the heart of the matter. The hegemony of the premise that only a universal, non–Nation-State actor can provide legitimacy and moral depth to international action can be explained only on the basis of an inarticulately shared intellectual *weltgeist* grounded ultimately on premises that have over the last 100 years been steadily losing philosophical credibility and cannot be put back on their feet again.

It goes without saying that sophisticated international action and diplomacy will use alliances as much as possible. To isolate oneself from other nations in the world is not a sound approach. And prudence may dictate that having a forum where multilateral discussions can be held can help avoid the inconvenience of a series of disjointed and disconnected ongoing one on one interactions. But any diplomacy, or exercise of political prudence, is blind if it does not clearly and articulately grasp its ultimate end. That end simply can no longer be—especially when the premise remains inarticulately held—a movement toward the philosophically discredited notion of a world state, resting as it does on the philosophically indefensible notion of linear History, and the parallel possibility of full transparency existing in a universal state. Beyond these issues lies the indefensible moral presupposition that an ultimate international universality, homogeneity and unity would in fact produce the good.

Granted, self-interest is always a significant part of international action. But especially for Americans that has never been enough.[2] The historical action of the American Republic could never seriously be written on the basis of self-interest alone, especially since the beginning of the twentieth century. American action has always been moved by ideas, ideals and philosophical goals. To grasp what should now be the defining ideas, ideals and goals we will need to rise beyond—although never simply leave behind—the practical issue that I have used to set this discussion in motion.[3] We start from the questions that **present themselves**, and always present themselves somewhere specific at a specific time, and make a dialectical ascent that leads us to consider central philosophical questions. In this case the question is, what premises inarticulately condition the belief that only the U.N. can provide morality and legitimacy in international affairs? Are those premises philosophically plausible? What alternatives exist?

THE POSTMODERN GLOBAL FUTURE

Have we definitively entered a new age? What transpired on September 11, 2001 may well have been more than just one event among many in recent history. It may have been a defining moment, a happening that changes everything. Such events can break into what might otherwise have been a more seamless movement of history and create a discontinuity. Is that the case now? Perhaps; we will have to see. Nothing is inevitable. If nothing else, 9/11 should have awakened both Americans and others to a present and future reality to which there may previously have been insufficient attention given and toward which we may still not be adequately attuned. It is not just that we have become aware that the world is a dangerous place, we vaguely knew that all along. September 11, 2001 should have made us aware of the extraordinarily thin veneer of our late modern technological civilization. Beyond the civilization and order that now exists—no matter how we praise or vilify it according to our ideological inclinations—lies the hegemony of a postmodern, barbaric chaos. Beyond our modern technological civilization there are no forces of order presently existent or on the immediate horizon. And beyond the United States there are almost no serious bases of order that can recall a chaos let loose if it is allowed to break out.[4]

In New York City, within minutes of the twin towers falling, we saw in microcosm what can happen in the late modern world. Panic can break out; cell phones, utilities, public transportation and all the accoutrements of modern civilization upon which we depend can so easily be taken from us in the blink of an eye. None of us can function any longer without those accoutrements, to say nothing of what would happen if we lost access to energy resources, food, supplies of water, medicine, and on and on.

Not only our daily lives could be disrupted in an instant, but our economy and our very capacity for defense could be corrupted within seconds. Computer viruses, attacks on power grids, mass epidemics, dirty bombs can make our technological civilization collapse while we take a sip of coffee. We late moderns all too smugly presume a higher level of independence vis-à-vis those of the past when in reality we are more dependent than anyone has ever been in ways never before imagined. **We have not conquered Chance, we have heightened its potential efficacy and unleashed new manifestations of it never before viable**. This newly heightened power of Chance will accelerate into the future. That is the ironic outcome of the modern project to conquer Chance. If we are attentive, 9/11 will teach us this sobering fact.

Were it to collapse, our tenuous civilization would dissolve much more quickly than the Roman, British or even Soviet empires, where the declines took generations and could be seen coming. Even with that limited list, one can see that collapse times are accelerating. There should be no mistake, we are not on the eve of the inevitability of universal peace, tranquility and predictability. We walk a perilous tightrope below which is an abyss of chaos and an age of technological barbarism the likes of which have never been seen and from which humanity might not re-emerge. That is not hyperbole, it is simple fact. We already possess the means to easily destroy all life on this planet with everything from nuclear weapons to chemical and biological agents. Just as frighteningly, we are coming into the possession of biological technologies that will allow us to transform and destroy the very fabric of human nature. In the hands of unscrupulous tyrants that technology can dwarf any of the experiments and aspirations of the Nazi scientists of our recent past. It is justly frightening to contemplate the Ayatollahs armed with nuclear weapons; but at worst we die as human beings. What of the Ayatollahs armed with biological technology? They could extinguish our very humanity. Hyperbole? I think not.

The dawning postmodern moment we occupy is a moment of the disintegration of old empires, power constellations and valued alliances. This occurs at a moment of not only political, but moral and intellectual balkanization as well. "High" European thought, which a couple of generations ago was still pursuing the enlightenment faith in the universal and the cosmopolitan openly and with a good conscience, has ceased to do so. It has given itself over to an abstract intellectual dilettantism that is a clear parallel to the political decadence that underlies it. This intellectual climate, which began with the powerful philosophical assaults on modernity of Nietzsche and Heidegger, the two greatest thinkers of the last 120 years, will have global consequences just as surely as the political balkanization we are witnessing.

The universal and cosmopolitan inclinations of past modern thought—admittedly those longings still retain an entropic momentum in some circles—can be traced to philosophical premises that have largely, for better or worse, lost credibility in the last century. Those premises can now be retained only as useful myths. But a rationalist civilization cannot with a good conscience proceed **consciously** on the basis of myths. This is especially true if that civilization simultaneously loses the basis for any political will maintainable over decades and generations.

We have conquered the great **modern** totalitarian experiments, born of the universalist (and counter-universalist) aspirations of the Soviets and Nazis. Postmodern balkanization and the all too real possibility of a descent into chaos and barbarism may be the yields of a West no longer able to stand fast against new enemies. Our situation has become more perilous at the dawning of the postmodern age than it was at the beginning of the modern. It is necessary to impress new forms upon the present formlessness. Both political and intellectual forms will be required. I am going to argue that on the political level that can only be done by the actions of a Nation-State, and that the U.S. is the only plausible present alternative.[5]

It is not presently plausible to believe that Europe or any possible European union can provide Western leadership. The long-term efficacy of any united Europe in fact rather than mere aspiration remains an open question, as the recent attempts of Germany and France for disproportionate hegemony have shown. Even with a European Union, we cannot expect Europe to stand as a future civilizational bulwark with its bloated individual national economies, lack of political will and philosophical disintegration. Our skepticism about the role of a rising Chinese empire should be as great as that regarding any rising Islamic empire. And Russia with its new oil and gas bonanzas has hardly become a sanguine international actor. While India may become a serious economic competitor, it is not culturally unified enough to become a major political actor in its own name. Few other alternatives exist.

I will argue that the moral legitimacy of the actions of any Nation-State actor can only be judged based upon the substantive high purpose to which those actions are to be put. That means that those actions can only be judged against a vertical standard rather than according to the horizontal standard of an alleged linear History, which implies inevitability, and points toward a universal outcome. The actor effectively capable of global actions will have to be the judge of the moral status of its actions in the present—pointing toward a hoped for future, civilized humanity to judge the nobility of those endeavors. No alternative in fact or in principle exists. The grandeur of one's purposes alone can vouch for their morality and legitimacy. That is what follows in the aftermath of the collapse of the philosophical credibility of modern universalist principles and the constructivist philosophy upon which they are based.

Yet contemporary America, the only Nation-State actor with any plausible ability to act morally on the global scale presently needed, hardly proceeds from a position that is unproblematic. We are a modern regime and modern political thought led if not inevitably then at this point irreversibly in the direction of the linear idea of History with its at least implied universal culmination. If any modern principles are questioned, our own principles will have to be subjected to that questioning as well and therein lies a problem. But, I will suggest, already existing **within** our political, moral and intellectual life we have other resources upon which to draw than the merely modern—e.g., classical and Scriptural.[6] I am going to argue that we can also draw from the best of what I will call the high postmodern premises that are emerging and fashion them into a new standpoint that avoids the worst of European postmodernism. We should not be too proud, and thereby scorn, the philosophically postmodern if it can offer resources for our use. **As the intellectually most open of nations, we will be determined by those ideas one way or another anyway.**[7]

I may now seem to have betrayed my argument that what is at stake is primarily a philosophical issue. As I have already admitted, I openly begin these dialectical reflections from the position of being an American. I fail to see how I have any other place to begin. Again, let the person who thinks he or she does explain that Archimedean point to the rest of us. The seeming betrayal is only true from the perspective of the modern philosophical premises I have been in the process of questioning above and elsewhere. In effect, I am going to argue that a postmodern philosophy can, having quit modern theoretical Constructivism, only begin dialectically from what is given, part of which is found in already given philosophical premises, but a significant part of what is given in the political constellation of reality as it presents itself. If the philosophical can, as I argue, only rise dialectically from the given, the political and philosophical cannot be abstracted from each other so as to be hermetically sealed off. We start from the one to get to the other, then move back again in an ongoing dialectical circle that cannot be broken.

Below I will argue that from high postmodern thought we can salvage a post-linear conception of history that will be consistent not only with the need to pursue high moral purpose, but with the Natural Right, Scriptural and classical elements embedded within American thinking, and the modern institutions that inform our practice as well. **Present** thinking must proceed from **present** realities and **present** resources. I will argue that that is always the Socratic, dialectical point of departure. Romantic longings, mere antiquarian attachments, utopian aspirations, hypothetical constructions, and so on, must be sacrificed because our present task of imposing new forms is daunting and the realities of our potential failure, all too chilling.

THE MODERN MYTHS OF
LINEARITY AND TRANSPARENCY

For the sake of conceptual clarity, in what follows I am going to juxtapose two alternative philosophical understandings. There is no present purpose served by considering a string of caveats before the central notions are in place. The caveats can be considered on another occasion. I am designating the two alternatives "linear" and "event horizon."

The idea of a linear human "History," leading toward a predictable and perhaps inevitable (and if not inevitable certainly wish-worthy) outcome rests upon a variety of assumptions that arose within modern political philosophy. Roughly speaking, the modern philosophic project rests on the coming together of the new political science founded by Machiavelli and the new natural science conceptualized by Descartes and Bacon. Machiavelli proposed a political science that abstracted from the high moral purpose that had animated ancient and medieval thought. **The major transformations of modern political philosophy thereafter can be traced to repeated attempts to return high moral purpose to the political equation: e.g., beginning with Rousseau.**

While remaining **within** the modern philosophical perspective, the thought, for example, of Rousseau, Kant, Hegel and Marx attempted to reintegrate the moral into the modern equation. Those authors, and scores of other lesser lights, all laid the foundation for a belief in a linear movement toward a high moral plateau achievable and maintainable in the future. But with those grand theoretical attempts the door was simultaneously opened to the politics of the transformation of man that led to the barbarous totalitarianisms of the twentieth century.

The modern formulation of a notion of linear History can be traced to those modern thinkers who postulated a movement toward, or "progress" toward, a moral high ground that was to arrive with more or less future inevitability and could be maintained thereafter in perpetuity. Eventually this strand of Modernity was intertwined with the underlying premises of the new science that likewise attempted to lay the foundations for cumulative linear progress in the knowledge of natural regularities. When that intertwining was finally consummated, the high moral ground longed for was increasingly conceptualized in apolitical (perhaps post-political) terms, indeed implying if not requiring the abolition of the political. In this regard Marx's thought was perfectly consistent with the inner logic of the strivings of Modernity. That apolitical longing remains embedded in most of late modern thought and even in permutations of postmodern**ism**.

Underlying the new science, in the competing conceptualizations of Bacon and Descartes, was an understanding that the greatest evils incident upon the human condition were primarily related to 1) natural scarcity, 2) the idea that humans were the pawns of Chance, and 3) the painful consciousness of human mortality. The founders of modern science saw the political as primarily growing out of the need to collectively garner scarce resources and defend against violent death—not, for example, the defense of our very humanity or the possibility of human excellence. A new science that could emancipate man from natural scarcity and the malignancy of Chance, and at the very least from the ongoing **consciousness** of death—by making conditions more pacific as well as by extending mortality to a more indefinite future—could allegedly produce the human good.

Implicit, therefore, in the new science was the perception that the good for man could be attained without the necessity of moral and political action, indeed it could go hand in hand with the eventual abolition of the political. Both the moral/political and scientific components of Modernity posited a possible linear History moving toward an end that could radically transform the human condition. When the two dispensations were conjoined, one could posit that the end toward which History moved involved the abolition of the political, the actualization of high moral purpose and a technical foundation for the human good simultaneously. This represents the completed manifestation of the modern idea of linear history. In the thought of Hegel, and in a less consistent fashion in Marx, this outcome was finally given the patina of inevitability and not mere desirability.

The idea of a linear history conceptually requires that History must have two termini. There has to be a beginning point and an end point. A conceptual frame has to be projected to give meaning to the seeming flux of actual events. Without philosophically positing two termini it is impossible to posit that history is not cyclical, repetitive or simply random. The empirical data of history itself is always approached in the present and on the surface displays itself as chaotic.

In effect, the first movement toward a linear understanding of history was to be found in the Christian conception of time. For the Christian, history is seen as stretched out between the creation and the Second Coming. History, like the cosmos, comes into Being and until it ends is an unchanging horizontal stage for the deeds of sinners who themselves might be redeemable by their actions even if History itself is incapable of such redemption.

The possibility of a line that in effect has a direction other than changelessly uniform and horizontal requires other premises. One finds those premises in the thought of authors like Kant, Hegel and Marx who posit a linearity of ascent. Postmodern authors like Nietzsche and Heidegger, and scores of their epigones, posit a more or less linear descent from the origins of the West to the present. The Greeks by comparison could not arrive at a linear understanding of history. Philosophically, with notable exceptions, they were committed to the eternity of the cosmos, without beginning and without end. While they prophesized cyclical cataclysms, they did not prophesize the end of the cosmos. Without a beginning or end, for the Greeks history had no termini, hence linearity was out of the question.

Seeing the **philosophical enterprise** as primarily individual and speculative, the Greeks did not prophesize the possibility of a cumulative approach, over time, to wisdom. They understood **political history** to be a manifestation of the endless risings and fallings of nations and empires. Hence they saw no basis upon which to believe that any generation could necessarily start from a higher political, moral or philosophical promontory than that which went before. Finally, for the Greeks, and the pre-moderns more generally, high individual moral excellence had to be re-achieved by each generation **through deeds**. The collective efforts of one's ancestors could not, therefore, offer a higher standpoint from which successive generations could begin. And unlike the Christians and Moderns, neither mere purity of intentions nor a universal form of willing was seen as a basis for moral excellence

The new science, as both Bacon and Descartes make explicitly clear, tried to find a basis upon which to create a cumulative, cross-generational advance in knowledge. But to do so, that knowledge **had to be de-ontologized and stripped of any pretensions relating to an ultimate explanation of the whole.** The new science was to lead toward increasingly minute knowledge of regularities in nature and repeatable cause and effect relationships. **It was never intended to lead to cosmological or ontological wisdom in the older sense.** In effect, mankind, in the name of controlling nature, had to eschew interest in the unavoidable existential questions about the whence and whither of existence and the ultimate nature of the whole. Those questions of course never go away, the questioning merely becomes substantively thinner and thinner as time passes. Eventually we are armed with immense technical sophistication as to means, and childish *naïveté* and innocence as regards ends. But in the process, the idea of cumulative progress in knowledge was launched. There was an obvious and straightforward cost to this project. In the intervening years, we have largely lost sight of what that cost was. It needs to be made present for our inspection if we are to relate to modern science in the future in a non-mythological fashion.

What the modern political and moral thinkers did was to turn the linear notion of History, which **was borrowed from Christianity and the scientific dispensation of modernity**, into a goal for a cumulative, linear, moral and political progress comparable to the cumulative advance of technical knowledge aspired to by the new science. Under the legitimizing cover of the obvious progress in technical knowledge of the new science, the assumption of possible moral and political progress gained some plausibility and allowed late modernity to try to inject high moral purpose back into the realism of otherwise fundamentally Machiavellian modernity. That this notion has retained philosophical plausibility long after it has lost empirical credibility—the barbarity of the twentieth century and the realization of the dark side of modern technology hardly represent mere linear progress—and long after its premises have been philosophically discredited, is one of the scandals of contemporary thought.

The philosophical premises that attempted to ground a moral and political linearity stretch back somewhat paradoxically to Rousseau. Rousseau's thought experiment involved positing that man was primarily a malleable, historical being who changed over time under the auspices of what amount to accidentally changing circumstances. Rousseau admitted, somewhat sheepishly, that the best he could do was to posit the beginning of man's historicality in some accident, and at that an implausible accident that required prelinguistic man to speak. But he can be forgiven because he was, as he says explicitly, merely following the modern physicists in theoretically constructing his point of departure, not engaging in historical analysis. This is the classic, modern, hypothetical Constructivism transferred from physics to moral and political life.

Rousseau's main point was that the changes in mankind over the past ages could be posited as accidental. Hence what man had become could likewise be posited as an accident which, once this was realized, could be transcended and transformed. Once this was accepted, the transformation of man could be **self-consciously** undertaken. **With this notion was launched the disastrous politics of the transformation of humanity.** If the goal is as grand as the utter transformation of man, almost no interim means can be morally objectionable. From this moral numbness proceeded the greatest barbarity, aided and abetted by the greatest and most technically sophisticated mass slaughter humanity has yet seen. The modern Holocausts, whether in Nazi Germany, the Soviet Union or Communist China, were not accidents. They were committed in the service of a theoretical understanding. But that can be as nothing compared to what lurks in the future. And given the dawning skills of our biologists, we must eschew the politics of the transformation of man before we lose not merely an untold mass number of lives but our very humanity.

What Kant extracted from Rousseau was the notion that the essence of man was to be found in his "metaphysical freedom," his ability to master, and perhaps—in some permutations of the argument—significantly transcend the hegemony of "Nature." For Kant, the essence of man was not to be found in his Nature, but in his Freedom. But this was a Freedom that conceptually went far beyond political liberty. For Kant, only as a metaphysically free being, free from any natural determination or natural diversity, could man became a moral being by giving laws to himself, laws that would to a greater or lesser extent take the place of the hegemony of natural laws, if not actively attempting to negate them.

To prove that those laws were not furtive manifestations of mere self-interest, natural inclination, or cultural particularity, the end of individual actions had to be completely abstracted from all manifestations of particularity. Given these premises, the only basis of action that could prove that man was a free and thereby rational actor was if the laws he gave to himself took the form of universality. Every maxim one applied to oneself needed to have the form of being applicable to everyone regardless of any natural or cultural particularity. Willing the universal was the only thing that could give truly human, high moral purpose to man's actions.

Unlike Rousseau, Kant did not envision that underlying human nature could be transformed. But it could increasingly and progressively be held at bay by following the precepts of universalizable laws. Kant concluded that the efficacy of this holding of human nature at bay could be advanced in an environment of universal Republics held together in a global federation in which all individuals followed universal moral precepts that they allegedly gave themselves. To that end, Kant proposed his great "as-if." One should act as-if by advancing the hegemony of the universal one could advance the hegemony of the free and rational essence of our humanity and with it a universal Republican outcome. **Variants of this premise lurk under all liberal understandings of international relations as well as under the notion that only the United Nations can be the basis of international morality.**

At one point Kant observed that he was in effect merely supplying a hypothesis, and, as he put it, leaving it to nature to bring forth someone to prove that it was true. Nature brought forth Hegel. Hegel did not just argue that there were moral and political advantages to proceeding as-if History were morally and political progressive. And he went beyond Kant's still somewhat commonsensical understanding that saw a federation of Republics as the best international political outcome. Hegel prophesied an impending bureaucratic World State and posited it as good. But he continued to agree with Kant that the natural in man could not be totally defeated or eradicated. For Hegel, a State apparatus remained necessary to subdue the natural in the name of the free and the rational. But the State, and hence the political, was to be reduced to a bureaucratic, administrative application of universal laws because a coercive legal element was still needed in the name of Freedom. It was left to Marx to combine Hegelian inevitability and Rousseaunian malleability and prophesize the withering away of the State. Hence Marx finally arrived at the inevitability of the abolition of the political that lurked within the interstices of Modernity from the beginning.

For Hegel, the engine of inevitability was two-fold. There was 1) an underlying psychological drive for "recognition" and 2) an ongoing materialist/technical transformation of the external world that would eventuate in its finally becoming the external manifestation of man's hitherto merely internal ideas. At the point at which universal recognition and the total transformation of the external world—thereby "humanizing" it—arrived, **a complete philosophical, moral and political "transparency" could allegedly be achieved.** The inherent opacity of human existence could be transcended once and for all. There need be no more than the most minimal accident or Chance in human affairs. We could all become fully self-conscious actors, transparent to ourselves and others.

Neither of Hegel's engines of History could account for inevitability alone. But with their eventual convergence, the twin engines of History pointed toward a terminus that would come to pass in a technologically transformed world in which man would allegedly be at home because the entire world would have become an "outered" manifestation of man himself—or of the World-God made manifest to itself, depending on the credence one gives Hegel's theological reflections. There is certainly no environmentalist ethic lurking here if that requires some respect for self-standing Nature—and that includes, of course, human nature. Hegel's terminus presupposed a universal outcome where each and all could attain **fully transparent recognition** as universal, abstract citizens following universal laws that they allegedly would have willed for themselves if they did not already exist. By this latter canard, choice and coercion could overlap. It opened the door not just to Rousseau's "forcing man to be free" but to such mind-boggling concepts as the "dictatorship of the proletariat" in the name of metaphysical Freedom. This opened the door to the arguments of the Leninists and Maoists that their tyranny was consistent with Freedom—only, of course, of the metaphysical variety of Freedom. That there was nothing at all of political freedom lurking in any of this was clear to anyone with eyes to see—and it was stunning just how many sophisticated blind men there were.

Hegel's argument stands or falls by whether the technically transformed world he posits is one we are alienated from or at home in. And it stands or falls as well based on whether human beings can find satisfaction and meaningful recognition in an abstract, formal universalizable recognition to be consummated in a suffocating global homogeneity in which moral and political action, in any substantive sense, have ceased to exist.

Marx merely substituted a different engine for inevitable linear History. Armed with his Rousseauian premise of human malleability, he could prophesize the abolition of the political in a universal, stateless condition. That the actual concrete Marxism we were forced historically to witness and endure was never even remotely stateless now seems beside the point. That Marx made what he claimed were "scientific" predictions of how History would necessarily evolve, which have been proven in almost every substantial fashion to be wrong, also now seems beside the point. No sensible observer thinks that Marxism in any form is the political wave of the future and is likely to capture any future world historical global state actor. Marxism had its moment on the political stage; but that moment has irreversibly passed.

Likewise, no sensible observer should, in the aftermath of the philosophical critiques of linearity and transparency of the last hundred years, believe that the idea of linear history can be revived as anything but an "as-if," which is to say, as a myth. Was it really ever anything more than a myth? But without that myth there is absolutely no possible way to give any serious philosophical credence to the notion that the U.N. is the only basis of moral authority in international action. Only with unspoken universalist and cosmopolitan premises that underpin a belief that we both are **and should be** on the way to a World State—"international community," cosmopolitan culture, global civilization are all just arcane or cowardly formulations for World State—can that premise gain any credibility. It is time to jettison the notion of linear history and inevitable transparency and with it all of the underlying premises that have in fact been the basis for **modern** barbarism and slaughter.

AN EVENT-HORIZON THEORY OF HISTORY

Even given the reduced American military capacity in the aftermath of the Cold War, the United States remains, in relative terms, militarily strong. In a politically balkanized world that strength is imperative if we are to impose form on an increasingly formless world. But the **intellectual** balkanization we face leaves us far more defenseless. Put simply, modern rationalism—based as it has been on a thoroughgoing theoretical Constructivism—has collapsed and ceased to have any true binding power. Many still long for the ends modern rationalism strived for—we can see this even in the anarchistic cosmopolitanism that informs the efforts of so many postmodernists and "deconstructionists"—but most admit that their ends no longer have philosophical "foundations."

If one wishes to be in any way philosophically consistent—i.e., have a philosophical conscience—one cannot simply will a smorgasbord of one's wishes, especially if one is philosophically incapable of grounding the idea of self-consciousness and the autonomy of the will, for then one cannot explain the basis of that willing. At this point the modern notion of self-grounded willing can lead only to groundless willing and that can lead only into a cacophony of voices speaking simultaneously and a political and moral din, which will make any resolute, collective action over time impossible.

Philosophically, we can no longer begin in constructivist mid-air, with a mere wishful willing, which is indistinguishable from myth making. We have to begin from where we are and use the resources we have, both materially and intellectually. We exist in a specific moral and political situation and an equally determinative intellectual situation. With the philosophical collapse of the plausibility of modern, constructivist reason goes the linear notion of History and the notion of the fully transparent self. This is all well and good in one sense. In the process we become freed from the narcotic effect of a belief in inevitability that saps moral resoluteness and long-range unity of purpose. Without the reassurance of inevitability we are forced to face the very real possibility of a future technological barbarism and to reflect on the prerequisites for avoiding it.

As is always the case, the intellectual horizon of our time is dominated by the most powerful thinkers of the recent past. They may not in the end be the ones we would have wished for, but that is beside the point. One can no more choose the thinkers who determine the thought horizon of the day than one can choose one's political foes. Both are thrust forward before the fact—Heidegger used the rather useful term "thrownness." One must begin where one finds oneself.

The two greatest thinkers of the last 120 years were Friedrich Nietzsche and Martin Heidegger. Their thought simply determines the parameters of all present thinking, frequently without individuals knowing it. And their thinking has, in a myriad of ways, philosophically destroyed the underpinnings of the linear, cosmopolitan myth of modernity. But without the linear notion of history, we run the risk of an enervating descent into seeing History as random, chaotic, without measure or purpose.

But that can be avoided by the "event-horizon"[8] notion of history I wish to suggest, especially when supplemented by a **vertical** rather than a linear or merely horizontal criterion for judging the actions we must take in response to events. I am suggesting that consistent with the philosophical premises we are now forced to work within, we are simultaneously forced to see history as moved by unpredictable "events" that nonetheless offer the possibility for the pursuit of the high and avoidance of the low—which is what I mean by verticality.[9]

Our distinctive moment, caught within the political balkanization following the Cold War, also exists within an environment of intellectual balkanization that is dominated by powerful critiques of long held modern philosophical premises. We cannot ignore any of the features of our dawning postmodern moment. They all affect us and we can move beyond their total hegemony only **dialectically** by starting from **within**. Thus, we must start from within the dominant thought of our time, and that means the thought of Nietzsche and Heidegger. What one can do is dialectically cull and "deflect" that dominant thought in a variety of directions, as there is never one determinative direction that has hegemony, unless we refuse to act.[10] A dialectical theory of deflections allows one someplace to actually stand to make a beginning, rather than the constructivist mid-air tap dance of modern thought. I intend to suggest an understanding of "thrownness" together with an "event horizon" understanding of history and a "vertical" standard for judgment. I see these as consistent postmodern possibilities.

While we cannot avoid starting dialectically from what is given, if we stood only within the thought of Nietzsche and Heidegger, or only within the thinking of their derivative postmodernist descendents, we would have radically circumscribed and limited options. That circumscribed horizon increasingly defines the intellectual landscape of contemporary Europe. Our European friends have fewer intellectual options than we Americans.[11] Americans can also deflect classical, Scriptural and Natural Right elements of thought that by and large no longer lurk prominently within the interstices of the contemporary European situation or that of any other global actor at present. Americans can draw from a much more vibrantly diverse intellectual set of life-giving resources than anyone else. That fortuitous fact is one of the most compelling arguments against seeing universal homogeneity as a good to be wished for—especially once it is stripped of philosophical inevitability.

I am arguing that philosophically there is no Archimedean point, in some theoretical mid-air, from which one may pick and choose their point of departure. Contrary to modernity, and in line with the critiques of Nietzsche and Heidegger, **reason is not self-grounding.** Reason must ground itself dialectically in its phenomenological given. Ours is the dawning postmodern moment and that is where we must begin. Mine is the American moment and that is where I must begin. But this is precisely a Socratic understanding and a Socratic point of departure. To begin from what is **already given** in concrete circumstances and the reigning intellectual environment is the Socratic understanding of how to engage in discourse. One begins by working within and questioning what is given.

This point of **departure** does not mean we cannot transcend the beginning dialectically and to some degree glimpse something that is beyond it. But our beginning will always determine any possible angle of approach to what may transcend the given. And the openness of any world to what is beyond it will determine how quickly it can dialectically ascend and how long that moment of openness will last.[12] We need make no initial ontological or epistemological assumptions regarding the possible status of what may transcend the given. We simply have enough empirical evidence to assert that human beings can and do think their way **beyond** the hegemony of their present circumstances. That is a phenomenon that should be accepted and need not be proven any more than we need to prove the existence of the color green.

In a similar vein, while eschewing modern Constructivism it would also be useful to jettison the fashionable Western self-flagellation that emanates from high European thought, and I would argue has no real philosophical basis. That self-defeating and enervating undertaking has two sources. One is the modern notion of linear history that always allows one to criticize the present from the perspective of the allegedly inevitable forthcoming future end. Given the questionableness of global uniformity as a choice worthy end, only a surreptitious belief that linear inevitability is **possible** can still condition the faith that its pursuit would be **good**. Without linearity and inevitability one must explain why a suffocating uniformity would conduce to the good, and I assume that would be a difficult argument.

The more fashionable contemporary basis of Western self-flagellation, that determines much of the left's reaction to any resolute Western action, especially American, is the equally linear idea that descends from the thought of

Nietzsche and Heidegger that all Western History represents a descent to a present which is then pilloried as dominated by all manner of this-centric and that-phobic excrescences. But if one jettisons the philosophically indefensible notion of linearity one undermines both its ascending and descending, progressivist and postmodernist permutations.

Contrary to the lurking linearity in elements of their thought, Nietzsche, and especially Heidegger, offer a basis for a non-linear, postmodern, event-horizon understanding of human historicality. This event-horizon understanding is more philosophically consistent with the essential core of their thought than the linear notions that frequently dominate. What I am calling an event-horizon understanding is based on the premise that History turns upon unpredictable galvanizing "events," and how one responds resolutely and self-consciously to those events.

An event-horizon understanding proceeds on the following premise: Pivotal historical events—some political, some moral, some philosophical—move history in no inevitable direction. Further, history cannot be seen as simply cyclical or even as necessarily repetitive. I am arguing that **the present postmodern moment is unique and unprecedented** and that the various possible futures embedded within it are unique as well. What remains constant and historically unchanged throughout all transformative events is **the ongoing possibility of maintaining our very humanity and of pursuing excellence.**

The discontinuous events that condition human History can represent vertical leaps upward or downward from the perspective of excellence but there is no horizontal, linear movement. Human greatness and the preservation of our humanity or barbaric chaos are equally possible at any moment, now more than ever. And chaos, as the path of least resistance, is always the most likely, especially now that we have so enlarged the arena of Chance.

One can judge the responses to unpredictable galvanizing events only vertically—e.g., the verticality of civilization versus barbarism, humanity versus inhumanity, discipline versus self-indulgence, nobility versus ignobility, etc. Recent events have made it hard for us to miss these vertical distinctions between the high and the low despite the fashionable reigning relativism of the day. The high and the low can only be judged in relation to the possibilities of **human** excellence. And the actualization of those possibilities emerges from our responses to unique, galvanizing events. The response to such events makes our morality and humanity possible. Hence on one level, we should be thankful for galvanizing events.

It is Heidegger's philosophical notion of *Ereignis,* or "event of appropriation," that comes closest to the vicinity of capturing what I am presenting as an event-horizon understanding, although elements of Nietzsche's understanding ("monumental" history) move in the same direction.[13] Heidegger, however, takes the notion of *Ereignis* in a radical **theoretical** direction that I do not think is necessary. He argues that every human act and perception is determined by an underlying, almost always inarticulate, understanding of Being. For Heidegger, those notions of Being are thrust forth in mysterious and unpredictable ways that can never be made transparent but are determinative of all human understanding and action.

For Heidegger, the reigning notion of Being can never be rationally mastered as everything that passes for reason is determined by it in advance. Hence no ultimate transparency is ever possible and apparently no conscious control of history is possible. The risings and fallings in revelatory power of these epochal dispensations of Being are the great "events" that determine human existence for Heidegger. This is Heidegger's version of Nietzsche's observation that the greatest events are ideas and like all seminal ideas they arrive on "dove's feet." While great ideas can be determinative, I am arguing that equally transformative can be moral and political events, at least as long as they are understood to be events out of the ordinary. One need not decide, for present purposes, whether ideas or concrete events have causal priority. That is a theoretical conundrum that need never detain us as it is theoretically derivative of the phenomenological revelation of reality.[14]

For Heidegger, each dispensation of Being comes on the scene with great fecundity and reigns for a while and then tends in the direction of a declining ability to light up reality. According to Heidegger, we live in an age where a longstanding dispensation of Being has lost all of its revelatory power and we are therefore left surrounded by moribund beings and bereft of genuine, unique possibilities. Herein Heidegger betrays his own notion of *Ereignis,* or event driven history, in the direction of a linear conception of History qua decline.

But given Heidegger's central philosophical understanding about the impossibility of ultimate philosophical transparency, any idea of a linear history—even one of descent—should be seen to rest on a rational intellectual mastery of History that Heidegger is intent upon showing cannot exist because of history's unpredictable event driven nature.

Despite its greatness, there are deep-seated inconsistencies in Heidegger's thought. What one notices is that despite the fact that he provides a theoretical basis for the most thoroughgoing historicism, Heidegger's corpus is littered with judgments about the high and the low, ascent and descent, the essential and the inessential, authentic and inauthentic, and on and on. Whether one considers his allegedly "early" or "late" writings, these judgments inform all of his efforts. That his theoretical premises cannot ultimately support these judgments does not detract from the fact that his ability to make them is what differentiates him from a trivial thinker. Judgments regarding the high and the low—that Heidegger cannot philosophically ground on his principles—approach from a perfectly straightforward direction. They arrive from out of our shared humanity for which such distinctions regarding the high and the low are imperative. Our shared humanity is the only basis for any vertical appreciation of what are otherwise random events and actions.

One benign outcome fostered by Heidegger's philosophical critique is the profound demonstration of why reason cannot and should not be its own ground. The modern self-grounding notion of reason, which is necessary for any linear conception of History, is also inextricably linked to the modern notion of possible total moral, political and philosophical transparency. Neither collectively nor individually is a total philosophic transparency presupposed in any Socratic, phenomenological, dialectical understanding, or any event driven understanding of history. The Socratic approach presupposes the **possibility** of transcendence, but does not posit what it consists of before the fact. Doubtless any experience of transcendence would have to be conveyed in poetic terms and hence in principle would be incapable of the apodictic transparency for which modern reason longed.

For Heidegger, the ground of reason surfaces mysteriously in history and then withdraws. Hence reason can never master itself let alone history. For Heidegger there is no transcendence other than in the direction of the Nothing. That said, I would argue that Heidegger's critique of modern self-grounding reason is so profound that it is impossible to recover a belief in linear History, or the necessary faith in transparency that goes with it, except by positing those concepts as useful myths.

Unfortunately, Heidegger, along with Nietzsche, brings a critique of modern reason that threatens a descent into meaninglessness. But it is the modern notion of hypothetical, constructivist reason that is primarily attacked and I do not believe that the critique need go further than that. For example, Heidegger's attempt to trace the origins of the modern conception of reason back to classical antiquity can be confronted and shown to be inadequate. Hence a different understanding of reason than the modern—i.e., the Socratic dialectical approach—remains open. But the critique of **modern, constructivist** reason is devastating. It cannot be ignored. Without that modern notion of reason no linear conception of History can be constructed. Without theoretical constructivism, actual history can hardly be assumed to be predictable or inevitable. There was no inevitability that the Nazis or the Soviets would be vanquished. That required clarity of purpose, sacrifice and resolute and determined action over an extended period of time especially by a specific world historical democratic people and its leaders. What is predictable is the need for virtue, resoluteness and the longing for human greatness, individually and collectively, together with an arena within which it can operate.

An event-horizon understanding of the nature of history and human historicality need not lead to historicism or the emasculation of serious action if linked to a Socratic dialectical point of departure and an openness to the phenomenon of moral verticality **built into human existence itself.** I have obviously been implying those "higher" vertical standards all along when I have invoked such terms as high moral purpose and the civilizing necessity of avoiding a descent into barbaric chaos. There is no real response to the person who does not see that civilization is a good, or that a life devoted to a good beyond one's own narrow self-interest is noble. In the end one cannot teach a blind man colors, or the morally myopic to see the difference between the high and the low. But even those committed **theoretically** to relativism proceed on a myriad of judgments of the high and low in their daily lives. It is hard enough to consistently maintain relativist premises theoretically; it is impossible to do so in one's everyday life.

The difference between the high and the low is built into the fabric of humanity; it cannot, and need not, be philosophically constructed. We will find it in the wishes and aspirations of, for example, the American people, or not at all. One wastes one's time, not to mention moral and intellectual energy, with those who are determined to assert that the obvious does not exist. It is obvious that liberty is preferable to tyranny, that the openness of the mind is preferable to closure and darkness, that a life devoted to high purpose is superior to one devoted to trifling self-indulgence, that the Taliban's treatment of women is inhumane, that the insanity of Al-Qaeda is not divinely inspired, that tyrants and democratically elected statesmen are two different things, that resolute self-defense is not brutality, that weakness and allowing events to drift are not moral virtues, that magnanimity is only possible from a stance of strength, and on and on. These things are, for anyone who has not been theoretically talked out of them, self-evident. Equally self-evident is that the high is never won or passed down to future generations without effort and cost.

The postmodern future, when robbed of the calming myth of inevitability, presents a very sobering prospect that should occasion anxiety. That is undoubtedly the state in which we will have to remain henceforth if we are to maintain our humanity. What occurred on 9/11 may have been a galvanizing "event" which awakens us not just to our vulnerability but to our higher purposes individually and as a historical nation. Or it may be a fleeting occurrence from which we fall away into a kind of sleepwalking forgetfulness. Whether our future moral, political and intellectual lives are put to high purpose or trivial self-indulgence, whether we shape events or merely drift into them, will depend on courage and leadership. Nothing is inevitable, to believe so is folly.

In the most powerful manifestation of the doctrine of linear history, presented in the thought of Hegel, at the "End of History" things like anxiety, discipline and leadership drop out of the human scene. Hegel posited a notion that human beings, moved by a desire for universal recognition, were driven toward a future moment of collective and individual self-transparency that would bring with it a genuine human satisfaction. In that moment the global concrete laws and the individual wills of "rational" human beings would converge. The actual laws would allegedly become precisely what self-transparent individuals would will. This in turn was supposed to bring with it a more or less perfect manifestation of universal satisfaction. But it was a satisfying life that could be had without engaging in any of the most demanding forms of human endeavor, from political life, to resolute self-defense, to the dialectical encounter with the ideas of one's time, to the anxiety of reflecting on the whence and whither of our existence historical and otherwise.

It was alleged by Hegel that a satisfying life could be had **without struggle, self-discipline, high effort, anxious concern, the deployment of critical acumen, the longing for unique future possibilities.** One could abolish the political and the philosophical—especially as dialectical—and have universal satisfaction. If the dignity of ideas is measured by the magnitude of the aspiration, perhaps this was a noble longing. But the homogeneity and dull indifference to life to which it pointed could never be anything but ignoble in practice.

There are two issues lurking here. First, can a life not in the service of high purpose, which has every chance of possible failure, be satisfying? Second, even if it is satisfying for some number of individuals, how possible is it without the perfect self-transparency posited for both collectives and individuals by a thinker like Hegel? Philosophically, the inevitability of linearity and transparency is no longer the issue for us as late moderns or early **post**-moderns; it is their desirability that is at stake. In an event-horizon world, the arena of morality is not some transparent arena of the application of abstract universal rules, where intention alone trumps outcome, but is determined by the ongoing, fluid necessity of generating the personal and collective discipline to be prepared to respond to unpredictable events. In a non-linear world, one must make preparation and provision for incoming tidal waves the existence of which are assured, even if the precise nature of which will never be transparent before the fact. Such preparation requires precisely political engagement in the shaping of those events and the pursuit of high purpose by a specific Nation-State capable of world historical action.

In the lack of clarity that is mortal life, and the high responsibility that is needed to face that ongoing lack of clarity, lie the greatest possibilities for both excellence and satisfaction. We must reflect on the possibilities for greatness in the future world that has been left without all manner of reassuring modern myths. We must come to see that morality needs to be grounded in the political understood as an arena for world historical action. **Morality and politics must again be brought together.** And the philosophical, when dialectical—and I argue that that now requires an event-horizon understanding of history—needs to be put in the service of securing the basis for the ongoing pursuit of the high and avoidance of the low. At the very least that requires clearing away many modern philosophical impediments, which is to say, modern myths.

There is ultimately no true ground of satisfaction to be found outside engaging in the human acts that are themselves transformative and responsive to transformative events. There will never be a present historical moment that can be made to hold still without ongoing actions of this kind—moral, political and philosophical. And those actions must be in the service of a vertical ascent from low to high that is anything but inevitable.

An event-horizon understanding is consistent with present and future philosophical resources and contemporary moral and political needs. And when linked with the phenomenon of human verticality it is in no way historicist. This understanding can, therefore, remain dialectically open to **the classical, Scriptural and Natural Right elements of verticality** already deeply embedded within the American political horizon and the souls of its citizens. We Americans, perhaps alone at this moment of history, have the point of departure that supplies the means for a dialectical, vertical ascent that leads in the direction of a possible, at least partial, transcendence of the opacity of mere, everyday existence in the direction of greatness. But we cannot get to that possible transcendence by taking a running leap that starts off from constructivist thin air. Man is a historical being, a being who in response to events and in pursuit of excellence makes History. We are history-making beings at a time when the possibility of future history itself hangs in the balance.

What we now need to see is that the perfection of the political and not its abolition is what is needed. And that requires submitting the political to high purpose. What occurred on 9/11 may have been an event that can make that possible if we can avoid dissipating not only the moral energy that flowed from it but the insight it opens into our postmodern future. It could have been the moment in which everything changes—including the philosophical *weltgeist* of the time—or in which nothing changes at all, in which case events will carry us away wither they will, most likely into a barbaric vortex.

POSTMODERN LEGITIMACY

We have dialectically moved back and forth from the concrete issue that initiated our reflections to related theoretical issues. This is consistent with my understanding of philosophy as intrinsically dialectical rather than Constructivist. In conclusion we need to return to our specific point of departure. Concluding that the U.N. is the only basis of international morality and legitimacy can only be supported on the basis of a series of philosophical premises that have little contemporary philosophical credibility and even less possible future philosophical plausibility: 1) A linear notion of History; 2) A faith in historical inevitability; 3) A rejection of the vertical validation of moral purpose; 4) The presumed goodness of global homogeneity and a cosmopolitan outcome; 5) The presumed goodness of laws that impose the universal; 6) A belief in the possibility of individual and collective historical transparency; and other lesser premises.

The alternate view I am presenting is that moral legitimacy in international relations is based on a combination of the hierarchy of the purposes pursued and the possibility of actually being able concretely to pursue those purposes by being a world historical, Nation-State actor. My view suggests that a belief in inevitability, linearity and transparency are narcotics that sap political and moral will making it impossible to be forearmed against the unpredictable events—and some that are perfectly predictable—that can undermine civilization in the postmodern future.

What I am suggesting also holds that the homogeneity that the linear understanding of History aims at is not only not inevitable but not good or wishworthy. Such homogeneity would destroy the political ground upon which high moral purpose can in fact be pursued and made actual by deeds—and not just by private, abstract intentions or the mere form of one's willing.

The principles of the event-horizon understanding I am proposing include among others: 1) Reason is not self-grounding; 2) One must begin dialectically from what is given in the present; 3) History is driven by unpredictable events that make full future transparency impossible; 4) There are embedded within human existence itself vertical criteria of judgment; 5) There can be greater transparency regarding those vertical standards than regarding linear events in time; 6) Morality requires for its stage the possibility of concrete, historical, political action; 7) Taking concrete action requires Nation-State actors; 8) Global homogeneity and the hegemony of the universal are evils and not goods; and other lesser premises.

The question legitimately arises, cannot this event-horizon understanding apply with equal force to Nation-State actors other than the United States? In principle, Yes; in practice, at this moment of history, No. One need only look at the risings and fallings of once and future empires to see this. Europe's moral, political and intellectual energies were exhausted in the wars, hot and cold, of the twentieth century. Russia remains in historical limbo with little substantive focus other than trying to negate American influence. While there is much talk about the clash of civilizations, with Islam being one of the competitors, it is hard to see how a unified Islamic "civilization" emerges in the near future, on any level as a possible **single** actor. This is especially true while we await a philosophically sensible Islam that would not threaten the planet in the name of a glorious entry into heaven. It would, of course, be foolish to ignore, and fail to control, the immoderate medieval manifestations of Islam we have seen until we see a re-emergence of the grand and philosophically open Islam of the great days of Baghdad and Cordoba now long past. And while China, with its immense economic potential, remains ruled by the iron fist of the butchers of Tiananmen Square, it is hard to be sanguine about their leading the planet into the postmodern future. Only those lost in a blind ideological desire to flagellate the United States as the source of all evil could reasonably find a viable alternate source of high moral purpose in the present and forthcoming world.

A final thought as we move back toward the particular: The only way to overcome the frequently perceived spiritual emptiness and fascination with baubles of what Zbigniew Brzezinski has called America's "permissive cornucopia" is to submit collective action to a high moral purpose to be pursued over time by generations to come. In that fashion, to transcend moral laxness one need not succumb to the ongoing antipathy to capitalism of many of our elites. The mere fact that capitalism to some extent inevitably commits one to the pursuit of consumption need not by itself be morally corrupting unless that pursuit is divorced from a simultaneous commitment to high purpose. Only if consumption becomes an end in itself, and indeed the highest end, is it inevitably corrupting. After all, the pursuit of high moral purpose, by a world historical people, on a global basis requires significant national resources. It is hoped that our experience with communism has taught us that it is ultimately impossible for a nation to be wealthy in any sense without any wealthy citizens.[15] We should not be led astray by the absolutely low and vulgar motivations of envy and resentment.

The West, as the United States represents it, is more than commerce and consumption and we should not succumb to the ideological assaults that try to convince us to the contrary. We frequently forget that the principles of our commercial Republic are linked to the very possibility of personal independence and human dignity, as well as to the political liberty that makes any morally serious action possible. We must get over our own self-flagellation if we expect others to do so as well. Still, sacrifices and self-discipline will be required. We can ultimately justify our prosperity best by the dignity of the tasks we assume because no one else can. Indeed, in the end, no one knows the true sweetness of liberty, humanity and human excellence like those who have fought for them. And the highest things, given as empty gifts by others—including past generations—will not last long. Only one thing is certain, the future is not inevitable. It will be shaped by our actions in the present, or by our inaction.

NOTES

1. I want to argue that this particular issue is just one among many practical issues from which we could dialectically begin in an attempt to rise to the theoretical issues I want to enjoin. My ultimate point will be that philosophy must always begin dialectically in this fashion from a phenomenological point of departure.

2. Without remorse I openly begin these dialectical reflections from the position of being an American. I fail to see how I have any other place to begin. Let the person who thinks he or she does explain that Archimedean point to the rest of us. Starting with what presents itself, and presents itself phenomenally **somewhere**, is what is implied in a dialectical, phenomenological political philosophy as I have been articulating it.

3. I am going to argue that philosophy can never simply abstract from its phenomenological roots, its thrownness, except to its detriment.

4. It would be hard to predict that a source of order could be found in the Europe that is led by a France and Germany that are in economic decline and utterly lacking any moral or political will. To expect it to be forthcoming from some Islamic empire, Russia or China is sheer blindness.

5. The Nation-State is threatened from "below" by ethnic balkanization and from "above" by supra–Nation-State institutions. In one argument the Nation-State is also threatened by nebulous "civilizations." I am going to argue that it is just as significantly threatened by certain philosophical premises.

6. The matter is both complicated and fortuitous as we are also heir to pre-modern and Christian principles as well as open to the postmodern possibilities I am suggesting. It is precisely that diversity that gives us multiple well-springs from which to draw and thereby the possibility of standing outside the modern without jettisoning what is valuable and life-giving that has emerged in the modern era.

7. I have dealt with these issues in my *Nietzsche, Heidegger and the Transition to Postmodernity* (Chicago: University of Chicago Press, 1996), and *Martin Heidegger: Paths Taken, Paths Opened* (Lanham, MD: Rowman & Littlefield, 2006), as well as in the essays above.

8. There is no magic to this particular locution; it was adopted *faux de mieux*.

9. Even from a Christian perspective, one can suggest that no Christian should arrogantly think he or she knows in its entirety, let alone even in general outlines, God's plan for historical man. One of the central Christian virtues is humility, and there is no humility in thinking we know the things that in principal we cannot. Nor should we allow ourselves to think that retreating from resolute historical action is what is required of a person of faith. That would be to grant victories to radical barbarity and tyranny or any number of other evils regardless of their source. It should be an article of faith that God does not intend us to stand by while His creation is destroyed. Part of that creation is our natural humanity, its possibilities for excellence, and our

responsibility to hand down to those who come after us at least as good as we received from the past.

10. One fashionable move of the contemporary intellectual left tries to reject the need to start dialectically from where one finds oneself philosophically by arguing that there are no possibilities, for example, in the thought of Heidegger but National Socialism. But that argument is fatuous and intellectually lazy. It rests on an attempt to dismiss a powerful philosophical critique one has no serious way to contest on actual philosophical grounds. I have dealt with this in my *Martin Heidegger: Paths Taken, Paths Opened*. See also my *Nietzsche, Heidegger and the Transition to Postmodernity*.

11. Consistent with my dialectical understanding, I begin with the givens of my own fellow citizens because I am arguing philosophy must begin with "one's own."

12. It would be useful if Islamic thinkers would recall those days when the greatest cities and greatest university towns were Baghdad and Cordoba. In those cities the greatest Jewish, Christian and Islamic thinkers (children of the Book) met to discuss and cross fertilize each other with their ideas. Islam was not always a "closed" society intellectually and philosophically. We would do well to foster the reemergence of that possibility for others while primarily being concerned to never lose it for ourselves. But in that regard, the narrowness and ideological one-sidedness of our elite universities is becoming very disturbing, so we have no reason to be smug if openness is our aim. We, like Islam, are fostering our own forms of narrowness, parochialism and forgetfulness.

13. See my *Nietzsche, Heidegger and the Transition to Postmodernity* for an elaboration of these themes, and for further elaboration on Heidegger see my *Martin Heidegger: Paths Taken, Paths Opened*.

14. It is a conundrum that can ultimately be solved by a phenomenological/dialectical approach which shows that the problem is theoretically derivative from a prior and determinative practical showing.

15. Let detractors who castigate the United States for its economic success match the dignity of the ends of our global action. And let us maintain an understanding of what makes our end dignified. They will certainly never match the national largesse, human and material, we have spent defending the possibility of civilization from one barbaric force after another, Nazi, Communist, radical Islamic. We will as a people fall short morally only by the paucity of our purposes, not by the superfluity of our national wealth, for which we should feel no guilt. Even if we do control and expend a significant percentage of the world's wealth, we simultaneously assume more than that percentage of the world's moral and political burdens. Those burdens cannot be assumed without national wealth. And let us worry on another occasion about whether our way of life is universally exportable. For now we need to have more modest expectations of simply maintaining the order necessary as a prerequisite for anything resembling civilization.

Chapter Nineteen

Jerusalem and Washington: Political Philosophy and Theology

Muhammad brought down from heaven and put into the Koran not religious doctrines only, but political maxims, criminal and civil laws, and scientific theories. The Gospels, on the other hand, deal only with the general relations between man and God and between man and man. Beyond that, they teach nothing and do not oblige people to believe anything. That alone, among a thousand reasons, is enough to show that Islam will not be able to hold its power long in ages of enlightenment and democracy, while Christianity is destined to reign in such ages, as in all others.[1]

We are children of Western Civilization, shaped and determined by it. That is the reality into which we are thrown. That means that not only are we Westerners determined by a Rationalist longing that can be traced back to Socrates but also by ethical and theological premises that can be traced back to the Revelations associated with the life and death of Jesus Christ. We can disinter our roots until the end of time, but they cannot be jettisoned if we are to remain true to ourselves and what we are at the deepest level. Those roots — and more than a few of the branches that grow from them — must repeatedly be re-fashioned in creative ways consistent with our present and future. That fashioning is the task of what I have designated as political philosophy.

But during the period dominated by modern political philosophy, there has been an antagonism between philosophy and Christianity, and for perfectly legitimate reasons. The longings of the medieval Church for a total society with itself at the top, a longing stretching back to Augustine, eventually created a situation that made a break both necessary and inevitable. The ramifications of the two cities of Caesar and God announced by Christ, or the "two swords" in the Gospel of Luke, had been abandoned and the outcome had become problematic. But an either/or confrontation between religion and the city or between religion and philosophy should not have been necessary and certainly is not necessary now.

At the end of the medieval period, the competing claims of the Western Church and secular States, with the ambiguous third claims of the Holy Roman Empire thrown in, led not so much to a total state as to political, and even moral and spiritual fragmentation together with artificial causes for internecine squabbling. Proto-modern authors like Machiavelli saw these schisms between multiple sovereigns as one of the causes of the political weakness that was the situation of the West in his time, with an encroaching Ottoman Empire to the south and east.

To that resultant political weakness could be added concern regarding the effects of deflecting the longing for immortality from great deeds in this world to a life in another and thereby an indifference to the goods that were perfectly possible in this world. And to all of this could be added a perceived softening of mankind by a morality of turn the other cheek and walk the second mile. And then the modern natural philosophers launched their project by turning God into a mathematician determined by mathematical and physical laws that His will could not master. This carried the modern assault on Christianity onto another plane.

If modernity ends in the thought of individuals like Nietzsche and Heidegger, as they thought, and as I have been arguing, we are left with a diminished faith in the competence of Reason, certainly of the modern constructivist variant. With that diminution we see an inevitable, simultaneous increase in the relative status of Faith, and with it, various "religious" claims to autonomy. As Nietzsche observed, while the theistic satisfactions of the past might decline, religiosity itself would likely increase in the future. But as the examples of Nietzsche and Heidegger show, that increased religiosity is perfectly consistent with a longing for the continuation of religion in some ambiguous post-Scriptural form.

What was undoubtedly necessary at the outset of modernity, a diminution of the place of religion in political life, has led potentially, toward its end, to an ambiguous, dangerous, largely untenable future set of possibilities where religion may increase its autonomy and hegemony. If one thinks through the matter clearly, we should not expect the modern, all too modern, longing for universal atheism to be forthcoming in the future. Leaving aside the fact that such an outcome would be inconsistent with the good, it is simply highly unlikely, if for no other reason, because the assault on modern Rationalism that has already occurred opens the door to an enlarged arena for Faith, not some version of universal, atheistic Enlightenment based on self-grounding constructivist Rationalism. Public atheism would only open the door to the reign of ignorance, all manner of irrationality, and the hegemony of Chance. What is needed is to rethink the relation between Reason and Faith.

As to the high reflections of thinkers like Nietzsche and Heidegger that lead to a longing for a post-Scriptural religiosity, we meet the Nietzschean longing for the hegemony of Chance in the form of the blind Will-to-Power under the auspices of some new Dionysian dispensation, and/or the Heideggerian hopeful waiting for new gods who would approach from heaven only knows what direction. Nietzsche's longed for future religion was symbolized by a Dionysus who it was alleged also pointed toward a greater affirmation of the earthlike and physical aspects of life—especially sensuality and sexuality, which Nietzsche argued Christianity intrinsically destroyed. Heidegger's longed for altogether new gods (plural) as well were alleged to be highly affirmative of the Earth and the earthlike as it rises up in us as individuals. But Heidegger's gods were so mysterious and amorphous in form, and their arrival so indeterminate, that he was forced into a hopeful waiting that could only be called irresponsible inertia and with it moral and political indifference to what was happening all around in the present.

At least Heidegger understood that one does not invent religions or gods as acts of self-conscious Will. And he realized that one cannot predict the comings and goings of religions—as did Machiavelli. I would argue that one may not will away the religion into which one is thrown, one that has already been determinative for what "we" are as Westerners. Fortunately, there is no inevitability that the Scriptural God is dead. He has risen from the grave before. And the evidence of another "awakening" is as clear in America as the opposite is clear in Europe. The present, attempted reawakening of Islam, primarily as a political force that will be the support for a new Caliphate, is also all too clear.

I dismiss universal public atheism as a preposterous longing in the first place and one that will not occur in "our" future given either the present intellectual constellation or our past determinations. Besides, one can find no greater dogmatists than atheists who presume to know what cannot be known on the basis of Reason—i.e., God's existence or non-existence. Even Rationalists must know the limits of reason as Socrates taught us so long ago. All those who look for possible, future, philosophical openings in the vicinity of atheists look in precisely the wrong direction.

On a more interesting plane, I will argue that not only is wishing and hoping for new gods a pointless and escapist undertaking but that Christianity, which is "our own" already, is replete with philosophical possibilities that can be tapped. And it is what we already are, as statesmen like Churchill and Roosevelt still understood right down to World War II when they characterized that battle as one for the soul of Christendom—as quaint as that phrase may now seem to us.

Christianity will remain part of us in the West as long as the West remains viable. I am not one of those rooting for the West's "going under." And in light of present confrontations that will afflict the West for some time to come, we should reflect on the words of Tocqueville above that Islam will have considerable difficulty making its peace with modernity and democracy. If we care for those things we should not be confused about where we must take our stand. Nor should we be confused about where the tradition of political philosophy has avoided extinction for two millennia.

Christianity is one of the three Scriptural dispensations. As Christians we are among the descendants of Abraham. But "monophysite" Islam is not an option for us in the West no matter how tolerant we are determined to be, and we may not simply will a return to the Hebrew Old Testament on the assumption that it offers a politically and morally sterner teaching and a more natural and carnal understanding of the status of the senses. For all of our talk about our Judeo-Christian heritage, the West is not now and will not become in the future Hebraic nor move increasingly toward an incorporation of the details of the Law in the Hebrew Bible, which we call the Old Testament. Albeit, from this fairly straightforward fact in no way follows something hateful like Anti-Semitism.

We need not be opposed to the Old Testament tradition, for we should be continually reminded that the Christian Bible, from almost the beginning of its existence, incorporated what we call the Old Testament. Christianity always admitted openly that it was the heir and descendent of the Old Testament tradition, as did Christ himself. And yet we see ourselves as an heir by way of perfecting the legacy of our ancestor and by way of moving beyond the prior detailed Law, as Paul makes clear in the *Letter to the Romans*.

The great advantage of Christianity is suggested by Tocqueville. Christianity is based on a few theological articles of Faith and a few very broad moral principles. It does not present a complete Law as do Judaism and Islam nor a "science," metaphysic, doctrine of the best regime, and so on. Hence it opens the door for and positively points toward reflections upon those other questions, and that means opens the door to political philosophy. What is peripheral at best in the other Scriptural dispensations—the need for political philosophy—is central within Christendom.

Even the moral principles that descend from the Gospels or the Sermon on the Mount are so broad that they have to be filled in and completed. There are broad outlines for our moral reflections, but no specifics. As regards political questions, there are not even broad outlines. At most there are negatives that must be avoided. Again, I would go so far as to say that only within Christendom could a tradition of political philosophy have survived in the first place and continue to evolve into the future. Indeed, Christianity itself, as a concrete institution, has been an evolving historical religion in a way Judaism and Islam cannot be. And that is a great virtue. Christianity is both a model for the ecstatic temporality that informs political philosophy itself as I have presented it, and a basis for ongoing human historicality and history making, which I have argued is of the essence of our humanity.

In this regard, we should learn an important lesson from the early Christians who were positive that the second coming was imminent—and this included even Paul—and avoid the lack of humility that believes we can know what we cannot. Being positive that the Second Coming was imminent allowed early Christians to believe that they could ignore all manner of political and moral necessities. After more than two millennia we should now admit that we do not know the mind of God and hence do not know when his son Christ will return. To believe that we have this knowledge is utterly at odds with the central Christian virtue of humility.

Humility as a virtue, both morally and intellectually, is for the Christian what "great souledness" was for the pagans. And humility is consistent as well with Socratic Rationalism in its knowing what it cannot know. We cannot know the date of the second coming; it may be imminent, another two millennia away, or 50,000 years in the future. We must assume active responsibility for the moral, the just and the noble until we are relieved of duty. And that is precisely our mission as Christians.

Added to these reflections is what I take to be the fact that Christian theology is distinct among the Scriptural traditions in that it is not primarily a deductive enterprise, i.e., deductive from already present legal and/or ontological premises. It has been precisely a historical phenomenon, emerging and evolving over time with the first great brushstrokes supplied by Paul and others in the first four hundred years after the death of Christ. Christian theology was carved out to meet its surroundings in the Roman Empire, transformed in the Carolingian age and the confrontation with the triumphant Germanic tribes, reassessed with the advent of modernity and so on down to our unique present. The good news is that there are no necessary last brush strokes that have already found their way to the canvas. Nothing is fixed, nothing is closed, the future is open, and much will always be possible. There is no reason to expect as many, or indeed any, unique possibilities from some vague post-Scriptural dispensation. That could be believed only on the basis of unfounded hope combined with an antipathy to what we are that can only be captured by Nietzsche's understanding of the "spirit of revenge."

Finally, the central doctrine of the Trinity offers significant philosophical resources that do not exist in Islam or Judaism. And the doctrine of the Trinity can easily be defended against the claim of the Koran that it is an attack on monotheism and close to a recurrence to polytheism. There has already been an extensive historical debate within Christian theology itself on that subject. Finally, throughout the Christian era, from the very beginning, there has always been a Rationalist dispensation, and I would argue that it is not only the essential dispensation but that Christian mysticism and emotivism were always the aberration. Reason and Revelation need not part ways. For them to do so would be non-Western. We may lovingly refashion both.

In the brief remarks that follow, I will begin by sketching what I see as some of the central modern criticisms of Christianity. After that I will turn to some equally brief reflections upon whether Christian thought has resources to meet these criticisms. I will sketch some lines of thought projected into the future that could be pursued. What follows will be at most suggestions that others could follow in greater detail. In conclusion I will return to the thematic issue of theology and political philosophy.

Machiavelli's criticisms of Christianity were both political and, somewhat more surprisingly, moral. The political criticisms have already been dealt with in chapter 4. The division of political loyalties, or of political sovereignty, fostered, according to Machiavelli, a version of the "divide and conquer" dynamic. When Machiavelli discussed "ecclesiastical principalities" in *The Prince*, he made it clear that as institutional regimes they succeeded or failed for the same reasons as secular ones. Hence there was no reason to complicate matters by engaging in duplication.

But for Machiavelli, Christianity also undermined the status of the pursuit of ambition and of immortal fame that Machiavelli, here in a rare instance actually following the pagan Romans, thought was, along with fear, a perfectly reliable basis for a sound political teaching. One must have an incentive to act in this world and not be seduced away from it by the hegemony of otherworldly aspirations. And hence for Machiavelli political ambition was a perfectly legitimate longing that was also easily manipulable precisely because it led to behavior that was as predictable as actions motivated by fear.

Of course, the history of the Western Christian era is not the history of actual political softness, nor is it lacking in expansionist tendencies. One could argue that this was because the institutional Church came to be and evolved within the Roman Empire and after the Empire collapsed it had to carve out its place among the victorious Germanic tribes and accede to their instincts and customs as well. Even the Eastern Church was hardly pacific in its institutional behavior, albeit it should be remembered that it was the Eastern Church that politically succumbed to the Ottomans, not the Western Church. And it is the West about which we are primarily concerned. The status and future of the Eastern Church, or of Christian ecumenical movements more generally, is a story for another time.

Given the actual history of Western Europe, we should keep in mind that the fragmentation and political impotence Machiavelli tried to confront had more than one cause, and Christianity may not have been the primary one. Machiavelli's deeper and more substantial attack on Christianity was part of his critique of ancient philosophy as well. The critique of the inculcation of virtue as the primary end of political life, with a variant of that undertaking pointing toward the immortality of the soul as the highest end, was Machiavelli's primary goal. Machiavelli wished to build on the now famous "low but firm" base, fostering and manipulating human inclinations like fear, ambition and greed. These characteristics had been vices within both Christian thought and Greek moral philosophy. To be fully useful, these inclinations had to be emancipated from pre-modern moral opprobrium, and Machiavelli launched that modern undertaking. He was aided and abetted in that undertaking by everyone from Hobbes and Locke to Adam Smith, Montesquieu and beyond.

Yet as Leo Strauss has pointed out, Machiavelli did admire one thing about Christianity. Machiavelli asserted in *The Prince* that unarmed prophets always fail. But he knew perfectly well that this was false. Christianity had been victorious as an idea long before it possessed the sword in any interesting fashion. It insinuated itself into the world, spread and conquered by means of what Strauss called "propaganda." Machiavelli clearly intended to succeed in the same fashion. An army of ideas will always defeat an army of swords. In the long run, an army without ideas cannot succeed and that will be even truer in the future than it has been in the past.

For the moment, it is my primary intention to reflect only upon the modern moral and political attack on Christianity. Ultimately one would also have to consider the way in which the new science proposed by modern philosophy started by representing God not as an involved, providential, willful, vengeful or loving God but as a knowable, predictable, rational, which is to say determined, mathematician who, as Einstein was to say, does not play dice with the universe. Those initial moves supplied an opening for thinkers like Locke and Kant who were to present Christianity as entirely reasonable in its moral and theological prescriptions when properly pared down to the limited theological dimensions they would suggest. Thereby there ceased to be any tension between Reason and Revelation. But there simultaneously ceased to be a providential, Scriptural God who was worth praying to.

For the moment I intend to pass over that part of the modern story and move to an author who in fact does not initially seem to be a critic of Christianity. I have in mind Alexis de Tocqueville. It is true that there is some debate regarding Tocqueville's commitment to what amounts to modernity, but I am prepared to stipulate that at the very least he was determined to make the best of what he saw as inevitable and irreversible. Tocqueville saw that America, in being the first true Democracy—Athenian Democracy was after all an

Aristocracy of a few who ruled built on the back of majority slavery—was the first true modern regime.

Tocqueville also saw that America was a secular regime which fairly quickly broke the back of any pretensions to a total state that presumed to combine or synthesize Church and State in a unity. In this he saw clearly that early Puritan New England was not going to be the model for the future. Yet Tocqueville pointed out that as a Protestant country America accepted that there was a bond between religion, liberty and republican principles. America was not the first Protestant country, but in Germany, or more to the point, Prussia, Lutheranism had been a state religion and hence the idea of the total state had remained. Such was not the case in America.[2]

Tocqueville saw many virtues in the unique American experiment, and several lurking dangers. The greatest danger was what Tocqueville was first to designate as "individualism." Americans were, he asserted, without knowing it, closet Cartesians. The victory of the democratic principle of equality had brought with it a belief that each person was to be the sovereign basis of his own opinions. Therefore, instead of looking "out" to authoritative opinion makers in the State, social order or Church for beliefs one was left to look "within"; thus, the Cartesian element. But when they got "inside" they found nothing. Hence they were projected back "out" again in search of opinions, but not toward authoritative opinion makers.

Armed with a belief in equality and sovereign individuality one looked instead to the crowd of equals like oneself. Yet all the others were doing the same thing. By this route everyone was led toward the quiet tyranny of "public opinion," the amorphous opinion that somehow emerged from the interactions of equal individualists. But public opinion ruled in a fashion that could never be held responsible, thereby sapping the moral wellsprings of individual action. One was left open to being carried along on the stream of public opinion, indeed tyrannized by it.

This quiet tyranny lined up with the danger of "soft despotism." A general commitment to materialism and a more or less total pursuit of material well-being, or comfortable self-preservation, exacerbated the personal isolation. Both individually and collectively there was the danger of quitting the public arena. This was the danger intrinsic to the dynamic of equality and individualism as they would play themselves out in America and more generally in the democratic epoch that was forthcoming. Democratic citizens tended to get wrapped up in their own narrow universe, concerned with their own private material pursuits. The mind never turned to grand and inspiring thoughts, and collective decision making passed inevitably toward a central administrative nanny State that administered to needs that citizens were no longer willing to attend to themselves. As a result, the wellsprings of will and self-determination were increasingly sapped making men fit primarily for a new democratic form of slavery.

Tocqueville looked with some optimism to the American colonial and frontier habit of forming "voluntary associations" to take care of public needs. But the dynamic of centralization, bureaucratization, individualism and soft despotism would, it was fair to predict, ultimately impinge on the efficacy of that ameliorative. Tocqueville also pointed toward religion, especially a uniquely configured Protestant religion as an alternate ameliorative. Religion alone might, in an environment of equality, materialism and individualism, be able to draw the mind out of itself, beyond its narrow attachments and project it "out" in the only remaining ennobling fashion. Tocqueville went so far as to assert that precisely in a democratic environment religion was more important than in any other form of society—"aristocratic" being his generic term for the alternatives that were not simply one person tyrannies.

Precisely because they are hierarchical and based on the principle of inequality, aristocratic societies give preference to greatness and ladders of rank. Hence they reproduce the same in their theater, literature, poetry and even religion. These ladders of rank give the mind ready-made objects for aspiration and emulation that could draw it out of itself and become the cause of ennoblement and spiritual invigoration. By this means, in an aristocratic society, one could overcome the tendency to the narrowness of scope and vision Tocqueville saw as intrinsic to democratic societies.

But these ennobling aristocratic objects of thought would not for long be available in a democratic age. Even the literature, theater and poetry of the age would inevitably focus on presenting figures like the majority, average and everyday rather than grand. As is true in aristocracies, the dominant element in democratic societies likes to see representations of itself on the stage and on the page. Hence Tocqueville concluded that in short order the only lofty object of ennoblement left outside the hegemony of the equal crowd would be the divine.

Tocqueville concluded that giving up thought of the most important things enervates the soul, making it ready for a bondage that silently works in the interstices of democratic life. Contemplation of the divine could be, Tocqueville reflected, the only remaining object of thought that could lift the mind out of its narrow compass, beyond the narrowness of scope that so enervates the soul, relaxes the springs of the will and prepares men for slavery. **In a democratic age, religion could become, therefore, the best defense of liberty.**

In an aristocratic age, religion would frequently side with the dominant political and social forces in being a danger to liberty. And just as aristocratic societies like to present a long hierarchical ladder of rank, so religion in an aristocratic age had a tendency to have a long ladder of gradations between divine master and humble servants—e.g., priests, bishops, cardinals, popes, angels, archangels, saints, the Virgin Mary. Tocqueville's advice was that these intermediary levels would have to be sacrificed because it was imperative to save the primary relation between God and man. Religion in a democratic age would need to focus on God and his relation to man, man's duties and obligations to God and other men. The myriad of small forms and rituals that had come to dominate the medieval Church would have to be jettisoned to save the core phenomenon of religion, man's mysterious relation to God.

Departing somewhat from Tocqueville, I might observe that his logic should point us toward the necessity of associating this culling of intermediary beings and their attendant rituals with a continuation of grandeur in other areas, like weekly services and architecture. The great cathedrals with their vaulted ceilings accomplish precisely what their designers desired; they unavoidably draw the eye aloft, and increase the chance that the mind will be carried aloft with the eyes.

There is something of the opposite effect operating as regards ennoblement in churches with flat ceilings, cinderblock walls, folding chairs, a pulpit and altar at the same level as the congregation, no adornment or even candles on the altar, if there is an altar. Some attempts at democratizing church architecture have all the ennobling appeal of the rooms one occupies for PTA meetings at the local high school. In a similar vein, undoubtedly it has become necessary in the late modern world to perform services in the vernacular, yet that something as regards grandeur and mystery is lost in the move from conducting services in Latin is clear and may require compensation elsewhere.

One can go so far in removing obstacles to the one to one relation between God and man that the relation itself loses some of its grandeur and ability to inspire, leaving a relation and experience similar to a bull session with a friend. Some mystery needs to remain precisely as part of what Tocqueville is hoping to achieve. The divine needs to be mysterious and remain at some distance. And hence the centrality of the mystery of the Trinity may be more essential now than ever in the Christian era.

Opposed to the aristocratic alternative of making the distance between God and man too great is the democratic tendency toward pantheism against which Tocqueville rightly warns. Pantheism makes God so close that He is in everything around us. In the process, pantheism plays into the characteristic vices of a democratic age. Again the doctrine of the Trinity addresses the problem with only the Holy Spirit still actual in the world after Christ's ascension.

An age of idolatry for equality leads one to be obsessed not with uniqueness but with similarity. Individualism forces one into oneself and then into the arms of a silent majority public opinion. Any form of distinctiveness will likely be taken as an assault on the primacy of equality. When they come face to face, equality always wins out over liberty, the concrete manifestation of which longs for uniqueness. Simultaneously, democratic individuals become convinced that History is moved by large impersonal forces beyond the control of individuals or even nations. In the modern democratic age we are first thrown back on our own powers and then dominated and overcome by unseen forces.

Tocqueville predicted that in a democratic age History would be written with increasing emphasis on the underlying movement of invisible and irresistible forces over which one could gain no control. These massive forces would be seen to take priority over individual action, rendering Republican government impotent. There would be a waning faith in resolute, self-conscious action and hence in individual and collective responsibility.

Eventually, in the forthcoming democratic age one would forget the defining role of individuals in the making of human history and look to peoples or classes or the movement of the entire species as the underlying force acting in all things, and finally to blind Fate. There would be an unavoidable determination to attempt to link everything that occurs to a single cause. And then, paradoxically, as a last ditch effort to save intentionality, that single cause would become in some fashion an unconscious cause (perhaps if one is Hegel, striving for self-consciousness in History, or if one is Nietzsche, the blind movement of the Will-to-Power).

By this means the movement of God, the universe and human history would become part of a single whole—Hegel's *Weltgeist*. It is not just that the Holy Spirit was in the world, or Christ for a short period, but God himself would come to be seen as the moving cause of history in this world, beyond which there is nothing. In pantheism there is no gap between God and what had previously been seen as his external creation. God is simply in the world and in all things. Ironically, a moment later, God would be replaced by blind Fate. God would be transformed from providential, concerned creator, to mathematical principle, to blind Fate operating in the World.

For Tocqueville there is a straightforward path by which we arrive at the inevitability of a pantheistic teaching like Hegel's in which history is the process by which God becomes manifest to Himself in the world. And then we would move from that to the various permutations of blind Fate depicted by Nietzsche and Heidegger. This is the culmination of the pantheism prefigured in the prior thought of modern authors like Spinoza and Leibnitz, to name but two.

For Tocqueville, pantheism is not only especially likely in a democratic age, but it is morally and spiritually debilitating as it denies us any transcendent object for drawing ourselves out of the narrow compass of our everyday domestic existence. There would cease to be any ennobling object to attach thought to "beyond" the world that so belittles and enervates. And hence the enervating march of equality and individualism would be crowned with no possibility of transcendence and little prospect for the will to remain vigorous and assertive of liberty. "I let my regard wander over this innumerable crowd composed of similar beings, in which nothing is elevated and nothing lowered. The spectacle of this universal uniformity saddens and chills me, and I am tempted to regret the society that is no longer."[3]

But this tide that leads toward pantheism has to be fought. Religion properly understood is the necessary tool in that fight. But that requires a transcendent God. In a democratic age, a providential, transcendent God, who is not so transcendent as to be indifferent, is necessary for the cause of liberty. "I am not unaware that several of my contemporaries have thought that peoples are never masters of themselves here below, and that they necessarily obey I do not know which insurmountable and unintelligent force born of previous events, the race, the soil, or the climate. Those are false and cowardly doctrines that can never produce any but weak men and pusillanimous nations."[4] Strong, free and outward looking men and women need a transcendent God who nonetheless is, in some fashion, caring, loving and in the world. **The doctrine of the Trinity is perfect for this need.**

Well into that democratic age that Tocqueville considered in its beginnings, we arrive, with Nietzsche and Heidegger, at the most thoroughgoing critique of not only democracy but Christianity. The groundwork had been laid for centuries, now one could openly pronounce that God is dead. It is a surprisingly small number of years from the writings of Tocqueville to those of Nietzsche, yet a sea change has occurred. We have moved from guarded optimism about the dawning democratic age to thoroughgoing pessimism—not just about modern civilization, but about Western Civilization more generally traced back to its twin wellsprings in Socrates and Christ. Nietzsche openly attacks both Socrates and Christ.

And as he does so often in his various critiques, Nietzsche psychoanalyzes Christianity by trying to get at what he sees as the psychological basis that leads individuals toward Christian belief. He asserts that at the core of Christianity is a love of the "afterworldly" in preference to an attachment to this world. This redirection of attachment is the result of a weakness and weariness on the part of masses of individuals who no longer desire to desire. It is the sign of the desire to quit life and run away.

According to Nietzsche, this afterworldly longing is the work of the weak and suffering (actually, weak and suffering **bodies**) who long to look away from themselves and forget themselves. Or put only slightly differently, the afterworldly longing is the product of a weak and enervated will. With this weakness comes a "No-saying" despising of the Earth and the earthlike in us (the body and its passions). There is an inability to affirm life on the part of a weak body with a weak will. Nietzsche concludes that those longing for the afterlife despise the Earth and the body. They are No-saying to life and can find no joy and can never take an affirmative stance to life. And "Yes-saying" or affirmation of this life is what Nietzsche presents as his main aim, his highest goal.

Lurking beneath the inability to affirm Earth and body is a distinctive flight from human temporality. The passing of time becomes unbearable in its relentless and meaningless movement. Those who are tired and want to want no more flee the relentless passing of time. But in this they fall into a "spirit of revenge" against "time and its 'it was'." They can no more affirm the past than they can affirm their present or remain affirmatively open to the future. This spirit of revenge spreads out into resentment against everything affirmative, distinctive, high-spirited and grand.

Hence Nietzsche asserts that what came to be called virtues in the West are all dark, nay saying and revengeful—both Socratic and Christian understandings allegedly show this resentment against human temporality. Instead of high-spirited virtues, cancerous emotions like pity rise to centrality and become core "values." But to pity someone is show that you are better than they are and look down upon them. For Nietzsche, pity is just a backhanded way of asserting superiority that should be affirmatively asserted out in the open. It also shows a lack of regard for the other; one should have a concern for the other person's sense of shame. Pity is a back handed way of shaming others. Likewise, turning the other cheek is in fact an overt attempt to shame rather than confront one's enemy. Subterranean, cancerous, resentful, revengeful inclinations become the core of virtue. And our souls are destroyed and made small.

And ultimately, all of virtue becomes mercenary as it demands rewards and punishments. Nothing can be affirmatively pursued in a noble fashion as an end in itself. This desire for rewards leads either to a vulgar utilitarianism or to a longing for an ultimate reward in the afterworld. Hence Christianity, built on fear of divine retribution, is quintessentially ignoble and foul, moved by pity, shame, furtiveness, resentment, revenge and all manner of mercenary tendencies. Everything beautiful is sullied. Everything noble is corrupted. Hence nothing in this life can be affirmed.

With no ability to affirm temporal existence there is no basis for joy, and all of life becomes ruled by a "Spirit of Gravity" that weighs down the soul. Life is a grave and depressing matter to be quit as soon as possible; the only longing that can be sanctified is longing for the grave. All joy and laughter are expunged. Nietzsche asserts that he could only pray to a god who dances, who can affirm life; not one who died an ignoble death. Christianity had made all the wellsprings of joy, laughter, dancing and nobility dry up. What remained was unendurably ugly, grey and lifeless.

Let us leave matters at the moment by observing that Nietzsche never let an opportunity for hyperbole pass him by. Still, an affirmative stance to life is what he sought, and he thought he had found it in his doctrine of the eternal recurrence. By this doctrine, time is neither created, nor will it ever end. The only eternity is the endless circling eternity of human temporality, not the linear movement of temporality from creation to *parousia*. For Nietzsche, the eternal return was supposed to be inspiriting because man would again take his temporal existence seriously and seek the noble and beautiful in this life. But one might also argue that the notion could quite easily be altogether enervating, especially in the environment sketched by Tocqueville. It could just as easily foster the debilitating effects Tocqueville attributed to equality and individualism. And the aristocratic tendencies for which Nietzsche hoped could hardly have purely republican implications.

While Nietzsche's teaching always presents problems because of his hyperbole, overstatement and misstatement, Heidegger's deepest relation to Christianity is perhaps even more difficult to discern, perhaps impossible except at great length, leading finally to a speculative leap. But his longing for new gods, his statement that "only a [new] god can save us now," clearly express a longing for a post-Christian religiosity. This impression is fortified by his critique of what he calls "onto-theo-logos."

Heidegger claims that all of Western metaphysics, and Christianity as well, has a doctrine of Being qua Presence. Where the pre-Socratics understood Being as both present and absent, coming into unconcealment while simultaneously remaining concealed, Plato allegedly first presented Being as a form of full presence in the so-called Platonic Ideas that were allegedly fully present to the mind. Likewise, the mysterious Old Testament God became fully present in the world through Christ and thereafter much less mysterious than his willful, vengeful, angry predecessor. This led on a path to a more predictable God, one who became a mathematician and finally fully present in the world in the teaching of Hegel. It was that fully present God who could then easily be killed, leading to the "death of God." **The lack of absence and mystery kills everything high and grand.**

But the matter becomes more complicated. It is clear that the "ecstatic temporality" that Heidegger sets forth as the key to "resoluteness" in *Being and Time* has as its model his understanding of the intense, caring existence of primordial Christianity.[5] The primordial Christian was projected back toward the virgin birth/death/resurrection and forward toward the Second Coming. It is this ecstatic temporal projection toward the past and the future, informing an intensely lived, caring present, that Heidegger wants to recapture. The primordial Christian experience was allegedly lost both in the evolution of early Christian theology but especially in that variant of Christian theology, which became "infected" by Aristotle and Greek metaphysics more generally. Hence for Heidegger it is Christian mystics who are always more appealing than the rationalist component of Christianity, which would include Aquinas and even the Duns Scotus toward whom some have thought him favorably disposed. Heidegger seems better disposed to everyone from Paul to Meister Eckhart to Luther and Schleiermacher.

The final Heideggerian argument of immediate interest to us in the present context is his discussion of "the Fourfold." The elements of Heidegger's Fourfold are Divine, Human, Earth, Sky. Heidegger asserts that they must always be phenomenologically kept together in a poetic synthesis. There are basic phenomena that present themselves to us that determine all possible thought. These phenomena can never be "cleansed" or separated from any later theoretical thinking. They are determinative. They must be kept together and "in" things in the World. For example, one cannot understand the human except in light of the divine. The earth and sky should not be allowed to fly apart.

Related to this discussion of the Fourfold is Heidegger's theme of the interpenetration of Earth and World. By World Heidegger means the cultural and spiritual World that always determines existence but is always a background phenomenon that should not yield to total unconcealment, for then it loses its life giving efficacy. Heidegger asserts that no cultural or spiritual World should allow itself to fly too far above the Earth, and that means above the unity of the Fourfold. One must respect the determinacy of the distinctive indigenous earthly settings that condition the openness of man to Being. This is Heidegger's way of dealing with the issue of the concrete Earth and the earthlike elements in us, in short, the body. The divine cannot be separated from the Earth and the body and attached only to the ghostlike and afterworldly, as Nietzsche would put the matter. Beyond that, all of the elements of the Fourfold must, Heidegger asserts, be kept "in things." For our purposes, the major ramification of this doctrine is that the Divine must be kept in things. The Divine must not become totally present; that leads to the death of God, but it must not fly off so far away from the human things that it becomes detached and irrelevant. This is Heidegger's version of Nietzsche's attempt to affirm the Earth and the earthlike in us, the body. It is also Heidegger's way of dealing with the issue Christianity deals with by the doctrine of the Trinity, and especially with the Holy Spirit as opposed to the Father.

Above I observed that there are resources within Christianity that allow it a philosophical response to its critics. But the question is always, what is essential to Christianity and what is peripheral, epiphenomenal and even ephemeral? What is essential and what is historically contingent? Do we find the core of Christianity in the sayings and parables of Christ reported in the Gospels? Do we find it in the deeds and actions of Christ that call for an *imitatio Christi*? Or do we look to the teachings of Paul, especially in the *Letter to the Romans,* the Paul without whom it is arguable there would never have been an institutional Christianity? Do we look to the early teachings of Ambrose, Jerome and Augustine and others who vanquished the early Montanists, Pelagians, Donatists, Arians etc., and carved out the early dogmas of the Western Church?[6] Do we look to the statement of the Nicene Creed or the pre-Nicene doctrine in the Athanasian Creed? What about the history of the institutional Church up until the Reformation or its definitive statements and papal encyclicals? Or do we as Americans, and following Tocqueville's advice, look to Protestantism; and if so, the Protestantism of Calvin, Luther, Erasmus or some other thinker?

Even if we try to be purists and get to the heart of the matter and limit ourselves to the Gospels and the Letters of Paul we are not without problems, for it is not clear that Christ's parables and Paul's teachings are simply identical. And without the institutional Church, and Christ himself seems to have pointed to the need for institutional arrangements in his instructions to his disciples, there would not have been Christianity even if a recorded history of Christ the historical figure had survived. So we cannot simply disentangle pure doctrine from institutional manifestation. In brief form, this train of questions presents our problem: Where do we begin?

Obviously choices have to be made. Mine, I admit, is a historical choice, but not one that I think is optional. And that is true because we always must begin in the present. We have no choice but to begin where we are "thrown." Nonetheless, in the present, we always "are" our past. Hence we must be projected toward that past and cannot will it away. But we must also, always, be projected toward what is possible in the future. As I have argued above repeatedly, we must bind together past, present and future. This is the necessary temporal stance of political philosophy, but also, I would argue, is especially true of Christian theology, which must be "ecstatic" in this fashion. This "ecstatic temporality" is the stance of Christianity itself. At its core, Christianity cannot lose its relation backwards to the resurrection and forward toward the promised Second Coming. That relation between past, present and future is central to Christianity, and only to Christianity among the Scriptural dispensations. Without it, one has a different phenomenon than Christianity.

We have to begin where we have arrived. America, in its fundamentally Protestant, republican manifestation, is now the heart of Christianity. Europe is increasingly atheist; its church attendance has dwindled dramatically. The Catholic Church is strongest in Central and South America, not its homeland of Europe, but even there congregations are hardly growing rapidly. There has been very little Christian penetration of Asia—whether we are talking about India, China, Japan, or Southeast Asia. The Christian penetration of Africa has been idiosyncratic and yielded syntheses that are frequently hard to recognize as Christian.

We must look where it is most likely, and indeed necessary, for Christianity to remain strong if it is to have a future in the face of the fastest growing religion, Islam. **Islam will not be confronted and stopped by atheism.** And we must keep in mind that in the American context, as Tocqueville suggested long ago, even Catholicism and Judaism have been protestantized. It is not immediately obvious that the same can happen with even an indigenous Islam, let alone Islam as a global phenomenon. For all of these reasons, I look therefore to the necessary bases of the distinctive form of Christianity crafted in America.

Christianity in America is voluntary and separates Church and State—and that separation was seen by America's Christian founders as precisely the best means to craft both religious freedom and republican liberty into a workable whole. American Christianity accepts the central doctrine of the Trinity, but follows Tocqueville in applying Ockham's razor to many rituals and peripheral theological doctrines. It follows Paul in seeing the primacy of "conscience" to the old Law and eschews legal rigidity.

While Christianity needs an institutional manifestation, that need not be the total state longed for by everyone from Augustine to the medieval Church to Luther and Calvin. Let us then follow the advice of Tocqueville and strip Christianity of its peripheral rituals and forms and try to get to the core articles of Faith without which we no longer have anything distinctively Christian. Here, it seems to me, much of the job has already been done for us by Paul. Again, there likely would not be an institutional Christianity without Paul.

At the heart of Paul's teaching, in all of his letters, and it is echoed in all of the Gospels, is the clarion call that what he has to report is "good news," a matter for joy and rejoicing. One simply must begin there. What appears at first blush to be the most horrific of events—the crucifixion of Christ—is in fact a cause for rejoicing because in rising above death, Christ redeemed us mortals, and all of creation, from original sin. Through Christ's resurrection man's entire relation to creation is transformed. **Contrary to Nietzsche, only after the resurrection can man affirm his mortal life and the created world.** To God's original injunction to go forth, be fruitful and multiply can now be added that we can do so joyously and affirmatively. On this level, Paul's teaching puts the lie to Nietzsche's assertions. Nietzsche's criticisms apply far better to the teachings of everyone from Ambrose, Jerome and Augustine down to Calvin, the pessimists and determinists for whom life is anything but a grand affair and creation anything but good and worthy of affirmation.

Paul makes it clear that with the resurrection the previous Law has been superseded. **Faith now replaces the Law.** We must have Faith in the forgiveness of sins, including original sin. By Faith, not by indulgent acts of the clergy or through various rituals or simple lawabidingness, circumcision or even baptism alone are we saved. We must have Faith that Christ is Lord and divine, God is King and raised Christ from the dead. Faith in the resurrection saves us from original sin and God's prior anger and supersedes the prior covenants and laws. We must have Faith in the immortality of the soul and that the Holy Spirit remains in the world as God's messenger after Christ's ascension and until the promised Second Coming. The Holy Spirit speaks to us in the world through Faith and conscience and the use of our God given ability to think and Reason. There is the core of Christianity. It consists of articles of Faith, not dogmas or laws or rituals.

In the place of legalism and dogmatism we have articles of Faith and the "speech" of the Holy Spirit addressed to our "conscience" **that we must repeatedly re-articulate for ourselves in rational speech publicly over time.** This ongoing re-articulation is mandatory because conscience always speaks to specific issues in the present. But even the addresses we receive from the Holy Spirit lack anything resembling legal specificity. Paul goes so far as to argue that the Ten Commandments themselves are either amended or reduced to the formula "love thy neighbor as thyself," or the even simpler injunction "love one another." (*Romans* 13:8) **In the process, love (*agapé*) replaces fear at the heart of both Christian theology and morality.** God, man and creation are reconciled. That is the joyous good news. Love replaces compulsion and fear. Hence the high can have hegemony over the low in dealing with human affairs. This is why Christianity intrinsically agrees with classical antiquity in a way the Old Testament and Koran do not. Fear, the low, has lost its hegemony.

Mere lawabidingness or mechanical acts like circumcision and baptism are no longer adequate. Christ's teaching is not another Law. One must now have Faith that God sent His Son to redeem His creation and thereby moved beyond His initial covenant with but one tribal entity or people. His covenant is now with all of mankind who have Faith that Christ was man, but also Divine in a mysterious fashion that defies definition or understanding. Christ died, transcended death, was resurrected. Remaining in the world is the Holy Spirit as the spokesman for Christ in the World after his return to the Godhead. Resurrection, Trinity, redemption of God's creation from original sin and the possibility of eternal life through Faith—that is the core of Christian theology. Love, affirmation, joy and neighborly sociality are the core of Christian morality. As Tocqueville observes, beyond that, everyday law is left to Reason to discern within the general outlines of Christian theology and morality so understood.

The great virtue of Christianity is that it has its basis in Faith rather than legal doctrines. **Articles of Faith still have to be applied in a changing historical context, but are far more flexible in that regard than minute mandated laws, doctrines and dogmas.** When Islam arrived seven centuries after Christ, it signaled not only a move back to the centrality of law, but a move back to a theological doctrine of non-complex unity that reproduced the gulf between man and God of Judaism as well as again lowering the status of the created world. It moved back as well to the centrality of fear and retribution and a conception of an angry God who is not reconciled to his creation.

Unlike Judaism, Islam returned to the centrality of law, but now the law presumed to have a universal scope that it did not previously have where the Law was seen as part of a covenant with a single people. Now the law could be armed with a mission for its universal spread not as an idea or through Faith alone, but politically. **While universal in scope, no such political injunction necessarily exists within Christianity.** It need not impose a law politically, with one conception of the best regime; it can reign victorious by the spread of a glorious idea and articles of Faith. And for Christians a respect for and need to preserve God's creation is central, until we are relieved of duty at the Second Coming.

The Christian doctrine of the Trinity, and here I approach the matter entirely from a philosophical perspective, is by comparison to non-complex doctrines of unity and Oneness, a tour de force. The doctrine of the Trinity overcomes the unbridgeable gulf between man and God without introducing pantheism. While the Old Testament God was not the inert One of Parmenides or neo-Platonism, there was still the problem of the relation between the One and the many. The intervening link became prophets. With the notion of prophets we open the problem of differentiating between true and false prophets and hence true and false linkages. Not only must one differentiate between Moses and David Koresh or Jim Jones, but there is the clear problem that the collection of the accepted prophets will, as it did, leave a legacy of a very mixed message and the possibility of more prophets to come and yet more confusion.

With Christianity, prophecy and law are no longer central; and as a result, all manner of moral, political and theological problems disappear. Christians can move from the dangerous arena of competing future prophets to the arena of Faith and Reason. **Let us hope the future is not dominated by competing would-be prophets** whose first move will assuredly be to try to disable our God given capacity to think and Reason. We will get far more David Koreshes than those who resemble Moses. That can be predicted by any sensible person. As an aside, contrary to Farabi, I see no reason why future political philosophy will want to come forth into the public arena in the guise of prophecy or assuming the mantle of prophet. A far better image would be that of a publicly open and accessible, fellow discussant qua *primus inter pares*.

The Trinitarian doctrine avoids the philosophical problems of seeing the One or Ultimate as so far from mankind as to become an indifferent One, or thought thinking itself, or of becoming a God who is an indifferent and powerless mathematician, or even God as an angry and sometimes unjust tribal God. In Christianity we have the hidden God who reveals himself in history, albeit not completely, and promises to do so again. We have a God who bridges the gap between himself and his creation, but not in the Hegelian fashion where he obliterates that gap. The Christian God remains present but never completely, absent but never completely, approachable by passion and love, but also by Reason and thought. God remains transcendent, yet in the world, things and man through the Holy Spirit. God is the present yet transcendent, loved yet mysterious Three in One both concealed and unconcealed, to co-opt Heidegger's terminology to use it against him.

This Christian teaching beautifully confronts the Heideggerian issue announced in the doctrine of the Fourfold, without the danger of pantheism warned against by Tocqueville. God is in man and things but not in such a fashion that he succumbs to total presence. The Christian God cannot fall into the problems Heidegger associates with "onto-theo-logos," i.e., a doctrine of Being as fully present. And as Machiavelli was aware, God the Three in One is a God who wins by ideas, not primarily by armies—albeit armies may be needed at times. Christianity came forth and spread as an idea before it had any institutional manifestation, and any access to an army. It will continue to do so if we give it a home.

On the political level Christianity has manifest advantages as well. There is no doctrine of the best constitution or the best laws in Christ's teachings, the Gospels or the letters of Paul. There is an intrinsic doctrine of the separation of Church and State in the doctrine of rendering to Caesar what is Caesar's and to Christ what is Christ's.[7] What Christ demands is acceptance of articles of Faith. Matters regarding the State are not dealt with and hence are matters for Reason, aided by the broad outlines of Faith, to work out. Aristotelian prudence has, therefore, a large arena in which to operate. And prudence always knows that the best regime depends on the changing times and indigenous circumstances.

Unlike modern political philosophy which increasingly relied on low but sure foundations like fear, **fear is not at the heart of the Christian teaching.** Love and the injunction to sociality and neighborliness take that place. This gives political philosophy a large arena in which to operate but also some guidance about where to begin—e.g., **not the posited fearful, a-sociality of constructivist state of nature theories.** The Christian need not begin with the competitive lowness of proto-modern political philosophy; yet the Christian can still admit that there exists evil in the world.

Again, it is probably only within Christianity that the tradition of political philosophy could have been maintained and continued. Only Christianity needs to be open to political philosophy and its entire Tradition, to fill in what is left open by the centrality of Faith. In fact, if not for the Christian translations of the texts of the Tradition it is unlikely that the Tradition of political philosophy would have come down to us preserved as it is, open for loving inspection. Faith may or may not precede Reason; it does not and cannot simply replace it.

Again, just as the Christian Church itself has been a historical institution evolving to meet the times, Christianity in its core is historical and so is political philosophy. The Christian God reveals himself in stages—first in covenants and laws, then finally through Christ. The Christian God reveals himself in history, promises to do so again, and leaves the Christian always in the ecstatic relation between present and future out of which ongoing History emerges and becomes possible. Only Christianity of the major Scriptural dispensations is in its core historical and hence open to historical change, including the changes that have brought modernity, enlightenment, democracy and an openness to Reason within a creation that has to be respected because it has been redeemed.

One should reflect on the fact that any environmental ethic has to presuppose a redeemed Earth or Nature. A creation that is not so redeemed would not as easily imply the injunction to preserve the Earth. One worries that in the name of a political Islam that goes over to the side of a fanaticism that justifies itself to followers on the basis of an alleged quick trip to immortality, the Earth could easily be sacrificed for the longed for afterworldly reward. There is immense danger in that political equation. It is a danger that Christianity has confronted before the fact. The creation is redeemed; we must love the Earth along with our neighbor. Christianity is in principle open to the interpenetration of Reason and Faith and a loving of creation on this Earth.

The interpenetration of Reason and Faith of historical Christianity cannot part ways. Indeed Reason must be applied even to the interpretation of Scripture. The Bible is not a book in a traditional sense. A traditional book has a single author with a single intention. And while we may assume God's hand operates in the background, the actual books of the Bible are penned by human hands. If there were one human author of the Bible, that author's inclusions and omissions, seeming contradictions and changes of heart could be traced either to an esoteric intention or carelessness. But the Bible is a set of compilings and witnessings by various authors which, even when divinely inspired, have to be passed through human speech to find their way into the world. It is to be expected in a "book" like the Bible that there will be repetitions and at times seeming contradictions that cannot be traced to authorial intention, but to the simple **human** necessities of speech and writing as well as the changing circumstances of **human** existence.

But the matter is more complicated still. The Bible simply is not intended to be read literally. This is not to say that there is no teaching that can be discerned, it is to say that that teaching will only yield to sustained effort rather than casual perusal. These reflections lead us of course to one of the issues at the heart of the Reformation. Not only interpretation but the very reading of the Bible had, prior to the Reformation, become the right of a select few in the caste of priests. The Protestant movement was forged on the premise that the Bible was also the property of the laity and all persons of Faith and hence should be open to lay interpretation. Of course people like Luther never intended that doctrine to include the frivolous notion that the Bible, whatever it means, should yield to the vagrant interpretations of every reader no matter how assiduous and careful they might be in their reading.

This raises another issue like the one that requires us to differentiate between true and false prophets. Interpretation, like wood-working or any other art requires skill and practice. **The Bible is not self-interpreting**, and a doctrine of private judgment that reduces to making all judgments equal is simply as silly as asserting before the fact that all wood-workers are equal. We do not consider all wood-workers equal. Neither are all interpretations of the Bible. And yet one must avoid making the Bible a private document that is the preserve of some self-chosen caste. It must be interpreted in public in the full light of day. Let us have the Faith in Reason wherein the best interpretations will survive that public confrontation. **Let us not long for closed castes of priests again.** For example, as regards interpretation of the Bible, the creation story in *Genesis* is on occasion interpreted literally, leading to the conclusion that the cosmos is only four or five thousand years old. There is ample straightforward evidence that this is nonsense. Faith does not call upon us to believe manifest nonsense.

Genesis tells us that on the first day God created light, then the heavens, the earth, the seas and vegetation. On the fourth day He created the sun, moon and stars, and made them move. On the fifth day He created water animals and birds, and on the sixth land animals and man. On the seventh day He rested. Obviously "days" are on one level determined by the rotation of the earth as regards the face it turns toward the sun. But before God created the earth and sun there could be no days in this present solar sense. "Days" are being used in *Genesis* in some other sense. One author has suggested the difference between divine creation days and temporal sun days. But divine creation days could easily be eons in temporal sun days. And hence we have no way of calculating the time in question in temporal sun days. One might even note that the order in which living things come to be—seas, water animals, birds, land animals, man—is consistent with the temporal sequencing in the account of contemporary evolutionary biology. Be that as it may, the point at present is that even this central Biblical teaching cannot be interpreted literally, nor was it ever intended to be.

If we jump ahead to the Gospels, the same is clearly true for Christ's teachings. Christ's speeches are symbolic and allegorical, simultaneously simple and mysterious with multiple layers. His parables are figurative and celebratory, admonitory and inspiriting. All of which is to say that Christ's teachings always need both interpretation and completion by way of filling out and application to concrete instances. And again, none of Christ's teachings are even remotely like the law in Judaism or Islam.

The Gospels make the allegorical nature of Christ's teachings abundantly clear. Christ repeatedly is quoted in the Gospels as explaining why he spoke in parables. This occurs in each of the Gospels. The reason given repeatedly reduces to the fact that everyone cannot receive the Word equally in rational speech. Some must receive the Word in another fashion. And that is why the Holy Spirit speaks to the "heart" as well as to Reason. But none of this is to say the Word should not be made articulate in rational speech. Again, for the Christian Faith may precede Reason; it does do away with the need for Reason, interpretation and the public articulation of the Word. **And the Christian Word, and an unchanging Law, are two entirely different things.** The Word is most definitely both revealed and mysterious, unconcealed and concealed.

We must keep in mind that if the central virtue for pre-Scriptural man was what Aristotle termed *magalopsychia*, greatness of soul, or magnanimity in the Latin sense, for a Christian it is most certainly humility. It is the humility to know that one cannot attain final Wisdom in this world. Socrates had concluded precisely the same thing. One must have the humility to know what we cannot know. That applies to having a final wisdom regarding the Word, the Word to which we must remain continually open as we try to bring it to speech for our time. That humility should certainly be applied to interpreting the Bible and not just *Genesis*, but especially books like *Revelations* which almost every Christian scholar admits included secret messages for early Christian readers in the grip of persecution. For example, to presume to knowledge of when the second coming is near, or the end of mortal temporality is coming—or even what that would mean—is totally lacking in humility. Likewise to believe one has final wisdom regarding what is required in day-to-day political affairs on the basis of a quotation taken out of context from a book of the Bible, let us say *Revelations*, is the absolute height of arrogance and utterly at odds with the core tenets of Christian Faith. Christian humility must spill over to our understanding that in political matters we do not have final wisdom and never will. Paul is clear in Romans (13:1) that we must obey the state and that means obey secular laws, which we must hope are reasonable and just. This is all the more true in a time when laws have been self-consciously crafted rationally at a specific founding publicly accessible to all and at a time when the laws are largely rational in intent, if occasionally not in application. Christian Faith does not substitute for the need for political institutions nor the need to apply Reason to understand how to accomplish the just in this world.

This leaves us to say a few brief, at best suggestive and prefatory, words about one of the major issues in the attacks on Christianity we sketched above. There is a drumbeat of repeated criticisms of what is taken to be the necessary Christian relation to the Earth (God's creation) and the earthlike in us, the body and its passions and functions. This is then related to practical issues dealing with marriage, sexuality and celibacy. At first blush one might conclude that here someone like Nietzsche may have a point. The institutional history of the Church certainly gives him leverage on this issue. **But ultimately I believe Nietzsche has it wrong, and so had much of the institutional Church.**

Throughout his letters, Paul makes much of the distinction between body and Spirit. He asserts that Spirit is higher, just as soul was asserted to be the legitimate ruler of the body in Greek thought. That did not lead the Greeks to an anti-body teaching. Neither need it lead in that direction for Christians. **The body as part of the physical creation of God is redeemed by Christ's death and resurrection just as the rest of creation.** Redeemed from original sin the body cannot be intrinsically evil for a true Christian.

One might point out that Paul is frequently quoted regarding his remarks on marriage that reduce to the injunction "marry if you must," but married to the Church on the level of Spirit is better. An implication drawn early on was that the best life is not just one devoted to the Spirit but one which includes celibacy as well. But when he announces this position explicitly in 1st Corinthians (7:25–30) he makes it clear that this is **not advice that he received in any Revelation**, as with that on the road to Damascus, but that it is simply his opinion. It represents a manifestation of Paul's mortal prudence applied to how to be "happy." Paul is entirely clear on this matter.

Paul is also clear that he is not attempting to project any necessary restrictions for Christians. One must consult the force of Paul's reasons for thinking celibacy leads to happiness and consider whether they are sound. His reflections on the subject of sexuality, marriage and happiness were taken in a specific context and make sense only in that context. It is a context where Paul expected the imminence of the Second Coming.[8] After 2000 years of being told by different individuals that the Second Coming is imminent, it is time to admit we mortals have no direct wisdom on this subject and must prepare to live justly and preserve God's creation for as long as it takes, which could quite easily be at least 2000 more years. Paul simply thought that the preservation of the species was not a major concern, nowhere near as important as the redemption of the soul. Without his belief in the imminence of the Second Coming he would most assuredly have had to reconsider.

Beyond that, much of the anti-body, anti-senses and anti-sensuality dogmas of the early Church come not from the teachings of the Gospels or of Paul but from early Christian thinkers like Ambrose and Jerome as well as the increasingly pessimistic Augustine. All of their teachings and their doctrines are simultaneously anti-body, anti-joy, anti-intellectual, anti-Reason and grossly pessimistic. All of this is completely at odds with the "good news" of the Gospels and Paul's central teachings as well as the necessary place that Reason must play where Faith is silent. The pessimism of the early Church has contextual reasons. And that pessimism continued to link up with the belief that the Second Coming was near. Consequently, early Christian thinkers had no compelling need to consider issues like marriage, family and reproduction.

Beyond that, the doctrine of celibacy that emerged in the early Church can be traced to a combination of accident **and political calculation far more than theological necessity.** When the Church began to institutionalize and approached recognition by the Roman Empire, it wanted to separate itself from the problems and entanglements that would make the Empire suspicious of it. That included trying to argue that unlike pagan priests, Christian priests would not form a hereditary caste. Celibacy was the proof. This fell in line with an evolving tradition of monastic life that stretched back to the example of various Jewish sects all of whom took exception to the priestly temple hierarchy. In a time of hardship for Christians during the first three hundred years, withdrawal into monastic enclaves had its appeal. That evolving monastic tendency, together with a political necessity, conjoined with an interpretation that deduced far too much from the virgin birth—which as a miracle had no bearing on the normal course of events within the rest of creation—formed the argument for celibacy.

Paul's teaching that the death and resurrection of Christ substitutes Faith for the previously promulgated Law, and thereby rests on the injunction Love your neighbor as yourself, or just love one another, presumably even affects the operative clauses regarding sexuality in the Ten Commandments. This leads me to conclude that the dogmas of historical, institutional Christianity dealing with the body, sexuality and marriage are not part of the central core of the Faith and hence belong to the realm of the State to be worked out by Reason. And the entire ethic of pessimism and the mortification of the flesh is at odds with the Pauline spirit of love, hope, high spirits, good news and humility. Christ's life, for all its trials and passion, is replete with joyous expressions of life. His first miracle was to turn water into wine for a party. He has frequent meals with family and disciples, wished to have the joyous children come unto him and surround him—and hence was pleased with the production of children as a good thing—and on and on.

As to this issue of joy and affirmation more generally, while there is limited reliance on dance in the Scriptural tradition, albeit there is more than a little mention of the practice, there is great reliance, especially in Christianity, on song and singing. If one wished to put it this way in response to Nietzsche, song and music are at least as central to the Dionysian as dance. We could change Nietzsche's injunction that he could only pray to a God who loves song, and there is no intrinsic problem with Christianity.

But beyond that, the Christian God is in general a God of passion, of love in particular, personally concerned in the world, not one of anger, detachment, tranquility or simple withdrawal. We are called to the same passionate engagement in the world, open to the transcendent, protecting and preserving the creation for generations of souls yet to come. We can quite legitimately dispense with the debilitating combination of Augustinian pessimism and Calvinist determinism, which have given more than a little free reign to angry, resentful would-be tyrants. Joyous good news and pessimism are at odds with each other. And a belief in determinism (that one knows the first things about the cosmos) is utterly inconsistent with Christian humility and at odds with the entire teaching of the centrality of "choosing" our Faith. We need to affirm life and protect God's creation **through our freely chosen lives in this world**. Our existence on this Earth simply need not be one of pointless drudgery.

My suggestions above are not intended to represent anything like a dogmatic position. I have offered only some suggestions of what is possible in light of modern criticisms of Christianity. I have done so with an eye to linking the Christian past with what is hoped will be a Christian future. **But no one should see that future as inevitable.** It must be secured by those of us in the present. The defense of the West demands a defense of Christianity because one will be hard put to define what one is defending if they eschew one of the main bases of Western Civilization. And that Civilization is and will continue to be under attack both from within and without for as far into the future as a mortal being can now see.

As in so many other things, the defense of the West is at this moment a distinctly American task. In America we stand for a Christianity that is voluntary, accepts the centrality of articles of Faith that include the resurrection and the Trinity, the possibility of life everlasting, the separation of Church and State, the need for reason to apply itself to the things pertinent to the State, and belief that the Reason that allows us to undertake many tasks is one of God's gifts to us. And for Americans there has always been **an intimate link, from the beginning, between religion, republican principles, and a love of liberty.** We have also had the great good fortune to have a doctrinal diversity on matters outside the core principles of Faith that keeps energy and thought alive, and the mind open. An open reasoning mind, ennobled and pointed aloft to the mystery of creation, redemption and salvation is, as Tocqueville observed, precisely what is needed in the modern, democratic age. It will be even more necessary in the postmodern future that is coming.

As a historical religion, that is ecstatically historical in its very core, Christianity alone offers the hope that we can remain open to the adaptations that a fast changing future will require of us. One should expect nothing of the kind from the post-scriptural longings of Nietzsche and Heidegger. Man is mortal and fallible and must be humble—we should not long to be gods, to rival God by recreating His creation nor presume to have fathomed His wisdom. Mortal wisdom needs to be ever impressed with the extent of our mortal limitations.

My central point throughout has been that one may not will away Christianity and remain Western. Further, only within Christianity was a tradition of political philosophy possible, and it is still possible as an architectonic undertaking. The basis for political philosophy does not exist in other Scriptural dispensations, in Hinduism, Buddhism, Nietzsche's Dionysianism, or Heidegger's amorphous post-Christian gods. The Doctrine of the Trinity is philosophically rich and can be tapped in creative ways. The historical nature of Christian theology itself is fruitful and useful and helps us see that many of the things criticized by everyone from Machiavelli to Nietzsche and Heidegger are historically contingent and far from the essential core of Christianity.

NOTES

1. Alexis de Tocqueville, *Democracy in American*, trans. by George Lawrence, (New York: Harper and Row, 1969), p 445.

2. On the issue of Church/State relations let us be clear. Our founders were Christians. They intended to create a Christian nation. But they purposely created a secular State having concluded that it would provide the best defense of religious liberty.

Chapter Nineteen

But they certainly never intended that their secular State had to be openly hostile to religion, a position several generations of scholars have tried to read into the "establishment" clause of the First Amendment. Apparently, those ideological partisans would have us forget not only our history but the "free exercise" clause of the same Amendment.

3. Alexis de Tocqueville, *Democracy in America*, trans. Harvey C. Mansfield and Delba Winthrop (Chicago: University of Chicago Press: 2000), p. 674.

4. *Democracy in America*, trans. by Mansfield and Winthrop, pp. 675–76.

5. For a fuller treatment of Nietzsche and Heidegger see my *Nietzsche, Heidegger and the Transition to Postmodernity*, and *Martin Heidegger: Paths Taken, Paths Opened*.

6. For this history see Paul Johnson, *A History of Christianity* (New York: Simon and Schuster/Touchstone Books), 1995.

7. See Romans 13:1–7, Mathew 22:16–21, Luke 20:25, Mark 12:17, 1st Timothy 2:1–4, 1st Peter 2:13–17.

8. Another pertinent textual support from the Old Testament which is frequently cited is Genesis 38:8–10. It deals with a man named Onan. The Lord had slain his brother for disobedience and it was Onan's responsibility under the Law to lie with his brother's wife and conceive. He refused and spilled his seed on the ground. For this the Lord slew him as well. But it utterly misinterprets the story to make it into a teaching regarding human sexuality. It is quite clearly a lesson on obeying the commands of the Lord as expressed in the Law—a Law that for Christians has been superseded. Of obeying the older Law after it has been superseded, we must consult what Paul says about the injunctions against pork, or for that matter wine: Do as you see fit and follow what your beliefs dictate. God loves you for sticking to your beliefs even if they are no longer mandatory injunctions.

Chapter Twenty

Ontology, Technology, Poetry or Mandarin Pastime? Theoretical Physics in the Postmodern Age

Modernity's public self-perception is substantially built upon the premise of the superiority of modern science as an ontological explanation of reality to the various forms of myth and religious parables that the pre-modern world offered. The sober search for experimentally demonstrable explanations, arrived at by tireless, multi-generational efforts, especially as backed by the precision of mathematics and novel technical instruments, gives an appearance of solidity to the modern picture of reality unknown to pre-moderns.

A further appearance of solidity comes from the technological successes that modern science has made possible. That appearance leads to a largely unshakable public Faith that the scientific picture of reality is simply a true depiction of the nature of the cosmos. The public perception, shared by many practitioners as well, is that modern science is ontology and not primarily hypothetical, mathematical *poiesis*. I want to argue that this view becomes far less obvious when it comes to contemporary theoretical physics and speculative cosmology than with prior manifestations of modern physics. I then want to reflect upon what would happen publicly if we were to take this into account. My assumption will be that almost nothing would change technologically.

My primary object of reflection is the situation of early twenty-first century theoretical physics and speculative cosmology, the physics that in hardly more than one hundred years has moved from the paradigm of Newton, to Quantum Mechanics, to Relativity Theory, to String Theory. A generation ago discussions of these "paradigm shifts" within physics was cutting edge thinking.[1] It confronted the traditional public understanding of science as a cumulatively evolving, seamlessly progressive undertaking. It substituted the idea, and indeed offered considerable evidence, that what one saw in theoretical physics was a series of paradigms that dealt with different things, none of which was capable of dealing with all questions and none was capable of giving a complete picture of the whole. Indeed, it was pointed out, in some cases we were left giving different explanations of the same things using different theories simultaneously.

The paradigm shift argument culminated in the notion that one simply chooses the paradigm that is most useful—and that ultimately can only mean technologically useful—and applies that theory with considerable indifference to any competing theories.[2] One was not particularly upset to have competing contradictory theories of the same phenomena—e.g., light—as long as they were useful for different technical predictions and applications. Technology, not ontology understood as a comprehensive grasp of reality (or as is now fashionable, T.O.E., a theory of everything), drove the choice. **The basis of the choice between competing scientific theories was not itself scientific.**[3] This affront to traditional *public* understandings of the nature of modern physical science had far reaching ramifications. But these discussions never really percolated down to the public arena to change the public dogma that modern theoretical physics was ontology.

Still, in the academic world, this notion of paradigm shifts, and its ontological ramifications, was seen as a marvelous discovery. But that modern physics was never intended to eventuate in ontology or cosmology in the older sense is, without too much effort, clear already in the work of a philosophical founder like Descartes. It is overtly clear in Copernicus's *On the Revolutions of the Celestial Spheres* as we see in the Preface by his student Osiander:

> Then, in turning to the causes of these motions or the hypotheses about them, he must conceive of a device, **since he cannot in any way attain to the true causes.** He must conceive of and devise **such hypotheses as**, being assumed, would enable the motions to be calculated correctly from the principles of geometry, for the future as well as the past. . . . For **these hypotheses need not be true nor even probable**; if they provide a calculus consistent with the observations, that alone is sufficient. . . . And if any causes are devised by the imagination as indeed very many are, **they are not put forward as if they were** *true*, but merely to provide a correct basis for calculations.[4] [my emphasis]

What was fairly straightforward at the origins of modern science was still straightforward when, more than three hundred years later, Nietzsche announced that it was finally dawning on a few that even modern physics is just an interpretation.[5] Perhaps slightly more novel was Nietzsche's observation that with different motives, which is to say different aesthetic, sociological and moral tastes, one could give an aristocratic rather than democratic explanation of things.

"Nature's conformity to law," of which you physicists talk so proudly, . . . it exists only owing to your interpretation. . . . It is no matter of fact, no "text," but rather only a naïvely humanitarian emendation and perversion of meaning, with which you make abundant concessions to the democratic instincts of the modern soul! . . . [But] somebody might come along who, with opposite intentions and modes of interpretation, could read out of the same "nature," and with regard to the same phenomena, rather the tyrannically inconsiderate and relentless enforcement of claims of power. . . . "[T]yranny" itself would eventually seem unsuitable, or a weakening and attenuating metaphor—being too human—but he might, nevertheless, end by asserting the same about this world as you do, namely, that it has a "necessary" and "calculable" course, *not* because laws obtain in it, but because they are absolutely *lacking*, and every power draws its ultimate consequences at every moment.[6]

What Nietzsche was suggesting is that at their core the various theories generated by modern physics had moral and political biases built in, a theme to which I will return below—in this case democratic and egalitarian biases. On a different level, if the choice of scientific theories is not itself scientific—as our more recent paradigm shift argument suggests—why must the basis of the choice be limited to considerations like mere technological advantage or based on mathematical aesthetic tastes? Again, **a technological basis for the choice between scientific theories is already based on the premise that the technology chosen produces some good**. Hence an idea of the Good is always lurking in the background. So a moral basis is already built into choices of technologies. But the same is true of theories that presume to be ontological. On the deepest level, I am suggesting that there is a more comprehensive and self-conscious deployment of Reason than that which we see in modern theoretical physics. It is this more comprehensive deployment that I have been suggesting throughout the chapters above is indicative of political philosophy in its holistic and architectonic manifestation.

Ultimately what is at stake here is the issue of the possible autonomy of postmodern theoretical physics. I do not mean by this primarily the autonomy from political and moral control. I take for granted that that is an issue we have already publicly decided. We should, for example, exercise moral and political control over biological and nuclear technologies that can be weaponized. We do decide whether building a super accelerator is the best use of limited public resources. This issue is already decided, and quite correctly in my view.

I am more concerned to reflect on the possibility of the intellectual and philosophical autonomy of theoretical physics and the extent to which it should be taken as ontology and form our public perceptions of reality. If modern theoretical physics is not ontology, and its technological products should not simply be autonomously disseminated—Bacon accepted as much in his *New Atlantis*—then what is the status of theoretical physics in its onto-logical and cosmological reflections and pretensions? What would happen if these reflections were no longer taken as ontological in the public arena?[7] What other factors should then be taken into account in self-consciously choosing between competing theories?

I am prepared to be called quaint by observing that long ago Plato as much as predicted what has transpired in contemporary physics. By that I have in mind his presentations, in dialogues like the *Sophist* and *Parmenides*. In those dia-logues and others Plato showed how the mind intrinsically and unavoidably would be unwilling to rest content that it possessed an adequate understand-ing of reality until it had arrived at something that deserved to be called a "One." The mind searches "downward" for the ultimate small One and "up-ward" to comprehend the whole as a One. Then the problem is to understand how those two Ones—we can call them the micro and the macro—are con-nected and how those Ones inform the "middle realm" of the many phenom-ena surrounded by which we carve out our everyday lives. And then there is the final conundrum of how these two Ones are reducible to an ultimate One.

Plato went on to point out that there are certain conceptual necessities im-posed by human thought when directed to reflections upon the "first things." I will maintain that modern theoretical physics, right down to String Theory, has not transcended these conceptual necessities and still gets entangled in them. I will make the same point in the following chapter on contemporary biology.

As to the issue of the search for Ones, in contemporary terms, quantum me-chanics deals with the ultimate small things on the micro level. Relativity Theory deals with the cosmos taken as a whole on the macro level. Only a generation ago, at the time of talk about "paradigm shifts," it was believed that these two theories could not be synthesized. One chose whether he or she wished to deal with the micro or the macro and thereby chose the theory most useful. It appeared that Einstein's longed for "unified field theory" would not be forthcoming.[8] But there is now a claimant to the throne: "String Theory." This was predictable. Equally predictable is that it will forever be thus, the enthusiasm of the present claimants to the throne to the contrary notwith-standing, there will be other claimants who will grow from the ashes of the burnout of ongoing claimants, and for reasons we can articulate.

The paths by which our contemporaries are led to ever-new levels of theo-retical deductions from deductions are interesting. Let us just for one moment think Black Holes, for they obviously present no phenomenal evidence for their existence no matter what anyone says—Stephen Hawking to the con-trary notwithstanding. Black Holes were posited as an adjunct to Einstein's theory of curved space which was theoretically posited to solve yet other prior problems—I will return below to the conceptual conundrum that space being curved causes for us. It was assumed that for space to curve, a very significant force would have to be applied. Of the four posited forces, for a variety of reasons, gravity was chosen as the operative curving force.

To be adequate to the task, the gravitational force had to be immense, hence the mass and density of the gravitational object had to be almost unimaginable. Yet it had to be small since no one had seen it. Voila, very small, dense Black Holes that bend space as well as the light that is not simply absorbed into them. Nothing was left to do but work out the math, even though in another sense the math was the cause of positing their existence in the first place.[9]

Wait several decades and Stephen Hawking enters. He takes Black Holes as given and deduces their qualities. We learn of the "event horizon," that Black Holes are not as black as first thought, that there is some radiation that emerges from them, even more surprisingly that entropy occurs within them, and so on. And then emerge new forms of mathematics to support the posited premises, or already generated ideal mathematical forms are co-opted to do the job. The choice of the mathematical (linguistic?)[10] forms to be deployed (or invented) is itself, however, not mathematical. This is an element of groundless choice unless the ground is technological, but that implies the primacy of the good.

What we have are deductions from deductions, not to be despised by any means. Such theories represent some of the finest ingenuity, inventiveness and creativity of the human mind. Eventually we arrive at a point where we have a string (sorry) of deductions largely unsullied by the phenomena or the possibility of experimental validation. This is where we arrive with String Theory. Keep in mind, we have still not seen a Black Hole, directly or indirectly. Yet they form part of the web to which String Theory attaches its deductions, together with the Big Bang theory, plus the discoveries of particle physics and the notion of curved space gone wild, and on and on. Ideal, symbolic, mathematical languages are merged with other disparate ideal languages to create a novel form of poetry.

Having waited a couple of decades, eventually the creative intuition of man offered the possibility that if the micro and the macro, quantum mechanics and relativity theory, are to be unified, Black Holes may be in some sense central or even paradigmatic for the effort. Black Holes are both macro in the sense that they come into being, as it were, as part of relativity theory and its explanation of the cosmos as a whole, and micro in that they are the size of sub atomic particles (and hence belong to the realm explained by quantum mechanics). Hence the conclusion: a unified theory would have to explain Black Holes, their coming to be, their passing away if they do, their qualities and effects. In the process one would unify all past theories by finding a theoretically "prior" theory that accounts for them all. Thus enters, String Theory.

Now obviously the story is more complicated than this, and String Theory is as much a product of the imagination as it is a deduction from other theories; but nothing said so far is misleading. We have arrived at the evolving theory of strings as the ultimate building blocks of the cosmos, which is the object of my present reflections. Herein we are confronted with a theory that absolutely did not emerge through an interrogation of empirical phenomena, in principle has no experimental basis of validation, and has a particularly difficult time even presenting itself phenomenologically through metaphors, pictures and analogies.[11] One of the things the theory can explain best is precisely why no experiments will be fruitful in corroborating its truth value—e.g., one would need an accelerator the size of the known universe to disentangle the miniscule strings from the six-dimensional "space" around which they are allegedly wound.

At the heart of my present concerns is the relation between String Theory and the phenomena in the world in which we live, i.e., the things that appear and show themselves publicly to all—what I call the "middle realm" between the small Ones and One conceived as a whole. Modern physics set out to "explain" such publicly appearing phenomena so that regularities could be found and predictions and manipulations undertaken. Until recently, modern physics remained inextricably attached to the phenomena even if it thought it needed prior theoretical constructions to set up its experiments. But it knew those constructions to be hypothetical while taking the appearing phenomena to be the given.

Like its classical modern predecessors, String Theory is still posited as a potentially cumulative undertaking that is projected to evolve over generations, albeit primarily generations of mathematicians rather than experimental physicists—keep in mind **experimental** physicists cannot quit the phenomena. Further, in String Theory it is not primarily a projected progress of technical mastery that is posited, but a progress in actual ontological understanding. There is vague talk about all manner of speculative technologies that might be forthcoming, but of those speculations a thoughtful person should remain very skeptical.

Like its predecessors, String Theory communicates through a symbolic language, actually several increasingly rarefied symbolic languages and the ideal "realities" they posit. But String Theory differs from its predecessors in that it culminates in theories that in principle yield no experiments and hence it points toward no phenomena that can be made available to all—as phenomena in the true sense must. Phenomena are a problem for String Theory, yet it must nonetheless try to give phenomenal representations of its understanding. And therein we approach the problem.

String Theory is a massive exercise of the imagination, but the imagination is always, ultimately, determined by self-showing phenomena in its beginnings and must repeatedly recur to the phenomenal to bring itself to speech. **The intervening move to symbolic speech changes nothing.** The increasingly problematic link to phenomena in String Theory is unique and a worthy object of interrogation as to its consequences and especially its public ramifications. Make no mistake, modern physics has long since become a public phenomenon itself. This will remain true throughout the history of postmodern theoretical physics as it has been true in the past.[12]

It is not newsworthy to observe that modern physics is conducted in the language of mathematics. This was true from the beginning. The names of Copernicus, Kepler, Newton, et al make this clear. It was true of Ptolemy. But they used mathematics in attempts to explain pre-given phenomena available to all. Their hope was to discover regularities and make predictions about, and eventually manipulations of, those pre-given phenomena. What happens if that link to phenomena ceases to be the origin of theories as well as their goal? What happens if the theories are primarily explanations aimed at solving problems in previous theories in an ever expanding fashion and the move back to phenomena on any level becomes problematic, if not in principle impossible? And what are the public ramifications? Those are my central questions in what follows.

Hence it is not my intention to approach String Theory with an eye to the credibility of its mathematical presentation. That I leave to others. My issue is its relation to phenomena. I will pursue my interrogation through a reflection upon a popular treatment of the subject by one of the participants in the evolving theoretical position, Brian Greene in his *The Elegant Universe*. This approach is doubly to the point in that Greene's treatment was not only a popular success as a book but spawned a public television series. Hence we have access to the issue of the public face of modern physics as itself a phenomenon in the everyday world. Put another way, I want to reflect not only upon the question of the relation between modern physics and phenomena, but upon modern physics as itself a **public** phenomenon.

Green is alert to my central issue. He observes before launching his synopsis of String Theory and its predecessors:

> When extracted from their technical incarnation, the themes of modern physics are, quite literally, universal.
>
> Of late, this has become increasingly clear with physics' **ever more visible cultural presence**—there is a growing body of theatrical, musical, and artistic works that have drawn their inspiration from modern science. . . . While more speculative, [than relativity theory or quantum theory] superstring theory is now

generating major revisions once again. It is little wonder that artists, writers, composers, and film-makers are finding resonance between their work and these scientific challenges to the status quo. . . .
And it's not a one-way street. **Integrating the discoveries of physics into our collective worldview is a slow process . . . The arts may well be the perfect medium to fully integrate science into the world's conversation.** We may even find that the art world's scientifically inspired works will provide new stimulus to the scientific imagination and, in some possibly intangible way, prepare us for the next step in understanding the universe. Certainly, shifting the sharp spotlight illuminating science from the purely rigorous, numerical, and cognitive, to one with the **softer, more ambiguous glow of human sensibilities**, is enormously potent. . . . **Truly science is the thread that weaves us all into the fabric of reality.**[13] [my emphasis]

As regards the last observation, someone with a slightly flip attitude might wonder, "Says who?" But that is the central question I am raising. The primary question is: Who legitimized theoretical physicists as responsible for shaping our "worldview?" And do the physicists even know that "worldview" talk is metaphysically and philosophically loaded? And are physicists unaware that their own theory creation is shaped **by their prior, cultural "worldview?"** Where do they think that prior worldview came from? **What gives modern theoretical physics its cultural pretensions**, first, that it is actually engaged in ontology, and second, that it can and should inform the public, phenomenological world, or as Greene puts it, our "worldview?" There is only one basis upon which this pretension can be built, and it is not superior knowledge of the everyday phenomenological world we occupy, nor ontological "truth," but technology and technological sophistication. That is what gives modern physics public credibility.

As those who have had the patience to follow *Between Eternities* to this point will realize, what I have called political philosophy is the architectonic undertaking that can weave all of the parts of the whole together self-consciously using public speech, which is always a form of *poiesis*. My question is, by what right do modern, theoretical, mathematical physicists presume to that architectonic status, as so many do, as Greene clearly does, and as, by and large, the public unconsciously accepts?

In what I have argued above, I have presented political philosophy as a form of Reason that can operate in the public arena of phenomena, using public speech. It is not to be confused with the mystifying efforts of the medieval priests and theologians against whom modern philosophy and science, and that means against which modern political philosophy, cut its teeth. Priests and theologians are no longer the primary enemies of Reason any more than the primary contemporary enemy of modern liberal constitutionalism is the convergence of throne and altar against which liberalism cut its teeth. To aim one's cannons in those directions is now a pointless exercise.

My point will be that modern theoretical physics is not and never has been the only, or the best, exemplar of architectonic Rationalism, especially as it can never achieve autonomy let alone provide for its own foundations, or even self-consciously understand them. More than one person has remarked that the theoretical physicists of our day, with their arcane symbolic languages, are reminiscent of the medieval priests who determined the public worldview of yesteryear by mystifying everyday man with their rarified speech and exclusive access to the most important texts. Indeed there is at the very least this similarity—contemporary theoretical physicists cannot go any farther in public speech than yesterday's arcane theologians without eventual recurrence to the phrase "trust me."

One repeatedly hears permutations of the argument, "the proof is difficult, the mathematics complicated, it is very deep and arcane, trust me." And that means trust me when I tell you that our symbolic languages with their ideal realities do in fact correspond phenomenologically with everyday, historically determined speech and hence correspond with the world we all experience publicly. But it is precisely this correspondence that is in question. "You must trust me" that what I am telling you with pictures, analogies and metaphors from everyday speech and everyday phenomenal reality re-present or correspond with my symbolic speech and ideal realities.

But for the average sensible person a degree of healthy skepticism should enter here so that this latest version of "trust me" does not end up being comparable to trusting the medieval priest or an accountant at Enron. There is the real danger that the pretensions of some physicists to be ontologists will simply prey on public credulity. A higher Reason must defend against that outcome.

Of course one is in great danger here of being depicted as being quaint and curious and old-fashioned in taking on one of the icons of the age. But this simply will not do because the proof of the ontological status of what the physicists offer is something the physicists cannot provide. What is required is a philosophical critique. But this will not be forthcoming from the physicists because to their disadvantage, philosophy is as much anathema to most physicists as theology and this despite the number of articles of pure Faith upon which they proceed—of the latter more below.

There is more than a little trust and Faith wrapped up in the interstices of modern theoretical physics not only for the public but on the part of the physicists themselves. For now, simply recall Einstein's observation that "God does not play dice with the Universe." But that is a pure act of Faith; Chance and Accident could rule the Cosmos. Furthermore, Einstein's Faith clearly descends from the early modern positing of God as a mathematician rather than as a willful, personal and providential Being. And as regards Faith, who has not heard a version of the argument, "the mathematics are so beautiful that it must be true of the universe." Nonsense; beauty has nothing to do with it unless one has a faith that Truth and Beauty (and hence why not Justice as well?) necessarily go together.

On a more sophisticated level, it is an act of pure Faith to believe in a simple correspondence between the ideal entities of mathematics and the entities we encounter in the phenomenal world. It is one of the fundamental questions, enjoined in antiquity and still open today, to wonder about the relation between the ideal entities, whether of metaphysics or mathematics, and the phenomenal world in which we live. This is especially true of modern mathematics, which has broken with the ancient mathematical idealities, which were presumed to be self-subsisting ontological monads, essences and "Identities." Modern mathematics is a pure symbolic speech that presumes nothing of the kind.[14] And if we make the Derridean move of making symbols equivalent to signs and see signs as signifying nothing but other signs, we get close to the place modern theoretical physics increasingly now occupies.

Without ever entering the debate, "correspondence" and "representation" are presumed by all but the most sophisticated theoretical physicists. Their enthusiasm is charming, but their *naïveté* is a matter of concern when they presume to possess the philosophical autonomy and moral and political insight to shape our public view of reality as does Greene, and that means shaping our public view of the Good.

This issue of the autonomy of contemporary physics cuts even deeper than we have seen so far. Modern science was not, in its beginnings, self-consciously aware, and is even less aware today, of its embeddedness in prior pre-scientific perceptions. For example, even Einstein was prepared to admit that the cosmos could be eternal and unchanging. But modern physics has since its inception been predominantly committed to a belief that the cosmos had a temporal origin. But this is primarily because modern theoretical physics is a phenomenon of the West, which is heir to the Scriptural legacy of creation, which presents far more theoretical conundrums than does the idea of an eternal cosmos. Without that act of Faith, modern physics could have just as easily provided mathematical explanations consistent with an eternal universe.

Nietzsche suggested even more radically that modern physics is enslaved to political and moral perceptions that are primarily democratic. This issue of the primacy of the pre-scientific perceptions that emerge from everyday phenomena could be developed at length. But the physicist has no right to complain one way or the other unless he or she can provide the philosophical proof of the immaculate generation of their fundamentally phenomenal, theoretical ideas and imaginings, which cannot be done. Passing originally phenomenal origins for concepts through symbolic forms of speech in no way purges contemporary theories of their phenomenal origins.

All that need be said at present is that contemporary theoretical physics is in no way capable of enjoining this issue. Hence it can never prove its autonomy; it can only take it on Faith. So for all the physicist knows, one forms one's theories on a prejudiced basis one cannot command. The physicist then abstracts from the phenomena that determined the original acts of imagination to pass the resultant intuitions through some form of symbolic speech that one has to assume corresponds and represents the original phenomenally determined intuitions. The theoretical physicist then leaps back to the pre-scientific realm where one is forced to use poetic speech to try to explain the yield publicly, and that even means to oneself and fellow physicists.

Through this necessary move back to public speech, the process is repeated, picking up yet new pre-scientific determinations on the basis of analogies, models and pictures, and burying the original foundations under deeper and deeper levels of allegedly autonomous symbolic sedimentation. How is the outcome autonomous? Why should an undertaking so lacking in self-conscious awareness inform our public "worldview," especially when it arrives at a point where it cannot have a technological yield? Make no mistake, in what follows **I will disagree mightily with Heidegger that technology is the great postmodern problem.** Modern science is far better served by retaining its technological link for that simultaneously links it to phenomena and limits its ontological pretensions. **The mythic faith in autonomy and ontology is the far greater problem.**

In what follows I will primarily be interested in pointing out some of the conceptual conundrums that plague contemporary speculative physics and show its lack of clarity and philosophical underpinnings. I will also try to point out some of the problems that emerge from the unavoidable, yet disconnected moves back and forth from the phenomenal to the ideal realm of modern, symbolic mathematics—a split, incidentally, that rather straightforwardly reproduces the relation between the sensible and supra-sensible realms that emerges in textbook accounts of Platonism.[15] The ideal/real, sensible/supra-sensible splits keep reproducing themselves in different ways and always will. In this vein, I will suggest some of the ways in which contemporary theoretical physics keeps reproducing fundamental conceptual conundrums that go back to the Greeks who first self-consciously grasped them. **These conundrums will never be transcended.**

Let me reduce to a formula what I will be suggesting. At present I will be able to give only the briefest of examples to indicate why I reach these conclusions. I will be giving suggestions not proofs. But that is of the nature of the subject matter. As with Aristotle's *arche*, some things one must just "see" and grasp directly. 1) There is something unique about the latest moves in theoretical physics; they are derivative not of direct attempts to explain readily "visible" phenomena, but of attempts to synthesize and solve the problems of prior competing theories which still had, if not a primary at least a secondary, relation to phenomena. 2) Almost in principle no confirming or validating rigorous experimental tests can verify a theory like String Theory, hence it has to be validated on other grounds. 3) Yet even in this most speculative of theories there remains the necessity to move back and forth from an ideal language to everyday language and the related need to take ideal realities and give them phenomenal representations. 4) All manner of conceptual nightmares are introduced in these moves back and forth from the ideal to the phenomenal. 5) Eventually what we see is that speculative physics loses sight of what it is doing, is unaware of its philosophical and metaphysical commitments and of how many purely phenomenal elements it carries with it unawares. 6) All of this leads to the conclusion that contemporary speculative physics, despite its frequent self-perception, cannot be ontology and absolutely is not and cannot be an autonomous activity because it cannot conquer and master its foundations in the phenomenal. Only political philosophy can rise to a higher level of self-conscious clarity.

Let us now commence more or less at the beginning. When I first encountered geometry as a boy I was undoubtedly one of the few concerned by the fact that a point was posited as having no dimensionality, while an obviously extended line was posited as made up of points. My teacher was philosophically unaware that the appropriate answer to my concern was that we were dealing with ideal realities and not phenomenal ones and therefore I should just get over it. She should have told me that as with the triangle, the "real" one exists only in the ideal realm. There are no pure triangles in the phenomenal world; the phenomenal triangles are hardly worth calling even approximations. We have my boyhood conundrum reproduced in String Theory with a vengeance.

In the latest theory, everything that "is" is posited as being composed of strings. The strings in turn are posited as one-dimensional closed loops. We have Euclid's line curved back on itself achieving closure. A rubber band is "sort of" a phenomenal analogy, except that a rubber band is a three dimensional phenomenal object while our string is an ideal mathematical "object." We have a first indication of the difficulty of moving from the ideal to the phenomenal.

Everything, from the elemental particles—including the various quarks that form protons, electrons and neutrons and so on—to the four forces—strong, weak, electromagnetic, gravity, including the corresponding "messenger" particles, gluons, bosons, photons, gravitons —are posited as made up of strings. What differentiates the strings is not something intrinsic to the "stuff" of which the string is composed—yet ultimately strings are clearly represented as forms of matter even though that is not strictly possible for an ideal entity—but to the varying motions, vibrations or "harmonies" to which the strings give manifestation. With the last term of the three (harmonies), we have clearly entered not just the realm of phenomenal representation but the arena of metaphor and poetry (in the strict sense of Greek *poiesis*). And it is a poetic metaphor already used by the Greeks long ago.

Let us simply presume for the present that something one-dimensional can vibrate, and that terms like frequency and amplitude can be made metaphorically useful in our one-dimensional world. We have an issue not unlike the one that emerges when we ask if my non-dimensional point from plane geometry can "move" in three dimensional space—how many dimensions are needed to account for motion? Try as one might, can one conceptualize vibrating as anything but a motion? Can an ideal, one-dimensional "thing" actually move?

According to the theory, the nature of the various, presumably quantitatively more than qualitatively distinct vibrations, accounts for whether we are dealing with a particle (i.e., "matter"—and henceforth "matter" and "extension" and "space" and like terms have to be bracketed) or a force ("energy"). At the core of all that is one finds vibrating, one-dimensional strings which are 10^{-20} the size of a nucleus, hence in principle incapable of any empirical manifestation, presumably not even the indirect manifestation of a trail in a cloud chamber by which we infer the existence of much larger particles. Hence almost in principle the existence of strings cannot be verified by rigorous, or any, experimental tests. To claim that this is only true now pending the invention of some fabulous new measuring tool strains one's patience.

The idea of vibrating strings as the ultimate building blocks of the universe takes the place of the traditional "point particle" notion that holds sway in everything from the atoms of Lucretius to the quarks of the day before yesterday. That said, today's strings are still conceptualized as most decidedly "One" for they cannot be divided and are not made of anything smaller. Strings, like rubber bands, may have a hole in the middle but they are like all past point particle notions in still being indivisible, or One. But why is it, since I would assert that it is true, that it is easier to represent a point particle as One rather than a string; for to my mind it simply is conceptually easier?

Despite being represented as extension, the ultimate "stuff" that gives reality or substance to our one-dimensional strings is left ambiguous by the move to vibrations or motions as determinative. What is the actual stuff that vibrates? What qualities does it have? And yet if we think about it, the metaphors used to explain the vibrations also imply qualitative difference[16]—different vibrations almost necessarily have to be phenomenally represented tonally. The vibrations are likened to notes and it is suggested that there are also harmonies (call them "symmetries" if you like but nothing thereby changes) operating in the smallest interstices of the cosmos. Of course this notion taps into a very old poetic intuition. For me that is not embarrassing for I assert that there are a finite set of such notions that cannot be transcended and in various permutations repeat.

For example, we are reminded of the "myth of Er" that Plato puts in Socrates's mouth at the end of the *Republic*. In that depiction, at the core of the cosmos, its engine room as it were, there are multiple sirens overseeing spinning whorls that produce notes that combine into a harmony. Motion and notes and harmony are at the core of all that is. Again, as I will suggest throughout, there is a finite set of primordial conceptual notions that get reused throughout time. And they can be combined only in certain ways without the outcome being a conceptual nightmare.

Still lurking behind all String Theories, which posit motion as a building block—and I used the plural because unfortunately at present there are at least five different String Theories that still need to be combined or synthesized into one "M theory"—are the ultimate primordial questions of what supplied the original motion to cause the strings to vibrate, will that motion wear down, will the primordial force that caused it be reapplied, and like questions. We are forced to ask for an external cause for the initial coming to be in motion of anything because the idea of self-motion is for a physicist simply a philosophical cop out. What would it mean to say that the cosmos is self-caused—would that imply it was a form of Will, of self-conscious Will? Physicists dare not go to these environs which will land one fairly quickly in the lap of something like Hegel's philosophy of Nature or some version of Theology—so why open the door in the first place? But even if the cosmos and/or its motion was self-caused, would that not mean that it was eternal rather than commencing at a certain moment? Questions like this indicate that at best String Theory cannot get at the ultimate first things or an explanation of them. That is obvious. That alone is reason not to presume to ontology.

How do we get at the issue of what caused the initial motion in the cosmos, or the "stuff" in which the motion takes place, or is all motion determined by something that only "is" external to primordial "stuff?" Can one conceptualize motion without matter? One cannot say that strings are not in some sense "stuff" and still say that they vibrate, because a Nothing or void cannot move and vibration is a motion. There are conceptual conundrums beyond which we cannot get and no mathematical ideality will move us beyond them. If one can live with conceptual nightmares one might as well just side with the worst of the worst theologians in some of their more preposterous speculation, or just say that everything is mysterious.

But let us give String Theory its due. It responded to a prior situation that was itself problematic. For all its genius, relativity theory operated on such a macro level that it had almost no predictive value in the world we occupy, let alone the world of microscopic things. And as individuals like Hawking pointed out, on some things Einstein was just wrong. On the microscopic level dominated by quantum mechanics and particle physics more generally there was a veritable riot of particles coming to be and a microscopic frenzy that was disquieting—for example, quantum frenzy was an immense problem from the perspective of chemistry where electrons moved predictably in various orbit-like shells.

As we continued to search for the ultimate point particle, it was found that the basic, original three subatomic particles were composed of quarks of different kinds. Electrons were formed of quarks 2 up/1 down, protons of quarks with an up and a down, neutrons by quarks 2 down/1 up. Then there were four other quarks—charm, strange, bottom, top. Beyond this there were seemingly unattached particles zipping about, really small neutrinos, really heavy electrons called muons, and other heavy electrons called tau, and then tau-neutrinos and muon-neutrinos, and the four messenger force particles and then each had an anti-particle cousin and then the positing of dark matter composed of literally God knows what. Many of the particles existed only momentarily and not as part of anything we encounter in our world, coming to be in large accelerators due to powerful collisions duplicating, it was alleged by an act of pure Faith, what happened at the alleged Big Bang. This riot of particles was not intellectually satisfying. The fundamental longing of the mind to reduce multiplicity to a One, and to find a One as the ultimate explanatory principle came into play. And it will come into play over and over again. The old Greek preoccupation with attempting to explain the many in relation to a One is an intellectual necessity that will ever reproduce itself.

Then there was the issue of the microscopic frenzy itself that was predicted by quantum mechanics. When the microscopic world was depicted, compared with the world we occupy, its seemed utterly bizarre. Further, what seemed like mass and matter to past physicists, when pushed far enough, actually became bundles or lumps of energy. And these bundles were then conceptualized as waves. But matter as a wave phenomenon was only capable of probabilistic explanations, due to being limited to predicting the probability of where to find, for example, any given electron. We arrived at Heisenberg's Indeterminacy Principle. Where there had been the orderly rotation of electrons in various shells—the explanation still relied upon by modern chemistry, which has significant technological applicability—now there was in the frenzy and indeterminacy at the microscopic level a huge door through which a dreaded element of Chance could enter the cosmos.

And the fungibility of the relation between matter and energy that crept in was reminiscent of classical Greek debates over whether the ultimate building blocks of the cosmos were matter/stuff or motion/energy. Einstein was, in the thinking that led to $e=mc^2$, still fairly traditional in positing the two as different even if convertible back and forth. But transforming matter into bundles of energy reduced a two to a One. Matter as traditionally understood became something of an epiphenomenon.

And therein we were back to the same conceptual discussions and difficulties of the Greeks. At the bottom of all things do we find One, Two or Many building blocks that are irreducible? Must we be monists, dualists, pluralists? A monist like Lucretius, following out Epicurean atomism, posited a materialistic monism. Everything is reducible to One, to matter understood as atoms, understood as indivisible Ones. Yet even he had to sneak in elements into the account to take the place of energy. The atoms were eternally "falling," only God knows where. But that accounted for motion. Combination was more difficult. One of the parallel falling atoms had to "swerve," hitting others and starting the chain reactions that created a cosmos. Therein, like quantum mechanics, an element of Chance sneaked in.

Anaxagoras tried to be a Mind (*nous*) monist. Mind or will, like energy was a first cause. But what did it move; because of that problem, even Anaxagoras got hung up in materialism. Plato's Socrates reports that he liked Anaxagoras's monistic idealism better than monistic materialism, but was disappointed when Anaxagoras then sneaked in discussions of the four elements, which is to say matter. This matter/energy, One/Two/Many issue is as old as thought. It is reproduced in different permutations in modern theoretical physics and it will forever be reproduced, for no experiment and no mathematical sophistication will eliminate the need to operate within basic concepts that are prior to any experiment and any attempt at a pure symbolic language. There is a finite set of basic primordial concepts to which the mind inevitably returns. And there are only so many plausible and non-contradictory ways to combine them.

The energy/mass dichotomy cannot be transcended. Hence that leaves us stuck with an untranscendable Two. If so, the conceptual attempt to reduce matter to bundles of energy (as a primordial One) will lead to conundrums. Take the following as the briefest of examples. If the various particles are quanta of energy and the various forces can be explained by "messenger" particles[17] what one has attempted to do is reduce a Two to a One. Let us call this One that accounts for the seeming Two the Same. Let us call this Same, whatever it is, X. Therefore, in the formula $e=mc^2$, both $e=X$, and $m=X$. The famous formula $e=mc^2$ can therefore be rewritten as $X=Xc^2$. Now if we divide each side by X we end up with the formula $1 = c^2$. In my cosmos that is an absurdity and would cause us to go back and conceptually rethink.

Recall again that Einstein was positing that energy and mass were convertible into each other, that they were a Two. Quantum mechanics looked for a One but got instead incredible multiplicity. String Theory hoped to transcend Quantum multiplicity by suggesting another One. But it gets caught in the twoness of the matter/energy duality. This is an age old conundrum, one that String Theory simply reproduces on a new level. But the unsatisfying nature of where physics had arrived before String Theory was increasingly bizarre from a phenomenal as well as conceptual point of view. And the profusion of particles was quite aesthetically displeasing. This forced the mind to think anew. But rather than going back to the phenomena and starting with new assumptions, String Theory co-opted its premises from the competing theories already in the field. It is derivative of those theories not in any sense directly related to phenomena. In co-opting prior premises it simply co-opted the attendant conundrums.

Greene depicts the sociological situation arrived at before the emergence of String Theory as one that caused young physicists ennui. "The success of [some of the founders of String Theory] finally trickled down even to first-year graduate students, and an electrifying sense of being on the inside of a profound moment in the history of physics displaced the previous ennui." (*Elegant Universe*, 139) Both the ennui and the excitement are human all too human. And physics is a human undertaking bound by the limitations of our shared, phenomenal humanity. Unfortunately, those who think they are on the verge of the final theory, like those who long for the End of History, fail to take into account that ennui and longing for the new will endlessly repeat themselves as human phenomena. No matter what theory gains momentary hegemony, this longing for the new will continually repeat itself. That is predictable. We will always long for the finished understanding, and always long for the new. The two operating together will lead to endless theorizing around a finite number of predictable conundrums. **Technology can progress, theorizing will only change within predictable parameters.**

To return to our sketch of String Theory, why there was an incentive for a new theory is clear. But what is posited in String Theory is ultimately no more conceptually clear than anything that went before. But we do get notions that seem novel until they are reduced to their core components, concepts and primordial elements. At its most bizarre, String Theory posits that there are in fact ten dimensions within which primordial strings operate. If one wants to call Time a dimension, as did Einstein, then in the theories that predate String Theory there were four dimensions, the three dimensions of Space plus Time.

In String Theory we have Time plus nine spatial dimensions (in one per-mutation of String Theory there are ten spatial dimensions). Yet the traditional three dimensions of Space retain a certain unity, and I would argue priority, within the alleged nine spatial dimensions. In effect, and the conceptual nightmares abound at this point, at the moment just after the alleged Big Bang—and we would still need to think about the origin of Time in any sense, did Time exist before the Bang—only three of the spatial dimensions expanded. The other six, or seven, did not expand but got "curled up," folded and constricted in unique ways because the very tiny strings that are the building blocks of everything were wound around them. At this point it is necessary to think rubber bands wound around some elaborate piece of incredibly elastic origami constricted in its ability to expand. One must simultaneously think this notion 1) on the scale of 10^{-20} the size of a nucleus, with 2) one-dimensional strings wrapped around the six dimensional origami, but with 3) the unique six dimensions extended within the traditional three dimensions (and if you can do all that I would like to sell you . . . Oh never mind). The actual configuration of the strings in the traditional three dimensions of space is at this point impossible to conceptualize phenomenally any more than how the new six spatial dimensions are extended within the traditional three dimensions of space.

The strings are posited as the building blocks of everything, matter as well as energy. But in the theory, what energy "is," for example, is due to both the unique vibrating of the strings and the unique windings of the strings around the six non-tradition dimensions of space. The winding causes a tension, as it were, that "releases" energy. (Obviously this implies a winder.) How something wound so tightly as to cause this tension can also vibrate is a bit mysterious. But perhaps that is not as mysterious as how this six-dimensional Space is being conceptualized such that it can provide a "resistance" that makes the winding and tensing possible. Space so understood is being conceived to have solidity of some kind. Further, why the traditional three dimensions of space were exempted from winding/folding/compressing/tensing is not clear. And "where" the six new dimensions of space "are" other than "in" the traditional three dimensions of space is equally mysterious.

I defy anyone to sort this out conceptually, let alone phenomenally represent it. Greene argues that one of the prime factors in favor of String Theory is that it is "elegant" and aesthetically beautiful. These kind of conceptual nightmares are not my idea of elegant or beautiful. **But why aesthetics should be the criteria of validity is not at all clear.** And to be able to empirically test these symbolic forms of poetry would require translating this explanation into some form of phenomenal representation that I would argue is impossible without picking up all manner of pre-theoretical presuppositions and assumptions.

Following the presumptions accepted and posited by String Theory, let us say that at the first nano-second before the Big Bang we have everything that "is" in a state that is compacted into the mother of all Black Holes.[18] That initial cosmic Black Hole in principle must be all that "is." "Surrounding" it therefore, must be Nothing. Can there be Space where there is Nothing? (Never mind the small problem of whether we want to say that Space "is.") Obviously not. But can the mother of all Black Holes be conceptualized as extended, and hence as itself having Space? It is hard to say, but probably not. Can there at this primordial moment "be" Time? No. Because unless one wants to posit some theologically primordial time, Time is linked to motion and motion implies movement from one place in Space to another and where there is no Space there is Nothing. And there really is no Space in a Black Hole which is so dense that it is seamlessly One. If it is not seamlessly One it is not a Black Hole. Conceptual difficulties like this cannot be solved by any experiment nor by any mathematical language.

Our first issue is at what point can it be said that Space and Time "are." Certainly not at the "time" of the mother of all Black Holes qua inert Parmenidean One which is surrounded by Nothing because it qua One is all that "is." We have something that is infinitely dense, and therefore totally One, and surrounded by Nothing because it is by definition every**thing** that is (of course one notices that the word "thing" is problematic here). If surrounded by Nothing, our primordial Black Hole cannot move because that would be to go from nowhere to nowhere, and nothing could move within it as it is totally dense. So before the Big Bang there was no Space, no motion, no Time. What could cause the primordial Black Holes to "explode" or expand is as mysterious as why the Scriptural God, if He was perfect, needed to create a cosmos.

Are we not just playing conceptual games with theoretical physics when we try to force the products of mathematical imagination into conceptual form, never mind that that is what the physicists do whenever they try to explain themselves publicly, using public speech? No, for we have no other tools to work with than those public concepts that emerge in public speech. I will further insist that the imagination, whether that of the physicist or anyone else, always takes off from finite concepts and always simultaneously takes off from a phenomenal basis and can never transcend the hegemony of the phenomenal any more than the hegemony of the conceptual. And this is true of all ideal languages, mathematics included. If we are limited by a finite set of concepts that we can push our images into, and there are conceptual necessities in the way those concepts can relate to each other, there are some things that simply cannot be thought and it is not a manifestation of Reason to ignore that fact. But theoretical physics frequently ignores that fact and that is why it is not the highest manifestation of Reason.

Leaving aside what I believe are insurmountable problems already encountered, I return to our primordial Black Hole, which expands suddenly, and necessarily from an external force if it is a seamless One. In principle as coming from "outside," that force comes from out of Nothing and Nowhere because that force cannot come from within if a Black Hole is by definition actually dense and One and we dispense with the notion of self-cause as a philosophical cop out.[19] Even the notion "expand" has to be metaphorical if what we have is a motion that moves from nowhere to nowhere precisely because we are expanding into Nothing. Likewise our One was originally "in" Nothing and hence it could not be anywhere either.[20]

An allegedly expanding universe cannot be posited as infinite for as expanding it is always in principle expanding into Nothing and hence always surrounded by Nothing. But what I would ask here is, is it not clear that Nothing is now being conceived as Space qua void? Is not one of the ways that physics conceptualizes space—as opposed to its conceptualization as extended three dimensions—as a void, vacuum or Nothing? Can a Nothing be three-dimensional; how many dimensions does Nothing have? One can see why some philosophers concluded long ago that there might be fewer problems in assuming the Cosmos was eternal and infinite, or in conceiving Space not as a void but as a plasma or gel. I would suggest in fact that while the Big Bang implies expanding into space qua Nothing, String Theory comes close to conceptualizing space as a plasma or gel around which things can wind and gain tension.

Where there is expansion there is a form of motion. Motion must take place in Space. Where there is Space and Motion there can be Time. Is it possible to think Time as in any way "existent" except where there is motion? The relation of Time and Space to Motion is still retained by relativity theory; the bending and warping of both Time and Space changes nothing substantial on the conceptual level. Motion requires "open" spaces if it is to avoid resistance or even deflection. So maybe motion requires space understood as a void. Can there be motion in less than the traditional three dimensions? Further, motion must be the motion of something, of matter. Can the thing that moves be one or two dimensional, or must it in principle be three dimensional and moving in three dimensionality?

Time is the time it takes for some "thing" or other to move from one place to another. If so, can there be Time in the dimensions that are curled up and provide no room to move because of the constricting strings wrapped around them (unless they and the strings are somehow "in" the other three spatial dimensions)? I will not belabor the matter further; the Big Bang theory, as extended by String Theory, is a conceptual nightmare. And all of these reflections abstract from Heidegger's assertion that the notions of Time and Space that physics uses are derivative from a phenomenologically prior showing of spatiality and especially of temporality as "ecstatic."

So let us forget about Black Holes and Big Bangs for the moment and back up and see if we can sort out this notion of six or seven more or less non-traditional dimensions of space all "curled up" on each other but nonetheless presumably existing in the traditional three dimensions of space — and do not underestimate the conundrums this causes if the nine or ten total dimensions are not on some level equal, and that means equal in terms of the conceptualization of the traditional three. This takes us back to Einstein and some purely ideal mathematical positings that come from so-called Calabi-Yau mathematics.

Traditionally, for physicists Space was seen as everywhere uniform and was conceptualized by a uniform three-dimensional grid. Likewise Time was conceptualized as a uniform passing of quantifiable nows understood on the basis of the duration of uniform motion from one place to another. Relativity theory argues that Space is not simply uniform as traditionally understood because it can be curved by large and dense objects. Furthermore, Time is not uniform because it can be affected or likewise "warped" by motion, especially acceleration and deceleration. At high speeds, and especially at accelerating or decelerating speeds, in the vicinity of the speed of light, Time bends or warps by which is meant it speeds up or slows down, although these latter notions require a frame of reference like normal earth time and certainly imply a fixed point outside the motion. Under certain circumstances involving immense speeds and immense densities it is posited that Space and Time also merge in such a fashion that their union creates Space/Time.

The warping of Space yields a fairly straightforward phenomenal representation. We can from such a representation see that objects that travel through curved space travel a greater distance than they would if it were possible to draw a straight line from any point A to any point B along a curved space. But if space itself is curved, nothing can in fact travel on that straight line. It is more difficult to give a phenomenal representation to warped time but even there a common-sensical explanation can be given. The representation of the melding of Space and Time presents all manner of phenomenal difficulties. But to present the lurking conceptual conundrums let me stick to the warping of Space.

The Greeks had at one time conceptualized Space as a plasma or gel, which is what held the planets in place, and kept them from "falling." The moderns of course ridiculed this notion and presented Space as a void, indeed a vacuum. It was the interplay of gravitational forces and centrifugal forces that kept bodies not so much suspended but in their orbits and relative relations to other bodies. **But a void is a Nothing, and you cannot warp a Nothing.** Not only to represent, but to think space as curved requires thinking it as a substance of some kind, e.g., like a plasma or gel. Let us say that if space is curved it must be a plasma-like something or other. If so it must have mass. Maybe this explains the posited "dark matter" that is supposed to exist throughout space, which we had not previously taken it into account because we had not taken into account the plasma-like nature, and attendant mass, of space itself. Or have we created a conceptual problem precisely because of the need to move from an ideal mathematical reality to a phenomenal representation? But that move is necessary if we are to undertake any validating experiment of any theory, which has to take place in the phenomenal not the ideal realm.[21] It is also necessary if we wish to speak in public about our findings.

Let me suggest that we know no more now what Space "is" than we ever have or ever will. Is it a void, a Nothing or a plasma? Is it "extended," uniform, curved, warped, etc.? Likewise we do not know what "matter" or "energy" or Time or anything else really "are." In fact, no one has ever actually explained how something as central as Gravity works or why it is a force that is different, say, than magnetism. Relativity theory does not provide an explanation of what Space and Time "are," and it simply represents Gravity using the picture of something like the motion of a marble moving through curved space with the curve drawing it toward the larger object that warped space in the first place. In this understanding, Gravity "is" curved/warped Space/Time. That definition is every bit as mysterious as saying that Gravity is an intrinsic force of attraction, which is not however magnetic or electromagnetic but is an independent force.

And under relativity theory, with all of the competing gravitational forces, there have to be multiple curves in space, and explaining how they relate to each other, let alone phenomenally representing the matter, really is not possible. So in actuality, in explaining gravity, relativity theory has made no advance over Newton who simply posited it and came up with a mathematical constant to predict it. Ontologically, we still do not know what it "is," any more than Space or Time or Matter or Energy or anything else.

But to return to String Theory, it builds on the intuition that space is not a uniform matrix without substance, not a Nothing or vacuum as traditionally conceived. The "folded" curvatures of six-dimensional Space have a substance like quality. Still, the three unfolded dimensions that did expand presumably still have to be understood in the older matrix/void fashion.

Prior to the emergence of String Theory, two mathematicians had already worked out the ideal mathematics for multi-dimensional geometrical shapes in an ideal, symbolic language operating in its purest form with no attempt at phenomenal representations. The mathematics of especially six-dimensional geometrical shapes proved useful for String Theory, but without marrying that ideal work with the intuition of curved space as offered by relativity theory, this ideal mathematics would probably have remained precisely that, ideal.

The allegedly six-dimensional shapes that String Theory hangs its hat on, Calabi-Yau shapes or spaces, were named for the two mathematicians who developed the original mathematics. But the problem becomes how to phenomenally represent such a thing or how it relates to predictions in the phenomenal world. When one looks at the phenomenal representations that Greene supplies, one sees intricately inter-wound curved and folded plane surfaces that are alleged to give six dimensions, which are nonetheless unbelievably minute as opposed to the three dimensions that allegedly expanded at the time of the Big Bang.

From the phenomenal representations provided in Greene's book, one can see that to get from one point to another in this six-dimensional sub-space would require movement along a very complicated and convoluted path that is massively longer than what common sense would take to be the straight line path. To say as Greene does that "you must bear in mind that the image has built-in limitations" is an understatement. Nothing is solved by the observation that "we are trying to represent a six-dimensional shape on a two-dimensional piece of paper, and this introduces significant distortions." (*Elegant Universe*, 207) What we have is yet another sign of the conundrums we introduce when moving from the ideal to the phenomenal.

The conceptual problem that emerges from the representation of six-dimensional Calabi-Yau space is that we can see that the complicated, alleged six dimensions have "shape," which implies substance, plasma or gel of some form. This is not a void or Nothing. Even if these unbelievably micro "spaces" around which strings allegedly wind themselves are in fact within traditional, three-dimensional Space, we see that there have to be spatial "places" or "spaces" that are nonetheless void and empty within which the other six exist. If the small folded six dimensions are not "in" traditional three-dimensional space it is impossible to grasp "where" they are supposed to be. And it then becomes a mystery how the old three dimensions and the new six (or seven) dimensions are supposed to be related. And does Time only transpire in the traditional three-dimensional matrix or only in the compact folded six dimensions or in both?

But my central concerns can be solved quite easily, can they not? Let us just admit that the naïve enthusiasm of our theoretical physicists that they are engaged in ontology should be put aside. And then it becomes clear that if they are not explaining the actual fabric of reality they certainly have no basis for informing our "worldviews." And the public would be better off if it knew that. But if twenty-first century theoretical physics, and postmodern physics more generally, is not ontology it might at least still be technologically useful. But String Theory of all theories seems the least technologically useful precisely because of its distance from the phenomena of our world and its inability to generate plausible phenomenal representations, which are the prerequisite for useful experiments. So it appears that we cannot judge such theories ontologically or technologically. The only remaining criterion of validity seems to be beauty, which is to say aesthetics: "The mathematical structure of string theory was so beautiful and had so many miraculous properties that it had to be pointing toward something deep." (137; Greene is quoting John Schwarz)

Here, perhaps, even more than anywhere else, beauty is in the eye of the beholder. **One wonders why the physicists think their aesthetic "eyes" are better than any others.** I would find a more beautiful criterion to be an explanation that "saves the phenomena," the phenomena the explanation of which set the effort in motion in the first place. **Why is not saving the phenomena a better criterion for judging theories than a physicist's conception of beauty?** I would argue that that is the best criteria.

String Theory's beauty is an article of Faith to add to many other articles of Faith upon which it and theoretical physics more generally are based. This is true especially of the central article of Faith of physicists that the laws governing phenomenal change are fixed. Greene admits that without this article of Faith, "the simplest acts [in the phenomenal world] would be an adventure, since random variations would prevent you or anyone else from using past experience to predict anything about future outcomes. . . . Such a universe is a physicist's nightmare. Physicists—and most everyone else as well—rely crucially upon the stability of the universe. . . . Rather it means that the laws governing such evolution are fixed and unchanging. **You might ask whether we really know this to be true. In fact we don't.**" (168) [my emphasis]

The premise seems to be: "if it must be then it is," therefore, we will proceed "as if" this and many other things are true. But even here, this Faith operates in the phenomenal realm. And in this context, what is meant by "must be"? Is it flippant to conclude that the answer is "so that physicists do not have nightmares"? Is one a curmudgeon to observe that the sleep habits and mental stability of physicists may not be a cosmically high priority for the rest of us?

As yet another article of Faith we get the acceptance of the "intrinsic aesthetic appeal of [an] **egalitarian treatment of all motion.**" (170) [my emphasis] Here we can refer back to the Nietzsche quote above. That we are well disposed to the egalitarian elements of democracy does not mean that those principles operate in the cosmos as a whole unless we are determined that our physics supports our democracy and is determined by it as the highest value. In the process physics loses all autonomy. I for one would also find more beautiful those theories that are aware of their presuppositions and confront them most openly and self-consciously.

Despite the centrality of aesthetic attachments, there is the problem that while the total applicability of physical laws would require the hegemony of iron Necessity, the seeming need for Chance is the basis of the imagination and creativity that lies at the heart of theoretical physics. The age old problem of Freedom and Necessity cannot be dismissed in theoretical physics anymore than anywhere else. As a counter article of Faith and aesthetic taste I would assert that I follow Nietzsche in concluding that the existence of a little bit of Chance is not only a reassuring fact, but one that makes the cosmos more loveable and beautiful because it makes choice and Freedom and imagination and philosophy itself, not to mention physics, possible.

Many contemporary physicists allow the possibility of Chance. It is enshrined in the indeterminacy at the heart of quantum mechanics. But even String Theory admits of the possibility. Greene admits that to date the mathematics of String Theory only yields "approximations." As such it is a form of "perturbation theory." But rather than simply accept that as a given why does Greene yield to another article of Faith: "given the recent tremendous progress in non-perturbative methods and their successful application to . . . aspects of black holes, string theorists have high hopes that it won't be long before the mysteries residing at the center of black holes start to unravel." (344) Which is the bigger act of Faith, the faith in a future non-perturbative precision, the faith in the ontological existence of Black Holes themselves, the Faith in Chance, the Faith in God as an external first cause?

Of String Theory as a whole one could say what Greene says of an imaginary four-dimensional beach ball, that "it's pretty close to impossible to picture such a [thing] in your mind's eye." (322) Quite true. I would suggest that this is a sign that twenty-first century theoretical physics is close to transforming itself into a game for a small club of individuals working out derivative puzzles using an arcane language and asking us to "trust them." It is an undertaking that presumes to ontology, and thereby the right to inform our public doings, but actually can't even explain the phenomena of the world in which we live. Theoretical physics as a cultural phenomenon has fostered the belief that it is doing ontology in the mind of the public. **In this, today's theoretical physicists simply play on the credulity of the public in precisely the same way that priests and theologians did in the past.** And keep in mind that they are committed believers with their articles of Faith just like those past theologians.

The reason physicists get away with a public faith in them as ontologists is that in the background as proof of the status of their knowledge is the premise, "we gave you bombs and microwaves, rockets to Mars and lasers and a whole panoply of useful gadgets." But technology and ontology are two different things. Plumbers, electricians and engineers never presume to be ontologists. My premise is that postmodern physicists will be best served by tying their efforts to technology, and experiment and speech in the phenomenal realm. Physics will be best served by keeping its feet on the ground of phenomena and its imagination close to its feet.

As technology, postmodern Physics can avoid a descent into parochial aesthetics, bad poetry and what amounts to a Mandarin pastime for a few which is not unlike a sophisticated form of chess. An experimental physics that remains tied to the phenomena can be all to the good. Non-phenomenal theoretical physics masquerading as ontology is not good for Physics or for the public understanding, and should be reined in. The physicists themselves should come to see why this self-discipline is to their advantage, and that requires that they get a more comprehensive education than they do now. **Contemporary physicists tend to be some of the least liberally educated among all contemporary professions.** The rest of us should maintain toward physics masquerading as ontology the same healthy skepticism we direct to medieval theology.

If the connection to technology is lost, contemporary physics will publicly begin to look like the arcane, Mandarin pastime it is becoming. Or perhaps the analogy would be to the extremely prescient "glass bead game" of Hermann Hesse.[22] If as is absolutely predictable, there will continue to be differing products of the imagination offered by physicists as ontology, and at times differing theories implying different ontological commitments that explain the same phenomena, there are only limited bases for choosing among theories: 1) technical applicability, 2) pure taste and aesthetics, or 3) the unself-conscious ideological presuppositions of the individual practitioners (why are so few physicists conservatives?), or 4) The Good for man. But the Good is the object of political philosophy, not physics, and I see no basis upon which the physicists can stake a claim to priority when it comes to knowledge of the Good.

Physics has at best a subsidiary claim to preeminence precisely because it is not ontology. Its subsidiary claim is that its technical products are good, and even then good understood in the limited sense that they produce utility or comfort. But as weaponized versions of even useful techniques show, they are not all good.

Even if the claim is made that theoretical physics leads to prediction—and there is no reason to believe String Theory will—and that predictability itself is good, that claim has to be defended. The implied general pacification and routinization that such predictability would offer is to say the least not an unmitigated good. Or perhaps a claim can be made that the highest good is the life of the mind and physics is one of the highest manifestations of that undertaking. Never mind that the priority of the life of the mind is the conclusion of **ancient political philosophy**, largely presumed to be transcended by modern philosophy, which launched modern physics.

But how is it that one could claim that physics is the highest manifestation of the life of the mind? The highest manifestation of the life of the mind would have to be that which is clearest about its own activity, its presuppositions and what is possible, including a grasp of the limits of knowledge. That clarity is simply not to be found in contemporary theoretical physics with its conceptual conundrums and blindness as to its own roots and conceptual bases. Hence a higher clarity and form of understanding must supervene over physics and its poetry as well as its pretensions to ontology and even as regards the goodness of its technological products. That higher understanding is political philosophy as I have presented it.

NOTES

1. See Thomas S. Kuhn, *The Structure of Scientific Revolutions*, 2nd edition (Chicago: University of Chicago Press, 1970).

2. The theory went beyond this to also suggest that in many cases the reasons for choosing one theory over another were primarily sociological, having to do with things like contemporary public perceptions and ideological views, funding necessities, demographic facts about scientists themselves and even such vulgar phenomena as the operation of majority tyranny.

3. If the choice was technological it depended on the belief that the technology would produce an outcome that was good. With any technological application we always have the primacy of the good, either explicitly or surreptitiously.

4. Quoted in "The Copernican Revolution" by Jacob Klein, in *Lectures and Essays* (Annapolis: St John's College Press, 1985), pp. 103–4.

5. See Nietzsche, *Beyond Good and Evil*, trans. by Walter Kaufmann (New York: Vintage Books, 1966), #14. "It is perhaps just dawning on five or six minds that physics, too, is only an interpretation and exegesis of the world (to suit us, if I may say so!) and *not* a world-explanation; but insofar as it is based on belief in the senses, it is regarded as more, and for a long time to come must be regarded as more—namely, as an explanation."

6. Nietzsche, *Beyond Good and Evil*, #22.

7. For example, despite the fact that no one has seen or ever will see one, and that their existence is based on theoretical deductions from deductions from deductions that ultimately rest on symbolic mathematical languages, Black Holes are publicly taken as simple givens, and not just by Disney studios. First, is this fact of any interest, and secondly, what would be the ramifications of public skepticism about the ontological foundations of such theories if the public was informed of the more subtle truth?

8. A true unified field theory would have to combine not just the various theories within physics, including the Newtonian classic thermodynamics and others, but chemistry, geology, psychology and biology as well. Combing chemistry and quantum mechanics seems impossible all by itself as I will observe.

9. At the risk of offending the Disney Studios and science fiction fans everywhere, even at this early point in the discussion it is necessary to point out and keep in mind the hypothetical nature of Black Holes. They are not ontological givens.

10. When we observe that mathematics is a form of language, we have already implied that it is a form of *poiesis* without however grasping what is implied in that fact. We will have to explore this further.

11. And make no mistake, when the most theoretical and mathematical physicist moves to the realm of metaphor, picture and analogy, we have entered the realm of both public speech, publicly sharable phenomena and *poiesis*, and the rules of public speech and poetry then take precedence to the rules of any ideal, symbolic language. It may very well be that the only real point of connection or overlap between the realm of theoretical physics and the phenomenological realm of *poiesis* is technology. So what are we to make of a physics that pretends to ontology rather than aiming simply at technology but cannot co-opt everyday speech? More interestingly, what happens to physics that almost in principle can have no technological application or experimental validation? **I will maintain throughout that no physical theory can or ever will dispense with a link with the phenomenal and all the entanglements that implies.**

12. Very little of what I will conclude here applies as easily to classical modern, self-consciously "hypothetical," physics or to what even its contemporary practitioners differentiate from theoretical physics and call "experimental physics" or "applied physics."

13. Brian Greene, *The Elegant Universe* (New York: Vintage Books, 2000), p. xi.

14. For an understanding of this issue see Jacob Klein, *Greek Mathematical Thought and the Origin of Algebra*, trans. by Eva Brann (Cambridge: MIT Press, 1968).

15. I have already signaled above my rejection of this textbook understanding of Plato.

16. Yet only the quantitative differences which will involve ideas like amplitude and frequency can be mathematically operationalized. But these can be differentiated only because they can be related to something phenomenal. For example, we know the wavelength green only because we first experience green phenomenally.

17. Notice that the move to turn the four forces (energy) into particles (matter) does the reverse of quantum mechanics but shares with it the attempt to reduce a two to a One. As the problem of light shows, this never quite works and ultimately it must be conceptualized as both an energy or wave phenomenon and a particle or mass phenomenon. To argue that the particle is massless, yet still a particle as opposed to a wave, is a sleight of hand.

18. At more or less this point we get all manner of pure speculation about what "was" before the Big Bang and regarding the origins of the cosmic Black Hole, and daydreams about parallel universes and even that there is a movement back and forth from the smallest and lightest of components like strings into and out of Black Holes

in a fashion likened to the "phase shift" of water from a solid to a liquid to a gaseous state. I repeat, this is pure unmitigated poetry and speculation, albeit useful for science fiction sales.

19. Notice why it becomes almost inevitable at some point to posit an external cause and why if one is to avoid an infinite regress "It" must be posited as a self-cause.

20. I am hoping that it is beginning to be clear that I have been and will be reproducing elements of the dialectical presentation offered by Plato in the *Parmenides*. See chapter 15 on the *Parmenides*.

21. This split between Ideal/Real, Ideal/Phenomenal, Sense/Supra-sensible is one that keeps reproducing itself, and always will. It is not surprising that it reproduces itself yet again in contemporary theoretical physics.

22. See in this regard Hermann Hesse, *Magister Ludi: The Glass Bead Game*, translation of *Das Glasperlenspiel* by Richard and Clara Winston (New York: Bantam Books, 1970).

Chapter Twenty-One

The Queen of the Sciences:
Political Philosophy or Biology?

We expect miracles, and in everything from electronics to medicine they ap-pear with increasing rapidity. They appear so frequently that we may be be-coming numb to their miraculous character. Whether in awe or indifference we are determined by these modern scientific miracles, or the shadows they cast, that shape our lives. In a different way we are determined by the scien-tific theories that make their way into the public arena as much as by the tech-nological transformations of nature they make possible. Unfortunately, not all of those public manifestations of science foster what deserves to be called En-lightenment. Many, in a vein similar to what I suggested in the last chapter, are quite mythical.

Not surprisingly, some of those myths form the self-understanding of prac-ticing scientists themselves. This can be forgiven due to the day-to-day situ-ation of practicing scientists as specialists engaged in specific detailed re-search within narrow areas of concern. They can be excused if they do not have the time to step back and reflect on the philosophical, *nee* ontological, nature of their undertaking. But in the true spirit of "science" (*sophia*), we are better served to grasp the real rather than the mythic. That longing for clarity is central to our Western commitment to Enlightenment as the highest good. Know the truth and the truth shall set you free. We would be ill served to give up commitment to that premise.

Let us begin with a central myth: Modern science is one rather than many. The reality is that there are geology, biology, chemistry, physics, botany and so on. They are bodies of knowledge and theory that are largely independent. Despite repeated longings for a unified field theory, it can be predicted that there will never be any simple synthesizing of the theories or bodies of knowledge of the various sciences into one body of knowledge and theory. I will deal with this issue below. Even the individual sciences are not one and unified. For example, the situation of contemporary, speculative, professional physics, which for many is *par excellence* the exemplar of modern science, is one of competing explanatory theories that I argued above in principle will not be synthesized—e.g., theories about the whole—relativity theory—and theories about the smallest—quantum mechanics.[1]

To this multiplicity in contemporary physics can be added that we have moved to higher and higher realms of theoretical conjecture where empirical validation becomes impossible in principle. That leaves one to wonder when scientific theorizing dissolves into poetry, with mathematical forms for the poetry taking the place of forms like the sonnet. What is the understanding that allows us to choose the appropriate form for our *poiesis*? That understanding is certainly not scientific in the modern sense. I will continue to argue that that understanding is political philosophy as I have defined it.

Be that as it may, one might expect to find a different situation within contemporary professional Biology, i.e., one of greater theoretical unity. And one might especially expect to find an undertaking tied almost exclusively to empirical validation. Put in my terms, one might expect to see contemporary Biology remain closer to the "phenomena" the explanation of which might be thought to set the sciences in motion in the first place.[2] In this case the phenomenon in question is "life." If modern Biology were more phenomenological than say physics, it might mean that contemporary Biology would be forced to remain openly teleological since this is how the phenomena of life present themselves. But only in the most marginal ways would any of these expectations be met when one looks at contemporary professional Biology as a discipline, especially at its self-understanding.

Whether at the micro or the macro level, what one finds in the enterprise of contemporary Biology is an increasingly heuristic, theoretically driven undertaking that is every bit as paradigm contentious as contemporary physics. That raises the question, does contemporary Biology lead to ontological knowledge, or primarily toward technical knowledge, for example in the genetic engineering of corn or in various medical applications? Is it "truth" or "utility" that ultimately validates its theorizing?

Our expectation that professional Biology, like the phenomenon "life," might be teleological is dispelled by a look at work at the micro level in contemporary Biology which is almost completely reductionist. Molecular Biology increasingly refuses to take its bearings on the basis of entities above the molecular level, whether that be cells, whole organisms, groups of organisms or the interrelated whole of life itself. This reductionism frequently opens the door to the vice of jumping to grand architectonic conclusions to which one is not entitled on the basis of limited phenomenal evidence. This in turn frequently leads to sophomoric intrusions into the realm of political philosophy—in this regard consider everything from "Sociobiology," to *The Selfish Gene,* to believing everything **human** can be explained in relation to bacteria, from which humans allegedly evolved.[3]

Given the speculative tensions within contemporary Biology, it is curious that we have also seen attempts by political philosophers to build on selected biological premises—primarily taken from the macro level which is dominated by evolutionary theory—to support their political and philosophical positions, or more generally—and even more questionably— to ground the activity of political philosophy itself. But even in taking off from distinctive permutations of evolutionary theory, those students of political philosophy try to ground their efforts on only a part of a body of theory which at best is given to its own fundamental disputes. This has in some instances produced better political philosophy than that of the reductionist biologists, but at the expense of taking evolutionary theory as either the entirety of contemporary Biology, or as if it were a finished body of knowledge—or at least is a science progressing toward a finished body of knowledge, rather than itself forever evolving. The alternative understanding is that modern science primarily eventuates in useful techniques and evolves rather than progresses toward a finished body of final knowledge. **Science as leading toward a finished and final body of knowledge is another myth.**

Presumably one cannot exempt evolutionary theory from the mechanics posited by evolution itself, hence how can it ever in principle be a finished body of ontological theorizing? Evolutionary theory itself, like everything else in the theory, must be conditioned by its environment. As such, why would evolutionary theory offer political philosophy a useful, allegedly fixed and finished ontological foundation given that the ethical and political are part of every environment and they change to meet changing circumstances?[4] The political and the moral, as part of the environment, would in fact be prior and condition evolutionary theory itself. And that is what I will argue below.

On the basis of evolutionary theory itself, no finished state of theorizing can be reached—since neither the inquirer nor the environment will ever reach a finished state. We must also keep in mind that "evolution," which implies only "change," and "progress" are, according to the theory, two different things. Further, deductive attempts by political philosophers to ground their efforts in Biology, as if that discipline were unified or offered some simple ontological given, fail to see the fundamentally heuristic nature of evolutionary theory—as well as micro theories—within professional Biology. And indeed, deductive attempts by political philosophers fail to grasp that evolutionary theory is not the focal point of contemporary Biology, which is found increasingly—in a reductionist and entirely non-teleological fashion—on the micro level.

Taking contemporary biological theorizing as an ontological ground for political philosophy is based on several misunderstandings. First, there is a misunderstanding of the nature of contemporary professional Biology and its theorizing. Second, there is a misunderstanding of the nature of political philosophy. Third, there is an inability to see that taking Biology as a point of departure rests on a choice that cannot be explained scientifically, and so far has not been explained in any fashion. Why choose the theorizing of professional Biology rather than that of contemporary physics, or for that matter Theology, as one's foundation or point of departure? Why choose one body of theorizing within Biology rather than others? One must see that a choice for one science over another or one body of theorizing over another is a choice that proceeds from a form of knowing that is not scientific in the modern sense. The only serious basis for that choosing is a political philosophy that is phenomenological, not the constructivist theory of modern science in any of its forms. Constructivism holds sway in Biology every bit as much as in physics.

In what follows I will start with some general reflections on two of the more sophisticated attempts to deduce the foundation of political philosophy from Biology, those of Roger Masters and Larry Arnhart.[5] Then I will have some remarks on contemporary biological theory at both the macro and micro levels. I will in the process include some ongoing reflections on the architectonic relation between political philosophy and modern science, especially Biology.

Both Arnhart and Masters, each originally trained in political philosophy, argue for a "naturalistic ethics" based on contemporary biological theory. Both focus on evolutionary theory albeit Arnhart more than Masters. Arnhart specifically argues that Darwin has a "Natural Right" teaching. Masters, apparently agreeing with George Simpson, argues that henceforth Biology should be the "queen of the sciences"[6] by which I take it he means that it is architectonic in the sense I apply to political philosophy. For both, political philosophy must turn to contemporary Biology for an ontological foundation, from which it should then deduce political and moral conclusions. In the process, political philosophy becomes not only subsidiary to some other undertaking but is conceptualized as a primarily deductive enterprise—with no conscious, originary element of *poiesis* which for me is an essential component of political philosophy.

Both Arnhart and Masters refer to Leo Strauss's observation regarding the "problem of modern science":

[In the modern world] the issue seems to have been decided in favor of the non-teleological conception of the universe. Two opposite conclusions could be drawn from this momentous decision. According to one, the nonteleological conception of the universe must be followed up by a nonteleological conception of human life. But this "naturalistic" solution is exposed to grave difficulties: it seems to be impossible to give an adequate account of human ends by conceiving of them merely as posited by desires or impulses. **[This is a position that Arnhart and Masters come close to offering despite their teleological pretensions-fundamental]** Therefore, the alternative solution has prevailed. This means that people were forced to accept a fundamental, typically modern, dualism of a nonteleological natural science and a teleological science of man. . . . The fundamental dilemma, in whose grip we are, is caused by the victory of modern natural science. An adequate solution to the problem of natural right cannot be found before this basic problem has been solved.[7]

Both Masters and Arnhart presume to "solve" this problem by saying that if we turn to Biology rather than physics as our exemplar of modern science, the problem disappears. **This is because Biology, they assert, is teleological where modern physics is not.** But the center of gravity of contemporary Biology is molecular Biology and it is thoroughly reductionist, not teleological. Further, since molecules are made of atoms, and atoms of subatomic particles, there is no way whatsoever that molecular Biology ultimately emancipates itself from physics. The solution to Strauss's "problem of modern science" will be found only after we view science for what it really is, and what it is not. What modern science is not is ontological explanation; it is beyond that myth that the solution to Strauss's "problem of modern science" is to be found. Ultimately, the power of modern Biology, like that of modern physics, is not found in its ontological explanatory power, but in its technical applications. We are always in danger of being seduced by the competence of technique into thinking we are confronted with something ontological.[8]

Masters is well disposed to a biological foundation for political philosophy because he seems to see the only alternative is the idea that ethics, and political philosophy more generally, should be based on the modern notion of the autonomy of the Will. For Masters there appears to be an either/or operating: either we are "naturalists" and understand that we are "in" Nature or we rely on the ungrounded autonomy of the Will that stands "outside" Nature and we become nihilists because we can find no guidance for the Will. Masters sees a great danger in a reliance on that staple of modern political philosophy, "metaphysical freedom." It is true that that notion, in various permutations, informs the thinking of Rousseau, Kant, German Idealism and even the reflections of an alleged materialist like Marx on "species being."

It is true that for those moderns who believe in the possibility of metaphysical freedom, and it rests on an act of Faith, man "stands" on the ground of a self-legislating autonomous Will that traces its lineage to Descartes's self-legislating ego. In other words, it has the same philosophical foundation as modern science itself, modern Constructivism. Standing "outside" of Nature, the modern Will is posited as capable of emancipating man from natural determination. From the stance of the self-legislating Will, man can change his moral and political world, a premise shared with modern science which aims to transform the natural world. Modern biological theory rests on the same premise.

Masters thinks we are better off ethically seeing ourselves as "in" Nature rather than "outside" it. He has concluded that the doctrine of the autonomy of the Will inevitably leads to Nietzsche's groundless competition of Wills for mastery, and this is nihilism. But Masters never explains the way in which we are "in" Nature but not so "within" it that we cannot understand it and master it, which we clearly do. Modern science itself is a sign that somehow we bracket Nature and stand "outside" it to understand it, or at least to gain the leverage that allows us to change it. The ability to change what we posit as determining us is a fairly clear sign of freedom or autonomy on some level. No monkey or ape ever developed a vaccine or microwave oven, not to mention nuclear technology and genetic engineering. Those activities must be explained and I would suggest simply cannot be explained if we are totally "in" Nature in the same fashion as a planet or a beaver.

But for Masters we should turn to "Nature" as a standard for ethics rather than to the Will. Yet Masters never gets away from implying the autonomy of thought no matter how often he invokes "naturalism." If our behavior is totally determined by Nature, then it is not clear why it would matter what we believe about ethics or the constitution of our own nature or the more comprehensive nature of Nature itself. Different understandings could make no difference. If we are only naturally determined beings it does not matter to our behavior if we are naturalists, nihilists or relativists. It certainly does not matter to chimpanzees.

Yet for Masters it seems to make a great deal of difference what we believe, hence ideas must have some causal autonomy. Ideas are part of our environment, and thus their causal nature is compatible with evolutionary theory and must be given their due because they have their effects. They are part of what determines us and no one can explain their effect in any simple "naturalistic" fashion or ever will. Otherwise, how could the modern project to conquer nature have had the profound effects it has, and bring with it the frightening prospects it might unleash if unchecked by ethical considerations? The unavoidable implication of Masters's undertaking is that ideas matter and hence we humans are not "in" nature in the same fashion as inanimate objects and other living beings.

If ideas matter, phenomena like the "absent" ends of our actions determine our behavior as much as, if not more than, our "present" genome or genotype structure. Otherwise, why choose ethical naturalism? Indeed, consider this statement: "A new naturalism suggests not only that biology replace physics or mathematics as the 'queen of the sciences' . . . but that nature thereby should be revalued [interesting Nietzschean term] as the source of meaning and purpose in the world."[9] But all of this requires a choice. Must there not be some autonomy to that act of choice for it to be interesting and efficacious?[10]

While Masters rightly criticizes the naturalistic theorizing that eventuated in Social Darwinism with its crass defense of *laissez-faire* capitalism, he does something suspiciously similar in ending up biologically "proving" the correctness of the politics of modern, Western, liberal states. He even throws in a contemporary respect for politically correct "diversity" on the basis of an appeal to bio-diversity, albeit conceptualized as a version of liberal individualism.

In an odd and ironic way, Masters uses evolutionary theory to arrive at a defense of what looks like a version of the End of History thesis, with Biology explaining why that end is both inevitable and just. The irony is somewhat softened by Masters's assumption that our species has been more or less fixed for fifty thousand years and little of interest will change in the vast foreseeable future. But this seems to overlook the massive, rapid and accelerating changes brought by modern science that are altering the very basis of political and moral existence such that we must creatively adapt to our environment with increasing rapidity—an environment which is itself changing. What we see in our present environment is an utter paucity of any thinking forward toward how we will provide for ourselves novel yet needed political and ethical forms to deal with a novel future.

To be fair to him, for Masters contemporary Biology supports what amounts to a synthesis of modern liberalism and Aristotelian politics and ethics as the final wisdom of historical evolution. Aristotle offers the contours of the best regime understood as a "polity" for all men in all places at all times henceforth—pending a transformation of our species into something new.[11] That polity, however, becomes in Masters's account a large modern republic informed by Lockean individualism. It is an interesting, if not altogether unheard of synthesis, to bring together the ancient Aristotle and the modern Locke.

Masters argues that contemporary Biology teaches us that our behavior is determined by both innate and acquired characteristics (habits), selfish and cooperative inclinations and causes that are instinctively similar to those operating in other species yet unique. This elaborate synthesis may be an attempt to square the circle. While this posited multiplicity of causes for our phenotype behavior helps avoid doctrinaire political and moral outcomes, it leaves us in a position that is somewhat vague and fails to explain the "practical wisdom" (phronesis) or poiesis by which we balance these competing drives and inclinations. We hardly seem to get beyond the categories of past political philosophy to any basis for how to choose from competing potential causes of behavior. And despite various bows in the direction of teleology, all of Masters's causes are conceived as operating almost exclusively as efficient causality. Both Arnhart and Masters share a conception of teleology that operates as efficient causality. And given that Masters's ideal political and ethical situation is based on options taken from past political philosophy, how does contemporary Biology help us choose what will be needed in the novel future environment that is coming all too soon?[12]

Given the understanding of political philosophy I have been pursuing throughout, which is not deductive in nature, Masters presents a picture of political philosophy that is neither consistent with its Platonic beginnings nor its post-Heideggerian intellectual situation in the present. As I have been arguing, it is political philosophy itself that is architectonic and hence the "queen of the sciences," and includes ontology within itself as a part but not as a foundation.

While contemporary Biology can unleash, for example, magnificent medical technologies, that does not prove the ontological status of its theoretical constructs and hence of its foundational status for political philosophy. I would offer the formula that medicine, for example—a form of technology— can progress, but that Biology as an explanation of the whole will, like evolutionary theory and evolution itself, only evolve, and around foci that are predictable. One of the predictable foci around which Biology, like Physics, will always revolve is found in the search for a One as the only persuasive basis for explanation, with the One being repeatedly conceived both as the whole and as an indivisible small unit. This split necessarily reproduces itself in both physics and Biology as I will discuss in the next chapter.

Arnhart is another scholar trained in political philosophy who wants to arrive at a "naturalistic" political philosophy. Arnhart deduces ten propositions he takes as proven by modern biology and then twenty natural desires he takes as given.[13] From these ten premises he then deduces the outlines of what would be needed to discuss a doctrine of the best regime. For Arnhart, a definition of the best regime is one that is not arbitrary, which means it does not run in the face of "Nature," or have as its end the desire to transcend or negate "Nature." Obviously there is circularity operating here but we can let it pass for the moment. Arnhart argues that his ten premises do not determine a specific regime to be applied everywhere and always, but they certainly constrain one's choices within a very narrow orbit which, again, looks like various permutations of what Aristotle meant by a "polity."

As is true for Masters, Arnhart's approach to the traditional question of the best regime rests on a view of Biology as supplying ontological givens and of political philosophy as a deductive enterprise that is subordinate to some architectonic knowledge found outside itself. What this approach cannot do is account for political philosophy as projective, as future oriented, as thrown toward future possibilities except to project the future as identical to the present, or past. Political philosophy becomes locked in the present with at best an eye cast to the past. This understanding cannot present political philosophy as an enterprise that links past and future as I have argued it must.

This a-historicality of Arnhart's view of political philosophy is, ironically, based on Darwinian Evolution. But it cannot account for man as a historical being always caught between past and future; it certainly cannot explain the priority of the future for human beings. It cannot explain why the future might present something novel. For Arnhart the tradition of political philosophy as ongoing and unique appears to be over. Even more than Masters, Arnhart arrives at the conclusion that in the history of political philosophy the one author who more or less got it right once and for all was Aristotle. **No other future political philosophy is required. The final wisdom has arrived.** On that premise, the tradition could have stopped long before we ever got to Darwin.

To be fair to Arnhart, philosophically he goes beyond Aristotle and offers a synthesis of ancient and modern elements, as does Masters. He accepts Darwin's teaching, and in doing so accepts "natural selection" as the moving principle of evolution, with all its Hobbesean implications. He accepts the existence of Hume's teaching regarding a "natural moral sense." If such a "sense" exists, it would be a "phenomenon" in my sense. But for Arnhart, Aristotle seems to be the author who properly articulates what is broadcast by the moral sense that Hume, not Aristotle, posits. And Arnhart accepts that Nature must be understood as a manifestation of Aristotle's four forms of causality. **What he does not tell us is where he stands philosophically to construct this synthesis, what it status is, how it manifests or shows itself.** A synthesis requires that one stand at some philosophical point outside the things synthesized. Where is that point for a Darwinian?

When Arnhart is finished we get a synthesis of the fundamentally nominalist Hume, who stresses the place of custom, habit and tradition as the basis of even philosophy, with the teleology and naturalism of Aristotle and the fundamentally Hobbesean teaching of the non-teleologist Darwin. The end of the synthesis is called "Darwinian Natural Right."[14] For Arnhart, Darwin becomes more Humean than Hobbesean despite the centrality of "natural selection." Hume's "natural moral sense" is explained in Aristotelian terms that come close to making Hume a teleologist. And the Aristotle of eternal species is ignored and the Darwin who relies almost exclusively on efficient causality becomes a teleologist.

Arnhart sees Darwinianism as a form of "naturalism." Using naturalism in the sense he does implies that what we have is an ontological foundation to evolutionary theory despite the extent to which its various theoretical formulations are based on inferences, from indirect evidence and all manner of creative filling in the blanks. Even Arnhart says, "With Darwin's help, we can "see" [Arnhart's emphasis] the evolution of species only by inference from indirect evidence such as the fossil record. As Darwin concedes, his arguments depend on plausibility rather than proof."[15]

But the central issue is, what counts as "plausibility?" Is it not determined by the political and philosophical environment of the time and the quality and perspicacity of the argumentative *poiesis* with which it is presented within that environment? Plausibility is always "thrown." Following the logic of that observation will lead one to my position which sees ontology as part of political philosophy, not an activity outside and prior to it.

For Aristotle, while all four of the causes—final, formal, material and efficient—operate together, final causality nonetheless takes precedence.[16] And for Aristotle final causality does not operate as fundamentally mechanical, efficient causality, it operates through conscious choice.[17] For Darwin it is perfectly clear that it is efficient causality that is primary as the driving force of evolution, even though in his species typologies he sneaks formal causality in the side door.[18] Darwin may even allow a bit of teleology to sneak in even more furtively on the level of individuals, but for the species, or the whole of life, there is primarily the moving force of efficient causality. Darwin had almost no conception of material causality. For example, he had no notion of "genes" or even how heredity worked at the material level. Darwin operated on the macro level.

Arnhart's Darwinian Natural Right is presented as if it is teleological, but upon closer inspection it is clear that his treatment focuses on efficient causality as does Darwin's. Furthermore, Arnhart relies on the natural traits of the species in general and as a whole more than those of unique groups of individuals who, as Plato shows, can form "tribes" of distinctive types of different individuals who transcend the more generic traits of the species as a whole. But we should keep in mind that for actual biologists those species traits operate only as statistical probabilities. Statistical probabilities work in the abstract rather than on the phenomenal level. Put another way, they are ontological only by inference. I would argue that the phenomena show themselves more as Plato suggested rather than as species wide generic traits.

To get from the statistical level to the phenomenal level, Arnhart's Natural Right has to operate in individuals through natural desires and instincts that incline all human beings toward certain fixed ends.[19] This is not final causality in Aristotle's sense. This is efficient causality operating, and to make the point one last time, Arnhart repeatedly proceeds as if final causality operated as efficient causality. ˙

The jump from statistical probabilities to ontological givens creates one set of problems. The move from the abstract "species" to individuals presents other problems. Nothing is solved by trying to rely on equally abstract, nonphenomenal terms like "gene pools," which can likewise only be given statistical articulations. Leaving aside the ontological status of the allegedly operative "instincts" (and the ends they point toward) those instincts clearly operate as efficient causality in "inclining" individuals toward ends. To go from statistical probabilities, to "instincts" operating efficiently to a teleological naturalism in ethics makes all manner of logical skips and jumps.

Leaving aside all of these problems, the outcome we arrive at with Darwinian Natural Right is not Aristotelian, for whom "Nature" only marginally operates through instinct, but something much closer to modern authors like Hobbes and Locke. Indeed, some instincts have to be opposed to each other in Aristotle's *Ethics* to bring about the ethical, "natural" end. That implies choice, which is how teleology operates. Understanding, choice, and the consequent habits and laws they imply, play a far greater role for Aristotle than for Darwin, or Locke and Hobbes. For Aristotle the end is made actual by choice but it is "absent" until chosen in a way that instinct is not. For Arnhart the end is always "present" in instincts and inclinations. This is altogether modern reductionism as is Darwinianism.

For Aristotle, natural inclinations and natural ends do not line up in some linear causal fashion. For Aristotle, final causality operates through choice, through human beings choosing the beautiful, the excellent or the perfect. These ends are somehow "given" and somehow "natural," yet they change; just as justice is natural for Aristotle even though it changes. For Aristotle, the ends change in a way "instincts" and "inclinations" do not for either Darwin or Arnhart. Without choice—and for some those choices are determined by the choices of others, like great statesmen who form the habits of citizens— outcomes would not come to be through efficient causality alone as they do for Locke and Hobbes.

Like Masters, Arnhart gets caught on the horns of the determinism/freedom issue. He wants natural determinism in ethics to avoid arbitrary choices, but then when stuck with that determinism will never be able to explain why it makes a difference to our behavior that we choose Darwinian Natural Right over Nietzschean nihilism, to use one of his fundamental dichotomies—a dichotomy that is far too simple. Yet it is predictable how proponents of this "naturalistic" view will respond. They will argue that without an ontological grounding, in this case in contemporary biological theory understood onto-logically, one will be thrown into relativism and nihilism. The matter is presented as an either/or choice.

I do not accept the necessity of that dichotomy nor the need to be limited to those two choices—and again, where Arnhart presumes to stand to make that choice is never clear. I have argued explicitly throughout *Between Eternities* that political philosophy must be rooted in the phenomena as they show themselves. That phenomenological rootedness is how one avoids arbitrariness. I will stipulate that a political philosophy that ignores phenomena is without limits and is a mistake.

Ultimately, contemporary Biology, like contemporary physics, is determined by the phenomena in ways both ignore and that ultimately shows the ways in which neither undertaking is capable of being autonomous. Both are forms of constructivist theory, which is why neither should presume to be ontology. One should keep in mind the ontology/methodology distinction. The constructivist is always a methodologist, and distinct from an ontologist.

It seems to me that thinkers like Masters and Arnhart are inadequately aware, or at least inadequately stress, how tenuously connected to actual phenomena contemporary physics and Biology have become and hence how determined by free floating theoretical projections (*poiesis*) those sciences are ultimately becoming. That may be technologically efficacious; it is not ontologically compelling.

In what follows I hope to indicate, in a preliminary fashion, the status of the theorizing in contemporary Biology just as I previously tried to suggest what is taking place in contemporary physics. I see no reason to believe that any of the sciences can become more phenomenological without ceasing to be what they are, in other words, fundamentally technological, constructivist undertakings. But even as technological they retain a phenomenological link.

For some time, we have heard about the "Two Cultures" and the need to bring them together. The Strauss quote above presented the split of the two cultures, ethical and scientific, as an unresolved dilemma. An approach to a resolution of that dilemma will only happen through a renovation of our understanding of the sciences wherein it is admitted that they are simply technological rather than ontological. That will in turn allow for our public understanding of the sciences to become more realistic. Unfortunately, I am not expecting either of those things to happen any time soon. But that outcome is a future toward which we can move. And this is an example of how political philosophy opens future possibilities.

Both Arnhart and Masters "solve" Strauss's problem by saying that if we turn to Biology rather than physics as our exemplar of modern science the problem disappears because contemporary Biology is not only ontological but teleological where contemporary physics is not. This is a misunderstanding of contemporary Biology. Evolutionary theory is teleological only by making efficient and final causality collapse. But beyond that fact, the center of gravity in contemporary professional biology is molecular biology and it is thoroughly reductionist, not teleological.

What is the present state of Biology as a profession? The short answer is that it is the same as that in contemporary physics. Like physics, Biology is a field of competing theoretical edifices that cannot be synthesized. It is true that molecular biology and bio-chemistry now take the lead within the profession. I would argue, however, that the reasons why studies at the micro level have become the focus of contemporary Biology are sociological and technical rather than ontological. Those studies predominate because they get the majority of contemporary funding and that is because they offer the most technical promise, not because they have the most ontological explanatory power.

But even microbiology seems to take evolution as the ultimate thing that must be explained, hence microbiology points beyond itself. And evolutionary theory, which operates at the macro level, has increasingly tried to explain microelements like "genes" and "heredity" and "inheritance" with molecular tools, i.e., using material causality. Each points beyond itself to the other without being able to provide the synthesis that is needed to supply a whole theory. The parts are not autonomous and there is no whole.

As far as I can see, no one working at the micro level can explain why, having moved "down" in search of the ultimate building blocks of "life" that they never go below the molecular level to the level of atoms and subatomic particles. Once one starts down the reductionist path toward the One qua smallest as if this would give one the ultimate explanatory principle, by what wisdom—certainly external to actual Biology as a professional undertaking—does one stop before getting to the ultimate indivisible One? If one sees the ultimate explanation for life at the smallest level why stop at the molecule rather than subatomic particles?

There are far more substantial reasons for stopping one's descent above the molecular level at the level of the cell, if the explanation of "life" is our primary end. Nothing at the molecular level ultimately explains the existence of cells or cell division, or explains eventual cell differentiation or anything related to the existence and operation of cells. It is an axiom of contemporary Biology that only cells cause or produce other cells, not molecules or proteins or amino acids or compounds of any kind. **And cells are the smallest things that are accepted as being alive.**

At the molecular level we confront objects of study that everyone agrees are not alive. At the level of the cell we have an entity that everyone agrees is alive. Somewhere in the gulf between molecule and cell that great mystery called "life" breaks out. Why not start with the smallest thing that has life if our main intention is to give a *logos* about *bios*? By what mysterious principle does one add together a number of entities that are not alive and get one that is? Literally no one can explain this.

On the other hand, we do not know what a cell "is" except in light of the fully developed organism toward which it points. **A cell "is" something not yet present.** Hence the ontological reality of any cell, its being, is always absent in some sense and therefore incapable of a materialistic explanation. **A cell is determined in its being far more by something absent than it "is" the chemical/molecular matter present in it.** Without knowing the finished organism first, any given cell tells us nothing about what it "is" or how it "should" develop correctly, or even that it will develop.

Further, we do not know what counts as a finished organism without looking at a manifestation of a specific group or species of organism, and members of that group, which have reached their completion, end or perfection (*telos*). That end shows itself in a finished or perfected member or excellent (*aretē*) manifestation of that species (i.e., in light of the good (*agathon*). But we cannot know what a perfect manifestation of the thing toward which a cell points is until we first know what such a thing "looks" like (*eidos*). Hence the form of the thing takes priority over its end or *telos*. And the forms of the various things are things that only show themselves publicly to a group of individuals in the public arena using public speech. That prior showing is always determinative, even for Biology.

Therefore, why not openly take our bearings by the "phenomena" that show themselves as sovereign, even, or especially, when dealing with cells—to say nothing of the dead molecules of which they are composed? In short, neither molecules nor cells can explain themselves without pointing away from themselves at something else, a something in this case which most assuredly appears in the realm of phenomena, the *eidos* of the various groups of living things.

The human genome project, and there are similar "maps" for other species, gives us unbelievable mountains of data but in principle cannot help us explain what happens in cells let alone what life "is." We can state, in a temporal fashion, what happens in mitosis. We can likewise temporally state that cells divide, and that mitochondria reproduce separately from mitosis and much more of a similar kind. We cannot explain cell differentiation or development or anything else except backwards from the whole organism toward which these processes point. Only the end (which is in a very real sense absent at the beginning, certainly in a materialistic sense) can in principle explain the beginning and intermediate steps.

Only in light of the *telos* of a thing can we offer an explanation, and that always means an explanation of what "is" happening, and indeed of what a thing "is." But that requires that we first have a grasp of the form (*eidos*) that allows us to know what kind of thing we are dealing with. It is only formal causality that allows us access to final causality and hence it takes priority. Microbiological reductionism can give us a mountain of facts but it can explain just exactly nothing regarding what "is," i.e., **it presupposes "being." It cannot therefore lead us up to ontology.**

If we must look to the fully developed thing to understand the smallest things, we are determined by the whole thing or organism as it presents itself as a phenomenon. And, it should be clear that one cannot understand an organism as a complete whole without concepts like fully developed, healthy, good, excellent, perfect.

One cannot know what a cell "is" except in light of the "species" of which it is a proto-manifestation. Those species are themselves phenomena that show themselves publicly in shared looks (*eidē*). Biology as a science is simply speechless without relying on those looks which "are" phenomena determined by how they present themselves to all in a publicly shared fashion. **Those public phenomena are prior to any scientific speaking.** The public looks always take priority, and that is why formal causality takes priority. In turn, that undertaking that studies publicly displayed phenomena as its primary task takes priority, and that is political philosophy. This is why phenomenological political philosophy, which is architectonic, is the "queen of the sciences."

We have several issues therefore. First, on the micro level, why not start with subatomic particles? Second why not start with cells rather than molecules as they are the smallest things that are alive? Third, why not take the fully developed organism, which exists on the macro level of phenomena, as the focus of analysis given that it is ruling even for analysis of the ultimate small things whatever they may be?

In the study of "life" we have various levels at which the *logos* can be engaged. We have sub-atomic particles, atoms, molecules, cells, individual organisms, groups of organisms, species, complete ecosystems that link species, and the planet-wide phenomenon of life as a whole. What is the appropriate primary object of analysis for those who allegedly, if we take the name Biology seriously, are attempting to provide a *logos* about *bios*? For a variety of reasons that will appear below I would argue that the most fruitful levels are individuals, groups and species, if our end is explanation. If our end is technical manipulation, this may not be true.[20]

To repeat an example, the human genome project is just a long list of catalogued facts which by themselves "explain" nothing. Lists of facts and explanations are two entirely different things. The medical techniques we have produced with accelerating frequency, and more that are coming, raise all manner of political and ethical concerns for which we do not presently have a political philosophy equipped to be of assistance in lending guidance. But those are not my concerns at present. I am concerned with the status of biological explanation as allegedly autonomous and as ontological, especially such that political philosophers must start from biological "facts" as a body of ontological givens. I do not accept that modern professional Biology offers us a corpus of ontological "fact" so understood.

Switching to reflections on the macro level, more or less everyone agrees that life has evolved, that it is not fixed and static. But to say that there is a consensus on one uniform evolutionary theory about the nature of the **mechanism** that operates or how long it takes for that mechanism to operate or on what level it operates is simply false. Evolutionary theory is usually associated with the name of Darwin. But it is hard even to pin down a core theory in Darwin's written works; and now we increasingly hear of "neo-Darwinianism," an equally protean body of theorizing.

Do the changes evolutionary theories posit come gradually or in a flash that yields a qualitative change followed by a stasis that terminates only with the extinction of a species—this possibility is referred to as "punctuated equilibrium"? That still leaves open the question of whether we are primarily dealing with catastrophic events/chance occurrences on the phenomenal level or something else that causes the punctuating events, perhaps at the micro level. Or is the mechanism of change a gradual "natural selection," whose operation can be explained in any number of ways—e.g., a more or less Hobbesean contest, the winner of which is crowned "fittest"?

Does gradual evolutionary change take place due to "survival of the fittest," or only "survival of the fit" who have reached some minimum threshold of fitness? Or is the causal venue for change primarily at the cellular level and caused by mutations due to invading rays, or by invading organisms as in "symbiotic" explanations, or something else altogether? The theoretical mechanism of change in evolution is as far from clear as is the amount of time required for qualitative change within a species or the alleged change from one species to another.

The issue of symbiosis, which has attracted much recent attention, raises the question of whether all trait inheritance is "vertical," coming only from a parent to an offspring—as is assumed in what might be called classical Darwinian theorizing—or is there also "lateral" trait inheritance coming from outside the mechanisms of parentage—e.g., by an invasion of another species at the micro level, usually posited at the level of bacteria. That mechanism would vouch for "acquired traits" at the micro level. And as far as I can see, we have in no definitive theoretical way even to put to rest the possibility of acquired traits gained at the macro level. Most of our reasons for dispensing with that possibility are aesthetic, moral and political rather than empirical.

The same is probably true of the prior theoretical rejection of "vitalism." I am not saying that LaMarckism or vitalism are true, just that the empirical evidence for rejecting them is far thinner, and far more ideological, than is usually assumed. It is theoretical majority tyranny in the profession that is primarily operating here.

There is an even more fundamental theoretical ambiguity lurking within evolutionary theory. What counts as a "trait" and how are so-called traits related to "genes" or DNA? This "relationship" is anything but simple to explain and not even remotely "linear." There is no straight-line relationship between "genes" and phenotype "traits." What a trait "is" and how it is passed on or acquired is usually posited in a variety of easygoing fashions and is rarely confronted at anything other than a statistical level. Again, to see evolutionary theory as some unproblematic ontological given, or as some monolithic unity, is as false as to believe that evolutionary theorizing can be easily synthesized with theorizing produced at the micro level.[21]

Presumably every evolutionary thinker, Darwinian or otherwise, must proceed on the assumption that life is somehow shaped by its external environment as much as by its internal material and that the relationship is mutual and reciprocal. It is the external environment that changes most clearly and frequently. And environmental changes are frequently determined by Chance, e.g., meteors hitting the earth, political or economic upheavals, massive changes in ideas and ideals. Even the "fittest" individual of a species can be struck down by lightning before reproducing. Even the fittest can be overcome by a rapidly changing political and moral environment—otherwise one's definition of "fittest" becomes tautological. We must never forget, in some reductionist blindness, that for some thousands of years now, a significant part of every human environment has been the environment of ideas.

In this latter vein, original Darwinianism itself presupposed that already existing in the intellectual environment of Darwin's time was the philosophical discovery of the idea of "History." Without that idea already floating in the intellectual air within which Darwinianism came into being, there would never have been the idea of evolution within Biology. As regards the issue of Chance and contingency, the origin and antecedents of the idea of History are matters of some debate, and the evidence becomes thinner and thinner once one gets much earlier than before Rousseau, with various originary antecedents being proposed from Vico to Joachim of Floris. The deeper point is that unless one is Hegel, and thinks the evolution of ideas was necessary, or Marx and thinks ideas are materially determined, we have an environmental element of Chance in the evolution of ideas. And ideas are environmentally determinative for human existence.

There would have been no Darwinianism without the prior philosophical notion of History, and its antecedents are themselves "thrown." Darwin co-opted an already ready-to-hand philosophical notion and Biology does this repeatedly. Without the philosophical notion of history Darwin literally would have had nowhere to begin. Without that prior theoretical intuition, no "data" would have "said" anything to Darwin or anyone else.

Theories precede even the recognition of what counts empirically as "facts." The facts never simply cry out a necessary theory. In Biology especially, and less visibly in the other sciences, there are always prior philosophical presuppositions whether operating primarily at the micro or macro level. Hence no modern scientific theory can be taken as simply autonomous. The sciences always arrive on the scene far too philosophically late, not to mention politically, morally and culturally late. And since most of the central theories, especially in evolutionary Biology, are borrowed from past, primarily modern, political philosophy there is no way that Biology can ever be prior to political philosophy.

When one looks at actual phenomena they do not cry out "History" or "Evolution," quite the contrary. The phenomena, **which always appear for us in the present,** present themselves to an honest observer as chaotic and random. It is a theory that imposes order. Keep in mind the phenomena for Biology, as is true of all phenomena, are ones we see around us in the present. There is no such thing as a past phenomenon. The past comes down to us only in and through present phenomena—i.e., present fossils, present texts, second hand accounts given in the present. Only in the present can we see "life." Everything else that counts as a phenomenon is a dead object left from the past, or an indirect indication of such an object that no matter how compelling and lively it may appear from a scholarly point of view is in fact dead. A conclusion about these dead objects as living requires an inference from something we experience as living, and that means in the present.

The idea of History or of Evolution requires a theoretical interpretation imposed on things that are dead and do not move. For example, as support for evolutionary Biology we primarily have fossils. And they are few and far between. We have no way of knowing anything about the ancestors or descendants of any specific fossil. We can rely on other evidence like carbon dating to try and date these objects but even then once we get back a decent interval of cosmic time we can only date things to within a period of 500,000 years one way or the other.

When we are lucky enough to have an actual skeleton, rather than an imprint in sand or stone or something that has over time congealed and hardened, we still have no remnant of soft tissue. In some instances we can extract DNA, in many instances it is impossible. As all life shows similarities in DNA, at best we are left to draw inferences even if we have DNA evidence that shows the existence of similarities across time. From these limited resources we are left to build our theory of evolution. To believe that we are working in the realm of certainties, with a mass of evidence, is simply not consistent with the facts.

For the rest of the evidence that is used within evolutionary theory—and ultimately this is true at the micro level of analysis as well—we rely on typologies and morphologies to build up classificatory systems. But those classifications are entirely dependent on the form or "look" (*eidos*) of the various phenomenal things that make up the operative groupings in the present. From various collective "looks" we infer things about the relations among species, we rank and separate them in various ways, ways that do not simply cry out from the looks themselves but require our interpretative efforts. To say that there is no imagination, creativity or interpretation in the human activity known as Biology is simply false in the extreme. And when we are in the realm of creativity we are in the realm of *poiesis*. And modern science itself is by no means the best arbiter of what counts as compelling, not to mention "good," *poiesis*.

Modern science, in all its diverse forms, is a human activity, and not primarily a body of facts or finished ontological knowledge about the whole. And it is a dynamic and ongoing activity which will never divorce itself from its environment. Hence, science will always evolve, and "evolution" and "progress" are two different things. And it will always require *poiesis* and that means it will always be dependent upon a tool it borrows from the public world it occupies. And it will always be dependent upon public standards of persuasiveness for *poiesis*.

I am not trying to argue that human life did not evolve; in fact it seems to me that there is more than a little intuitive phenomenal support for this premise. I am not on the way to a creationist argument. What I am suggesting is that we need to see evolutionary theory for what it is: heuristic, dominated by conjecture, creative, poetic, dynamic, interpretative, contentious, an ongoing discussion that will not yield a finished explanatory outcome because there is no linear, representational relation between the limited "facts" upon which the theorizing is built, and the resultant theories.

Evolutionary theory, or theorizing on the macro theory more generally, will always be a necessary part of biological theorizing because of the unavoidable intellectual necessity to account for the whole as a One. To that extent it corresponds with relativity theory in physics, with molecular Biology lining up roughly with quantum mechanics in its desire to grasp the ultimate small building block as One.

The human mind will not be satisfied until it arrives at a One as an explanation, either the ultimate comprehensive One, or the ultimate small One. But this means, of course, that we arrive at a Two, not a One. It would still be necessary to reduce these Two to a One, that is, synthesize the micro and macro accounts. For a variety of reasons this desire will never be met. As Plato showed in the *Parmenides*, the two Ones can never be brought together into an ultimate One. Contemporary Biology is certainly nowhere in the vicinity of that synthesis any more than contemporary physics, and I will follow Plato and predict neither will ever get there. The same prediction can be made of any synthesis of Biology and physics.

And it should not be surprising that neither micro nor macro theory in Biology has yielded a simple, fixed understanding. Evolutionary theory by definition should never arrive at closure. Still, there are premises that evolutionary theory probably cannot avoid. All life must itself have emerged from a single source, a One, and thought must try to think back to that source. In some fashion that One has to go through a process of differentiation into Many. The account then confronts several predictable conceptual dilemmas. Is the cause of the initial One becoming Many in the One or outside it? If outside it, we actually have a Two. If the cause of differentiation is inside the One, do we really have a One after all?

By itself, Evolutionary theory cannot even approach the question of the beginning and therefore relies on micro theory which in turn would ultimately have to accept the speculations of physics on the Black Holes to get to an ultimate originary One. But physics confronts the same problem of trying to explain how an initial One (ultimate black hole?) becomes Many (rudimentary detached atoms). Was the cause of the first bang in the One or outside the One, with the same problems reproducing themselves? For example, thought cannot posit an expanding universe without asking how an alleged initial One ceased to be One and began to expand. Was the cause internal to the One— in which case it was not One after all—or external to it in which case we have a Two?

Getting from some originary One to a multiplicity of atoms poses serious theoretical problems. Getting from initial free floating atoms to living bacteria poses all sorts of other problems. One still hasn't explained how what doesn't have life "causes" life or transforms itself into something living. Equally inexplicable is how we could have gotten from rudimentary prokaryotic cells which have no nucleus—bacteria and green slime algae are the only two examples in this category of cells—to complex eukaryotic cells with nuclei that account for the rest of the more complex living organisms in our world. And cells themselves "are" primarily "sites" where proteins that originate elsewhere congregate and come together to form a functional One. And yet, even primarily as a site, it is cells that reproduce, have effects and cause outcomes, not genes or DNA which strictly speaking cause nothing and are really just inferences or figures of speech rather than "things." The attempts to explain these things that I have seen are pure speculation, conceptual nightmares and bad poetry. And even as bad poetry, those speculations are determined by the ideological presuppositions of the speculators.[22]

Must we not ultimately conclude that for biological theory the issue of the first cause is beyond discussion? The story must always be taken up in progress. But can one really take up the story of causality in progress anymore than one can stop before getting to an ultimate explanatory One?

Evolutionary theory posits change in all living things. That means there must be some change at the level of the genotype. Theoretical problems arise from the beginning if what we mean by the concept "genotype" is the sum total of all of our "genes" taken together. Further, it is clear that there is no one to one linear relationship between any given genotype and its phenomenally occurring phenotype. And if phenomena always remain controlling for our thinking, the phenotype has its own independent status and ultimately is probably at least as causative for the genotype as vice versa. Beyond that, evolutionary theory positively requires that what happens to the phenotype has causal ramifications for the genotype. What I am going to suggest is that the concept genotype is the far more ambiguous and problematic concept than that of phenotype.

The "disconnect" between genotype and phenotype can be explained in any number of ways. For example, our phenotype may be either over or under determined. If it is over-determined there are multiple possible "genetic" determinants operating and it becomes difficult to explain which wins out in a given circumstance and why. Eventually, over-determinism becomes indistinguishable from Chance, for there can be no other way of explaining which allegedly deterministic principle operates at any given moment. If our phenotype is under-determined, unpredictable environmental factors play at least as big a role as "genes" and LaMarckism will fairly quickly come charging back into the room. My prediction is that it will prove impossible to resolve either this over/under determined dilemma, or to silence once and forever some form of LaMarckism.

As regards the causal control of genotype over phenotype we also have the very real problem of what "is" a gene. Is it chemical "matter," or is it primarily a "code" or "information" or "instructions" for various activities? If a gene is more of a code or instructions rather than matter, we are left with the issue of who (as it were) gives instructions to whom? How does one conceptualize this? What is the status of the instructor and the instructed respectively? From a materialistic perspective, both the information is absent and the end toward which it points is equally absent. Absence controls all presence.

If a gene "is" primarily a code or information and not matter it has no extension, hence no place; thus it is not present in the way matter can be posited as present. A gene "is" therefore primarily absent—especially if we take matter as what is truly present. Hence absence is mysteriously the cause of all presence. That outcome is something with which the sciences will never be able to deal qua science.

How do we "map" something that "is" in its essential being not matter and hence would have no extension and no "place" in the way that matter does? This is a problem. And then how do we conceptualize our "genotype" as the sum total of our genes if our genes are not primarily matter and are in their essence materialistically absent? How do we relate genes to DNA, which as composed of chemical molecules, is matter? Would that mean that we "are" the sum total of all codes and information? Or are we the sum total of our chemical molecules? There are multiple irresolvable difficulties with the concept "gene" and this is but one indication of why no "materialism" will ever be adequate to explain "life." Hence no materialistic reductionism will ever prove satisfactory as ontological explanation.

I would argue that ultimately, what a gene "is," is only determinable in relation to the phenotype that it "informs" in advance and hence "causes" in a fashion that cannot be conceptualized as either material or efficient causality. We can only grasp what a gene "is" by looking backward from its phenomenal manifestation. What a "gene pool" is therefore becomes even more abstract, not to say mysterious.

Beyond that, the causal relation between individual "genes" and phenomenal "traits" is anything but clear. Perfectly clear is that only rarely can one gene appear to theoretically line up in a linear fashion with one trait. Frequently, any given trait is posited as requiring the "actions" of multiple genes. And frequently, any one "gene" is posited as implicated in "causing" more than one trait. And on the technological level, even when we think we have isolated one gene causing one trait—take Huntington's disease—we still cannot explain why what happens was produced or what to do about it. It is not obvious that this inability is because of a momentary lack of insight that technical progress will eventually resolve.

Leaving aside these, to my mind, insurmountable theoretical problems regarding the causal relations between genotypes and phenotypes, and hence what the basis of evolutionary change could possibly be, we are left with the problem of how what happens on the phenomenal level (the level of interaction with the "environment") impacts the level of the genotype. We are left therefore with the eternal nature/nurture debate that has from the beginnings moved political philosophy and always will. **This is not a debate Biology can resolve**; it is a debate that is built into the interstices of biological reflections because those reflections are always impacted by the surrounding philosophical environment and by the phenomena themselves. For evolutionary theory, somehow transformations must take place at the micro level, and yet everything at the micro level makes sense only in light of the macro level toward which it points. And the macro level simply has to have some causal relationship to the micro level or the theory of evolution collapses.

We should grant that despite discussion of "cooperation" and "altruism," most evolutionary theory is dominated by the competitive, Hobbesean model: There is no other way to conceptualize "survival of the fittest." Over and over again we will see that it is political philosophy that has supplied the models for most biological theorizing. But to what extent is the Hobbesean model any more persuasive than the "cooperative" or "altruistic" model which implies the need for the survival of groups? It is groups that reproduce; solitary individuals do not. **Why is it not survival of the fittest group that shapes evolution**, and why does that not imply cooperative sociality as Aristotle argued?[23] And why does that not in turn imply the necessity of the political, with the form of the political resting on choice, not instinct?

Certainly at the time when the human genetic die was initially (allegedly) being cast it was small groups that carried the gene pools and they could be wiped out in groups. Throughout all of early human social and political history it was groups who strove to survive. It was cities like Athens that held out against the Persians, with the price of failure being obliteration. If a city was wiped out by another city it would not reproduce, so traits like heroism and nobility may have been important traits. Does one trace those traits primarily to "genes" or to habit and training provided by great statesmen?

Let us now shift to a final issue, the increasing abstractness of modern science and its seeming detachment from phenomena. I have already suggested that contemporary Biology remains dependent upon formal causality, public "looks," and hence phenomena, even when it is unaware of this fact. But is contemporary Biology, like physics, increasingly relying on thought experiments that are detached from phenomenal validations? For example, are the objects of study for a microbiologist, on a day to day basis, things that deserve to be called phenomena? Phenomena are things that publicly show themselves to all in the public arena (at least potentially). For example, are cells phenomena? One can see them, they show themselves, if only with the aid of an optical microscope. This is an extension of public seeing that leaves what one sees as a phenomenon that shows itself. But do electron microscopes simply extend our phenomenal "seeing?" My answer to that question is no.

To see a cell under an electron microscope it first has to be massively manipulated: e.g. one has to dye it and prepare a thin cross-section. In every instance, the necessary manipulations kill the cell. Hence one never knows if what then presents itself is something true about the cell or an "artifact" introduced by the investigator. There is only so much we can know on the level of what is truly phenomenal, as opposed to on the basis of creative surmise and conjecture (*poiesis*). This is true of cells, and parts of cells like mitochondria—which have become so important in theories regarding symbiosis—not to mention other "organelles." We can study protein synthesis and nucleic acids and DNA transfer from mitochondria to the nucleus and many more manifestations of biochemistry but this is not the same as studying the phenomenon "life." This move away from phenomena is also true of the study of "things" like "genes" which are far more like codes and information than matter. What a gene "is" cannot be "seen."

As an example, I would accept the two kinds of cells as phenomena—prokaryotic and eukaryotic. I would accept the similarity between bacteria and mitochondria in eukaryotic cells as a phenomenon in the true sense. I would admit the similarity between mitochondrial DNA and nuclear DNA as a phenomenon. But that mitochondria are descended from primordial bacteria that invaded eukaryotic cells which already had nuclei is pure speculation. That two prokaryotic bacteria somehow mysteriously merged and evolved a nucleus is equally speculative. That does not mean that we cannot get to all manner of technical manipulations of cells on the basis of these theories. But speculation always presupposes *poiesis* and that in turn presupposes environmental presuppositions, i.e., publicly disseminated ideas that are phenomena, which shape what will be "persuasive" speculations and what will not.

I have argued that modern science can never emancipate itself from the everyday, public, appearing phenomena except through a total forgetfulness, which will occasion a descent into all manner of conundrums in whose grip it will remain. **Consequently modern science is not autonomous and cannot provide the ground or basis for political philosophy.** In fact, it is informed by prior political philosophy without knowing it and should be informed by it for the sake of an account of the whole that has hopes of being persuasive. Political philosophy should grasp, therefore, the full comprehensiveness of its task, the need to fashion a comprehensive phenomenological account of the whole.

I have suggested some of the ways in which the phenomena are essential to evolutionary Biology but also to microbiology as well. For example, one cannot compare the DNA of monkeys and human beings without first having phenomenal awareness of what counts as a man and what counts as a monkey any more than one can explain the wavelength of the color green without first having experienced the phenomenon green. As another example, one can do nothing in embryology without prior knowledge of the phenomenal end toward which a cell is moving. Without that knowledge one could not explain what was going on in cell development, cell differentiation, or anything else. One cannot talk about the presumed ancestry of man from *homo erectus* without first having present phenomenal acquaintance with man and how man differs from quadrupeds, another phenomenal category. One cannot talk about the evolution of one species into another without first having a phenomenal grasp of what differentiates different species.

Attempts at explanation will always remain bound to the phenomena and that means phenomena in the present and that implies the "environment" in the largest sense including the environment of ideas. This is true even as the backdrop for modern science as primarily a technological phenomenon as opposed to an ontological one, even though most modern scientists themselves, and this too is a phenomenon, do not see themselves engaged simply in manipulation and transformation of phenomena; they see themselves engaged in explanation. But they are unclear about what explanation (ontology) requires. And as scientists they are incapable of ever gaining that clarity.

Political philosophy is prior to Biology, and the tradition of political philosophy is not over. It may be just beginning in a postmodern form, a form that can conquer some of the accidents that determined the past history of political philosophy. Changes in ideas change behavior, which changes the environment that has the evolutionary effects that biological theory posits. When we realize that we are forced to take seriously the central place of "punctuated equilibrium"—now understood in a broader sense than usual—and see how that is linked to great tidal shifts in ideas, we grasp the discontinuity that is likely in future biological theorizing. I have argued, both in *Between Eternities* and elsewhere, that we are at the beginning of one of those great tidal shifts in ideas, comparable to what happened at the dawn of modernity.

Transformations of ideas can have more profound effects at this stage of human evolution than posited transformations on the level of genes or gene pools—or "matter" in any sense. Those tidal shifts of ideas condition, before the fact, the interpretation of biological "facts," but also what we "are," and how the *eidē* present themselves. We must give up the mythical hope that some autonomous, to say nothing of reductionist, scientific, ontological explanation of thought will ever be possible. And that is because, among other reasons, genius is unpredictable, and it will have its effects whether those effects are "horizontal" or "lateral." The priority of the phenomena in all thought plus effects like "random drift" and "punctuated equilibrium" should dissuade us from ever succumbing to the soporific effects of opiates like materialism and determinism. Life is now, has been, and always will be, unpredictable. It is not, however, entirely lived out beyond the realm of choice.

Political philosophy always begins with an interrogation of the phenomena; hence as Socrates understood, it has a dialectical component. One of the phenomena is the environment that always includes the climate of opinion (the coming together of *ethos* and *doxa*). Opinions, linked as they are to phenomena, always carry an element of truth, and almost always a larger element of falsity. One of the phenomena of our time is modern science itself. Its public image is part of the *ethos* and *doxa* of our time. Modern science "is" primarily technology not ontology. To understand what science "is" we must again see that, as its founders at the beginning of the modern era understood quite clearly. This differentiation between technology and ontology will not solve all problems, as Heidegger's discussions of the possibility of autonomous technology show. But at least it can help us focus on the real problems not false ones. And at least we will realize that it is political philosophy that takes priority in the examination of phenomena and *doxa*. And as I have argued from the beginning, we see the place of ontology **as part of** an architectonic, proto-philosophy qua political philosophy and not as an autonomous prior activity.

NOTES

1. I have suggested above why String Theory will not become the unified field theory in physics that its proponents hope. But one might also reflect upon the problem that quantum mechanics seems to pose theoretically for chemistry as a science. Among other things, quantum mechanics argues that one cannot know the position of electrons in any given atom. Traditional theories in chemistry explain the possibility of creating compounds by presuming to know the number of electrons in the alleged outer shell of an atom. According to this understanding, with its electrons neatly spinning in various quite predictable orbits, the outer orbit that is posited to hold only a maximum number of electrons determines the possibility of atoms combining to form various compounds. This neat predictability is gone in quantum mechanics. Yet quantum theory has hardly brought the enterprise of modern chemistry to a halt. There are significant matters for reflection here, for example, regarding the relation between "pure science" and technical applications of that allegedly pure ontological knowledge.

2. Or, is modern science set in motion by the desire to manipulate nature rather than simply understand it? Does one need to understand the whole to manipulate it; does a plumber need to know the nature of the whole to manipulate it in his distinctive fashion? If manipulating nature for the sake of improving man's condition is the goal of modern science, as founders like Bacon and Descartes thought, then it is in the service of and determined by an end outside itself—the Good, however conceived.

3. See for example, Edward O. Wilson, *Sociobiology: The New Synthesis* (Cambridge: Harvard University Press, 1975), Richard Dawkins, *The Selfish Gene* (New York: Oxford University Press, 1989), and Lynn Margulis and Dorion Sagan, *Microcosmos: Four Billion Years of Evolution from Our Microbial Ancestors* (New York: Summit Books, 1986).

4. It might offer a useful foundation for *poiesis*, but that is a matter for further reflection at another time. Ultimately biology, like physics or political philosophy, must

be grounded in phenomena. The question is, which undertaking has the self-consciously clearest grasp of the phenomena. My answer is political philosophy as I have been describing it.

5. Roger Masters, *The Nature of Politics* (New Haven: Yale University Press, 1989) and Larry Arnhart, *Darwinian Natural Right: The Biological Ethics of Human Nature* (Albany: SUNY Press, 1998).

6. Masters, p. 248. See also George Simpson, *Biology and Man* (New York: Harcourt, Brace & World, 1969).

7. Leo Strauss, *Natural Right and History* (Chicago: University of Chicago Press, 1968), p. 8.

8. I have been arguing throughout that ontology is *part* of political philosophy, not prior to it.

9. Masters, p. 248.

10. I would be the first to admit that standing entirely "outside" Nature, **outside the present phenomena as they present themselves,** is a preposterous notion. We are thrown beings in a variety of ways, but our genotype is only one of those modes of thrownness. But there is no way to conceptualize being entirely "in" Nature, as a noncomplex unitary whole, in any fashion that is consistent with the phenomena. Again, if the core of modern Biology is molecular biology, and molecules are made of atoms, on what basis does Biology succeed in making itself independent of physics? And if evolutionary biology is the core of Biology, on what basis do we choose it over molecular biology, and even if we do, **why do not ideas condition the environment?**

11. Arnhart is more subtle in this regard arguing that the environment will determine what is just even though human nature narrows the limits within which choice is reasonable. It is not only a subtler conclusion but also more Aristotelian. Still, both Masters and Arnhart see contemporary Biology as justifying some permutation of what Aristotle called a "polity" as the best regime and that contemporary liberalism offers a permutation of a polity.

12. I accept, as do Masters and Arnhart, the need to reject the fact-value dichotomy as artificial and incapable of being sustained. But my rejection is not "naturalistic," it is phenomenological. As one example, as phenomena present themselves they always "are," in their essential being, determined by what they are for, and whether they are well or poorly suited to that end. Stripping away their "value" components in an attempt to get down to something normatively neutral destroys what they "are" and comes too late anyway. Things have already revealed themselves at the point at which we step back from them and try to strip them of some of their attributes. Since I do not believe that any intellectual undertaking from political philosophy to physics or biology can ultimately transcend or stand somewhere outside the phenomena, I see the fact-value dichotomy as an utterly artificial piece of chicanery. The phenomena always dominate and they are evaluative in their very being, in the way they present themselves.

13. The ten propositions are on pp. 6–7 and the twenty desires are on pp. 31–36 in Arnhart, *Darwinian Natural Right.*

14. Perhaps we can begin to see the issue this synthesis poses by asking why Arnhart did not choose to call his synthesis "Aristotelian Evolution," or "Humean Naturalism," instead of "Darwinian Natural Right."

15. Arnhart, 234.

16. The issue is what form of causality takes precedence even if they all operate together. I would summarize it this way: For Darwin, efficient causality takes precedence, for Aristotle, final (implying choice), for microbiology, material causality, for my understanding of phenomenology, it is formal causality that takes precedence. This is not to say that formal causality has no place in Darwinianism or even in contemporary microbiology for I maintain that the sciences never succeed in emancipating themselves from the phenomena which show themselves, and always do so, formally. I will return to this issue below.

17. Consider the following from the *Politics*, Book I: "[I]t is by looking at how things develop naturally from the **beginning** that one may best study them. First, then, there must of necessity be a conjunction of persons who cannot exist without one another: on the one hand, male and female, for the sake of reproduction (**which occurs not from intentional choice** but—as is also the case with the other animals and plants—from a natural striving to leave behind another that is like oneself) . . ." (1252a25–30) This is the operation of material and efficient causality without choice. Compare this to: "Every city, therefore **exists by nature**, if such also are the first partnerships. For the city is their end, **and nature is an end**: what each thing is—for example, a human being, a horse, or a household—when its coming into being is complete is, we assert, the nature of that thing. . . . For it is peculiar to man as compared to the other animals that he alone has a perception of good and bad and just and unjust and other things [of this sort] . . . Accordingly, there is in everyone by nature an impulse toward this sort of partnership. And yet **the one who first constituted [a city] is responsible for the greatest of goods.**" [my emphasis] (1252b30–12253a30) This is the operation of final causality and it requires choice, in this instance the choice of a statesman who grasps a conception of the good. And of things good and just, in the *Nichomachean Ethics*, Aristotle famously albeit mysteriously asserts that while they are natural, they change. The good must be first consciously grasped and then put into operation by choice. Final causality does not operate by efficient causality as it would have to for Darwin. Aristotle, *The Politics*, trans. by Carnes Lord (Chicago: University of Chicago Press, 1984).

18. See Arnhart, pp. 242–48. There is very little in the way of material causality in Darwin's own account. Darwin had no explanation of the mechanics of heredity or genetics. He simply inferred that some mechanism must be operating. For Darwin the makeup of the whole organism is his smallest object of analysis. For Aristotle, a thing "is" what it is primarily as manifest in its finished, indeed perfected, manifestation. This is why final causality takes precedence. **But in every interesting manifestation of the end as it operates in human beings it must be chosen and supported,** perhaps not by each individual, but by legislators and their laws, parents and their raising of their young, and then finally by fully responsible adults and their choices. Arnhart Aristoteleanizes Darwin to get to his Darwinian Natural Right. But even then, even when talking about teleology and final causality, Arnhart has the end operating efficiently in drives and instincts. Aristotle does not.

19. See Arnhart, p. 231.

20. Like cells, manipulative techniques always point beyond themselves to the absent good that determines their activities. Those goods are themselves phenomena

that show themselves and the good in the human arena requires choice; it does not actualize itself through efficient causality. Any theorizing in Biology is always determined before the fact by phenomena which are shaped by publicly appearing *eidē*. The *eidē* always only show themselves in relation to the good. Biology can never be autonomous ontology because it is determined by factors it cannot master. Hence biology cannot be some autonomous given on which political philosophy grounds itself and from which political philosophy deduces prescriptions. Political philosophy as phenomenological is always closer to the source of all meaning and understanding than any other undertaking.

21. None of this questionableness I am raising seems to me to point necessarily to "creationism" by default. As I have suggested in my brief discussion of Theology above, Revelation always implies the need for responsible interpretation and that seems to me to rely upon the same phenomenological presuppositions that shape any responsible biological theorizing. We may grant the fact of Revelation, but it is present for almost all of us only indirectly through texts. Those texts operate as the primary phenomena for Theology. And in the operative texts we are quite literally always presented with parables, allegories and metaphors that have to be interpreted. That raises the issue of competent versus incompetent interpretations. The only available arbiter here is political philosophy which in that respect stands prior to both Theology and modern science and that is one of the reasons why it is architectonic.

22. Consider the reflections of Stephen Webster in *Thinking About Biology* (Cambridge: Cambridge University Press, 2003), especially p. 19 and surrounding material. See also Jan Sapp, *Genesis: The Evolution of Biology* (New York: Oxford University Press, 2003).

23. Evolutionary theory seems to me to rest primarily on premises drawn from modern political philosophy and that includes everything from man's fundamental a-sociality to the idea of History. But some permutations of evolutionary theory not only co-opt the pre-modern notion of a cosmic origin in time, taken from the Scriptural dispensation, but also co-opt variants of the Greek notion of natural sociality, but without seeing that this points to the priority of the political which in turn implies choice. It is unlikely that a consistent *poiesis* can ultimately be constructed from modern and pre-modern elements pasted together in this fashion. This is especially true when the premises exist at the level of unconscious presuppositions.

Chapter Twenty-Two

Political Philosophy and Environmentalism: Recovering the Phenomenon "Nature"

What seemed to be an eternal, impenetrable, awe-inspiring, broad-bosomed Earth to pre-modern humanity **no longer presents itself as such** a phenomenon to late moderns who stand before a natural whole that now seems increasingly weak and vulnerable against the willfulness of modern technology. It is also a natural whole that now shows itself only as modern technological science allows it to come to presence. But like a real estate developer unimpressed with the antiquity of a neighborhood or wilderness, our scientists now stand before the natural whole ready to demolish an old dwelling and build a replacement from scratch. But what is the status of that envisioned replacement now that we no longer stand before a natural whole so threatening to us that we can take our bearings simply by negating it? If we cannot take our bearings by the negative stance of modernity to nature, how do we generate a positive vision of our relationship?

Perhaps most thought-provoking, with increasing technical and ideological intensity we now stand before our own humanity in the same fashion we have stood for so long before the rest of nature, ready to dominate and transform it. Our concern that we have gone too far seems to come too late. Our desire to willfully master our will to mastery presents us with one philosophical conundrum after another. Philosophically, nature itself has increasingly become a vaporous concept for us at precisely the moment that the natural whole seems to be losing the autonomous rhythms that many think it so important to recover, at least in their non-human manifestations. Yet almost no one sees the need to recover the natural within our own humanity. Ethically, almost universally, nature is taken as the problem; metaphysical Freedom is the solution. We are locked in a modern, all too modern, opposition at a time that the momentum of the modern technological project appears to permit no exit. But as a point of departure it is always available to us to remember where we entered.

Non imperium in imperio asserted the great proto-modern political philosopher Spinoza—let there be no belief that there is a human kingdom within the
larger natural whole. Being is One. But modern philosophy substantially ignored that sentiment and set about carving out a human kingdom not so much
within as "outside" and in opposition to the nonhuman part of the natural
whole. We late moderns are left with the ramifications of that decision,
among them most of the concrete issues that are usually addressed by the
amorphous body of thought called "environmentalist" theory. In environmentalist theory we have what I have posed above as one of the unavoidable
questions for political philosophy understood as a holistic undertaking, the relation between human nature and the larger natural whole. The modern conceptualization of this issue opposes Nature and Freedom, but I would suggest
that it is no longer tenable. On the one hand, to remain human, the human
cannot be seamlessly integrated into the larger natural whole. Yet the human
cannot exist outside the larger whole either as modern political philosophy
has come to conceptualize the matter. Contemporary environmentalist
thought gives us our most efficient access to the issue of nature because there
is at least initial respect for the natural on some level.

   While various conservation movements have roots going back at least
into the last century, *environmentalism* as I am using the term is a phenomenon that can be traced back no further than the 1960s. Its primary debt is
to the constellation of ideas that can be designated "New Left." Needless to
say, contemporary environmentalist thought has gone beyond its beginnings. But its instincts remain clear in its repeated attempts to harness for
its use everything from critical theory, Marxism, neo-Marxism, socialism,
feminism and anarchism, to the thought of Nietzsche and Heidegger, and
most problematically, deconstructionism.[1] Ultimately, all of these dispensations are straightforwardly modern phenomena, descended from modern
political philosophy—I have argued above that even an allegedly postmodern phenomenon like deconstructionism is a simple extension of modernity.
I will argue that with modern tools environmentalism will never escape the
confining grip of the modern, which is where the origin of the real problems lies.

   Our contemporary "problem of nature" and most "environmentalist" cures
descend from the same premises, the modern moral and political project as it
is incorporated within both the new science and modern political philosophy.
Far from inoculating us with a therapeutic antibody, contemporary environmental thought injects a virulent new strain of the same virus. This would not
be the first time in modern thought we have seen intensified doses of what
caused an illness proposed as its cure. To avoid such repeated exercises, we
need philosophical clarity more than immediate, concrete policy prescriptions

because the central and unavoidable issue is ultimately not technical nor simply a matter of political will. The fundamental question is: What should be the relation between humanity and the rest of the natural whole? It was the specifically modern understanding of the articulation of the natural whole and the place of humanity within it that led to the problems that contemporary environmentalism tries to confront.

The problem presented by environmentalism is identical to the problem of modernity: its solution lies beyond modernity. I will argue that that "beyond" is to be found in a possible **post**-modernity. But I differentiate what I mean by **post**modernity from what is customarily discussed under the rubric postmodern**ism**, which, as I have argued above and elsewhere, is an all too modern phenomenon.

Given my central premise, I must direct at least a few initial words to the much-vexed question of the meaning of modernity.[2] I accept the conventional wisdom that modern philosophy begins with Descartes and modern political philosophy begins with Machiavelli. They, and other proto-modern authors, share the self-understanding that they were making a conscious break with past thought and concrete reality, and that this was required to actualize the human good.[3] In every case, the archimedean point from which they hoped to quit the past and raise a categorically different future was a self-legislating, self-grounding conception of reason. In Machiavelli's thought this is consciously deployed in the service of the "conquest of Chance" through a new political science. For Descartes it is deployed to generate a new physical science that can manipulate and dominate nature. In each case there was an understanding that the human good was to be constructed outside the natural whole rather than through an appropriate integration into it.

According to Machiavelli, humanity remains in the clutches of Chance whenever it is not ruled by consciously constructed "modes and orders." Hence the traditional world had to be replaced by a consciously projected world. It was necessary to quit the relatively small, homogeneous communities ruled by custom that Aristotle had praised and that Machiavelli admitted were "natural."[4] Humanity could become master of its fate only in a consciously constructed kingdom, one consciously constructed by "theorists" like Machiavelli who manipulate "new" princes, and eventually see to it that they become obsolete.[5]

What one sees in Machiavelli is a manifestation of modernity's distinctive anti-nature animus. The natural condition, here understood as Chance, is seen as at odds with human well-being. Through a conscious application of reason one constructs an artificial arena that is allegedly superior in producing human well-being. In the process, reason is transformed into a manifestation of human will, no longer to be confused with the pre-modern tool used to contemplate an order of nature that presents itself—or so the conventional presentation of antiquity would have it. In Machiavelli we already see the first manifestation of the modern dichotomy Reason (conceived as Will)/Nature (conceived as Chance, later as Necessity). Reason became a tool used to stand outside the rest of the natural whole. Eventually, the natural world came to be presented as if it could be conceptualized as a whole despite the expulsion of one of its parts, humanity.

With Machiavelli we also see the emergence of the distinctive modern relation to temporality. The past is delegitimized. The present is put in the service of a transition to the future. From the very beginning, modern humanity has been "on the way." And hence from the beginning modern humanity has been expelled from the present because it had no reason to take the past seriously except as a problem to negate. I will assert that only by recapturing the present will we be able to confront the problems encountered in environmentalism. But as I suggested above, that can only be done in a stance like that of "ecstatic temporality" that holds the three ecstasies of temporality together, affirming the past and opening rather than constructing and projecting the future in detail. That is the stance of an architectonic, phenomenological political philosophy.

While Machiavelli's transition to a better human future required primarily a political program, Descartes sounded one of the first overt notes of the modern longing for the sublimation, indeed extirpation, of the political.[6] For Descartes, political competition was primarily conditioned by natural scarcity and the fear of death. Transcend those natural limitations, and what passes for the political might no longer be needed. What was required was a new physical science, not a new political science.

Eventually, to transcend natural limits, one must first engage in the famous Cartesian suspension of belief in Tradition, common sense, and the data of the senses, and bracket everything that in the past passed for knowledge or was at least seen as the entree to knowledge. As with Machiavelli, the past as a repository of wisdom is delegitimized. But this time the entire world as it appears for us in everyday life—all "phenomena"—is de-legitimized as well. Modernity never accomplishes a rapprochement with the world as it appears phenomenologically in common for all: indeed, as time passes, modern thought radicalizes the rift between the world of appearance and the one that is posited as the "real" world.

The empty, unencumbered self-consciousness of the abstract Cartesian ego became the abode of a Reason whose end is the manipulation and domination of Nature for the sake of overcoming natural limits. And that project is understood as the means to actualizing the human good. In the process, an a-historical, traditionless, worldless self came to dictate what would count as Being via the projection of "clear and distinct" ideas as the ultimate substratum. Reality thereby became a creation of a self-conscious mind now openly understood as self-projecting, self-legislating, self-grounding Will. As with Machiavelli, one sees in Descartes **the fundamental autonomy of the master theorist**—the existence of subaltern theorists should never divert the gaze from the grand paradigm setter.

The same fundamental principles resurface in the poetry of the state of nature theorists who bring proto-modernity to its culmination. Again the natural state is seen as inimical to human well-being. Reason discovers laws that allow us to quit that state. In Hobbes's version, reason is posited as a trained capacity (presupposing primarily shared names and a shared method) for deducing what follows from the sovereign names that are dependent on a founding theorist like Hobbes. Reason rests, therefore, on the legislative efforts of a name-giver or definition-creator—albeit this does not really account for Hobbesean *poiesis*. Armed with laws of Reason so derived, it was hoped that humanity could leave the natural state behind and launch a progressive transition toward the creation of a human world that had reached an accommodation with the larger natural whole. Once again, Reason is Nature's "Other," the tool for the great escape from Nature.

With Hobbes we also see modernity's egalitarian bias emerge with singular clarity. In Hobbes's case, this egalitarianism is purchased through an open assault on natural difference. Various types of human beings had to be simply suppressed. For example, the laws of Reason tell us that the natural love of honor—a manifestation of which, we are told, occurs even in laughter—must be sublimated if the human good—understood as involving the universal search for peace, comfort, considerable material consumption, and a relatively predictable existence—is to be ensured. Once again, to accomplish this a historically and naturally unencumbered Reason constructs its point of departure, which obviously carries within it the final destination. The whole enterprise is circular from the very beginning.[7] Modern egalitarianism is purchased at the price of a radically disencumbered, abstract self that is completely alienated from Nature and natural difference. Put another way, deep within the interstices of modernity is what Nietzsche would later call the "Spirit of Revenge"; a subject to which I will return.[8] Locke merely made the same core premises more publicly palatable.

Proto-modernity was deflected by thinkers such as Rousseau and Kant onto a different but still altogether consistently modern path. For example, although Rousseau rejected the "bourgeoisification" of modern human beings by proto-modernity, his critique of proto-modernity continued to use altogether modern theoretical tools by directing proto-modernity in the direction of "metaphysical freedom"—an idea that in one permutation or another underlies almost all contemporary thought, including most environmentalist thought. For Rousseau, man is metaphysically free to the extent that he is the one animal with a malleable, evanescent nature. What humanity "is" at any moment depends on what it has become, by imitation as well as a result of various historical accidents—and according to Rousseau all of prior human history was an accident.

Rousseau's insight was that if humanity changes over time, that process of change can eventually be consciously shaped, and hence all past accidents could give way to an artifact that is entirely the product of human Will—the Will, of course, of individuals such as Rousseau. Rousseau is explicit that one of the ways to accomplish this is to try to induce new forms of behavior and belief on the basis of hypothetically constructed histories—or the now more fashionable term, *narratives*. One would act as if certain fables were true. As Nietzsche would observe, eventually all of life becomes a fable, actually a competition between fables. Should one be surprised that modern science in conjunction with competing fables would produce a vaporous world of mere "traces?"

The altogether modern insight of the theorists of metaphysical freedom implies that the truly human is not to be found in natural characteristics but is based on self-legislating self-consciousness—that is, the arena in which we give laws to ourselves, where "we" means the great philosophical legislators. This is the human realm of Freedom; the natural realm is now reduced to the realm of blind necessity. We must stand "outside" Nature so conceived to be human. The venue of this "outside" is a self-grounding Reason that has been transformed into Will. The modern Reason/Nature split and transformation of Reason into Will is given a novel twist in Rousseau such that the genuinely "human" good rests on moral and political progress in "metaphysical freedom" rather than primarily technical progress. But Rousseau in no way dismissed the discoveries of modern science; he simply wanted them to remain the domain of a few rather than be publicly disseminated.

The idea of metaphysical freedom ran the risk of devolving into the nihilism of competing ungrounded fables from the very beginning. Rousseau makes it clear that the primary Will at stake in proving our Freedom was that of the theorist and "legislator" like Rousseau, who posits the hypothetical histories that would be instrumental in founding new nations, thereby reshaping humanity. What lurks here is a potential battle of theorist titans to re-create humanity in their respective images. Who is to say which titan is correct? The only limit to the potential free-for-all that Rousseau offers is the "General Will," that is, subordination to a shared, national *Volkgeist*. What simultaneously supports and limits Reason as Will is public myth. Without that there is no limit for the seemingly unlimited power that Rousseau has unleashed.

Rousseau's vision was too morally and politically demanding for most. Metaphysical freedom had to be made more palatable to the increasingly bourgeois tastes, egalitarian and hedonist sentiments, and universalistic tendencies latent in modernity. In that light, Kant's work was a *tour de force* (although Kant, as well, would have desired a far sterner morality than was his ultimate effect). For Kant, self-grounding, self-legislating Reason had to dictate both what would count as Nature and Freedom for us and simultaneously eschew the attempt to know the "thing-in-itself." We had to simply accept that we cannot grasp the underlying whole of reality except as Necessity, but that allegedly does not prove that Nature is in reality in the grip of Necessity rather than constant becoming or simple Chance and indeterminacy. We will allow ourselves to "view" Nature in only one way; but thereby we may act "as-if" we are free beings because we cannot prove anything to the contrary about the ineffable thing-in-itself. We can, however, prove to ourselves that an act is free only if we can show that it is not a response to natural inclination. The only way to do that is to will moral laws universally applicable without regard to natural determinations based on the place and time we inhabit, its climate, or our natural inclinations.

The price paid for this maneuver is that both the natural realm of appearance and phenomena and the human realm of "values" lose ontological foundations. If successful in deploying Reason in this fashion, it was hoped we would **come to live in a human realm outside the natural whole—the great modern myth.** For Kant even more than for Hobbes, if this myth was successfully deployed, the concrete ramification for which we then could hope was perpetual peace consummated on a bed of universal, cosmopolitan, egalitarian, commercial republicanism made possible by modern science and technology. That is the modern longing in a nutshell.

Kant was not the end of modernity to date, but from the present perspective nothing that is simultaneously novel and thoroughly modern has announced itself since. Hegel tried to give ontological credibility to the transforming march of self-actualizing Will through History. Marx tried to rethink the means to metaphysical freedom on allegedly materialist grounds. Nietzsche stripped the Will of the need to will the universal. Now one could openly and with good conscience re-create humanity and the natural world through an unlimited exercise of the creative Will-to-Power. In the process, for Nietzsche, history ceased to be progressive or meaningful, and human existence was delivered back to the contingency that Machiavelli and Descartes set out to master. Heidegger further stripped the Will of the possibility of self-consciousness and left us with the reign of a mysterious contingency and fate that we could no longer master. In the process the way was paved for the "antifoundationalism" and praise of blind, contentless "difference" of postmodern*ism*. Therein modernity circled back on itself to will Chance. I would argue that there are no more novel modern moves to play in the game. As I suggested above and elsewhere, we arrive at closure.

Having delineated modernity in this fashion, what would deserve to be called genuinely *post*modern? A genuinely *post*modern alternative 1) would have to be beyond metaphysical freedom. It 2) would have to position itself beyond modernity's anti-nature animus. It 3) would have to be beyond the glorification of rationality as autonomous, unencumbered self-legislating Will conceptualized as Nature's Other. Postmodernity 4) would have to open itself to affirming the present, and that, I will argue shortly, 5) will require emancipation from what Nietzsche called the Spirit of Revenge against "time and its 'it was.'" In short, *post*modernity would have to quit the revenge against what shows itself that holds throughout modernity and simultaneously negates the past as nothing but error and **leaves us always in transition standing nowhere.**

*Post*modernity would have to open itself to the spontaneous occurrence of natural difference in all its manifestations—although that need not imply a blind immersion in or total acceptance of all material and efficient causality. Part of that essential difference that makes us human, I have argued, is to be history making beings. And *post*modernity would have to find for itself a place to stand other than the gravity-defying, mid-air tightrope dance of modern, self-legislating Reason. Finally, it would have to find a way to grasp the whole as a complex whole of which humanity is a part. To understate the matter, this is easier said than done, but is not thereby unworthy as an object of philosophical reflection.

The characteristics of the genuinely postmodern to which I have pointed would have little in common with what customarily asserts itself under the rubric postmodern*ism*. As noted above, my understanding implies a distinction between **post**modernity and postmodern**ism**.[9] Postmodernism as it is associated with such names as Rorty, Derrida, Foucault, Vattimo, and others, and as it is used in conjunction with discussions in architecture, the social sciences, art, literature, and cultural criticism, is a decidedly post-Enlightenment, late modern phenomenon. It rejects the possibility of the self-conscious, self-grounding, self-legislating self of modern thought. Given that there is no longer a self-conscious ego—and likewise no self-presenting natural Other—it becomes impossible for postmodernism to posit the possibility of a linear, unidirectional motion for human history. Therefore, the central modern idea of progress must be jettisoned as chimerical.

Throughout postmodern*ism* we hear the assertion that reality is totally fluid, evanescent, and ultimately unknowable. That is true of both knower and known, "subject" and "object." Reality, human and nonhuman, is constituted by our attempts to use, describe, and understand what is. The phenomenological concept of Nature, that which is *self*-presenting rather than dependent on man, is jettisoned entirely—although it is repeatedly brought in surreptitiously through the back door whenever a concrete political or moral prescription is made. I do not accept this rejection of phenomenology. There are things that present themselves.

For postmodern*ism*, because reality is not fixed, it is a mistake to believe we can consciously or "rationally" control it. The modern dream of control slips away as do any worries about historical closure or the "end of history," which can be dismissed without being confronted. Life exists primarily on a surface that constantly reconstructs itself in unpredictable ways. There is no source or foundation; what passes for presence is determined exclusively by absence. When anything begins to ossify or gain rigidity in reality, it is the duty of the deconstructionist to step forward and take it apart so that it can no longer be an object of attachment. But this "moral" prescription cannot be justified using postmodernist premises as it implies a self-presenting understanding of the Good. Be that as it may, for the postmodernist this deconstructing must be constant, hence it never points toward reconstruction. What is needed is an urbane appreciation of "difference" even though all difference is entirely contingent. All of reality dissolves into an endless, arbitrary, contingent play of differences that occupy a surface beneath which there is nothing.[10]

It is entirely predictable that this understanding be frequently conjoined with an ironic stance toward life. But with that irony usually comes cynicism as well. We bide our time, jaded and indifferent, the perfect citizens of the posthistorical age, knowing that nothing is worthy of passion or commitment. It is not clear how one could construct a useful environment ethic from such a stance except by sneaking in altogether modern political and moral commitments to which postmodernists are not theoretically entitled—although they do it all too often.

As I have argued above and elsewhere, postmodernism is an altogether consistent extension of modernity. It is the kind of understanding that presupposes that natural limits have been pushed back by a manipulative science and that natural scarcity is not an inevitable given. It presupposes a world where human labor has been increasingly successful in supplanting the natural realm and where human labor has been increasingly stripped of any rhyme or reason other than ongoing transformation. The entire ensemble of postmodern commitments from antifoundationalism to an-archic pluralism not only presuppose the liberal bourgeois world but represent the coming together of Marx's longed-for "withering away of the state" and Nietzsche's understanding that all of life is interpretation (which is nothing but an extension of the proto-modern understanding that we can only know what we make). It is only the shortest of steps from middle modernity's faith in the malleability and manipulability of nature, and metaphysical freedom's positing of the moral irrelevance of the natural to the evanescence of a world of traces where everything is dominated by absence and nothing presents itself.

Where can we look to find the first notes out of which we might fashion something genuinely postmodern that can address our needs? To my mind the most promising elements are to be found in the works of Nietzsche and Heidegger. I would be the first to admit that both thinkers remain within the orbit of modern thinking; for example, consider Nietzsche's all too modern glorification of the Will. But each author also articulates elements that open genuinely postmodern possibilities. I will briefly focus on those elements, knowing the danger involved in abstracting them from their context.[11]

In Nietzsche's thought the modern transformation of Reason into Will is raised to its highest power. Nietzsche merely wills the inversion of various modern dichotomies. He wills the priority of the instinctive animal over the metaphysically free "human," mere consciousness over self-consciousness, the realm of appearance over the true or ideal realm. But in the doctrine of the "eternal occurrence," which he asserted was his central and highest thought, Nietzsche intended a metaphor for a new human relation to reality. Nietzsche's Zarathustra says of the eternal recurrence that it should be seen as his "last will." By that he meant it was necessary to will the cessation of willing. Future humanity could then cease to operate in the realm of and under the hegemony of the Will. What this pointed to for Nietzsche was the "reintegration of man into nature."[12]

For Nietzsche, as for Rousseau, all of past human history had been an accident. Nietzsche asserted that this becomes the ground of great distress for moderns because something eludes their will. Because the present is a product of a past that we did not consciously will, we inevitably rebel against it and are never satisfied. We always resent the past and with that comes a dissatisfaction with the present that makes opening the future impossible. Hence we repeatedly re-create the same rebellion and resentment endlessly. There is only one solution; we must will that the past transpired precisely as we would have willed it. Then the past will cease to be an object for our anger and resentment, and the present that follows from it can be affirmed.

To prove that the past is just as we would have willed it, we must will that the future be a repetition of the past. In more concrete terms, we must will the return of unself-conscious instinct or immediate "nature" over the autonomous, self-conscious, self-legislating ego. And we must will that the abode of truth come to reside in the realm of appearance and not in some "real" or "ideal" realm that is "beyond." Thereby Nietzsche attempted to overcome metaphysically free, modern man, who, like pre-modern man, longs for something beyond nature (the "meta"). We will the overcoming of the Realm of Freedom in favor of the hegemony of the Realm of Chance.

In Nietzsche's understanding, what is concretely required is the unleashing of a new dialectic of the strong and the weak, of master and slave, as well as new dialectics of male and female, nation and nation, wise and foolish, in short, the unleashing of hierarchical "difference" and an acceptance of the spontaneous outcomes that unimpeded interactions would imply. Needless to say, the implications could be harsh, and Nietzsche was by no means squeamish in this regard. Like a good Machiavellian, Nietzsche thought that foundings were always harsh. But upon a harsh foundation a new world could be erected. That new world would help humanity avoid the impasse characterized by the victory of the "last man," that is, the End of History.

Nietzsche characterized the modern refusal of the Will to accept the past—resentment against "time and its it was"—as a manifestation of the "spirit of revenge." For Nietzsche, all of past history, especially as it is conditioned by Christianity and Socratic rationalism—but also by their descendants who launched modern science, politics, and ethics—was resentful and revengeful. **All of Western history had been sullied by a revengeful relation to phenomenal, temporal reality.** Never yet had humanity been able to accept reality as it presents itself, to accept that the whole is and must be constructed out of a balance of competing contradictory parts. Hence humanity had throughout time exacted a revenge against phenomenal reality. It became necessary to reject the world as it presents itself and eventually "rationalize" and transform it, bringing it in line with the wishes of the Will. Hence we have never yet affirmed life. On the contrary, we have willfully and revengefully destroyed all manner of natural oppositions, clashes, and confrontations. In the process, we have threatened to destroy life itself.

According to Nietzsche, it is a mere prejudice to believe that the good is caused only by the good, that the beautiful is caused only by the beautiful, that justice only emerges from a just cause and foundation. For example, using Nietzsche's understanding of art, the most beautiful and magnificent artistic creations are responses to the ugly, the threatening, and the frightening. Human greatness in all its forms is born of facing challenges, overcoming hardships, confronting the base and the low, enduring the painful and the ugly. If we revengefully remove all obstacles, humanity is not enhanced but diminished. Life is reduced to an at-best subhuman banality.

To truly affirm life and be freed from the spirit of revenge, Nietzsche thought that one must affirm life in all its sorrow and joy, beauty and ugliness, strength and weakness, sickness and health, tyranny and magnanimity. To affirm *all* of life in a revenge-free fashion was to affirm the eternality of what is and to will that one would want it no other way for all of time. Hence one must be freed from the desire for a future that obliterates the past, a future that rests on a progressive change and transformation of reality, which aims at what Nietzsche designated the "Sabbath of all sabbaths."

Modern man had to eschew faith in linear History and affirm life in its infinite, mysterious, unfathomable circling and recurrence. To say yes to life, to affirm it in all of its diversity, is the human equivalent of affirming and nurturing what environmentalists call bio-diversity. **My suggestion is that a postmodern environmental ethic will have to be affirmative in this fashion** and cease not only its revengeful assaults on the nonhuman part of nature, but fall back from the intensifying force being brought against the human part as well. Needless to say, if this cannot be accomplished without the element of barbarity Nietzsche thought unavoidable, we are presented with an unattractive set of options. But I believe we can proceed on the assumption that this is not necessary. As I have argued throughout, the truly human is not to be found in the merely instinctive and materialist side of the ledger. Man "is" the history making being.

It is my contention that Heidegger, despite his critique of Nietzsche as the last metaphysician, broadens and deepens Nietzsche's analysis of the "spirit of revenge" in a useful fashion.[13] Even when on the surface he overtly parted company with Nietzsche's rhetoric, Heidegger pursued an end similar to Nietzsche's, a rapprochement with a world that could be seen as *self*-presenting, which could be **lovingly affirmed in all its genuine diversity and mystery.**

A central ontological intuition reigns throughout Heidegger's thought: Being is conceived as *physis*, that which sends forth out of concealment into unconcealment, while simultaneously holding back something in concealment. In more customary parlance, Being and the realm of appearance, the realm of the self-showing phenomena, are intimately connected. But Being never completely reveals itself, and it reveals itself in a succession of different ways that are beyond our control. Heidegger—in a way that philosophically deepens the mere willful Nietzschean inversion of the real and the apparent—gives ontological grounding to what appears for all, and grounds it on something other than the human, positing Will. Unlike the modern understanding in which what counts as Being is determined in advance by a human construction projected by the Will, for Heidegger, Being presents *itself* if we open ourselves to it; albeit it does not present itself in a static fashion, and it is incapable of being grasped or mastered by us in its entirety.

According to Heidegger, the nihilism that engulfs late modern life—at least in one permutation of his argument—is due to the fact that we have turned away from openness to that which presents itself. We live in the "Age of the World Picture," **imposing our self-grounded viewpoints on the world,** and as a result we live in a time of competing "worldviews." The world has become no more than our picture, and it has lost the dignity it gains when it is imbued with a relation to Being which is more than our invention. As a result, both nature and human nature have become fundamentally evanescent and valueless for modern humanity. Man is transformed into a mere laborer-consumer and nature is transformed into inert material—both man and nature become raw material—to be manipulated at will and kept "standing by" for future manipulations. Hence we feel no real qualms about imposing various projects for transformation, manipulation, and domination of what amounts to ontologically valueless material. The modern "Age of the Worldview," as Heidegger presents it, is the ultimate manifestation of what Nietzsche called the Spirit of Revenge. **Any postmodern environmental ethic would have to stand beyond the belief that the world is of value only after we impose our view upon it.** We must stand beyond constructivism.

But according to Heidegger, emancipating ourselves from the modern age of worldviews will be very difficult. In principle this cannot be accomplished by an act of the self-conscious, self-grounding Will, for that simply reproduces the problem. Herein lies Heidegger's deepest criticism of Nietzsche. One cannot transcend the hegemony of the revengeful, positing human Will by an act of Will. We are so determined by the spirit of the revengeful technological world that it is a myth to believe that we can stand beyond or outside it. Everything that surrounds us, as well as how we relate to ourselves, is revealed in the modern, revengeful technological fashion. All we can do is step back from willfulness, step back from projecting and positing worldviews, and await a new dispensation of Being, a new revelation of the realm of appearance: but we cannot predict when that new dispensation will be forthcoming. Unfortunately, this latter conclusion led Heidegger in the direction of a mere hopeful waiting. We must assume that something more proactive is possible.

Where do these intimations leave us? They certainly do not leave us in a position to move immediately in the direction of a specific program ready for concrete adoption. In a significant way, the explosion of policy alternatives and theoretical perspectives—and the general faith that enough clarity exists to move immediately to projecting more or less grand, consciously constructed transformations of reality—is at the heart of the problem. What is needed is a new way of relating to the whole of which we humans are a part, not a laundry list of prescriptions littered freely with our ideological wishes.

It may be true that a new relation to Nature will be adopted only after some unpredictable occurrence or happening makes it necessary. But an arena of already opened possibilities must be available before the fact, to be tapped when the moment is right. That is how a postmodern political philosophy correctly opens out the future. It opens spaces that can be filled in, in the future, when needed. We must open those spaces. To do so we must accept that the world that appears is not merely our creation and is an abode of truth, ceasing thereby to continually transport truth to some other realm—whether that be some presumed "real" world that transcends the one we occupy or a constellation of human statements ordered in an allegedly incontestable fashion by human logic or any of the myriad of other attempts to dirempt the ideal and the real.

With very few exceptions, environmentalism as we have seen it up to now is but another manifestation of the spirit of revenge that simultaneously argues for forcing humanity to step back from nonhuman nature, allowing it an unfettered arena in which to operate spontaneously—for example in its "wilderness" manifestation—and for projecting all manner of transformative contructions and manipulations on contemporary humanity. But this man versus the natural whole dichotomy is simply modern, all too modern, and carries with it the underlying basis of the problem that needs to be solved. The problem of nature requires us to rethink nature as a complex whole that always already includes man within it.

Further, beyond the fact that what we can loosely call environmentalism almost always rests on a view of the natural whole that does not include man, it also has a view of nature that is far too static. Part of the movement of nature includes the movement of humanity, the ongoing movement of history making man. To fail to appreciate that what humanity is and does is as important to the whole and the ever-changing "balance" of that whole as the actions of a whale or snail darter or the movement of the continents is to fail to understand the whole of nature as it presents itself as a phenomenon—and not as an idea or concept. Historical man is as "natural" as a whale or a snail darter and part of the movement of the natural whole. It is utterly inappropriate—although entirely modern—to view humanity as something external to the natural whole and to see an environmental solution that unleashes some static conception of an allegedly non-human natural whole while thoroughly destroying the natural in man.

It is difficult to find a contemporary manifestation of environmentalism that does not go hand in hand with a longing for a conscious, willful transformation of moral and political culture by an autonomous ego. But that longing for transformation remains altogether within the revengeful modern manipulative longing that threatens nature as a whole. Further, we must come to realize that a "culture," "world" or "*ethos*" in any meaningful, comprehensive sense, is a background phenomenon that loses its function precisely when we disinter it and bring it to the foreground. *Ethoi* "grow," they are not self-consciously projected or constructed. Constructivism destroys the very possibility of unique *ethoi*. That is why modern humanity does not have a "culture" but instead merely lives eclectically—in the mode of postmodernist pastiches and collages—off the cultural capital of the past. Cultures grow out of an indigenous experience of life, shared by a distinct group of people in a distinct place with a distinct history that is still open and history making. **That is part of what is natural for human beings and it has been or is rapidly being lost as a possibility.** We praise wilderness on the one hand while being willing to totally self-consciously and revengefully construct the human on the other.

The cultural capital from the past that comes down to us late moderns, while ennobling and invigorating to inspect, cannot be expected to be a living experience for individuals immersed in a present that is entirely different than the ones in which that cultural capital was generated. Attempting to resurrect past *ethoi* will not do, and the ultimate modern longing for the hegemony of the cosmopolitan and the abstract universal destroys the rootedness that makes the growth of *ethoi* possible. What is required is that we step back from the modern universalist, dogmatic faith that there is only one correct and just way to do things everywhere and always. But we must also cease lambasting our own Western heritage so that we may ecstatically affirm *our* past and link it in a non-constructivist fashion with *our* future. The Western tradition represents the only roots "we" have. To transcend the spirit of revenge, *both* past and future must be affirmed and linked. Otherwise, one has no present in which to live.

What is required is a "step back" from those self-hating forms of modern constructivism to encounter the conditions under which the kinds of positive and frequent interactions among individuals occur that allow living additions to our traditions to emerge and take root. At the same time, we need to step back from the attempt to bureaucratically plan existence from the top down at a public level, as well as from privately deconstructing everything that does not please our groundless ideological wills. Perhaps then we could **find our way beyond the divisive and destructive contemporary ideological politics** which makes any sensible long range staying power for a people impossible. It took the Romans centuries to finish their aqueduct system. Can we imagine such long range projects in our time? What are the conditions for such a possibility? Certainly not bureaucratic and ideological tyranny. But that kind of resentful imposing of a future on those as yet unborn is the first thought that will come to most contemporary minds poisoned by modern constructivism. But that kind of tyranny will not allow spontaneous interactions on the part of those to come. We can open the spaces for that interaction; we should not impose our will upon the free interactions of those not yet born.

We will have to reconsider our modern prejudice against what we call "traditions," although given our distinctive traditions, that would not mean giving up a commitment to Reason. The modern Reason/Tradition split is a false dichotomy. It is build on a false, constructivist view of Reason and a false view of man as something other than a history making being who needs the room to be allowed to let novel interactions emerge.

Hence what is required is a new postmodern understanding of Reason, not a pointless choice for the alleged fecundity of irrationality in any of its many forms. My suggestion is that what is implied is the emancipation of Reason from the willfulness and hubris of modern, abstract, constructivist theoretical reason. The *modern,* Enlightenment prejudice against a form of Reason that was at peace with various traditions as traditions rested on the belief that traditions were intrinsically bad because they limited "self-realization" understood as self-creation out of nothing. That notion in turn rests on the modern longing to denaturalize human beings while commanding and torturing the rest of nature.

Traditions, as they emerge from an ecstatic binding together of past and future that is not revengeful, which is to say, traditions correctly understood, are not reducible to the dead weight of blind, oppressive, past accidents and prejudices. Traditions are more closely linked with the distinctive way of doing things of a group in a certain place, whose members have shared experiences over an extended, ongoing period of trial and error shaped by shared appearance and phenomena **and shared discussion and reasoning together.** That process involves considerable reasoning interaction and the need to publicly give reasons to each other. Participation in that dialectical process of reasoning is where philosophy should enter the picture. Philosophy should not, in modern fashion, be reduced to abstract, resentful, theoretical constructivism.

Correctly understood, a dialectical, phenomenological philosophy qua political philosophy is a necessary adjunct to ongoing public discussion. It is through an ongoing process of discussion that the glue that binds together individuals and generations can he fashioned, thereby making cross-generational perseverance possible, while allowing us to lovingly affirm our past and present in all their self-presenting diversity.

We must eschew faith in the totalitarian belief that it would he efficacious to impose a new culture, one which, according to our theoretical lights, is more in line with the prospering of either humanity or some presumably autonomous, nonhuman, natural whole, at the expense of our humanity. Nature is not so static that its preservation requires the destruction of our humanity and our transformation into totally administered pets with an all powerful State as the pet owner. **Reason and Liberty are perfectly compatible historical companions.**

If we are to have a future reality that is not, for example, totally a consumer culture—as so many environmentalists assert is necessary to save the planet—we in the present must step back from the willful modern attempts that have transformed humanity into an increasingly uniform herd of laborer-consumers, which rests on the distinctively modern attempt to suppress and ultimately transform the natural diversity of types of human beings ("tribes" or *eidē*) that present themselves whenever we step back from revengeful projects for their suppression. The natural diversity of humanity will reassert itself in the same fashion as the wilderness reclaims the asphalt if we step back from willful constructivism. If we are to unleash the natural from the revengeful theoretical transformations of modernity we cannot do it selectively, according to our various ideological priorities and agendas—which, both Right and Left, as products of the modern Will, are equally counterproductive. Ideological politics is the necessary outgrowth of modern constructivism.

Under the rubric "the Tragedy of the Commons," environmentalists have argued—and this is a quintessential instinct of contemporary environmentalism—that the individualism that will ensue if human nature is given full scope, in an environment of modern consumerism, will inevitably lead to ruin. Therefore, according to this modern, all too modern, inarticulate inclination, individualism must be limited by elite cadres of modern theorists and bureaucratic managers, and "communal" outcomes must, paradoxically, be consciously manufactured. By this argument popular sovereignty must likewise be radically limited, if not jettisoned completely.

The mechanics by which these tyrannical limitations will be administered are never made entirely clear, but the specter of self-selected and self-appointed elites imposing their constructions on reality is never far from the surface. The specter becomes even more menacing when it is asserted that the primary problems confronting us are global and hence will require global administration beyond the sovereignty of the nation-state. In that regard, the name of Greenpeace is often repeated with almost religious reverence.[14] The need for radical transformations imposed by an elite is assumed by many to be the only available option for contemporary humanity given that present manifestations of individualism and popular sovereignty will lead to universal consumerism, which it is assumed will in turn make accelerated demands for economic growth, requiring the transformation and depletion of limited natural resources. It is argued that there is no other way out of the vicious cycle that leads to inevitable ruin than through elite-imposed limitations on freedom and consumption.

But there is another way out of this presumed impasse that is consistent with individualism and popular sovereignty, but which the antidemocratic strains of contemporary environmentalism never consider because of their modern frame of reference. Further, the anti-growth bias of environmentalism overlooks possibilities that can quite plausibly allow for economic growth without environmental ruin. We need not turn to the frequently mentioned palliative of enforced equality of possessions—again implying greater centralized bureaucratic oversight and administration. **If over-consumption is the primary problem, then what is required is that we give modern individuals something to love other than consumption.** Actual human beings, **by nature**, are inclined to a variety of other ends beyond comfortable self-preservation if given the opportunity to pursue their natural diversity. Forcibly constraining and administering individual patterns of consumption is not the only imaginable way to proceed.

Modernity was founded on the premise that universal, material progress toward perpetual peace and comfortable self-preservation—as the only legitimate ends—together with political progress toward greater equality could only be had if various human inclinations and potentialities were suppressed and morally delegitimized. This is the basis of modernity's reductionist, revengeful, universalistic tendencies. **If consumerism is the problem, it is because of the victory of the modern, unitary vision of the good.** What is needed is to relegitimize other ends beyond the pursuit of predictable, comfortable self-preservation. For example, to wealth and physical comfort could be added honor, piety, or any other version of the pursuit of excellence—and there is an entire pantheon of excellences that correspond with the various human capacities and potentialities: courage, artistic excellence, the pursuit of knowledge, friendship, spirited competition, to name but a few.

Modernity rests on an ever-increasing revengeful attack on natural, human diversity and an attempt to reduce humanity to one universal Whole. What is needed is to unleash actual human diversity, not the radically constricted, *faux* brand to be constructed by many postmodernists and "environmentalists" under their banner of "diversity." This respect is not tantamount to accepting a free-for-all, or a back-door entry for neo-social Darwinism. Human diversity can be balanced in a variety of philosophical, ethical, and constitutional ways. But the sublimation, transformation, and elimination of what presents itself is an entirely different matter.

Human diversity must be part of any interesting conception of biodiversity. Any "balance of nature" implies the functioning of all the parts—the human included. Why, for example, is the spirited, honor-loving human being any less important to the whole than the spirited bald eagle? The one is the object of preservationist concern, the other the object of Constructivist scorn and attack. A postmodern environmental ethic will have to wean itself of the inclination to impose a unitary view of the nature of the human—which is part of the natural whole—in the name of the alleged well-being of the diversity of the supposedly autonomous nonhuman part of the natural whole.

A postmodern environmental ethic must also wean itself from seeing the "problem of nature" as a problem regarding the well-being of everything nonhuman and non-manmade. Why is an anthill natural (it is a product of labor, not of biological reproduction), while a human temple is not? Why is a fishpond a mini-ecosystem, while a human community rooted in a specific indigenous place is not? Reflect on the cliff dwellers of the American Southwest in this regard, but also on the ancient Greeks and Persians, or even the ancient and contemporary Californians. Why does the "balance of nature" require anthills and not human communities as they emerge and present themselves when allowed to do so? More to the point, why do we begin by considering them to be different? The answer is simple: because we are still operating under the sway of modern prejudices—most specifically the modern Reason/Nature, Will/Nature, Freedom/Nature and "human"/Nature dichotomies. We assume that to willfully construct the natural whole is an outrage, while willfully constructing the human things is necessary. Our problem lies in unwarranted modern assumptions.[15]

Take as another example of this point the debate within environmentalism over whether one should adopt an "ecocentric" or "anthropocentric" perspective. It makes no sense to choose for the human or the natural unless they are somehow separate and different already. There is no choice that needs to be made if they are part of the same, complex whole.[16] If nature is not nature until the last part is added—the human—then this issue never arises. One should also keep in mind that the posited choice can only be made by the modern, self-grounding ego. And that notion has now most assuredly run its course and can henceforth only be maintained on a mythological level.

As yet another example, take the approach known as "deep ecology." Projecting the need to integrate humanity "back" into nature as a less self-conscious animal with closer ties to natural rhythms once again implies that humanity is already outside nature.[17] It implies as well that we are only natural as unself-conscious animals. Nietzsche understood all too well what followed from this approach, instinctive barbarity. Our easygoing, environmentalist, egalitarian, deep ecologists simply lack clarity. And how do we get to the egalitarianism the deep ecologists always demand on the level of purely natural animals who show all manner of natural difference? The massive contradictions built into positions like deep ecology are truly embarrassing.

Why is not humanity part of nature precisely when all of our diverse human capacities, which are the ground of our essence as history making beings, are actualized? **Why is not humanity precisely natural when it is rational, historical, cultural, individual and free, and especially when it is political?** Those are elements of our essential nature, as any unbiased view of history and human nature shows quite amply.

Arguments for stepping back and allowing a natural whole that does not include the human to reassert its own alleged changeless rhythms make all manner of assumptions that are also descended from modern conceptualizations. The most significant assumption operating here is that the natural whole from which the human has been expelled is fundamentally static, and it is ruled by a discernable Necessity that relies on a chain of causes into which Chance never intrudes. How would one prove that? Is an asteroid hitting earth and causing the destruction of the dinosaurs Chance or Necessity? It will be hard to argue that it is Necessity without Theological presuppositions. Many contemporary physicists of the first rank no longer accept the proto-modern, Newtonian view of nature from which Chance has been expelled—quantum mechanics enthrones Chance and indeterminacy. Why should our environmentalists underestimate the place of Chance occurrences over which we will never have any control—like "global warming"? Keep in mind, if the human is part of the natural whole, in the movement of actual human historicality—not the constructed linear History of modern theory—we have a basis for the intrusion of indeterminacy into the future whole. Man as part of the natural whole is precisely why nothing is ever simply necessary.

When it is asserted that humankind "should" be integrated into nature as unself-conscious, a-historical beings like other animal species, it is assumed that simultaneously some primordial, prior, natural state can reassert itself. Does that mean we go back to the point when Europe and North America were one continent? If not that "prior" then how far back is it that we are being advised to go? When is the quintessential prior moment that is truly natural? Instead of some static view of nature from which the human has been expelled, is not nature an ever-changing, ever-rebalancing phenomenon that must be seen as it presents itself as far from static and as far from having only one manifestation?

Does it make any sense to say that the "balance" of nature that existed at the time of the dinosaurs is the yardstick for all time? **Why assume that there is some primary or primordial nature to return to, rather than an ever-reconstituting whole of which humanity—as rational, historical, cultural, and political—is not only a part but the quintessential part?** As historical and reconstituting, would not human existence be by far a better microcosm for understanding the natural whole than any other physical entity or event, and certainly better than the "history" of any other species?[18]

We should rid ourselves of the modern, fundamentally romanticist, longing for Arcadia. Were we to do that, the poeticizing of the wilderness as a wonderful. refreshing, static place that would offer the eternal equivalent of a get-away weekend would fade away. And the frequently associated daydream that nature in some simple wilderness manifestation is unmitigatedly supportive of human existence—especially if humanity is "deeply" immersed in it without any cultivation through habits and laws—will slip away as well. **The phenomenon Nature is omnipresent in every present moment.** We need not go "back" to find it.

Most contemporary environmentalist approaches are nothing but extensions of altogether modern fables—like the State of Nature—or they are born of conceptualizations that were reactions that arose at the dawn of modern industrialization and urbanization. By comparison, a postmodern approach to the issue of nature must affirm that nature is nature only when humanity is part of it, and humanity is human only by being genuinely historical, cultural, and political in a way freed from modern Constructivism. Nature is not static but it is self-presenting. The phenomenon Nature is not "our" picture, projection or construction.

As I have argued above, humanity can be truly historical and cultural only if we step back from the modern revengeful assault on natural human diversity that attempts to reduce humanity to universal laborer-consumers or to abstractly identical and equal citizens of a global *polis* ruled by a politically and environmentally "sound" elite. If one opens oneself to true human diversity, beyond the modern spirit of revenge, the only meaningful basis of that diversity is the pursuit of different ends by different types of human beings—Plato's different "tribes" of human beings.[19] The attempt to reduce humanity to the uniform pursuit of one end is to denature humanity and make it less fruitfully a part of the ever reconstituting natural whole.

Any genuine, reasonably unfettered play of a diversity of ends would necessarily include excellence in some manifestation as an end in itself. This inevitably implies that we would have to be publicly mindful of the distribution of honors for various excellences rather than dispensing honor for utility alone. Such an environment would have an element that was aristocratic, understood resolutely as implying a relation to *aretē*. Yet that is perfectly consistent with genuinely republican outcomes.

I do not doubt that the word aristocratic will in and of itself raise hackles. First, this is partly because we are inclined to make the conceptual mistake of collapsing the terms aristocratic and oligarchic. Strictly speaking, the one implies love of excellence, the other love of wealth as the highest end and greatest good. Second, our modern world was carved out in conscious opposition to a manifestation of a decaying oligarchy that called itself an aristocracy. But the aristocratic need not align itself with the oligarchic, nor need it become inextricably linked with economic class divisions, especially in a postmodern environment.[20] We must recognize that the world that is coming will be increasingly classless by any historical standards, it will be a manifestation of the victory of an increasingly universal middle class. That does not mean that we cannot have an aristocratic component in the coming world, or that that world cannot be very diverse in the only way that diversity is interesting, a diversity of understandings of the good. But for that outcome we will have to take seriously the primacy of the Good. I have argued that that is what a postmodern, phenomenological political philosophy will do.

What I am describing, under the admittedly broad rubric of an aristocratic postmodern environmentalist ethic, is what would also make possible the stability under which indigenous postmodern additions to living traditions could emerge and cross-generational perseverance become possible. It is the most logical way to assure a concern for the future and for the well-being of future generations that still affirms the present and the past, accepts individuality and makes **a democratic discussion that has not prejudged the outcome** of the discussion, rather than elite rule, possible.

Only by giving individuals a present they can affirm rather than revengefully attack can they have a past they revere and a future for which they are passionately concerned. That "ecstatic" relation to temporality is fundamentally aristocratic and antimodern. In short, if our tastes and aspirations change, our patterns of consumption will begin to become more environmentally friendly. If we quit the abstract kind of individualism and egalitarianism that go hand in hand with asocial atomism, abstract universalism and mindless consumerism, a fundamental reintegration of human beings into nature could occur that does not require sacrificing everything that is unique about human nature and everything that is open and democratic about modernity.[21] To become postmodern we do not have to cast off the concrete moral and political yield of modernity. As the common saying goes, been there, done that. The modern moral and political yield already presents itself. On that level, in the phenomenal present, it has about it an element of the natural.

I am not encouraging any specific changes, and I am certainly not arguing that changes should be imposed. I am simply observing that if our natural human diversity is unleashed, our aspirations will change, and all manner of different forms of economic and social interaction are plausible. Actual human history is replete with them. Unleashing that difference does not require a construction imposed from the top down, and there does not need to be one universally valid pantheon of virtues or ordering of the ones that present themselves. That ordering will present itself from within.

As far as I can see, what is required on some level is the legitimizing of diverse aspirations and tastes that will hierarchically order themselves in different ways. That kind of ordering, released from constructivist willing, intrinsically carries with it an element that is aristocratic. Legitimizing diverse, ranked outcomes will take care of itself if we step back from the modern revengeful assault on human diversity as it presents itself. There is no reason that the problem of environmentalism has to be solved by giving in to the totalitarian temptation, unless we are determined to continue to impose a modern, all too modern, universality on humanity. And that there is a multitude of phenomenal ends that the various tribes of human beings pursue is not relativism, it is natural diversity presenting itself.

Further, the implication of these reflections is that the primary locus of our human activities would increasingly become *praxis* rather than *technē*—in the original Greek sense rather than that used by modern authors such as Marx and neo-Marxists armed with their modern prejudices. In other words, we would again become genuinely political beings who have not reduced all discussion to primarily economic issues.[22]

A genuinely political situation is one in which different individuals with different ends interact. The dynamic of that interaction could work itself out in a great variety of ways, as any unbiased look at actual human history will show—as opposed to a history theoretically constructed as seamless, linear or progressive. When we simply compete over distributional issues we prove that we all pursue the same end. Such interaction is economic, not political in any serious sense. Economic interaction points toward universal consumption, conjoined with bureaucratic administration and the technical domination of nature. Political interaction points toward face-to-face participation at some indigenous level capable of sustaining such interaction within a variety of differently ordered situations, many of which can be legitimate.

The outcome of any genuinely political interaction cannot be judged in advance as regards all of its particulars. Novelty, on some level, is a human possibility that will grow out of an incalculably large number of individual interactions rather than outcomes that are created self-consciously by an individual artist. When the arena within which individuals play out their existence enlarges the political and contracts the economic, the technical and utilitarian bases for honor could inevitably decline, and we could have a locus for human existence that is far less devastating to the environment.

The movement of nature can proceed with man's historical existence moving naturally in concert with the movement of the continents and the ice ages. That is the model for the phenomenon of nature that we must recover in the postmodern world. Recovering the phenomenon of nature would help us overcome the destructive consequences of the modern anti-nature animus.[23]

Environmental concerns offer a powerful new opening for political philosophy precisely because they force us to re-open the question regarding nature, which modernity was intent upon closing and which contemporary movements of thought, from deconstructionism to environmentalism, continue to assert out of existence as one of their opening premises.

A truly *post*modern environmental ethic will have to recover and articulate a consistent concept of nature that includes the human as part of the whole. Needless to say, we will be forced to recover a complex and dynamic view of nature into which humanity has been "reintegrated." If the argument is to be artful and internally consistent,[24] it seems to me to point to an accentuation of face to face interaction at venues that are not primarily global and cosmopolitan.[25] It would have an aristocratic component—it would be concerned with *aretē* and reward something other than utility. It would open itself to the interaction of genuine natural diversity. It would allow for evolving traditions—the only plausible, nontotalitarian way to create concern for the future that is not stale and imposed from the top down. It would be political in the full, architectonic sense rather than administrative and bureaucratic, and it would take as a given that the natural whole is distorted when the natural diversity of its human component is expelled.

What is needed is to emancipate the love of ends other than utility, consumption, and a quiet, predictable existence. When we stop seeing the good for humanity in static, universalistic terms, we can stop seeing the good for nature as a whole in equally static, to say nothing of artificial, terms. Being is eternal and presents itself, but it changes. Truly enlightened and emancipated humanity is a part of the whole, not a kingdom within a kingdom. Only when we see this will we quit the modern manipulative stance, shared by most contemporary environmentalist thought, which still believes we must will a cultural change upon humanity from the top down, pursue enforced redistribution, and willfully transform existing power relations to save a static conception of nature.[27] Crafting a new, persuasive understanding of a complex natural whole is part of the task for a postmodern political philosophy.

NOTES

1. In almost every permutation of environmentalism we see a commitment to most of the following tenets: (1) an almost universal commitment to egalitarianism (of a particular, abstract, modern metaphysical variety), (2) a critique of modern liberal culture, (3) a distaste for commerce, (4) a faith in the legitimacy and beneficence of social and political experimentation by elites (usually self-selecting elites), (5) a belief in the necessity of transcending almost all manifestations of tradition and natural difference, (6) a belief that the sovereignty of the modem democratic state must be transcended; the list could be expanded. A useful, if partisan, survey of the landscape can be found in Robin Eckersley, *Environmentalism and Political Theory: Toward an Ecocentric Approach* (Albany: SUNY Press, 1992)

2. See in this regard the debates surrounding Hans Blumenberg's *The Legitimacy of the Modern Age* (Cambridge: MIT Press, 1991). One should also consider Amos Funkenstein's influential *Theology and the Scientific Imagination* (Princeton, NJ: Princeton University Press, 1986). I have already touched on this issue above in part 1 of *Between Eternities.*

3. I reject Karl Löwith's contention that this self-understanding is a self-deluded myth. See Löwith's *Meaning and History* (Chicago: University of Chicago Press, 1949).

4. See the discussion of old or "natural" principalities in chapter 2 of Machiavelli's *The Prince.*

5. See the Machiavelli chapter.

6. What I mean here by the "political" is not to be confused with the economic competition over who gets what, when, and how. Political competition is between genuinely, not atavistically, diverse individuals pursuing different ends.

7. With Hobbes we see a perfect manifestation of the hypothetical nature of the modern deployment of reason. For example, Hobbes makes clear that his definitions or names do not correspond necessarily with anything in the natural world or ordinary speech. True and false are terms related to speeches, not things; they are as artificial as Hobbes's polity. Further, the possibility of the greatest good—peace, predictability and material progress—requires that reason impose the same artificial whole universally. Hobbes purchases the human good, as he sees it, at the price of a dogmatic universalism—only one morality and one set of political arrangements are desirable everywhere and always. This dogmatic universalism rules in increasingly virulent forms throughout all later modern thought until Nietzsche.

8. Locke further develops modernity's anti-nature animus. For Locke, nature is posited as thoroughly valueless. Human, transforming labor is the source of all value; we must produce our existence. Nature does not bestow well-being, or even survival, as a birthright. We must carve out a human arena with our labor—an understanding shared completely by Marx. Marx merely added that as the "objectivizing" process of labor proceeds, alienation occurs. Marx's discussion of alienation requires a twist derived from Kant; it is ultimately "self"-alienation—or alienation from our universal, rational "species-being"—that is the primary problem, not alienation from "external" nature which for Marx is all to the good. For both Locke and Marx, the production of the human good becomes primarily a technical problem, not a phenomenon requiring appropriate moral perfection or healthy *praxis*, in the traditional sense. Hence both Locke and Marx presuppose the unleashing of an unlimited transforming technology, and a more or less self-conscious pursuit of material progress.

9. I have dealt with this issue at length in my *Nietzsche, Heidegger and the Transition to Postmodernity* (Chicago: University of Chicago Press: 1996) (Ch. 1).

10. In Derrida's version of the argument, all of reality is a text, constantly rewritten in the very act of reading. Consequently nothing in reality is really present in the traditional sense—as with texts as conventionally understood—what is in the "margins" and between the lines carries meaning as much as the words. And a web of words is all that ever is present for us no matter how frequently we delude ourselves on this topic. All we are ever confronted with is "traces" of an intrinsically absent

source or foundation—traces which continually reconstitute themselves and while seeming to point toward something substantive in fact never do. See chapter 6 on Derrida.

11. For a more complete analysis of Nietzsche and Heidegger, see my *Nietzsche, Heidegger and the Transition to Postmodernity*, especially parts 2 and 3; and *Martin Heidegger: Paths Taken, Paths Opened* (Lanham, MD: Rowman & Littlefield, 2007).

12. See in this regard, Nietzsche's *Beyond Good and Evil*, no. 230.

13. For a discussion of this subject see my "Heidegger's Postmodern Politics?", *Polity* (Fall 1991), and my *Nietzsche, Heidegger and the Transition to Postmodernity* and *Martin Heidegger: Paths Taken, Paths Opened*.

14. See for example William E. Connolly, *Identity/Difference: Democratic Negotiations of Political Paradoxes* (Ithaca, NY: Cornell University Press, 1991). The prospect of a self-selecting, environmentalist global tyranny conducted in the name of a static understanding of nature from which history making humanity has been expelled should, in my view, cause a determination to rethink the premises that lead to such frightening conclusions arrived at without much in the way of democratic qualms. **This is one of the most dangerous specters of the modern, resentful instinct for control that is at the heart of the problems we need to confront.** I agree with Connolly that what is required is a postmodern approach; but his is in fact modern, all too modern, despite postmodernist buzzwords like "Identity" and "Difference" and the feint toward the word "democratic." It is amazing how undemocratic some calls for "democracy" can really be.

15. It is easy to construct an altogether predictable response at this point. To question the modern is to be a proponent of one version or another of atavistic, prejudiced and appalling pre-modern options. But this response is also modern, all too modern. It assumes the modern linear view of human history. History moves seamlessly and in only one direction. To question the modern is to wish to go back because that is the only alternative. I reject the core premise; far from being seamless and one directional, history is discontinuous and determined by qualitative breaks. This is what I have called an "event-horizon" view of human history. For the modern there can be no unique forthcoming break or discontinuity, hence there cannot be anything qualitatively unique like the postmodern. All there can be is reactionary movements backward. Hence, any alternative can be judged reactionary before the fact. **It is a wonderful, self-serving, mythical prejudice.**

16. For an unparalleled discussion of just such a complex view of nature into which human beings have been integrated as the concluding part, see Joseph Cropsey, "Political Life and a Natural Order," in *Political Philosophy and the Issues of Politic,* (Chicago: University of Chicago Press, 1977), pp. 221–30.

17. One should not miss the clear Hegelian assumption that the natural, as it operates in "humans," goes hand in hand with the unconscious and the subconscious and that the human goes hand in hand with self-consciousness. This unquestioned assumption is, like so many, modern, all too modern.

18. It may very well be true that beavers evolved from some prior form, but there is a good reason why no one would ever write a book on the history of beaver society. Yet geologists write what amounts to the history of the movement of continents

and the creation of mountains and valleys and the coming and going of ice ages and on and on. It is that ongoing change that is natural, not some fixed and primordial state. And throughout multiple changes in what we call natural history, beaver society has remained unchanged. Not so with human society. Why is not human historicality the measure for nature as a complex whole? Are we not as history making beings the microcosm of the whole?

19. If one assembles a group of ten people, of various melanin levels and dominant chromosomes, and they all pursue the same end—utility, wealth, consumption, manipulation and domination of nature—one has hardly accomplished diversity in any interesting sense.

20. To approach this issue from another direction, if we open ourselves to ends other than utility, then we will inevitably open ourselves to the pursuit of what Aristotle called the basis of the noble—the pursuit of the beautiful and the useless, that which is desired as an end in itself. Surely there is enough wealth and technical skill available in the modern world to make this pursuit possible, and for more than a small few, if they should freely choose it, and if the society rewards it with honors. Without the addition of the latter, all contemporary activity will have to be deflected onto the plane of utility by anyone with an even rudimentary acquaintance with contemporary reality and in possession of any appropriate and healthy degree of self-love.

Just to be clear, I reject the altogether modern, Marxist reduction of all human ends to mere epiphenomena of economics. This is so at odds with how human reality presents itself that it requires a willful blindness to the actual phenomena of life to reach this constructivist conclusion. For the person who keeps asserting this understanding as if it was a primary truth like grasping the color green, all I can say is that ultimately one cannot teach a blind man colors.

21. Genuine political interaction freed from the spirit of revenge will not eventuate in the kind of abstract egalitarianism that modernity has pursued, which much contemporary environmentalism is still determined to impose in the name of nature. But this does not mean that we are forced to give up the belief—a correct one I believe—that the concepts of justice and equality are inextricably linked in complicated ways. Long ago, Aristotle asserted that necessary link. The issue of equality need only be disentangled from the desire to impose abstract universal identity; it needs to be made truly consistent with genuine diversity. Political and economic equality and genuine difference are not mutually exclusive unless the pursuit of the former is made to rest on **a constructivist determination to impose an outcome rather than appreciate what emerges dialectically.**

22. One is reminded of Rousseau's observation that all moderns talk about is business and commerce while the ancients talked about honor and virtue. The latter is part of how nature presents itself.

23. I have arrived at a point where I reach a conclusion that is in some respects parallel to that reached by Strauss. He concluded that the possibility of political philosophy required the recovery of the **"idea of nature."** But I am arguing that the possibility of a postmodern, phenomenological political philosophy requires openness to the **"phenomenon of nature."** The central difference between these two approaches is that an "idea" and a "phenomenon" are not identical. The one is static, not subject

to change, the other is dynamic and has a strong element of Heidegger's understanding of *physis*. I refer the reader to the essays on Strauss above. I am also arguing that phenomenon nature includes mankind and its essential human doings as the culminating part of the natural whole.

24. I am not here trying to make some theoretical point drawn from an allegedly autonomous discipline like logic. My underlying premise is more simple: thinking is an art form. Every jury-rigged rhetorical contraption held together by ideological duct tape does not deserve to be called a philosophy. No one other than a tendentious fool confuses a sculpture crafted by Rodin and a clay flower pot made by a child at summer camp. In a similar vein, a philosophical position rife with internal contradiction cannot be beautiful, elegant or eloquent. More to the point, it will not be publicly persuasive. This is a fact wrapped within the everyday nature of public persuasiveness as it presents itself. It is irrelevant whether this was equally true before Socrates as it is now, or in the Ming dynasty or pre-historical, sub-Saharan Africa. That is how things present themselves now. That is the nature of public persuasiveness now. Hence, it is natural.

25. It is surprising how many self-proclaimed postmodern*ists* speak in favor of the local only to move immediately to will various manifestations of the universal and the cosmopolitan as applicable everywhere and always. What is needed is to allow significant, novel additions to local traditions to emerge, not use the local as the latest venue for the modern imposition of the abstract and the universal.

26. And "power" is almost always conceptualized in proto-modern Newtonian fashion. Seeing the natural whole as moved in a fashion that contemporary physicists would reject as old-fashioned forces such thinkers to conceive of human relations as primarily power relations in an altogether simplistic manner.

Chapter Twenty-Three

Conclusion: Is There a Future?

Either the tradition of political philosophy is at an end—having become a relic or museum curiosity with no novel possibilities left—or it still has a future that could conceivably be far longer than its past. Was the past tradition just a preamble? Likewise, either the civilization of the West is nearing its culmination, with no more possibilities other than slow decline, or it has a future that could easily be longer than its past. The two issues are related for what is most distinctive about the West is traceable to the tradition of political philosophy. And it is only political philosophy that can now open an ongoing future.

It is not reasonable to rely on blind Chance and hopeful waiting to save our humanity. But what are the necessary conditions under which it is possible for there to be a continuing tradition of political philosophy? Clarity on this issue is necessary since there is no historical inevitability operating now or into the future any more than it operated in the past. Clarity and resolute choice are required.

I am prepared to be so bold as to suggest that the engine of Western uniqueness and novelty has been the tradition of political philosophy. Is there a future for the tradition of political philosophy that is more than a repetition of the past, or the stagnant freezing in place of one past moment of the tradition? If there is to be a genuine future for the Tradition it needs to recur to the fundamental sources and wellsprings from which the tradition initially grew. To do that we will have to relinquish a great deal of the encrusted theoretical baggage that has built up within the past tradition.

The only wellsprings from which an ongoing tradition can draw are the phenomena, which show themselves. The phenomena are not always and everywhere identical, albeit in many ways they are always and everywhere similar. For example, the original Greeks who founded our Tradition were not thrown into a world informed by Christianity, modern science, modern commercialism, or modern republicanism. And that is just to name a few of the novel phenomena we confront from which we must begin our reflections. Yet like our Greek predecessors, we must begin from the phenomena as they present themselves.

This is especially true as one of the phenomena unique to us late moderns, as Nietzsche pointed out so clearly, is our "historical sense." It was Christianity which first gave us a linear conception of history, rather than the cyclical vision that was predominant in antiquity, or a view that all temporal movement was random and Chance driven. Only with the Christian linear notion already in place could modernity posit history as directional in the sense of progressive. But linearity and inevitable progress are not how the phenomena now present themselves to any honest observer, nor are those ideas consistent with the possibility of an ongoing novel future.

At the end of the modern age that we occupy, the philosophical presuppositions used to support linearity and progress either as an "as-if" or as inevitable have **deconstructed themselves**. Whether or not this is regrettable is beside the point. And that awareness of what has occured has yet to filter down to the everyday street is marginally interesting, but of no philosophical import.

There is simply no modern dispensation that can do without a linear conception of history, but a postmodern political philosophy will have to do without it. The phenomena do not now present themselves as linear, cyclical or repetitive. The phenomena present themselves, when freed from the encrustation of modern theoretical projections, as discontinuous and event driven. This differs from a view of simple randomness as there is considerable predictability within the arena determined by epochal events. We will be determined by an "event/happening" understanding of history (it can no longer be "H"istory in the modern sense) because this is how the phenomena do and will present themselves.[1]

This is but one suggestion about how a future oriented political philosophy can begin to build, taking off from the phenomena that now show themselves. A future tradition can build upon an articulation of an event/happening view of history while still affirming the past that has led to this unique present moment. Such an event/happening is indeed implied in the break with the modern tradition and its view of history, and that break has already occurred. It need not be willed or constructed by an autonomous ego. It is a phenomenon that shows itself to those with the eyes to see.

The modern notion of "History" can henceforth be maintained only on the level of myth. Modern Constructivism as a whole can henceforth only survive on the level of mythology. It is no longer possible to believe in the autonomous self-grounding ego. Necessary History and the self-grounding ego go hand in hand, they stand and fall together.

The event horizon view of history is itself a novel phenomenon that will open the future in a novel way and help allow the future to present itself from within. I can give an intimation of what I mean by the phrase "create itself from within" with the help of the non-metaphysical Plato I presented above. If we look at the Platonic dialogues with openness and care, we do not primarily see ontological or metaphysical doctrines. We see articulations of what is implied in the phenomena that present themselves, especially the human phenomena. The so-called "doctrine of ideas" has precisely this phenomenological status.

Plato shows us that phenomenologically we always grasp the world as a world of discrete "things" that simultaneously sort themselves out into various groups or tribes of things. And individual things as they present themselves are always a unity of a manifold. As they present themselves, things point toward necessary reflection upon the One or principle of unity that makes it possible for them to present themselves publicly for all. Some basis for Oneness has to be articulated to explain the phenomena as they present themselves. That One is the tribe or "form" which shows itself to all in the public arena. Further, individual things never present themselves as discrete or autonomous but everywhere and always present themselves as not only members of groups but as intricately interwoven phenomenal wholes with many other forms or tribes. The same is true of individual human beings. They too present themselves as manifestations of unique tribes of individuals with these tribes linked into other larger wholes. Those wholes may be "nations," but they may be constituted into other ways as well, forming smaller tribes across national boundaries.

In the Platonic dialogues we see that humanity is not projected as a uniform whole, with a single essence, but as consisting of a variety of discrete types of human beings. Those types or tribes of human beings transcend nations or "civilizations" or any other form of whole. That panoply of diversity and multiplicity informs what we are as human beings more than a uniform humanity.

We also see the Platonic dialogues presenting a conspectus and interrogation of the reigning most powerful ideas of the day in such a fashion that Plato isolates the underlying core ideas that determine them. Those core ideas are recurrent fundamental intellectual notions that do not go away, and to which very little in the way of addition or subtraction over time occurs. Yet there is some addition and subtraction over time to these fundamental concepts and ideas.

Throughout the Platonic dialogues, as in the phenomena themselves, we see a multiplicity that has to be articulated, and as the metaphor of Plato's Trilogy *Theaetetus/Sophist/Statesman* presents the matter, "woven" together with a creative *poiesis*. The phenomena present themselves, but they must still be articulated and woven together by political philosophy to present a publicly available whole.

To the contemporary phenomena that present themselves, and the recurrent phenomena as presented by Plato, "we" in the present can add the conspectus of the phenomena introduced by Christianity and modernity, and modern science among other novel phenomena. We can see many of the same fundamental ideas Plato isolated recur, as I have shown above in my reflections on contemporary physics and biology. And we can see that many of the human tribes recur. But we can also see that the whole is not simply static. By "we" I mean informed phenomenological observers in the present.

What a postmodern, phenomenological political philosophy can do is open the horizon for the dialectical interplay of diverse tribes of human beings (freed from the tyranny of the abstract universal)—and here I absolutely do not mean by "tribe" a nation or a "race" or anything of the kind, but different groups of individuals who pursue different ends as the highest. And we can see the interplay of fundamental, recurrent ideas interacting with the novel phenomena that have opened in the ongoing tradition through past historical theoretical/poetic articulations of phenomena that now determine us. From these phenomena that show themselves we can weave a whole that can open new spaces for the dialectical interaction of future human beings to play out their humanity with some degree of freedom and novelty.

What can be unleashed in the present is a novel set of dialectical interactions that can occur within the future and which will yield a novel showing that can be articulated by a phenomenological/poetic political philosophy on an ongoing basis. There will be novelty, yet underlying predictability because the fundamental phenomena, ideas and human types do not change that radically even if the situation in which they present themselves does. The predictable can be channeled into novel categories and articulations. But that throwing forward of a future must remain grounded in phenomena that are allowed to show themselves. The postmodern future must be given its freedom from the tyranny of past modern, Constructivist projecting so that it may constitute itself from within in the future.

This kind of phenomenological opening of the future is indicative of the holistic political philosophy I am suggesting. It is entirely distinct from the Constructivist projecting of frames upon the future. Through persuasive **public** articulations—and political philosophy must be a public rather than private undertaking—of the whole freed from past theoretical prejudices, one "opens" arenas that will be filled in by the dialectical interactions of those living in the future. They will be freed from past theoretical tyranny so that they may possess their own present.

This is most assuredly not a manifestation of modern Constructivism or even of some kind of Nietzschean philosopher-kings ruling the future world.

That reading of Nietzsche just raises to the highest power the modern notion of the Constructivist theorist as legislator. That cannot be the model for political philosophy in the future if there is to be an ongoing tradition. Everyday individuals must be granted a space to dialectically determine their own world. That space is the work of the weaving of a phenomenological political philosophy.

This kind of opening and reopening must be constantly reenacted for and within its unique situation. And that is why there can be no final political philosophy or any end to its tradition. Finality would also imply the possibility of a final apodictic representational speech. But all speech in the public arena always has a poetic element. I have tried to show how this poetic element even operates in contemporary theoretical physics and biology. I have tried to show how in the Platonic dialogues a necessary interpenetration of *logos* and *poiesis* is consciously deployed as a corrective of the Socratic longing for autonomous, linear, representational *logos*. A holistic, phenomenological political philosophy, which must operate in the public arena of phenomena and public speech, has to use an element of *poiesis* in its articulations of the whole.

We are entering a future situation that will be unique and unprecedented. Our thinking will have to match the unprecedented nature of that unavoidable future. Otherwise we can lose our essence as history making beings, and thereby lose our humanity. Antiseptic phrases like "post-human condition" should not insulate us from the chilling nature of that prospect.[2] I am arguing that only an architectonic, holistic, phenomenological political philosophy can open a future beyond the endless modernity that could be an end for the West, and humanity more generally. I realize how many will be smugly dismissive of that conclusion. But I believe the argument has its own force and inevitability if one will only follow it.

When all is said and done, what differentiates man from other sentient beings is his ability to create novel historical worlds.[3] That is something no other social species can do. All other species remain determined by the same categories and rhythms of biological life throughout time. That is why they are not history making beings. Man is the history making being. The material and biological substratum of our existence is background; it is not of the essence of our humanity. The biological substratum of our existence is an important phenomenon, but does not get to the essence of our being as human. It is only because of our essence as history making beings that we are in a position to open the future for ourselves in novel ways.

I have argued that political philosophy must start from the ensemble of phenomena into which it is always thrown. But the further we push "back," or "down," lurking behind almost all of the dominant phenomena of our late modern age is the issue of man's relation to "nature." This is especially true at a time when modern science, another major determining phenomenon in our time, seems so competent to do and make of the natural whatever is desired. For all of our snowballing technical competence, the fundamental issue remains: On what basis does one decide what should be desired, what should be changed, what should be left alone in the natural as it presents itself?

As fundamentally technological rather than ontological—and that is how science in the postmodern age will present itself—modern science can never be more than a means to an end. We still need clarity about the end, and that end will always be the good for man as truly human. And central to our humanity is the ability to be history making beings. We cannot deny that possibility to those yet to come.

We are confronted with the sobering and awe-inspiring question of how man should stand before the natural whole, understanding that we too are a part of that natural whole. This question regarding the status of nature, and how the natural is related to the human good, has not been enjoined with any kind of directness or clarity for hundreds of years. During that period our technical competence has far outpaced our moral and philosophical clarity about how to deploy that competence. Our response so far to the "problem of nature" has been focused on a concern for the importance of maintaining or recovering the natural as it displays itself "outside" the human. This way of looking at things is imposed upon us by the overall anti-nature animus of modernity which conceives of the truly human as existing only outside and opposed to the natural. This central modern diremption between man and nature cannot stand. Man must be reintegrated into nature and nature must be seen as a complex whole that includes man as a history making being.

Contemporary thinkers seem determined to argue for the autonomy of a static conception of the external natural whole while simultaneously remaining committed to the moral expulsion of man from that natural whole. As regards the human things, we continue to see the need to de-nature man in the name of freedom and morality. In the process, our conception of the human becomes increasingly a-historical, static and pointing toward an unchanging a-historical stagnancy that is out of touch with our understanding of natural history. It is almost as if the external natural world, with man expelled is what has become historical, while human existence becomes static—e.g. determined by an abstract universal—like our older conception of nature. Once we give up the myth of the self-legislating ego existing totally outside of nature all of this will have to be rethought.

But man as human, as history making, is part of the natural whole. The truly human is indeed a microcosm for the understanding of dynamic Nature as a whole. While we valorize the maintenance of the natural in the non-human part of the natural whole, it is a natural whole from which we somehow repeatedly expel human beings.[4] It is no accident that we are facing a preposterous either/or where in the minds of some either the natural whole will be substantially destroyed or it will be saved only by the expulsion of the human which is cast off to some tyrannically determined stasis.

As a "phenomenon," nature presents itself as a complex whole that includes the human. The whole that includes man and non-man is dynamic, not static, it constitutes and reconstitutes itself. At one time the earth had only one continent which over time drifted apart into the multiple continents that now present themselves. Neither situation is more "natural" than the other. Something similar is true of the way in which nature displays itself in the human arena and in the complex whole that includes man. Nature "is" and "shows itself" but it is dynamic not static.

That complex whole that is nature can be best understood in a way that is consistent with the Heideggerian notion of *physis*, that which emerges and shows itself, but not completely, not statically, not always in the same fashion and not primarily as an idea or concept. Humanity is not simply "in" nature any more than it is "outside" nature. **Humanity is linked with the larger whole as the site where nature rises to phenomenal consciousness. Man in his essential being is central to the ability of the natural whole to show itself.** What is needed is a relation to nature that understands it as a self-presenting, but not static, complex whole which includes history making humanity. The articulation of this understanding is a task for a holistic, phenomenological, poetic, postmodern political philosophy.

In the chapters above I have explored some of what is involved in this understanding of political philosophy. In the process I have argued that **we must understand man's historical doings, and history making, as the culminating part of the natural whole and not as something that occurs outside the natural at some imaginary Archimedean point beyond nature.** Man is by nature a history making being and the natural whole includes man so understood within it as the last and indeed culminating part.

To return from the underlying phenomenon nature—to say that it is "underlying"—is to say that it both shows itself and in some fashion conceals itself, to phenomena closer to the surface. Another of the central phenomena of late modernity is modern science in both its public showing and self-understanding. That showing takes "modern science"—understood as a whole and not as individual sciences—as both an autonomous and ontological undertaking. This opens a door to the conclusion that modern science is primarily "factual" and progressing toward an end state of perfect knowledge of the whole, using a form of *logos* that is unsullied by any element of *poiesis*.

But this is not the reality of late modern science anymore than it was the understanding of those who launched the modern scientific project in the first place. In the postmodern situation, science will need to see itself more in line with its non-ontological technological reality than in its mythical ontological presentation. And that new, less mythical understanding must come to shape in the public understanding of science. Since a truer understanding is unlikely to originate from within modern science itself, it will have to come from "without," in fact, from "above." That venue outside the sciences is political philosophy.

Yet another phenomenon of our time is the unique way in which modern science and religion confront each other. In his discussion of Nietzsche's *Beyond Good and Evil*, Strauss observed that for Nietzsche it was imperative that future philosophy have priority over religion, apparently expecting that the political would decline in importance and hence as in any way being a limiting factor.

> Philosophy and religion, it seems, belong together—belong more closely together than philosophy and the city. . . . The fundamental alternative is that of the rule of philosophy over religion or the rule of religion over philosophy; it is not, as it was for Plato or Aristotle, that of the philosophic and the political life; for Nietzsche, as distinguished from the classics, politics belongs from the outset to a lower plane than either philosophy or religion.[5]

Throughout I have been suggesting something that is in one way similar to what Strauss says about Nietzsche and yet substantively different. Political philosophy is architectonic, hence in one very real fashion rules over all other possibilities: science, religion and politics. But as phenomenological, political philosophy is grounded in and grows out of phenomena, which are always already intrinsically morally, religiously and politically shaped. As thrown, political philosophy is always tied to what already presents itself while projecting future possibilities in an unbreakable circle. That said, to open new public spaces for future human beings is to reinvigorate the political, while realizing it will always have moral and religious components built in. Political philosophy is architectonic, but the political retains self-standing status.

In antiquity the issue confronting philosophy involved ameliorating and dealing with the danger presented to it by the city which was not only prior but at that point autonomous from philosophy. Philosophy needed to craft a rapprochement with city. It is not clear to me that Strauss follows antiquity in this regard; he seems to follow his Nietzsche in thinking the relation between philosophy and religion will be the primary concern in the future, with the political declining. My argument is that political philosophy must be architectonic and have hegemony over all other possibilities as the only undertaking capable of being holistic and of fashioning a whole out of the parts and doing so **in publicly accessible speech**. But it does not and cannot overcome the parts. Thus there is no either/or choice between philosophy and religion or modern science and religion or philosophy and the city. Political philosophy is architectonic and bound in a circular relationship with the phenomena that intrinsically condition its thrownness, and those are moral, religious and political.

The central issue for modern political philosophy was to reverse the hegemony of religion over philosophy that had taken root in the post-classical period. But why would that be the primary concern for political philosophy now or in the foreseeable future any more than the situation that confronted philosophy at its birth? The situation has changed. If political philosophy is architectonic it will be so over both religion and modern science or any other possibility. And in the name of the phenomena, political philosophy, if it is to save our essence as historical beings, will have to take up the defense of the city rather than carve out a defensive posture against it as was true at the time of its origins. Our situation is unique.

I have tried to suggest that, proceeding from the present phenomena as they show themselves, **the future will necessarily be both religious and scientific.** And I have suggested that in the aftermath of faith in linear history and the hegemony of the abstract universal, the primary political actors will for the foreseeable future be large nations and the primary basis of morality will be "vertical" rather than "horizontal," substantive rather than abstract or deontological—which is to say things like intentionality will not take precedence in future moral discourse.[6] I would also suggest that the political and the moral will be reintegrated as they have not been since classical times. The postmodern situation will be unique.

Postmodernity, as the outgrowth of what shows itself in the present rather than as mythology and constructivist wishful thinking, will be naturalistic in a unique sense, religious—with modern science understood as primarily technological rather than ontological—and will remain political with large states as primary international actors. The postmodern world will be in need of a new holistic view of nature as complex and that will be a view that has reintegrated that man into Nature. I will not now elaborate further on this summary of what I have discussed above. But a word is required about what I mean by the somewhat unique terms I have injected regarding "vertical" and "horizontal" morality.

By the distinction "vertical" versus "horizontal" I am suggesting that a phenomenological approach to morality will have to pay attention to how the moral phenomena present themselves in everyday action and perception. In everyday perception the phenomena present themselves as higher and lower. One can transcend the phenomena and ignore them only with a horizontal/linear view of history for support. I take ethical verticality as a given, and furthermore as compatible with republican and democratic political forms. Even if we do not always get the highest individuals as our leaders, almost all of us would loathe choosing them by lot or without prior scrutiny of their lives and behavior. This is because we have standards of higher and lower even if, precisely if, we dialectically disagree about those standards.

In the same vein, we do not send our poorest students to our best universities and most famous teachers even though they need more creative remedial training. We will not pay the same for tickets to every ballet dancer or opera singer regardless of merit. This is because we have standards of higher and lower. Beauty may be in the eye of the beholder, but no sensible person doubts that there is such a thing as beauty. This is because we have standards of higher and lower. Even in our choice of food and beverage we have conceptions of higher and lower and pay accordingly. However we initially derived these hierarchical conceptions, they "are" and we must begin from them. **It is not the task of thought to make them go away in the name of some artificial construction which leaves us standing in an ambiguous "everywhere and nowhere."**

We begin with what is always already given around us, with phenomena that show themselves. Our task becomes one wherein we must refine and articulate rather than projecting from some presumed autonomous stance something that can never be other than revengeful constructions that try to negate what is already in some sense given. We need to articulate what is given precisely because of the fact that while it shows itself, it never shows itself completely. Phenomenology transcends the spirit of revenge that rules in Constructivism by accepting the things that already show themselves. To attempt to dismiss the phenomena before we articulate them is a mistake, for we have no other place to begin. Once we begin to articulate the everyday phenomena we are already underway. We must **begin** from the fact that our everyday phenomena "are." We should take them seriously, not dismiss them.[7] And when we do so, the watchword for morality will be attention to verticality and hierarchy. That in turn means we will again have to take seriously, and indeed be guided by, notions like "nobility" which shows itself everywhere in everyday life. The high and the noble versus the low and the vulgar is how the phenomena of morality present themselves in everyday action and judgment.

This leaves us with the very interesting question of whether a phenomenological postmodern political philosophy that views the phenomena hierarchically as they present themselves will inevitably see the world teleologically. My suggestion is that it will not inevitably do so even if that notion is somehow embedded in everyday life. Instead, a truly phenomenological approach will be forced to see the priority not of final causality but of formal causality. This is entirely different than saying it will be teleological, which would require the priority of final causality. Formal causality can operate in abstraction from final causality. This is one of the more substantial differences between Plato and Aristotle in my understanding. Teleology ultimately requires religious presuppositions. Political philosophy as architectonic begins from the priority of formal causality, that is the insight of Plato. It is the basis of why he is the more clear-sighted phenomenologist than Aristotle.

I am arguing that formal causality takes complete priority to the other three forms of causality in a phenomenological account. For example, the phenomena can present themselves vertically only after first having presented themselves as what they "are," and what they are is due to belonging to this or that tribe or category of phenomena. That requires formal causality. That things present themselves vertically does not require that we know why they do so, or what the ground of that showing is. That is, it does not require final causality. There can be phenomenological verticality without presuming teleology.

That something is and why it is what it is are two different issues, and the "that" is always prior. As a **point of departure**, phenomenology, as I understand it, requires only that there are phenomena that present themselves. In any articulation of the whole as I have presented political philosophy, one will eventually get to the questions about "why" but one does not begin there.

In the chapters above I tried to show the silent hegemony of formal causality even in contemporary biology. I have argued that it takes priority in all phenomenological/dialectical approaches as well, for example, in Socratic questioning and in the Platonic dialogues. A "what is" question can only be answered by presupposing a grasp of a common form or tribe shared by many particulars. To presume that we know how or why things show themselves as they do is almost always to presume too much. This is especially true of every manifestation of Constructivist philosophy, which is always already determined by formal causality before it starts its allegedly autonomous projecting. Presuming to know the how and the why implies unmediated, direct knowing. Phenomenology assumes the existence of only mediated and dialectical knowing. It shows moderation and modesty, it knows what it does not know. There are many things about which we cannot help but speculate. And that speculation can be more or less phenomenologically rich and sound. But it is best to keep in mind the difference between knowing and speculating. I take that to be the central Socratic instinct regarding knowing what one cannot know.

To return to the issue of the relation between religion and modern science, as we look forward beyond the now ending late-modern world, I would argue that there are already prejudices built into, for example, modern physics that descend from Christianity. And I would also argue that Christianity is the philosophically most useful of the Scriptural dispensations, and as that into which we are thrown already will have hegemony even if we try to invent some post-Scriptural alternative.

Christianity is not just the philosophically most useful Scriptural dispensation but it is far better than paganism, or any form of polytheism, as Socrates and Plato already made clear two millennia ago. Religions are not invented by self-legislating autonomous egos, they emerge and show themselves. In light of these facts, we need to fashion a new understanding of the relation between religion and modern technological science, not try to make one victorious over the other.

But what this really means is that we need therefore to fashion a new understanding of the relation between Reason and Revelation with political philosophy as the prime exemplar of fully self-conscious Reason. Reason understood as modern science and Revelation must both be lovingly reinterpreted as the ground for a healthy future dialectical engagement which will open new possibilities.

Previous attempts at fashioning a relation between Reason and Revelation occurred in decidedly different situations. For example, in one early form this tension was between an early Christianity still overly dominated by the idiosyncratic pessimism of Ambrose, Jerome and Augustine on the one hand and a non-phenomenological theoretical Reason as depicted by Aristotle on the other. The synthesis of those two competitors was not necessary for all time. Our situation is radically different.

For the reasons I have presented above and elsewhere, we in the present are in a position to fashion together something that descends from Plato, understood as dialectical phenomenology. Plato can be taken as the exemplar of phenomenological Reason, and a Christianity that after two millennia should no longer predict the immediacy of the Second Coming, nor assume the early-Christian pessimistic and negative relation to the world. A Christianity freed from early preoccupations with the immediacy of the Second Coming will have an entirely different relation to the present and will need to rethink everything from issues regarding the necessity of the family to the basis of community to the preservation of God's natural creation and the natural in us. That means, among other things, that we can now accentuate the "good news" elements of Christianity, where Christ has redeemed God's creation from original sin. And Plato, correctly recovered—not through the totally foreign neo-Platonism that infected, for example, Augustine[8]—and Christianity as optimistic and loving life, have never really been woven together before.

Something like that weaving together could open all manner of future dialectical interactions which in turn could produce new situated realities in the future, not ones tyrannically and revengefully projected from the past **or determined by present and future elites from the top down.** My suggestion would be that we absolutely do not need anything resembling philosopher-kings. That is not the model for a future, phenomenological/dialectical, holistic political philosophy.

Once we see that we have the chance to find ourselves beyond the hegemony of intrinsically elitist Constructivist Reason which can only be reduced to a form of tyrannical logic, with its reliance on correspondence theories of truth and representational thinking, all manner of opportunities open for us. As I have suggested above, the Platonic understanding of Reason represents a significant alternative to the one that descends from Aristotle which points forward toward modern Constructivism.

In this vein, I offer a final thought on what follows from political philosophy understood as phenomenological. In *Thus Spoke Zarathustra*, the future is designated by a child who represents "innocence and forgetting." I have argued for the absolute importance of a postmodern political philosophy having a necessary element of *Andenken* or Remembrance. I have argued for the necessity of this Remembrance precisely because there is no Archimedean stance for an autonomous ego. Remembrance is an imperative part of the ecstatic temporality that I have argued is central for any ongoing tradition of political philosophy. Concern for the future and memory of the past go hand in hand. It is not possible to have one without the other. We need not revengefully negate the past. We cannot will the future *ex nihilo*.

The belief that the future can be healthy only if revengefully cut off from the past, or any of the various permutations of "innocence and forgetting" which lurk in so much contemporary thought, is a dangerous chimera. Innocence and forgetting are not the means to the good for fully human, historical beings. It only opens the door to one form of tyranny or the other. Being able to open ourselves to the phenomena of our present requires that we know how we got here and also how the future is determined by what we do now. Past and future must be eternally bound together to allow a vibrant and healthy present in which to live as human beings. We have an obligation to leave such a vibrant, alive and healthy future to those yet to come. That is the task of political philosophy now.

NOTES

1. We may learn one thing from the great proto-modern authors. They attacked not primarily concrete institutions as much as core premises that were the underlying, if publicly unseen, cornerstones that supported the reigning institutional structures and theoretical positions. Remove the cornerstone, and the edifice collapses. Many modern cornerstones have already removed themselves. We need now merely take **public** note of the fact and proceed accordingly.

2. For some interesting introductory reflections of this subject see Francis Fukuyama, *Our Posthuman Future: Consequences of the Biotechnology Revolution* (New York: Farrar, Straus and Giroux, 2002). After reading this work with some care, it is not clear to me whether Fukuyama ultimately sees the "posthuman" condition as inevitable or as something that can be avoided. If the latter, I do not see what Fukuyama presents as the presuppositions for transcending the inevitability of the posthuman condition. In light of his published corpus since *The End of History and the Last Man*, (New York: Free Press, 1992), I remain unclear whether Fukuyama is or is not still a proponent of a version of the "End of History." I have argued that the presuppositions for avoiding the End of History and a possible posthuman condition include both the continued existence of the tradition of political philosophy and of our human essence as history making beings. The End of History that Fukuyama seemed to accept at one time would be the end of man in his essential humanity.

3. Let it be understood what I am suggesting here. Man's essence is to be found not in being the "rational animal" (a fundamentally animal being to which is pasted alongside something called reason). Nor is man essentially the "social or political animal," a notion that requires the same kind of paste job. And we can ignore all of the tedious attempts to differentiate man from all other social species or "rational" species like dolphins, or political/hierarchical species like chimps. These attempts do not get to our essential humanity. Man is the one being that is history making. And man is the being that can consciously articulate and project the space for his historical existence. Man is the being who can stand between past and future.

4. Above, I chose to enter the issue of nature as a complex dynamic whole through discussions of the environment for this and yet a second reason. I have concluded, agreeing with Strauss, that political philosophy requires a recovery of "nature." This is especially true of a postmodern political philosophy. But contrary to Strauss's treatment of the "origin of the idea of nature" in *Natural Right and History*, what is required is a recovery of the "phenomenon" nature, and not as Strauss would have it, the "idea" of nature. For now I would simply make the following observation. Strauss once observed that the idea or concept of nature is never to be found in the Bible. Perhaps. However, the phenomenon nature is displayed in that text and everywhere around us. But that phenomenon may not now show itself precisely as it did to pre-modern humanity. At the very least, one should not begin from the prejudice that it does.

5. Leo Strauss, *Studies in Platonic Political Philosophy* (Chicago: University of Chicago Press, 1983), p. 176.

6. Cf. Nietzsche, *Beyond Good and Evil*, #32, on the place of intentionality—past, present and future.

7. To begin from some permutation of the difference between nature and convention is denied to almost all of our philosophical contemporaries as a basis for sorting through everyday perceptions. They do not believe in nature, so in effect nothing can be a mere convention. But the nature/convention distinction should be suspended by phenomenologists. The phenomenologist begins from the premise that the phenomena "are" and moves on from there. One may rediscover the nature/convention distinction, but only if it shows itself in the phenomena themselves as they show themselves. This distinction may reemerge from the phenomena, perhaps in different form

than at the time of the origins of the tradition. But we should not **begin** from something that is at best derivative from the phenomena.

8. I admit that I find Augustine to have been one of the more pernicious influences in the Tradition. Many turn to him for his doctrine of freedom and free will. But that early teaching seems completely at odds with his influence in the early church, which was tyrannically determined to not only create a total church ruled from the top down, but a total society ruled by the church in the same top down fashion. Together with his general pessimism Augustine's influence has been to foster all the life negating, spirit benumbing, Puritanical influences that have repeatedly popped up within Christian civilization. It is hoped that we can now relegate those influences to the dustbin of history. And I say that from within the perspective of Christianity itself. The future can offer us a Christianity without Ambrose, Jerome, Augustine, Calvin and his descendants, Puritanism in every form, etc.—a very hopeful prospect. A more joyous and affirmative Christianity is entirely possible.

Index

absolutism, 217

Adorno, Theodore, 171

ambition: Machiavelli's treatment of, 80; pursuit of, 67–68

anarchism, self-regulating, 123

Anaxagoras, moistic idealism of, 544

anxiety, 25, 297, 493–94

appearance: Aristotle on, 446; of historical change, 91, 98; Nature brought to, 440–41; truth in, 183n7

architectonic unity, postmodernist fragmentation v., 42

Arendt, Hannah, 5

aristocracy, 459, 609–10

Aristophanes, 173, 435

Aristotle: appearance and, 446; on Being, 438, 440; on biology, 445; on causality, 438–40; on cities, 445–46; on desire, 450–51; on economic institutions, 447–48; on education, 458–60; on family, 441–42, 447, 450; on fourfold causality bringing Nature to appearance, 440–41; on friendship and virtue, 446–47; on great-souled man, 457–59; on household management, 447–48; on justice, 460–61; on laws, 451–52; on leisure, 453; on *logos/praxis* required by happiness, 442; metaphysics and,

333; misogyny of, 467n23; on moral virtue, 98; on natural inclinations/ends, 569; on Nature of philosophy, 459–60; on *nomos/physis* distinction, 437–38; on peaks of virtue, 458; phenomenological element in approach of, 436–37; phenomenological presentation of Nature by, 438; on philosopher, 460–61; philosophy as influenced by, 309–10; in Plato's works, 372–73, 393n6; Plato v., 397–98; on *polis,* 441–43, 456; on political community, 438; practical works of, 436–37; on reason, 438, 449, 463–64; on reason's application, 443; on regimes, 462–63; regimes as investigated by, 452–55; on rulers, 444–45; on slavery, 443–45; on Socrates, 449; on soul, 443; theoretical/logical works of, 4; on unity, 449–50; on virtue, 456–57, 457, 461; on wisdom, 445; women as treated by, 444–46. *See also Politics* (Aristotle)

Arnhart, Larry: a-historicality of political philosophy view of, 567–68; approach of, 567; on best regime, 566; biology's ontological givens for, 567; on Darwinian Natural Right,

633

v. non-political men as rulers in work of, 82; positive proto-modernity of, 69; on Principalities, 69–71; on principality, 74–78; on radically new as possibility, 74; regimes for, 68–69; on self-sufficiency, 75–76; value-free teaching and, 68; on wisdom, 81. *See also The Prince* (Machiavelli)

Maimonides, Moses, 153, 168, 169

Marcuse, Herbert, 171

Margins of Philosophy (Derrida), 119

Marxism: Derrida and, 126–27; modern technology in, 127

Marx, Karl: on abolition of political, 485, 486; Derrida's relation to, 126–27; on good, 49; materialism and, 126; metaphysical freedom as rethought by, 595–96

Masters: on biological foundation for political philosophy, 563–64; on contemporary biology, 565–66; on evolutionary theory, 562–63, 565; on ideas' causal autonomy, 564–65; on naturalistic ethics, 562; on naturalistic theorizing, 565; on Nature as ethics' standard, 564

materialism, 126, 323

mathematics: Calabi-Yau, 549; modern, 538

Medieval Church, 501

memory, 407

metaphysical freedom, 34n24

metaphysics: Aristotle and, 333; Heidegger and, 3–4, 44, 115; in Husserl's work, 115; logocentric, 119; origin of tradition of, 422; Plato and, 3–4; as redefined, 115; Socrates and, 4

miracles, 559

modernity: anti-political bias of, 472; beginning of, 13, 235; Christian ecclesiastical authority v., 253; closure of, 14; concerns of, 104; Constructivism as essential to, 13, 149; core phenomenon of, 472–73;

Cropsey on, 259–60, 268–69; Descartes on, 154–55, 170; detachment from phenomena in, 14; dissolution of, 108–9; egalitarian bias of, 594; ego in, 15; emancipation through thought in, 275n26; endless, 15, 94–95; end of, 500; essence of, 13, 108–9, 149; fundamental questions of, 30, 472–73; good life in, 154, 170; high intellectual perceptions disconnect from everyday perceptions in, 93; Idealism and, 90; longing of, 472; Machiavelli and Descartes sharing essential, 65–68; meaning of, 591; moral change in, 2, 154, 170–71; morality of, 473–74; myth of, 488; natural science in, 472; Nature/convention relation in, 259–60; Nature in, 8; outcomes of, 108–9; phenomena of, 471; as phenomenologically saved, 104; philosophical notions central to, 15–16; Plato linked with, 308; political/moral yield of, 2; premise of, 606; *The Prince* (Machiavelli), and essence of, 65–83; problems of, 259–60; proto, 593–94; public self-perception of, 529; as rational, 15; rationality of, 95; religion in, 472; shared premises in, 66; split within, 259, 274n24; Strauss on, 169–75, 170, 183n5, 235–36, 283; thought as moving, 66, 261; three waves of, 148, 153, 155, 171, 255–56; uniqueness of, 102; unity/diversity in, 259; world as artificial in, 88

modern physics: autonomy of, 538, 552–53; biology v., 570–71; chance in, 553; multiplicity in, 560; Nietzsche on, 538–39; phenomena's relation to, 535; as public phenomena, 535–36

modern science: abstractedness of, 581–82; as activity, 577;

About the Author

Gregory Bruce Smith is professor of political philosophy, affiliated with the Departments of Political Science and Philosophy at Trinity College, Hartford, CT. He received his B.A. with honors from the Maxwell School at Syracuse University and his M.A. and Ph.D. degrees from the University of Chicago. Among other venues, he had taught at the University of Pennsylvania, Carleton College and the University of Michigan. He is the author of *Martin Heidegger: Paths Taken, Paths Opened* (Rowman & Littlefield, 2007), *Nietzsche, Heidegger and the Transition to Postmodernity* (University of Chicago Press, 1996), and dozens of articles on the tradition of political philosophy.